Neue Horizonte
A Brief Course

David B. Dollenmayer

Worcester Polytechnic Institute

Thomas S. Hansen

Wellesley College

Houghton Mifflin Company   Boston   New York

Director, World Languages: New Media and Modern Language Publishing   Beth Kramer
Development Editor and Project Editor   Harriet C. Dishman, Elm Street Publications
Editorial Associate   Melissa Foley
Senior Production/Design Coordinator   Carol Merrigan
Senior Cover Design Coordinator   Deborah Azerrad Savona
Senior Manufacturing Coordinator   Sally Culler
Marketing Manager   José A. Mercado

Cover design   Deborah Azerrad Savona
Cover image   Germany, Cologne, Altstadt at night. Tony Stone Images.

Printed in the U.S.A.

Library of Congress Catalog Card Number: 00-104948

Student Text ISBN: 0-618-09860-7
Instructor's Annotated Edition ISBN: 0-618-09861-5

123456789-VH-04 03 02 01 00

About the Authors

David B. Dollenmayer is Professor of German at the Worcester Polytechnic Institute (Worcester, Massachusetts). He received his B.A. and Ph.D. from Princeton University and was a Fulbright fellow at the University of Munich. He has written on the 20th-century writers Alfred Döblin, Joseph Roth, Christa Wolf, and Ingeborg Bachmann, and is the author of *The Berlin Novels of Alfred Döblin* (Berkeley, CA: University of California Press, 1988).

Thomas S. Hansen is Professor of German at Wellesley College (Wellesley, Massachusetts). He received his B.A. from Tufts University, studied six semesters at the University of Tübingen, and received his Ph.D. from Harvard University. His current research focuses on the 20th-century writer Arno Schmidt and on German-American literary relations. He is the author (with Burton R. Pollin) of *The German Face of Edgar Allan Poe: A Study of Literary References in His Works* (Columbia, SC: Camden House, 1995).

Ellen W. Crocker is Senior Lecturer in German at the Massachusetts Institute of Technology (Cambridge, Massachusetts). She received her B.A. from Skidmore College and the Magister Artium from the University of Freiberg, Germany. She is co-author (with Claire J. Kramsch) of the intermediate-level workbook for conversational management, *Reden, Mitreden, Dazwischenreden* (Boston: Heinle and Heinle, 1985). Currently she is working on multimedia projects for foreign language and culture studies.

Contents

Kapitel 2

Familie und Freunde   43

Kapitel 3

Jugend und Schule   64

Kapitel 4   Land und Leute   87

Kapitel 5   Arbeit und Freizeit   111

Kapitel 6

An der Universität   136

Kapitel 9

Unsere Umwelt   216

Kapitel 10

Deutschland im 20. Jahrhundert   240

Kapitel 11

Deutschland nach der Mauer   266

Kapitel 12

Erinnerungen   294

Kapitel 13

Die Schweiz   323

Preface

Neue Horizonte: A Brief Course is a complete first-year German program for college and university students. Its contents reflect both the approach used successfully by the original *Neue Horizonte* for over twenty years, but also a clear understanding of the practical needs of today's classes. *Neue Horizonte: A Brief Course* can be comfortably completed in two semesters or three quarters. It can be used in courses meeting three or more days per week or in programs with short (twelve- or thirteen-week) semesters.

You will learn the basic structures and vocabulary of German by practicing the four skills of speaking, listening, reading, and writing. In addition, you will learn about the cultures of the contemporary German-speaking world. The goal of the program is to help you achieve a basic level of linguistic proficiency in German. Such proficiency includes both communicative competence—that is to say, speaking the language in order to communicate thoughts, ideas, and feelings—and grammatical accuracy. The program prepares you either to continue with an intermediate course in German or to go directly to a German-speaking country. There, after a period of acclimatization, you will be able to communicate in most everyday situations and to continue to build on what you have already learned.

In addition, the text aims to excite your curiosity and help you view your own culture through the prism of another, thereby expanding your intellectual horizons in the spirit of the Austrian philosopher Ludwig Wittgenstein when he wrote, "Die Grenzen meiner Sprache sind die Grenzen meiner Welt." (*The boundaries of my language are the boundaries of my world.*)

The Student Text

Neue Horizonte: A Brief Course consists of an introductory chapter and fourteen regular chapters.

Einführung (Introductory chapter)

From the very first day of the course, you begin talking with your fellow students in German. In this chapter you will learn greetings and farewells. You will also learn basic vocabulary such as the names of classroom objects, the days of the week, and the months of the year. In addition, you will learn how to spell, count to twenty, tell time, talk about the weather, and tell how you feel and where you are from.

Chapter Organization

Each of the fourteen regular chapters contains the following sections:

Dialoge und Variationen (Dialogues and Variations)

The **Dialoge** introduce new vocabulary and structures through idiomatic conversations in everyday situations. There are two or three dialogues per chapter, most short enough to be memorized, with English translations printed on the following page. The

Variationen follow up with activities that encourage you to build on and vary the material in the dialogues. When a dialogue is closely related to the *Neue Horizonte* video, this is signaled by a video icon that appears in the margin.

Wortschatz 1 und Wortschatz 2 (Vocabulary 1 and Vocabulary 2)

Each chapter contains two lists of words and phrases for you to learn. **Wortschatz 1** (*Vocabulary 1*) comes early in the chapter, following the dialogues. **Wortschatz 2** comes later, just before the reading selection. Words are arranged alphabetically by parts of speech. In addition, nouns are arranged by gender to facilitate learning. Each **Wortschatz** also includes useful expressions (**Nützliche Ausdrücke**), antonyms (**Gegensätze**), as well as a section called **Mit anderen Worten** (*In other words*). Here some of the colorful idioms frequent in the everyday speech of native Germans are defined using German you already know. These include, for instance, intensified forms of adjectives such as **blitzschnell** (*quick as lightning*) and colloquialisms such as **prima** (*great!*). By the end of the course you will have acquired a total active lexicon of about 1,500 words and phrases.

Lyrik zum Vorlesen (Poetry for reading aloud)

Each chapter includes a poem related to its cultural theme. This may be used both for pronunciation and intonation practice and for simple interpretive discussion. Unfamiliar vocabulary is glossed in the margins.

Grammatik (Grammar)

Grammar explanations in *Neue Horizonte: A Brief Course* are concise but complete and do not presuppose familiarity with English grammatical terms. So that class time can be devoted to communication, you should study the grammar carefully outside of class.

The sequence of in-class activities moves from theory to practice. The **Übungen** (*Exercises*) are directed by your instructor and briefly reinforce the grammar you have studied on your own. These are followed by activities called **Gruppenarbeit** and **Partnerarbeit** (*Group work* and *Work with partners*) in which you use German with more freedom and creativity on your way toward communicative competence.

Vor dem Lesen (Before the reading)

This pre-reading section offers tips for learning and expanding your German vocabulary. Lists of easily recognized cognates (e.g., **Universität**) are given under the heading **Leicht zu merken** (*Easy to remember*). Strategies for approaching the reading selection that follows are also provided.

Lesestück (Reading selection)

The **Lesestück** is the core of the cultural presentation of each chapter. In Chapters 1–8 it provides basic information on daily life in the German-speaking countries. Topics include the family, secondary schools, geography and climate, work and professions, university study, travel, and urban life. The readings of Chapters 9–14 address important topics in twentieth-century German history and culture. These include the Weimar era, the legacy of World War II, and German reunification, as well as issues of intense current concern such as the environment. The readings in Chapters 13 and 14 are devoted to Switzerland and Austria, respectively. Chapters 12 presents an authentic, unedited nonfiction text by the modern writer Anna Seghers. In each chapter, the section **Nach dem Lesen** (*After the reading*) includes content questions as well as a variety of activities related to the topic of the reading.

Situationen aus dem Alltag (Situations from everyday life)

This section contains activities and optional vocabulary that emphasize "survival skills" for everyday situations such as using public transportation, eating in restaurants, introducing oneself in various social situations, and expressing feelings. When these situations are the subject of a ***Neue Horizonte*** video module, this is indicated by the video icon (shown on the left).

Almanach (Almanac)

The final section provides more detailed information in English on the cultural topic of the chapter or presents authentic material in German related to the chapter's theme. For example, in Chapter 3 you will learn more about the school system in German-speaking countries, while in Chapter 8 you will work with a city bus brochure.

Student Annotations

Student annotations are printed in black in the margins. These annotations serve several purposes. They not only provide cross-references to the Workbook/Laboratory Manual/Video Manual and Cassette Program, but also offer learning hints, cultural and historical notes, contrasts and similarities to English, interesting word histories, and statements of communicative and cultural goals.

Reference Section

A table showing the principal parts of the strong and irregular verbs introduced in the book is included at the end of the book. Both the German-English and the English-German end vocabularies include all the active vocabulary in the **Wortschatz** sections, as well as the optional vocabulary from the **Situationen aus dem Alltag** sections. For quick reference, the book ends with a comprehensive index to grammatical and communicative topics included in the text.

The Workbook/Laboratory Manual/Video Manual and the Audio Program

The Workbook/Laboratory Manual/Video Manual and the Audio Program for ***Neue Horizonte: A Brief Course*** are fully integrated with the Student Text. The textbook includes extensive cross-references to the ancillary components. The Audio Program and its coordinated Laboratory Manual are an integral part of the program. The audio program is available for individual purchase on either cassettes or audio CDs at a special student price.

In order to use the Workbook/Laboratory Manual/Video Manual to best advantage, follow the sequence suggested in the marginal cross-references in your Student Text. Each cross-reference is identified by an icon referring to the appropriate component section.

The pen icon directs you to written exercises in the Workbook. These offer further practice of the vocabulary and grammar presented in each chapter.

The headphone icon directs you to the Audio Program and the Laboratory Manual. All the **Dialoge**, **Lyrik zum Vorlesen**, and **Lesestücke** from the Student Text are recorded on the audio program, which also includes numerous grammar exercises. Some of these are identical to exercises in the Student Text, while others are variations on them.

The video icon directs you to the Video Manual and to the *Neue Horizonte* Video. The video consists of eight modules and the Video Manual is made up of eight corresponding **Videoecken** that provide vocabulary and activities to enhance your comprehension and enjoyment.

An especially valuable feature of the Workbook is the **Zusammenfassung und Wiederholung** (*Summary and review*) section located after every three to four chapters. This section contains condensed grammar summaries and reviews useful vocabulary expressions. It includes a self-correcting test called *Test Your Progress* that you can use to review the preceding quarter of the textbook.

The Neue Horizonte *Video*

Shot entirely on location in Berlin, the *Neue Horizonte* video contains eight modules. Each module opens with scenes of Germany related to the module's cultural theme. There follow several minutes of a continuing story, performed by German actors using idiomatic language. Each module concludes with a **Welle Magazin** segment in which further footage shows aspects of German culture and life. For students who wish to view the video at their own convenience, the *Neue Horizonte* video is available for purchase at a special discount price.

The eight **Videoecken** in the Video Manual are designed for use with the eight modules of the *Neue Horizonte* video. In addition, when a video module is particularly closely related to a dialogue or a **Situation aus dem Alltag** section in the Student Text, a video icon (shown here on the left) signals that fact and alerts you to the possibility of viewing this module again at this point.

Computer Study Modules 2.0 to Accompany Neue Horizonte: A Brief Course

Available on a dual-platform CD-ROM for both Macintosh® and Windows®, this text-specific software offers additional, computer-aided practice of the structures and vocabulary of the Student Text. It also provides helpful error correction.

Neue Horizonte *NOW! CD-ROM*

Developed in collaboration with Transparent Language, Inc., and Windows® and Macintosh® compatible, the *Neue Horizonte* **NOW!** CD-ROM is a learning tool that helps you to work at your own pace, practicing listening, speaking, reading, and writing through interactive games and activities. This program includes text dialogues, vocabulary, and cultural notes and is correlated by chapter with the textbook.

Neue Horizonte *Web Site*

Look for this icon next to the **Almanach** headings in the **Contents**.

The multifaceted, text-specific *Neue Horizonte* **Web Site** features a self-testing section for practice and a task-based activity section. It also links you to contemporary material on the language and cultures of the German-speaking countries available on the World Wide Web.

Acknowledgments

We wish to express our special gratitude to Ellen Crocker of the Massachusetts Institute of Technology for countless suggestions for improvement of the text and better coordination with the Workbook/Laboratory Manual/Video Manual and Cassette Program. We wish to express our special gratitude to Harriet C. Dishman and Katherine Gilbert of Elm Street Publications for their unfailing attention to detail, as well as the editorial team at Houghton Mifflin Company. Thanks also to our colleagues and students at Worcester Polytechnic Institute, Wellesley College, and Massachusetts Institute of Technology who have used, along with us, *Neue Horizonte* over the years. Without their comments, criticisms, and suggestions, *Neue Horizonte: A Brief Course* would not have been possible.

We wish to thank especially the following colleagues and institutions for their advice and help.

Prof. Jutta Arend, College of the Holy Cross and Worcester Polytechnic Institute

Prof. John Austin, Georgia State University and the Deutsche Schule, Washington, D.C.

Prof. Sharon DiFino, University of Florida at Gainesville

Prof. Wighart von Koenigswald, Universität Bonn and the Hessisches Landesmuseum, Darmstadt, Germany

Prof. Jean Leventhal, Wellesley College

Prof. Thomas Nolden, Wellesley College

Prof. Michael Ressler, Boston College

Prof. Ute Trevor, Arbeitskreis DaF in der Schweiz

Prof. Margaret Ward, Wellesley College

In addition, we would like to thank the following colleagues who reviewed the manuscript at various stages of its development:

Prof. Margaret Klopfle Devinney, Temple University

Prof. Monika R. Dressler, University of Michigan

Prof. Enno Lohmeyer, University of Kansas

Prof. James R. McIntyre, Colby College

Prof. Guenter Georg Pfister

Prof. Ann Ulmer, Carleton College

Prof. Gretchen Van Galder-Janis, Johnson County Community College

Prof. Elizabeth I. Wade, University of Wisconsin at Oshkosh

We welcome reactions and suggestions from instructors and students using *Neue Horizonte: A Brief Course*. Please feel free to contact us.

Prof. David B. Dollenmayer
Department of Humanities and Arts
Worcester Polytechnic Institute
Worcester, Massachusetts 01609-2280
E-mail: dbd@wpi.edu

Prof. Thomas S. Hansen
Department of German
Wellesley College
Wellesley, Massachusetts 02482
E-mail: thansen@wellesley.edu

Communicative Goals

- Greeting people and asking their names
- Identifying classroom objects
- Saying good-bye
- Learning the days of the week and months of the year
- Spelling in German
- Describing how you feel
- Talking about the weather
- Counting to 20
- Telling time
- Telling where you are from

Stufe 1 (Step 1)

■ **Guten Tag!** (Hello!)

The shaded boxes in this **Einführung** (*Introduction*) contain useful words and phrases that you should memorize. You will find a complete list of this vocabulary on p. 19.

German speakers greet each other in various ways. What greeting you use depends on the time of day:

Guten Morgen!	*Good morning!* (until about 10:00 A.M.)
Guten Tag!	*Hello!* (literally: "*Good day.*" Said after 10:00 A.M.)
Guten Abend!	*Good evening!* (after 5:00 P.M.)

where you live:

Grüß Gott!	*Hello!* (in southern Germany and Austria)

and how well you know each other and what the social situation is:

Hallo! **Tag!**	*Hi!* (informal greetings)

Lab Manual
Einführung, dialogues in Stufe 1 and The Sounds of German.

■ **1** ■ **Gruppenarbeit: Guten Tag!** (Group work) When German speakers meet friends and acquaintances, they not only greet each other, but they also shake hands. Greet the students next to you in German. Don't forget to shake hands!

■ **2** ■ **Partnerarbeit: Was sagen diese Leute?** (Work with partners: What are these people saying?) With a partner, complete the following dialogues by saying them aloud.

German has no equivalent to English *Ms.* One can avoid **Fräulein** by using **Frau** for all young women. In restaurants a waitress is frequently called by saying **Bedienung, bitte!** (*Service, please!*).

Herr	=	*Mr.*
Frau	=	*Mrs. or Ms.*
Fräulein	=	*Miss*

1. _____ , Herr Lehmann!
   _____ , Frau Schmidt!

2. _____ , Brigitte!
   _____ , Heinz!

3. _____ , Fräulein Schröder!
_____ , Frau Königstein!

4. _____ , Peter!
_____ , Ute!

5. _____ , Franz!
_____ , Joseph!

■ Wie heißen Sie? (What's your name?)

You: *du* or *Sie*?

German has two forms of the pronoun *you*. If you're talking to a relative or good friend, use the familiar form **du**. University students often call each other **du** even when they're meeting for the first time. If you're talking to an adult whom you don't know well, use the formal **Sie**.

When you meet people for the first time, you want to learn their names. Listen to your instructor, then repeat the following dialogue.

A: **Hallo, ich heiße Anna. Wie heißt du?**   *Hello, my name is Anna. What's your name?*

B: **Hallo Anna. Ich heiße Thomas.**   *Hello Anna. My name's Thomas.*

A: **Freut mich, Thomas!**   *Pleased to meet you, Thomas.*

You can hear these dialogues on the tape accompanying the **Einführung**.

If you're meeting an adult who is not a fellow student, the dialogue would go like this:

A: **Ich heiße Schönhuber und wie heißen Sie?**

B: **Guten Tag, Herr Schönhuber. Ich heiße Meyer.**

A: **Freut mich, Herr Meyer.**

> ## *heißen:* _____'s name is
>
> German verbs have endings that must agree with the subject of the sentence:
>
> | | |
> |---|---|
> | ich heiß**e** | *my name is* (literally: *I am called*) |
> | du heiß**t** | |
> | Sie heiß**en** | *your name is* |
> | er heiß**t** | *his name is* |
> | sie heiß**t** | *her name is* |
> | **Wie heißt du?** | *What's your name?* (literally: *How* |
> | **Wie heißen Sie?** | *are you called?*) |

wir heißen
ihr heißt

■3■ Partnerarbeit: Wie heißt du? Practice the first dialogue at the bottom of p. 3 with a partner. Substitute your own names for Anna and Thomas, and don't forget to switch roles.

■4■ Gruppenarbeit: Ich heiße ... Now introduce yourself to three or four people in class you don't know. Use **du** and don't forget to shake hands.

Wie heißt du?

Wie heißt er?

Wie heißt sie?

5 **Gruppenarbeit: Wie heißt ... ?** Your instructor will ask you the names of other students. If you can't remember someone's name, just ask that person, **Wie heißt du?**

■ **Wie geht's?** (How are you?)

dir or *Ihnen*?		
informal	Wie geht's **dir**?	(literally) *How goes it for*
formal	Wie geht es **Ihnen**?	*you?*

After you've said hello, you want to find out how someone is. With a relative or fellow student, the conversation goes like this:

A: **Wie geht es dir, Franz?** *How are you, Franz?*
B: **Sehr gut, danke. Und dir?** *Very well, thanks. And you?* for you
A: **Prima, danke.** *Great, thanks.*

With other adults, the exchange goes like this:

A: **Wie geht es Ihnen heute,** *How are you today, Mrs.*
   Frau Müller? *Müller?*
B: **Leider nicht so gut.** *Unfortunately, not so well.*
A: **Oh, das tut mir Leid.** *Oh, I'm sorry.*

6 **Partnerarbeit: Wie geht's?** With a partner, practice the two preceding dialogues several times until you can say them with books closed.

7 **Partnerarbeit: Wie geht's dir?** Complete this dialogue with a new partner. You're both students or good friends and so say **du** or **dir** to each other.

A: Hallo! Wie geht's dir heute, _____ ?
B: _____ , danke. Und _____ ?
A: _____ , danke.

8 **Partnerarbeit: Wie geht es Ihnen?** Now you have a more formal relationship. Use **Ihnen** instead of **dir**.

A: Guten Tag, Frau/Herr _____ . Wie geht es _____ heute?
B: Leider _____ .
A: Oh, _____ .

■ Was ist das? (What is that?)

In items 1–4, the first word refers to a university classroom (professor and student), while the second word in parentheses refers to a secondary school classroom (teacher and pupil). **Student** in German *always* means *university student*.

1. der Professor
   (der Lehrer)
2. die Professorin
   (die Lehrerin)
3. der Student *college, univ.*
   (der Schüler) *school*
4. die Studentin
   (die Schülerin)
5. die Tafel
6. der Tisch
7. die Uhr
8. die Wand
9. das Fenster
10. der Stuhl
11. die Tür
12. die Landkarte
13. das Poster
14. die Kreide
15. der Wischer

1. das Buch
2. das Heft
3. das Papier
4. der Bleistift
5. der Kugelschreiber *der Kuli*
6. der Radiergummi

A: **Was ist das?**	*What is that?*
B: **Das ist der Tisch.**	*That's the table.*
das Buch.	*the book.*
die Tafel.	*the blackboard.*

The = *der, das,* or *die*

Every German noun belongs to one of three classes, traditionally called *masculine, neuter,* and *feminine.* The form of the definite article (**der, das, die** = *the*) shows which class each noun belongs to. This article *must* be learned with each noun.

masculine	**der** Mann	*the man*
	der Stuhl	*the chair*
neuter	**das** Kind	*the child*
	das Buch	*the book*
feminine	**die** Frau	*the woman*
	die Tafel	*the blackboard*

A:	**Wer ist das?**	*Who is that?*
B:	**Das ist Thomas.**	*That's Thomas.*
	die Professorin.	*the (female) professor.*
	der Professor.	*the (male) professor.*
	die Studentin.	*the (female) student.*
	der Student.	*the (male) student.*

The **-in** suffix denotes a female.

■ 9 ■   Partnerarbeit: Was ist das?

Work together and see how many people and things in the room you can identify.

A:	Was ist das?	A:	Wer ist das?
B:	Das ist der/das/die _____.	B:	Das ist _____.

> **Question words**
>
> **wie?**   *how?*
> **was?**   *what?*
> **wer?**   *who?*

Auf Wiedersehen!

■ Auf Wiedersehen! (Good-bye!)

There are several expressions you can use when leaving.

Auf Wiedersehen!	*Good-bye!*
Tschüss!	*So long!* (informal, among friends)
Schönes Wochenende!	*(Have a) nice weekend!*
Danke, gleichfalls!	*Thanks, same to you! (You too!)*
Bis morgen!	*Until tomorrow!*
Bis Montag!	*Until Monday!*

Tschüss is derived from Spanish *adiós*.

In Austria, the informal expression **Servus** means both *hi* and *so long*. In Switzerland, instead of **Guten Tag**, one says **Grüezi** formally and **Hoi** informally.

Lab Manual
Einführung,
The Days of the Week.

■ Die Wochentage (Days of the week)

der **Montag**	*Monday*
Dienstag	*Tuesday*
Mittwoch	*Wednesday*
Donnerstag	*Thursday*
Freitag	*Friday*
Samstag (in southern Germany)	
Sonnabend (in northern Germany	*Saturday*
Sonntag	*Sunday*

The letter **ß** represents the unvoiced *s*-sound. It follows long vowels and diphthongs. In Switzerland **ss** is used instead of **ß**.

■ 10 ■ Gruppenarbeit: Auf Wiedersehen! At the end of class, turn to your neighbors and say good-bye until next time. Tell your instructor good-bye too.

Stufe 2

Lab Manual
Einführung, The Alphabet.

In addition to this alphabet, German also has three vowels modified by a symbol called the **Umlaut: ä, ö, ü**.

■ Das Alphabet

The name of almost every letter in German contains the sound ordinarily represented by that letter. You should memorize the German alphabet. Listen to the alphabet on the tapes and to your instructor.

a	ah	**j**	jot	**s**	ess
b	beh	**k**	kah	**t**	teh
c	tseh	**l**	ell	**u**	uh
d	deh	**m**	emm	**v**	fau
e	eh	**n**	enn	**w**	weh
f	eff	**o**	oh	**x**	iks
g	geh	**p**	peh	**y**	üppsilon
h	hah	**q**	kuh	**z**	tsett
i	ih	**r**	err	**ß**	ess-tsett

Notes on capitalization:

- All nouns are capitalized, wherever they occur in the sentence.

- Adjectives denoting nationality are *not* capitalized.

deutsch	*German*	**kanadisch**	*Canadian*
amerikanisch	*American*	**schottisch**	*Scottish*

Lab Manual
Einführung,
Variations on dialogues in Stufe 2.

■ 11 ■   **Partnerarbeit: Wie schreibt man das?**   (How do you spell that?)

A.   Ask each other how you spell your names. Write the last name as your partner spells it, then check to see whether you've written it correctly.

A: Wie heißt du?
B: Ich heiße Jay Schneider.
A: Wie schreibt man Schneider?   *How do you spell "Schneider"?*
B: Man schreibt das S-C-H-N-E-I-D-E-R.   *You spell it . . .*

B.   Now turn to the classroom objects pictured on p. 6. One partner spells four or five of the objects pictured; the other partner says each word as it is spelled. Then switch roles.

BMW = Bayerische Motorenwerke (*Bavarian Motor Works*), **MP** = Militärpolizei, **ISBN** = Internationale Standardbuchnummer, **EKG** = Elektrokardiogramm, **BASF** = Badische Anilin- und Sodafabrik (*Baden Aniline and Soda Factory*).

■ 12 ■   **Gruppenarbeit: Wie sagt man das?**   (How do you say that?)   Here are some abbreviations used in both English and German. Take turns saying them in German:

VW	BMW	ISBN	BASF
IBM	MP	EKG	TNT
USA	PVC	CD	

■ 13 ■   **Gruppenarbeit: Wie spricht man das aus?**   (How do you pronounce that?)

A.   Let's move from individual letters to pronouncing entire words in German. Here are some well-known German surnames. Take turns saying them aloud.

Fahrenheit	Kissinger	Nietzsche	Bach
Jung	Freud	Luther	Schönberg
Diesel	Ohm	Zeppelin	Schwarzenegger
Beethoven	Röntgen	Bunsen	Goethe
Hesse	Mozart	Schiffer	Pfeiffer

B.   Now here are some words that English has borrowed from German. Caution: in English, their pronunciation has been anglicized. Be sure to pronounce them in German, and see if you know what they mean.

Angst	Kindergarten	Spiel
Ersatz	Kitsch	Strudel
Flak	Leitmotiv	Wanderlust
Gestalt	Poltergeist	Weltanschauung
Gesundheit	Rucksack	Zeitgeist
Hinterland	Schmalz	Zwieback

Flak = acronym for **Fliegerabwehrkanone** (*anti-aircraft gun*).

■ Wie geht's?

Now let's move beyond the basics of "How are you?" "I'm fine" and find out more detail about how you're feeling.

A: **Wie geht's heute? Bist du guter Laune?**   *How are you today? Are you in a good mood?*

B: **Nein, ich bin nicht guter Laune. Ich bin schlechter Laune.**   *No, I'm not in a good mood. I'm in a bad mood.*

You will learn the complete present tense of **sein**, including plural forms, in **Kapitel 1**.

---

sein to be

The most frequently used verb in German is **sein**. It is very irregular in the present tense.

ich	**bin**	*I am*	*wir sind*
du	**bist**		*ihr seid*
Sie	**sind**	*you are*	
er	**ist**	*he is*	*Sie sind*
sie	**ist**	*she is*	

■ Negation

Nicht (*not*) is placed in front of the adjective it negates:

A: Bist du müde?   *Are you tired?*
B: Nein, ich bin **nicht** müde.   *No, I'm not tired.*

Wie geht's?

Es geht mir gut. (*I'm fine.*)   **Es geht mir nicht so gut.** (*I'm not so well.*)

Ich bin ...
    guter Laune (*in a good mood*).
    munter (*wide-awake, cheerful*).
    fit (*in good shape*).

Das freut mich! (*I'm glad!*)
(freuen)

Ich bin ...
    schlechter Laune (*in a bad mood*).
    müde (*tired*).
    krank (*sick*).
    sauer (*ticked off, sore*).

Das tut mir Leid. (*I'm sorry.*)

Er *(oder)* sie ist _____ .

1. *muenter, guter Laune*
2. *müde*
3. *krank*
4. *fit*
5. *Schlechter Laune*
6. *sauer*

■15■   **Partnerarbeit**   With a partner, complete the following dialogues.

GERTRUD: Grüß Gott, Melanie! Wie geht's *dir* heute?
MELANIE: Hallo, Gertrud. Leider geht's mir *nicht* gut. Ich bin heute *krank*.
GERTRUD: Oh, *das tut mir Leid*.

FRAU PABST: Guten Tag, Herr Hauser! Wie geht es *Ihnen*?
HERR HAUSER: Guten Tag, Frau Pabst! Sehr gut, danke. Ich bin heute *guter Laune / munter*!
FRAU PABST: Oh, _____ !
das freut mich

■16■   **Gruppenarbeit: Bist du ... ?**   Form groups of three or four for this guessing game. Each person in turn acts out one of the adjectives listed on page 10. The others ask questions until they guess what the mood is.

A: Bist du müde?
B: Nein, ich bin nicht müde.
C: Bist du ... ?
B: Ja, ich bin ...

■ Das Wetter (The weather)

The weather is a frequent topic of conversation everywhere.

> A: Wie ist das Wetter heute?
> B: Es ist **herrlich** (*great, terrific*).   ODER (*or*)
>   Es ist **furchtbar** (*terrible*).

Es ist kühl.   Es ist warm.   Es ist kalt.   Es ist heiß.

Scheint die Sonne heute?   *Is the sun shining today?*

Ja, die Sonne scheint.   *Yes, the sun is shining.*

Nein, es regnet.   *No, it's raining.*

■ 17 ■   Partnerarbeit: Wie ist das Wetter heute?   Chat briefly with a partner about today's weather. Use the words and phrases above.

More Weather Words

Es ist heute wolkig.	*Today it's cloudy.*
neblig.	*foggy.*
sonnig.	*sunny.*
windig.	*windy.*
Es regnet.	*It's raining.*
Es schneit.	*It's snowing.*

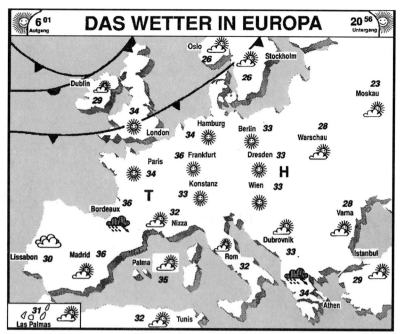

Guess the meaning of **Aufgang** and **Untergang**. What season is this?
Ist es heiß oder kalt? (Die Temperatur ist Celsius!)

| sonnig | heiter | wolkig | bedeckt | Regen | Gewitter | Nebel | Schnee |

cheerful?   ?   Stormy?

Wie ist das Wetter in Berlin?
Ist es Sommer oder Winter?

Wie ist das Wetter in ...

Oslo? *Es schneit*

Cannes? *Die Sonne scheint*

Boston? *Es ist neblig*

Berlin? *Es ist windig*

Hamburg? *Es regnet*

Stufe 3

■ **Wie viele?** (How many?)

Lab Manual
Einführung, The Numbers from 0 to 20.

0	null	11	elf
1	eins	12	zwölf
2	zwei	13	dreizehn
3	drei	14	vierzehn
4	vier	15	fünfzehn
5	fünf	16	sechzehn
6	sechs	17	siebzehn
7	sieben	18	achtzehn
8	acht	19	neunzehn
9	neun	20	zwanzig
10	zehn		

19 Gruppenarbeit: Wie ist die Telefonnummer? (What is the telephone number?) Read these business telephone numbers aloud.

Two of these numbers include an area code beginning with 0. When dialing German numbers from abroad, the zero is omitted. For example, to dial the Dortmund number from the U.S., dial 011 (international operator), 49 (country code), then the area code 231 (without zero), and then the local number 82 34 45. 49 is the country code for Germany, 43 for Austria, 41 for Switzerland.

mitfahr zentrale **Berlin 15** 030-8827606

NATURKOST · NATURKOSMETIK
bellad☀nna
BERGMANNSTR. 101 694 3731

SCHALLPLATTEN + CD's
ANKAUF · VERKAUF · TAUSCH
Ständiger Barankauf von LP's + CD's (Sammlungen)
Mo–Fr 12.00–18.30
Sa 10.00–14.00
Bergmannstraße 10
Telefon: 6 93 19 98

LP's ab 4 DM
Sl ab I DM

Dortmund
☎ **0231/82 34 45**
82 20 67

EIGENER ABSCHLEPPDIENST
K. Walter
VORM. ZINNEKER
1230 WIEN, BREITENFURTERSTR. 213
☎ 804 21 42
Autokosmetik
KAROSSERIE-FACHWERKSTÄTTE
Einbrenn- und Sonderlackierung

Lab Manual Einführung, dialogues in Stufe 3.

20 Kettenreaktion: Wie ist deine Telefonnummer? (Chain reaction: What's your telephone number?) Follow the model. One student asks the next.

BEISPIEL: A: Wie ist deine Telefonnummer?
(Example) B: Meine Telefonnummer ist _____ . Wie ist *deine* Telefonnummer?
C: _____ .

■ **Wie spät ist es bitte?** (What time is it, please?)

Wieviel Uhr

Es ist drei Uhr.

Es ist Viertel nach sieben.

Es ist Viertel vor zehn.

Es ist ein Uhr. *or* Es ist eins.

Es ist elf (Minuten) nach
zehn.

Es ist vierzehn vor acht.

The half hour is counted in German in relation to the following full hour, not the
preceding hour as in English.

Es ist halb acht.
(literally) *It is halfway
to eight; that is, it is 7:30.*

Wieviel Uhr ist es?

„Wie spät ist es?" (Turmuhr
[*tower clock*] und Sonnenuhr
in Würzburg)

■ 21 ■ **Partnerarbeit: Wie spät ist es bitte?** Take turns asking each other for the time.

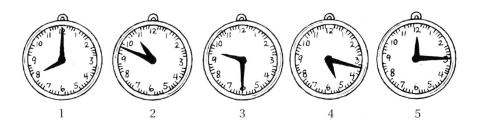

1   2   3   4   5

■ **Persönliche Fragen** (Personal questions)

Question words

| woher? | *from where?* (origin) |
| wo? | *where?* (location) |

When you meet people, you usually want to find out some basic facts about them, such as where they come from. Listen to the following dialogue and repeat it after your instructor.

Woher kommst du?
connotes *Where were you born?*

The only American states with separate German names are **Kalifornien** and **Pennsylvanien**, and states beginning with **Nord-** or **Süd-**, as in **Südkarolina**.

A: **Woher kommst du?**   *Where do you come from?*
B: **Ich komme aus Minnesota.**   *I come from Minnesota.*
A: **Wo wohnst du jetzt?**   *Where do you live now?*
B: **Ich wohne jetzt in Kalifornien.**   *I'm living in California now.*

kommen		*to come*	wohnen		*to live*
ich	komm**e**	*I come*	ich	wohn**e**	*I live*
du	komm**st**	*you come*	du	wohn**st**	*you live*
Sie	komm**en**		Sie	wohn**en**	
er	komm**t**	*he comes*	er	wohn**t**	*he lives*
sie	komm**t**	*she comes*	sie	wohn**t**	*she lives*

ihr

■ 22 ■ **Gruppenarbeit: Woher?** Walk around the classroom and find out what cities, states, or foreign countries your classmates are from. Your instructor can help you with the German names of other countries. Then find out where your classmates live, on campus or otherwise.

A: Woher kommst du?
B: Ich komme aus _____ .
A: Wo wohnst du jetzt?
B: Ich wohne in Davis Hall.

Question word

| wann? | *when?* |

Listen to the dialogue and repeat it after your instructor.

A: Wann hast du Geburtstag?   *When is your birthday?*
                                  (literally: *When do you have birthday?*)

B: Ich habe im Januar   *My birthday is in January.*
   Geburtstag.

haben		*to have*
ich	**habe**	*I have*
du	**hast**	*you have*
Sie	**haben**	
er	**hat**	*he has*
sie	**hat**	*she has*

Lab Manual
Einführung, The Months.

The stress is on the second syllable in **Apríl** and **Augúst**.

Die Monate (The months)

(der) im Januar	im Juli
im Februar	im August
im März	im September
im April	im Oktober
im Mai	im November
im Juni	im Dezember

■ 23 ■ **Kettenreaktion**   Find out in what months your classmates were born.

BEISPIEL: A: Wann hast du Geburtstag?
           B: Ich habe im _____ Geburtstag. Wann hast *du* Geburtstag?
           C: _____ .

Lab Manual
Einführung, Useful
Classroom Expressions.

■ Useful classroom expressions

Wie sagt man „the book" auf Deutsch?	*How do you say "the book" in German?*
Man sagt „das Buch".	*You say "das Buch."*
Übersetzen Sie bitte.	*Please translate.*
Wiederholen Sie bitte.	*Please repeat.*
Üben wir!	*Let's practice!*
Machen Sie Nummer drei, bitte.	*Please do number three.*
Alle zusammen, bitte.	*All together, please.*
Sie sprechen zu leise.	*You're speaking too softly.*
Sprechen Sie bitte lauter.	*Please speak more loudly.*
Sie sprechen zu schnell.	*You're speaking too fast.*
Sprechen Sie bitte langsamer.	*Please speak more slowly.*
Wie bitte?	*I beg your pardon? What did you say?*
Antworten Sie bitte auf Deutsch!	*Please answer in German.*
Das ist richtig.	*That's correct.*
Das ist falsch.	*That's incorrect.*
Verstehen Sie das?	*Do you understand that?*

This is useful classroom vocabulary. You need not memorize these expressions.

Wortschatz (Vocabulary)

The following list contains all the words and expressions from the **Einführung** that you need to know.

Greetings

Grüß Gott! Hello! (*in southern Germany and Austria*)
Guten Abend! Good evening!
Guten Morgen! Good morning!
Guten Tag! Hello!
Hallo! } Hi!
Tag!

Partings

Auf Wiedersehen! Good-bye!
Bis morgen. Until tomorrow.
Schönes Wochenende! Have a nice weekend!
Danke, gleichfalls! Thanks, same to you!
Tschüss! So long!

Days of the week

Montag Monday
Dienstag Tuesday
Mittwoch Wednesday
Donnerstag Thursday
Freitag Friday
Samstag/Sonnabend Saturday
Sonntag Sunday

Courtesy titles

Frau Mrs./Ms.
Fräulein Miss
Herr Mr.

Question words

wann? when?
was? what?

wer? who?
wie? how?
wie viele? how many?
wo? where?
woher? from where?

Personal questions, feelings, and emotions

Wie heißen Sie? / Wie heißt du? What's your name?
Wie geht es Ihnen? / Wie geht es dir? How are you?
Ich bin guter / schlechter Laune. I'm in a good / bad mood.
Ich bin munter / müde. I'm wide-awake, cheerful / tired.
   fit in good shape
   krank sick
   sauer ticked off, sore
Das freut mich. I'm glad.
Das tut mir Leid. I'm sorry.

Time and place

Wie spät ist es bitte? What time is it, please?
Woher kommst du? Where do you come from?
Wann hast du Geburtstag? When is your birthday?

Classroom words

der Lehrer, die Lehrerin (school) teacher
der Professor, die Professorin professor
der Schüler, die Schülerin pupil, student (*pre-college*)
der Student, die Studentin (university) student
der Bleistift pencil

der Kugelschreiber ballpoint pen
der Radiergummi rubber eraser
der Stuhl chair
der Tisch table
der Wischer blackboard eraser
das Buch book
das Fenster window
das Heft notebook
das Papier paper
das Poster poster
die Kreide chalk
die Landkarte map
die Tafel blackboard
die Tür door
die Uhr clock, watch
die Wand wall

Months of the year

Januar	**Juli**
Februar	**August**
März	**September**
April	**Oktober**
Mai	**November**
Juni	**Dezember**

The weather

Wie ist das Wetter heute? How's the weather today?
Es regnet / schneit. It's raining / snowing.
Es ist herrlich / furchtbar. It's great / terrible.
   heiß hot
   kalt cold
   kühl cool
   warm warm
   neblig foggy
   sonnig sunny
   windig windy
   wolkig cloudy

Profile of the Federal Republic of Germany

Area: 357,000 square kilometers; 138,000 square miles

Population: 82 million, or 230 people per square kilometer (595 per square mile)

Currency: Deutsche Mark; 1 DM = 100 Pfennige. By 2002, the euro will completely replace the Deutsche Mark. 1 euro = 1.955 DM

Major Cities: Berlin (largest city, official capital, pop. 3.5 million); Hamburg (pop. 1.7 million); Munich (pop. 1.2 million); Cologne (pop. 964,000); Frankfurt am Main (pop. 647,000); Stuttgart (pop. 585,000); Düsseldorf (pop. 571,000); Leipzig (pop. 500,000); Dresden (pop. 481,000); Bonn (pop. 298,000)

Religions: Protestant: 38%; Catholic: 34%; Muslim: 1.7%; unaffiliated: 26.3%.

In 1945 the victorious Allies divided defeated Germany into four zones of occupation: American, British, French, and Soviet. Their original intention was to denazify and reunite Germany. But by 1949 the ideological tensions of the Cold War led to the creation of two German states. The Federal Republic of Germany in the West and the German Democratic Republic in the East existed side by side for 41 years. The reunification of 1990 merged one of the most affluent capitalist countries with one of the most prosperous socialist countries from the Eastern bloc. The former GDR was divided into five new states (*Länder*) of the Federal Republic.

Today, the unified nation has an area slightly smaller than Montana. The Federal Republic is the most populous and economically one of the strongest countries in the European Union.

But the revolutionary changes in Germany are still difficult to assess. Forty years of state ownership and lack of competition left eastern Germany's industry obsolete and unable to compete in the Western marketplace. The infrastructure of the former GDR is being modernized and its industry privatized, a process that has caused inflation in the entire country and high rates of unemployment in the former East German workforce. Unification has thus come at a high price to German taxpayers. Germans east and west must continue to make economic sacrifices to resolve their differences and achieve genuine national unity.

Wie geht es Ihnen?

Communicative Goals

- Making statements
- Asking yes/no questions
- Asking for information: when, why, who, where, what, etc.

Cultural Goal

- Understanding the social implications of German forms of address

Chapter Outline

- **Lyrik zum Vorlesen**
  Kinderreime, Zungenbrecher

- **Grammatik**
  Personal pronouns
  Verbs: Infinitive and present tense
  Noun gender and pronoun agreement
  Noun plurals
  Nominative case
  The sentence: German word order
  The flavoring particle *ja*

- **Lesestück**
  Wie sagt man „you" auf Deutsch?

- **Situationen aus dem Alltag**
  Sie oder *du*?

- **Almanach**
  Where Is German Spoken?

In colloquial German **guten Morgen!,** **auf Wiedersehen!,** and **guten Tag!** are often shortened to **Morgen!,** **Wiedersehen!,** and **Tag!**

In Eile

HERR LEHMANN:	Guten Morgen, Frau Hauser!
FRAU HAUSER:	Morgen, Herr Lehmann. Entschuldigung, aber ich bin in Eile. Ich fliege um elf nach Wien.
HERR LEHMANN:	Wann kommen Sie wieder zurück?
FRAU HAUSER:	Am Mittwoch – also dann, auf Wiedersehen!
HERR LEHMANN:	Wiedersehen! Gute Reise!

Die Mensa

KARIN:	Tag, Michael!
MICHAEL:	Hallo, Karin! Wie ist die Suppe heute?
KARIN:	Sie ist ganz gut. – Übrigens, arbeitest du viel im Moment?
MICHAEL:	Nein, nicht sehr viel. Warum fragst du?
KARIN:	Ich gehe heute Abend zu Horst. Du auch?
MICHAEL:	Ja, natürlich.
KARIN:	Prima! Also tschüss, bis dann.

Typisch für September

FRAU BACHMANN:	Guten Tag, Frau Kuhn! Wie geht's?
FRAU KUHN:	Tag, Frau Bachmann! Sehr gut, danke, und Ihnen?
FRAU BACHMANN:	Danke, auch gut. Was machen die Kinder heute?
FRAU KUHN:	Sie spielen draußen, das Wetter ist ja so schön.
FRAU BACHMANN:	Ja, endlich scheint die Sonne. Aber vielleicht regnet es morgen wieder.
FRAU KUHN:	Das ist typisch für September.

„Wie ist die Suppe heute?"

Wortschatz 1 (Vocabulary 1)

Verben (Verbs)

arbeiten to work
fliegen to fly
fragen to ask
gehen to go; to walk
kommen to come
machen to make; to do
regnen to rain
scheinen to shine; to seem
sein to be
spielen to play
wohnen to live; to dwell

In this book, nouns are grouped by gender for easier learning. Always learn the article and the plural along with the singular of each noun. Don't just learn **Kind** = *child*, but rather **das Kind, die Kinder**.

Substantive (Nouns)

der **Herr, -en** gentleman
   Herr Lehmann Mr. Lehmann
der **Morgen, -** morning
der **September** September
der **Tag, -e** day

das **Büro, -s** office
das **Kind, -er** child
das **Wetter** weather
(das)**Wien** Vienna

die **Frau, -en** woman; wife
   Frau Kuhn Mrs./Ms. Kuhn
die **Mensa** university cafeteria
die **Sonne** sun
die **Straße, -n** street, road
die **Suppe, -n** soup

City names are neuter in German but are seldom used with the article. In such cases, the article is given in parentheses in the **Wortschatz**.

Nachnomen
Vornamen

Adjektive und Adverbien (Adjectives and adverbs)

auch also, too
da there
dann then
draußen outside
endlich finally
gut good; well
   ganz gut pretty good; pretty well
heute Abend this evening, tonight
hier here
morgen tomorrow
natürlich natural(ly); of course
schön beautiful(ly)
sehr very
typisch typical(ly)
vielleicht maybe, perhaps
wieder again

German has no equivalent for the English adverbial ending -*ly*. For example, the German word **natürlich** can mean both *natural* and *naturally* (similarly, **gut** means both *good* and *well*).

Andere Vokabeln (Other words)

aber but *(as)*
also well
bis until; by
   bis dann until then; by then
danke thanks
für for
in in
ja yes; *untranslatable "flavoring particle," see p. 36.*
nach to (*with cities and countries*)
nein no
nicht not
übrigens by the way
um (*prep.*) at (*with expressions of time*)
und (*conj.*) and
usw. (= **und so weiter**) etc. (= and so forth)

There is a complete list of abbreviations on p. 373.

viel (*pron.*) much, a lot
warum? why?
wie (*conj.*) how; like, as
zu (*prep.*) to (*with people*); too (*as in* "too much")
zurück back

Nützliche Ausdrücke (Useful expressions)

am Mittwoch (Donnerstag usw.) on Wednesday (Thursday, etc.)
→ **Entschuldigung!** Pardon me! Excuse me!
Gute Reise! (Have a) good trip!
im Moment at the moment
in Eile in a hurry
Prima! Terrific! Great!

Gegensätze (Opposites)

gut ≠ schlecht good ≠ bad
hier ≠ da here ≠ there
schön ≠ hässlich beautiful ≠ ugly
der Tag ≠ die Nacht day ≠ night
viel ≠ wenig much, a lot ≠ not much, little

Study hint: learn antonyms in pairs. They are all active vocabulary.

Mit anderen Worten (In other words)

prima = sehr gut
wunderschön = sehr schön

ausgezeichnet = exc.
sehr gut
so la la
nicht besonders gut
   (particularly)
schlecht
aberscheidt

In a Hurry

MR. L: Good morning, Ms. Hauser.
MS. H: Morning, Mr. Lehmann.
Entschuldigung Forgive me, but I'm in a hurry. I'm flying to Vienna at eleven.
MR. L: When are you coming back again?
MS. H: On Wednesday. Well then, good-bye.
MR. L: Bye. Have a good trip!

English translations are idiomatic, not always word-for-word.

The University Cafeteria

K: Hi, Michael!
M: Hello, Karin! How's the soup today? _übrigens_
K: It's pretty good. By the way, are you working a lot at the moment? _ganz_
M: No, not very much. Why do you ask?
K: I'm going to Horst's tonight. You too?
M: Yes, of course. _natürlich_
K: Great! Well, so long until then.

Typical for September

MRS. B: Hello, Mrs. Kuhn. How are you?
MRS. K: Hi, Mrs. Bachmann. Very well, thanks, and you?
MRS. B: Thanks, I'm fine too. What are the kids doing today?
MRS. K: They're playing outside—the weather is so nice. _draußen_
MRS. B: Yes, the sun is finally shining. But maybe it will rain again tomorrow.
MRS. K: That is typical for September.

Variationen (Variations)

■ A ■ Persönliche Fragen   (Personal questions)

1. Wo wohnen Sie?
2. Wie geht es Ihnen heute?
3. Arbeiten Sie viel im Moment?
4. Was machen Sie heute Abend?

Asking for information is a communicative goal.

■ B ■ Partnerarbeit   (Work with a partner)   Now ask each other the same questions as in **Variation A**. Use the **du**-form.

■ C ■ Partnerarbeit: Wann fliegst du?   The clock faces show departure times from the Frankfurt airport. Ask each other when you're flying to various places.

BEISPIEL: Wann fliegst du nach Sydney?
Ich fliege um halb acht. _nach Prague, etc._

1. nach Prag

2. nach Moskau

3. nach Kopenhagen

4. nach Madrid

5. nach Toronto

6. nach Singapur

■ **D** ■ **Übung** (Exercise)   Respond to these greetings and farewells.

1. Guten Morgen!
2. Wie geht es Ihnen?
3. Guten Tag!
4. Auf Wiedersehen!
5. Gute Reise!

6. Tschüss, bis dann.
7. Tag!
8. Hallo!
9. Schönes Wochenende!

■ **E** ■ **Übung: Und Sie?**   To each question, respond that you feel the same way.

BEISPIEL: Richard ist heute guter Laune. Und Sie?
Ja, *er* ist guter Laune und *ich* bin es auch.

1. Maria ist fit. Und Sie?
2. Herr Schrödinger ist krank. Und Sie?
3. Frau Bachmann ist munter. Und Sie?   *wide awake*
4. Christian ist guter Laune. Und Sie?
5. Wir sind schlechter Laune. Und Sie?   *Sie sind*
6. Ich bin heute sauer. Und Sie?

outdoor
alles für draußen

Lyrik zum Vorlesen   (Poetry for reading aloud)

In each chapter this section presents some short selections of original German poetry (**Lyrik**), rhymes, or song texts for your enjoyment. Read them aloud. Don't worry about understanding everything. The emphasis here is on the *sound* of German.

Lab Manual Kap. 1, Lyrik zum Vorlesen.

Kinderreime   (Children's rhymes)
Traditional counting-out rhymes

Eins zwei drei,
du bist frei°.   free
Vier fünf sechs,
du bist weg°.   out
Sieben acht neun,
du musst's sein°.   you are it

Ich heiße Peter, du heißt Paul.
Ich bin fleißig°, du bist faul°.   hard-working / lazy

Children's alphabet rhyme

A b c d e f und g,
h i j k l m n o p,
q r s t u v w,
x y z und o weh°,
jetzt kann ich das ABC°.

o weh = oh my
now I know the ABC

Zungenbrecher°

Tongue twisters

In Ulm, um Ulm°
und um Ulm herum°.

In Ulm, around Ulm,
and round about Ulm.

Fischers Fritz fischt frische Fische.
frische Fische fischt Fischers Fritz°.

Fischer's (boy) Fritz fishes fresh fish.
Fresh fish is what Fischer's Fritz fishes.

Ulm lies on the Danube River in the southern state of Baden-Württemberg. Its famous Gothic church has the highest spire in the world at 161.6 meters (530 ft.).

Grammatik

(Grammar)

Personal pronouns

Personal pronouns as the subject of a sentence:

	Singular			Plural	
1st person	**ich**	*I*		**wir**	*we*
2nd person	**du**	*you* (familiar)		**ihr**	*you* (familiar)
	Sie	*you* (formal)		**Sie**	*you* (formal)
3rd person	**er**	*he, it*			
	es	*it*		**sie**	*they*
	sie	*she, it*			

„Tag, Frau Breitenkamp! Wie geht es Ihnen?"

■ The three ways to say *you* in German

Understanding the social implications of German forms of address is the cultural goal of this chapter.

German has three words for the subject pronoun *you*: **du**, **ihr**, and **Sie**.

The familiar pronouns **du** (*singular*) and **ihr** (*plural*) are used when addressing children, family members, close friends, animals, and the deity. Members of certain groups (students, blue-collar workers, soldiers, athletes) converse among themselves almost exclusively with **du** and **ihr**. People on a first-name basis usually use **du** with each other. In conversation with German speakers, allow them to establish which form is used.

The formal **Sie** is used when addressing one or more adults who are not close friends of the speaker. In writing, **Sie** meaning *you* is distinguished from **sie** meaning *they* by always beginning with a capital letter.

The pronoun **ich** is not capitalized except when it is the first word in a sentence.

Verbs: Infinitive and present tense

■ The infinitive

German verbs are found in a dictionary in the infinitive form. In English the infinitive is usually preceded by *to*.

to play   *to hike*

In German, the infinitive consists of the verb stem plus the ending **-en** or **-n**.

spiel-	**spielen**	*to play*
wander-	**wandern**	*to hike*

■ Present-tense endings

A German verb has various endings in the present tense, depending on its subject.

Das Kind spiel**t** draußen.	*The child plays outside.*
Die Kinder spiel**en** draußen.	*The children play outside.*

In order to form the present tense of a German verb, first find the stem by dropping the infinitive ending **-en** or **-n**:

komm- ~~en~~

Then add the personal endings:

Stem + Ending		Present Tense		
ich	komm-**e**	ich	komme	*I come*
du	komm-**st**	du	kommst	*you come* (familiar singular)
er, es, sie	komm-**t**	er, es, sie	kommt	*he, it, she comes*
wir	komm-**en**	wir	kommen	*we come*
ihr	komm-**t**	ihr	kommt	*you come* (familiar plural)
sie, Sie	komm-**en**	sie	kommen	*they come*
		Sie	kommen	*you come* (formal singular and plural)

The verb ending will help you distinguish between **sie** = *she* (**sie kommt**) and **sie**, **Sie** = *they*, *you* (**sie**, **Sie kommen**). The verb ending for third-person plural and the polite *you*-form is always the same. From now on they will be listed together in verb paradigms: **sie**, **Sie kommen**.

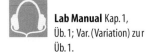

Lab Manual Kap. 1, Üb. 1; Var. (Variation) zur Üb. 1.

Workbook Kap. 1, A.

exercise

■ 1 ■ **Übung: Wer kommt morgen?**   Say who is coming tomorrow, using the pronouns cued.

BEISPIEL: ich
Ich komme morgen.

1. er
2. Sie (*you*)
3. wir
4. sie (*they*)
5. sie (*she*)
6. du
7. ich
8. ihr

chain reaction

■ 2 ■ **Kettenreaktion: Wo wohnst du?**   Say where you live and then ask the next student.

BEISPIEL: Ich wohne in Atlanta. Wo wohnst du?
Ich wohne in _____ .

■ Regular variations in personal endings

Verbs with stems ending in **-d**, **-t**, or a consonant cluster such as **-gn** require an **-e-** before the **du**, **er**, and **ihr** endings to make them pronounceable.

arbeiten	stem: arbeit-			regnen	stem: regn-
ich	arbeite	wir	arbeiten		
du	arbeit**est**	ihr	arbeit**et**		es regn**et**
er, es, sie	arbeit**et**	sie, Sie	arbeiten		

■ 3 ■ **Übung: Wer arbeitet heute?** Tell who is working today, using the cued pronoun or name.

> BEISPIEL: wir
>
> Wir arbeiten heute.

1. ich
2. Herr Lehmann
3. sie (*they*)
4. du

5. ihr
6. Sie (*you*)
7. wir
8. Michael

■ 4 ■ **Gruppenarbeit: Was machst du heute?** (*4 Studenten*) Ask each other what you're doing today.

> A: Was machst du heute, Katrin?
> B: Ich fliege nach Wien. Was machst du heute?
> C: Ich _____ . Was machst du heute?

■ English and German present tense compared

German present tense is equivalent to three English forms:

$$\text{ich gehe} \begin{cases} \textit{I go} \\ \textit{I am going} \\ \textit{I do go} \end{cases}$$

du gehst
er geht
wir gehen
ihr geht
Sie gehen

■ Present tense with future meaning

In German the present tense often expresses future meaning, especially when another element in the sentence makes the future meaning clear.

> Ich fliege um elf nach Wien.   *I'm flying to Vienna at eleven.*
> Mittwoch bin ich wieder   *I'll be back Wednesday.*
>   zurück.

Note that English often uses the present progressive (*I'm flying*) for the same purpose.

■ The verb *sein*

Like *to be* in English, the verb **sein** is irregular; its forms must be memorized.

ich	**bin**	*I am*		wir	**sind**	*we are*
du	**bist**	*you are*		ihr	**seid**	*you are*
er, es, sie	**ist**	*he, it, she is*		sie, Sie	**sind**	*they, you are*

Prima leben und sparen

Noun gender and pronoun agreement

You have learned that German has three genders for nouns, shown by the definite article (**der**, **das**, **die**). When a pronoun replaces a noun (*the chair = it*), it must have the same gender.

Wo ist **der** Stuhl?	**Er** ist hier.	*It's here.*
Wo ist **das** Buch?	**Es** ist hier.	*It's here.*
Wo ist **die** Tafel?	**Sie** ist hier.	*It's here.*

Note that **er**, **es**, and **sie** can all mean *it*.

Note also the similarities between the definite article and its corresponding pronoun.

d**er** Stuhl → **er**
da**s** Buch → e**s**
die Tafel → s**ie**

Plural forms do not show gender. The definite article **die** is used with all plural nouns, and the pronoun **sie** replaces all plural nouns.

Wo sind **die** Stühle?
Wo sind **die** Bücher?   **Sie** sind hier.   *They are here.*
Wo sind **die** Tafeln?

Lab Manual Kap. 1, Üb. 5; Var. zur Üb. 5.

Workbook Kap. 1, B–D.

■ 5 ■ Übung   Answer the questions affirmatively. Use a pronoun.

BEISPIEL: Ist Rolf heute guter Laune?   *of good mood (gen.)*
   Ja, er ist heute guter Laune.

1. Ist das Buch gut?
2. Ist Frau Schmidt sehr müde?
3. Spielen die Kinder draußen?
4. Ist das Wetter typisch für September?
5. Scheint die Sonne heute?
6. Sind Karin und Michael Studenten?
7. Ist die Suppe gut?
8. Ist der Tag schön?

■ 6 ■ Partnerarbeit: Hier oder da?   Partner A asks where the things in the left-hand column are. Partner B answers with the correct pronoun, pointing to the object. Reverse roles for the right-hand column.

BEISPIEL: A: Wo ist die Tafel?
    B: Sie ist da.

das Buch	der Radiergummi
das Heft	das Fenster
die Tür	der Professor/die Professorin
der Bleistift	der Tisch
die Wand	der Stuhl
die Landkarte	das Poster

Here are the nouns you learned in the
→ **Einführung** with their plurals:
der Lehrer, - / die Lehrerin, -nen
der Professor, -en / die Professorin,
    -nen
der Schüler, - / die Schülerin, -nen
der Student, -en / die Studentin, -nen
der Bleistift, -e
das Buch, ⸚er
das Fenster, -
das Heft, -e
der Kugelschreiber, -
das Poster, -
der Stuhl, ⸚e
die Tafel, -n
der Tisch, -e
die Tür, -en
die Uhr, -en
die Wand, ⸚e
    Landkarte

Noun plurals

The most common plural ending for English nouns is -s or -es: chair, chairs; dish, dishes. Some nouns have irregular plurals: man, *men*; mouse, *mice*; child, *children*; sheep, *sheep*.

German has a much greater variety of plural forms. There is no one basic rule, nor is any one form the most common. The following list gives examples of all the plural forms.

	Singular	Plural
No change	der Lehrer	die Lehrer
Umlaut added to stem vowel	die Mutter	die Mütter
Add ending **-e**	der Tisch	die Tische
Umlaut + ending **-e**	der Stuhl	die Stühle
Add ending **-er**	das Kind	die Kinder
Umlaut + ending **-er**	das Buch	die Bücher
Add ending **-en**	die Frau	die Frauen
Add ending **-n**	die Straße	die Straßen
Add ending **-s**	das Büro	die Büros

Dictionaries and vocabulary lists customarily use an abbreviation to indicate the plural. An umlaut above the hyphen indicates that the stem (stressed) vowel is umlauted in the plural.

Dictionary entry	You must learn
der **Lehrer, -**	der **Lehrer**, die **Lehrer**
die **Mutter, ⸚**	die **Mutter**, die **Mütter**
der **Tag, -e**	der **Tag**, die **Tage**
der **Stuhl, ⸚e**	der **Stuhl**, die **Stühle**

Lab Manual Kap. 1, Üb. 7, 8.

Workbook Kap. 1, E.

■ 7 ■ Übung Look at the following nouns and say aloud both the singular and plural forms with their articles.

1. das Kind, -er
2. das Büro, -s
3. der Tisch, -e
4. die Mutter, ⸚
5. die Tafel, -n
6. die Straße, -n
7. der Stuhl, ⸚e
8. die Frau, -en

Turn to the German–English Vocabulary at end of book, pp. 373–391, for more practice with plurals.

■ 8 ■ Übung Make the subjects plural. Change the verbs accordingly.

DAS **BEISPIEL:** *Der Herr kommt* um elf.
       Die Herren kommen um elf.

1. Das Büro ist sehr schön.
2. Die Frau fliegt nach Wien.
3. Das Kind kommt heute Abend.
4. Die Straße ist sehr schön.
5. Das Buch ist gut.
6. Der Lehrer arbeitet morgen im Büro.
7. Der Tag ist schön.

Nominative case

The definite article in German, unlike English *the*, shows the *gender* (masculine, neuter, or feminine), *number* (singular or plural), and *case* of the noun it is used with. As a result, German has many forms that all correspond to *the* in English.

The case of a noun or a pronoun signals its function in the sentence. German has four cases: nominative, accusative, dative, and genitive. The article used with the noun shows its case.

Der Schüler fragt den Lehrer.   *The pupil asks the teacher.*
Der Lehrer fragt **den** Schüler.   *The teacher asks the pupil.*

Nominative case		*Accusative case*
der Schüler		**den** Schüler
subject	vs.	*direct object*
person asking		*person being asked*

This chapter uses only the nominative case, which is the case for the subject of a sentence and for a predicate nominative (see page 33).

■ Definite article in the nominative case

You have already learned the definite articles (*the*) in the nominative:

	Singular	*Plural*
masculine	**der** Mann	**die** Männer
neuter	**das** Kind	**die** Kinder
feminine	**die** Frau	**die** Frauen

■ Indefinite article in the nominative case

Like the definite article, the indefinite article (*a, an*) shows the gender, number, and case of the noun it is used with. Here are the indefinite articles in the nominative:

	Singular	*Plural*
masculine	**ein** Mann	Männer
neuter	**ein** Kind	Kinder
feminine	**eine** Frau	Frauen

Note: Masculine and neuter singular indefinite articles are identical in the nominative: **ein** Mann, **ein** Kind. The indefinite article has no plural:

Ein Kind ist hier. → Kinder sind hier.

The personal pronouns you have learned in this chapter (**ich**, **du**, *etc.*) are all in the nominative case.

■ 9 ■   **Übung: Was ist das?**   Say what your instructor is pointing to. Use the indefinite article.

     BEISPIEL: PROFESSORIN: Was ist das?
                STUDENTIN: Das ist **ein** Fenster.

■ Use of the nominative case

The subject of the sentence is always in the nominative case. Notice that the subject does not have to come at the beginning of the sentence.

Der Herr ist in Eile.	*The gentleman is in a hurry.*
Endlich kommt **die Suppe**.	*The soup is finally coming.*
Morgen fliegt **sie** zurück.	*She's flying back tomorrow.*

Other linking verbs (**bleiben** *to remain;* **heißen** *to be called;* **werden** *to become*) also take the predicate nominative. You will learn them later.

A predicate nominative is a noun that refers to the same person or thing as the subject of the sentence. It follows the subject and the linking verb **sein**.

Das ist **Frau Schmidt**.	*That is Mrs. Schmidt.*
Paul ist **ein Kind**.	*Paul is a child.*

Remember to always use nominative case after the verb **sein**.

Lab Manual Kap. 1, Var. zur Üb. 10.

Workbook Kap. 1, F.

■ 10 ■ **Gruppenspiel** (Group game)**: Was ist das? Wer ist das?** One student leads the game. The rest are divided into two teams. The leader points to an object or a person in the room and asks:

Wer/Was ist das?
Das ist ein(e)/der/das/die _____.

Teams answer alternately. The team with the most correct answers wins.

The sentence: German word order

Making statements is a communicative goal.

■ Statements: Verb-second word order

In declarative sentences (statements) in English, the subject almost always comes immediately before the verb phrase.

subject verb
We are going to Richard's tonight.

Other elements may precede the subject-verb combination:

Tonight **we are going** to Richard's.

In German statements, only the verb has a fixed position. *The verb is always the second element.*

1	2	3	4
Wir	**gehen**	heute Abend	zu Richard.

This is an ironclad rule that must be learned well. If an element other than the subject begins the sentence, the verb *remains* in second position and the subject then *follows* the verb. Note the difference from English, where the subject always precedes the verb.

1	2	3	4
Heute Abend	**gehen**	wir	zu Richard.
Zu Richard	**gehen**	wir	heute Abend.

A time phrase (**heute Abend**) or a prepositional phrase (**zu Richard**) may consist of two or more words, but counts as *one* grammatical element.

Initial **ja**, **nein**, **und**, and **aber** do *not* count as first elements.

0	1	2	3
Ja,	wir	gehen	zu Richard.
Aber	wir	gehen	zu Richard.

First position is generally used to restate what's being talked about. A new element with information value—the answer to a question, for instance—is usually placed at the end of the statement.

Was machen wir?	Wir gehen **zu Claudia**.
Was machen wir heute Abend?	Heute Abend **gehen wir zu Claudia**.
Wann gehen wir zu Claudia?	Zu Claudia gehen wir **heute Abend**.

Workbook Kap. 1, G.

■ 11 ■ **Übung** Restate the sentences, beginning with the word or phrase in italics.

> **BEISPIEL:** Ich arbeite *übrigens* viel. *by the way*
> *Übrigens* arbeite ich viel.

1. Die Lehrerin geht *morgen* zu Frau Bachmann.
2. Die Sonne scheint *endlich* wieder.
3. Es regnet *heute*.
4. Wir fliegen *um elf* nach Wien.
5. Das ist *vielleicht* die Straße.
6. Ich arbeite viel *im Moment*.
7. Die Suppe ist *heute* ganz gut.
8. Es regnet *natürlich* viel.

■ Questions

Asking yes/no questions and asking for information are communicative goals.

There are two main types of questions in German:

- Yes/no questions are answered by **ja** or **nein**. In a yes/no question, the verb is always the first element.

Ist Andrea hier?	*Is Andrea here?*
Arbeitet sie in Berlin?	*Does she work in Berlin?*
Kommst du wieder zurück?	*Are you coming back again?*

- Questions asking for information start with a question word (*what, how, when, etc.*) and have the same verb-second word order as statements.

1	2		
Was	macht	er?	*What is he doing?*
Wie	geht	es Ihnen?	*How are you?*
Wann	kommen	Sie wieder zurück?	*When are you coming back again?*

Here are some question words:

Wohin is introduced in Kap. 3.

wann	*when*	**Wann** kommt sie zurück?
warum	*why*	**Warum** fragst du?
was	*what*	**Was** macht er?
wer	*who*	**Wer** ist das?
wie	*how*	**Wie** geht es dir?
wo	*where*	**Wo** wohnen Sie?
woher	*from where*	**Woher** kommt ihr?

Do not confuse **wer** (*who*) and **wo** (*where*)!

Lab Manual Kap. 1, Üb. 12.

Workbook Kap. 1, H, I.

■ **12** ■ **Übung** Change these statements to yes/no questions.

BEISPIEL: Stefan arbeitet in Stuttgart.
Arbeitet Stefan in Stuttgart?

1. Das ist typisch für September.
2. Ihr geht wieder zu Karin.
3. Es regnet.
4. Herr Hauser fliegt nach Berlin.
5. Frau Kuhn kommt auch.
6. Du arbeitest viel im Moment.
7. Er ist sehr in Eile.
8. Der Herr kommt am Mittwoch zurück.

■ **13** ■ **Übung** Ask the questions for which the following statements are answers:

BEISPIEL: Das ist der Professor.
Wer ist das?

1. Er fliegt um elf.
2. Die Lehrer sind im Büro.
3. Das ist Frau Bachmann.

4. Das ist die Mensa.
5. Die Suppe ist gut, danke.
6. Sie kommt aus Deutschland. *woher kommt sie?*

■ **Time before place**

In German, adverbs like **heute** and adverbial phrases like **nach Wien** *must* come in the sequence *time before place*. The usual sequence in English is exactly the reverse: *place before time*.

	time	place		place	time
Sie fliegt	morgen	nach Wien.	*She's flying to*	*Vienna*	*tomorrow.*
Wir gehen	heute Abend	zu Horst.	*We're going to*	*Horst's*	*tonight.*

■ 14 ■ **Übung: Heute oder morgen?** Answer with a complete sentence, using either **heute** or **morgen**. *adverbs (no caps)*

> **BEISPIEL:** Wann gehen Sie zu Stefanie?
> Ich gehe heute zu Stefanie.

1. Wann fliegt Stefan nach Wien?
2. Wann geht Frau Bachmann zu Frau Kuhn?
3. Wann spielen die Kinder draußen?
4. Wann kommt Herr Lehmann zurück?

The flavoring particle ja

German adds various kinds of emphasis to sentences by using intensifying words known as "flavoring particles." These can seldom be directly translated into English, but it is important to become familiar with them and understand the intensity, nuance, or "flavor" they add to a sentence.

One flavoring particle frequently used in declarative sentences (i.e., statements) is **ja**. As a flavoring particle, **ja** does not mean *yes*, but rather adds the sense of *after all, really*.

In the third dialogue at the beginning of this chapter, Frau Kuhn says about her children:

> Sie spielen draußen, das Wetter ist **ja** so schön.
>
> *They're playing outside—the weather really is so beautiful.*

The flavoring particle **ja** is usually placed immediately after the verb and personal pronouns. Here is how **ja** might be added to some other sentences from the dialogues:

> Ich bin **ja** in Eile.
> Ich gehe **ja** heute Abend zu Horst.
>
> *I'm in a hurry, after all.*
> *I'm going to Horst's tonight, you know.*

Lesestück

Vor dem Lesen (Before the reading)

Tipps zum Lesen und Lernen (Tips for reading and studying)

■ **Tipps zum Vokabelnlernen** (Tips for learning vocabulary)

The feminine suffix -in You've learned that German has two different nouns to distinguish between a male and a female.

Professor/Professorin	Lehrer/Lehrerin
Schüler/Schülerin	Partner/Partnerin
Student/Studentin	

The suffix **-in** always denotes the female, and its plural is always **-innen**.

-in	*-innen*
die Studentin	die Studentinnen

■ ■ ■ **Partnerarbeit: Wie heißt der Mann, wie heißt die Frau?** With a partner, fill in the blanks. Say the words aloud as you write them.

Mann	*eine Frau?*	*zwei Frauen?*
1. Amerikaner	*Amerikanerin*	*Amerikanerinnen*
2. Tourist	Touristin	Touristinnen
3. Nachbar (*neighbor*)	Nachbarin	innen
4. Lehrer	Lehrerin	
5. Professor	Professorin	
6. Schüler	Schülerin	
7. Student	Studentin	
8. Partner	Partnerin	

Note the stress shift: **Profes'sor / Professo'rin.**

Lab Manual Kap. 1, Üb. zur Betonung.

■ **Leicht zu merken** (Easy to remember)

German has many words that look so much like their English equivalents that you can easily guess their meanings. Both languages have borrowed many of these words from Latin or French. When such words occur in the readings, they are previewed in this special section called **Leicht zu merken**. If the German word is stressed on a different syllable than the English, this will be indicated to the right. You should have no trouble guessing the meanings of these cognates:

formell	formell
die **Solidarität**	Solidarität
der **Tourist**	Tourist

These pre-reading exercises help you to acquire the skill of reading a text in a foreign language. Always work through them carefully before beginning to read the **Lesestück**. The most valuable technique is *re*-reading a foreign language text as many times as possible.

■ **Einstieg in den Text**   (Getting into the text)

Here are some tips to help you get the most out of the reading (**Lesestück**) in each chapter.

- Read the title. How does it anticipate the text? The title "Wie sagt man *you* auf Deutsch?," for example, lets you know that the text is about the various forms of second-person address. You have already used these.

- Read out loud the new active vocabulary for the reading (**Wortschatz 2**). Try to identify similarities between English and German forms that will help you remember the words; for example, **grüßen** (*greet*), **Haus** (*house*), **Gruppe** (*group*); **freundlich** (*friendly*), **oft** (*often*).

- Read the text once aloud without referring back to the vocabulary. Do not try to translate as you read. Your purpose is to get a rough idea of content from the key words you recognize in each paragraph. For example, in the first paragraph of the following reading, you will recognize the words **Touristen**, **Deutschland**, and **Amerikaner**. A good working assumption is that the paragraph deals with tourists in Germany.

- Once you have a general idea of the content of each paragraph, read the text at least one more time, again without trying to translate. Your objective this time is to begin to understand the text on the sentence level. The marginal glosses (marked by the degree sign°) will help you to understand words and phrases not for active use.

- Read and try to answer the **Nach dem Lesen** questions that follow the reading. Refer back to the text only if necessary.

200.000 Bücher ** über Nacht
schwarz auf weiß
BUCHHANDLUNG
24-Stunden-Bestellservice: Telefon 0511/452 453
Montag-Freitag 10-13 und 15-18 Uhr, Samstag 10-13 Uhr, Lindener Marktplatz 5, 30449 Hannover, Telefon 0511/452 453

Wortschatz 2

Verben

bedeuten to mean, signify
  Was bedeutet das? What does
    that mean?
duzen to address someone
  with **du**
grüßen to greet, say hello
meinen to be of the opinion,
  think
sagen to say; to tell
siezen to address someone
  with **Sie**
(stimmen) das stimmt that's right,
  that's true
studieren to attend a university; to
  study (*a subject*); to major in

Substantive

der **Amerikaner, -** American
  (*m.*)
der **Deutsche, -n** German (*m.*)

Note the abbreviations *m.* (for *masculine*) or *f.* (for
feminine) after **Amerikaner**, **Deutsche**, and other
nouns. There is a complete list of abbreviations on
p. 373.

der **Schüler, -** primary or secondary school pupil (*m.*)
der **Student, -en** university
  student (*m.*)
der **Tourist, -en** tourist (*m.*)

(das) **Deutschland** Germany
das **Haus, ⸚er** house

die **Amerikanerin, -nen**
  American (*f.*)
die **Deutsche, -n** German (*f.*)
die **Gruppe, -n** group
die **Klasse, -n** class; grade
die **Schule, -n** school
die **Schülerin, -nen** primary or
  secondary school pupil (*f.*)
die **Studentin, -nen** university
  student (*f.*)
die **Touristin, -nen** tourist (*f.*)

Note the plural form of **Haus—Häuser**: the first
vowel of a diphthong is umlauted.

Adjektive und Adverbien

freundlich friendly
höflich polite(ly)
immer always

oft often
so so; like this
viele many
wahrscheinlich probably
ziemlich fairly, quite

Andere Vokabeln

einander (*pron.*) each other
man one (*indefinite pronoun*)
miteinander with each other
oder (*conj.*) or
zueinander to each other

Note on **man**: This pronoun is often best translated
with *we, you, or they*: **Das sagt man oft.** = *They
(people) often say that.* See p. 78 for a complete
explanation.

Nützliche Ausdrücke

zum Beispiel for example
auf Deutsch in German

Gegensätze

immer ≠ nie always ≠ never
oft ≠ selten often ≠ seldom

Wie sagt man „you" auf Deutsch?

Lab Manual Kap. 1,
Lesestück.

Touristen in Deutschland sagen oft, die Deutschen sind sehr freundlich und höflich. *[polite]*
Das stimmt, aber wahrscheinlich meinen viele Amerikaner auch, die Deutschen sind *[verb] [rather]*
ziemlich formell.

    Frau Bachmann und Frau Kuhn sind zum Beispiel Nachbarinnen°. Sie wohnen im   neighbors
5 selben° Haus und sind auch miteinander befreundet°, aber Frau Bachmann fragt   **im selben** = in the same / on
nicht: „Wie geht es dir, Gisela?" Nein, sie sagt: „Wie geht es Ihnen, Frau Kuhn?" Sie   friendly terms
grüßen einander formell.

    Wie ist es in der Schule? In allen° Klassen – von Klasse eins bis Klasse dreizehn –   all
duzen die Lehrer ihre° Schüler. Die Schüler siezen die Lehrer natürlich immer.   their

10   Das Du ist auch ein Ausdruck der° Solidarität. Für die Studenten bedeutet es: Wir   **Ausdruck der** = expression of
sind eine Gruppe. Karin und Michael, zum Beispiel, studieren.[1] Sie sagen von Anfang   **von** ... = from the beginning
an° „du" zueinander. *[study at university]*

In **Kapitel 5** you will learn why line 8
reads **in der Schule** even though
Schule is feminine.

---

1. Note that **studieren** means to attend college or university and is not used to describe a student's daily activity of studying. Thus, *I'm studying* (i.e., doing homework) *tonight* is translated as
Ich *arbeite* **heute Abend,** or **Ich** *lerne* **heute Abend.**

Diese Studenten sagen „du"
zueinander.

Nach dem Lesen   (After the reading)

■ A ■   Richtig oder falsch?   (True or false?)

1. Lehrer duzen die Schüler bis Klasse zehn.   *13 Studenten*
2. Karin und Michael sind Schüler.
3. Frau Kuhn und Frau Bachmann sagen „du" zueinander.   *Nein*

■ B ■   Antworten Sie auf Deutsch.   (Answer in German.)

1. Was meinen Touristen: Wie sind die Deutschen?
2. Duzen die Schüler die Lehrer in Deutschland?
3. Siezt Karin Michael?
4. Was bedeutet das Du für Studenten?   *mean*

■ C ■   Was sagt man?   (What do you say?)   Sie sind Student oder Studentin. Zu
wem (*to whom*) sagen Sie „Sie", zu wem sagen Sie „du"?

Lab Manual Kap. 1,
Diktat.

Workbook Kap. 1, J–N.

Situationen aus dem Alltag

(Situations from everyday life)

■ ■ ■ **Partnerarbeit:** *Sie* oder *du*?

Frau Professor   Herr Kuhn   Karoline und   Niklas Schuhmacher
Ullman   Dieter Flessner

1. Take turns asking the people pictured
   a. what their names are.
   b. whether they're working at the moment.
   c. whether they're tired today.   *müde*
   d. where they live.
   e. where they work.

2. Partner A plays one of the people pictured above and responds to Partner B's
   questions. Then Partner B plays another of these people and answers Partner A's
   questions.

   BEISPIEL: A: Wo wohnen Sie, Herr Kuhn?
                 B: Ich wohne in Wien.

3. Now ask each other three personalized questions using the **du**-form.

Mit Inter Rail eröffnen sich neue Horizonte.

Almanach

Where is German Spoken?

German is the language of the Federal Republic of Germany, Austria, Liechtenstein, and portions of Switzerland, Luxembourg, the South Tyrol in northern Italy (until 1919 part of Austria), and Belgium. Linguistic enclaves of German speakers in the U.S.A. (notably the Amish in Pennsylvania), Canada, Brazil, Africa (especially in Namibia, once the German colony of South West Africa), and Australia bring the number of native German speakers to around 121 million. In 1993, 20 million people were studying German as a second language. Of these, 13 million were eastern Europeans.

The following statistics on the world's major languages include both native and second-language speakers in 1994. Notice that the names of almost all languages in German end with **-sch**.

Chinesisch	1 Milliarde 18 Millionen	**eine Milliarde** = (American) *billion;*
Englisch	470 Millionen	**eine Billion** = (American) *trillion.*
Hindustani	418 Millionen	
Spanisch	401 Millionen	
Russisch	288 Millionen	
Arabisch	219 Millionen	
Portugiesisch	182 Millionen	
Japanisch	126 Millionen	
Französisch	124 Millionen	
Deutsch	121 Millionen	
Italienisch	63 Millionen	

Familie und Freunde

Communicative Goals

- Talking about the family
- Saying what belongs to whom
- Counting above 20

Cultural Goal

- Learning about German family life

Chapter Outline

- **Lyrik zum Vorlesen**
  „Du bist mein"

- **Grammatik**
  The accusative case
  More on verbs in the present tense
  Possessive adjectives
  Cardinal numbers above 20

- **Lesestück**
  Die Familie heute

- **Situationen aus dem Alltag**
  Die Familie

- **Almanach**
  Die ganze Familie

Dialoge

Lab Manual Kap. 2, Dialoge, Fragen, Hören Sie gut zu!, Üb. zur Aussprache [z/s].

Listen carefully to the tapes and your instructor for the difference in the pronunciation of **denn** (short vowel) and **den** (long vowel).

The video screen icon signals that related material appears in the video program. *quite*

Pronunciation of **hab'**: **b** becomes unvoiced **p**.

Wer liest die Zeitung?

VATER: Kurt, ich suche meine Zeitung. Weißt du, wo sie ist?
SOHN: Deine Zeitung? Ich lese sie im Moment.
VATER: Was liest du denn? *"flavoring particle" = interest on part of speaker*
SOHN: Ich lese einen Artikel über unsere Schule.

Ich hab' eine Frage

ANNETTE: Katrin, ich hab' eine Frage. Kennst du den Mann da drüben?
KATRIN: Wen meinst du denn?
ANNETTE: Er spricht mit Stefan. Ich sehe, er kennt dich.
KATRIN: Natürlich kenn' ich ihn – das ist mein Bruder Max!
ANNETTE: Ach, du hast auch einen Bruder! Ich kenne nur deine Schwester.

Georg sucht ein Zimmer

GEORG: Kennst du viele Leute in München?
STEFAN: Ja, meine Familie wohnt da. Warum?
GEORG: Ich studiere nächstes Semester dort und brauche ein Zimmer.
STEFAN: Unser Haus ist ziemlich groß. Sicher haben meine Eltern ein Zimmer frei.
GEORG: Fantastisch! Vielen Dank! *certainly*
STEFAN: Bitte, bitte. Nichts zu danken.

Notes on Usage: **Unstressed *e* and *denn***

***Dropping unstressed* e** In informal conversation, Germans often drop the unstressed ending **-e** in the first-person singular.

> Katrin, ich **hab'** eine Frage.
> Natürlich **kenn'** ich ihn.

***The flavoring particle* denn** Probably the most frequently used flavoring particle is **denn**. It adds an element of personal interest to a question. **Denn** is never stressed and usually comes immediately after the verb and personal pronouns.

> Was liest du **denn**?
> Wen meinst du **denn**?
> Wer ist **denn** das?

■ Wortschatz 1

Verben

brauchen to need
essen (isst) to eat
haben to have
heißen to be called
   Er heißt Max. His name is Max.
kennen to know, to be acquainted
   with
lesen (liest) to read
   lesen über (+ *acc.*) to read
    about
meinen to mean
nehmen (nimmt) to take
sehen (sieht) to see
sprechen (spricht) to speak, to talk
   sprechen über (+ *acc.*) to talk
    about
suchen to look for; to seek
wissen (weiß) to know (*a fact*)

Substantive

der **Artikel, -** article
der **Bruder, ⸗** brother
der **Freund, -e** friend
der **Mann, ⸚er** man; husband
der **Sohn, ⸚e** son
der **Vater, ⸗** father

das **Fleisch** meat
das **Gemüse** vegetables
das **Obst** fruit

das **Semester, -** semester
das **Zimmer, -** room

die **Familie, -n** family
die **Frage, -n** question
die **Schwester, -n** sister
die **Zeitung, -en** newspaper

die **Eltern** (*pl.*) parents
die **Leute** (*pl.*) people

Adjektive und Adverbien

(da) drüben over there
dein (*fam. sing.*) your
dort there
frei free; unoccupied
groß big; tall
mein my
nur only
sicher certain, sure
unser our

Andere Vokabeln

ach oh, ah
bitte you're welcome
denn *flavoring particle, see p. 46*
mit with
über (+ *acc.*) about
wen? whom?
wessen? whose?
wie viele? how many?

The preposition **über** means *about* with verbs like *to say, tell, write, read, laugh,* etc.

Nützliche Ausdrücke

Fantastisch! Fantastic!
vielen Dank many thanks, thanks
   a lot
nächstes Semester next semester
Nichts zu danken! Don't mention
   it!

Gegensätze

danke ≠ bitte thank you ≠ you're
   welcome
groß ≠ klein big; tall ≠ little; short

nach ≠ aus   to + from

Who's Reading the Newspaper?

FATH.: Kurt, I'm looking for my
       newspaper. Do you know where
       it is?
SON: Your newspaper? I'm reading it
       at the moment.
FATH.: What are you reading?
SON: I'm reading an article about our
       school.   *über*

I Have a Question

A: Katrin, I have a question. Do you
    know that man over there? *da drüben*
K: Whom do you mean? *meinst*
A: He's talking with Stefan. I see he
    knows you.
K: Of course I know him—that's my
    brother Max!
A: Oh, you have a brother too! I only
    know your sister.

Georg Is Looking for a Room

G: Do you know many people in
    Munich?
S: Yes, my family lives there. Why?
G: I'm studying there next semester *dort*
    and need a room.
S: Our house is pretty big. I'm sure my
    parents have a room free.
G: Fantastic! Thanks a lot!
S: You're welcome. Don't mention it.

Variationen

■ A ■ Persönliche Fragen

1. Wie viele Studenten kennen Sie hier? Wie heißen sie?
2. Stefans Haus ist ziemlich groß. Ist Ihr Haus auch groß oder ist es klein? Wie viele Zimmer hat es?
3. Stefan kommt aus München. Woher kommen Sie?
4. Kurt liest die Zeitung im Moment. Lesen Sie auch eine Zeitung? Oft oder nur selten? Wie heißt sie?

■ B ■ Partnerarbeit: Wie heißt ...? Help each other recall the names of other students in the class.

A: Wie heißt die Studentin (*oder* der Student) da drüben?
B: Sie/er heißt ...

■ C ■ Partnerarbeit: Wen kennst du hier? Ask your neighbor whom he or she knows in class and how well.

A: Wen kennst du hier?
B: Ich kenne ...
A: Kennst du ihn (*oder* sie) gut?
B: Ja, sehr gut. (*oder*: Nein, nicht sehr gut.)

Vielleicht sprechen die Frauen über das Wetter. Was sagen sie zueinander?

■ D ■   **Partnerarbeit: Was suchst du?**   Tell what you're looking for. Try to remember the correct gender of these nouns, then put them into the corresponding column.

n Buch   *m* Stuhl   *m* Professor
m Bleistift   *m* Kugelschreiber   *f* Professorin
n Heft   *f* Landkarte   *f* Zeitung
f Uhr

Ich suche:

meinen (masculine)	**mein** (neuter)	**meine** (feminine)
Bleistift	Buch	Uhr
Stuhl	Heft	Landkarte
(Kuli) Kugelschreiber	_____	Professorin
Professor	_____	Zeitung
_____	_____	_____

Now use each of these objects in the following conversation.

A: Was suchst du?
B: Ich suche meinen/mein/meine _____ .
A: Er/es/sie ist nicht hier.

■ E ■   **Gruppenarbeit: Was brauchen wir?** (*4 Studenten*)   You and three friends are going to Munich to study. Decide together on some things you'll need.

Wir brauchen:

einen (masculine)	**ein** (neuter)	**eine** (feminine)
einen Kugelschreiber	ein Zimmer	eine Landkarte
einen Professor	_____	eine Uhr
_____	_____	_____
_____	_____	_____

Lyrik zum Vorlesen

Lab Manual Kap. 2, Lyrik zum Vorlesen.

This is one of the earliest surviving love poems in German. It was found in the Latin text of a letter written ca. 1160 A.D. by a lady to her lover. The original medieval German has been translated into modern German.

Du bist mein

Du bist mein, ich bin dein.
Des sollst du gewiss sein°.   **Des ...** = of that you can be certain
Du bist verschlossen°   locked up
In meinem Herzen°,   heart
Verloren° ist das Schlüsselein°:   lost / little key
Du musst immer drinnen° sein.   inside

The accusative case

Grammatik

In **Kapitel 1** you learned the forms and functions of the nominative case. In this chapter you will learn the accusative case. The direct object of a verb is in the accusative.

■ The direct object

The direct object is the thing or person acted upon, known, or possessed by the subject.

Subject (nominative)			*Direct object (accusative)*	
Sie	lesen	→	das Buch.	*They're reading the book.*
Anna	kennt	→	meine Eltern.	*Anna knows my parents.*
Karl	hat	→	einen Bruder.	*Karl has a brother.*

The accusative is identical in form to the nominative *with the exception of the masculine singular articles.*

The indefinite article **ein** has no plural form. Therefore, the possessive adjective **mein-** (*my*) is used to show the plural endings.

	Nominative	**Accusative**
masc:	Hier ist **der** / ein Bleistift.	Ich habe den / **einen** Bleistift.
neut:	Hier ist **das** / ein Zimmer.	Ich habe **das** / ein Zimmer.
fem:	Hier ist **die** / eine Zeitung.	Ich habe **die** / eine Zeitung.
plur:	Hier sind **die** / meine Bücher.	Ich habe **die** / meine Bücher.

Workbook Kap. 2, A, B.

■ 1 ■ **Übung: Wer hat ein Deutschbuch?** Your instructor asks who has various things. Say that you have them.

> BEISPIEL: Wer hat ein Deutschbuch?
> Ich habe ein Deutschbuch.

Lab Manual Kap. 2, Var. zu Üb. 2, 3.

■ 2 ■ **Übung: Was sehen Sie?** Name five things you see in the picture.

> BEISPIEL: Ich sehe einen Tisch.

■ 3 ■   **Kettenreaktion: Was brauchst du?**   Ask other students what things they need.

> **BEISPIEL:**   A: Was brauchst du?
> B: Ich brauche den/das/die _____ . Und was brauchst du?
> C: Ich brauche …

Fragewort

The accusative form of the question word **wer** is **wen**:

Wen kennst du in München?   *Whom do you know in Munich?*

■ Accusative of the personal pronouns

Be sure to learn all forms of the accusative personal pronouns.

Singular			Plural		
nom.	acc.		nom.	acc.	
ich	**mich**	*me*	wir	**uns**	*us*
du	**dich**	*you*	ihr	**euch**	*you*
er	**ihn**	*him, it*			
es	**es**	*it*	sie; Sie	**sie, Sie**	*them; you*
sie	**sie**	*her, it*			

Workbook Kap. 2, C, D, E.

■ 4 ■   **Übung: Brauchen Sie etwas?**   Your instructor asks whether you need something. Say that you do need it.

> **BEISPIEL:** Brauchen Sie den Stuhl?
> Ja, ich brauche ihn.

Lab Manual Kap. 2, Var. zur Üb. 5.

■ 5 ■   **Partnerarbeit: Wen kennst du hier?**   Conduct the following dialogue with your partner, naming as many students in your class as possible.

> A: Wen kennst du hier?
> B: Ich kenne Barbara/Robert.
> A: Ich kenne sie/ihn auch.
> B: Wen kennst *du* hier?

■ 6 ■   Übung: Fragen   Answer the questions affirmatively.

> **BEISPIEL:** Suchst du mich?
> Ja, ich suche dich.

1. Kennst du mich?   *dich*
2. Brauchst du uns?   *Sie*
3. Seht ihr uns?   *dich*
4. Kenne ich dich?   *mich*
5. Kenne ich euch?   *uns*

6. Fragst du mich?   *dich*
7. Brauche ich dich?   *dich*
8. Brauche ich euch?   *uns / mich*
9. Kennen Sie mich?   *Sie Sie*
10. Kenne ich Sie?   *uns*

More on verbs in the present tense

■ Contraction of *du*-form: *heißen*

Verbs with stems ending in **-s**, **-ß**, or **-z** contract the **du**-form ending **-st** to **-t**. In these verbs, the **du**-form and the **er**-form are identical. You used some of the forms of **heißen** in the **Einführung**. Here is the complete conjugation in the present tense.

heißen	*to be called*		stem: **heiß-**
ich	heiße	wir	heißen
du	**heißt**	ihr	heißt
er, es, sie	heißt	sie, Sie	heißen

■ Verbs with stem-vowel change *e* to *i* or *ie*

Some German verbs change their stem vowel in the **du**- and **er**-forms of the present tense.

e → i		**sprechen**	*to speak*
ich	spreche	wir	sprechen
du	**sprichst**	ihr	sprecht
er, es, sie	**spricht**	sie, Sie	sprechen

e → ie		**sehen**	*to see*
ich	sehe	wir	sehen
du	**siehst**	ihr	seht
er, es, sie	**sieht**	sie, Sie	sehen

e → ie		**lesen**	to read
ich	lese	wir	lesen
du	**liest**	ihr	lest
er, es, sie	**liest**	sie, Sie	lesen

Stem-vowel change will be indicated in the **Wortschatz** sections by inclusion of the **er**-form: **sehen (sieht)** *to see*. Two other verbs in this group are **essen,** *to eat*; and **nehmen**, *to take*. Note that **nehmen** changes not only its stem vowel but also some consonants.

essen	*to eat*	nehmen	*to take*
ich	esse	ich	nehme
du	**isst**	du	**nimmst**
er, es, sie	**isst**	er, es, sie	**nimmt**

Lab Manual Kap. 2,
Var. zur Üb. 7.

Workbook Kap. 2, F.

■ 7 ■　**Kettenreaktion**

1. Say what you eat, then ask the next person.

   BEISPIEL: Ich esse Fleisch, was isst du?

n Fleisch — Käse *m* — der *Kohl* — Gemüse *N* — Möhre, Karotte *F* — Suppe *f* — Obst *N* — Brot *n* — Wurst *F* — *m+n* Joghurt

2. Say what you read, then ask the next person.

   BEISPIEL: Ich lese den *Spiegel*, was liest du?

Die Zeit — einen Artikel — *Den* den Spiegel — die Zeitung — *die Zeitung* — ein Buch — einen Brief

3. Say what languages you speak and then ask the next person.

   BEISPIEL: Ich spreche _____ , was sprichst du?

   H
Chinesisch	Französisch	*Latein*
Italienisch	Englisch	
Polnisch	Japanisch	
Schwedisch	Spanisch	
Deutsch	Russisch	

4. Say what you see. The next student repeats what you see, then adds something new.

   BEISPIEL: A: Ich sehe ein Fenster.
   　　　　　　B: Sie sieht ein Fenster und ich sehe eine Tafel.

■ The verb *wissen*

The verb **wissen** (*to know*) is irregular in the present singular. Its forms must be memorized.

ich	**weiß**	wir	wissen
du	**weißt**	ihr	wisst
er, es, sie	**weiß**	sie, Sie	wissen

Both the first-person singular and the third-person singular lack endings: **ich weiß**, **er weiß**.

Ich weiß.

The difference between **wissen** and **kennen** parallels that between French **savoir** and **connaître** and Spanish **saber** and **conocer**. Cf. Scots English *ken: to know* (a person or thing); also "beyond my ken": *beyond my knowledge*.

wissen vs. *kennen*   Both **wissen** and **kennen** may be translated as "to know," but **wissen** means "to know a fact" and **kennen** means "to be familiar, acquainted with" and is used when the direct object is a person or place.

Weißt du, wer das ist?
  Ja, ich **kenne** ihn sehr gut.
Kennen Sie Berlin, Herr Brandt?
  Nein, nicht sehr gut.

Do you know who that is?
  Yes, I know him very well.
Do you know Berlin, Mr. Brandt?
  No, not very well.

Workbook Kap. 2, G.

■ 8 ■   Übung: *Wissen* oder *kennen*?

BEISPIEL: ich / Georg
        Ich kenne Georg.

k 1. er / Michael
k 2. wir / Berlin
weiß 3. Katrin / wo ich wohne
weißt 4. ihr / was sie macht
k 5. ich / Stefan und Annette
 6. du / München
weiß 7. ich / wer das ist *who*   *Wen = acc.*
wissen 8. die Schüler / was der Lehrer meint

SPIEGEL-Leser wissen mehr
DER SPIEGEL

■ The verb *haben*

The verb **haben** (*to have*) is irregular in the present singular.

ich	habe	wir	haben
du	**hast**	ihr	habt
er, es, sie	**hat**	sie, Sie	haben

Lab Manual Kap. 2, Var. zur Üb. 9.

■ 9 ■ **Übung: Wer hat die Zeitung?** Your professor asks you who has the newspaper, while pointing to somebody. Say that that person has the newspaper.

> **BEISPIEL:** Wer hat die Zeitung? (*points to Sean*)
> Sean hat sie.

Possessive adjectives

Learn all forms of the possessive adjectives.

Singular			Plural		
personal pronoun	possessive adjective		personal pronoun	possessive adjective	
ich	**mein**	*my*	wir	**unser**	*our*
du	**dein**	*your*	ihr	**euer**	*your*
er	**sein**	*his; its*			
es	**sein**	*its*	sie; Sie	**ihr; Ihr**	*their; your*
sie	**ihr**	*her; its*			

Note that formal **Ihr** (*your*), like formal **Sie** (*you*), is always capitalized.

Possessive adjectives must agree with the nouns they modify in case, number, and gender. This agreement is shown by endings. As the following table shows, the endings of the possessive adjectives are the same as the endings of **ein**. Possessive adjectives are therefore called **ein**-words.

Ending of **ein**-words				
	masc.	neut.	fem.	plur.
nom.	ein	ein	ein**e**	(*no plural*)
	mein	mein	mein**e**	mein**e**
	ihr	ihr	ihr**e**	ihr**e**
	unser	unser	unsr**e**	unsr**e**
	euer	euer	eur**e**	eur**e**
acc.	ein**en**	ein	ein**e**	(*no plural*)
	mein**en**	mein	mein**e**	mein**e**
	ihr**en**	ihr	ihr**e**	ihr**e**
	unsr**en**	unser	unsr**e**	unsr**e**
	eur**en**	euer	eur**e**	eur**e**

The **e** *must* be dropped from **euer** (→ **euren**) and *may* be dropped from **unser**.

Note: The **-er** on **unser** and **euer** is *not* an ending, but part of the stem. When **euer** and **unser** take endings, the second **-e-** of the stem is dropped.

Das ist unser / euer Bruder.   Das ist unsre / eure Schwester.

Note: The endings for nominative and accusative possessive adjectives are identical *except in the masculine.*

Das ist mein Bruder. Und das
ist meine Schwester.

Masculine nominative

Das ist mein Bruder.
Das ist ihr Bruder.
Das ist unser Bruder.
Das ist euer Bruder.

Masculine accusative

Ich sehe mein**en** Bruder.
Sie sieht ihr**en** Bruder.
Wir sehen unsr**en** Bruder. *(unseren)*
Ihr seht eur**en** Bruder.

Fragewörter	
wer?	*who?*
wen?	*whom?*
wessen?	*whose?*

Lab Manual Kap. 2, Var.
zu Üb. 10, 11.

Workbook Kap. 2, H–K.

Saying what belongs to whom is a
communicative goal.

■ **10** ■ **Übung: Wessen Buch ist das?**   Tell your instructor whose book is being
pointed to.

> **BEISPIEL:** Wessen Buch ist das?
> Das ist *mein* Buch.

■ **11** ■ **Übung: Wessen Freund kennen Sie?**   Tell your instructor whose friend
you know.

> **BEISPIEL:** Wessen Freund kennen Sie?
> Ich kenne *seinen* Freund.

Cardinal numbers above 20

The English nursery rhyme "Sing a Song of Sixpence" contains the phrase "four-and-twenty blackbirds." German forms the cardinal numbers above twenty in the same way: 24 = **vierundzwanzig**.

Counting above 20 is a communicative goal.

20	zwanzig	30	dreißig
21	einundzwanzig	31	einunddreißig (usw.)
22	zweiundzwanzig	40	vierzig
23	dreiundzwanzig	50	fünfzig
24	vierundzwanzig	60	sechzig
25	fünfundzwanzig	70	siebzig
26	sechsundzwanzig	80	achtzig
27	siebenundzwanzig	90	neunzig
28	achtundzwanzig	100	hundert
29	neunundzwanzig	1 000	tausend

4 982   viertausendneunhundertzweiundachtzig

German uses a period or a space where English uses a comma to divide thousands from hundreds, etc. German numbers above twelve (**zwölf**) are seldom written as words, except on checks. When they *are* written out, each number is one continuous word.

German	*English*
4.982 oder 4 982	4,982

German uses a comma where English uses a decimal point. The comma is read as **Komma**.

0,5	0.5
(null Komma fünf)	(zero point five)

■ 12 ■   **Übung**   Read these numbers aloud in German.

26	1 066	3 001
69	533	0,22
153	985	3,45
4 772,08	48	71
1992	1971	1800

Was kostet das?

Wie weit ist es nach Garmisch-
Partenkirchen?

Vor dem Lesen

Lesestück

Tipps zum Lesen und Lernen

■   **Tipps zum Vokabelnlernen**

Compound nouns A characteristic feature of German is its formation of compound
nouns from two or more nouns. You should get used to analyzing these words and
should learn to identify their component parts. You will frequently see similarities to
English compound nouns.

Hausfrau	*housewife*
Hausarbeit	*housework*

Often a connecting -**(e)s**- or -**(e)n**- is inserted between the components.   *genitive ?*

das **Eigentum** + die **Wohnung** = die **Eigentumswohnung**
   (*property*)   (*apartment*)   (*condominium*)

der **Bund** (*federation*) + die **Republik** = die **Bundesrepublik**

die **Familie** + die **Diskussion** = die **Familiendiskussion**

The gender of the *last* component noun is *always* the gender of the entire compound.

das **Haus** + die **Frau** = die **Hausfrau**

das **Wort** + der **Schatz** = der **Wortschatz**
   (*word*)   (*treasure*)   (*vocabulary*)

■ Leicht zu merken

die **Alternative, -n**	Alternative
der **Konflikt, -e**	Konflikt
(das) **Nordamerika**	
normal	normal
relativ	
sozial	sozial
traditionell	traditionell

■ Einstieg in den Text

- Review the tips for reading on page 38 in **Kapitel 1**.

- The following text is entitled "Die Familie heute." This gives you a good idea of what sort of information to expect.

- Before reading, recall the vocabulary you already know that relates to the topic of family, e.g., **Bruder**, **Schwester**, etc.

- *Guessing from context* The first sentence of a paragraph—the topic sentence—announces the primary topic of what follows. Look at page 59, line 8 of "Die Familie heute." **Die typische Familie** is the topic of this paragraph. Later in the paragraph comes this sentence:

   Fast alle Familien besitzen ein Auto und einen Fernseher.

   The words that are probably immediately comprehensible to you are **alle Familien** and **Auto**. Knowing the topic, you can make an educated guess at the meaning of **fast** and **besitzen**. Such educated guessing, or finding context clues, *own* is very important when reading texts with many unfamiliar words.

◼ Wortschatz 2

Verben

besitzen to own
bleiben to stay, remain
finden to find
geben (gibt) to give
kochen to cook
leben to live; to be alive
verdienen to earn

Substantive

der **Beruf, -e** profession, vocation
der **Fernseher, -** TV set
der **Großvater, ⁚** grandfather
der **Onkel, -** uncle

das **Auto, -s** car
das **Essen** food; meal
das **Geld** money
das **Klischee, -s** cliché
das **Problem, -e** problem

die **Arbeit** work
die **Bundesrepublik (Deutschland)** the Federal Republic (of Germany)
  die **BRD** the FRG
die **Diskussion, -en** discussion

die **Großmutter, ⁚** grandmother
die **Hausfrau, -en** housewife
die **Mutter, ⁚** mother
die **Rolle, -n** role
die **Stelle, -n** job, position
die **Tante, -n** aunt
die **Tochter, ⁚** daughter

die **Großeltern** (*pl.*) grandparents

Adjektive und Adverbien

anders different
berufstätig employed
deutsch German
fast almost
jung young
manchmal sometimes
mehr more
  nicht mehr no longer, not any more
noch still
  noch ein another, an additional
sogar even, in fact
überall everywhere
wenigstens at least
wichtig important

Andere Vokabeln

alle (*pl.*) all; everybody
niemand nobody, no one
zwischen between

Nützliche Ausdrücke
useful expressions

es gibt (+ *acc.*) there is, there are
das sind (*pl. of* **das ist**) those are
zu Hause at home

Gegensätze

jung ≠ **alt** young ≠ old
niemand ≠ **jemand** no one ≠ someone
wichtig ≠ **unwichtig** important ≠ unimportant

Mit anderen Worten

Kinder sagen:
  Vati = Vater
  Mutti = Mutter
  Oma = Großmutter
  Opa = Großvater

Die Familie heute

„Der Vater hat einen Beruf und verdient das Geld; die Mutter ist Hausfrau. Sie bleibt zu Hause, kocht das Essen und versorgt° die Kinder." Die Klischees kennen wir schon. Heute stimmen sie aber nicht mehr, wenigstens nicht für junge[1] Familien in Deutschland. Dort ist die Rollenverteilung° oft anders. Viele Frauen sind berufstätig

5   oder suchen eine Stelle, Tagsüber° ist manchmal niemand zu Hause. Oft machen der Mann und die Frau die Hausarbeit gemeinsam° und in Familiendiskussionen haben die Kinder heute auch eine Stimme°.

     Die typische Familie ist relativ klein: Ein oder zwei Kinder, das ist normal. Manchmal wohnen auch die Großeltern mit ihnen zusammen°. Viele Familien in der

10 Bundesrepublik haben ein Haus oder eine Eigentumswohnung°. Fast alle Familien besitzen ein Auto und einen Fernseher. Ihr Lebensstandard° ist sogar oft höher als° in Nordamerika.

     Aber gibt es denn keine° Probleme? Natürlich! Man findet in Deutschland, wie überall, Konflikte zwischen Eltern und Kindern. Nach dem Schulabschluss° suchen

15 junge Leute manchmal Alternativen wie das Zusammenleben° in Wohngemein-schaften°. Aber für die Mehrheit° bleibt die traditionelle Familie – Mutter, Vater und Kinder – noch die wichtigste° soziale Gruppe.

takes care of

assignment of roles
during the day
jointly
voice

mit ... = with them
condominium *"apt. that you own"*
standard of living / **höher**
  als = higher than
no *"conclusion of school" = graduation*
Nach ... = after secondary
  school / living together
communal living groups /
  majority / most important

Learning about German family life is the
cultural goal of this chapter.

Workbook Kap. 2,
M–O.

Junge Familie aus Eibelstadt. Wie alt sind die Kinder?

Nach dem Lesen

■ **A** ■   **Partnerarbeit: Fragebogen**   (Questionnaire)   You are a German sociologist studying American family life. Use the questionnaire below to interview your partner. Be ready to report the information that you collect to the class.

1. **Großeltern**: Leben sie noch?   ja / nein
2. **Mutter**: wie alt? _____ berufstätig? ja / nein Beruf? _____
3. **Vater**: wie alt? _____ berufstätig? ja / nein Beruf? _____

1. Line 3 **junge**: When German adjectives are used before nouns they have endings, most often **-e** or **-en**. You will learn how to use these endings actively in **Kapitel 9**.

4. **Geschwister**: wie viele Brüder? _____ *1* wie alt? _____ *29*
   wie viele Schwestern? _____ wie alt? _____
5. **Autos:** wie viele? _____
6. **Fernseher**: wie viele? _____
7. Wer kocht das Essen? _____
8. Wer macht die Hausarbeit? _____ *Putzfrau, Raumkosmetikerin*
9. Wer liest die Zeitung? _____
10. Besitzt Ihre Familie ein Haus?   ja / nein

Lab Manual Kap. 2,
Diktat.

Workbook Kap. 2,
P–S.

■ **B** ■   **Antworten Sie auf Deutsch.**

1. Was sind die Klischees über die traditionelle Familie?
2. Was suchen heute viele Frauen?
3. Haben Familien in Deutschland viele Kinder?
4. Besitzen alle Familien in Deutschland ein Haus?
   viele

Situationen aus dem Alltag
everyday life

Talking about the family
is a communicative goal.

■ **Die Familie**

Here is some useful vocabulary for talking about your family. Words you already know
from **Wortschatz** sections are listed without English equivalents; new supplementary
vocabulary is listed with definitions.

This vocabulary focuses on an everyday
topic or situation. Your instructor may
assign some supplementary
vocabulary for active mastery.

die **Großeltern**
die **Großmutter, ¨**
   die **Oma, -s**
der **Großvater, ¨**
   der **Opa, -s**
die **Eltern**
die **Mutter, ¨**
   die **Mutti, -s**
der **Vater, ¨**   *der Mann = husband*
   der **Vati, -s**   *die Weibe*   *?*
der **Sohn, ¨e**
die **Tochter, ¨**

die **Geschwister** (*pl.*)	siblings, brothers and sisters
der **Bruder,** ⸚	
die **Schwester, -n**	
der **Onkel, -**	
die **Tante, -n**	
die **Kusine, -n**	cousin (f.)
der **Vetter, -n**	cousin (m.)

der Cousin, -s

der Enkel, die Enkelin, das Enkelkind   grandson, -dau, -child

■ **A** ■   **Übung: Wer ist in der Familie?**   Answer the questions about Sylvie, Felix, and their families.

geb. = geboren (*born*)

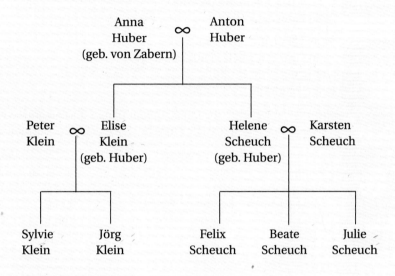

Anna Huber (geb. von Zabern) ∞ Anton Huber

Peter Klein ∞ Elise Klein (geb. Huber)

Helene Scheuch (geb. Huber) ∞ Karsten Scheuch

Sylvie Klein   Jörg Klein

Felix Scheuch   Beate Scheuch   Julie Scheuch

1. Das ist Sylvie Klein. Sie hat eine Mutter und …
    Wer ist Peter Klein? … Er ist ihr Vater.
    Wer ist Elise Klein?
    Wer ist Jörg?
    Wer sind Anna und Anton Huber?
2. Das ist Felix Scheuch. Er hat einen Vater und …
    Wer sind Beate und Julie? Karsten Scheuch? Helene Scheuch? Elise Klein?
3. Machen Sie einen Stammbaum (*family tree*) für Ihre Familie.

■ **B** ■   **Gruppenarbeit: Familienfotos** (*4 oder 5 Studenten*)   Bring to class photographs or your own drawing of some of your family members. Tell the others in the group about the people in the picture.

View Module 1 of the ***Neue Horizonte*** video (00:00) and do the activities in **Videoecke 1** in your Workbook/Laboratory Manual/Video Manual.

Die ganze Familie (The whole family)

Der Vater, der heißt Daniel,
der kleine Sohn heißt Michael,
die Mutter heißt Regine,
die Tochter heißt Rosine.

Der Bruder, der heißt Kristian,
der Onkel heißt Sebastian,
die Schwester heißt Johanna,
die Tante heißt Susanna.

Der Vetter, der heißt Benjamin,
die Kusine, die heißt Katharin,
die Oma heißt Ottilie—
nun kennst du die Familie!

In 1997, these were the most popular names for newborn children according to the
Gesellschaft für deutsche Sprache (Society for the German Language):

Namen für Mädchen			*Namen für Jungen*		
Sarah	Julia	Maria	Christian	Michael	Daniel
Marie	Lisa	Laura	Lukas	Felix	Alexander
Anna / Anne	Sophie	Vanessa	Tobias	Kevin	Maximilian
Lena	Jessica	Michelle	Tom	Marcel	Jan
			Philipp	Paul	Florian
			Erik		

Parents do not have absolute freedom in choosing names for their children.
A name may be rejected by the government registry office if it does not clearly
indicate the child's sex or if it is deemed to "endanger the well-being of the child."

Die Familie ist zusammen.
Sie trinken Kaffee und
sprechen miteinander.

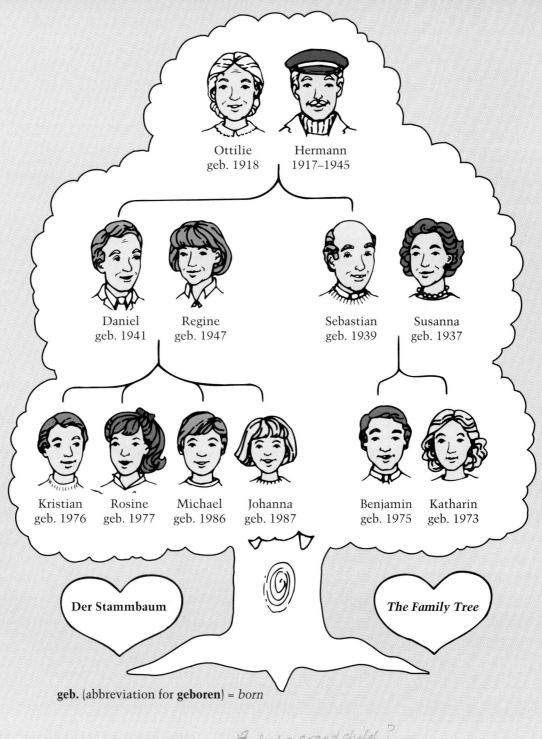

Ottilie
geb. 1918

Hermann
1917–1945

Daniel
geb. 1941

Regine
geb. 1947

Sebastian
geb. 1939

Susanna
geb. 1937

Kristian
geb. 1976

Rosine
geb. 1977

Michael
geb. 1986

Johanna
geb. 1987

Benjamin
geb. 1975

Katharin
geb. 1973

Der Stammbaum

The Family Tree

geb. (abbreviation for **geboren**) = *born*

Enkel = grandchild?

Jugend und Schule

Communicative Goals

- Negating statements and questions
- Contradicting someone
- Requesting confirmation
- Expressing opinions
- Talking about clothing

Cultural Goal

- Learning about German schools

Chapter Outline

- **Lyrik zum Vorlesen**
  „Bruder Jakob" und Rätsel

- **Grammatik**
  The predicate
  Modal verbs
  Verbs with stem vowel change *a* to *ä, au* to *äu*
  Negation with *nicht* (not)
  Negation with *kein*
  Expecting an affirmative answer: *nicht wahr*?
  Contradicting a negative statement or question: *doch*
  The indefinite pronoun *man*

- **Lesestück**
  Eine Klassendiskussion

- **Situationen aus dem Alltag**
  Kleidung und Farben

- **Almanach**
  A Note about Schools in German-speaking Countries

🎧 **Lab Manual** Kap. 3, Dialoge, Fragen, Hören Sie gut zu!, Üb. zur Aussprache [o/ö].

Two cities in Germany are named Frankfurt. They are distinguished by the rivers on which they are situated: Frankfurt am Main (Frankfurt a. M. or Frankfurt/Main) in the state of Hessen; and Frankfurt an der Oder (Frankfurt a. d. O. or Frankfurt/Oder) in the state of Brandenburg.

Innsbruck is the capital city of the mountainous Austrian province of Tyrol (German **Tirol**). German place names often have topographical significance. **Die Brücke** = *bridge*; this city was originally a settlement at "the bridge over the Inn River." See the map in the front of the book.

Um Gottes Willen! Although **Gott** means *God*, this exclamation is not offensive in German, but is the social equivalent of *For heaven's sake* or *Oh, my gosh.*

Du hast es gut!

Renate besucht ihre Freundin Monika. (visits)

MONIKA: In Frankfurt hast du es gut, Renate! Hier in Hinterwalden ist es stinklangweilig. (v.v. boring!)
RENATE: Dann musst du mich bald besuchen. Oder hast du keine Lust?
MONIKA: Doch, ich möchte schon nach Frankfurt, aber ich habe leider kein Geld.
RENATE: Das verstehe ich schon, aber bis Juni kannst du sicher genug verdienen. (really)

Eine Pause

Kurt und Stefan fahren nach Innsbruck.

KURT: Wir müssen noch eine Stunde nach Innsbruck fahren.
STEFAN: Können wir eine Pause machen? Ich möchte ein bisschen laufen. (walk)
KURT: Ich auch. Da drüben kann man halten, nicht wahr?
STEFAN: Ja. (*Sie halten.*) Mensch! Der Berg ist wahnsinnig steil! (v.v. steep)
KURT: Was ist denn los? Bist du nicht fit?
STEFAN: Doch! Das schaff' ich leicht. (manage easily)

Heute habe ich leider keinen Wagen

CAROLA: Klaus, wie spät ist es denn?
KLAUS: Um Gottes Willen! Es ist schon halb zwölf.
CAROLA: Musst du jetzt nach Hause?
KLAUS: Ja, und ich muss zu Fuß gehen. Heute habe ich leider keinen Wagen.
CAROLA: Warum denn nicht?
KLAUS: Mein Mitbewohner hat ihn heute Abend. Er hat viel zu tun.

Note on Usage: **The flavoring particle *schon***

As a flavoring particle, **schon** is often used to strengthen, confirm, or reinforce a statement. It adds the sense of *really, indeed.* In the first dialogue, Monika protests:

Ich möchte **schon** nach Frankfurt, aber ich habe leider kein Geld.	*I really would like to go to Frankfurt, but unfortunately I don't have any money.*

Renate answers:

Das verstehe ich **schon** ...	*I certainly understand that ...*

Wortschatz 1

Verben

besuchen to visit
dürfen (darf) may, to be allowed to
fahren (fährt) to drive; to go (by vehicle)
halten (hält) to stop (intrans.); to hold
können (kann) can, to be able to
laufen (läuft) to run; to go on foot, walk (colloq.)
ich möchte I would like to
müssen (muss) must, to have to
schaffen (colloq.) to handle, manage; to get done
schlafen (schläft) to sleep
sollen (soll) should, to be supposed to
tragen (trägt) to carry; to wear
tun to do
verstehen to understand
wollen (will) to want to

Berg: cf. English *iceberg*.

Substantive

der **Berg, -e** mountain
der **Wagen, -** car
der **Mitbewohner, -** roommate (m.)
die **Freundin, -nen** friend (f.)
die **Minute, -n** minute

die **Pause, -n** break; intermission
 eine Pause machen to take a break
die **Stunde, -n** hour; class hour
 die **Deutschstunde** German class
die **Mitbewohnerin, -nen** roommate (f.)

Adjektive und Adverbien

bald soon
fit in shape
genug enough
jetzt now
langweilig boring
leicht easy; light (in weight)
leider unfortunately
schon already, yet
spät late
steil steep
wahnsinnig (colloq. adv.) extremely, incredibly
wahr true

Andere Vokabeln

doch yes I *do*, yes I *am*, etc. (contradictory, see p. 86)
kein not a, not any, no
nichts nothing
wie lange? how long?
wohin? where to?

Kein has the same endings as **ein**. See p. 76.

Nützliche Ausdrücke
useful expressions

ein bisschen a little; a little bit; a little while
Ich habe keine Lust. I don't want to.
Mensch! Man! Wow!
nach Hause home (as destination)
 Ich fahre nach Hause. I'm driving home.
nicht (wahr)? isn't it?, can't you?, doesn't he?, etc.
Um Gottes Willen! For heaven's sake! Oh, my gosh!
Was ist los? What's the matter?; What's going on?
zu Fuß gehen to go on foot, walk

Gegensätze
opposites

langweilig ≠ interessant boring ≠ interesting
leicht ≠ schwer light; easy ≠ heavy; difficult, hard
nichts ≠ etwas nothing ≠ something
spät ≠ früh late ≠ early

Mit anderen Worten

stinklangweilig = sehr, sehr langweilig
wahnsinnig (colloq.) **= sehr, sehr**

You've Got It Made!

Renate is visiting her friend Monika.

M: You've got it made in Frankfurt, Renate. It's really boring here in Hinterwalden.
R: Then you have to visit me soon. Or don't you want to?
M: Sure I do. I really would like to go to Frankfurt, but unfortunately I don't have any money.
R: I certainly understand that, but surely you can earn enough by June.

A Break

Kurt and Stefan are driving to Innsbruck.

K: We still have an hour to drive to Innsbruck.
S: Can we take a break? I'd like to walk a bit.
K: Me too. We can stop over there, can't we?
S: Yes. (*They stop.*) Man, the mountain is really steep!
K: What's the matter? Aren't you in shape?
S: Sure! I can manage that easily.

Unfortunately, I Don't Have a Car Today

C: Klaus, what time is it?
K: Oh, my gosh! It's already 11:30.
C: Do you have to go home now?
K: Yes, and I have to walk. Unfortunately I don't have a car today.
C: Why not?
K: My roommate has it tonight. He has a lot to do.

Variationen

■ A ■ Persönliche Fragen

1. Wo sind Sie zu Hause? *at home*
2. Gibt es da viel zu tun oder ist es langweilig?
3. Brauchen Sie heute einen Wagen oder gehen Sie zu Fuß?
4. Besitzen Sie einen Wagen? *own*
5. Sind Sie fit oder nicht?
6. Haben Sie genug Geld?

exercise

safety

example

■ B ■ Übung

1. Kurt möchte ein bisschen laufen. Ich möchte zu Hause bleiben. *walk*
   Was möchten Sie denn machen?
   Ich möchte ___ ein bisschen laufen ___

2. Kurt und Stefan wollen da drüben halten. Ich will nach Hause laufen.
   Was wollen Sie denn machen?
   Ich will _____ .

3. Klaus muss morgen arbeiten. Ich muss kochen.
   Was müssen Sie denn morgen machen?
   Ich muss _____ .

■ C ■ Partnerarbeit: Doch!   Contradict what your partner says, using **doch**.

BEISPIEL: Du besuchst mich nicht!
           Doch, ich besuche dich!

1. Du bist nicht fit!
2. Der Tourist kommt nicht aus Amerika!
3. Du verstehst mich nicht!
4. Wir arbeiten heute nicht!
5. Die Studenten gehen nicht nach Hause!
6. Robert ist nicht dein Freund!
7. Der Berg ist nicht steil!
8. Es ist nicht spät!

Lab Manual Kap. 3,
Lyrik zum Vorlesen.

Bruder Jakob

This round for four voices comes originally from France, but is sung by children all over the world. In German, **Frère Jacques** is called **Bruder Jakob**.

Bruder Jakob, Bruder Jakob!
Schläfst° du noch? Schläfst du noch?   sleep
Hörst du nicht die Glocken°?   bells
Hörst du nicht die Glocken?
Ding, ding, dong. Ding, ding, dong.

Rätsel   (Riddles)

Rhyming riddles are very old forms of oral popular literature. The solutions to these two are shown by the accompanying illustrations.

(der Hummer)

Rot° und gut,   red
hat Fleisch° und kein Blut°.   flesh / blood

(die Schnecke)

Ich gehe alle Tage° aus   every day
und bleibe doch in meinem Haus.

The predicate

In both German and English, all statements and questions contain a subject (S) and an inflected verb (V):

S   V   S V
Ich arbeite viel.   *I work a lot.*

  V   S   V   S
Schläfst du?   *Are you sleeping?*

The verb by itself, however, is not always adequate to express the entire action or condition in which the subject is involved. For example, consider the simple statement:

Stefan ist jung.

Stefan is the subject and **ist** is the verb. When taken by themselves, however, the words

Stefan ist

are not a meaningful utterance. The verb **sein** must be completed, in this case by the adjective **jung**. **Sein** may also be completed by a noun in the nominative case.

Stefan ist **mein Bruder**.

In both cases, the verb and its complement together make up the entire verbal idea, or predicate. That's why adjectives and nouns that follow the verb **sein** are called *predicate adjectives* and *predicate nominatives*.

Various kinds of words and phrases can complement verbs to form the complete predicate. For instance, in the sentence

Ich trage Jeans.

the verb **trage** is completed by the direct object **Jeans.** In the sentence

Ich möchte laufen.   *like to walk*

the modal verb **möchte** is completed by the infinitive **laufen**. You will learn about modal verbs like **möchte** in the following section.

Modal verbs

The English modal system has no past tense for verbs like *must* and *may*; instead, English speakers say *had to* and *was allowed to*. The German system is much more regular.

There is a group of six verbs in German called *the modal verbs*. They do not express an action or condition by themselves, but rather the subject's *attitude* or *relation* to the action expressed by another verb.

Wir **müssen** noch eine Stunde **fahren**.   *We still **have to drive** for an hour.*

Bis Juni **kannst** du genug **verdienen**.   *By June you **can earn** enough.*

The modal verb **müssen** (*have to*) indicates that it is *necessary* for the subject (**wir**) to perform the action of driving (**fahren**). **Müssen** is the first part of the predicate, and the infinitive **fahren** is the second part of the predicate. The German modals are:

		Expresses
dürfen	*to be allowed to, may*	permission
können	*to be able to, can*	ability
müssen	*to have to, must*	necessity
sollen	*to be supposed to, should*	obligation
wollen	*to want to; to intend to*	desire; intention
(ich) **möchte**	*(I) would like to*	inclination, desire

Möchte (*would like to*) is a subjunctive form of the modal verb **mögen** (*to like*), which you will learn in the next chapter.

Lehrer und Schüler

The modal auxiliaries take no endings in the **ich-** and **er-**forms, and most have a changed stem vowel in the singular.

dürfen	*to be allowed to*		
ich	**darf**	wir	dürfen
du	**darfst**	ihr	dürft
er, es, sie	**darf**	sie, Sie	dürfen

Darf ich draußen **spielen**?
May I play outside?

können	*to be able to*		
ich	**kann**	wir	können
du	**kannst**	ihr	könnt
er, es, sie	**kann**	sie, Sie	können

Wir **können** da drüben **halten**.
We can stop over there.

	müssen	*to have to*		
ich	**muss**		wir	müssen
du	**musst**		ihr	müsst
er, es, sie	**muss**		sie, Sie	müssen

Heute **muss** ich zu Fuß **gehen**.
Today I have to go on foot.

	wollen	*to want to*		
ich	**will**		wir	wollen
du	**willst**		ihr	wollt
er, es, sie	**will**		sie, Sie	wollen

Willst du jetzt **essen**?
Do you want to eat now?

Notice that only **sollen** does not have a stem-vowel change in the singular.

	sollen	*to be supposed to*		
ich	soll		wir	sollen
du	sollst		ihr	sollt
er, es, sie	soll		sie, Sie	sollen

Sollen wir eine Pause **machen**?
Should we take a break?

Notice that **möchte** has endings different from the other modal verbs.

	ich möchte	*I would like to* (infinitive: **mögen**)		
ich	möchte		wir	möchten
du	möchtest		ihr	möchtet
er, es, sie	möchte		sie, Sie	möchten

Ich **möchte** dich **besuchen**.
I would like to visit you.

In contrast to German, some English modals require a dependent infinitive with *to* (*I want **to read***), while others do not (*I can **read***).

The modal verb is *always* the inflected verb in the sentence. The complementary infinitive (which is the second part of the predicate) comes at the end of the sentence. Note the difference from English, in which the dependent infinitive immediately *follows* the modal verb.

Wir **können** da drüben **halten**.	We **can stop** over there.
Das **muss** ich für morgen **lesen**.	I **have to read** that for tomorrow.
Marie **soll** ihre Eltern **besuchen**.	Marie **is supposed to visit** her parents.

It is important to get used to this two-part predicate, since it is a central structural feature of German sentences.

Lab Manual Kap. 3,
Var. zur Üb. 1.

Workbook Kap. 3, A–C.

■ 1 ■ **Übung: Was möchten Sie heute tun?**   Here are some things people in the dialogues on p. 65 are doing.

Monika besuchen   Geld verdienen
nach Frankfurt fahren   eine Pause machen
ein bisschen laufen   da drüben halten
nach Hause fahren   zu Fuß gehen

Choose from these activities to answer the following questions.

BEISPIEL: Was möchten Sie heute tun?
Ich möchte Monika besuchen.

1. Was können Sie heute tun?
2. Was müssen Sie heute tun?
3. Was möchten Sie heute tun?

■ 2 ■ **Gruppenarbeit: Was willst du machen?** (*4 Studenten*)   Ask each other about what you intend to do or be. This list will provide some ideas. What others can you find?

BEISPIEL: Was willst du denn machen?
Ich will in Deutschland studieren, und du?

eine Familie haben   Freunde in Europa besuchen
viel Geld verdienen   fit sein
berufstätig sein *employed* eine Pause machen
ein Haus besitzen *own*   in Deutschland studieren
nach Hause fahren

■ **Omission of the infinitive**

Certain infinitives may be omitted from sentences with modal verbs when they are clearly implied.

- **haben**

    Möchten Sie ein Zimmer   *Would you like (to have) a room?*
    [**haben**]?

- **machen, tun**

    Das kann ich leider nicht   *Unfortunately I can't (do that).*
    [**machen/tun**].

- verbs of motion (**gehen, fahren, fliegen, laufen**) when destination is expressed

    Musst du jetzt nach Hause   *Do you have to go home now?*
    [**gehen, fahren**]?

- **sprechen**, in the following expression:

    Kannst du Deutsch?   *Can you speak German?*
    Ja, ich kann Deutsch.   *Yes, I can speak German.*
    Ich kann auch Dänisch.   *I can also speak Danish.*

1. Wollen Sie jetzt nach Hause?
2. Er kann das noch nicht. *not yet*
3. Willst du meinen Bleistift? *(haben)*
4. Mein Vater will das nicht. *(tun)*

5. Sie können schon gut Deutsch. *already*
6. Möchten Sie das Geld?
7. Darf man denn das? *be allowed to*
8. Wann wollen Sie nach Amerika?

Wohin (*where to?*) is analogous to the question word **woher**? (*from where?*): **Woher kommst du?**

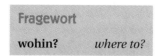

Fragewort	
wohin?	*where to?*

■ 4 ■   Partnerarbeit: Wohin wollen wir im Februar?   By the time the semester break comes in mid-February, many German students want to travel where it is warm. Use the map of Europe on the inside back cover to plan such a trip with your partner.

BEISPIEL: A: Wohin willst du im Februar?
               B: Ich will nach … Wohin willst du?
                          where

Lab Manual Kap. 3, Var. zur Üb. 4.

Verbs with stem-vowel change a to ä, au to äu

Some verbs change their stem-vowel in the following ways:

a → ä	fahren	*to drive; to go by vehicle*	
ich	fahre	wir	fahren
du	**fährst**	ihr	fahrt
er, es, sie	**fährt**	sie, Sie	fahren

halten	*to hold; to stop*		
ich	halte	wir	halten
du	**hältst**	ihr	haltet
er, es, sie	**hält**	sie, Sie	halten

Other verbs in this group are: **schlafen** (**schläft**), *to sleep;* **tragen** (**trägt**), *to carry, wear.*

au → äu	laufen	*to run*	
ich	laufe	wir	laufen
du	**läufst**	ihr	lauft
er, es, sie	**läuft**	sie, Sie	laufen

Lab Manual Kap. 3, Var. zur Üb. 5.

Workbook Kap. 3, D.

■ 5 ■   Kettenreaktion   *Chain*   Say how you get home, then ask your classmates how they get home.

BEISPIEL: A: Ich fahre nach Hause. Fährst du auch nach Hause?
               B: Nein, ich laufe nach Hause. Läufst du auch nach Hause?
               C: Ja, ich laufe auch nach Hause. Läufst du …

■6■ Kettenreaktion   Wie lange schläfst du?

BEISPIEL: Ich schlafe acht Stunden. Wie lange schläfst du?

■7■ Gruppenarbeit: Mit offenen Büchern   (With open books)   Tell one thing that you're wearing, then one thing the person next to you is wearing.

BEISPIEL: Ich trage _____ und er/sie trägt heute _____ .

accusative endings

(h) ein Hemd (shirt)

eine Armbanduhr

ein T-Shirt

Jeans *pl*

eine Brille

eine Jacke

Turnschuhe
Tennisschuhe

einen Rock

eine Mütze

einen Pulli
einen Sweater
Schall (scarf)

einen Rucksack

Negation with nicht (not)

Negating statements and questions is a communicative goal.

Nicht is used to negate a sentence.

Sabrina ist meine Schwester.	*Sabrina is my sister.*
Sabrina ist **nicht** meine Schwester.	*Sabrina is **not** my sister.*

*For a preview and summary of German negation, see **Zusammenfassung und Wiederholung I**, in the Workbook.*

In the preceding example, the position of **nicht** is exactly the same as the position of *not* in English. In most German sentences, however, this will not be the case. Here are some preliminary guidelines for the position of **nicht**.

In English, *not* almost always follows the inflected verb immediately.

- **Nicht** usually *follows* the subject, verb, direct object, and all personal pronouns.

Ich kenne deinen Freund **nicht**.	*I don't know your friend.*
Er sagt das **nicht**.	*He doesn't say that.*
Wir besitzen das Auto **nicht**.	*We don't own the car.*
Deine Schwester kennt mich **nicht**.	*Your sister doesn't know me.*

Some expressions of definite time: **jetzt, heute, heute Abend, morgen, am Mittwoch**.

- **Nicht** usually *follows* expressions of definite time.

Sie können heute Abend **nicht** kommen.	*They can't come tonight.*
Hans arbeitet jetzt **nicht**.	*Hans isn't working now.*

Lab Manual Kap. 3, Üb. 8, 9.

Workbook Kap. 3, E.

Review the explanations of the predicate on p. 69 and of predicate nominatives on pp. 32–33.

■ **8** ■ **Übung** Negate these sentences by adding **nicht**. *(at end of sentence)*

1. Kurt besucht seinen Bruder.
2. Ich kenne eure Mutter.
3. Frau Schmidt besucht uns morgen.
4. Monika macht das heute Abend.
5. Ich verstehe ihn.
6. Am Donnerstag kochst du.
7. Er liest sein Buch.
8. Mein Großvater schläft.
9. Das schafft er. *manage, handle, get done*

- **Nicht** *precedes* complements that constitute the second part of the predicate. These include:

  1. Predicate adjectives

Der Berg ist **steil**.	*The mountain is **steep**.*
Der Berg ist **nicht** steil.	*The mountain is **not** steep.*

  2. Predicate nominatives

Das ist **Herr Blum**.	*That is **Mr. Blum**.*
Das ist **nicht** Herr Blum.	*That is not Mr. Blum.*

  3. Adverbs of manner, indefinite time, and place

Margit geht **zu Fuß**.	*Margit is going **on foot**.*
Margit geht **nicht** zu Fuß.	*Margit is**n't** going on foot.*
Er besucht mich **oft**.	*He **often** visits me.*
Er besucht mich **nicht** oft.	*He doesn**'t** visit me often.*
Sie wohnt **hier**.	*She lives **here**.*
Sie wohnt **nicht** hier.	*She doesn**'t** live here.*

Some expressions of indefinite time: **bald, spät, früh, immer, oft**.

  4. Prepositional phrases that show destination (**nach Wien, nach Hause**) or location (**in Berlin, zu Hause**)

Sie geht **nach Hause**.	*She's going **home**.*
Sie geht **nicht** nach Hause.	*She's **not** going home.*
Er arbeitet **in Berlin**.	*He works **in Berlin**.*
Er arbeitet **nicht** in Berlin.	*He doesn**'t** work in Berlin.*

  5. Infinitives complementing modal verbs

Er kann mich **sehen**.	*He can **see** me.*
Er kann mich **nicht** sehen.	*He can**'t** see me.*

■9■ **Übung** Negate these sentences by adding **nicht**.

1. Das Wetter ist ~~nicht~~ schön.
2. Ich kann dich besuchen.
3. Ich möchte Berlin sehen.
4. Der Berg ist steil.
5. Wir wollen halten.
6. Frau Mackensen ist unsere Lehrerin.
7. Ich muss nach Hause gehen.
8. Margit läuft gut.
9. Er kann mich sehen.

■10■ **Partnerarbeit: Unsere neue Mitbewohnerin** You're both getting a new roommate. Take turns asking each other questions about her. Answer them all negatively.

> BEISPIEL: A: Kennt unsere Mitbewohnerin Berlin?
> B: Nein, sie kennt Berlin nicht.

1. Kommt sie aus Dresden?
2. Ist sie freundlich?
3. Arbeitet sie heute Abend? *nicht*
4. Studiert ihr Bruder in Leipzig?
5. Kennst du ihn?
6. Muss sie nach Hause? *(gehen)*
7. Fährt sie bald nach Hause? *nicht bald n. H*
8. Schläft sie viel? *nicht viel*
9. Ist das ihr Auto?
10. Ist sie oft schlechter Laune?

Negation with kein

Kein (*not a, not any, no*) is the negative of **ein**. It negates nouns preceded by **ein** or nouns not preceded by any article.

Morgen will ich ein Buch lesen.	*I want to read a book tomorrow.*
Morgen will ich **kein** Buch lesen.	*I don't want to read a book tomorrow.*
Hier wohnen Studenten.	*Students live here.*
Hier wohnen **keine** Studenten.	*No students live here.*

Kein is an **ein**-word and takes the same endings as **ein** and the possessive adjectives.

Das ist {
 ein Fernseher.
 kein Fernseher.
 unser Fernseher.
}

Er hat {
 einen Wagen.
 keinen Wagen.
 meinen Wagen.
}

Nicht and **kein** are mutually exclusive. In any given situation, only one will be correct. If a noun is preceded by the definite article or by a possessive adjective, use **nicht** rather than **kein** to negate it.

Ist das die Professorin?	*Is that the professor?*
Nein, das ist **nicht** die Professorin.	*No, that's not the professor.*
Ist das eure Professorin?	*Is that your professor?*
Nein, das ist **nicht** unsere Professorin.	*No, that's not our professor.*
Ist sie Professorin?	*Is she a professor?*
Nein, sie ist **keine** Professorin.	*No, she's not a professor.*

Lab Manual Kap. 3,
Var. zur Üb. 11; Üb. 11.

Workbook Kap. 3, F.

■ 11 ■   Übung   Negate the sentence, using **kein**.

1. Meine Familie besitzt einen Wagen.
2. Maria hat heute Geld.
3. Hier gibt es ein Problem.
4. Hier wohnen Studenten.
5. Morgen gibt es eine Diskussion.
6. Herr Meyer hat Kinder.

■ 12 ■   Übung   Respond negatively to these questions, using **kein** or **nicht**.

BEISPIEL: Hat Barbara einen Freund? Nein, sie hat keinen Freund.
Ist das ihr Freund? Nein, das ist nicht ihr Freund.

1. Haben Sie einen Freund in Oslo?
2. Haben Sie Freunde in Washington?
3. Ist das der Professor?
4. Verdient er Geld?
5. Sehen Sie das Haus?
6. Ist das seine Freundin?
7. Suchen Sie das Buch?
8. Suchen Sie ein Buch?

■ 13 ■   **Partnerarbeit: Meine Familie**   Ask each other about your families. (For family members, see pp. 62–63.)

BEISPIEL: A: Hast du einen Sohn?
B: Nein, ich habe keinen Sohn.

Expecting an affirmative answer: nicht wahr?

Requesting confirmation is a communicative goal.

Nicht wahr? can only follow positive statements.

Nicht wahr? (literally, "not true?"), when added to a positive statement, anticipates confirmation (English: *doesn't she? wasn't he? wasn't it? didn't you?* etc.). In spoken German, you may shorten it to **nicht**?

Heute ist es schön, **nicht wahr**?   *It's beautiful today, isn't it?*
Sie studieren in Freiburg, **nicht**?   *You're studying in Freiburg, aren't you?*

Gisela kennst du, **nicht wahr**?   *You know Gisela, don't you?*

■ 14 ■   Übung: Das ist ein Tisch, nicht wahr?   Contradict your instructor if necessary.

BEISPIEL: Das ist ein Tisch, nicht wahr?
Nein, das ist kein Tisch, das ist ein(e) _____ .

■ 15 ■   Übung: Wie sagt man das auf Deutsch?

1. You have a car, don't you?
2. You're learning German, aren't you?
3. You'll visit me soon, won't you?
4. He's in good shape, isn't he?
5. We can work today, can't we?
6. You can understand that, can't you?

Workbook Kap. 3, G.

Contradicting a negative statement or question: doch

Contradicting someone is a communicative goal.

To contradict a negative statement or question, use **doch** instead of **ja**.

Ich spreche nicht gut Deutsch.	*I don't speak German well.*
Doch, Sie sprechen sehr gut Deutsch!	*Yes you do, you speak German very well.*
Kennst du Ursula nicht?	*Don't you know Ursula?*
Doch, ich kenne sie sehr gut!	*Sure, I know her very well.*

Lab Manual Kap. 3, Var. zur Üb. 16.

■ 16 ■ Übung: Doch! Contradict these negative statements and questions, beginning your response with a stressed **doch**.

Initial **doch** does not count as the first element in determining word order. See p. 34.

BEISPIEL: Schaffst du das nicht?
Doch, ich schaffe das!

1. Wir wollen nicht halten.
2. Wir haben nicht genug Geld.
3. Hast du keinen Bruder?
4. Es ist nicht sehr spät.
5. Kannst du kein Deutsch?
6. Willst du nicht zu Fuß gehen?

■ 17 ■ Übung Contradict your instructor if necessary.

BEISPIEL: Das ist kein Tisch.
Doch! Natürlich ist das ein Tisch!

The indefinite pronoun man

The indefinite pronoun **man** refers to people in general rather than to any specific person. Although the English indefinite pronoun *one* may sound formal in everyday speech, **man** does not sound this way in German. It is used in both colloquial and formal language. It is often best translated into English as *people, they, you,* or even *we.*

You can use **man** only as the subject of a sentence, and only with a verb in the third-person singular.

In Deutschland sagt **man** das oft.	*They often say that in Germany.*
Das muss **man** lernen.	*You've got to learn that.*
Das weiß **man** nie.	*One never knows.*

Do not confuse **man** with **der Mann** (*the man*).

Der Mann spricht Deutsch.	Hier spricht man Deutsch.

18 **Übung** Change the subject to **man**.

1. In Hinterwalden können die Leute nicht genug verdienen.
2. Um elf Uhr machen wir eine Pause.
3. Hoffentlich können wir drüben halten.
4. Hier können Sie gut essen.
5. Dürfen wir hier schlafen?

19 **Übung: Wie sagt man das auf Deutsch?** Use **man** as the subject.

1. In America we don't say that.
2. You've got to stop here.
3. One has to do that.
4. People say there are problems here. es gibt Probleme hier
5. Can we go on foot?

Lesestück

Vor dem Lesen

Tipps zum Lesen und Lernen

Tipp zum Vokabelnlernen

Masculine nouns ending in **-er** have the same form in the plural.

Singular	*Plural*
der Lehrer	die Lehrer
der Amerikaner	die Amerikaner
der Schüler	die Schüler
der Europäer	die Europäer
der Pullover	die Pullover
der Computer	die Computer

Resist the temptation to add an **-s** as in the English plural (*two pullovers*). Remember that *very few* German nouns take **-s** in the plural.

Übung Answer your instructor's questions with the plural form.

1. Wie viele Computer besitzt die Universität?
2. Wie viele Amerikaner sind hier im Zimmer?
3. Wie viele Schüler kennen Sie?
4. Wie viele Europäer studieren hier?
5. Wie viele Pullover besitzen Sie?

Leicht zu merken

Lab Manual Kap. 3, Üb. zur Betonung.

international	international	der **Sport**	
die **Jeans** (*pl.*)		das **System, -e**	System
optimistisch	optimistisch	das **Schulsystem**	Schulsystem
pessimistisch	pessimistisch	das **Theater**	Theater

1. The speakers in the following **Klassendiskussion** express opinions about their recent trip. Notice how often they preface opinions with such phrases as **Ich finde**, … or **Man meint**, … *(I think . . . , People think . . .).*

2. Remember that word order in German is in some ways freer than in English. It is true that the verb must be in second position in statements. In place of the subject, however, an object, an adverb, or some other element can be in first position. You will often find sentences beginning with the direct object:

Das finde ich auch.   *I think so too.* (literally: *I find that too.*)
Das kann ich verstehen.   *I can understand that.*

The clue to understanding such sentences is the personal ending of the verb. Words like **habe** and **finde** are obviously first person and go with the subject pronoun **ich**.

■ Wortschatz 2

Verben

besprechen (bespricht) to discuss
entscheiden to decide
hassen to hate
hören to hear
lachen to laugh
lernen to learn
schreiben to write
singen to sing

Substantive

der **Europäer, -** European (*m.*)
der **Fuß, -̈e** foot
  zu Fuß on foot
der **Mantel, -̈** coat
der **Pullover, -** pullover, sweater
  also: der **Pulli, -s**
der **Schuh, -e** shoe
  der **Turnschuh** sneaker, gym shoe
(das) **Amerika** America
(das) **Deutsch** German (*language*)
(das) **Englisch** English

(das) **Europa** Europe
das **Gymnasium, die Gymnasien** secondary school (*prepares pupils for university*)
das **Hemd, -en** shirt
das **Kleid, -er** dress; *pl.* = dresses *or* clothes
die **Angst, -̈e** fear
  Angst haben to be afraid
die **Europäerin, -nen** European (*f.*)
die **Farbe, -n** color
die **Hausaufgabe, -n** homework assignment
die **Hose, -n** trousers, pants
die **Jacke, -n** jacket
die **Musik** music
die **Reise, -n** trip
  eine Reise machen to take a trip
die **Sprache, -n** language
  die **Fremdsprache** foreign language

Gymnasium derives from Greek for the place where athletes trained (**gymnos** = *naked*). The word was later generalized to mean *place of study*.

die **Umwelt** environment
die **Welt, -en** world
die **Zeit, -en** time
die **Pommes frites** (*pl., pronounced "Pomm fritt"*) French fries

Adjektive und Adverbien

ähnlich similar
also thus, for that reason
amerikanisch American
darum therefore, for that reason
dunkel dark
ehrlich honest
eigentlich actually, in fact
fremd strange, foreign
neu new
schnell fast
toll (*colloq.*) great, terrific
ziemlich = quite

Basic meaning of **toll**: *mad, crazy* (**das Tollhaus** = *madhouse*).

Angst from Latin *angustiae* = a narrow constriction. English has borrowed **Angst** from German and uses it to mean *anxiety, existential fear*.

Farben

blau blue
braun brown
bunt colorful, multicolored
gelb yellow
grau gray
grün green
rot red
schwarz black
weiß white

Nützliche Ausdrücke

bitte please
Das finde ich auch. I think so too.
gar nicht not at all
Stimmt schon. That's right.

Gegensätze

dunkel ≠ **hell** dark ≠ light
hassen ≠ **lieben** to hate ≠ to love

lachen ≠ **weinen** to laugh ≠ to cry
neu ≠ **alt** new ≠ old
schnell ≠ **langsam** fast ≠ slow
Stimmt schon. ≠ **Stimmt nicht.** That's right. ≠ That's wrong.

Mit anderen Worten

uralt = sehr, sehr alt
blitzschnell = sehr, sehr schnell

Eine Klassendiskussion

 **Lab Manual** Kap. 3, Lesestück.

Last spring class 12a from the Kepler Gymnasium in Hannover visited a high school in California. Now they are discussing their impressions of the States with their teacher, Herr Beck; they also plan to write an article for their school newspaper.[1]

Learning about German secondary schools is the cultural goal of this chapter.

Notice the flavoring particle **ja** (lines 2 and 6) conveying the meaning *after all*.

HERR BECK: Können wir jetzt unsere Amerikareise ein bisschen besprechen? Rolf, möchtest du etwas sagen? – Ach, er schläft ja wieder. (*Alle lachen.*)

ROLF: Meinen Sie mich? Entschuldigung! Unsere Reise? Sie war° doch toll.

KIRSTEN: Das finde ich auch. Die Amerikaner sind wahnsinnig freundlich und jetzt
5 weiß ich, die Schüler in Amerika sind eigentlich gar nicht so anders. Dort trägt man ja auch Jeans und Turnschuhe, hört Rockmusik, singt dieselben Schlager° und isst Pommes frites.

HERR BECK: Stimmt schon, aber haben die amerikanischen Schüler auch ähnliche Probleme wie ihr?

dieselben Schlager = the same hits

10 ANDREAS: Ach, wissen Sie, alle Schüler hassen Hausaufgaben! (*Alle lachen.*) Nein, aber im Ernst°, wir sind alle manchmal pessimistisch. Man meint, man kann später° keine Arbeit finden, und auch die Umweltprobleme sind heute international. Auch in Amerika haben die Schüler manchmal ein bisschen Angst.

seriously
later

15 HERR BECK: Das kann ich verstehen, muss ich ehrlich sagen. Aber gibt es denn keine Unterschiede° zwischen hier und dort?

KIRSTEN: Doch, natürlich! Dort besuchen° alle Schüler die Highschool, bis sie 18 sind. Mit zehn Jahren müssen wir aber entscheiden: Gymnasium, Realschule oder Hauptschule.[2] Die zwei Schulsysteme sind also ganz
20 anders.

differences
here: attend

1. The **Gymnasium** in German-speaking countries has 13 grades. Class 12a is one of several parallel 12th-grade classes in the **Gymnasium**. Students stay in the same group for several years and take all their classes together. German 13th-graders are between 18 and 20 years old.
2. See *Almanach*, p. 86.

Die Schülerin hat eine Frage. (Hannover)

CHRISTA: Ich finde, wir müssen hier mehr und schneller° lernen. Deutschland ist in Mitteleuropa° und hat viele Nachbarländer°. Darum müssen wir ja Fremdsprachen lernen. Viele Europäer können z.B. gut Englisch, aber relativ wenige Amerikaner lernen Fremdsprachen. Andererseits° macht
25   man an der Schule[1] in Amerika mehr Sport, Musik und Theater.

HERR BECK: Jetzt haben wir leider keine Zeit mehr. Aber morgen können wir unseren Artikel über die Reise für die Schülerzeitung schreiben. Auf Wiedersehen bis dann.

faster
Central Europe /
   neighboring countries
on the other hand

Nach dem Lesen

■ A ■ **Unterschiede und Ähnlichkeiten** (differences and similarities) Which statements apply to schools in Germany, which apply to schools in America, which apply to both (**beide**)?

	Deutschland	USA	beide
1. Die Schüler hören gern Rockmusik.			✕
2. Man trägt oft Jeans und Turnschuhe.			✕
3. Die Schule hat 13 Klassen.	✕		
4. Fremdsprachen sind sehr wichtig.	✕		
5. Sport, Musik und Theater sind sehr wichtig.			✕
6. Mit zehn Jahren müssen Schüler die Schule wählen (choose).	✓		

important

1. **an der Schule** = *at school*. The article **der** indicates that **Schule** is in the dative case, which you will learn about in **Kapitel 5**.

■ B ■ Ein Stundenplan   Fabian Becker ist ein Schüler in Klasse 13 im Keplergymnasium. Hier sehen Sie seinen Stundenplan für die Woche. Sie können sehen, ein Schüler in Deutschland hat viele Fächer (*subjects*). Wie viele Fächer hat er? *12* Wie viele Fremdsprachen und naturwissenschaftliche Fächer (*science courses*) hat er? *2, 2* Was hat er am Montag und Dienstag? Welche (*which*) Hausaufgaben muss er am *biologie* Mittwochabend machen? *B, R M E F*

Wie ist sein Stundenplan anders als (*different from*) der Stundenplan in amerikanischen Schulen?

Zeit	Montag	Dienstag	Mittwoch	Donnerstag	Freitag
7⁴⁵ – 8³⁰	–	–	Französisch	Biologie	–
8³⁵ – 9²⁰	Englisch	Mathematik	Französisch	Biologie	–
9³⁰ – 10¹⁵	Religion	Politik/Erdkunde	Deutsch	Mathematik	Mathematik
10²⁰ – 11¹⁵	Deutsch	Chemie	Deutsch	Religion	Politik/Erdkunde
11²⁵ – 12¹⁰	Sport	Biologie	Geschichte	Englisch	Englisch
12¹⁵ – 13⁰⁰	Sport	Biologie	–	Französisch	Geschichte
13⁰⁰ – 14⁰⁰	(Orchester)				
14⁰⁰ – 14⁴⁵	Biologie				
14⁵⁰ – 15³⁵	Französisch				
15⁴⁰ – 16²⁵	Französisch		Chemie		
16³⁰ – 17¹⁵			Chemie		
17²⁰ – 18⁰⁵					

Workbook Kap. 3, H–O.

Lab Manual Kap. 3, Diktat.

■ C ■ Antworten Sie auf Deutsch.

1. Sind die Schüler in Amerika sehr anders oder sind sie ähnlich?
2. Was trägt man zum Beispiel in Amerika und auch in Deutschland? *Jeans und Turnschuhe*
3. Was isst man auch dort?
4. Was hassen alle Schüler? *Hausaufgaben*
5. Warum sind viele Schüler manchmal pessimistisch? *keine Arbeit*
6. Warum müssen die Deutschen Fremdsprachen lernen?
7. Was schreibt die Klasse für ihre Schülerzeitung?

Situationen aus dem Alltag

Talking about clothing is a communicative goal.

■ **Was soll ich heute tragen?**

This vocabulary focuses on an everyday topic or situation. Words you already know from **Wortschatz** sections are listed without English equivalents; new supplementary vocabulary is listed with definitions. Your instructor may assign some supplementary vocabulary for active mastery.

You already know some of this vocabulary.

die **Kleidung**	clothing
1. der **Anzug, ⁻e**	suit
2. die **Bluse, -n**	blouse
3. die **Brille** (*sing.*)	glasses
4. der **Handschuh, -e**	glove
5. das **Hemd, -en**	
6. die **Hose, -n** (*use sing.*)	
7. der **Hut, ⁻e**	hat
8. die **Jacke, -n**	
9. das **Kleid, -er**	
10. die **Krawatte, -n**	tie
11. der **Mantel, ⁻**	
12. der **Pulli, -s**	
13. der **Rock, ⁻e**	skirt
14. der **Schuh, -e**	
15. die **Tasche, -n**	pocket; handbag, shoulder bag
16. das **T-Shirt, -s**	T-shirt
17. der **Turnschuh, -e**	
18. der **Regenschirm, -e**	umbrella
19. die **Mütze, -n**	cap

der Sweater
der Schal   *scarf, shawl*

Gruppenarbeit: Was tragen Sie heute?

BEISPIEL: PROFESSOR: Was tragen Sie heute, Mary?
STUDENTIN: Ich trage _____ und _____ .

■ B ■ **Partnerarbeit: Was trägst du heute?**

BEISPIEL: A: Was trägst du heute, Mary?
B: Ich trage _____ und _____ . Was trägst du?

■ C ■ **Gruppenarbeit: Was tragen Sie in diesen Situationen?**

BEISPIEL: Es regnet.
Dann trage ich ...

1. Es regnet. (Es schneit. Es ist windig.)
2. Die Sonne scheint und es ist sehr warm.
3. Sie müssen eine Stelle suchen.
4. Sie und Ihre Mitbewohner machen heute Abend eine Party.

■ **Welche Farbe hat das?**

The prefixes **dunkel** and **hell** may be added to the colors you have learned in **Wortschatz 2**.

dunkelblau = *dark blue*
hellgrün = *light green*

Three more colors that may be useful:

rosa *pink*
lila *violet, lavender*
orange *orange*

▮	Belgien
✚	Dänemark
▤	Griechenland
✖	Großbritannien
▭	Luxemburg
▭	Niederlande
◉	Portugal
▭	Spanien
▦	EU
✚	Finnland
✚	Schweiz
●	Japan
✦	Kanada
▤	USA

■ D ■ **Übung** Welche Farben haben diese Fahnen (*flags*)?

BEISPIEL: Frankreich: blau, weiß, rot

▮▮ Frankreich

Deutschland: _____ , _____ , _____ [*gold*]
Österreich: _____ , _____ , _____
Schweden: _____ , _____
Italien: _____ , _____ , _____
Irland: _____ , _____ , _____

▭ Deutschland
▭ Österreich
✚ Schweden
▮▮ Italien
▮▮ Irland

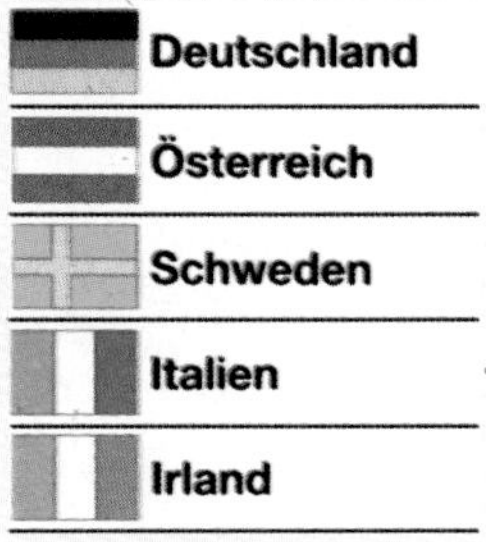

■ E ■ **Partnerarbeit** Ask each other about the colors of various things in the classroom and of clothing people are wearing.

BEISPIELE: Welche Farben hat die Landkarte?
Sie ist _____ .

Welche Farbe hat Peters Hemd?
Sein Hemd ist _____ .

A Note about Schools in German-speaking Countries

The public school systems in Germany, Austria, and Switzerland all differ from American public schools in the degree to which they track pupils. Relatively early in their schooling, children are steered toward apprenticeships, commercial training, or preparation for university study. In the Federal Republic of Germany, each **Land** (state) has authority over its own school system. In all **Länder**, children attend four years of elementary school (**Grundschule**) together. At the end of the fourth, fifth, or sixth grade (depending on the **Land**), they are then tracked into separate schools. The decision is made on the basis of grades and conferences between teachers and parents.

There are three possibilities: the **Hauptschule**, the **Realschule**, or the **Gymnasium**. The first two are oriented respectively toward trades and business and prepare the pupils for various forms of apprenticeship and job training. The **Gymnasium** is the traditional preparation for university study. After passing their final examination, called the **Abitur** in Germany and the **Matura** in Austria and Switzerland, pupils may apply to a university.

Since 1971, there has been some experimentation in the Federal Republic with **Gesamtschulen** (unified schools) comprising all three types of secondary schools. These schools resemble American high schools, in that pupils need not make their important decision at the age of ten, but can wait until they are sixteen. **Gesamtschulen**, however, comprise only a small percentage of the total number of secondary schools.

DUDEN
für
SCHÜLER

Land und Leute

Communicative Goals

- Making suggestions and giving commands
- Expressing likes, dislikes, and preferences
- Discussing weather, climate, and landscape

Cultural Goal

- Learning about the climate and geography of Germany

Chapter Outline

- **Lyrik zum Vorlesen**
  „Die Jahreszeiten"

- **Grammatik**
  Prepositions with the accusative case
  Suggestions and commands: The imperative
  The verb *werden*
  Negating *schon* and *noch*
  Equivalents of English *to like*
  Sentence adverbs
  Gehen + infinitive

- **Lesestück**
  Deutschland: Geographie und Klima

- **Situationen aus dem Alltag**
  Klima, Wetter und Landschaft

- **Almanach**
  The Common Origin of German and English;
  The German Spelling Reform

Lab Manual Kap. 4, Dialoge, Fragen, Hören Sie gut zu!, Üb. zur Aussprache [r].

Kitzbühel is a popular skiing and hiking resort in Tirol (Austria).

Das Frühstück originally meant the piece (**das Stück**) of bread eaten early (**früh**) in the morning.

Am See

FRAU MÜLLER: Wollen Sie noch einmal schwimmen gehen, Frau Brinkmann?
FRAU BRINKMANN: Nein, lieber nicht. Ich bin ein bisschen müde. Und das Wasser ist so wahnsinnig kalt. Gehen Sie doch ohne mich.
FRAU MÜLLER: Möchten Sie vielleicht lieber Karten spielen?
FRAU BRINKMANN: Ja, gerne!

Winterurlaub

RICHARD: Möchtest du im Winter nach Österreich?
EVA: Super! Fahren wir doch im Januar nach Kitzbühel.
RICHARD: Hoffentlich können wir noch ein Hotelzimmer bekommen.
EVA: Ich glaube, es ist noch nicht zu spät.

Morgens um halb zehn

ANITA: Also tschüss! Ich muss jetzt weg.
BEATE: Warte mal! Ohne Frühstück geht's nicht! Iss doch wenigstens ein Brötchen.
ANITA: Leider habe ich keine Zeit mehr. Mein Seminar beginnt um zehn und unterwegs muss ich noch ein Heft kaufen.
BEATE: Nimm doch das Brötchen mit. Später wirst du sicher hungrig.
ANITA: Du hast Recht. – Also, bis nachher!

Beim Bäcker kauft man frische Brötchen.

■ Wortschatz 1

Verben

beginnen to begin
bekommen to receive, *get*
frühstücken to eat breakfast
(etwas oder jemand) gern haben
    to like something or someone
glauben to believe; to think
kaufen to buy
mögen (mag) to like
schwimmen to swim
warten to wait
werden (wird) to become, to get
    (*in the sense of* "become")

Don't confuse **bekommen** (*to receive*) with **werden**
(*to become*).

Substantive

der **See, -n** lake
  am See at the lake
der **Urlaub, -e** vacation (*from a
    job*)
der **Winter, -** winter
  im Winter in the winter
das **Brötchen, -** roll
das **Frühstück** breakfast
  zum Frühstück for breakfast
das **Hotel, -s** hotel
(das) **Österreich** Austria
das **Seminar, -e** (*university*)
    seminar
das **Wasser** water
die **Karte, -n** card; ticket; map

Brötchen (called **Semmeln** in southern Germany
and Austria), crusty rolls baked fresh daily, are the
most common breakfast food.

Adjektive und Adverbien

einmal once
  noch einmal once again, once
    more
gern(e) gladly, with pleasure
Gott sei Dank thank goodness
hoffentlich I hope . . .
hungrig hungry
kalt cold
lang(e) long; for a long time
lieber (+ *verb*) prefer to, would
    rather
  Ich spiele lieber Karten. I'd
    rather play cards.
morgens (*adv.*) in the morning(s)
müde tired, weary
nachher later on, after that
noch nicht not yet
selbstverständlich it goes without
    saying that . . ., of course
später later
super (*colloq.*) super, great
unterwegs on the way; en route;
    on the go
weg away, gone
zusammen together

The final **-e** on **gerne** is optional; **gern** and **gerne**
mean the same thing.

Andere Vokabeln

doch (*flavoring particle with
    commands, see p. 104*)
durch through

gegen against
mal (*flavoring particle with com-
    mands, see p. 104*)
mit along (with me, us, etc.)
ohne without
um around; at (*with time*)

Nützliche Ausdrücke

Bis nachher! See you later!
Es geht. It's all right. It's possible.
    It can be done.
Es geht nicht. Nothing doing. It
    can't be done.
Lieber nicht. I'd rather not. No
    thanks. Let's not.
Recht haben to be right
  Du hast Recht. You're right.
Warte mal! Wait a second!
    Hang on!

Gegensätze

kalt ≠ heiß cold ≠ hot
kaufen ≠ verkaufen to buy ≠ to
    sell
lang ≠ kurz long; for a long time ≠
    short; for a short time
zusammen ≠ allein together ≠
    alone

Mit anderen Worten

todmüde = sehr müde
**super = fantastisch = prima =
    sehr gut**

At the Lake

MRS. M: Do you want to go
    swimming again, Mrs.
    Brinkmann?
MRS. B: No, I'd rather not. I'm a little
    tired. And the water is so
    awfully cold. You go without
    me.
MRS. M: Maybe you'd rather play
    cards?
MRS. B: Yes, gladly!

Winter Vacation

R: Would you like to go to Austria
    this winter?
E: Great! Let's go to Kitzbühel in
    January!
R: I hope we can still get a hotel
    room.
E: I don't think it's too late yet.

9:30 in the Morning

A: So long then. I've got to go now.
B: Wait a second! Not without
    breakfast! Eat a roll at least.
A: Unfortunately I have no more
    time. My seminar begins at ten,
    and on the way I still have to buy
    a notebook.
B: Take the roll along. Later you're
    sure to get hungry.
A: You're right . . . Well, see you later!

Variationen

■ A ■   Persönliche Fragen

1. Frau Brinkmann und Frau Müller spielen gern Karten. Was machen Sie gern?
2. Spielen Sie gern Karten oder gehen Sie lieber schwimmen?
3. Frau Brinkmann sagt, sie ist ein bisschen müde. Sind Sie heute müde?
4. Wohin wollen Sie im Winter?
5. Essen Sie immer Frühstück oder haben Sie manchmal keine Zeit?
6. Essen Sie gern Brötchen?
7. Wann beginnt die Deutschstunde?
8. Anita muss ein Heft kaufen. Was müssen Sie heute kaufen?

■ B ■   Gruppenarbeit: Gegensätze (*Mit offenen Büchern*)   Contradict each other.

> BEISPIEL: A: Fremdsprachen sind unwichtig.
> B: Nein, sie sind wichtig. *important*

1. 8.00 Uhr ist zu früh.
2. Dieses Buch ist langweilig. *interessant*
3. Dieses Zimmer ist schön. *hässlich*
4. Wir kennen jemand in München. *niemand*
5. Bernd hasst Rockmusik. *lieben*
6. Du trägst oft Turnschuhe. *selten*
7. Sie sind immer müde. *wach (aw ake)*
8. Ich esse sehr langsam. *schnell*

■ C ■   Partnerarbeit: Wie kann man antworten?   For each sentence in the left column choose appropriate responses from the right column.

1. Gehen wir noch einmal schwimmen!	Super!
2. Das Wasser ist zu kalt!	Du hast Recht.
3. Ohne Frühstück geht's nicht.	Stimmt schon.
4. Es gibt keine Hotelzimmer mehr.	Stimmt nicht.
5. Spielen wir zusammen Karten!	Das finde ich auch.
6. Das schaffst du leicht. *manage, get done*	Gar nicht!
7. Bist du hungrig?	Es tut mir Leid.
8. Ein Hotelzimmer mit Frühstück kostet 250 Mark!	Was ist denn los?
	Um Gottes Willen!
9. Du kommst wieder zu spät.	Nichts zu danken.
10. Mensch, bin ich müde.	Mensch!
	Fantastisch!
	Doch!
	Prima!
	Gerne!

Mensch, bin ich todmüde!

Now choose one of the exchanges above and expand it into a mini-dialogue. Prepare to say it for the whole class.

> BEISPIEL: A: Es gibt keine Hotelzimmer mehr.
> B: Um Gottes Willen! Was machen wir denn?
> A: Ich weiß nicht. Hoffentlich ...

Viele deutsche Kinder lernen dieses traditionelle Gedicht (*poem*) über die Jahreszeiten.

Lab Manual Kap. 4,
Lyrik zum Vorlesen.

Die Jahreszeiten°

	seasons
Es war° eine Mutter,	there was
Die hatte° vier Kinder:	who had
Den Frühling, den Sommer,	
Den Herbst und den Winter.	
Der Frühling bringt Blumen°,	flowers
Der Sommer bringt Klee°,	clover
Der Herbst, der° bringt Trauben°,	it / grapes
Der Winter bringt Schnee°.	snow

Grammatik

No German prepositions take nominative case, which is used only for the subject of a sentence and for predicate nominatives (see p. 33).

In spoken German, **durch**, **für**, and **um** often contract with the article **das**: **durchs**, **fürs**, **ums**.

Prepositions with the accusative case

Prepositions are a class of words that show relationships of space (*through* the mountains), time (*until* Tuesday), or other relationships (*for* my friend, *without* any money). A preposition with the noun or pronoun that follows it is called a prepositional phrase. German prepositions are used with nouns in specific grammatical cases. Here is the list of prepositions that are always followed by the accusative case. Learn this list by heart.

bis	*until, by*	Wir warten **bis Dienstag**.
		Ich muss es **bis morgen** lesen.
durch	*through*	Er fährt **durch die Berge**.
für	*for*	Sie arbeitet **für ihren Vater**.
gegen	*against*	Was hast du **gegen mich**?
	around, about (with times)	Karl kommt **gegen drei**. *(before, not after)*
ohne	*without*	Wir gehen **ohne dich**.
um	*around* (the outside of)	Das Auto fährt **um das Hotel**.
	at (with times)	Karl kommt **um drei**.

Workbook Kap. 4, A, B.

■ 1 ■ **Übung: Für wen?**

Sie suchen eine Karte. Für wen suchen Sie sie?
Ich suche sie für mein*en Bruder*.
Sie machen heute das Frühstück. Für wen machen Sie es?
Ich mache es für mein*en Mann*.

Lab Manual Kap. 4,
Var. zur Üb. 2.

■ 2 ■ **Übung: Ich mache das allein.** Your instructor asks if you do things with other people in your class. Say that you do everything without them. Use pronouns in your answer.

1. Spielen Sie mit Richard Karten? Nein, ohne *ihn* .
2. Arbeiten Sie morgen mit Ingrid zusammen? Nein, leider ohne *sie* .
3. Gehen Sie mit Robert und Susan schwimmen? *Nein, allein*
4. Frühstücken Sie am Mittwoch mit Patrick? *Nein, ohne ihn* .

■ 3 ■   **Übung: Wohin fährt Monika?**   ~~Where to~~   Monika is going to drive through various locations. Tell where she's driving. Use a complete sentence.

Sie fährt durch _____ .
Dann fährt sie durch _____ .

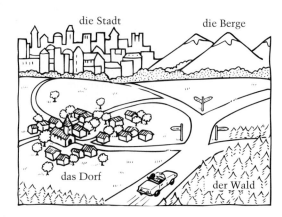

■ 4 ■   **Übung: Wie sagt man das auf Deutsch?**

1. Are you for me or against me?
2. I'd like to take a trip around the world.   *um die Welt*
3. I hope I can do it without my parents.
4. She's looking for a card for her grandfather.
5. Let's drive through the mountains.

Making suggestions and giving commands are communicative goals.

Suggestions and commands: The imperative

The imperative form of German verbs is used either to make suggestions ("Let's go swimming") or to give commands ("Wait!").

■ "Let's do something": The *wir*-imperative

Fahren wir nach Österreich.   ***Let's go** to Austria.*
Spielen wir Karten.   ***Let's play** cards.*

The **wir**-imperative has the same word order as a yes/no question, but at the end of the sentence, the voice drops instead of rising. Compare the following intonation curves:

Gehen wir nach Hause?   Gehen wir nach Hause!

In the first dialogue on page 88, Frau Brinkmann uses the **Sie**-imperative: *Gehen Sie* doch ohne mich.

■ "Do something": The *Sie*-imperative

Fahren Sie nach Österreich.   *Go to Austria.*
Bitte **besuchen Sie** mich im Mai.   *Please visit me in May.*

Bitte also turns an imperative into a
polite request: **Gehen Sie** *bitte* **nach
Hause.**

Note on punctuation: German uses an
exclamation mark to add emphasis to
commands.

Lab Manual Kap. 4, Üb. 5;
Var. zu Üb. 6, 7.

■ **5** ■   **Übung: Machen Sie das doch!**   Encourage your instructor to go ahead and
do something.

> BEISPIEL: Ich möchte eine Reise machen.
> Machen Sie doch eine Reise!

1. Ich möchte Brötchen kaufen.   *keine*
2. Ich möchte eine Pause machen.
3. Ich möchte nach Hause gehen.
4. Ich möchte Tennis spielen.   *kein*
5. Ich möchte Frau Klein besuchen.   *Besuchen Sie doch Frau Klein nicht*
6. Ich möchte meinen Wagen verkaufen.   *sell*   *Ihren*   *Verkaufen Sie Ihren Wagen nicht.*

■ **6** ■   **Übung: Nein, machen Sie das nicht!**   Now tell your instructor *not* to do
the things listed in **Übung 5**.

> BEISPIEL: Ich möchte nach Hause gehen.
> Nein, gehen Sie nicht nach Hause!

■ **7** ■   **Gruppenarbeit: Ja, machen wir das!**   Here are some activities you could
do today. Take turns suggesting them to each other.

> BEISPIEL: schwimmen gehen
> A: Gehen wir heute schwimmen!
> B: Ja, machen wir das! *oder* Nein, lieber nicht.

jetzt frühstücken	eine Reise machen
Karten spielen	eine Pause machen
eine Zeitung kaufen	nach Hause laufen
zu Hause arbeiten	den Wagen verkaufen

Now suggest other things to do today.

■ **8** ■   **Übung: Wie sagt man das auf Deutsch?** (*Mit offenen Büchern*)   Use the
Sie- or **wir**-imperative.

1. Let's go swimming.
2. Buy a notebook.
3. Let's discuss our trip.   *besprechen*
4. Learn a foreign language.   *eine Fremdsprache*
5. Please speak slowly.
6. Don't sleep now.   *jetzt nicht*
7. Let's walk a little bit.
8. Don't wear that.

Imperative forms for *du* and *ihr*

To give commands or make suggestions to people whom you address with **du**, you need to learn the forms of the **du-** and **ihr**-imperatives.

*The **du**-imperative* The **du**-imperative of most verbs is simply the verb stem without ending.

Geh ohne mich.	*Go without me.*
Frag mich nicht.	*Don't ask me.*
Fahr schnell nach Hause!	*Drive home quickly!*
Sei nicht so langweilig.	*Don't be so boring.*

Note: The pronoun **du** is *not* used with the **du**-imperative!

If the verb changes its stem vowel from **e** to **i(e)**, the *changed* stem is used:

Verb	*Statement*	*du-imperative*
lesen	Du **liest** das für morgen.	**Lies** das für morgen.
geben	Du **gibst** Peter das Buch.	**Gib** Peter das Buch.
essen	Du **isst** ein Brötchen.	**Iss** ein Brötchen.

Note that the stem-vowel change **a(u)** to **ä(u)** does *not* appear in the *du*-imperative:

fahren	Du **fährst** nach Hause.	**Fahr** nach Hause.
laufen	Du **läufst** zu schnell.	**Lauf** nicht so schnell!

Verb stems ending in **-d** or **-t** add an **-e** to the stem:

Arbeite nicht so viel.	*Don't work so hard.*
Warte doch!	*Wait!*

Lab Manual Kap. 4, Var. zu Üb. 9, 10; Üb. 11.

■9■ **Übung: Ja, tu das doch!**   Your instructor plays the part of your friend Beate. Tell her to go ahead and do the things she asks about.

> BEISPIEL: Soll ich da drüben halten?
> Ja, halte doch da drüben.

1. Soll ich Englisch lernen?
2. Soll ich mit Hans sprechen?
3. Soll ich Peter das Buch geben?
4. Soll ich schnell laufen?
5. Soll ich hier warten?
6. Soll ich Pommes frites essen?
7. Soll ich etwas singen?
8. Soll ich zu Fuß gehen?
9. Soll ich eine Zeitung lesen?
10. Soll ich eine Jacke tragen?

Gib Peter das Buch nicht, (handwritten note next to item 3)

lies (handwritten note next to item 9)

Wie bitte? Was sollen wir essen?

Reminder: **Sie-** and **wir-** imperatives include the pronoun; **ihr-** and **du-** imperatives do not.

■ 10 ■ **Partnerarbeit: Nein, lieber nicht.** Now tell your partner *not* to do the things listed in **Übung 9**. This time, do *not* use **doch**.

> BEISPIEL: Soll ich drüben parken?
> Nein, park nicht drüben. *over there*

The **ihr-***imperative* The **ihr-**imperative is identical to the present-tense **ihr-**form, but without the pronoun. *you - pl.*

Present tense	*ihr-imperative*
Ihr **bleibt** hier.	**Bleibt** hier.
Ihr **singt** zu laut.	**Singt** nicht so laut.
Ihr **seid** freundlich.	**Seid** freundlich.

■ 11 ■ **Übung: Sollen wir das machen?**

A. Your instructor plays one of a group of children and asks what they all should do.

> BEISPIEL: Sollen wir bald nach Hause kommen?
> Ja, kommt doch bald nach Hause.

1. Sollen wir Karten spielen?
2. Sollen wir das Buch lesen?
3. Sollen wir nach Hause laufen?
4. Sollen wir die Brötchen essen?

B. Now tell them what not to do.

> BEISPIEL: Sollen wir nach Hause kommen?
> Nein, kommt nicht nach Hause.

Tragt doch keine Jeans

1. Sollen wir Jeans tragen?
2. Sollen wir heute kommen?
3. Sollen wir hier bleiben?
4. Sollen wir das sagen?

■ **Imperative of *sein***

The verb **sein** is irregular in the **Sie-** and **wir-**imperatives (the **du-** and **ihr-**forms are regular):

Seien Sie bitte freundlich, Herr Kaiser.	*Please be friendly, Mr. Kaiser.*
Seien wir freundlich.	*Let's be friendly.*
Seid freundlich, Kinder.	*Be friendly, children.*
Sei freundlich, Rolf.	*Be friendly, Rolf.*

Lab Manual Kap. 4, Var. zur Üb. 12.

Workbook Kap. 4, C.

■ 12 ■ **Übung: Sei doch ...!**

A. Tell the following people to be honest.

> BEISPIEL: Richard
> Sei doch ehrlich, Richard!

1. Kinder *Seid*
2. Herr Bachmann *Seien Sie*
3. wir *Seien wir*
4. Barbara *sei*

B. Now tell them not to be so boring.

> **BEISPIEL:** Herr Stolze
> Seien Sie doch nicht so langweilig, Herr Stolze!

1. Ute *Sei doch nicht*
2. Frau Klein *Seien Sie*
3. Thomas und Beate *Seid*
4. wir *Seien wir*

■ **13** ■ **Übung: Wie sagt man das auf Deutsch?** (*Mit offenen Büchern*) Use the **du**-imperative.

1. Please be honest. *Bitte, sei ehrlich*
2. Wear your jeans. *Trag deine Jeans*
3. Please read the article. *Bitte, lies den A*
4. Give Anita your notebook. *Gib Anita deine Heft*

Now use the **ihr**-imperative.

5. Ask me later. *Frag mich später*
6. Please wait here. *Bitte wartet hier auf*
7. Work together. *Arbeitet zusammen*
8. Don't be so pessimistic. *Seid nicht so pessimistisch*

The verb werden

The only German verbs that are irregular in the present tense are **werden, sein, haben, wissen,** and the modal verbs. You have now learned them all.

Tell students that **werden** is another linking verb followed by the predicate nominative. Students tend to say: **Ich möchte einen Lehrer werden.**

The verb **werden** (*to become*) is irregular in present tense **du**- and **er**-forms.

ich	werde	wir	werden
du	**wirst**	ihr	werdet
er, es, sie	**wird**	sie, Sie	werden

Werden is a frequently used verb. Its basic English equivalent is to *become, get.* It can be translated in various ways, depending upon context.

Es **wird** kalt.	*It's getting cold.*
Ihre Kinder **werden** groß.	*Your children are getting big.*
Meine Schwester will Professorin **werden**.	*My sister wants to become a professor.*
Am Montag **werde** ich endlich 21.	*I'm finally turning 21 on Monday.*

■ **14** ■ **Übung: Wer wird müde?** Say who is getting tired.

> **BEISPIEL:** Barbara
> Barbara wird müde.

1. wir
2. die Kinder
3. meine Mutter
4. ihr
5. du
6. ich

■ **15** ■ **Übung: Wie sagt man das auf Englisch?**

1. Morgen wird es heiß.
2. Wann wirst du denn zwanzig?
3. Draußen wird es warm.
4. Das Buch wird endlich interessant.
5. Meine zwei Freunde wollen Lehrer werden.

Negating schon and noch

■ **Negation of schon**

The negations of **schon** (*already, yet*) are:

noch nicht	*not yet*
noch kein- [+ *noun*]	*not a* [+ noun] *yet*
	not any [+ noun] *yet*

Here are some examples of questions followed by negative answers.

Sind Sie **schon** hungrig?	*Are you hungry yet?*
Nein, **noch nicht**.	*No, not yet.*
Wollt ihr **schon** gehen?	*Do you want to leave <u>already?</u>*
Nein, wir wollen **noch nicht** gehen.	*No, we don't want to leave yet.*
Hast du **schon** Karten?	*Do you have tickets <u>yet?</u>* *already?*
Nein, ich habe **noch keine** Karten.	*No, I don't have any tickets yet.*
Kauft er **schon** einen Wagen?	*Is he already buying a car?*
Nein, er kauft **noch keinen** Wagen.	*No, he's not buying a car yet.*

 **Lab Manual** Kap. 4, Üb. 16, 17.

■ 16 ■ Übung: Nein, noch nicht. Answer the following questions about Katrin Berger negatively, saying that things haven't happened yet.

1. Ist Katrin schon da?   *Nein, K ist noch nicht da.*
2. Studiert sie schon in Berlin?
3. Kennt sie Frau Bachmann schon?   *kennt FB noch nicht.*
4. Beginnt das Semester schon?
5. Will sie schon essen?   *Sie will noch nicht essen*

■ 17 ■ Übung Say you don't have any of these things yet.

1. Haben Sie schon Kinder?   *noch keine Kinder*
2. Haben Sie schon eine Karte?   *„ keine Karte*
3. Haben Sie schon ein Hotelzimmer?
4. Besitzen Sie schon einen Wagen?
5. Haben Sie schon Angst?   *'noch keine Angst*
6. Besitzen Sie schon einen Computer?   *own*

In **Übung 17**, the short answers would all be **Nein, noch nicht.** Complete-sentence answers, however, must use **noch kein-** [+ *noun*].

■ **Negation of noch**

The negations of **noch** (*still*) are:

nicht mehr	*not any more, no longer*
kein- [+ *noun*] **mehr**	*no more* [+ noun], *not any more* [+ noun]

Here are some examples of questions followed by negative answers:

Regnet es **noch**?	*Is it still raining?*
Nein, **nicht mehr**.	*No, not any more.*

Studiert Rita **noch**?	*Is Rita still a student?*
Nein, sie studiert **nicht mehr**.	*No, she's no longer a student.*
Hast du **noch Geld**?	*Do you have any more money?*
Nein, ich habe **kein Geld mehr**.	*No, I haven't got any more money.*
Können wir **noch Karten** bekommen?	*Can we still get tickets?*
Leider habe ich **keine Karten mehr**.	*Unfortunately I have no more tickets.*

Lab Manual Kap. 4, Üb. 18, 19; Var. zu Üb. 18, 19.

■ **18** ■ **Übung**   Answer these questions negatively.

1. Wohnen Sie noch zu Hause?
2. Können Sie noch warten?
3. Ist es draußen noch kalt?
4. Ist Ihr Wagen noch neu?
5. Geht Ihre Uhr noch?
6. Können Sie uns noch besuchen?

Workbook Kap. 4, D.

■ **19** ■ **Übung**   Answer these questions negatively.

1. Hat er noch Arbeit?
2. Haben Sie noch Zeit?
3. Hat Ihre Großmutter noch einen Wagen?
4. Ist er noch ein Kind?
5. Gibt es noch Probleme?
6. Hören Sie noch Rockmusik?

Equivalents of English *to like*

Expressing likes, dislikes, and preferences is a communicative goal.

Gern is etymologically related to English *yearn*.

■   **Verb +** *gern(e)* **= to like to do something**

Ich **schwimme gern**.	*I like to swim.*
Sie **geht gern** zu Fuß.	*She likes to walk.*
Hören Sie **gerne** Musik?	*Do you like to listen to music?*

Gern(e) generally comes immediately after the subject and verb. The negation of **gern** is **nicht gern**.

Ich schwimme **nicht gern**.	*I don't like to swim.*

Lab Manual Kap. 4, Var. zu Üb. 20, 22.

■ **20** ■ **Partnerarbeit: Ich höre gern Musik.**   Take turns saying what you like to eat (**essen**), read (**lesen**), play (**spielen**), and listen to (**hören**). Here are some suggestions.

BEISPIEL: Ich höre gern Rockmusik. Und du?

Jazz	Fußball	Frühstück
Pizza	Brötchen	Volksmusik
Mozart	Zeitungen	Bücher
Tennis	Tischtennis	Lyrik (*poetry*)

■ **21** ■ **Kettenreaktion: Was machen Sie gern? Was machen Sie lieber?**

A: Ich spiele gern Tennis.
B: Sie spielt gern Tennis, aber ich lese lieber Bücher.
C: Er liest gern Bücher, aber ich _____ lieber _____ .
usw.

- *Mögen* or *gern haben* = to like someone or something

Ich **habe** dich sehr **gern.** ⎫
Ich **mag** dich sehr. ⎭ *I like you very much.*

Negation: Ich habe dich **nicht gern.**
Ich mag dich **nicht.**

Mögen is a modal verb. Its present-tense forms are:

mögen	*to like (something)*		
ich	**mag**	wir	mögen
du	**magst**	ihr	mögt
er, es, sie	**mag**	sie, Sie	mögen

cf. möchte

Unlike the other modals, it is usually used without an infinitive.

Ich **mag** Maria.   *I like Maria.*
Mögen Sie die Suppe nicht?   *Don't you like the soup?*

> Use **mögen** or **gern** + *verb* to say what you like to eat: **Ich mag die Suppe heute** and **Brötchen esse ich gern.** Do not use **gern haben** for food.

■ 22 ■   **Übung**   Tell who likes Frau Brandt. Use the appropriate form of **mögen.**

BEISPIEL: die Schüler
          Die Schüler mögen Frau Brandt.

1. du
2. wir
3. Franz
4. meine Eltern
5. ich
6. ihr

■ 23 ■   **Übung: Was haben Sie gern?**   Say which things and people you like or dislike. Here are some ideas. Add some of your own. Use **gern haben** or **mögen.**

meine Mitbewohner
das Mensaessen
den Winter *nicht gern*
Hausaufgaben

die Uni
meine Arbeit
meine Geschwister *siblings*
Fremdsprachen *foreign languages*

- **Summary: Three German equivalents for *to like***

Distinguish carefully among the three German equivalents for English *to like*:

- **Möchte** means *would like to* do something and is used with a complementary infinitive (which may sometimes be omitted, see p. 72):

Ich **möchte** Innsbruck besuchen.
Ich **möchte** nach Innsbruck (fahren).

- A *verb* + **gern** means *to like to do something.*

Ich spiele **gern** Karten.

Möchte expresses a wish for something, while a *verb* + **gern** makes a general statement about your likes or dislikes:

Ich **möchte** Karten spielen.   *I would like to play cards.*
Ich spiele **gern** Karten.   *I like to play cards.*

- **Mögen** or **gern haben** means *to like* people or things and is used with a noun or pronoun:

  Ich **mag** Professor Jaeger.
  Ich **habe** ihn **gern**.

■ 24 ■   Übung: Wie sagt man das auf Deutsch?

1. I like the soup.
2. I like to eat soup.   *Ich*
3. I would like the soup.
4. They would like to study in Germany.
5. Karl doesn't like to wait.   *wartet nicht gern*
6. Do you like Professor Lange?   *spielen*
7. Our children like to play outside.   *gern drausen*
8. We would like to drive home.
9. I don't like that.   *Ich habe das nichtgern*
10. I like her.   *{ Ich habe sie gern*
                    { Ich mag sie

8. Wir möchten gern nach Hause fahren

Sentence adverbs

Sentence adverbs modify entire sentences and express the speaker's attitude toward the content of the whole:

Natürlich bin ich morgens müde.	*Of course* I'm tired in the morning.
Du hast **sicher** genug Geld.	*You surely have enough money.*
Leider habe ich keine Zeit mehr.	*Unfortunately I have no more time.*
Gott sei Dank ist es nicht mehr so heiß.	*Thank goodness it's not so hot any more.*
Du kannst mich **hoffentlich** verstehen.	*I hope you can understand me.*
Selbstverständlich mag ich Pizza.	*Of course I like pizza.*
Übrigens habe ich kein Geld mehr.	*By the way, I don't have any more money.*

Lab Manual Kap. 4, Var. zur Üb. 25.

Workbook Kap. 4, E.

■ 25 ■   Übung: Selbstverständlich!   Answer these questions emphatically. Show that your answer is obvious by beginning it with **Selbstverständlich ...** or **Natürlich ...**

BEISPIEL: Lernen Sie Deutsch?
           Selbstverständlich lerne ich Deutsch!

1. Frühstücken Sie bald?
2. Sind Sie hungrig?
3. Haben Sie Zeit für mich?
4. Möchten Sie nach Österreich?
5. Schwimmen Sie gern?
6. Spielen Sie gern Karten?

■ 26 ■   Übung: Leider!   Answer these questions. Show that you regret having to answer "yes" by beginning your answer with **Ja, leider ...**

BEISPIEL: Regnet es noch?
           Ja, leider regnet es noch.

1. Schneit es noch?
2. Haben Sie viele Fragen?
3. Sind Sie sehr müde?
4. Ist der Berg sehr steil?
5. Gehen Sie ohne mich?
6. Ist das Wasser zu kalt?

Segelboot im Hafen von
Lindau (Bodensee)

Gehen + *infinitive*

The verb **gehen** is often used with an infinitive as its complement.

Sie **geht** oft **schwimmen**.	*She often goes swimming.*
Gehen wir noch einmal **schwimmen**!	*Let's go swimming again!*
Ich **gehe** mit Dieter **schwimmen**.	*I'm going swimming with Dieter.*

The complementary infinitive **schwimmen** is the second part of the predicate and comes at the end of the sentence.

Note what happens when the entire verbal idea **schwimmen gehen** (*to go swimming*) is used as the complement of a modal verb:

Wir wollen heute **schwimmen gehen**.	*We want to go swimming today.*

■ **27** ■ **Partnerarbeit: Dann geh doch …!** Partner A reads the sentences on the left. Partner B then tells partner A what to do, choosing an appropriate activity from the right-hand column.

> **BEISPIEL:** A: Ich bin müde.
> B: Dann geh doch schlafen!

1. Ich muss Geld verdienen.   arbeiten gehen
2. Ich bin hungrig.   schlafen gehen
3. Ich möchte gern fit bleiben.   essen gehen
4. Ich bin müde!   Tennis spielen gehen

Lesestück

Vor dem Lesen

Tipps zum Lesen und Lernen

■ Tipps zum Vokabelnlernen

- Note that all four compass points are masculine:

der Norden	der Osten
der Süden	der Westen

  Remember that the days, seasons, and the months are also masculine:

der Montag	der Januar
der Dienstag	der Februar
der Mittwoch	der März
der Donnerstag	der April
der Freitag	der Mai
der Samstag (oder Sonnabend)	der Juni
der Sonntag *(Norden)*	der Juli
	der August
der Frühling	der September
der Sommer	der Oktober
der Herbst	der November
der Winter	der Dezember

Haupt is derived from Latin *caput* (head).

- The prefix **Haupt-** is attached to nouns and adds the meaning *main, chief, primary, principal, most important.*

die **Haupt**regionen	*the principal regions*
die **Haupt**frage	*the main question*
die **Haupt**stadt	*the capital city*
die **Haupt**rolle	*the leading role*
die **Haupt**straße	*the main street*

Lab Manual Kap. 4, Üb. zur Betonung.

Kolonie: Both this word and the city name Cologne (German **Köln**) are derived from Latin *colonia*. The Roman emperor Claudius named the city Colonia Agrippinensis in A.D. 50 after his wife Agrippina. Its strategic position on the Rhine made it the capital of the Roman colony *Germania Inferior*.

■ Leicht zu merken

die **Alpen**	
barbarisch	
die **Geographie**	Geographie
geographisch	
die **Kolonie, -n**	Kolonie
der **Kontrast, -e**	Kontrast
die **Kultur, -en**	Kultur
mild	
die **Region**	Region
der **Rhein**	
wild	
zirka	

Rivers in German are generally **die**. Exceptions are **der Rhein, der Main, der Inn, der Lech, der Neckar**, and foreign rivers (**der Nil, der Mississippi**) except those ending in **-a** or **-e** (**die Themse, die Rhone**).

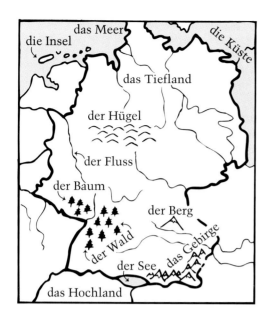

das Meer
die Insel
die Küste
das Tiefland
der Hügel
der Fluss
der Baum
der Berg
der Wald
das Gebirge
der See
das Hochland

■ **Einstieg in den Text**

The reading in this chapter builds on familiar vocabulary about the weather (**das Wetter**) and discusses climate and geography (**Klima und Geographie**).

Study this map and try to guess the meanings of the new words.

The word **Wein** is not of Germanic origin but was introduced by the Romans (Latin *vinum*) along with viniculture. The word **Bier** comes from Latin *bibere* (*to drink*). The Germanic word for beer is preserved in English *ale*, which was brewed without hops. The medieval cloister breweries first added hops to the beverage.

■ Wortschatz 2

Verben

beschreiben to describe
fließen to flow
liegen to lie; to be situated
trinken to drink
wandern to hike; to wander

Substantive

der **Baum, ⸚e** tree
der **Fluss, ⸚e** river
der **Frühling** spring
der **Herbst** fall, autumn
der **Hügel, -** hill
der **Norden** the North
der **Osten** the East
der **Schnee** snow
der **Sommer** summer
der **Süden** the South
der **Wald, ⸚er** forest

The obvious cognates in points of the compass and seasons (**der Herbst**, English *harvest*) recall common Germanic designations for time and space.

der **Wein, -e** wine
der **Westen** the West

das **Bier, -e** beer
(das) **Italien** Italy
das **Klima** climate
das **Land, ⸚er** country
das **Leben** life
das **Lied, -er** song
  das **Volkslied, -er** folk song
das **Märchen, -** fairy tale
das **Meer, -e** sea
das **Tal, ⸚er** valley

die **Landschaft, -en** landscape
die **Schweiz** Switzerland
die **Stadt, ⸚e** city

Adjektive und Adverbien

flach flat
hoch high
immer noch / noch immer still
  (*intensification of* **noch**)
modern modern
nass wet, damp

schrecklich terrible
sonnig sunny
trocken dry

Andere Vokabeln

von from

useful

Nützliche Ausdrücke

im Süden (im Norden usw.) in the South (in the North, etc.)
im Winter (im Sommer usw.) in the winter (in the summer, etc.)

Gegensätze

modern ≠ altmodisch modern ≠ old-fashioned
nass ≠ trocken wet ≠ dry

Deutschland: Geographie und Klima

Cultural goal: Learning about the climate and geography of Germany.

Lab Manual Kap. 4, Lesestück.

Für die alten Römer° war° das Leben in der Kolonie Germania nicht sehr schön. Der Historiker° Tacitus (zirka 55 bis 115 n.Chr.°) beschreibt das Land als° kalt und neblig°. Über die Germanen° schreibt er: „Sie sind ohne Kultur, haben keine Städte und leben im Wald. Sie sind wild und barbarisch, wie ihr Land."

5   Das moderne Deutschland liegt in Mitteleuropa und die „wilden Germanen" wohnen heute zum größten Teil° in der Stadt.[1] Es gibt keinen Urwald° mehr, aber der Wald ist immer noch typisch und wichtig für die Landschaft in Deutschland, Österreich und der Schweiz. Am Sonntag wandert man gern durch die Wälder und die Kinder hören auch heute noch gern Märchen wie „Hänsel und Gretel" oder

10 „Schneewittchen".[2] In solchen° Märchen und auch in deutschen Volksliedern spielt der Wald eine große Rolle.

    Auch das Klima in Deutschland ist Gott sei Dank nicht so schrecklich, wie° Tacitus meint. Selbstverständlich ist es nicht so warm und sonnig wie in Italien, aber das deutsche Klima ist eigentlich ziemlich mild. In den Flusstälern wird es zum Beispiel

15 im Winter nicht sehr kalt. Die großen Flüsse – der Rhein, die Weser, die Elbe und die Oder – fließen durch das Land von Süden nach Norden. Nur die Donau° fließt von Westen nach Osten. Am Rhein und an der° Donau trinkt man gern Wein; die Römer brachten° den Weinbau° nach Deutschland. Die Deutschen trinken also nicht nur Bier.

Romans / was
historian / **nach Christus** = A.D. / as / foggy / Germanic peoples

zum ... = for the most part of / primeval forest
important

such

so ... wie = as . . . as

actually quite mild

the Danube River
am and **an der** = on the
brought / viniculture

Familienwanderung im Regen

1. **Die Germanen** were the ancient tribes that the Romans called collectively *germani*. The word **Deutsch** comes from Old High German **diot** (*people*). The French applied the name of one tribe, the *alemanni*, to the whole people: *les Allemands*.
2. *Snow White.* Other folk tales are **Dornröschen** (*Sleeping Beauty*), **Rotkäppchen** (*Little Red Riding Hood*), **Aschenputtel** (*Cinderella*), and **Der Froschkönig** (*The Frog King*).

Burgruine (*castle ruin*)
Ehrenfels am Rhein

20   Es gibt in Deutschland drei geographische Hauptregionen. Im Norden ist das
Land flach und fruchtbar und ohne viele Bäume. Hier beeinflusst° das Meer – die
Nordsee und die Ostsee – Landschaft und Klima. Diese° Region nennt man das
Norddeutsche Tiefland°. In der Mitte des Landes° gibt es aber viele Hügel und kleine
Berge. Man nennt diese Region das Mittelgebirge°. Im Süden liegt das Hochgebirge° –
25 die Alpen. Hier gibt es natürlich viel Schnee im Winter, denn° die Berge sind sehr
hoch. Deutschlands höchster° Berg ist die Zugspitze (2 963 m). Man sieht also, in
Deutschland gibt es viele Kontraste: Stadt und Land, Wald und Feld°, Berge und Meer.

major

influences
this
North German lowlands /
In ... In the middle of the
country / central
mountains / high
mountains / because /
highest / field

Ostsee = Baltic

mtns

Nach dem Lesen

■ **A** ■   **Partnerarbeit: Märchen**   Take turns reading aloud these descriptions of
well-known **Märchen**. Then match the descriptions with the silhouettes on the next
page. Use context to help you guess unknown vocabulary.

1. Vier Freunde – ein Esel, ein Hund, eine Katze und ein Hahn – sind alt und können
   nicht mehr arbeiten. Also gehen sie zusammen nach Bremen. Dort wollen sie
   Straßenmusikanten werden und so ihr Brot verdienen.

   donkey

2. Eine Frau isst Rapunzeln (*lamb's lettuce, a leafy salad vegetable*) aus dem Garten
   ihrer Nachbarin. Diese Nachbarin ist aber eine Hexe. Die Hexe nimmt die
   erstgeborene Tochter der Frau und schließt sie in einen Turm.

3. Ein kleines Mädchen bringt ihrer kranken Großmutter Kuchen und Wein. Sie
   muss durch einen Wald, aber im Wald wartet ein Wolf. Der Wolf frisst die
   Großmutter und das Mädchen auf.

4. Eine Familie ist sehr arm und hat nicht genug zu essen. Die Stiefmutter zwingt
   den Vater, seine Kinder im Wald zu lassen. Bruder und Schwester finden dort ein
   kleines Haus aus Brot, Kuchen und Zucker. Dort wohnt aber eine böse Hexe und
   sie will die Kinder essen.

   evil

A.

B.

C.

D.

■ B ■   **Antworten Sie auf Deutsch.**

1. Wie beschreibt Tacitus die Kolonie Germania?
2. Was ist <u>noch immer</u> typisch für die Landschaft in Deutschland?
3. Was macht man gern am Sonntag?
4. Wie ist das Klima in Deutschland?
5. Ist es so warm und sonnig wie in Italien?
6. Wo trinkt man viel Wein?
7. Wie ist das Land im Norden?
8. Wo gibt es viel Schnee im Winter?
9. Wie heißen die drei geographischen Hauptregionen?

■ C ■ **Partnerarbeit: Tacitus modern – Gespräch** (conversation) **mit einem römischen Historiker** Tacitus has returned to modern Germany. Work in pairs. Correct his outdated impressions by completing the following dialogue, then perform it for your classmates.

TACITUS: Ihr Germanen seid alle furchtbar barbarisch. *(terribly)*

REAKTION: Das stimmt gar nicht mehr! Wir sind heute *zum großen Teil in der Stadt*.

TACITUS: Euer Klima ist schrecklich, immer kalt und neblig.

REAKTION: *Nein, das Klima ist eigentlich ziemlich mild*.

TACITUS: Ihr lebt ja alle im Wald wie die wilden Tiere (*animals*).

REAKTION: *Das stimmt nicht mehr. Wir leben in der Stadt, ohne Wald und wilden Tiere*.

TACITUS: Ihr trinkt nur Bier und keinen Wein. Das finde ich barbarisch.

REAKTION: *Das ist nicht wahr. Wir trinken viel Wein, und auch Bier*.

Lab Manual Kap. 4, Diktat.

Workbook Kap. 4, F–K.

Situationen aus dem Alltag

Discussing weather, climate, and landscape is a communicative goal.

This vocabulary focuses on an everyday topic or situation. Words you already know from **Wortschatz** sections are listed without English equivalents; new supplementary vocabulary is listed with definitions. Your instructor may assign some supplementary vocabulary for active mastery.

With this chapter you have completed the first quarter of **Neue Horizonte: A Brief Course.** For a concise review of the grammar and idiomatic phrases in chapters 1–4, you may consult the **Zusammenfassung und Wiederholung 1** (*Summary and Review 1*) of your Workbook. The review section is followed by a self-correcting test.

■ **Klima, Wetter und Landschaft**

You already know some of these words from the introductory chapter (see pp. 12–13).

Klima und Wetter

die **Luft** *air*
der **Regen** *rain*
  regnerisch *rainy*
  Es regnet.
der **Schnee**
  Es schneit.
der **Wind** *wind*
  Es ist windig.
wolkig *cloudy*
neblig
sonnig
windig
kalt ≠ **heiß**
warm ≠ **kühl**
nass ≠ **trocken**
mild

Landschaft

der **Baum,** ¨e
der **Berg,** -e
der **Hügel,**
  hügelig *hilly*
  bergig *mountainous*
der **Wald,** ¨er
das **Meer,** -e
das **Tal,** ¨er

■A■   Gruppenarbeit: Sprechen wir über Klima und Landschaft.   Beschreiben Sie die Landschaft in diesen Fotos.

1.

2.

3.

■B■   Partnerarbeit: Landschaft und Klima, wo ich wohne   Find out where your partner comes from and ask about the climate and geography there.

BEISPIEL: Woher kommst du denn?
Wie ist das Klima dort im Sommer?
Kannst du die Landschaft beschreiben?

View Module 2 of the *Neue Horizonte* video (5:29) and do the activities in **Videoecke 2** in your Workbook/Laboratory Manual/Video Manual.

In der Natur vergisst man den Stress des Alltags.

The Common Origin of German and English

Although Tacitus thought the Germanic tribes had "always been there," in fact, they originated in the Baltic region around the second millenium B.C. As the Roman Empire began to collapse in the fourth century A.D., the Germanic peoples migrated south, a movement that continued for nearly two hundred years. The **Germani** (as they were called by the Romans) displaced the Celts from the heart of the European continent, pushing them as far west as Ireland. The Romans temporarily halted Germanic expansion southward by establishing their own northern frontier, a series of fortifications called the **limes**, literally the "limits" or boundaries of their empire. Remains of the **limes** can be seen in Germany today. Contemporary dialects and regional differences within the German-speaking countries have their origins in the various Germanic tribes of the early Middle Ages.

Thanks to the migration of the Germanic Angles and Saxons to the British Isles in the fifth century A.D., the Germanic language that was to evolve into modern English was introduced there. German and English thus share a common origin. Some other languages included in the Germanic family are Yiddish, Dutch, Flemish, Norwegian, Swedish, Danish, and Icelandic. You will easily recognize cognates (words that have the same etymological root) in English and German, although different meanings may have developed. These words can be readily identified by some regularly occurring consonant shifts. Try guessing the English equivalents for the following words:

German	English	Related words
z	t	zehn = ten
		Herz =
ss	t	Wasser =
		groß =
pf	p	Pflanze =
ff	p or pp	Schiff =
		Pfeffer und Salz =
ch	k	machen =
		Milch =
t	d	Tag =
		Tür =
d	th	du =
		drei =
		Pfad =

Hochdeutsch (*High German*) is the official, standardized language of the German-speaking countries. It is the language of the media, the law, and education, and is based on written German (**Schriftdeutsch**). Educated native speakers are bi-dialectal, knowing their local dialect and High German, which they may speak with a regional accent.

The German Spelling Reform

English speakers are used to alternate spellings. In particular, most of us are aware that there are variant British and American spellings of a number of words (*jail/gaol, tire/tyre, theater/theatre*). Thus, you may be surprised that the German-speaking countries have an officially approved set of spelling rules. German spelling was codified in 1902 in a set of 212 rules. Compared to English, you will find that German spelling is very phonetic, that is, every letter stands for only one or at the most two sounds. For instance, German **o** represents the long or the short version of a single vowel sound, whereas English *o* represents a different sound in each of the following words: *to, woman, women, hold, world, long, got*. In German, it is almost always possible to sound out a new word correctly according to the pronunciation rules you have learned.

In spite of German's already straightforward spelling, however, language experts from the German-speaking countries have been working for the past 15 years or so on a reform aimed at making the orthography even more rational. After years of discussion and revision, the new spelling was agreed to by the governments of Austria, Germany, and Switzerland in July 1996. The new rules (112 instead of the 212 of 1902) have been taught in schools since 1998–1999, although the old spelling will continue to be allowed until 2005. You are learning the new spelling in *Neue Horizonte: A Brief Course*.

Although the spelling reformers during their deliberations solicited opinion from the general public and especially from professional writers, most German authors were caught off guard by the announcement of the new rules. Many of them signed a declaration of protest and call to resistance against the reform at the Frankfurt Book Fair in October 1996. But although some authors have threatened to refuse permission to reprint their works in the reformed orthography, the **Rechtschreibreform** appears to be inevitable.

In fact, the reform doesn't change German spelling very much. It has been characterized as a **Reförmchen**—*a reformlet*—by some critics. Many regret that the reformers were not able to agree on the elimination of noun capitalization and of the letter **ß**, the two major features that make German spelling different from that of other languages that use the Latin alphabet. The Swiss Germans have not used the diagraph-S for years and the reform allows them to continue to use **ss** instead.

Although you are learning German in the new spelling, you will inevitably encounter the old spelling as well when you travel in Europe or read German books and magazines printed before 1998. The main differences you will notice are the following:

1. In the new spelling, the letter **ß** is used only when an unvoiced, hissing *s*-sound (rather than a voiced, buzzing *s*-sound) follows a long vowel or diphthong:

   Klasse (short **a** followed by unvoiced *s*)
   Straße (long **a** followed by unvoiced *s*)
   Nase (long **a** followed by voiced *s*)

In the old spelling, **ß** occurred in other cases as well. You need only remember that this letter always represents the unvoiced *s*-sound, both in the old and the new spelling. Here are some examples of the changes:

New spelling	Old spelling
dass	daß
ich muss	ich muß
der Fluss	der Fluß

2. In the new spelling, several noun + verb combinations are written apart, whereas they used to be written together.

New spelling	Old spelling
Rad fahren	radfahren
Ski laufen	skilaufen

3. In unchanging idiomatic phrases, some nouns are now capitalized that used to be written lower case:

New spelling	Old spelling
auf Deutsch	auf deutsch
heute Morgen	heute morgen
morgen Abend	morgen abend

Arbeit und Freizeit

Communicative Goals

- Talking about work and professions
- Showing, giving, and telling things to people
- Asking about prices in shops
- Saying when and for how long things happen

Cultural Goal

- Learning about the world of work in Germany

Chapter Outline

- **Lyrik zum Vorlesen**
  Richard Dehmel, „Der Arbeitsmann"

- **Grammatik**
  Dative case
  Dative personal pronouns
  Word order of noun and pronoun objects
  Prepositions with dative case
  Verbs with separable prefixes
  Verbs with inseparable prefixes
  Time phrases in accusative case

- **Lesestück**
  Drei Deutsche bei der Arbeit

- **Situationen aus dem Alltag**
  Berufe

- **Almanach**
  Stellenangebote (*Help Wanted Ads*)

Dialoge

Lab Manual Kap. 5,
Dialoge, Fragen, Hören Sie
gut zu!, Üb. zur Aussprache **(I)**.

Der neue Bäckerlehrling kommt an

Morgens um 6.00. Georg macht die Bäckerei auf.

MARTIN: Morgen. Ich heiße Martin Holst. Ich fange heute bei euch an. *right away* / *start*

GEORG: Morgen, Martin. Mein Name ist Georg. Den Chef lernst du gleich kennen.

MARTIN: Ist gut. Seit wann arbeitest du denn hier?

GEORG: Erst seit einem Jahr. Komm jetzt mit und ich zeige dir den Laden. *shop*

Beim Bäcker

VERKÄUFERIN: Was darf's sein, bitte?

KUNDE: Geben Sie mir bitte sechs Brötchen und ein Bauernbrot.

VERKÄUFERIN: *(Sie gibt ihm das Brot.)* So, bitte sehr. Sonst noch etwas?

KUNDE: Sind diese Brezeln frisch? *pretzels*

VERKÄUFERIN: Ja, von heute Morgen.

KUNDE: Dann geben Sie mir doch sechs Stück. Wieviel kostet das bitte?

VERKÄUFERIN: Das macht zusammen DM 6,80, bitte sehr.

KUNDE: Danke. Auf Wiedersehen.

VERKÄUFERIN: Wiedersehen.

DM 6,80 is pronounced **sechs Mark achtzig.**

Schule oder Beruf?

VATER: Warum willst du denn jetzt die Schule verlassen? Deine Noten sind ja ganz gut und du hast nur noch ein Jahr.

KURT: Aber das Abitur brauch' ich nicht. Ich will ja Automechaniker werden. *exam*

VATER: Sei nicht so dumm! Als Lehrling verdienst du schlecht. *earn*

KURT: Aber ich hab' die Nase einfach voll. Ich möchte lieber mit den Händen arbeiten. *fed up*

VATER: Quatsch! Du schaffst das Abitur und ich schenke dir ein Motorrad. Einverstanden?

KURT: Hmmm.

Lehrling: apprentice in training, colloquially called **Azubi** (acronym for the official term **Auszubildender** = *person to be trained*).

Note on Usage: *Seit wann?*

Seit wann **arbeitest** du hier?   *How long **have** you **worked** here?*

English uses perfect tense (*have worked*) for a situation beginning in the past but still continuing. German uses present (**arbeitest**).

„bei *Heinz Holl* "
Spezialitäten Restaurant für Kenner
Geöffnet: Mo. - Sa. 19.00 -2.00 Uhr

1 Berlin 31
Damaschkestraße 26
Tel.: 32 31 404
Tischbestellungen erbeten!

Wortschatz 1

See p. 123 for an explanation of the raised dot in **an·fangen** and other verbs.

Verben

an·fangen (fängt an) to begin, start
an·kommen to arrive
an·rufen to call up
auf·hören (mit etwas) to cease, stop (*doing something*)
auf·machen to open
auf·stehen to stand up; to get up; get out of bed
kennen lernen to get to know; to meet
kosten to cost
mit·kommen to come along
schenken to give (*as a gift*)
stehen to stand
verlassen (verlässt) (*trans.*) to leave (*a person or place*)
zeigen to show

Substantive

der **Automechaniker, -** auto mechanic
der **Bäcker, -** baker
der **Bauer, -n** farmer
der **Chef, -s** boss
der **Kunde, -n** customer (*m.*)
der **Laden, ⸚** shop, store
der **Lehrling, -e** apprentice
der **Name, -n** name

das **Abitur** final secondary school examination
das **Brot** bread
das **Bauernbrot** dark bread
das **Jahr, -e** year
das **Motorrad, ⸚er** motorcycle
das **Stück, -e** piece
sechs **Stück** six (*of the same item*)

die **Bäckerei, -en** bakery
die **Brezel, -n** soft pretzel
die **Chefin, -nen** boss (*f.*)
die **Deutsche Mark (DM)** the German mark
die **Hand, ⸚e** hand
die **Kundin, -nen** customer (*f.*)
die **Nase, -n** nose
die **Note, -n** grade
die **Woche, -n** week

Adjektive und Adverbien

dumm dumb
einfach simple, easy
erst not until; only
fertig (mit) done, finished (with); ready
frisch fresh
gleich right away, immediately
heute Morgen this morning
voll full

Andere Vokabeln

als as a
als Lehrling as an apprentice
als Kind as a child
dies- this, these
dir (to *or* for) you
euch (to *or* for) you (*pl.*)
jed- each, every
wem? to *or* for whom?
wie viel? how much?

Dies- and **jed-:** These words (*this, every*) always take endings (**dieser, jede**, etc.).

Präpositionen mit Dativ

The eight prepositions below are followed by dative case. See **Grammatik**, p. 121.

aus out of; from
außer except for; besides

bei at; at the home of
bei euch with you, at your place (*i.e., where you work or live*)
mit with
nach after
seit since (*temporal*)
von from; of; by
zu to

Nützliche Ausdrücke

Ist gut. (*colloq.*) O.K.; Fine by me.
Was darf es sein? What'll it be? May I help you?
Bitte sehr. Here it is. There you are.
Sonst noch etwas? Will there be anything else?
Das macht zusammen ... All together that comes to . . .
Ich habe die Nase voll. I'm fed up. I've had it up to here.
Quatsch! Baloney! Nonsense!
Einverstanden. Agreed. It's a deal. O.K.

Gegensätze

an·fangen ≠ auf·hören to start ≠ to stop
auf·machen ≠ zu·machen to open ≠ to close
dumm ≠ klug dumb ≠ smart, bright
einfach ≠ schwierig simple ≠ difficult
voll ≠ leer full ≠ empty

Mit anderen Worten

das **Abi** = das Abitur (*Schülerslang*)
blöd = dumm

The New Baker's Apprentice Arrives

Six A.M. Georg is opening the bakery.

M: Morning. My name is Martin Holst. I'm starting here today.

G: Morning, Martin. My name is Georg. You'll meet the boss soon.

M: O.K. How long have you been working here?

G: Only for a year. Now come with me and I'll show you the shop.

At the Baker's

*CL: May I help you?

**CU: Give me six rolls and one loaf of dark bread, please.

CL: (*She gives him the bread.*) There you are. Anything else?

CU: Are these pretzels fresh?

CL: Yes, from this morning.

CU: Then give me six of those. How much is that, please?

CL: Together that comes to six marks eighty.

CU: Thank you. Good-bye.

CL: Bye.

*CL = Clerk
**CU = Customer

School or Profession?

F: Why do you want to leave school now? Your grades are pretty good and you've only got one more year.

K: But I don't need the **Abitur**. I want to be an auto mechanic.

F: Don't be so dumb. You won't earn much as an apprentice.

K: But I'm fed up. I'd rather work with my hands.

F: Nonsense! You pass your **Abitur** and I'll give you a motorcycle. Is it a deal?

K: Hmmm.

Variationen

■ A ■ Persönliche Fragen

1. Der Vater schenkt Kurt ein Motorrad. Was schenkt Ihnen Ihr Vater? Er schenkt mir _____ .

2. Kurt sagt, das Abitur braucht er nicht. Was brauchen *Sie* nicht?

3. Kurt hat nur noch ein Jahr und dann ist er mit der Schule fertig. Wie viele Jahre haben Sie noch an der Universität?

4. Kurt arbeitet gern mit den Händen. Arbeiten Sie auch gern mit den Händen?

5. Martin lernt den Chef gleich kennen. Wen möchten *Sie* kennen lernen?   *Whom?*

6. Sechs Brezeln und ein Bauernbrot kosten DM 6,80. Was kosten 12 Brezeln und zwei Bauernbrote?

"The Germans have an inhuman way of cutting up their verbs. Now a verb has a hard enough time of it in this world when it's all together. It's downright inhuman to split it up. But that's just what those Germans do. They take part of a verb and put it down here, like a stake, and they take the other part of it and put it away over yonder like another stake, and between these two limits they just shovel in German."

Mark Twain

Asking about prices in shops is a communicative goal.

■ B ■   Partnerarbeit: Was darf's sein? (*Mit offenen Büchern*)   Partner A spielt den Verkäufer oder die Verkäuferin, Partner B spielt eine Kundin oder einen Kunden. Für das Semester müssen Sie viel kaufen. Spielen Sie diesen Dialog zusammen. Hier sehen Sie, was man kaufen kann.

May I help you? What'll it be?

euro price = ½ of

A: Guten Tag. Was darf's denn sein, bitte?
B: Zeigen Sie mir bitte _____ .
A: Bitte sehr.   *(Here you are)*
B: Was kostet denn _____ ?
A: Das kostet _____ .
B: Ich möchte gern _____ , _____ und _____ kaufen.
A: Das macht zusammen DM _____ , bitte sehr.

Lyrik zum Vorlesen

Richard Dehmel worked as a journalist in Berlin and was active in progressive literary circles. The language of his revolutionary lyric poetry was influenced by the philosopher Friedrich Nietzsche. In this poem an **Arbeitsmann** (*day laborer*) contrasts his family's life of toil and deprivation with the freedom, beauty, and fearlessness of the swallows that he and his child see on a Sunday walk.

Lab Manual Kap. 5, Lyrik zum Vorlesen.

Der Arbeitsmann

Wir haben ein Bett°, wir haben ein Kind,	bed
Mein Weib!°	**mein Weib = meine Frau**
Wir haben auch Arbeit, und gar zu zweit°,	**und** ... = and even together
Und haben die Sonne und Regen und Wind.	
Und uns fehlt nur eine Kleinigkeit°,	**uns** ... = we lack only a small thing
Um so frei zu° sein, wie die Vögel° sind:	**um** ... **zu** = in order to / birds
Nur Zeit.	

Wenn wir sonntags° durch die Felder° gehn,
Mein Kind,
Und über den Ähren weit und breit°
Das blaue Schwalbenvolk blitzen sehn°,
Oh, dann fehlt uns nicht das bisschen
Kleid,
Um so schön zu sein, wie die Vögel sind:
Nur Zeit.

on Sundays / fields

über ... = above the grain far and wide
Das ... = see flocks of blue swallows
  flashing
lack, be missing

Nur Zeit! wir wittern° Gewitterwind°,
Wir Volk°.
Nur eine kleine Ewigkeit°;
Uns fehlt ja nichts, mein Weib, mein Kind,
Als all das, was durch uns gedeiht°,
Um so kühn° zu sein, wie die Vögel sind.
Nur Zeit!

smell / stormwind
common folk
eternity

Als ... = except for all that prospers
  through us
daring

Richard Dehmel (1863–1920)

Dative comes from **datus**, a form of the Latin verb **dare** (*to give*). The etymology highlights an important function of dative case: to designate the receiver of something given.

Grammatik

Dative case

The dative case is the case of the indirect object in German. An indirect object is the person or thing *for* whom an action is performed or *to* whom it is directed.

Sie gibt **ihm** das Brot.   *She gives him the bread.* (or)
                              She gives the bread to him.

English shows the indirect object by means of word order and in some cases also uses a preposition (*to* him, *for* the teacher).

■ 1 ■ **Übung**   Identify the direct object and the indirect object in the following English sentences.

  1. We owe him a debt of gratitude.
  2. I'm buying my father a necktie.
  3. Tell me what you think.
  4. We're cooking spaghetti for the kids.
  5. Peel me a grape.
  6. To whom did you say that?

Die Arbeit in der Bäckerei
fängt früh an.

■ German versus English indirect object

You can recognize the dative case by the form of the personal pronoun (e.g., **dir** = *to/for you*) or of the article or possessive adjective used with a noun (**dem** Lehrer = *to/for the teacher*, **ihrer** Tochter = *to/for her daughter*).

German does *not* use a preposition to show the indirect object. It is signalled by case alone.

Here are some verbs you already know that can take a dative and an accusative object in the same sentence: **sagen (Sag mir etwas); geben (Ich gebe dir 2 Mark); kochen; tragen; schreiben; singen; kaufen; verkaufen; beschreiben; schenken; zeigen.** *give gift*

      ind. obj.   *dir. obj.*
Ich kaufe **dir das Motorrad**.

{ *I'll buy you the motorcycle.*
{ *I'll buy the motorcycle for you.*

      ind. obj.   *dir. obj.*
Sag **dem Lehrer Guten Morgen**.

{ *Tell the teacher good morning.*
{ *Say good morning to the teacher.*

      ind. obj.   *dir. obj.*
Sie gibt **ihrer Tochter das Geld**.

{ *She's giving her daughter the money.*
{ *She's giving the money to her daughter.*

Showing, giving, and telling things to people are communicative goals.

The German case system allows more flexibility in word order than does English. The following sentences all say basically the same thing, with some minor shifts in emphasis.

Sie gibt **ihrer Tochter das Geld**.
Sie gibt **das Geld ihrer Tochter**.
Das Geld gibt sie **ihrer Tochter**.
Ihrer Tochter gibt sie **das Geld**.

By mastering the case endings, you can always find your way through such sentences and understand what they mean.

■ Forms of the dative case

The definite article, indefinite article, possessive adjectives, and **dies-** all share the same set of dative endings. The chart below shows these dative forms, as well as the nominative and accusative forms of the definite article (the cases you have already learned).

	masc.	neut.	fem.	plural
nom. acc.	der Vater den Vater	das Kind	die Frau	die Leute
dat.	-em **dem** Vater dies**em** Vater ein**em** Vater unser**em** Vater	-em **dem** Kind dies**em** Kind ein**em** Kind dein**em** Kind	-er **der** Frau dies**er** Frau ein**er** Frau sein**er** Frau	-en -n **den** Leuten dies**en** Leuten kein**en** Leuten mein**en** Leuten

Note: *All nouns* in the dative plural add an **-n** to the noun itself (**den** Leute**n**, **den** Hän-**den**), except those nouns already ending in **-n** (**den** Frauen) and those ending in **-s** (**den** Hotels).

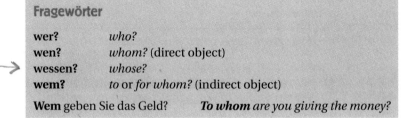

Fragewörter

wer?	*who?*
wen?	*whom?* (direct object)
wessen?	*whose?*
wem?	*to* or *for whom?* (indirect object)

Wem geben Sie das Geld?   ***To whom*** *are you giving the money?*

Übungen

Lab Manual Kap. 5, Var. zur Üb. 2.

Workbook Kap. 5, A.

To review family vocabulary, see pp. 60–61.

■2■ Übung: Wem soll sie es geben?   Beate kann ihr Brötchen nicht essen. Wem soll sie es geben?

> **BEISPIEL:** die Lehrerin
>   Sie soll es der Lehrerin geben.

Feminine
1. ihre Freundin *ihrer*
2. ihre Schwester *ihrer*
3. die Professorin *der*
4. die Chefin
   Boss (F)

Neuter and masculine
5. ein Kind · *einem*
6. ihr Freund *ihrem*
7. der Lehrer *dem*
8. mein Vater *meinem*
9. dieser Automechaniker *m*

Plural
10. die Kinder *n*
11. diese Leuten *n*
12. die Studenten
13. ihre Freunde *n*

■3■ Kettenreaktion: Wem schenkst du den Pulli?   Sie kaufen einen schönen Pulli für jemand in Ihrer Familie. Wem schenken Sie ihn?

> **BEISPIEL:** A: Wem schenkst *du* den Pulli?
>   B: Meiner Schwester. Wem schenkst *du* den Pulli?
>   C: Mein-_____ . Wem ... ?

Das gebe ich dir, aber was gibst du mir?

■ 4 ■ **Übung: Wie sagt man das auf Deutsch?** Benutzen Sie (*Use*) den du-Imperativ.

> BEISPIEL: Buy the child a book.
> Kauf dem Kind ein Buch.

1. Buy your [er] sister a book.
2. Give my parents the money.
3. Describe the problem to the mechanic.
4. Write your mother a card.
5. Cook the food for your friends.
6. Show my friend the city.

Dative personal pronouns[1]

The following table lists the dative personal pronouns and reviews their nominative and accusative forms as well.

	Singular [*direct* *indirect*]				Plural			
nom.	*acc.*	*dat.*			*nom.*	*acc.*	*dat.*	
ich	mich	**mir**	*to/for me*		wir	uns	**uns**	*to/for us*
du	dich	**dir**	*to/for you*		ihr	euch	**euch**	*to/for you*
er	ihn	**ihm**	*to/for him*		sie	sie	**ihnen**	*to/for them*
es	es	**ihm**	*to/for it*		Sie	Sie	**Ihnen**	*to/for you*
sie	sie	**ihr**	*to/for her*					

Note the similarities between the third-person dative pronouns and the dative endings of the articles and possessive adjectives.

> **ihm** → **dem** Mann, **meinem** Kind
> **ihr** → **der** Frau, **seiner** Schwester
> **ihnen** → **den** Freunden, **unseren** Kindern

■ 5 ■ **Übung: Kaufen wir Brot.** Sie wollen Brot kaufen. Ihre Professorin möchte wissen, **wem** Sie es kaufen. [*for whom*]

> BEISPIEL: Wem kaufen Sie das Brot? (*points to another student*)
> Ich kaufe es *ihm* / *ihr*.

■ 6 ■ **Partnerarbeit: Kaufst du mir etwas?** Taking turns and using the cues below, ask your partner what he or she will do for you.

> BEISPIEL: Kaufst du mir eine Brezel?
> Ja, ich kaufe dir eine Brezel *oder*
> Nein, ich kaufe dir keine Brezel.

> dein Motorrad verkaufen [sell]   Geld schenken
> deine Fotos zeigen [show]   eine Karte kaufen [card, map]
> deine Reise beschreiben [describe]   ein Brötchen geben (gibst)

Lab Manual Kap. 5, Var. zur Üb. 6.

Workbook Kap. 5, B, C.

---

1. Note that English pronouns do not have different forms for the direct object and the indirect object, whereas German pronouns (except **uns** and **euch**) do.

> *I see **him**.*   Ich sehe **ihn**.
> *I'm giving **him** the book.*   Ich gebe **ihm** das Buch.

Word order of noun and pronoun objects

Verbs such as **geben**, **schenken**, **kaufen**, **beschreiben**, **sagen**, and **zeigen** often have *describe* two objects. The first is usually the person (in the dative case) *to whom* something is given, shown, etc., or *for whom* something is done. The second object is the thing (in the accusative case) that is being given, shown, bought, etc.

Ich zeige **meiner Freundin den Laden**.	*I'm showing my girlfriend the shop.*

If one of the objects is a <u>pronoun,</u> it precedes the noun object.

Ich zeige **ihr den Laden**. *Dative*	*I'm showing her the shop.*
Ich zeige **ihn meiner Freundin**. *Acc.*	*I'm showing it to my girlfriend.*

If both objects are pronouns, the <u>accusative must precede the dative.</u> (Note the similarity to English word order.)

Ich zeige **ihn ihr**.	*I'm showing it to her.*

Any personal pronouns that are not in the first position are placed *immediately after the inflected verb.*

Note the third example: the direct-object pronoun (**uns**) even precedes the noun subject (**dein Opa**).

Ich gebe **ihm** mein Buch.	*I'm giving **him** my book.*
Ich gebe **es** meinem Bruder.	*I'm giving **it** to my brother.*
Kann <u>**uns**</u> dein Opa anrufen?	*Can your grandpa phone **us**?*

If more than one personal pronoun follows the verb, they come in the order *nominative, accusative, dative.* Again, this is just like English word order: *subject pronoun, direct-object pronoun, indirect-object pronoun.*

Ich gebe **es Ihnen** heute.	*I'm giving **it to you** today.*
Heute gebe **ich es Ihnen**.	*Today **I'm** giving **it to you**.*

Lab Manual Kap. 5, Var. zur Üb. 7.

Workbook Kap. 5, D.

■ **7** ■ **Übung: Wem schenken Sie das Buch?** You've bought copies of your favorite novel as presents. Your instructor will ask whom you're giving it to. Answer the questions affirmatively, using pronouns.

BEISPIEL: Wem schenken Sie das Buch? Schenken Sie es Ihrer Mutter?
Ja, ich schenke es <u>ihr</u>.

Schenken Sie es ...

1. Ihrem Vater? *ihm*
2. den Kindern? *ihnen*
3. Ihrem Freund? *ihm*
4. Ihrer Mitbewohnerin? *ihr*
5. mir?
6. uns?

MERIAN zeigt Ihnen die Welt.

As with the list of accusative prepositions (p. 91), you must learn this list until you can repeat it in your sleep.

sing to 'Blue Danube'!

Prepositions with dative case

The dative case is also used for the object of the following prepositions.

aus	*out of*	Sie sieht **aus** dem Fenster.	*She's looking out of the window.*
	from (native country, city or region)	Ich komme **aus** Amerika.	*I'm from America.*
außer	*except for*	**Außer** ihm sind wir alle hier.	*We're all here except for him.*
	besides, in addition to	**Außer** ihm wohnt auch sein Bruder hier.	*Besides him, his brother lives here too.*
bei	*in the home of*	Ich wohne **bei** meiner Tante.	*I live at my aunt's.*
	at	Er ist **bei** der Arbeit.	*He's at work.*
mit	*with*	Ich arbeite **mit** den Händen.	*I work with my hands.*
nach	*after*	**Nach** der Arbeit bin ich manchmal müde.	*After work I'm sometimes tired.*
	to (with country and city names)	Wir fahren **nach** England.	*We're going to England.*
seit	*since* (referring to time)	**Seit** dem Tag mag ich ihn nicht mehr.	*Since that day I haven't liked him.*
	for	Ich arbeite **seit** einem Jahr hier.	*I've worked here for a year.*
von	*from*	Das Buch habe ich **von** meiner Mutter.	*I got that book from my mother.*
	of	Er ist ein Freund **von** mir.	*He's a friend of mine.*
	by	Das ist ein Buch **von** Hermann Hesse.	*That's a book by Hermann Hesse.*
zu	*to* (people and some locations) *building*	Ich gehe **zur** Schule und dann **zu** meinen Freunden.	*I'm going to school and then to my friends' house.*

in die Schweiz
in die Türkei
in die Ver Staat (us)

■ Contractions

The following contractions are standard.

bei dem	→ **beim**	Brezeln kaufe ich immer **beim** Bäcker.
von dem	→ **vom**	Ich komme gerade **vom** Chef.
zu dem	→ **zum**	Ich muss schnell **zum** Professor.
zu der	→ **zur**	Ich gehe jetzt **zur** Schule.

Lab Manual Kap. 5,
Var. zur Üb. 8.

Workbook Kap. 5, E.

■ **8** ■ **Übung: Bei wem wohnen Sie?** Sie sind alle Studenten in Tübingen. Sie wohnen aber nicht im Studentenwohnheim (*dormitory*). Sagen Sie Ihrem Professor oder Ihrer Professorin, bei wem Sie wohnen.

> BEISPIEL: Bei wem wohnen Sie?
> Bei meinem Freund.

Tante	Freundin	Bruder	Großeltern
Familie	Vater	Freund	Frau König
			Herr König *(Herrn)*

■ **9** ■ **Kettenreaktion: Zu wem gehst *du*?** Say whom you are going to see, then ask another student.

> BEISPIEL: PROFESSOR/IN: Zu wem gehen Sie?
> A: Ich gehe zu meiner Familie. Zu wem gehst *du*?
> B: Ich gehe zum Bäcker. Zu wem ...

zum Automechaniker	*zur* Bäckerin	Lehrling *apprentice*
zur Professorin	Automechanikerin	Amerikaner
Professor	*zu den* Eltern	Familie
Chef	Amerikanerin	Bäcker

■ **10** ■ **Übung: Mit wem gehen Sie schwimmen?** Sie gehen mit Freunden aus der Deutschstunde schwimmen. Sagen Sie, mit wem Sie schwimmen gehen.

> BEISPIEL: PROFESSOR/IN: Mit wem gehen Sie schwimmen?
> STUDENT/IN: (*points to one or more other students in the class*)
> Mit ihr/ihm/ihnen.
> *3 ps f*

Verbs with separable prefixes

The meanings of many English verbs can be changed or modified by the addition of another word.

> to find → to find out
> to look → to look up
> to burn → to burn down
> to hang → to hang around

Likewise, the meanings of many German verbs are modified—or even changed completely—by the addition of a prefix to the root verb.

stehen	*to stand* → **auf**stehen	*to stand up; get out of bed*
kommen	*to come* → **mit**kommen	*to come along*
hören	*to hear* → **auf**hören	*to cease, stop*
fangen	*to catch* → **an**fangen	*to begin*

Similarly:

ankommen	*to arrive*
anrufen	*to call up*
aufmachen	*to open*
kennen lernen	*to get to know, meet*
zurückkommen	*to come back*

Note that although **kennen lernen** is written as two words, the first element **kennen** behaves like a separable prefix.

Ruf doch mal an!

Telekom

Such verbs are called *separable-prefix verbs*. Separable-prefix verbs have the primary stress on the prefix (**an**kommen, **auf**hören).

In the present tense and the imperative, the prefix is *separated* from the verb and placed at the end of the sentence or clause. It is the second part of the predicate.

Ich **stehe** morgen sehr früh **auf**.	*I'm getting up very early tomorrow.*
Wann **stehst** du **auf**?	*When are you getting up?*
Stehen Sie bitte **auf**!	*Please get up!*
Steht ihr denn bald **auf**?	*Are you getting up soon?*

When a verb with a separable prefix complements a modal verb, the separable prefix is again attached to the root verb infinitive at the end of the sentence or clause.

Without a modal	*With a modal*
Er **fängt** morgen **an**.	Er soll morgen **anfangen**.
Sie **kommt** bald **zurück**.	Sie möchte bald **zurückkommen**.

Note: Separable prefixes will be indicated in the **Wortschatz** sections by a raised dot between prefix and root verb: **an·fangen**. This symbol is often used in textbooks, though *not* in conventional German spelling.

Lab Manual Kap. 5, Var. zu Üb. 11, 12.

Workbook Kap. 5, F, G.

■ 11 ■ **Übung** Ihre [*Your*] Professorin sagt, Sie sollen etwas machen. Antworten Sie, Sie können es nicht machen.

BEISPIEL: Fangen Sie doch heute an.
Ich kann heute nicht anfangen.

1. Hören Sie doch auf.
2. Kommen Sie doch mit.
3. Machen Sie das Fenster auf.
4. Rufen Sie doch Ihre Mutter an.   *Ich kann meine Mutter nicht anrufen*
5. Stehen Sie bitte auf.
6. Kommen Sie bitte heute zurück.

■ 12 ■ **Übung** Ihr Professor sagt, Sie müssen etwas machen. Sie antworten, Sie sind einverstanden. [*agreed*]

BEISPIEL: Sie müssen um sieben aufstehen.
Einverstanden, ich stehe um sieben auf. [*Agreed*]

1. Sie müssen jetzt anfangen.
2. Sie müssen früh aufstehen.
3. Sie müssen um acht aufmachen.
4. Sie müssen Helena anrufen.
5. Sie müssen aufhören.
6. Sie müssen gleich mitkommen. [*right away*]

■ 13 ■ **Partnerarbeit: Mach das bitte für mich.**

1. **aufmachen** Partner A asks partner B to open various things, and B agrees.

BEISPIEL: A: Mach doch _____ auf.
B: Gut, ich mache _____ auf.

das Buch	Laden [M]	Rucksack [M]	Zeitung [F]
das Fenster	Tür	Tasche [F] *pocket, handbag*	

2. **anrufen** Partner B tells A to call up various relatives and friends. Partner A doesn't want to.

BEISPIEL: B: Ruf doch dein_____ *en* an.
           A: Aber ich will mein-_____ nicht anrufen.

Onkel	Tante	Freundin	Lehrer
Bruder	Schwester	Großeltern	Professorin
Mutter	Vater	Geschwister *pl*	

3. **Um 7 Uhr** Partner A wants to know when B is going to do various things. Partner B answers with the time.

BEISPIEL: A: Wann kommst du denn zurück?
           B: Um 7 komme ich zurück.

arrive   ankommen   mit deiner Arbeit aufhören *stop*
        zurückkommen   morgens aufstehen *get up*
begin anfangen (fängst ... an)   den Chef kennen lernen

Verbs with inseparable prefixes

There are also German verbs with *inseparable* prefixes. These prefixes *never* separate from the root verb. You can tell them from separable prefixes in these ways:

• They are *never* stressed.

• They have no independent meaning of their own, while separable prefixes resemble other parts of speech such as prepositions (**mit**kommen) and adverbs (**zurück**kommen).

The inseparable prefixes are: **be-, emp-, ent-, er-, ge-, ver-,** and **zer-.** Here are the verbs with inseparable prefixes that you have already learned: **bedeuten, beginnen, bekommen, beschreiben, besitzen, besprechen, besuchen, entscheiden, verdienen, verlassen, verstehen.**
describe *own* *discuss* *decide* *earn*
leave

■ 14 ■ **Übung**   Say these verb pairs aloud to practice the difference between stressed separable prefixes and unstressed inseparable prefixes. Then complete the following sentences with the appropriate verb.

Inseparable	*Separable*
verstehen	**auf**stehen
beschreiben	**auf**schreiben (*to write down*)
gehören (*to belong to*)	**auf**hören
bekommen	**mit**kommen
erfahren (*to find out*)	**ab**fahren (*to depart*)

1. Ich *verstehe* dich nicht.   (*understand*)
   Ich *stehe* um 7 Uhr *auf* .   (*get up*)

2. *Beschreiben* Sie es bitte!   (*describe*)
   Schreiben Sie es bitte *auf* !   (*write down*)

3. Harald *bekommt* heute ein Motorrad.   (*is getting*)
   Bernd *kommt* heute *mit* .   (*is coming along*)

Time phrases in accusative case

Saying when and for how long things happen is a communicative goal.

Here are some time phrases telling *when* or *how often* something occurs or *how long* it goes on. The nouns in these phrases are in the *accusative case*.

Remember that when a time phrase uses a preposition, that preposition will govern the case of the noun: **seit dem Tag** *since that day;* **nach einer Stunde** *after an hour.*

Wann?

diesen Freitag	dieses Semester	diese Woche
diesen Herbst	dieses Jahr	
diesen März		

Ich studiere **dieses Semester** in Konstanz.	*I'm studying in Konstanz this semester.*
Diese Woche ist Thomas krank.	*Thomas is sick this week.*

Wann / Wie oft?

jeden Morgen	jedes Semester	jede Minute
jeden Abend	jedes Jahr	jede Stunde
jeden Tag		jede Woche
jeden Montag		
jeden Mai		
jeden Sommer		

Remember that expressions of time (**jeden Tag**) precede expressions of place or destination (**zum Bäcker**).

Wir gehen **jeden Tag** zum Bäcker.	*We go to the baker's every day*
Er fährt **jedes Jahr** nach Amerika.	*He goes to America every year.*

Wie lange?

einen Tag	ein Jahr	eine Minute	drei Tage
		eine Stunde	zwei Semester

Wir bleiben **einen Tag** in London.	*We're staying in London for a day.*
Ich studiere **ein Semester** in Köln.	*I'm studying in Cologne for a semester.*

Note that the German equivalent of "*for* a day" is simply **einen Tag** without a preposition.

1. Wie oft stehen Sie um 7 Uhr auf?
   Ich stehe _jeden Tag_ um 7 Uhr auf. (*every day*)

2. Wann rufen Sie Ihre Eltern an?
   Ich rufe sie _diesen_ an. (*this Wednesday*)
   Mittwoch

3. Wie lange bleiben Sie in Tübingen?
   Ich bleibe _ein Jahr_ dort. (*a year*)
   eines

4. Wann arbeitest du denn mit Karl zusammen?
   Wahrscheinlich arbeite ich _diese_ mit ihm zusammen. (*this week*)
   Woche

5. Wie lange wartet ihr noch?
   Wir warten noch _einen_ vor der Bäckerei. (*for an hour*)
   Stunde

6. Hoffentlich kannst du lange bei uns bleiben.
   Nein, leider kann ich nur _ein Tag_ bei euch sein. (*one day*)

7. Wann ist das Klima bei euch besonders schön?
   Das Wetter ist _jeden_ mild und sonnig. (*every October*)
   Oktober

8. Wann kann ich Sie besuchen, Herr Wahrig?
   Jeden Dienstag um 9 Uhr bin ich frei. (*every Tuesday*)

Lesestück

Vor dem Lesen

Tipps zum Lesen und Lernen

■ **Tipps zum Vokabelnlernen**

Agent nouns Both English and German add the suffix **-er** to a verb stem to form a noun that denotes a person who performs the action (agent). In German, the additional ending **-in** indicates that the agent is female.

arbeiten	→ **der Arbeiter / die Arbeiterin**	*to work*	→ *worker*
lesen	→ **der Leser / die Leserin**	*to read*	→ *reader*

Sometimes an umlaut is added in the agent noun:

anfangen	→ **Anfänger**	*to begin*	→ *beginner*
tragen	→ **Briefträger**	*to carry*	→ *letter carrier*
backen	→ **Bäcker**	*to bake*	→ *baker*
handeln	→ **Buchhändler**	*to trade, deal*	→ *bookseller*

■ **A** ■ **Übung** Was machen diese Leute?

1. Herr Kropf ist Kaffeetrinker.
2. Frau Baumann ist Zeitungsleserin.
3. Wir sind alle Anfänger.
4. Albert ist Frühaufsteher.
5. Frau Hanselmann ist Buchhändlerin.

Lab Manual Kap. 5, Ex. on Professions.

Briefträgerin in Bielefeld
(Nordrhein-Westfalen)

Adverbs of time German adds an **-s** to the names of the days or parts of the day to form adverbs showing regular or habitual occurrence.

morgens	*in the mornings, every morning*
nachmittags	*in the afternoons, every afternoon*
abends	*in the evenings, every evening*
nachts	*at night, every night*
montags	*Mondays, every Monday*
dienstags	*Tuesdays, every Tuesday*
usw.	*etc.*

 Note: These words are *adverbs*, not nouns, and are therefore not capitalized.

■ **B** ■ **Übung** Wann machen Sie das?

BEISPIEL: Wann essen Sie Brötchen?
Morgens esse ich Brötchen.

1. Wann haben Sie Deutsch?
2. Wann trinken Sie Kaffee? *homework*
3. Wann machen Sie Ihre Hausaufgaben?

4. Wann gehen Sie zum Bäcker?
5. Wann rufen Sie Ihre Familie an?

Lab Manual Kap. 5,
Üb. zur Betonung.

Korsika (*Corsica*) is a French island in the Mediterranean. See map on the inside of the back cover.

■ **Leicht zu merken**

campen	(pronounced **kämpen**)
die **Industrie, -n**	Industrie
der **Journalist, -en**	Journalist
(das) **Kanada**	
der **Korrespondent, -en**	Korrespondent
(das) **Korsika**	
der **Partner, -**	
realistisch	
der **Supermarkt**	
die **Universität, -en**	Universität
die **USA** (*pl.*)	

The title "Drei Deutsche bei der Arbeit" lets you know that the reading will focus on three individuals and their work. What sorts of things would you expect to learn about people's personal and professional lives from such a reading? You can apply to this text the familiar question words that you have been using to ask about each other's lives.

Before reading the whole text, skim the third portrait and see if you can quickly find answers to the following questions:

Wie heißt dieser Mann?
Wie alt ist er?
Was macht er?
Wo wohnt er?
Wer sind die anderen (*other*) Menschen in seiner Familie?

Let these questions guide your reading for information as you work through the entire text.

■ Wortschatz 2

Verben

ab·holen to pick up, fetch, get
aus·sehen (sieht aus) to appear, look (happy, tired, fit, etc.)
  Du siehst schrecklich aus. You look terrible.
berichten to report
ein·kaufen to shop for; to go shopping
fern·sehen (sieht fern) to watch TV
reisen to travel
schließen to close
spazieren gehen to go for a walk
sterben (stirbt) to die
vergessen (vergisst) to forget
vorbei·kommen to come by, drop by

Substantive

der **Arbeiter, -** worker
der **Fußball** soccer
der **Reiseführer, -** (travel) guide book
der **Roman, -e** novel
der **Stadtplan, ⸚e** city map
der **Stress** stress

das **Bild, -er** picture; image
das **Dorf, ⸚er** village
(das) **Frankreich** France
das **Geschäft, -e** business; store
das **Mittagessen** midday meal, lunch
das **Schaufenster, -** store window
das **Wochenende, -n** weekend
  am Wochenende on the weekend
das **Wort** word (*2 plural forms:* die **Worte**: words in a context; die **Wörter**: unconnected words, as in a dictionary)
das **Wörterbuch, ⸚er** dictionary

die **Buchhandlung, -en** bookstore
die **Fabrik, -en** factory
die **Freizeit** free time
die **Mannschaft, -en** team
die **Muttersprache, -n** native language
die **Postkarte, -n** postcard
die **Stimme, -n** voice
die **Wanderung, -en** hike
die **Zeitschrift, -en** magazine

die **Lebensmittel** (*pl.*) groceries

The word **Frankreich** recalls the original empire of the Franks (**die Franken**), a Germanic tribe that settled mainly west of the Rhine. The greatest Frankish king was Charlemagne (**Karl der Große**), 747–814 A.D.

Adjektive und Adverbien

abends (in the) evenings
aktuell current, topical
besonders especially
bunt colorful
fleißig industrious, hard-working
französisch French
meistens mostly, usually

Gegensätze

fleißig ≠ **faul** industrious ≠ lazy

Mit anderen Worten

stressig (*colloq.*) = **mit viel Stress**

Remember that singular masculine nouns ending in **-er** have the same form in the plural: **der Arbeiter, die Arbeiter**. Feminine forms ending **-erin**, however, do have a plural ending: **die Arbeiterin, die Arbeiterinnen**.

Drei Deutsche bei der Arbeit

Lab Manual Kap. 5, Lesestück.

Learning about the world of work in Germany is the cultural goal of this chapter.

Man sagt über die Deutschen, sie leben für ihre Arbeit. Stimmt das heute noch? Unsere Beispiele zeigen ein anderes° Bild.

different

Christine Sauermann, Buchhändlerin

Christine Sauermann ist 35 Jahre alt, geschieden°, und hat einen jungen Sohn Oliver

5 (10 Jahre alt). Sie ist seit sieben Jahren berufstätig und besitzt seit fünf Jahren eine Buchhandlung in der Altstadt° von Tübingen.[1] Zwei Angestellte° arbeiten für sie im Laden.

divorced
owns (owns)
old city / employees

Das Geschäft geht gut, denn° viele Touristen gehen durch die Altstadt spazieren

und Studenten kommen auch jeden Tag vorbei. Mit den neuesten° Romanen sieht ihr

10 Schaufenster immer bunt aus. Den Studenten verkauft sie Wörterbücher und Nachschlagewerke°, aber die Touristen kaufen meistens Reiseführer, Stadtpläne und Postkarten von der Stadt.

business
because
newest   *aussehen = appear*
reference works

Morgens macht sie um 9 Uhr auf und abends um 6 Uhr zu. Von 1 Uhr bis 3 Uhr

macht sie Mittagspause°. Sie schließt den Laden, holt Oliver von der Schule ab und

15 geht mit ihm nach Hause. Dort kocht sie das Mittagessen und kauft später dann noch Lebensmittel im Supermarkt ein.[2]

midday break
groceries

Außer sonntags arbeitet Christine Sauermann jeden Tag sehr fleißig in ihrem

Laden. In ihrer Freizeit möchte sie also Erholung° vom Stress. Darum macht sie gern

Wanderungen mit ihrem Sohn zusammen. Diesen Sommer zum Beispiel gehen sie

20 zusammen in Schottland° campen.

hardworking
relaxation
Scotland

Es ist schon spät, aber die Buchhandlung ist noch offen. (München)

---

1. Most German cities and towns have an **Altstadt** (*old city*) in their centers, which may date from the Middle Ages. They are often pedestrian zones. **Tübingen** is a university town on the Neckar River about twenty miles south of Stuttgart. The university was founded in 1477.
2. Many small shops and businesses close from 1:00 to 2:30 or 3:00 P.M., but this practice is less common nowadays in large cities. The noon meal is traditionally the main meal of the day.

Jörg Krolow (22 Jahre alt), Fabrikarbeiter

Jörg Krolow arbeitet seit einem Jahr als Mechaniker in einer Autofabrik in Dortmund.[1]
Die Arbeit ist schwer, aber gut bezahlt°. Nach der Arbeit trinkt er oft ein Bier mit   paid
Freunden zusammen oder sieht fern. Am Wochenende spielt er im Sportverein°   sports club
25 Fußball.

      Wie die meisten° deutschen Arbeiter in der Schwerindustrie ist Krolow in einer   most
Gewerkschaft°. Sie sichert° jedem Mitglied° einen guten Lohn° und gibt den Arbeitern   union / assures / member /
eine Stimme im Aufsichtsrat.[2]   wage

      Krolow hat wie die meisten Deutschen° fünf Wochen Urlaub im Jahr. Dieses Jahr   **wie** ... = like most Germans
30 will er im Sommer mit seiner Freundin nach Korsika. Im Oktober fährt seine Fußball-
mannschaft nach Amiens,[3] der Partnerstadt von Dortmund, und spielt dort gegen
einen französischen Fußballklub.

Klaus Ostendorff (53 Jahre alt), Journalist

Klaus Ostendorff ist Korrespondent bei der Deutschen Presseagentur° in   wire service
35 Nordamerika. Seit fünfzehn Jahren berichtet er über die USA und Kanada für
Zeitungen und Zeitschriften in Deutschland. Seine Artikel geben den Lesern ein
realistisches Bild von beiden° Ländern.   both

1. An industrial city in North Rhine-Westphalia. See map on the inside of the front cover.
2. **Aufsichtsrat** = board of directors. Historically, the ability of West German trade unions to elect
up to 50% of the board of directors of large companies brought a high degree of cooperation
between management and labor, very few strikes, and a high standard of living for union members. West Germany's economic growth ensured low unemployment rates. Since German unification in 1990, however, unemployment in the new eastern **Bundesländer** has been high, and
many workers have left the unions.
3. Northern French city on the Somme River. Many such partnerships exist between European
cities.

Im Moment schreibt Ostendorff einen Artikel über das Waldsterben° in
Nordamerika. Dieses Problem ist in Deutschland besonders aktuell: Auch in Europa
40 bedroht° der saure° Regen die Wälder.

    Ostendorff lebt mit seiner Frau Martina und ihren drei Kindern in Washington.
Die Kinder sollen ihre Muttersprache nicht vergessen und darum spricht die Familie
zu Hause meistens Deutsch. Die Kinder besuchen das deutsche Gymnasium in
Washington und reisen im Sommer nach Deutschland. Dort macht die ganze° Familie
45 Urlaub bei den Großeltern. Sie wohnen in einem Dorf in den Bayerischen° Alpen.

death of the forests
especially
threatens / acid

whole
Bavarian

Nach dem Lesen

■ A ■   Antworten Sie auf Deutsch.

1. Wo arbeitet Christine Sauermann?
2. Wie lange ist sie schon berufstätig?
3. Wer sind ihre Kunden und was kaufen sie bei ihr?
4. Wie sieht ein typischer Tag für Frau Sauermann aus?
5. Was macht sie gern in ihrer Freizeit?
6. Was macht Jörg Krolow in seiner Freizeit?
7. Wohin fährt er im Urlaub?
8. Über was schreibt Klaus Ostendorff im Moment?
9. Wie ist seine Familie anders als die Familie von Christine Sauermann oder Jörg Krolow?
10. Warum sprechen Ostendorff und seine Frau zu Hause meistens Deutsch?

MIT FREUNDEN, SURFBRETTERN, PICKNICK-KOFFER, MOUNTAINBIKES UND EINEM HUND.

■ B ■   Wer macht was?   In the left-hand column are some jobs and professions; in the right-hand column are some statements about what people in these jobs do. For each job, find the statement that describes it best.

Bäcker, Bäckerin
Fabrikarbeiter, Fabrikarbeiterin
Hausmann, Hausfrau
Journalist, Journalistin
Lehrer, Lehrerin
Mechaniker, Mechanikerin
Professor, Professorin

Schreibt Artikel für Zeitungen und Zeitschriften.
Arbeitet schwer, verdient aber nichts.
Lehrt an einer Universität
Repariert Maschinen, z. B. Autos.
Bäckt Brote und Brötchen.
Unterrichtet (*teaches*) an einer Schule.
Arbeitet in einer Fabrik.

■ C ■ **Die Deutsche Schule Washington (DSW)** Klaus Ostendorffs Kinder besuchen die Deutsche Schule Washington. Hier sehen Sie Informationen über die Schule. Was ist die Unterrichtssprache (*language of instruction*)? Welche (*which*) Fremdsprachen kann man lernen? In welchen Klassen sind sie fakultativ (*elective*), in welchen sind sie Pflicht (*a requirement*)? An welchen Feiertagen (*holidays*) gibt es keine Schule? Wann haben die Schüler Ferien (*vacations*)?

Newsletter
Deutsche Schule Washington, D.C.

Deutscher Schulverein Washington, D.C.
Die Deutsche Schule Washington D.C. ist eine Privatschule und wurde 1961 gegründet. Ihre Zeugnisse und Abschlüsse sind in Deutschland und in den USA staatlich anerkannt.

certificates

Sprachen
- Deutsche ist Unterrichtssprache
- Englisch: (fakultativ:) Klasse 1–4; (Pflicht:) Klasse 5–13   *compulsory*
- Französisch: (Pflicht:) Klasse 7–11, nur für Gymnasium

TERMINE   TERMINE   TERMINE

3. Oktober 97	**Tag der deutschen Einheit** *(unity)*
	- keine Schule -
14. Oktober 97	PSAT Tests in der DSW, 8 Uhr 30
17. Oktober 97	Lesung für die Oberstufe, 1./2. Stunde *Reading* *(upper step?)*
20. bis 24. Oktober 97	**Herbstferien**
8. November 97	Bücherverkauf im Rahmen der Sprachschule *within the bounds*
15. November 97	Martinsfest in der DSW
20. November 97	Mitgliederversammlung des Schulvereins, 20 Uhr *members gathering*
27./28. November 97	**Thanksgiving - keine Schule -**
30. November 97	Weihnachtsoratorium in der Kirche "Lady of Mercy", 17 Uhr
22.12.97 bis 2.1.98	**Weihnachtsferien**

Situationen aus dem Alltag

This vocabulary focuses on an everyday topic or situation. Words you already know from **Wortschatz** sections are listed without English equivalents; new supplementary vocabulary is listed with definitions. Your instructor may assign some supplementary vocabulary for active mastery.

■ Berufe

Was sind Sie von Beruf?   *What is your profession?*

Here are some other professions you can use in the following exercises.

der **Arzt**, ¨e	die **Ärztin**, -nen	*physician*
der **Elektrotechniker**, -	die **Elektrotechnikerin**, -nen	*electrician* or *electrical engineer*
der **Geschäftsmann** (*pl.*) **Geschäftsleute**	die **Geschäftsfrau**, -en	*businessman/ business- woman*
der **Ingenieur**, -e	die **Ingenieurin**, -nen	*engineer*
der **Kellner**, -	die **Kellnerin**, -nen	*waiter/waitress*
der **Krankenpfleger**, -	die **Krankenschwester**, -n	*nurse*
der **Künstler**, -	die **Künstlerin**, -nen	*artist*
der **Landwirt**, -e	die **Landwirtin**, -nen	*farmer*
der **Politiker**, -	die **Politikerin**, -nen	*politician*
der **Rechtsanwalt**, ¨e	die **Rechtsanwältin**, -nen	*lawyer*
der **Schriftsteller**, -	die **Schriftstellerin**, -nen	*writer*
der **Verkäufer**, -	die **Verkäuferin**, -nen	*salesperson*

Wer arbeitet hier? Lesen Sie die Schilder (*signs*).

■ A ■ Fragen: Was wissen Sie über diese Berufe?

1. Wer braucht das Abitur?   *secondary school*
2. Wer muss für seinen Beruf studieren?   *diploma*
3. Wer macht eine Lehre (*apprenticeship*)?
4. Wer verdient gut? Wer verdient relativ schlecht?
5. Wer hat viel Freizeit? Wer hat nicht viel Freizeit?
6. Wer hat flexible Arbeitszeiten?
7. Wer arbeitet oft nachts / morgens / abends?
8. Wer arbeitet draußen?
9. Wer braucht vielleicht einen Computer bei der Arbeit?
10. Wer arbeitet meistens allein, wer mit anderen Menschen zusammen?

Mit Menschen
zu tun haben

Handwerklich
arbeiten

Im Labor
arbeiten

Note on Usage: Stating profession or nationality

| Ich will Automechaniker werden. | *I want to become **an** auto mechanic.* |
| Frau Gerhard ist Amerikanerin. | *Ms. Gerhard is **an** American.* |

German does not use an indefinite article before the noun.

■ B ■ Gruppendiskussion: Was willst du werden, und warum? (*4 Studenten*)

First tell each other what you want to do after college. Then ask questions about each other's career plans.

BEISPIEL: A: Ich möchte Lehrer werden.
B: Verdienen Lehrer genug Geld?
C: Sind deine Eltern Lehrer?
D: Wo möchtest du denn arbeiten?
usw.

■ C ■ Partnerarbeit mit dem Almanach: Suchen wir eine Stelle.   Sie und Ihr Partner brauchen Geld und suchen Stellen für den Sommer. Im Almanach (S. 135) sind einige Stellenangebote (*job offers, help wanted ads*) aus deutschen Zeitungen. Besprechen Sie sie zusammen. Was möchten Sie gern machen? Was möchten Sie lieber nicht machen?

Almanach

Stellenangebote (Help Wanted Ads)

job *offer / supply of*

These help-wanted ads from the German press range from unskilled labor (**Zeitungsträger/in**) to highly specialized professionals (**Statistiker/in**). Note the English business and computer jargon in the technical fields.

Nielsen *research*

Marketing Forschung

Marketing-Forschung und -Beratung der Markenartikelindustrie ist unser Tätigkeitsfeld. Die vergangenen Jahre waren durch eine stetige Expansion gekennzeichnet. Für die Zukunft haben wir uns ehrgeizige Ziele gesetzt.
Zur Erweiterung unseres Mitarbeiterstabes suchen wir jüngere Damen und Herren (auch Berufsanfänger) als:

STATISTIKER/IN

Der Caritasverband für die Stadt Köln e.V.
sucht eine(n) *co-worker* *collaborator*

qualifizierte(n) Mitarbeiter(in)

im

Sozialdienst für Italiener

Zur Aufgabe gehören die Beratung in sozialen Angelegenheiten italienischer Mitbürger und die Arbeit mit Gruppen und Vereinen.

Wir stellen uns vor, daß ein italienischer Mitarbeiter/in mit qualifizierter pädagogischer Ausbildung und sehr guten Deutsch-Kenntnissen für diese Aufgaben ebenso in Frage kommt wie deutsche Sozialarbeiter/Sozialpädagogen/innen mit sehr guten Kenntnissen der italienischen Sprache und der Kultur und dem Lebensstil Italiens.

Wir erwarten die Zugehörigkeit zur katholischen Kirche und aktive Teilnahme an ihrem Leben.

Caritasverband für die Stadt Köln e.V.
Große Telegraphenstr. 35, 5000 Köln 1

---

manager

Leitende/n
Ärztin/Arzt (Dr. med.)

Wir wünschen uns eine engagierte Persönlichkeit, die die Grundsätze unserer Organisation im Hinblick auf die Sorge und Verantwortung für behinderte Menschen mitträgt.

Für ein erstes Gespräch stehen wir Ihnen ab 3. 8. 87 gern telefonisch unter der Rufnummer 0421/23 83-211 oder 221 zur Verfügung.

Ihre Bewerbung erbitten wir an den **Geschäftsführer.**

REICHSBUND BERUFSBILDUNGSWERK GMBH
Kitzbühler Straße 1 · 2800 Bremen 33

Interatom GmbH
Postfach
5060 Bergisch Gladbach 1

INTERATOM

Sind Sie Frühaufsteher?

Wir bieten Ihnen — auch nebenberuflich — gute Verdienstmöglichkeiten als

newspaper delivery

Zeitungsträger(in)

Folgender Zustellbezirk ist zur Zeit unbesetzt:

Usingen-Eschbach

Bitte schreiben Sie uns, besuchen Sie uns, oder rufen Sie uns an unter Telefon-Nr. 06081/94 032.

Broadcasting

Frankfurter Rundschau

Vertriebsabteilung
Agentur Doris Görlich
Am Hebestumpf 11, 6393 Wehrheim 1

Wir suchen dringend eine
Haushälterin
die bei uns wohnen und unsere drei Kinder betreuen kann.
Herr und Frau Adda, privat 0211/61 4208,
Büro 0211/39 30 41.

STADT HERTEN

Die Stadt Herten (70000 EW), Kreis Recklinghausen, sucht zum baldmöglichen Eintritt eine(n)

STADTPLANER(IN)
– Bes. Gr. A 15 –

als Amtsleiter(in) des Stadtplanungsamtes.

Au-pair-Mädchen für 2 Kinder in Dublin gesucht, Tel.: 07391/2189.

Software-Engineering
Datenbanken
Informationssysteme

Informatiker
Mathematiker
Physiker
Ingenieure

n
bstän-
siert in
ganz-
ikolas-
)00 ab

t

Hilfe im
Betreu-

Niederlassun
nell expandie
n Vertrieb und
btechnologie.

ückflug,
)0,– DM

---

nöglichen Eintrittstermin suchen wir

Mikrobiologen/innen

als Spezialisten für die Sparte Fermentation bundesweit.

Wir erwarten: biochemische/mikrobiologische/molekularbiologische universitäre Ausbildung, gute

An der Universität

Communicative Goals

- Talking about events in the past
- Writing a letter in German

Cultural Goal

- Learning about German student life and the university system

Chapter Outline

- **Lyrik zum Vorlesen**
  Johann Wolfgang von Goethe, „Wanderers Nachtlied"

- **Grammatik**
  Simple past tense of *sein*
  Perfect tense
  Two-way prepositions
  Masculine N-nouns

- **Lesestück**
  Ein Brief aus Freiburg

- **Situationen aus dem Alltag**
  Das Studium; Das Studentenzimmer

- **Almanach**
  Universities in the German-Speaking Countries

Dialoge

Lab Manual Kap. 6, Dialoge, Fragen, Hören Sie gut zu!, Üb. zur Aussprache (**b**, **d**, **g** / **p**, **t**, **k**).

Dormitory space is scarce in Germany. Students frequently live together in apartments called **Wohngemeinschaften** (abbreviated **WG**).

German students buy their course catalogues every semester in local bookstores.

German students calculate time spent at the university in semesters rather than years.

Konstanz is a city on Lake Constance (**der Bodensee**) with a university founded in 1966.

Karin sucht ein Zimmer

STEFAN: Hast du endlich ein Zimmer gefunden?

KARIN: Nee, ich suche noch. Leider habe ich keinen Platz im Studentenwohnheim bekommen.

STEFAN: Du! Gestern ist bei uns in der WG die Helga ausgezogen. *ziehen* Also, jetzt ist ein Zimmer frei. Willst du zu uns? *move out*

KARIN: Super! Meinst du, das ist möglich?

STEFAN: Selbstverständlich!

Am Semesteranfang

CLARA: Wo warst du denn so lange?

EVA: In der Bibliothek und später in der Buchhandlung.

CLARA: Hast du mir ein Vorlesungsverzeichnis mitgebracht?

EVA: Ja, ich hab's auf den Schreibtisch gelegt.

CLARA: Ach ja, da liegt es unter der Zeitung. Wie viel hat's denn gekostet?

EVA: Vier Mark fünfzig, aber ich schenk's dir.

CLARA: Das ist wirklich nett von dir! Vielen Dank!

An der Uni in Tübingen

PETRA: Hast du den Peter schon kennen gelernt?

KLAUS: Ist das der Austauschstudent aus Kanada?

PETRA: Ja. Er kann fantastisch Deutsch, nicht?

KLAUS: Ich glaube, er hat schon zwei Semester in Konstanz studiert.

PETRA: Ach, darum!

Note on Usage: **Definite article with names**

In informal, colloquial speech, Germans often use the definite article with proper names. The dialogues contain two examples of this:

Gestern ist bei uns in der WG **die** Helga ausgezogen.

Yesterday Helga moved out of our apartment.

Hast du **den** Peter schon kennen gelernt?

Have you met Peter yet?

■ Wortschatz 1

Verben

aus·ziehen, ist ausgezogen[1] to move out
bringen, hat gebracht to bring
legen to lay, put down
mit·bringen, hat mitgebracht to bring along, take along
ziehen, hat gezogen to pull

Substantive

der **Anfang, ˙̈e** beginning
  am Anfang at the beginning
der **Austauschstudent, -en, -en**[2] exchange student
der **Mensch, -en, -en** person, human being
der **Platz, ˙̈e** place; space; city square
der **Schreibtisch, -e** desk
das **Bett, -en** bed
(das) **Kanada** Canada
das **Studentenwohnheim, -e** student dormitory

das **Vorlesungsverzeichnis, -se** university course catalogue
die **Bibliothek, -en** library
die **Universität, -en** university
  an der Universität at the university
die **Vorlesung, -en** university lecture
die **Wohngemeinschaft, -en** communal living group, co-op apartment

Adjektive und Adverbien

gestern yesterday
möglich possible
nett nice
so lange for such a long time
wirklich real; really

Präpositionen mit Dativ oder Akkusativ

an to, toward; at, alongside of
auf onto; on, upon, on top of
hinter behind

in into, to; in
neben beside, next to
über over, across; above
unter under; beneath
vor in front of
zwischen between

Gegensätze

am Anfang ≠ am Ende at the beginning ≠ at the end
ausziehen ≠ einziehen to move out ≠ to move in
möglich ≠ unmöglich possible ≠ impossible

Mit anderen Worten

die **Uni, -s** (*colloq.*) = **Universität**
die **WG, -s** (*colloq.*) = **Wohngemeinschaft**
nee (*colloq.*) = **nein**

Karin Looks for a Room

S: Have you finally found a room?
K: Nope, I'm still looking. Unfortunately I didn't get a place in the dorm.
S: Hey! Yesterday Helga moved out of our apartment. So now there's a room free. Do you want to move in with us?
K: Terrific! Do you think it's possible?
S: Of course.

At the Beginning of the Semester

C: Where were you for so long?
E: In the library and later at the bookstore.
C: Did you bring me a course catalogue?
E: Yes, I put it on the desk.
C: Oh yeah, it's lying under the newspaper. How much did it cost?
E: Four marks fifty, but I'll give it to you for free.
C: That's really nice of you! Thanks a lot.

At the University in Tübingen

P: Have you met Peter yet?
K: Is that the exchange student from Canada?
P: Yes. He speaks fantastic German, doesn't he?
K: I think he's already studied two semesters in Konstanz.
P: So that's why!

---

1. For an explanation of the form **ist ausgezogen**, see **Grammatik**, pp. 143–144.
2. For an explanation of the second ending, see **Grammatik**, p. 152.

Variationen

■ A ■ **Persönliche Fragen**

1. Wo wohnen Sie: im Studentenwohnheim, bei einer Familie, in einer WG oder zu Hause bei Ihren Eltern?
2. Stefan wohnt in einer WG. Kennen Sie Studenten in WGs? Was ist dort anders als im Studentenwohnheim?
3. Eva kauft ein Vorlesungsverzeichnis. *catalogue* Was müssen Sie am Semesteranfang kaufen?
4. Eva schenkt Clara das Vorlesungsverzeichnis. Was schenken Sie Ihrem Mitbewohner oder Ihrer Mitbewohnerin?
5. An der Uni in Tübingen gibt es viele Austauschstudenten. *exchange* Gibt es auch an Ihrer Uni Austauschstudenten? Woher kommen sie?

■ B ■ **Übung: Das möchte ich auch.**   Your instructor tells you something he has done. Say you would like to do that too.

BEISPIEL: A: Ich habe in Berlin gewohnt.
B: Ich möchte auch in Berlin wohnen.

1. Ich habe einen Sportwagen gekauft.
2. Ich habe um acht Uhr gefrühstückt.
3. Ich habe Karten gespielt.
4. Ich habe Russisch gelernt.
5. Ich habe eine Reise gemacht.

■ C ■   **Übung: Was meinen Sie?**   Antworten Sie mit dem Gegensatz.

> BEISPIEL: Finden Sie den Film *gut*?
> Nein, ich finde ihn *schlecht*.

1. Soll man *spät* aufstehen?
2. Ist dieses Klassenzimmer zu *groß*?
3. Sind Fremdsprachen *unwichtig*?   *unimportant*
4. Ist Deutsch *schwer*?   *leicht*
5. Soll man *immer* in Eile sein?   *nimmer*
6. Spricht der Professor zu *langsam*?   *schnell*
7. Soll man *allein* arbeiten?
8. Sind die Studenten hier meistens *faul*?   *fleißig*
   lazy

Lyrik zum Vorlesen

Lab Manual Kap. 6,
Lyrik zum Vorlesen.

Many composers have set this text to music. One of the most famous settings is Franz Schubert's Opus 96, No. 3 (D 768).

This brief poem from 1780 is perhaps the most famous in the German language. Goethe first wrote it on the wall of a forest hut where he was spending the night. The simplicity of its three main images (mountains, trees, and birds) and the evocative language of stillness make this a profound statement of the relationship between man and nature.

Der junge Goethe

Wanderers Nachtlied

Über allen Gipfeln°	mountain peaks
Ist Ruh°,	peace
In allen Wipfeln°	tree tops
Spürest° du	feel
kaum° einen Hauch°;	hardly / breath
Die Vögelein° schweigen° im Walde.	little birds / are silent
Warte nur, balde°	**balde = bald**
Ruhest° du auch.	rest

> *Johann Wolfgang von Goethe (1749–1832)*

NATIONALE FORSCHUNGS-
UND GEDENKSTÄTTEN DER KLASSISCHEN
DEUTSCHEN LITERATUR IN WEIMAR

**GOETHEHAUS
GOETHEMUSEUM**

209198 ❋

EINTRITTSKARTE 5,00

Grammatik

Talking about events in the past is a communicative goal.

Simple past tense of sein

Up to now, you have been using the present tense of verbs to talk about events in the present. To talk about events in the past, German has two tenses. One is called the *perfect tense* and the other, the *simple past tense*. In spoken German, the perfect tense is usually used to talk about the past. You will learn how to use it in this chapter. The frequently occurring verb **sein**, however, is used more often in the simple past than in the perfect. It is therefore very useful for you to learn the following conjugation.

ich	**war**	*I was*	wir	**waren**	*we were*
du	**warst**	*you were*	ihr	**wart**	*you were*
er, es, sie	**war**	*he, it, she was*	sie, Sie	**waren**	*they, you were*

Lab Manual Kap. 6, Var. zur Üb. 1.

Workbook Kap. 6, A.

■ 1 ■ **Übung: Wo waren sie?** You all traveled in Europe last summer. Turn to the map at the back of the book. Tell your instructor where people were.

BEISPIEL: Wo war Eva?
　　　　　Sie war in Belgien.

1. Wo war Clara?
2. Wo war Franz?
3. Wo warst du?
4. Wo waren die Studenten?

5. Wo war ich?
6. Wo wart ihr?
7. Wo waren wir?
8. Wo waren Sie?

Perfect tense

The perfect tense is composed of an *auxiliary verb* ("helping" verb) and a form of the main verb called the *past participle*. The auxiliary verb, either **haben** or **sein**, is conjugated to agree with the subject of the sentence. The past participle is a fixed form that never changes. The participle is placed at the end of the sentence or clause.

■ **Conjugation with *haben***

Most German verbs use **haben** as their auxiliary verb. Here is a sample conjugation:

aux.　　　　　*part.*
Ich **habe** das Buch **gekauft**.　　　　*I bought the book.* (or: *I have bought the book.*)

Du **hast** es **gekauft**.　　　　*You bought it.*
Sie **hat** es **gekauft**.　　　　*She bought it.*

Wir **haben** es **gekauft**.　　　　*We bought it.*
Ihr **habt** es **gekauft**.　　　　*You bought it.*
Sie **haben** es **gekauft**.　　　　*They bought it.*

■ Past participles of weak verbs

There are two basic classes of verbs in German: the *weak* verbs and the *strong* verbs. They are distinguished by the way they form their past participle.

The weak verbs form their past participle by adding the unstressed prefix **ge-** and the ending **-t** or **-et** to the verb stem. Here are some examples of weak verbs you have already learned:

Infinitive	*Stem*	*Auxiliary + past participle*
arbeiten	arbeit-	hat **gearbeitet**
kaufen	kauf-	hat **gekauft**
kosten	kost-	hat **gekostet**
legen	leg-	hat **gelegt**
meinen	mein-	hat **gemeint**

Verbs ending in **-ieren** are *always* weak verbs. They do *not* add the prefix **ge-** in the past participle, just a **-t** to the stem.

studieren → studier- → hat **studiert**

Er hat in Freiburg **studiert**.   *He studied in Freiburg.*

Lab Manual Kap. 6, Var. zur Üb. 2.

Workbook Kap. 6, B–C.

■ **2** ■ **Übung: Was haben Sie gekauft und was hat das gekostet?** You went on a shopping spree yesterday. Tell your instructor which of the things listed below you bought and what they cost.

1. eine Schreibmaschine (DM 949)
2. einen Taschenrechner (DM 39)
3. ein Vorlesungsverzeichnis (DM 4,50)
4. eine Espressomaschine (DM 129)

Solar-Digital Taschenrechner nur 39,-

> BEISPIEL: A: Was haben Sie gestern gekauft?
> B: Ich habe ein-_____ gekauft.
> A: Was hat das denn gekostet?
> B: Das hat DM _____ gekostet.

■ **3** ■ **Partnerarbeit: Austauschstudenten** Say where the exchange students come from and where they studied.

> BEISPIEL: Nicole kommt aus Frankreich und sie hat in Leipzig studiert.

Name	*Heimat (homeland)*	*Universitätsstadt*
Nicole	Frankreich	Leipzig
Yukiko	Japan	Tübingen
Pedro	Spanien	Zürich
Cathleen	Irland	Wien
Matthew	Kanada	Berlin
Beth	USA	Konstanz

Past participles of strong verbs

Beginning in **Wortschatz 1** of this chapter, the past participle (and present-stem vowel change, when applicable) of each new strong verb is given following the infinitive.

Strong verbs in English also form past tenses by changing their root vowels and sometimes add the ending *-n: give, gave, given; see, saw, seen; stand, stood, stood; drink, drank, drunk; do, did, done.*

The strong verbs form their past participle by adding the prefix **ge-** and the suffix **-n** or **-en** to the verb stem. In addition, many strong verbs change their stem vowel. Some verbs also change consonants in the stem. For this reason, *the past participle of each strong verb must be memorized.* Here are some examples of strong verbs you have already learned:

Infinitive	*Auxiliary + past participle*
geben	hat **gegeben**
sehen	hat **gesehen**
stehen	hat **gestanden**
trinken	hat **getrunken**
tun	hat **getan**

Lab Manual Kap. 6, Var. zur Üb. 4.

■ **4** ■ **Übung: Was haben Sie gesehen?** Was haben Sie gestern gesehen? Sagen Sie es der Gruppe.

> **BEISPIEL:** A: Sagen Sie uns, was Sie gestern gesehen haben.
> B: Ich habe _____ , _____ und _____ gesehen.

■ **5** ■ **Kettenreaktion: Was hast du getrunken?** You and your friends were thirsty yesterday. Each person says what he or she drank, then asks the next person.

> **BEISPIEL:** A: Gestern habe ich _____ getrunken. Was hast du getrunken?
> B: Ich habe _____ getrunken.

Kaffee   Milch   Tee

Conjugation with *sein*

Some German verbs use **sein** rather than **haben** as their auxiliary verb in the perfect tense.

> Gestern **ist** die Helga ausgezogen.   *Helga moved out yesterday.*

To take **sein**, a verb must fulfill two conditions:

1. It must be *intransitive* (i.e., it *cannot* take a direct object).
2. It must indicate *change of location or condition.*

Here are some examples of verbs with **sein** as their auxiliary:

	Infinitive	*Auxiliary + participle*	
move out	ausziehen	**ist ausgezogen**	
fly	fliegen	**ist geflogen**	
go	gehen	**ist gegangen**	*change of location*
hike	wandern	**ist gewandert**	
travel	reisen	**ist gereist**	
to get up	aufstehen	**ist aufgestanden**	
die	sterben	**ist gestorben**	*change of condition*
become	werden	**ist geworden**	

As you can see, verbs with **sein** may be either weak (**gereist**) or strong (**geflogen**).

Two frequently used verbs are exceptions to the second rule: **sein** itself and **bleiben**. In the perfect tense, these verbs use **sein** as their auxiliary even though they don't show change of location or condition:

Wo **bist** du so lange **gewesen**?	*Where were you for so long?*
Wir **sind** bei unseren Freunden **geblieben**.	*We stayed with our friends.*

Lab Manual Kap. 6, Var. zur Üb. 6.

■ 6 ■ **Kettenreaktion: Wohin bist du gereist?** Alle haben sicher Reisen gemacht. Wohin sind *Sie* einmal gereist?

BEISPIEL: A: Ich bin nach Mexiko gereist. Wohin bist du gereist?
B: Ich bin _____ gereist.
(usw.)

■ 7 ■ **Übung: Was ist sie geworden?** You've all lost touch with your old school friend Karoline. Tell your instructor what you think she became.

BEISPIEL: Was glauben *Sie*?
Ich glaube, sie ist Ärztin geworden.

Manchmal arbeitet man zusammen am Referat.

There are about 200 strong or irregular verbs in German, many of low frequency. In this course you will learn about 70 frequently used ones. The strong verb forms are the result of a linguistic development in the Germanic languages that was completed hundreds of years ago. New verbs coined in German today are always regular weak verbs, often borrowed from English: **interviewen**, **formattieren**.

■ Table of strong verbs

The following table contains all the strong verbs that you have learned so far.[1] Review your knowledge of the infinitives and stem-vowel changes in the present tense. Note that the verbs with stem-vowel change in the present-tense **du-** and **er-**forms are *always* strong verbs. *Memorize the past participles.*

Infinitive	Stem-vowel change	Aux. + participle	English
anfangen	fängt an	**hat angefangen**	*to begin*
anrufen		**hat angerufen**	*to call up*
beginnen		**hat begonnen**	*to begin*
besitzen		**hat besessen**	*to possess*
bleiben		*ist* **geblieben**	*to stay*
entscheiden		**hat entschieden**	*to decide*
essen	isst	**hat gegessen**	*to eat*
fahren	fährt	*ist* **gefahren**	*to drive*
finden		**hat gefunden**	*to find*
fliegen		*ist* **geflogen**	*to fly*
fließen		*ist* **geflossen**	*to flow*
geben	gibt	**hat gegeben**	*to give*
gehen		*ist* **gegangen**	*to go*
halten	hält	**hat gehalten**	*to hold; to stop*
heißen		**hat geheißen**	*to be called*
kommen		*ist* **gekommen**	*to come*
laufen	läuft	*ist* **gelaufen**	*to run*
lesen	liest	**hat gelesen**	*to read*
liegen		**hat gelegen**	*to lie*
nehmen	nimmt	**hat genommen**	*to take*
scheinen		**hat geschienen**	*to shine; to seem*
schlafen	schläft	**hat geschlafen**	*to sleep*
schließen		**hat geschlossen**	*to close*
schreiben		**hat geschrieben**	*to write*
schwimmen		*ist* **geschwommen**	*to swim*
sehen	sieht	**hat gesehen**	*to see*
sein	ist	*ist* **gewesen**	*to be*
singen		**hat gesungen**	*to sing*
sprechen	spricht	**hat gesprochen**	*to speak*
stehen		**hat gestanden**	*to stand*
sterben	stirbt	*ist* **gestorben**	*to die*
tragen	trägt	**hat getragen**	*to carry; to wear*
trinken		**hat getrunken**	*to drink*
tun		**hat getan**	*to do*
vergessen	vergisst	**hat vergessen**	*to forget*
verlassen	verlässt	**hat verlassen**	*to leave*
werden	wird	*ist* **geworden**	*to become*
ziehen		**hat gezogen**	*to pull*

1. Except for **anfangen**, **anrufen**, **besitzen**, **entscheiden**, **vergessen**, and **verlassen**, this list includes only the basic verb (e.g., **stehen** but not **aufstehen** or **verstehen**). See pp. 146–147 for the formation of past participles of verbs with separable and inseparable prefixes.

■ 8 ■ **Übung: Heute und gestern**   Sie hören etwas über heute. Sie sagen, auch gestern ist es so gewesen.

> **BEISPIEL:** A: Heute scheint die Sonne.
>
> B: Auch gestern hat die Sonne geschienen.

1. Heute trägt Thomas einen Pulli.
2. Heute liegt die Zeitung da.
3. Heute tun wir das.
4. Heute singt er zu laut.
5. Heute nimmt Vater den Wagen.
6. Heute schließe ich den Laden.
7. Heute steht Markus draußen.
8. Heute liest du einen Artikel.
9. Heute essen wir um sieben.
10. Heute Abend wird es kalt.
11. Heute finden wir die Vorlesung gut.
12. Heute schlafen wir bis acht.
13. Heute läuft Christian durch den Wald.
14. Heute kommt ihr um neun Uhr.
15. Heute geben wir dem Kind ein Brötchen.
16. Heute hält das Auto hier.

Workbook Kap. 6, D–F.

Lab Manual Kap. 6, Var. zur Üb. 8.

■ **Past participles of separable-prefix verbs**

Verbs with separable (stressed) prefixes form their past participles by inserting **-ge-** *between* the prefix and the verb stem.

anfangen   → hat **angefangen**
aufmachen → hat **aufgemacht**

Das Konzert hat um acht Uhr **angefangen**.	*The concert began at eight o'clock.*
Wann bist du denn **aufgestanden**?	*When did you get up?*
Wer hat den Laden **aufgemacht**?	*Who opened the store?*

Lab Manual Kap. 6, Var. zur Üb. 9.

■ 9 ■ **Übung: Ich habe das schon gemacht!**   Ihr Professor sagt Ihnen, Sie sollen etwas tun. Sagen Sie, Sie haben es schon getan.

> **BEISPIEL:** A: Machen Sie doch die Tür auf.
>
> B: Ich habe sie schon aufgemacht.

1. Fangen Sie doch an.
2. Hören Sie doch auf.
3. Stehen Sie doch auf.
4. Kaufen Sie doch ein.
5. Machen Sie doch die Tür zu.
6. Rufen Sie doch Robert an.

To review inseparable prefixes, see p. 124.

■ **Past participles of inseparable-prefix verbs**

Verbs with inseparable (unstressed) prefixes do *not* add the prefix **ge-** in the past participle.

berichten → hat **berichtet**
verstehen → hat **verstanden**

Sie hat uns über Amerika **berichtet**.	*She reported to us about America.*
Das habe ich nicht **verstanden**.	*I didn't understand that.*

146 ■ **Kapitel 6**

Lab Manual Kap. 6,
Var. zur Üb. 10.

■ **10** ■ **Übung: Ich habe das schon getan!** Ihr Professor sagt Ihnen, Sie sollen etwas tun. Sagen Sie, Sie haben es schon getan.

> BEISPIEL: A: Beginnen Sie bitte.
> B: Ich habe schon begonnen.

1. Beschreiben Sie die Landschaft.
2. Vergessen Sie das.
3. Besuchen Sie Ihre Großeltern.
4. Berichten Sie über Ihre Reise.
5. Besprechen Sie das Problem.
6. Verlassen Sie das Zimmer.

■ **Perfect tense of mixed verbs**

A handful of German verbs have the weak participle form **ge—t** but also change their stem. They are called "mixed verbs." The ones you have learned so far are:

bringen	hat **gebracht**
mitbringen	hat **mitgebracht**
kennen	hat **gekannt**
wissen	hat **gewusst**

Schon gehört? . . .
Nee, hab' ich nicht gewusst.

Lab Manual Kap. 6,
Var. zur Üb. 11.

■ **11** ■ **Partnerarbeit: Das habe ich schon gewusst!** Take turns telling each other things. Respond either that you did or did not know that already.

> BEISPIEL: A: Mark kommt aus Kanada.
> B: Das habe ich schon gewusst! (*oder*)
> Wirklich? Das habe ich nicht gewusst.

■ **12** ■ **Kettenreaktion: Was hast du heute mitgebracht?** Say what you've brought with you to class today, then ask what the next student has brought.

> BEISPIEL: A: Ich habe heute einen Bleistift mitgebracht. Was hast du mitgebracht?
> B: Ich habe ein-_____ mitgebracht.

■ **The use of the perfect tense**

The perfect tense is used much more frequently in German than it is in English. In spoken German, the perfect is the most frequently used tense for talking about events in the past. It is therefore often referred to as the "conversational past." English uses the simple past tense (one-word form) for the same purpose.

Sie **sind** gestern nach Berlin **geflogen**.	*They **flew** to Berlin yesterday.*
Ich **habe** die Zeitung um sieben **gelesen**.	*I **read** the newspaper at seven.*

There are no German equivalents for English past-tense progressive and emphatic forms.

$$\text{Ich habe } \mathbf{gesprochen.} = \begin{cases} \textit{I spoke.} \\ \textit{I have spoken.} \\ \textit{I was speaking.} \\ \textit{I did speak.} \end{cases}$$

Two-way prepositions

Review accusative prepositions, p. 91; dative prepositions, p. 121.

You have learned that some prepositions in German are always followed by an object in the accusative case, while others are always followed by an object in the dative case. A third group, called the "two-way prepositions," all show spatial relationships. They are followed by the *accusative* case when they signal *destination*, and by the *dative* when they signal *location*. In the example sentences in the table below, notice how the verb determines location or destination. Verbs like **stehen** and **sein** show location (*dative*); verbs like **fahren** and **gehen** show destination (*accusative*).

Memorize the list of two-way prepositions.

Some two-way prepositions can show non-spatial relationships, e.g., **über** + accusative = *about*: **Wir haben** *über* **unsere Amerikareise gesprochen.**

Preposition	Destination (accusative) Answers *Wohin?*	Location (dative) Answers *Wo?*
an	**to, toward** Hans geht **ans Fenster**. *Hans is walking toward the window.*	**at, alongside of** Hans steht **am Fenster**. *Hans is standing at the window.*
auf	**onto** Wohin legt Inge das Buch? Sie legt es **auf den Tisch**. *She's putting it on the table.*	**on, on top of** Wo liegt das Buch? Es liegt **auf dem Tisch**. *It's lying on the table.*
hinter	**behind** Das Kind läuft **hinter das Haus**. *The child is running behind the house.*	**behind** Das Kind steht **hinter dem Haus**. *The child is standing behind the house.*
in	**into, in** Wo gehen die Studenten hin? Sie gehen **in die Mensa**. *They're going (in)to the cafeteria.*	**in** Wo sind die Studenten? Sie sind **in der Mensa**. *They're in the cafeteria.*
neben	**beside, next to** Leg dein Buch **neben die Zeitung**. *Put your book next to the newspaper.*	**beside, next to** Dein Buch liegt **neben der Zeitung**. *Your book is next to the newspaper.*
über	**over, across** Wir fliegen **über das Meer**. *We're flying across the ocean.*	**over, above** Die Sonne scheint **über dem Meer**. *The sun is shining over the ocean.*
unter	**under** Die Katze läuft **unter das Bett**. *The cat runs under the bed.*	**under, beneath** Die Katze schläft **unter dem Bett**. *The cat sleeps under the bed.*
vor	**in front of** Der Bus fährt **vor das Hotel**. *The bus is driving up in front of the hotel.*	**in front of** Der Bus hält **vor dem Hotel**. *The bus is stopping in front of the hotel.*
zwischen	**between** Er läuft **zwischen die Bäume**. *He's running between the trees.*	**between** Er steht **zwischen den Bäumen**. *He's standing between the trees.*

Note: The prepositions **an** and **in** are regularly contracted with the articles **das** and **dem** in the following way:

an das → **ans**   in das → **ins**
an dem → **am**   in dem → **im**

Workbook Kap. 6, G–J.

■ 13 ■ **Übung:** *Wo* **oder** *wohin*?   Ihre Professorin fragt Sie, **wo** einige (*some*) Leute sind, oder **wohin** sie gehen. Antworten Sie mit **In der Mensa** oder **In die Mensa**.

1. Wo ist Karin?
2. Wo geht ihr jetzt hin?
3. Wo habt ihr gestern gegessen?
4. Wo sind Horst und Petra?
5. Wo hast du Wolf gesehen?
6. Wohin läuft Peter so schnell?

■ 14 ■ **Partnerarbeit:** *Wo* **oder** *wohin*? (*Mit offenen Büchern*)   Ask each other questions about where things are lying or where they are being placed. Answer with **Auf dem Tisch** or **Auf den Tisch** as appropriate.

1. Wo liegt meine Zeitung?
2. Wohin soll ich das Geld legen?
3. Wo liegen die Karten für heute Abend?
4. Wohin hast du das Buch gelegt?
5. Wo liegt denn das Vorlesungsverzeichnis?

■ 15 ■   **Übung: Wo war Martina heute?**   Martina war heute viel unterwegs. Sagen Sie, wo sie war.

BEISPIEL: Sie war in der Stadt.

Lab Manual Kap. 6, Var. zur Üb. 16.

■ 16 ■   **Gruppenarbeit (*Mit offenen Büchern*)**   Take turns replacing the verbs in the sentences below with new verbs from the list. Change the case of the prepositional object according to whether the verb you use shows destination or location. Choose three or four new verbs for each sentence.

gehen	liegen	warten	laufen	halten
arbeiten	fahren	lesen	wohnen	sein

1. Wir fahren in die Stadt.
2. Jutta steht hinter dem Haus.
3. Das Kind läuft unter den Tisch.
4. Hans steht am Fenster.
5. Wir sind im Zimmer.
6. Ich lese im Bett.

> Suche für meinen Sohn (Jura-Stud., NR) z. 1. 9. od. 1. 10.
> **Zimmer mit Bad**
> **od. 2-Zi.-App.** zu mieten.
> Tel. 02 11/40 03 76, Rückruf

NR = Nichtraucher.
Jura: See p. 159.

■   **Note on the prepositions *an* and *auf***

The prepositions **an** and **auf** do not correspond exactly to any English prepositions.

• **an** generally signals motion *toward* or location *at* a border, edge, or vertical surface.

Gehen Sie bitte **an die Tafel**.	*Please go to the blackboard.*
Wir fahren **ans Meer**.	*We're driving to the ocean.*
Sie steht **am Tisch**.	*She's standing at the table.*

• **auf** generally signals motion *onto* or location *upon* a horizontal surface.

| Leg das Buch **auf den Tisch**. | *Put (or lay) the book on the table.* |
| Das Buch liegt **auf dem Tisch**. | *The book is (lying) on the table.* |

■ 18 ■   **Übung:** *an* oder *auf*?   Complete each sentence with **an** or **auf** and the appropriate article.

Wohin? Antworten Sie mit Präposition + *Artikel im Akkusativ.*

1. Karl geht _____ Tafel.
2. Legen Sie Ihren Mantel _____ Stuhl.
3. Marga fährt im Sommer _____ Meer.
4. Ich habe die Zeitung _____ Schreibtisch gelegt.

Wo? Antworten Sie mit Präposition + *Artikel im Dativ.*

5. Das Kind steht _____ Stuhl.
6. Karl wartet _____ Tür.
7. Das Haus liegt _____ Meer.
8. Das Essen ist schon _____ Tisch.

Jetzt neu in Ihrer Stadt

Masculine N-nouns

A few masculine nouns take the ending **-en** or **-n** in all cases except the nominative singular. They are called "N-nouns."

	Singular	Plural
nom.	der Student	die Student**en**
acc.	den Student**en**	die Student**en**
dat.	dem Student**en**	den Student**en**

Dieser Student kennt München sehr gut.
Kennst du diesen Student**en**?
Ich habe diesem Student**en** einen Stadtplan verkauft.

A good rule-of-thumb is that a noun that is masculine, refers to a person or animal, and has the plural ending **-en** or **-n** is an N-noun. Here are the N-nouns you have already learned. The first ending is for all cases in the singular *except* nominative; the second ending is for all cases in the plural.

<table>
<tr><td>der Bauer, -n, -n</td><td>farmer</td></tr>
<tr><td>der Herr, -n, -en</td><td>gentleman; Mr.</td></tr>
<tr><td>der Journalist, -en, -en</td><td>journalist</td></tr>
<tr><td>der Kunde, -n, -n</td><td>customer</td></tr>
<tr><td>der Mensch, -en, -en</td><td>person, human being</td></tr>
<tr><td>der Student, -en, -en</td><td>student</td></tr>
<tr><td>der Tourist, -en, -en</td><td>tourist</td></tr>
</table>

When **Herr** is used as a title (*Mr.*), it also must have the N-noun singular ending: **Das ist Herr Weiß**; *but* **Kennen Sie Herrn Weiß?**

Lab Manual Kap. 6, Var. zur Üb. 19.

Workbook Kap. 6, K, L.

■ 19 ■ **Partnerarbeit: Wer ist das? Ich kenne ihn nicht.**   Partner A asks who one of these men is; partner B answers. Partner A says he/she doesn't know this person. Switch roles for the next man.

BEISPIEL: A: Wer ist das?
  B: Das ist ein Bauer.
  A: Ich kenne diesen _____ nicht.
  B: Wer ist das? (usw.)

Vor dem Lesen

Tipps zum Lesen und Lernen

Writing a letter is a communicative goal.

■ **Wie schreibt man eine Postkarte oder einen Brief auf Deutsch?**

Salutation: **-e** with a female name, **-er** with a male name

Place and date: day / month / year

Jena, den 20.5.99

Liebe Sabine, lieber Markus!

Hallo! Wie geht's euch denn? Gestern sind wir hier angekommen und haben schon eure Kusine Gertrud besucht. Sie und ihre Freunde sind wahnsinnig nett und haben uns sehr viel von Jena gezeigt.

Morgen fahren wir nach Berlin und sind dann Freitag wieder zu Hause.

Bis dann.

Viele herzliche Grüße von

Standard closing = *many cordial greetings* Tanja und Fabian

■ **Leicht zu merken**

automatisch
der **Film, -e**
finanzieren   finanzieren
das **Foto, -s**
das **Konzert, -e**   Konzert
die **Party, -s**
die **Philosophie**   Philosophie
praktisch
privat   privat
das **Programm, -e**   Programm

■ **Einstieg in den Text**

Einen Brief lesen The following text is a letter written by a German student named
Claudia in response to a letter from her American friend Michael, who is coming to
Germany as an exchange student. Such informal letters between friends are more
loosely structured and associative than formal prose. They tend to be halfway
between spoken and written style. In Claudia's letter, for instance, you'll find conversational phrases and slang (e.g., "Ich kann dir eine Menge erzählen" or "Da staunst du
wohl, oder?").

Claudia writes first about what she's studying, then tells a bit about student life in
Freiburg and compares it to America. Then she describes the difficulty of finding a
place to live and talks about the rich cultural life in Freiburg. It is clear that her letter is
a response to what Michael has written her. She refers to his letter with the following
phrases:

"Dein Brief ist gestern angekommen, ..." (line 6)

"Du schreibst, ... " (lines 6–7)

What do you think Michael wrote in his original letter? Claudia also asks some questions of him:

"Wie ist es denn bei dir? Bekommst du ... " (line 35)

How might Michael respond in his next letter to her?

In einer Vorlesung

Wortschatz 2

Verben

antworten (+ *dat.*) to answer (*a person*)
  Ich kann dir nicht antworten. I can't answer you.
aus·geben, hat ausgegeben to spend (*money*)
belegen to take (*a university course*)
bezahlen to pay for
enttäuschen to disappoint
erzählen to tell, recount
feiern to celebrate, have a party
schicken to send
sitzen, hat gesessen to sit
staunen to be amazed, surprised

Substantive

der **Ausweis, -e** I.D. card
  Studentenausweis student I.D.
der **Brief, -e** letter
der **Bürger, -** citizen
der **Krieg, -e** war
der **Termin, -e** appointment

das **Ende, -n** end
das **Glück** happiness; luck
  Glück haben to be lucky
das **Haar, -e** hair
das **Hauptfach, -̈er** major field (*of study*)
das **Kino, -s** movie theater
  ins Kino gehen to go to the movies
das **Nebenfach, -̈er** minor field (*of study*)
das **Referat, -e** oral report; written term paper
das **Stipendium, Stipendien** scholarship, stipend

Glück haben means *to be lucky*, but **glücklich sein** means *to be happy*.

das **Studium** (university) studies
das **Tempo** pace, tempo

die **Antwort, -en** answer
die **Geschichte, -n** story; history
die **Klausur, -en** written test
die **Kneipe, -n** tavern, bar
die **Wohnung, -en** apartment

die **Ferien** (*pl.*) (school or university) vacation
  die **Semesterferien** semester break

Der Urlaub is a vacation from a job. **Die Ferien** (always plural) is the term for school and university vacations.

Adjektive und Adverbien

billig inexpensive, cheap
gerade just, at this moment
je ever
kostenlos free of charge
lieb dear, nice, sweet
  Das ist lieb von dir! That's sweet of you!
niedrig low
schlimm bad
sofort immediately, right away
sonst otherwise, apart from that
verantwortlich (für) responsible (for)
wohl probably

Andere Vokabeln

alles (*sing.*) everything
einige some
ein paar a couple (of); a few
selber or **selbst** by oneself (myself, yourself, ourselves, etc.)

Remember: **alle** (*pl.*) = *everybody*.

Nützliche Ausdrücke

das heißt that means, in other words
  d.h. i.e. (= that is)
herzlich willkommen! Welcome! Nice to see you!
letzte Woche last week

Gegensätze

billig ≠ **teuer** cheap ≠ expensive
Glück haben ≠ **Pech haben** to be lucky ≠ to be unlucky
je ≠ **nie** ever ≠ never
der Krieg ≠ **der Frieden** war ≠ peace

Mit anderen Worten

die **Bude, -n** (*Studentenslang*) = das **Studentenzimmer**
eine **Katastrophe** = eine **schlimme Situation**
eine **Menge** (*colloq.*) = **viel**

Ein Brief aus Freiburg[1]

Claudia Martens hat gerade einen Brief von ihrem amerikanischen Freund Michael Hayward bekommen. Claudia war ein Jahr in Amerika als Austauschschülerin an Mikes Schule in Atlanta. Sie schickt ihm sofort eine Antwort.

Lab Manual Kap. 6, Lesestück.

Learning about German student life and the university system is the cultural goal of this chapter.

Freiburg, den 20.2.99

5 Lieber Michael,

    dein Brief ist gestern angekommen und ich möchte ihn sofort beantworten°. Du schreibst, du willst zwei Semester an der Uni in Freiburg Geschichte studieren. Das finde ich super! Ich studiere auch Geschichte, aber nur im Nebenfach. Mein Hauptfach ist eigentlich Philosophie. Letztes° Semester habe ich ein sehr interessantes
10 Seminar über den Ersten Weltkrieg belegt. Vielleicht können wir im Herbst zusammen in die Vorlesung über Bismarck und die Gründerjahre[2] gehen.

    Habe ich dir je über unser Universitätssystem und das Studentenleben bei uns berichtet? Die Semesterferien[3] haben gerade begonnen, also habe ich endlich ein bisschen Freizeit und kann dir eine Menge erzählen. Im Allgemeinen° ist das Tempo
15 bei uns etwas langsamer und das Studium weniger° stressig als bei euch. Wir schreiben nicht so viele Klausuren und Referate und man ist als Student mehr für sich selbst° verantwortlich. Das heißt zum Beispiel, du kannst abends zu Hause sitzen und Bücher wälzen° oder mit Freunden in die Kneipe gehen. Erst am Semesterende musst du für das Seminar ein Referat schreiben; dann bekommst du einen Schein°. Bei einer
20 Vorlesung gibt es weder Referate noch° Klausuren! Da staunst du wohl, oder°?

    Wie du vielleicht schon weißt, sind unsere Unis staatlich°; das bedeutet, sie sind für uns Studenten fast kostenlos. Die Studiengebühren° sind sehr niedrig. Ansonsten° muss man praktisch nur für Wohnung, Essen, Bücher und Kleidung Geld ausgeben. Außerdem° bekommen viele Studenten auch das sogenannte° Bafög.[4] Wie finanzierst
25 du eigentlich dein Jahr in Deutschland? Mit einem Stipendium, oder musst du alles selber bezahlen?

answer (*trans.*)

last

im Allgemeinen = in general
weniger = nicht so

für ... = for oneself
Bücher wälzen = hit the books
certificate of course credit
weder ... noch = neither ...
nor / = **nicht wahr?**

state-run

tuition fees / otherwise

in addition / so-called

---

1. City in Baden-Württemberg between the Black Forest and the Rhine. The Albert-Ludwigs-Universität was founded in 1457.
2. **Otto von Bismarck** (1815–1898): German statesman and Prussian Chancellor, under whose leadership the German states were united into the German Empire in 1871. **Gründerjahre**: the "Founders' Years" refers to the period of 1870–1900, when many German businesses were established.
3. The German academic year has a **Wintersemester** that begins in mid-October and ends in mid-February. The **Sommersemester** begins in late April and ends in mid-July. The **Semesterferien** come between the two semesters.
4. Inexpensive government loans for university students in Germany are mandated by the Federal Education Support Law, or **Bundesausbildungsförderungsgesetz** (**Bafög**). This acronym has entered the university vocabulary.

Wo möchte dieser Student wohnen?
Kann man ihn anrufen?

Jedenfalls° ist das Essen in der Mensa immer billig und relativ gut, aber mit dem Wohnen ist es manchmal eine Katastrophe. Es gibt nicht genug Studentenwohnheime für alle Studenten und private Buden sind wahnsinnig teuer geworden. Die Wohnungs-
30 not° ist besonders schlimm: Wir sind seit der Wiedervereinigung° überflutet von° Deutschen aus der ehemaligen° DDR und von den Aussiedlern aus Osteuropa.[1] Übrigens habe ich letztes Semester einigen Schulkindern aus zwei Aussiedlerfamilien Nachhilfestunden° in Deutsch gegeben, denn° diese neuen Bürger können oft nur wenig Deutsch.

35 Wie ist es denn bei dir? Bekommst du durch das Austauschprogramm auto- matisch einen Platz im Studentenwohnheim? Wenn nicht°, dann hast du Glück: Du kannst zu uns in die WG! Wir haben nämlich° nächstes Semester ein Zimmer frei und du bist herzlich willkommen. Michael, du bist immer so gern ins Kino und Konzert gegangen. Ich bin sicher, die Filme und Konzerte hier werden dich nicht ent-
40 täuschen°. Mit deinem Studentenausweis bekommst du im Theater, Kino und Museum immer eine Ermäßigung°.

Jetzt habe ich aber einen Termin beim Arzt und muss nachher für eine Party einkaufen. Wir feiern nämlich heute Abend das Semesterende. Also, genug für heute, aber ich schreibe dir bald wieder. Viele herzliche Grüße an dich und deine Familie.

45 Deine

Claudia

P.S. Ich hab' dir einen Stadtplan und ein paar Postkarten von der Altstadt beigelegt° und dazu° ein neues Foto von mir. Kennst du mich noch mit kurzen Haaren?

in any case

housing shortage /
reunification /
inundated by / former
tutoring / because

wenn nicht = if not
you see

werden ... = will . . .
disappoint
discount

enclosed
in addition

mit kurzen Haaren: The plural form is usually used to describe someone's hair: **Jetzt hat sie kurze Haare.**

1. Citizens of the former German Democratic Republic and the **Aussiedler** (*emigrants*, ethnic Germans from other Eastern European countries) have a constitutional right to German citizen- ship. Many of them have flooded the German housing and employment markets since the dissolution of the Soviet bloc in the late 1980s.

Nach dem Lesen

■ A ■ Antworten Sie auf Deutsch.

1. Wo hat Claudia Michael kennen gelernt?
2. Was will Michael in Freiburg studieren?
3. Wie ist das Tempo im Studentenleben in Freiburg?
4. Warum kostet das Studium in Deutschland nicht sehr viel?
5. Warum sind Studentenzimmer manchmal wahnsinnig teuer?
6. Was hat Claudia letztes Semester in ihrer Freizeit gemacht?
7. Wo kann Michael in Freiburg wohnen?
8. Was hat ihm Claudia außer einem Brief geschickt?
9. Was war für Michael neu auf dem Foto von Claudia?

■ B ■ Partnerarbeit: Michael und Claudia (*Mit offenen Büchern*)   Partner A
spielt die Rolle von Claudia. Partner B spielt Michael und stellt Fragen über ihr Leben
an der Uni. (Use the **Lesestück** for information but answer in your own words.)

Lab Manual Kap. 6,
Diktat.

Workbook Kap. 6, M–Q.

> Was studierst du denn?
> Was belegst du dieses Semester?
> Wann habt ihr Ferien?
> Was kostet das Studium bei euch?
> Was für ein Zimmer hast du?
> Sag mir bitte: Wo kann ich nächstes Jahr wohnen?
> Was gibt's denn zu tun in Freiburg?

Situationen aus dem Alltag

This vocabulary focuses on an everyday topic or situation. Words you already know from **Wortschatz** sections are listed without English equivalents; new supplementary vocabulary is listed with definitions. Your instructor may assign some supplementary vocabulary for active mastery.

Note stress: **Labór.**

■ Das Studium

Einige Wörter kennen Sie schon.

studieren an (+ *dat.*)	*to study at*
Ich studiere an der FU.	
(= **Freien Universität, Berlin**).	
die **Bibliothek, -en**	
das **Fach, ‥er**	*area of study, subject*
das **Hauptfach**, das **Nebenfach**	
die **Klausur, -en**	
das **Labor, -s**	*lab*
das **Referat, -e**	
ein Referat halten	*to give an oral report*
ein Referat schreiben	*to write a paper*
das **Semester, -**	
das **Sommersemester**	*spring term (usually April to July)*
das **Wintersemester**	*fall term (usually October to February)*
das **Seminar, -e**	
die **Vorlesung, -en**	
die **Wissenschaft, -en**	*science; scholarship; field of knowledge*

■ Einige Studienfächer

Note that most academic disciplines are feminine.

Additional vocabulary: **Völkerkunde** (or) **Anthropologie, Theologie, Amerikanistik** (*American studies*). In student slang, **WiWi** = **Wirtschaftswissenschaft** (*economics*). In Austria and Switzerland, **Jura** = **Jus**.

die **Anglistik**	Anglistik	*English studies*
die **Betriebswirtschaft**		*management, business*
die **Biologie**	Biologie	*biology*
die **Chemie**	Chemie	*chemistry*
die **Elektrotechnik**		*electrical engineering*
die **Germanistik**	Germanistik	*German studies*
die **Geschichte**		*history*
die **Informatik**	Informatik	*computer science*
Jura (used without article)		*law*
die **Kunstgeschichte**		*art history*
die **Landwirtschaft**		*agriculture*
die **Linguistik**	Linguistik	*linguistics*
die **Mathematik**	Mathematik	*mathematics*
die **Medizin**	Medizin	*medicine*
die **Musikwissenschaft**		*musicology*
die **Pädagogik**	Pädagogik	*education*
die **Philosophie**	Philosophie	*philosophy*
die **Physik**	Physik	*physics*
die **Politikwissenschaft**		*political science*
die **Psychologie**	Psychologie	*psychology*
die **Soziologie**	Soziologie	*sociology*
die **Wirtschaftswissenschaft**		*economics*

Talking about university life is a communicative goal.

■ A ■ Gruppenarbeit: Was studierst du denn? Was ist Ihr Hauptfach und was belegen Sie dieses Semester?

BEISPIEL: Mein Hauptfach ist _____ . Dieses Semester belege ich _____ , _____ und _____ . Was studierst denn du?

■ B ■ Partnerarbeit: Interview Interview each other in more detail about your studies. Take notes if necessary, and be prepared to report to the whole class. Ask each other questions such as the following:

1. Was tust du lieber: Referate schreiben oder Referate halten? Wie oft musst du das tun?
2. Schreibst du deine Referate auf einem Computer?
3. Arbeitest du oft in der Bibliothek oder mehr im Labor?
4. Was willst du nach dem Studium machen?
5. Brauchst du Deutsch für dein Studium oder für deinen Beruf?
6. Wie finanzierst du das Studium? Bekommst du ein Stipendium?
7. Wohnst du im Studentenwohnheim oder privat?

■ Das Studentenzimmer

Die Möbel (*pl.*)   *furniture*

Dieses Zimmer ist **möbliert** (*furnished*).

1. das **Telefon, -e**
2. das **Bett, -en**
3. die **Lampe, -n**
4. der **Teppich, -e**
5. der **Computer, -**
6. der **CD-Spieler, -**
7. die **CD, -s**
8. das **Radio, -s**

9. das **Bücherregal, -e**
10. das **Poster, -**
11. der **Spiegel, -**
12. der **Wecker, -**
13. der **Kleiderschrank, ̈e**
14. der **Schlüssel, -**
15. die **Decke, -n**
16. der **Boden, ̈**

■ C ■   **Gruppenarbeit: Beschreiben wir dieses Zimmer.**   Wie finden Sie dieses Zimmer? Ist es typisch für die Studentenzimmer bei Ihnen? Kann man hier gut wohnen? Wie sieht *Ihr* Zimmer aus? Was gibt es zum Beispiel *nicht* bei Ihnen?

> View Module 3 of the *Neue Horizonte* video (9:33) and do the activities in **Videoecke 3** in your Workbook/Laboratory Manual/Video Manual.

Universities in the German-Speaking Countries

The university system is similar in all the German-speaking countries and differs in fundamental ways from that in the United States. All institutions of higher learning (**Hochschulen**) in Austria, Germany, and Switzerland are state-run and financed by taxes. Successful completion of the **Abitur** examination (called **Matura** in Austria and Switzerland) entitles a student to enroll in any university in the country. German universities do not have the general education or distribution requirements common at American colleges and universities; students begin their studies in a particular major. Some specialized schools (e.g., **Musikhochschulen**, **Kunsthochschulen**) and majors in high demand (e.g., medicine and management) have restricted enrollments.

Educational reforms in the 1960s and '70s led both to an increase in the number of students and more diversity in their socio-economic backgrounds. In 1950, for example, only 6% of German pupils completed the **Abitur**, and they were mostly the children of the upper middle class whose parents also had a university education. Today, the percentage of students in any given year who go on to university varies from about 16% in Switzerland to about 30% in Germany. Moreover, students who have not attended a **Gymnasium** can obtain a kind of **Abitur** that allows them to study at **Fachhochschulen**, which emphasize applied knowledge rather than theory. For example, one can study electrical engineering but not physics at a **Fachhochschule**, while hotel management is offered at some **Fachhochschulen,** not at universities.

The biggest difference from the United States is the fact that students pay almost no tuition. While a university education is thus feasible for almost everyone, the system has no strong financial incentive for students to complete their education quickly. In the past few years, universities have been encountering increasing fiscal difficulties. State education spending has not kept up with the needs of expanding institutions: faculties have not grown nearly as fast as student bodies, lecture halls and laboratories are often overcrowded, and libraries are unable to keep up with demand. Widespread but peaceful student strikes in Germany in late 1997 reflected growing discontent. In the coming years, legislators in the German-speaking countries must address both the structure and financing of higher education in order to maintain its high quality.

KAPITEL 7

Auf Reisen

Communicative Goals

- Expressing opinions, preferences, and polite requests
- Making travel plans and talking about traveling
- Talking on the telephone
- Telling time with the 24-hour clock

Cultural Goal

- Learning about traveling in Germany and Europe

Chapter Outline

- **Lyrik zum Vorlesen**
  Wilhelm Müller, „Wanderschaft"

- **Grammatik**
  Der-words and *ein*-words
  Coordinating conjunctions
  Verbs with dative objects
  Personal dative
  Using *würden* + infinitive
  Verbs with two-way prepositions
  Perfect tense of modal verbs
  Official time-telling

- **Lesestück**
  Unterwegs per Autostopp oder mit der Bahn

- **Situationen aus dem Alltag**
  Reisen und Verkehr

- **Almanach**
  Jugendherbergen (*Youth Hostels*)

Lab Manual Kap. 7, Dialoge, Fragen, Hören Sie gut zu!, Üb. zur Aussprache [ü].

die Flasche: English cognate: *flask*.

der Straßenatlas: Most German drivers carry a bound road atlas of Western Europe rather than folding maps.

Am Bahnhof

Ein Student sieht eine alte Dame mit viel Gepäck und will ihr helfen.

STUDENT: Darf ich Ihnen helfen?
TOURISTIN: Ja, bitte! Würden Sie mir den Koffer tragen?
STUDENT: Gerne. Wohin müssen Sie denn?
TOURISTIN: Gleis drei. Mein Zug fährt um 15.00 Uhr ab.

Vor der Urlaubsreise
(Vacation)

MARION: Suchst du die Thermosflasche?
THORSTEN: Nein, nicht die Thermosflasche, sondern den Straßenatlas. Ich glaube, ich habe ihn auf den Tisch gelegt.
MARION: Ja, hier liegt er unter meiner Jacke.
THORSTEN: Häng die Jacke doch auf, dann haben wir mehr Platz. Wir müssen unsere Reise nach Venedig planen.

Am Telefon
(das)

Marion ruft ihren Vater an. Es klingelt lange, aber endlich kommt Herr Krogmann ans Telefon.

HERR KROGMANN: Krogmann.
MARION: Hallo Papa! Hier ist Marion. Warum hast du nicht gleich geantwortet?
KROGMANN: Ach, Marion, seid ihr wieder zurück? Ich habe auf dem Sofa gelegen und bin eingeschlafen.
MARION: Oh, tut mir Leid, Papa.
KROGMANN: Das macht nichts. Ich habe sowieso *(anyway)* aufstehen wollen. Wie war denn eure Reise?
MARION: Alles war wunderbar.

Am Bahnhof

Wortschatz 1

Verben

ab·fahren (fährt ab), ist abge-fahren to depart, leave (*by vehicle*)

danken (+ *dat.*) to thank

ein·schlafen (schläft ein), ist eingeschlafen to fall asleep

gefallen (gefällt), hat gefallen (+ *dat.*) to please
   Das Buch gefällt mir. I like the book.

gehören (+ *dat.*) to belong to (a person)

hängen, hat gehängt (*trans.*) to hang
   auf·hängen to hang up

hängen, hat gehangen (*intrans.*) to be hanging

helfen (hilft), hat geholfen (+ *dat.*) to help

klingeln to ring

planen to plan

reservieren to reserve

setzen to set (down), put

stellen to put, place

würden (+ *infinitive*) would (do something)

Substantive

der **Bahnhof, ⸚e** train station
der **Koffer, -** suitcase
der **Straßenatlas** road atlas
der **Zug, ⸚e** train

das **Gepäck** luggage
das **Gleis, -e** track
das **Telefon, -e** telephone
(das) **Venedig** Venice

die **Flasche, -n** bottle
die **Thermosflasche** thermos bottle

Adjektive und Adverbien

sowieso anyway
wunderbar wonderful

Andere Vokabeln

sondern but rather, but . . . instead
welch- which

Nützliche Ausdrücke

Es tut mir Leid. I'm sorry.
Das macht nichts. That doesn't matter.
Das ist (mir) egal. It doesn't matter (to me). I don't care.

Das macht (mir) Spaß. That's fun (for me).
Wie viel Uhr ist es? = Wie spät ist es?

Often shortened in spoken German: **Tut mir Leid; Macht nichts; Mir egal.**

Gegensätze

ab·fahren ≠ an·kommen to depart ≠ to arrive

auf·stehen ≠ ins Bett gehen to get up ≠ to go to bed

ein·schlafen ≠ auf·wachen to fall asleep ≠ to wake up

The verbs in **Gegensätze** illustrate the meanings of some separable prefixes: **ab** = *away from*; **an** = *at*; **auf** = (*here*) *up* .

Mit anderen Worten

Das ist mir Wurscht. (*colloq.*) = **Das ist mir egal.**

At the Train Station

A student sees an elderly woman with a lot of luggage and wants to help her.

S: May I help you?
T: Yes, please. Would you carry my suitcase?
S: Gladly. Where do you have to go?
T: Track three. My train leaves at 3:00 P.M.

Before the Trip

M: Are you looking for the thermos bottle?
T: No, not the thermos, but the road atlas. I think I put it on the table.
M: Yes, here it is, under my jacket.
T: Hang up the jacket, then we'll have more room. We've got to plan our trip to Venice.

On the Telephone

Marion is calling up her father. The phone rings a long time, but Mr. Krogmann finally comes to the telephone.

MR. K: Krogmann.
M: Hello, Dad. This is Marion. Why didn't you answer right away?
MR. K: Oh, Marion, are you back? I was lying on the sofa and fell asleep.
M: Oh, sorry, Dad.
MR. K: That doesn't matter. I wanted to get up anyway. How was your trip?
M: Everything was wonderful.

Variationen

■ A ■ **Persönliche Fragen**

With means of transportation **mit** = *by*: **Die Touristin fährt mit dem Zug.**

1. Sind Sie oft mit dem Zug gefahren? Wohin?
2. Fahren Sie gern mit dem Zug?
3. Die Touristin muss zu ihrem Zug. Wohin müssen Sie heute?
4. Thorsten und Marion brauchen einen Straßenatlas für ihre Reise. Was brauchen Sie für eine Reise?
5. Thorsten plant eine Reise nach Venedig. Planen Sie eine Reise in den Ferien? Wohin?
6. Schlafen Sie gern nachmittags wie Herr Krogmann?
7. Herr Krogmann schläft auf dem Sofa. Wo schlafen Sie lieber am Nachmittag, auf dem Sofa oder im Bett?

■ B ■ **Reaktionen**   Respond to the statements and questions on the left with an appropriate phrase from the right.

1. Ich kann den Koffer nicht tragen.	Einverstanden!
2. Würden Sie mir bitte helfen?	Doch!
3. Hast du das nicht gewusst?	Oh, das tut mir Leid!
4. Wo fährt denn Ihr Zug ab?	Das macht nichts!
5. Waren die Hausaufgaben besonders schwer?	Gerne!
6. Wie war die Reise?	Auf dem Tisch.
7. Wohin hast du den Atlas gelegt?	Gar nichts.
8. Wo liegt denn der Stadtplan?	Auf das Sofa.
9. Gehen wir zusammen einkaufen?	Das finde ich auch.
10. Was ist denn los?	Bitte sehr.
	Auf Gleis zehn.
	Nee, gar nicht.
	Wunderbar!

■ C ■ **Übung: Im Reisebüro** (At the travel agency)   Im Reisebüro fragt man, ob Sie etwas machen wollen. Antworten Sie, Sie würden das gerne tun.

BEISPIEL: A: Wollen Sie ein Hotelzimmer reservieren?
   B: Ja, ich würde gern ein Hotelzimmer reservieren.

1. Wollen Sie Ihren Mantel aufhängen?
2. Wollen Sie morgen abfahren?
3. Wollen Sie morgen Abend in Venedig ankommen?
4. Wollen Sie im Zug schlafen?
5. Wollen Sie mir Ihr Gepäck geben?
6. Wollen Sie Ihre Familie anrufen?

German Romantic literature uses nature images to evoke themes of yearning for the unknown, wandering, and love. The Romantic poets were obsessed with the illusory world of appearances expressed in moonlit nights, fog, and the forest. In the early 19th century **das Wandern** described the life of an itinerant journeyman. These were artisans who journeyed from town to town, gaining experience with different master craftsmen.

Wilhelm Müller's poem cycle "Die schöne Müllerin" (1820) is unified by the theme of the love of the journeyman for the miller's daughter. In this poem the youth is moved to **Wanderlust** by the mill itself with its rushing water and turning wheels. He ends by asking the miller and his wife for permission to depart.

Lab Manual Kap. 7, Lyrik zum Vorlesen.

Set to music by Franz Schubert, this poem is the first song in his cycle "Die schöne Müllerin," op. 5, no. 1 (D 795).

Wanderschaft°

journeying *wandering around*

Das Wandern ist des Müllers Lust°,
Das Wandern!
Das muss ein schlechter Müller sein, *bad*
Dem niemals fiel das Wandern ein°, *To whom*
Das Wandern.

des ... = the miller's desire

dem ... = who has never thought of wandering

Vom Wasser haben wir's gelernt, *We've learned it from the water*
Vom Wasser!
Das hat nicht Rast° bei Tag und Nacht,
Ist stets° auf Wanderschaft bedacht°,
Das Wasser.

rest
stets = immer / intent

Das sehn wir auch den Rädern ab°,
Den Rädern! *not at all stand still*
Die gar nicht gerne stille stehn
Und sich mein Tag nicht müde drehn°,
Die Räder.

sehn ... see also from the wheels

Und ... = never tire of turning

Die Steine selbst°, so schwer sie sind, *heavy*
Die Steine!
Sie tanzen mit den muntern Reihn°
Und wollen gar noch schneller sein, *even far*
Die Steine!

Steine selbst = even the stones

cheerful dance

O Wandern, Wandern, meine Lust, *desire*
O Wandern!
Herr Meister und Frau Meisterin,
Lasst mich in Frieden weiterziehn°
Und wandern!

Lasst ... = let me go in peace

Wilhelm Müller (1794–1827)

Grammatik

Der-*words and* ein-*words*

You have learned the definite and indefinite articles (**der** and **ein**) and similar words that precede nouns (**dies-, jed-, mein, kein, alle**). Such words are divided into two groups, the **der**-words and the **ein**-words, because of slight differences in their endings:

der-*words*		**ein**-*words*	
der, das, die	the	**ein**	a, an
dies-	this, these	**kein**	no, not a
jed-	each, every		
welch-	which	**mein**	my
all-	all	**dein**	your
jéner		**sein**	his, its
mancher		**ihr**	her, its
Solcher		**unser**	our
Welcher		**euer**	your
		ihr	their
		Ihr	your

Possessive adjectives (mein, dein, sein, ihr, unser, euer, ihr, Ihr)

Since the endings of the definite article (**der, das, die**) are slightly irregular, **dieser** is used here to review the **der**-word endings in the three cases you know so far.

der-word endings	masc.	neut.	fem.	plural
nom.	dies**er** Stuhl	dies**es** Buch	dies**e** Uhr	dies**e** Bücher
acc.	dies**en** Stuhl	dies**es** Buch	dies**e** Uhr	dies**e** Bücher
dat.	dies**em** Stuhl	dies**em** Buch	dies**er** Uhr	dies**en** Bücher**n**

The **ein**-words have the same endings as **der**-words *except in three cases* where they have *no* endings, as highlighted in the following table.

ein-word endings	masc.	neut.	fem.	plural
nom.	**mein** Stuhl	**mein** Buch	mein**e** Uhr	mein**e** Bücher
acc.	mein**en** Stuhl	**mein** Buch	mein**e** Uhr	mein**e** Bücher
dat.	mein**em** Stuhl	mein**em** Buch	mein**er** Uhr	mein**en** Bücher**n**

■ **1** ■ **Übung** Your instructor makes a statement. Student A asks which thing is meant. Student B answers.

> BEISPIEL: Das Zimmer ist klein.
> A: Welches Zimmer ist klein?
> B: Dieses Zimmer ist klein.

1. Das Hemd ist teuer.
2. Die Turnschuhe sind neu.
3. Der Lehrling heißt Martin.
4. Die Gruppe fährt nach Europa.
5. Der Pulli ist hässlich.
6. Die Brötchen sind frisch.

Lab Manual Kap. 7, Üb. 2.

Workbook Kap. 7, A.

■ 2 ■ **Übung** Respond to each statement as in the example.

BEISPIEL: Dieser Berg ist steil.
Ja, aber nicht jeder Berg ist steil.

1. Dieser Koffer ist schwer.
2. Dieses Studentenwohnheim ist neu.
3. Dieser Zug fährt pünktlich ab.
4. Dieses Telefon klingelt zu laut.
5. Diese Thermosflasche ist teuer.
6. Dieser Tourist kann Deutsch.
7. Diese Vorlesung ist langweilig.

■ 3 ■ **Übung** Your instructor wants to know what belongs to whom. Answer as in the examples.

BEISPIEL: A: Ist dieses Buch Ihr Buch?
B: Nein, dieses Buch ist sein Buch.
A: Welches Buch ist Ihr Buch?
B: Dieses Buch ist mein Buch.

Tempelhofer Ufer 32
10963 Berlin
Tel. 030 / 264 95 2-0
Fax 030 / 262 04 37

JUGENDHERBERGE

Coordinating conjunctions

A clause is a unit containing a subject and an inflected verb. A simple sentence consists of one clause; a compound sentence has two or more clauses.

Coordinating conjunctions are words that join clauses that could each stand alone as a simple sentence. The coordinating conjunction joins them into a compound sentence.

Christa ist achtzehn.   Ihr Bruder ist sechzehn.
Christa ist achtzehn **und** ihr Bruder ist sechzehn.

Kannst du das Fenster aufmachen?   Soll ich es machen?
Kannst du das Fenster aufmachen **oder** soll ich es machen?

Do not confuse the conjunction **denn** with the flavoring particle used with questions: **Wo bist du denn so lange gewesen?**

The most common coordinating conjunctions in German are

und	*and*
oder	*or*
aber	*but, however*
sondern	*but rather, instead*
denn	*for, because*

Remember the iron-clad rule: The verb is always in second position in German statements. A coordinating conjunction is *not* counted as being in first position in its clause. The word order of the second clause is *not* affected by the coordinating conjunction.

0   1 2

Ute kommt nicht zu Fuß, **sondern** sie fährt mit dem Auto.

0 1 2

Ich kann dich erst am Abend anrufen, **denn** ich bin bis 7 in der Bibliothek.

0 1 2

Klaus muss bis drei arbeiten, **aber** dann kann er nach Hause.

The coordinating conjunctions are also used to join units smaller than a clause.

Ich habe einen Bruder **und** eine Schwester.
Möchtest du Wein **oder** Bier?
Dieser Laden ist gut, **aber** sehr teuer.
Barbara ist nicht hier, **sondern** in Italien.

Note on punctuation: There is *always* a comma before **aber**, **sondern**, and **denn**.

Lab Manual Kap. 7, Var. zur Üb. 4.

■ 4 ■ **Partnerarbeit**   Use **und**, **aber**, **oder**, or **denn** to join each sentence from column A to one from column B. Try to find the most logical pairings. Compare results with other students.

A	*B*
Meine Eltern kommen morgen.	Ich möchte sie dort besuchen.
Bist du krank?	Willst du in einer WG wohnen?
Gisela studiert in Freiburg.	Ich zeige ihnen meine Wohnung.
Ich bringe das Buch mit.	Mein Bruder wohnt auf dem Land.
Ich wohne in der Stadt.	Du sollst es lesen.
Ich bin jetzt in Eile.	Sie hat mir nicht geantwortet.
Willst du in der Mensa essen?	Mein Zug fährt gleich ab.
Willst du allein wohnen?	Wollen wir bei mir etwas kochen?
Ich habe Sabine gefragt.	Geht es dir gut?

■ *Aber* versus *sondern*

Aber and **sondern** are both translated with English *but*. Both express a contrast, but they are *not* interchangeable. **Sondern** must be used when *but* means *but . . . instead*, *but rather*.

Er bleibt zu Hause, **aber** sie geht einkaufen.	*He's staying home, but she's going shopping.*
Er bleibt nicht zu Hause, **sondern** geht einkaufen.	*He's not staying home, **but** is going shopping **instead**.*

Sondern *always* follows a *negative* statement and expresses *mutually exclusive alternatives*. Note that the clause following **sondern** often leaves out elements it has in common with the first clause. Such deletion is called *ellipsis*.

Er bleibt nicht zu Hause, sondern [er] geht einkaufen.
Das ist kein Wein, sondern [das ist] Wasser.
Käthe hat es nicht getan, sondern die Kinder [haben es getan].

Lab Manual Kap. 7, Üb. 5.

■ 5 ■ **Übung:** *Aber* oder *sondern*?   Combine each pair of simple sentences into a compound sentence, using **aber** or **sondern** as appropriate. Use ellipsis where possible.

1. Sie fliegt nach Italien. Ihr Mann fährt mit dem Zug.
2. Sie hasst mich nicht. Sie liebt mich.
3. Es ist noch nicht sieben Uhr. Er ist schon zu Hause.
4. Ich fahre nicht mit dem Auto. Ich gehe zu Fuß.
5. Ich trage keinen Mantel. Ich trage meine Jacke.
6. Bernd mag dieses Bier nicht. Lutz trinkt es gern.

Mit dem Fahrrad (*bicycle*) kann man billig reisen und auch fit bleiben. Woher kommen diese Radfahrer?

■ **Word order:** *nicht x, sondern y*

Notice how the position of **nicht** shifts when it is followed by **sondern**.

Ich kaufe den Mantel nicht.	*but*	Ich kaufe **nicht den Mantel**, sondern die Jacke.
Johanna arbeitet heute nicht.	*but*	Johanna arbeitet **nicht heute**, sondern morgen.

Workbook Kap. 7, B, C.

■ **6** ■ **Übung: Nein, nicht x, sondern y.** Answer these questions negatively, using **sondern**.

> BEISPIEL: Wollen Sie *um sieben* frühstücken?
> Nein, ich will nicht um sieben frühstücken, sondern um zehn.

1. Suchen Sie *die Thermosflasche*?
2. Gehen Sie *am Mittwoch* ins Kino?
3. Gehen Sie *mit Ursula* in die Stadt?
4. Gehen Sie mit Ursula in *die Stadt*?   *auf das Land*
5. Wollen Sie mir *die Fotos* zeigen?
6. Waren Sie *gestern* in der Bibliothek?

Review dative endings for **der**-words, p. 118, and dative forms of the personal pronouns, p. 119.

Verbs with dative objects

A few German verbs require an object in the dative case rather than the accusative. Two of these are **helfen** and **antworten**.

Ich sehe den Mann.	*I see the man.*
but:	
Ich helfe **dem** Mann.	*I'm helping the man.*
Du fragst die Frau.	*You ask the woman.*
but:	
Du antwortest **der** Frau.	*You answer the woman.*

This chapter introduces the following verbs with dative objects:

antworten	*to answer* (someone)
danken	*to thank*
gefallen	*to please*
gehören	*to belong to*
glauben	*to believe* (someone)
helfen	*to help*

Glauben takes an accusative inanimate object, but a dative personal object: **Ich glaube das**, *but* **Ich glaube dir.** One can thus say: **Ich glaube dir das.** = I believe you when you say that.

The dative object is usually a person.

Marie dankt **ihrem Lehrer**.	*Marie thanks her teacher.*
Wem gehört dieser Wagen?	*Who owns this car?* (Literally: *To whom does this car belong?*)
Diese Stadt gefällt **mir**.	*I like this city.* (Literally: *This city pleases me.*)

Note that **gefallen** is another way of saying to *like something*. However, since its literal meaning is *to please* (*someone*), the subject and object are the reverse of English. Remember that the verb must agree in number with the subject.

Die Vorlesungen gefallen **mir**.   literally: *The lectures please me.*

*I like the **lectures**.*

Lab Manual Kap. 7, Var. zur Üb. 7.

Workbook Kap. 7, D, E.

■ 7 ■   **Übung: Was gefällt Ihnen?**   Your instructor asks if you like various things. Say whether you do or do not.

> **BEISPIEL:** Gefällt Ihnen das Wetter heute?
> Ja, es gefällt mir. (*oder*) Nein, es gefällt mir nicht.

1. Gefällt Ihnen diese Stadt?
2. Gefällt Ihnen Ihr Hauptfach?
3. Gefällt Ihnen mein Hemd?
4. Gefällt Ihnen das Wetter heute?
5. Gefallen Ihnen die Vorlesungen an der Uni?
6. Gefallen Ihnen diese Bilder?
7. Gefallen Ihnen meine Schuhe?
8. Gefällt Ihnen dieser Film?

■ 8 ■   **Übung: Wem helfen diese Leute?**   Diese Leute wollen heute helfen. Sagen Sie, wem sie helfen.

■ 9 ■   **Übung: Wem gehört das Buch?**   Say what belongs to whom.

> **BEISPIEL:** A: Wem gehört dieses Buch?
> B: Es gehört mir. Es ist mein Buch.

■ 10 ■   **Gruppenarbeit: Wer kann mir helfen?** (*Mit geschlossenen Büchern*)
Your instructor asks a general question. Redirect the question to a neighbor, who may answer positively or negatively.

> **BEISPIEL:** Wer kann mir helfen?
> A: Kannst *du* ihr helfen?
> B: Nein, ich kann ihr nicht helfen.

1. Wer glaubt mir?
2. Wer kann mir antworten?
3. Wem gehört dieser Rucksack?
4. Wem gefällt das Wetter heute?
5. Wer kann mir heute helfen?

Personal dative

The dative case is also used to indicate a person's involvement in or reaction to a situation. This *personal dative* is often translated by English *to* or *for*.

Ist es **Ihnen** zu kalt?	*Is it too cold **for you**?*
Es wird **mir** zu dunkel.	*It's getting too dark **for me**.*
Wie geht es **dir**?	*How are you?* (Literally: *How is it going **for you**?*)
Wie geht es **deiner Mutter**?	*How is **your mother**?*
Das ist **mir** egal.	*It's all the same **to me**.*
Das macht **mir** Spaß.	*That's fun **for me**.*

The personal dative may often be omitted without changing the basic meaning of the sentence.

When personal dative is omitted, a statement is more absolute. Contrast **Es ist zu dunkel** with **Es ist mir zu dunkel**.

Ist es zu kalt?   Es wird zu dunkel.   Wie geht es?   Das macht Spaß.

It may *not* be omitted in the following idiom:

Das tut mir Leid.   *I'm sorry about that.*

Lab Manual Kap. 7, Var. zur Üb. 11.

■ 11 ■ Übung: Ist es Ihnen zu kalt?   Your instructor asks how you feel about something. Give your opinion, then ask your neighbor for an opinion.

auch nicht = *not . . . either.*

BEISPIEL: Ist es Ihnen hier zu kalt?
A: Mir ist es nicht zu kalt. Und dir?
B: Mir ist es auch nicht zu kalt.

Workbook Kap. 7, F.

1. Ist es Ihnen zu dunkel hier?
2. Ist Ihnen dieses Zimmer zu heiß?
3. Ist Ihnen dieses Buch zu teuer?
4. Ist Ihnen dieser Stuhl hoch genug?
5. Macht Ihnen Deutsch Spaß?
6. Ist Ihnen der Winter hier zu kalt?

■ 12 ■ Partnerarbeit: Reaktionen   Make at least three statements (invented or real) about how things are going for you, what you're doing at the moment, etc. Your partner must decide whether to respond with indifference, sympathy, or enthusiasm. Then switch roles.

BEISPIEL: Ich habe morgen eine Klausur.
Oh, das tut mir Leid. (*oder*) Das ist mir egal.

Am Dienstag fahren wir nach Venedig.
Das finde ich toll!

Using würden + *infinitive*

Expressing opinions, preferences, and polite requests is a communicative goal.

To express opinions, preferences, and polite requests, **würden** is used with an infinitive.

Ich **würde** das nicht **machen**.   *I wouldn't do that.*
Was **würdest** du gerne **tun**?   *What would you like to do?*
Würden Sie mir den Koffer **tragen**?   *Would you carry my suitcase?*

Würden is the German equivalent of English *would*. It functions like a modal verb, with a dependent infinitive in final position. **Würden** is conjugated like **möchten** (see p. 71):

Ich **würde** sagen, ...   Wir **würden** sagen, ...
Du **würdest** sagen, ...   Ihr **würdet** sagen, ...
Er/sie **würde** sagen, ...   Sie/sie **würden** sagen, ...

■ 13 ■   **Gruppenarbeit: Würden Sie bitte ... ?**   Ask your instructor to do a favor for you. Some possibilities are listed below.

BEISPIEL: Würden Sie bitte das Fenster schließen? *bitte*

mir den Koffer tragen	für uns ein Foto machen
mir eine Brezel kaufen	Lebensmittel einkaufen *groceries*
das Mittagessen kochen	Ihre Arbeit beschreiben *describe*
mir den Bahnhof zeigen	mir den Straßenatlas geben

■ 14 ■   **Kettenreaktion: Ich würde gern ...**   Was würden Sie heute Abend gerne machen? Sagen Sie es und dann fragen Sie weiter.

BEISPIEL: Heute Abend würde ich gern _____ . Und du?
            Ich würde gern _____ .

Verbs with two-way prepositions

There is an important group of verb pairs used with the two-way prepositions. One verb shows destination and always takes the accusative case. The other shows location and always takes the dative case.

Destination (accusative)	Location (dative)
Weak transitive verbs	*Strong intransitive verbs*
legen, hat gelegt *to lay (down), put*	**liegen, hat gelegen** *to lie, be lying*
Ich lege das Buch **auf den Schreibtisch**. *I'm putting the book on the desk.*	Das Buch liegt **auf dem Schreibtisch**. *The book is (lying) on the desk.*
setzen, hat gesetzt *to set (down), put*	**sitzen, hat gesessen** *to sit, be sitting*
Sie setzt das Kind **auf den Stuhl**. *She's putting the child on the chair.*	Das Kind sitzt **auf dem Stuhl**. *The child is (sitting) on the chair.*
stellen, hat gestellt *to place (down), put* (upright)	**stehen, hat gestanden** *to stand, be standing*
Ich stelle die Flasche **auf den Tisch**. *I'll put the bottle on the table.*	Die Flasche steht **auf dem Tisch**. *The bottle is (standing) on the table.*
hängen, hat gehängt *to hang up*	**hängen, hat gehangen** *to be hanging*
Er hat die Karte **an die Wand** gehängt. *He hung the map on the wall.*	Die Karte hat **an der Wand** gehangen. *The map hung on the wall.*

Note that **hängen** has one infinitive form but a weak participle (**gehängt**) and a strong participle (**gehangen**).

Legen and **liegen** are used when objects are *laid down* or are *lying* in a horizontal position. **Stellen** and **stehen** are used when objects are *stood up* or are *standing* in a vertical position.

Ich **lege** das Buch auf den Tisch.	*I'm putting the book (down flat) on the table.*
but:	
Ich **stelle** das Buch ins Bücherregal.	*I'm putting the book (upright) in the bookcase.*

■ 15 ■ **Übung: Bei Frau Schneider zu Hause**   Frau Schneider is working around the house. Describe what she is doing in the left-hand pictures, then the results of her efforts in the right-hand pictures.

legen — put down lay
setzen . . . . , set

Perfect tense of modal verbs

You know that modal verbs are used with a dependent infinitive.

Ich muss meinen Freund **anrufen**.	*I have to call my friend.*
Wir wollen nach Hause **gehen**.	*We want to go home.*

Here are the same sentences in the perfect tense:

Ich habe meinen Freund **anrufen müssen**.	*I had to call my friend.*
Wir haben nach Hause **gehen wollen**.	*We wanted to go home.*

A modal verb with a dependent infinitive uses its own *infinitive* form instead of a past participle to form the perfect tense.[1] The infinitive of the modal verb *follows* the dependent infinitive. This construction is called a "double infinitive."

Note that the modal verbs always use **haben** as their auxiliary in the perfect tense, regardless of the dependent infinitive.

Wir **sind** nach Hause gegangen.	*We went home.*

but:

Wir **haben** nach Hause gehen wollen.	*We wanted to go home.*

Lab Manual Kap. 7, Üb. 16.

Workbook Kap. 7, I.

■ 16 ■ **Übung**   Change these sentences from present to perfect tense.

BEISPIEL: Wir dürfen nicht laut singen.
      Wir haben nicht laut singen dürfen.

1. Ich will meinen Stadtplan finden.
2. Meine Freundin muss ich heute anrufen.
3. Sie muss viel Geld ausgeben.
4. Ich kann den Bahnhof nicht finden. *können*
5. Darf man Fotos machen? *dürfen*
6. Ich muss kein Referat schreiben.
7. Ich will dich nicht <u>enttäuschen</u>. *disappoint*

Urlaub auf dem Bauernhof
Ferien auf dem Lande

Seite 140 Marlene Jensen, Steinbergkirche
Einzelhof, ruhig und schön gelegen, Spielplatz, Tischtennis, Fahrräder, 7 km zur Ostsee, BAB-Abfahrt Tarp, Bahnstation Sörup.

---

1. All the modal verbs are mixed verbs and have past participles on the pattern **ge-** + *stem* + **-t** (**dürfen–gedurft, können–gekonnt, mögen–gemocht, müssen–gemusst, sollen–gesollt, wollen–gewollt**). These past participles, however, are used *only* when there is *no* dependent infinitive.

Das hat er nicht **gekonnt**.	*He wasn't able to do that.*
Sie hat mich nicht **gemocht**.	*She didn't like me.*
Das habe ich nicht **gewollt**.	*I didn't want that (to happen).*

Official time-telling

You already know how to tell time in German (see p. 16). For official time-telling, however, there is another system. One gives the full hour and the number of minutes past it. In addition, rather than A.M. or P.M., the twenty-four hour clock is used. This is the way the time is given in the media, in train schedules, on announcements of events, etc. Subtract 12 to get the P.M. time as expressed in English.

Written	Spoken	English
1.40 Uhr	ein Uhr vierzig	*1:40 A.M.*
7.55 Uhr	7 Uhr 55	*7:55 A.M.*
13.25 Uhr	13 Uhr 25	*1:25 P.M.*
20.00 Uhr	zwanzig Uhr	*8:00 P.M.*

null Uhr

Midnight can be both **0 Uhr** and **24.00 Uhr**. However, one minute past midnight is **0.01 (null Uhr eins)**.

Telling time with the 24-hour clock is a communicative goal.

Brokerage 24

21.45 ist in Deutschland Schlafenszeit, in New York Börsenzeit, bei uns immer noch Orderzeit.

Workbook Kap. 7, J.

Lab Manual Kap. 7, Üb. 17.

Wann kann man Dr. Mehler donnerstags in der Praxis besuchen?

■ 17 ■ Übung: Wie viel Uhr ist es? Sagen Sie die Uhrzeit auf Deutsch.

BEISPIEL: 11:20 P.M.
     Es ist 23.20 Uhr (dreiundzwanzig Uhr zwanzig).

1. 1:55 P.M.   3. 11:31 A.M.   5. 10:52 P.M.
2. 6:02 P.M.   4. 9:47 P.M.   6. 2:25 A.M.

Dr. med. Ulrich Mehler
prakt. Arzt
Sprechzeiten:
Mo - Fr: 9 - 12 Uhr
Di + Fr: 16 - 18 Uhr
und nach Vereinbarung
Tel. 06031/12150
Praxis - Eingang

Lesestück

Vor dem Lesen

Tipps zum Lesen und Lernen

■ Tipps zum Vokabelnlernen

***Translating English* to spend**   The reading passage in this chapter talks of spending time and money. Note the different verbs that German uses to distinguish between these two kinds of spending.

Zeit: verbringen

Wir **verbringen** unsere Ferien in den Alpen.
We're spending our vacation in the Alps.

Sie hat den Nachmittag zu Hause **verbracht**.
She spent the afternoon at home.

Sparen (*to save*) is used with both time and money.

Geld: ausgeben

Wie viel muss man für ein Zimmer **ausgeben**?
How much do you have to spend for a room?

Wir haben sehr viel Geld **ausgegeben**.
We spent a lot of money.

Note the verbal noun in Wilhelm Müller's poem on p. 190: ***Das Wandern ist des Müllers Lust.***

Verbal nouns   Any German infinitive may act as a noun. It is then capitalized and is always neuter.

reisen → **das Reisen** (*traveling*)

Das Reisen ist heutzutage leicht.
Traveling is easy nowadays.

These verbal nouns correspond to English gerunds (the form ending in **-ing**); some have additional, more specific meanings. For instance, **das Essen** means *eating* but also *food* and *meal*. Here are some other examples:

das **Fliegen**   *flying*
das **Lernen**   *learning, studying*
das **Leben**   *living; life*
das **Sein**   *being; existence*
das **Wissen**   *knowing; knowledge*

Lab Manual Kap. 7, Üb. zur Betonung.

Das Ticket has been borrowed from English and is used mainly for airline tickets and international train travel. In a train, however, the conductor will say **Fahrkarten, bitte** (*Tickets, please*).

■ Leicht zu merken

hektisch
der **Horizont, -e**   Hori<u>zont</u>
das **Instrument, -e**   Instru<u>ment</u>
die **Kamera, -s**
packen
spontan
das **Ticket, -s**
die **Wanderlust**

"Unterwegs per Autostopp oder mit der Bahn" describes how German young people travel in Europe. To gain a first impression of this text, simply skim it, do not read it. Look for familiar vocabulary that is related to travel. In addition, watch for context clues that point to new travel-related vocabulary. As you skim, also keep an eye out for obvious cognates such as **Instrument**.

After skimming the text, go back and read it through once completely. Use the following questions as a guide to highlight some main ideas. See whether you can answer them after a first reading.

Wie kann man durch Europa reisen?
Warum reisen diese Menschen gern?
Wie kann man beim Reisen Geld sparen?
Wo kann man unterwegs Menschen kennen lernen?
Wo kann man auf der Reise übernachten?

■ Wortschatz 2

Verben

aus·steigen, ist ausgestiegen to get out (*of a vehicle*) *cf. einsteigen*
benutzen to use
hoffen to hope
mit·nehmen (nimmt mit), hat mitgenommen to take along
quatschen (*colloq.*) to talk nonsense; to chat
sparen to save (*money or time*)
trampen (*pronounced „trämpen"*), **ist getrampt** to hitchhike
übernachten to spend the night
verbringen, hat verbracht (+ *time phrase*) to spend (*time*)

Substantive

der **Abend, -e** evening
  am **Abend** in the evening
der **Platz, ⸚e** seat
der **Rucksack, ⸚e** rucksack, backpack

das **Ausland** (*sing.*) foreign countries
  im **Ausland** abroad (*location*)
  ins **Ausland** abroad (*destination*)
das **Ding, -e** thing
das **Flugzeug, -e** airplane
das **Foto, -s** photograph
  ein **Foto machen** to take a picture
das **Ziel, -e** goal
  Reiseziel destination

die **Bahn** railroad; railway system
die **Fahrkarte, -n** ticket (*for means of transportation*)
die **Freiheit, -en** freedom
die **Jugendherberge, -n** youth hostel
die **Tasche, -n** pocket; hand *or* shoulder bag

Adjektive und Adverbien

bequem comfortable
pünktlich punctual, on time

so so
sympathisch friendly, congenial, likeable
verrückt crazy, insane

Nützliche Ausdrücke

useful

in der Nähe von near, nearby
egal wohin (**wer, warum** usw.) no matter where (who, why, etc.)

Gegensätze

aus·steigen ≠ ein·steigen to get out ≠ to get in

Mit anderen Worten

per Autostopp reisen = trampen

Unterwegs — en route, on the go, on the way

Unterwegs per Autostopp oder mit der Bahn

🎧 **Lab Manual** Kap. 7, Lesestück.

Mit dem Sommer kommt wieder die Wanderlust. Dann packt man den Koffer oder den Rucksack und macht eine Reise. Viele Menschen fahren mit dem eigenen° Wagen oder mit dem Flugzeug. Aber junge Leute mit wenig Geld in der Tasche wollen nicht so viel ausgeben. Sie fahren lieber mit der Bahn oder reisen per Autostopp. Ein paar

5 erzählen uns hier von ihren Reiseerfahrungen°.

own

travel experiences

Adrienne, 18, Azubi° aus Kaisersaschern

„Trampen erweitert° den Horizont. Ich bin in den Sommerferien mit meinem Freund Markus nicht nur in Deutschland, sondern auch im Ausland getrampt. Wir haben Glück gehabt: Überall waren die Menschen sympathisch und wir haben auch eine

10 Menge Geld gespart. In Italien war es einfach super. Ein Autofahrer hat uns von Venedig nach Florenz[1] mitgenommen. Er hat ein bisschen Deutsch verstanden und wir haben dann drei Tage bei seiner Familie gewohnt. Mit meiner Kamera habe ich ein paar schöne Fotos von seinen Kindern gemacht. Das hat uns Spaß gemacht und ich hoffe, wir können sie nächstes Jahr wieder besuchen. Ja, im Zug lernt man die Men-

15 schen einfach nicht so gut kennen."

= **Lehrling**
broadens

a lot of money

Learning about traveling in Germany and Europe is the cultural goal of this chapter.

fun

easy

Thomas, 21, Student aus Tübingen

„Ich trampe schon in der Nähe von Tübingen, aber für eine lange Reise würde ich immer ein Interrail-Ticket kaufen. Das kostet unter DM 500 für vier Wochen und man kann durch ganz Europa reisen. Mit diesem Ticket habe ich viel Freiheit: Da kann man

20 spontan weg, egal wohin.

Tramper in der Nähe von Heidelberg.

---

1. Florence: city in Tuscany famous as a center of Italian Renaissance culture.

Freunde von mir benutzen den Zug als ‚rollendes° Hotel'. Am Tag besuchen sie eine neue Stadt. Am Abend steigen sie wieder ein und schlafen dann im Zug unterwegs zum nächsten° Reiseziel. Dieses Tempo ist mir aber zu hektisch. Ich übernachte lieber in der Jugendherberge und verbringe ein paar Tage in jeder Stadt."

rolling *use*

next

25 *Herbert, 29, Assistenzarzt° aus Ulm*

resident (physician)

„Früher bin ich viel per Autostopp gereist, aber heute würde ich das nicht mehr machen. Die Unsicherheit° ist mir zu stressig und ich habe nicht mehr so viel Freizeit. Das Reisen mit der Bahn gefällt mir, denn es ist sehr praktisch und bequem. Man geht einfach zum Bahnhof, kauft eine Fahrkarte und steigt in den Zug ein. Und man weiß,
30 man kommt pünktlich an.

uncertainty

arrives

Im Abteil quatsche ich gern ein bisschen mit den Mitreisenden° über viele Dinge. Letztes Wochenende bin ich zum Beispiel nach Berlin gefahren. Neben mir hat ein Musikstudent aus Leipzig gesessen. Er ist in Wittenberg¹ ausgestiegen und ich habe ihm mit seinem Gepäck geholfen. Er hatte° nicht nur einen Rucksack und einen Koffer
35 mit, sondern auch eine Bassgeige°. Für sein Instrument hat er einen zweiten° Platz reservieren müssen. Verrückt, nicht?"

fellow passengers

had
double bass / second

Unterwegs mit der Bahn

vacation
m ⌃ *pl.*
Urlaub vs *Ferien*
job *school*

Nach dem Lesen

■ A ■ Antworten Sie auf Deutsch.

1. Wie kann man im Urlaub Geld sparen?
2. Wohin ist Adrienne getrampt?
3. Hat es ihr Spaß gemacht? Warum?

1. The composer Johann Sebastian Bach (1685–1750) spent the greater part of his life in **Leipzig** (in the state of Saxony). The church reformer Martin Luther (1483–1546) is buried in **Wittenberg** (in the state of Saxony-Anhalt).

4. Wo kann man Menschen unterwegs kennen lernen?
5. Wie kann man mit der Bahn billig reisen?
6. Wie kann man den Zug als „rollendes Hotel" benutzen?
7. Wo kann man billig übernachten?
8. Warum würde Herbert heutzutage nicht mehr trampen?

■ **B** ■ **Urlaub am Mittelmeer**   Nach dem langen kalten Winter machen viele Deutsche gern Urlaub am Mittelmeer, wo es warm und sonnig ist. Lesen Sie diese Beschreibungen von beliebten (*popular*) Urlaubszielen und dann suchen Sie diese Orte auf der Europakarte am Ende des Buches.

Kreta: die größte griechische Insel.   Der Berg Ida erreicht eine Höhe von 2 456 m. Von 3000 bis 1200 v. Chr. war Kreta der Mittelpunkt der minoischen Kultur.

Korsika: französische Insel im Mittelmeer.   Bergige Landschaft. Mildes Klima, <u>Anbau</u> von Kastanien, Oliven, Orangen und Wein. Bevölkerung spricht italienisch. Napoleon 1769 auf Korsika geboren.

Workbook Kap. 7, K–O.

Tunesien: eine Republik in Nordafrika.   Landessprache: Arabisch. Im Norden Gebirge, im Süden Wüste mit Oasen. Viele Urlaubsorte an der Küste.

Lab Manual Kap. 7, Diktat.

Türkei.   Hauptstadt, Istanbul. Viele Türken wohnen und arbeiten in Deutschland und viele Deutsche machen gern Urlaub an der türkischen Mittelmeerküste.

TUNESIEN Djerba

Hotel Miramar Cesar Palace ■■■■■
—— **Komforthotel mit sehr guter Ausstattung** ——

Lage: Nur ca. 100 m bis zum weitläufigen, feinen Sandstrand, ca. 5 km bis Midoun und ca. 16 km nach Houmt Souk (Linienbushaltestelle am Hotel).
Ausstattung: Komfortable, elegant ausgestattete und vollklimatisierbare Hotelanlage mit Haupthaus und mehreren bungalowähnlichen Wohngebäuden, gepflegtem Garten, hübschem Swimmingpool mit Sonnenterrasse, Liegen (Auflagen gegen Geb.) und Schirmen, Pool-/Snackbar. Im Haupthaus schöne Empfangshalle im orientalischen Stil mit Rezeption. Ansprechend gestaltetes Speiserestaurant mit Nichtraucherzone, à la carte-Restaurant, Bar. Hallenbad. Tun. Kat.: 5 Sterne, 112 Zimmer. 1-2 Etagen. Kreditkarten: Euro-/Mastercard, Visa, Diners, Amex.

1 Wo. HP ab DM **1051,-**

☆☆☆☆

HOTEL
OBAKÖY
MODERNE FERIENANLAGE

LAGE:
Durch die Hauptstraße (Unterführung) vom weitläufigen Sandstrand getrennt und ca. 3 km vom Ortskern Alanyas entfernt (Dolmusverbindungen).

AUSSTATTUNG:
Empfangshalle mit Rezeption, Aufenthaltsraum, TV-Ecke (Sat.-Empfang), Mietsafe, Bar, Geschäfte, Speiserestaurant mit Terrasse, Swimmingpool, sep. Kinderbecken, Sonnenterrasse (Liegen u. Schirme inkl.) und Pool-/Snackbar.

corner →

ZIMMER:
Freundlich ausgestattete Zimmer mit Klimaanlage, Telefon, Sat.-TV, Radio, Fön, Minibar (gegen Gebühr), Bad oder Dusche/WC und Balkon.

VERPFLEGUNG:
Frühstück und Abendessen in Buffetform.

SPORT:
Beachvolleyball, Tischtennis und Fitness inkl., Billard, Sauna, Massage und Türkisches Bad gegen Gebühr.

UNTERHALTUNG:
Tagesanimation, abends gelegentlich Unterhaltungsprogramme.

ZUSATZINFORMATIONEN:
Landeskategorie 4 Sterne; 181 Zimmer, 6 Etagen, 1 Lift; Kreditkarten: Visa, Amex, Mastercard; Reinigung: täglich, Handtuch- und Bettwäschewechsel: 5 x pro Woche; Babybetten inkl.;
Tel.: 0090 242-5140700

1 WOCHE HALBPENSION AB DM **815,-**

TIP

Situationen aus dem Alltag

This vocabulary focuses on an everday topic or situation. Words you already know from **Wortschatz** sections are listed without English equivalents; new supplementary vocabulary is listed with definitions. Your instructor may assign some supplementary vocabulary for active mastery.

■ **Reisen und Verkehr** (Travel and traffic)

Some of these words are already familiar.

Verben

ab·fahren ≠ **an·kommen**
ein·steigen ≠ **aus·steigen**
um·steigen   *to transfer, change (buses, trains, etc.)*

Substantive

der **Bahnhof**, ¨e	
der **Bus**, -se	*bus*
der **Flughafen**, ¨	*airport*
der **Verkehr**	*traffic*
der **Wagen**, -	
der **Zug**, ¨e	*train*
das **Auto**, -s	
das **Flugzeug**, -e	
die **Autobahn**, -en	*expressway, high-speed highway*
die **Fahrkarte**, -n	

ERHOLUNG AUF DEM RHEIN.
DIE BAHN BRINGT SIE ZUM SCHIFF.

K·D Köln-Düsseldorfer ▥ **Deutsche Bundesbahn**

Debate continues about whether to impose a speed limit on the **Autobahn**. Many claim the present lack of a speed limit contributes to Germany's high accident rate.

Nützliche Ausdrücke

Ich fahre	**mit dem Wagen.**	. . . *by car.*
	mit dem Bus.	. . . *by bus.*
	mit der Bahn.	. . . *by train.*
Ich fliege.		

der Zug?

■ **A** ■ **Partnerarbeit: Was habe ich zuerst gemacht?** Here are eight statements about a train trip. Number them in the order that the events most likely happened. Then read them aloud in order.

  7/8 Ich habe im Zug mit der Frau neben mir gequatscht.
  5 Ich habe mir eine Fahrkarte gekauft.
  7/8 Ich habe im Zug einen guten Roman gelesen.
  1. Ich habe eine Reise ins Ausland machen wollen.
  6 Ich bin in den Zug eingestiegen.
  2 Ich habe mir eine Landkarte gekauft.
  3 Ich bin zum Bahnhof gegangen.
  4 Ich bin pünktlich angekommen.

■ B ■ Gruppenarbeit: Planen wir unsere Reise. (*4 Personen*) Planen Sie eine Reise nach Europa. Besprechen Sie diese Fragen zusammen. Benutzen Sie die Landkarte.

Welche Länder wollen wir besuchen?
Wie lange wollen wir bleiben?
Wie wollen wir durch Europa reisen? Mit der Bahn? Per Autostopp?
Wo wollen wir übernachten? In einer Jugendherberge? Im Hotel?
Was wollen wir mitnehmen? Machen wir eine Liste.
Haben wir etwas vergessen?

Jetzt berichtet jede Gruppe über ihre Pläne.

■ C ■ Partnerarbeit: Rollenspiel Spielen Sie diese Situation mit Ihrem Partner. Partner A spielt den Autofahrer, Partner B spielt den Tramper. Der Tramper steht seit einer Stunde im Regen. Endlich hält ein Auto. Der Tramper steigt ein und spricht mit dem Fahrer über das Trampen und die Ferien.

Sie können Ihr Gespräch (*conversation*) dann der ganzen Klasse vorspielen.

■ D ■ Partnerarbeit: Wann kommt der Zug an? Sie arbeiten am Hauptbahnhof in Mannheim und geben Auskunft über die Züge. Eine Touristengruppe bittet um (*asks for*) Auskunft. Sie müssen die Antworten auf dem Fahrplan finden.

> **BEISPIEL:** A: Entschuldigung, wann kommt der Zug aus Hamburg in Mannheim an?
> B: Er kommt um 14.22 Uhr an.
> A: Um wie viel Uhr fährt er in Hamburg ab?
> B: Um 9.33 Uhr.

Mannheim Hbf (Hauptbahnhof)					
	Ankunft (*arrivals*)			**Abfahrt (*departures*)**	
Zug-Nr.	*ab*[1]	*an*[1]	*Zug-Nr.*	*ab*	*an*
6342	Hamburg 9.33 Uhr	Mannheim 14.22 Uhr	1338	Mannheim 5.42 Uhr	Zürich 8.12 Uhr
7422	München 10.03 Uhr	Mannheim 13.10 Uhr	2472	Mannheim 6.06 Uhr	Nürnberg 9.33 Uhr
1387	Frankfurt 11.20 Uhr	Mannheim 12.01 Uhr	6606	Mannheim 7.55 Uhr	Straßburg 8.40 Uhr
7703	Wien 10.10 Uhr	Mannheim 17.56 Uhr	2203	Mannheim 10.12 Uhr	Innsbruck 15.46 Uhr
9311	Berlin 11.05 Uhr	Mannheim 19.16 Uhr	3679	Mannheim 13.23 Uhr	Prag 20.09 Uhr

1. **ab**: time and place of departure; **an**: time and place of arrival.

Jugendherbergen (Youth Hostels)

There are about 670 **Jugendherbergen** in Germany, 110 in Austria, 85 in Switzerland, and 13 in Luxembourg. They are meeting places for young travelers from all over the world. In addition to providing inexpensive food and lodging, they offer a variety of courses and organized trips.

Membership in the AYH (American Youth Hostels) entitles the cardholder to privileges in hostels all over the world. Membership costs as of 1995: under 17 years of age, $10.00; 17–54, $25.00; over 54, $15.00. In Bavaria you must be under 26 years of age to stay in a youth hostel. To apply for membership, write to:

American Youth Hostels, Inc.
P.O. Box 37613
Washington, D.C. 20013–7613
(202) 783–6161

Here are some excerpts from the Youth Hostel handbook for Germany.

Berlin, Jugendgästehaus Berlin 15, E 3

Anschrift: JGH Berlin, Kluckstraße 3, 10785 Berlin, ☎ 030/2611097, Fax: 030/2650383.
Herbergsväter: Hans-Martin Schwarz und Ingolf Keil.
Anreise: Auto: Stadtautobahn (Richtung Wilmersdorf/Schöneberg: Ausfahrt Innsbrucker Pl.), links, über Hauptstr. und Potsdamer Str. bis Lützowstr., dort links, Kluckstr. rechts einbiegen. Bahn: Bahnhof. Zoo-U-Bahn-Linie 1 (Richtung Schlesisches Tor) bis Kurfürstenstr. und 5 Min. Fußweg oder Bhf. Zoo und Bus 129 ab Haltestelle Kurfürstendamm/Joachimstaler Str. (Richtung Hermannplatz) bis JGH, Haltestelle "Gedenkstätte".
Lage: Innenstadt, am Rande des Tiergarten, nahe des Kulturforums.
Geeignet für: Familien (bedingt), Seminare, Tagungen, Lehrgänge (nach Absprache), Gruppen, Einzelgäste.
Raumangebot: 364 Betten, 5 Tagesräume, 6 Familienzimmer.
Freizeitmöglichkeiten: Fahrradausleihe (500 m entfernt), TT-Platten, Spaziergänge durch den Tiergarten mit Reichstag, Brandenburger Tor, Siegessäule, Kulturforum. Stadterkundungen auf kulturellem und historischen Gebiet, Gedenkstätte: Widerstand im 3. Reich,

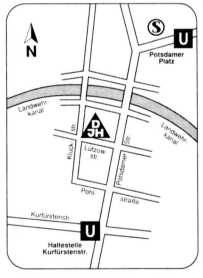

"Alternativszene" Kreuzberg, Berlin-Ost: historisches Zentrum (Nikolai-Viertel, Unter den Linden, Museumsinsel, Pergamonmuseum).

Erklärung der Piktogramme

Icon	Bedeutung	Icon	Bedeutung
	Sportplatz		Fußball
	Sporthalle		Volleyball
	Basketball		Tennis
	Kegeln		Reitsport
	Fahrrad-Verleih am Ort		Flugsportarten
	Leichtathletik		Wintersport
	Segeln/Surfen		Hallenbad
	Kanu/Kajak/Rudern		Freibad/Gewässer

	Sportplatz	Sporthalle	Fußball	Volleyball	Basketball	Kegeln	Tennis	Reitsport	Fahrrad-Verleih am Ort	Leichtathletik	Flugsportarten	Wintersport	Segeln/Surfen	Kanu/Kajak/Rudern	Hallenbad	Freibad/Gewässer	Besonderes:
Bayern																	
Bayerisch-Eisenstein	◆	◆										◆				◆	
Bayreuth	◆	◆													◆	◆	
Bayrischzell	◆	◆	◆			◆						◆				◆	
Benediktbeuern "Don-Bosco"	◆	◆	◆				◆		◆					◆		◆	Billard
Bodenmais	◆	◆										◆				◆	
Furth im Wald	◆	◆							◆					◆	◆	◆	
Garmisch-Partenkirchen												◆		◆	◆	◆	Bergsport
Berlin																	
Berlin, JGH Wannsee													◆	◆		◆	

187

Das Leben in der Stadt

Communicative Goals

- Talking about food and shopping
- Discussing city life
- Asking for directions
- Ordering in a restaurant

Cultural Goal

- Learning about life in German cities

Chapter Outline

- **Lyrik zum Vorlesen**
  Heinrich Heine, „Die Loreley"

- **Grammatik**
  Subordinate clauses and subordinating conjunctions
  Infinitive constructions with *zu*
  Genitive case
  Nouns of measure, weight, and number
  Equivalents for English *to*

- **Lesestück**
  Aspekte der Großstadt

- **Situationen aus dem Alltag**
  Unterwegs in der Stadt; In der Konditorei

- **Almanach**
  Mit dem Bus durch Berlin

Dialoge

Lab Manual Kap. 8, Dialoge, Fragen, Hören Sie gut zu!, Üb. zur Aussprache [e/er].

Remember: **DM 25,80** is spoken **fünfundzwanzig Mark achtzig**. Note on tipping: German restaurants automatically add 15% for service to the bill. When paying, however, it is customary to round up the bill.

Im Restaurant: Zahlen bitte!

KELLNERIN: So, hat es Ihnen geschmeckt?

GAST: Ausgezeichnet!

KELLNERIN: Möchten Sie noch etwas bestellen?

GAST: Nein, danke, ich möchte zahlen, bitte.

KELLNERIN: Sie haben Schnitzel, Pommes frites, einen Salat und ein Bier gehabt, nicht wahr?

GAST: Ja, und auch eine Tasse Kaffee.

KELLNERIN: Das macht zusammen DM 25,80, bitte sehr.

GAST: (*Gibt ihr DM 30*) 27 Mark.

KELLNERIN: Danke sehr, und drei Mark zurück.

Hat es Ihnen geschmeckt? (*How was everything?*) means literally *Did it taste good to you?*

Most Germans eat a hot meal at noon and a simple supper of cold cuts, bread, cheese, and salad in the evening.

Was brauchen wir noch?

DORA: Heute Morgen habe ich Max zum Abendessen eingeladen. Weißt du, ob er kommt?

FRANZ: Ja, aber er hat mir gesagt, dass er erst um halb sieben kommen kann. Wie viel Uhr ist es jetzt?

DORA: Halb sechs. Also muss ich noch schnell zum Supermarkt, um ein paar Sachen einzukaufen. Was brauchen wir noch?

FRANZ: Ein Kilo Kartoffeln, 200 Gramm Leberwurst, Käse, eine Flasche Rotwein und Obst zum Nachtisch.

DORA: Ist das alles?

FRANZ: Ich glaube schon.

Ein Stadtbummel

Marianne besucht ihren Freund Helmut in Köln. Er hat ihr die Stadt noch nicht gezeigt, weil es geregnet hat.

Du is used here as an attention-getter, equivalent to *hey, look*.

HELMUT: Du, der Regen hat endlich aufgehört! Hast du jetzt Lust einen Stadtbummel zu machen?

MARIANNE: Ja gerne. Aber ich hab' jetzt Hunger. Können wir zuerst essen?

HELMUT: Selbstverständlich! In der Nähe des Doms gibt es ein Lokal, wo wir griechisch essen können.

MARIANNE: Hmm, das klingt lecker!

HELMUT: Nachher können wir dann den Dom besuchen und von da ist es nicht mehr weit zum Kunstmuseum.

Wortschatz 1

Verben

bestellen to order
ein·laden (lädt ein), hat eingeladen to invite
klingen, hat geklungen to sound
schmecken to taste; to taste good
  Wie schmeckt es dir? How does it taste? How do you like it?
zahlen to pay

Substantive

der **Bummel, -** stroll, walk
  einen Stadtbummel machen to take a stroll through town
der **Dom, -e** cathedral
der **Durst** thirst
der **Gast, ˸e** guest; patron
der **Hunger** hunger
der **Kaffee** coffee
der **Kellner, -** waiter
der **Liter** liter
der **Nachtisch** dessert
  zum Nachtisch for dessert
der **Salat, -e** salad; lettuce
das **Abendessen** supper, evening meal
  zum Abendessen for dinner
das **Gebäude, -** building
das **Glas, ˸er** glass
das **Gramm** gram
das **Kilogramm** (or das **Kilo**) kilogram
(das) **Köln** Cologne
das **Lokal, -e** neighborhood restaurant or tavern
das **Museum, Museen** museum
das **Restaurant, -s** restaurant
das **Schnitzel, -** cutlet, chop

Dom comes from Latin *domus ecclesiae* (*house of the congregation*).

die **Kartoffel, -n** potato
die **Kellnerin, -nen** waitress
die **Kunst, ˸e** art
die **Sache, -n** thing; item
die **Tasse, -n** cup
die **Wurst, ˸e** sausage
  die **Leberwurst** liverwurst

Adjektive und Adverbien

ausgezeichnet excellent
griechisch Greek
lecker tasty, delicious
weit far; far away
zuerst first, at first

Andere Vokabeln

dass (*sub. conj.*) that
noch etwas something else, anything more
ob (*sub. conj.*) whether, if
um ... zu in order to

Nützliche Ausdrücke

Durst haben to be thirsty
Hunger haben to be hungry
Lust haben (etwas zu tun) to want to (do something)
griechisch (italienisch, französisch usw.) essen to eat Greek (Italian, French, etc.) food
Ich glaube schon. I think so.
in der Nähe (+ *gen.*) near, nearby
Zahlen bitte! (May I have the) check please!

You already know **in der Nähe von** (+ *dat.*).

Gegensätze

Ich glaube schon. ≠ Ich glaube nicht. I think so. ≠ I don't think so.
weit ≠ nah(e) far ≠ near
zuerst ≠ zuletzt at first ≠ finally, last of all

Mit anderen Worten

der **Kram** (*colloq.*) = die **Sachen;** alte Sachen

ich möchte zahlen, bitte

In a Restaurant: Check please!

WAIT.: How was everything?

P: Excellent!

WAIT.: Would you like to order anything else?

P: No thanks. I'd like the check, please.

WAIT.: You had a cutlet, French fries, a salad, and a beer, right?

P: Yes, and also a cup of coffee.

WAIT.: All together that comes to 25 Marks 80, please.

P: (*Gives her DM 30*) 27 Marks.

WAIT.: Thank you, and three Marks change. (*back*)

What Else Do We Need?

D: This morning I invited Max to supper. Do you know if he's *ob* coming?

F: Yes, but he told me that he couldn't come until 6:30. What time is it now?

D: 5:30. So I need to make a quick trip to the supermarket to buy a few things. What else do we need?

F: A kilo of potatoes, 200 grams of liverwurst, cheese, a bottle of red wine, and fruit for dessert. *Nachtisch*

D: Is that all?

F: I think so.

A Stroll Through Town

Marianne is visiting her friend Helmut in Cologne. He hasn't shown her around town yet because it's been raining.

H: Hey look, the rain's finally stopped! Do you want to take a stroll through town now?

M: Sure. But I'm hungry now. Can we eat first?

H: Of course. Near the cathedral there's a place where we can eat Greek food.

M: Hmm, that sounds delicious!

H: Then we can visit the cathedral afterwards, and from there it's not far to the art museum.

Variationen

■ A ■   Persönliche Fragen

1. Haben Sie heute gefrühstückt? Was haben Sie denn gegessen? Hat's Ihnen geschmeckt?
2. Kennen Sie ein Lokal, wo man sehr gut essen kann? Wie heißt es?
3. Essen Sie gern griechisch? italienisch? französisch? deutsch?
4. Trinken Sie viel Kaffee? Was trinken Sie sonst?
5. Was essen Sie gern zum Nachtisch?
6. Laden Sie oft Freunde zum Abendessen ein?
7. Kaufen Sie im Supermarkt ein? Wie oft? *zweimal*
8. Marianne hat Lust einen Stadtbummel zu machen. Haben Sie Lust heute etwas zu machen? Was denn?
9. Gehen Sie gern ins Kunstmuseum? Welche Künstler (*artists*) mögen Sie?

Käse des Monats:

Echter Käse aus Holland
holländischer Schnittkäse, 30% Fett i.Tr., 100 g *1.99*

Granny Smith Äpfel
Chile, Kl. I, neuerntig
1 kg   **2.99**

Unser SB-Wurst-Angebot:
Pfälzer Leberwurst
400-g-Packung   *3.49*

Obstabteilung!

Griech. Victoria-Trauben
Hkl. I
1 kg   **2.99**

Südafrik. Outspan-Orangen
Hkl. I
7er Netz   **2.99**

oatmeal = Haferschrot (m)
juice = Saft (m) but Apfelsine
ice cream = Speiseeis (n)

Übung: Raten Sie mal! (Take a guess!) Marianne und Helmut wollen einen Stadtbummel machen. Das heißt, sie haben ein bisschen Freizeit und können langsam durch die Stadt gehen. Um einen Bummel zu machen braucht man also Zeit. Raten Sie mal, was diese Wörter bedeuten:

window shopping 1. Sie machen einen **Schaufensterbummel**.

shopping trip 2. Ich hab' ein bisschen Geld in der Tasche. Machen wir doch einen **Einkaufsbummel**.

milk train 3. Der Zug hat an jedem kleinen Bahnhof gehalten. Ich fahre nie wieder mit diesem **Bummelzug**!

perpetual student 4. Fritz studiert seit 13 Semestern an der Uni und ist immer noch nicht fertig. Er ist ein **Bummelstudent**!

slow down 5. Die Arbeiter arbeiten immer noch, aber sehr langsam. Sie machen einen **Bummelstreik**.

Talking about food is a communicative goal.

■ C ■ **Partnerarbeit: Schmeckt es dir?** Fragen Sie Ihren Partner, ob ihm etwas schmeckt.

BEISPIEL: A: Isst du gern Tomatensuppe?
B: Nein, das schmeckt mir nicht. (*oder*)
Ja, das schmeckt mir.

der Käse   Kaffee
das Bier   Brot
die Pizza   Salat
fl Kartoffeln   *das* Wiener Schnitzel
u Pommes frites   griechisches Essen
fl Leberwurst   *der* Wein (*trinken*)

eine Portion Pommes

Papa kocht das Abendessen.

The cliff called the Loreley is on the Rhine River at its deepest spot. Heinrich Heine's famous poem "Ich weiß nicht, was soll es bedeuten" (1823) is a retelling of a Romantic legend invented by his contemporary Clemens Brentano (1778–1842). It recounts the tale of a siren who lures boatmen to their deaths at this place. Set to music by the composer Silcher, it achieved the status of a folk song.

Lab Manual Kap. 8, Lyrik zum Vorlesen.

Ich weiß nicht, was soll es bedeuten („Die Loreley")

Ich weiß nicht, was soll es bedeuten,
dass ich so traurig° bin;   sad   *ur = very old times*
ein Märchen aus alten Zeiten,   *ur*
das kommt mir nicht aus dem Sinn°.   **das ... = das kann ich nicht vergessen**

Die Luft ist kühl und es dunkelt°,   **es dunkelt = es wird dunkel**
und ruhig° fließt der Rhein;   peacefully
der Gipfel° des Berges funkelt°   mountain top / glistens
im Abendsonnenschein.

Die schönste Jungfrau° sitzet°   most beautiful maiden / **sitzet = sitzt**
dort oben° wunderbar,   high above
ihr goldenes Geschmeide° blitzet°,   jewelry / glistens
sie kämmt° ihr goldenes Haar.   combs

Sie kämmt es mit goldenem Kamme°,   comb
und singt ein Lied dabei°;   while doing so
das hat eine wundersame°,   = **wunderbare**
gewaltige° Melodei.   powerful   *Melodie*

Den Schiffer° im kleinen Schiffe°   sailor / boat
ergreift es° mit wildem Weh°;   is gripped / longing
er schaut° nicht die Felsenriffe°,   = **sieht** / submerged rock
er schaut nur hinauf in die Höh°.   up to the heights

Ich glaube, die Wellen° verschlingen°   waves / swallow
am Ende Schiffer und Kahn°;   boat
und das hat mit ihrem Singen
die Loreley getan.

Heinrich Heine (1797–1856)

Heinrich Heine

Subordinate clauses and subordinating conjunctions

Subordinating conjunctions, like coordinating conjunctions, join two clauses together. The clause beginning with a subordinating conjunction, however, is *subordinate to*, or *dependent on*, the main clause. A subordinate clause is *not* an independent sentence.

main clause   *subordinate clause*
    I know   *that they still remember me.*

In the example above, the subordinate clause "that they still remember me" is not a complete sentence. In this chapter you will learn the following subordinating conjunctions:

bis	*until*
da	*since* (causal, not temporal)
dass	*that*
ob	*whether, if* (when it means *whether*)
weil	*because*
wenn	*if*

...für meine Familie tu' ich alles.
Aber was passiert, wenn mir was passiert?

■ Verb-last word order in the subordinate clause

Unlike coordinating conjunctions, which do not affect word order, subordinating conjunctions *move the inflected verb to the end of the subordinate clause.*

Wir essen um halb sieben.

Ich glaube, **dass** wir ▬ um halb sieben essen.
I think that we're eating at 6:30.

Brauchen wir noch etwas?

Weißt du, **ob** ▬ wir noch etwas brauchen?
Do you know whether we need anything else?

Ich habe gerade gegessen.

Ich habe keinen Hunger, **weil** ich ▬ gerade gegessen habe.
I'm not hungry because I've just eaten.

Ich habe Zeit.

Ich helfe dir, **wenn** ich ▬ Zeit habe.
I'll help you if I have time.

WENN ALLES EGAL IST...

Lab Manual Kap. 8,
Üb. 1, 2; Var. zur Üb. 3.

Workbook Kap. 8, A–D.

■ **1** ■ **Übung: Ich weiß, dass ...**   Sie planen miteinander ein Abendessen. Ihre Professorin sagt Ihnen etwas. Sagen Sie, dass Sie das wissen.

> **BEISPIEL:** Die Wurst ist teuer.
> Ich weiß, dass sie teuer ist.

1. Wir essen um sieben.   *Ich weiß, dass wir um sieben essen.*
2. Wir brauchen Rotwein.
3. Der Käse schmeckt gut.
4. Die Kinder wollen essen.
5. Tante Marie kommt zum Abendessen.
6. Wir haben keinen Salat.
7. Wir brauchen etwas zum Nachtisch.   *dessert*
8. Tante Marie trinkt keinen Kaffee.

if/whether

■ **2** ■ **Übung: Ich weiß nicht, ob ...**   Ihr Professor ist neu in dieser Stadt. Er hat viele Fragen, aber Sie wohnen auch nicht lange hier und können ihm keine Antworten geben.

> **BEISPIEL:** Ist dieses Restaurant teuer?
> Ich weiß nicht, ob es teuer ist.

1. Gibt es hier einen Automechaniker?
2. Ist dieses Hotel gut?
3. Ist die Uni weit von hier?   *far*
4. Gibt es eine Buchhandlung in der Nähe?
5. Kann man den Dom besuchen?
6. Kann man hier einen Stadtplan kaufen?

■ **3** ■ **Partnerarbeit: Warum lernst du Deutsch?**   Ask each other why you do the things listed below. Give your reason, then ask the next question.

> **BEISPIEL:** Warum lernst du Deutsch?
> Ich lerne Deutsch, *weil* es interessant ist. Warum ... ?

- Reiseführer (m)

Deutsch lernen	einen Rucksack tragen
zur Buchhandlung gehen	bis 9.00 schlafen
trampen	draußen sitzen
jetzt essen	keine Leberwurst essen
viel Kaffee trinken	früh aufstehen

nächstes Sommer ich in Deutschland wohnen gehe

das gefällt mir nicht.

Das Leben in der Stadt   ■   **195**

■ Conditional sentences: If *x* is true, then *y* is true

A clause introduced by **wenn** is called a *conditional clause* because it states a condition. The main clause is then called the *result clause* because it states the expected result of the condition. The result clause may begin with an optional **dann** which does not affect word order.

> Wenn ich Zeit habe, helfe ich dir.
> Wenn ich Zeit habe, **dann** helfe ich dir.

■ 4 ■ Übung: Wenn ... , dann ...

A. Complete these sentences by supplying a result clause:

1. Wenn wir Hunger haben, dann ...
2. Wenn du griechisch essen willst, dann ...
3. Wenn du mich morgen einlädst, dann ...
   invite

B. Now supply the conditional clause:

1. Wenn ... , dann können wir einen Stadtbummel machen.
2. Wenn ... , dann kannst du einen Nachtisch bestellen. *order*
3. Wenn ... , dann müssen wir noch schnell einkaufen.

der Abendessen zu Ende ist,

■ Question words as subordinating conjunctions

The question words (**wann**, **warum**, **was**, **wer**, etc.) act as subordinating conjunctions when they introduce an indirect question (i.e., a question restated as a subordinate clause).

question: Was **brauchen** wir zum Abendessen?

indirect question: Weißt du, was ▬▬ wir zum Abendessen **brauchen**?
Do you know what we need for supper?

question: Wer **ist** das?

indirect question: Ich kann Ihnen nicht sagen, wer ▬ das **ist**.
I can't tell you who that is.

■ 5 ■   Übung: Die Tramper *(hitchhikers)*   Ein Freund von Ihnen will mit anderen Studenten eine Reise per Autostopp machen. Ihr Professor hat Fragen über ihre Reise, aber Sie wissen die Antworten nicht.

Lab Manual Kap. 8,
Var. zur Üb. 5.

> **BEISPIEL:** Wer plant die Reise?
>   Ich weiß nicht, wer die Reise plant.

1. Wohin fahren die Tramper?
2. Wo wollen sie übernachten?
3. Warum trampen Ihre Freunde?
4. Wen wollen sie besuchen?   *visit*   *(whom)*
5. Wann kommen die Tramper zurück?
6. Was packen sie in den Rucksack?
7. Welche Städte besuchen sie?

■ Verbs with separable prefixes in subordinate clauses

You know that when a verb with a separable prefix is used in a main clause, the prefix is separated from the verb and placed at the end of the clause.

> Dort **kaufe** ich immer **ein**.   *shop*

In a subordinate clause, the verb moves to the end of the clause and the prefix is attached to it.

> Weißt du, warum ich ▬▬▬ immer dort ein**kaufe**?

■ 6 ■   Partnerarbeit: Wie lange müssen wir warten?   Sie warten zusammen vor der Mensa. Sagen Sie einander (*each other*), bis wann Sie warten müssen. (*Use the cues below.*)

> **BEISPIEL:** Wie lange müssen wir noch warten?
>   (der Bus / ankommen)
>   Wir müssen warten, bis der Bus ankommt.

1. der Regen / aufhören
2. Max / uns abholen   *pick up*
3. unsere Freunde / ankommen
4. die Vorlesung / anfangen   *lecture*
5. die Buchhandlung / aufmachen

■ **7** ■ **Übung: Was hat sie gefragt?** Die Professorin spricht zu leise (*quietly*).
Student A hört sie nicht richtig und fragt Studentin B, was sie gesagt hat. Studentin B
antwortet.

BEISPIELE: Wann stehen Sie auf?
    A: Was hat sie gefragt?
    B: Sie hat gefragt, wann du aufstehst.

    Kommt Bernd vorbei?
    A: Was hat sie gefragt?
    B: Sie hat gefragt, ob Bernd vorbeikommt.

1. Wann fängt das Semester an? *begin*
2. Kommt Ingrid vorbei?
3. Warum geht Regine weg?
4. Bringt Maria die Kinder mit?
5. Hört die Musik bald auf? *stop* *ob*
6. Mit wem geht Hans spazieren?
7. Wo steigt man in die Straßenbahn ein?
8. Wo steigen wir aus?
9. Wer macht das Fenster zu?

■ **Order of clauses in the sentence**

Subordinate clauses may either follow or precede the main clause.

    1   *2*
Ich spreche langsam, da ich nicht viel Deutsch gelernt habe.

              1   *2*
Da ich nicht viel Deutsch gelernt habe, spreche ich langsam.

When the subordinate clause comes first, the *entire* subordinate clause is considered
the first element in the sentence. The verb of the main clause therefore follows it
immediately in second position. The two inflected verbs are directly adjacent to each
other, separated by a comma.

    subordinate clause   main clause
    Wenn ich Zeit **habe**, **gehe** ich ins Museum.
    Ob er sympathisch **ist**, **weiß** ich nicht.

■ **8** ■ **Übung** Ihr Professor hat Fragen, aber Sie wissen die Antworten nicht.

BEISPIEL: Wie ist das Wetter?
    Wie das Wetter ist, weiß ich nicht.

1. Wer ist das?
2. Wem gehört das? *belong*
3. Wohin fährt er?
4. Was kostet das?
5. Wie heißt sie?
6. Warum ist er müde?
7. Wessen Koffer ist das?
whom 8. Wen kennt sie?

„Wie ich wirklich bin, weiß niemand!"

■ 9 ■ **Übung: Ich mache heute keinen Stadtbummel.** You've decided not to take a stroll through town today. Use the cues below to explain why.

BEISPIEL: Es regnet noch.
Da es noch regnet, mache ich keinen Stadtbummel.

1. Ich habe keine Zeit.
2. Das Wetter ist schlecht.
3. Ich brauche nichts in der Stadt.
4. Ich gehe nicht gern allein.
5. Ich bin heute spät aufgestanden.
6. Ich habe zu viel Arbeit.

Infinitive constructions with zu

When used in a sentence, the German infinitive is frequently preceded by **zu**. For the most part, this construction parallels the use of the English infinitive with *to*:

Was gibt's hier **zu sehen**?   *What's there to see here?*
Hast du Zeit diesen Brief **zu lesen**?   *Do you have time to read this letter?*

Note especially the second sentence above. In German, the infinitive with **zu** comes at the end of its phrase. In English, the infinitive with *to* comes at the beginning of its phrase.

 When a separable-prefix verb is used, the **zu** is inserted between the prefix and the stem infinitive.

ab**zu**fahren   spazieren **zu** gehen

Ich hoffe bald **abzufahren**.   *I hope to leave soon.*
Hast du Lust mit mir   *Would you like to go for a walk with me?*
    spazieren zu gehen?

Here are some cases in which the infinitive with **zu** is used:

- as a complement of verbs like **beginnen, anfangen, aufhören, helfen, hoffen, lernen, planen, scheinen,** and **vergessen.**

  Ich fange an **einen Brief zu**   *I'm starting to write a letter.*
      schreiben.
  Sie hofft **Geschichte zu**   *She's hoping to study history.*
      studieren.
  Ich habe vergessen **dir von**   *I forgot to tell you about my trip.*
      meiner Reise zu erzählen.

- as a complement of constructions like **Lust haben, Zeit haben,** and **Spaß**   *have fun*
  machen.

  Hast du Lust **einen**   *Do you want to take a walk*
      Stadtbummel zu machen?   *through town?*
  Ich habe keine Zeit   *I have no time to go shopping.*
      einkaufen zu gehen.

- as a complement of many adjectives such as **dumm, einfach, schön,** and **wichtig.**

  Es ist sehr wichtig **das zu**   *It's very important to*
      verstehen.   *understand that.*
  Es ist schön **dich**   *It's nice to see you again.*
      wiederzusehen.

Lab Manual Kap. 8,
Var. zur Üb. 10.

Workbook Kap. 8, E, F.

■ 10 ■ Übung: Es macht mir Spaß ... _fun_ Ihr Professor fragt, ob Sie etwas gerne machen. Antworten Sie ja oder nein.

> BEISPIEL: Gehen Sie gern ins Museum?
> Ja, es macht mir Spaß ins Museum zu gehen. (_oder_)
> Nein, es macht mir keinen Spaß ins Museum zu gehen.

1. Trampen Sie gern?
2. Reisen Sie gern mit der Bahn?
3. Essen Sie gern im Restaurant?
4. Quatschen Sie gern am Telefon? _chat_
5. Spielen Sie gern Tennis?
6. Leben Sie gern in der Stadt?

■ 11 ■ Kettenreaktion: Was hast du vergessen? Sie haben alle vergessen etwas zu tun. Sagen Sie, was Sie vergessen haben, dann fragen Sie den nächsten Studenten.

> BEISPIEL: A: Ich habe vergessen meine Hausaufgaben zu schreiben.
> Was hast du vergessen?
> B: Ich habe vergessen ...

Diese Liste gibt Ihnen einige Möglichkeiten (_possibilities_):

to invite my friends _einzuladen_	to shop _einzukaufen_
to order tickets _die Karten zu bestellen_	to buy potatoes _Kartoffeln zu kaufen_
to order dessert _den Nachtisch zu bestellen_	to show you my photographs _dir meine Photos zu zeigen_

kaufen = by
einkaufen = shop (for)

■ **Infinitives with _um ... zu_ and _ohne ... zu_**

um ... zu = _in order to_

> Ich muss in die Stadt, **um Lebensmittel einzukaufen.**
> _I have to go to town (in order) to buy groceries._
>
> Ich fahre nach Deutschland, **um Deutsch zu lernen.**
> _I'm going to Germany in order to learn German._

ohne ... zu = _without . . . -ing_

> Sie ist abgefahren, **ohne mich zu besuchen.**
> _She left without visiting me._
>
> Ich habe das Buch gelesen, **ohne es zu verstehen.**
> _I read the book without understanding it._

■ 12 ■ Übung Restate each sentence, changing the **weil**-clause _because_ to an **um ... zu** phrase and eliminating the modal verb and its subject.

> BEISPIEL: Ich gehe in die Stadt, weil ich einkaufen will.
> Ich gehe in die Stadt _um einzukaufen._

1. Ich gehe ins Lokal, weil ich etwas essen will.
2. Sie sitzt am Fenster, weil sie die Straße sehen möchte.
3. Oft trampen Studenten, weil sie Geld sparen wollen.
4. Manchmal fährt man ins Ausland, weil man mehr lernen möchte.

■ 13 ■   Übung   Sagen Sie, warum Sie etwas machen.

die Vorlesung= lecture

BEISPIEL: Warum gehen Sie zum Supermarkt?
Um Brot zu kaufen.

1. Warum gehen Sie zur Uni?
2. Warum gehen Sie nach Hause?
3. Warum arbeiten Sie diesen Sommer?
4. Warum sparen Sie Geld?
5. Warum rufen Sie Ihre Eltern an?
6. Warum gehen Sie ins Museum?

■ 14 ■   Übung   Combine these sentences, changing the second one to an **ohne ... zu** phrase.

BEISPIEL: Er hat den Koffer genommen. Er hat mich nicht gefragt.   *(nehmen)*
Er hat den Koffer genommen, ohne mich zu fragen.

1. Sie sind abgefahren. Sie haben nicht Auf Wiedersehen gesagt.
2. Ich arbeite in einem Geschäft. Ich kenne den Chef nicht.
3. Karin hat ein Zimmer gefunden. Sie hat nicht lange gesucht.
4. Geh nicht spazieren. Du trägst keinen Mantel.
5. Geh nicht weg. Du hast kein Frühstück gegessen.
6. Sie können nicht ins Konzert. Sie haben keine Karten gekauft.

Genitive case

The genitive case is the fourth and last case to be learned. It expresses possession (***John's*** *books*) or a relationship between two nouns marked in English by the preposition *of* (*the color **of your eyes***). Here are some examples of genitive phrases:

der Wagen **meiner Mutter**	***my mother's*** *car*	
die Freunde **der Kinder**	***the children's*** *friends*	
das Haus **meines Bruders**	***my brother's*** *house*	
das Ende **des Tages**	*the end **of the day***	
Egons Freundin	***Egon's*** *girlfriend*	

pl.
N die
G der
D den
A die

Review **der**- and **ein**-words on p. 167.

■ **Forms of the genitive case**

The **der**-words and the **ein**-words all share the same set of genitive endings. Nominative, accusative, and dative—the cases you have already learned—are included in the following table for comparison and review.

Genitive Case			
	masc.	**neut.**	**fem.**	**plural**
nom.	der Mann	das Kind	die Frau	die Leute
acc.	den Mann			
dat.	dem Mann	dem Kind	der Frau	den Leuten
gen.	-es -(e)s	-es -(e)s	-er	-er
	des Mannes	**des** Kindes	**der** Frau	**der** Leute
	eines Mannes	**eines** Kindes	**einer** Frau	**keiner** Leute
	meines Mannes	**eures** Kindes	**Ihrer** Frau	**unserer** Leute
	dieses Mannes	**jedes** Kindes	**welcher** Frau	**dieser** Leute

In addition to the genitive ending of the **der**- or **ein**-word, in the masculine and neuter singular *the noun itself adds the ending* **-s** (**des** Bahnhof**s**). Monosyllabic nouns such as **Mann** and **Kind** usually take the ending **-es** (**des** Mann**es**).

Review N-nouns on p. 152.

The masculine N-nouns, however, do *not* add an **-s** to the noun, but rather the same **-en** or **-n** ending as in the accusative and dative.

Kennen Sie die Freundin **meines Studenten**?	*Do you know my student's friend?*
Kennen Sie die Frau **dieses Herrn**?	*Do you know this gentleman's wife?*

■ **Use of the genitive case**

In German, the genitive generally *follows* the noun it modifies, but in English, the possessive precedes the noun: **das Haus meines Bruders** (*my brother's house*). Proper names and kinship titles used as names, however, usually *precede* the nouns they modify, as in English: **Egons Freundin** (*Egon's girlfriend*), **Muttis Wagen** (*Mom's car*). Proper names simply add **-s** without an apostrophe in the genitive.

German uses the genitive case for both persons and things, whereas English usually reserves the possessive ending *'s* for people and animals and uses *of* for things.

das Haus **meiner Großmutter**	*my grandmother's house*
die Häuser **der Stadt**	*the houses of the city*

260.000 Langzeitarbeitslose eingestellt.

Nicht das Ende aller Probleme.

Aber ein wichtiger Schritt.

important   Step

Lab Manual Kap. 8, Üb. 15; Var. zur Üb. 16.

■ 15 ■ Übung Change these noun phrases from nominative to genitive.

> **BEISPIEL:** der Zug
> des Zuges

1. ein Arzt _es_	7. jede Uni _f._
2. mein Freund	8. deine Mutter
3. unser Vater	9. der Student _en_ — weak masc nouns Herr Junge President
4. die Lehrerin	10. dieser Herr _-n_
5. das Kind	11. das Essen
6. die Leute	12. diese Zimmer _n.pl._

Workbook Kap. 8, G.

> **Note on Usage:** *von* + dative
>
> German uses **von** + *dative* where English uses **of** + *possessive*:
>
> | | |
> |---|---|
> | *a friend of my brother's* | **ein Freund von meinem Bruder** |
> | *a cousin of mine* | **eine Kusine von mir** |
> | *Is Max a friend of yours?* | **Ist Max ein Freund von dir?** |

■ 16 ■ Übung: Wie sagt man das auf Deutsch?

> **BEISPIEL:** *your girlfriend's sister*
> die Schwester deiner Freundin

1. the walls of my room _Wände Zimmers_	10. the rooms of the house _die Zimmer des Hauses_
2. the end of the week _das Ende der Woche_	11. Maria's students _Marias Studenten_
3. Karl's major _Karls Hauptfach_	12. the cities of Europe _die (Städte Europas)_
4. the children's pictures _die Bilder der Kinder_	13. the windows of this room _die Fenster dieses Zimmers_
5. the history of the war _des Krieges_	14. your mother's car _das Auto deiner Mutter_
6. his brother's house _seines Bruders_	15. the history of these countries _die Geschichte diesen Länder_
7. her sister's boyfriend	16. Grandpa's clock _die Uhr des Grandpas_ (Opas Uhr)
8. the cities of Switzerland	17. a friend of yours _ein Freund von mir_
9. a student's letter _eines Studenten_	18. a student of mine _ein Student " "_

■ Prepositions with the genitive

You've already memorized the accusative, dative, and two-way prepositions on pp. 91, 121, and 148. Remember that no prepositions take the nominative case.

There is a small group of prepositions that take the genitive case.

statt or **anstatt**	*instead of*	Schreib eine Karte **statt eines Briefes**.
trotz	*in spite of, despite*	**Trotz des Wetters** sind wir ans Meer gefahren.
während	*during*	**Während der Woche** fährt er oft in die Stadt.
wegen	*because of, on account of*	**Wegen meiner Arbeit** kann ich nicht mitkommen.

Note: **Statt** and **anstatt** are interchangeable and equally correct.

■ 17 ■ Übung Form prepositional phrases with the elements provided and give English equivalents. Then complete the sentences in your own words.

> **BEISPIEL:** während / Sommer
> während des Sommers (*during the summer*)
> Während des Sommers habe ich gearbeitet.

Workbook Kap. 8, H.

1. trotz / Wetter
2. während / Ferien
3. statt / Stadtplan *s*
4. wegen / mein / Mutter
   because
5. wegen / mein / Studium   *because of* (*h*)
6. trotz / Arbeit
7. während / Tag
8. anstatt / Hotel (*h*)
   instead

■ 18 ■ Übung: Warum tun Sie das? Ihre Professorin möchte wissen, warum Sie etwas tun. Sagen Sie es ihr. Die Liste von Gründen (*reasons*) hilft Ihnen.

> **BEISPIEL:** Warum arbeiten Sie so viel?
> *because* (Wegen) meines Studiums.

das Studium   *die* Eltern   *das* Wetter
die Klausur (*test*) *der* Schnee   *das* Klima
die Arbeit   *der* Regen   *der* Stress (*es*)

1. Warum bleiben Sie heute zu Hause?
2. Warum wollen Sie im Süden wohnen?
3. Warum dürfen Sie heute Abend nicht mitkommen?
4. Warum brauchen Sie Ferien?
5. Warum brauchen Sie manchmal Aspirin?
6. Warum wollen Sie heute draußen sitzen?

Nouns of measure, weight, and number

```
      15-08-90 #0000

GAST/TISCH # 161
2 PAELLA VAL.  *40.00
1 SCHNITZEL PA *14.00
1 KINDERTELLER  *9.00
1 FL WASSER     *3.50
1 FL LIMO       *3.50
1 MÄRZEN 0.5    *2.80
1 WEIZEN        *3.50
1 MÄRZEN 0.3    *1.80
BROT            *2.00
BAR          *80.10
ENTH.MWST14%    *9.59

BESTEN DANK
COSTA DEL SOL
```

German noun phrases indicating measure and weight do not use a preposition. Equivalent English phrases use *of*.

ein Glas Bier	*a glass **of** beer*
eine Flasche Wein	*a bottle **of** wine*
eine Tasse Kaffee	*a cup **of** coffee*
ein Kilo Kartoffeln	*a kilo **of** potatoes*
ein Liter Milch	*a liter **of** milk*
ein Stück Brot	*a piece **of** bread*
eine Portion Pommes frites	*an order **of** French fries*

Masculine and neuter nouns of measure *remain in the singular*, even following numerals greater than one.

drei **Glas** Bier	*three glass**es** of beer*
zwei **Kilo** Kartoffeln	*two kilo**s** of potatoes*
vier **Stück** Brot	*four piece**s** of bread*

Feminine nouns of measure, however, *do use their plural forms.*

zwei Tass**en** Kaffee	*two cups of coffee*
drei Flasch**en** Wein	*three bottles of wine*
drei Portion**en** Pommes frites	*three orders of French fries*

*Pommes ¢/used
w/out frites!*

Ordering in a restaurant is a communicative goal.

■ 19 ■ **Übung: Im Lokal** Sie reisen mit einer Studentengruppe durch Deutschland und essen in einem Lokal. Die anderen in der Gruppe können kein Deutsch. Sie müssen der Kellnerin sagen, was sie bestellen wollen.

BEISPIEL: *I'd like a cup of coffee.*
Bringen Sie uns bitte eine Tasse Kaffee.   *zwei*

1. ... a glass of wine and two cups of coffee.
2. ... three glasses of water and two glasses of beer.
3. ... a bottle of wine and two orders of French fries.
4. ... three glasses of beer, two glasses of wine, and a cup of coffee.

Equivalents for English *to*

The all-purpose English preposition indicating destination is *to:* We're going *to Germany*, *to the ocean*, *to the train station*, *to the movies*, *to Grandma's*. German has several equivalents for English *to*, depending on the destination:

Workbook Kap. 8, I.

- Use **nach** with cities, states, and most countries.

  Wir fahren **nach Wien.**
  　　　　　nach Kalifornien.
  　　　　　nach Deutschland.
  　　　　　nach Europa.

  and in the idiom: **nach Hause.**

Remember also that **an** + *acc.* signals motion toward a border, edge, or vertical surface: **Ich gehe ans Fenster/an die Tafel/an die Tür. Wir fahren ans Meer/an den See.** (Review p. 150.)

- Use **zu** with people and some locations.

  Ich gehe **zu meinen Freunden.**   *zu meine Familie*
  　　　　zu meiner Großmutter.
  　　　　zum Arzt.   *-ung = fem.*
  　　　　zum Bahnhof.
  　　　　zur Buchhandlung.   *oder in die Buchhandlung*
  　　　　zur Post (*to the post office*).

- Use **in** with countries whose names are feminine or plural, and with some locations.

  Ich fahre **in die Schweiz.**
  　　　　in die Bundesrepublik.
  　　　　in die USA.

  Wir gehen **ins Kino.**
  　　　　ins Bett.   *oder zu Bett = to go to bed*
  　　　　ins Konzert.
  　　　　ins Museum.
  　　　　ins Restaurant/ins Lokal.
  　　　　ins Theater.
  　　　　in die Stadt (*downtown*).
  　　　　in die Kirche (*to church*).
  　　　　in die Mensa.

Here is a rough rule-of-thumb for deciding whether to use **zu** or **in** with a destination within a city: **in** is usually used with destinations where one will spend a relatively long time (**ins Kino, in die Kirche, ins Bett**); **zu** is usually used with destinations involving a briefer visit (**zum Bahnhof, zur Post**).

■20■   **Übung: Wohin gehen Sie?**   Antworten Sie auf Deutsch.

> BEISPIEL: Wohin gehen Sie, wenn Sie einkaufen wollen?
> Ich gehe in die Stadt.

1. Wohin gehen Sie, wenn Sie krank sind?
2. Wohin gehen Sie, wenn Sie mit der Bahn reisen?
3. Wohin gehen Sie, wenn Sie müde sind?
4. Wohin gehen Sie, wenn Sie Musik hören wollen?
5. Wohin gehen Sie, wenn Sie ein Buch kaufen wollen?
6. Wohin gehen Sie, wenn Sie Ihre Familie besuchen wollen?
7. Wohin gehen Sie, wenn Sie Hunger haben?
8. Wohin gehen Sie, wenn Sie einen Film sehen wollen?
9. Wohin gehen Sie, wenn Sie einen Brief schicken wollen?   *send*
10. Wohin gehen Sie, wenn Sie Kunst sehen wollen?

Lesestück

Vor dem Lesen

Tipps zum Lesen und Lernen

■ Tipp zum Vokabelnlernen

The topic of this chapter is **die Stadt**. Compound nouns with **Stadt** define various kinds of cities. You have already encountered, for example, **Altstadt**, the "old city" or medieval core of modern German cities. In the following reading, other kinds of cities are mentioned: **Großstadt**, **Kleinstadt**, and **Hafenstadt** (*port city*).

■■■   **Übung**   Try to describe in German the following kinds of cities:

> BEISPIEL: Industriestadt
> Eine Stadt mit viel Industrie. (*oder*)
> Eine Stadt, wo es viel Industrie gibt.

Touristenstadt
Universitätsstadt
Kulturstadt
Weltstadt
Ferienstadt

Lab Manual Kap. 8, Üb. zur Betonung.

■ Leicht zu merken

der **Aspekt, -e**	Aspekt
elegant	elegant
die **Generation, -en**	Generation
historisch	
katastrophal	katastrophal
die **Restauration, -en**	Restauration
der/die **Sozialarbeiter/in**	Sozialarbeiter
die **Tour, -en**	

■ Einstieg in den Text

The following reading is called **Aspekte der Großstadt**. In it, an American exchange student, a German social worker, and a German stone cutter talk about their lives in Hamburg, Munich, and Dresden. Before reading it, think about your own experiences in or impressions of cities. Write a few sentences in German about what you find good or bad about big cities.

Das Stadtleben

Das gefällt mir:

Kultur (Musik, Kunst)
Essen

Das gefällt mir nicht: _Luft_
Trafik, die (Verschmutzing

Wortschatz 2

Verben

ärgern to annoy, offend
bauen to build
Rad fahren (fährt Rad), ist Rad gefahren to bicycle
Ski fahren (fährt Ski), ist Ski gefahren (*pronounced „Schifahren"*) to ski
steigen, ist gestiegen to climb
zerstören to destroy

Substantive

der **Alltag** everyday life
der **Eindruck, ⸚e** impression
der **Fußgänger, -** pedestrian
der **Hafen, ⸚** port, harbor
der **Preis, -e** price

das **Jahrhundert, -e** century
(das) **München** Munich
das **Rad, ⸚er** wheel; bicycle
   das **Fahrrad, ⸚er** bicycle
(das) **Russland** Russia

die **Ecke, -n** corner
   an der Ecke at the corner
   um die Ecke around the corner
die **Fußgängerzone, -n** pedestrian zone closed to vehicles
die **Großstadt, ⸚e** large city (*over 500,000 inhabitants*)
die **Kleinstadt, ⸚e** town (*5,000 to 20,000 inhabitants*)
die **Luft** air
   die **Luftverschmutzung** air pollution

Adverbien

geradeaus straight ahead
links to *or* on the left
rechts to *or* on the right
trotzdem in spite of that, nevertheless

Andere Vokabeln

gar kein ... no ... at all, not a ... at all

obwohl (*sub. conj.*) although
viele (*pl. pronoun*) many people

Nützliche Ausdrücke

auf dem Land in the country (i.e., rural area)
aufs Land to the country
im Gegenteil on the contrary

Mit anderen Worten

riesengroß = sehr sehr groß

Links, **rechts**, and **geradeaus** are adverbs, *not* adjectives.

Aspekte der Großstadt

Learning about life in German cities is the cultural goal of this chapter.

Lab Manual Kap. 8, Lesestück.

Die meisten° Deutschen leben in Städten mit über 80 000 Einwohnern. Welche Vorteile und Nachteile° gibt es, wenn man in einer Großstadt wohnt?

Eindrücke eines Amerikaners

Mark Walker, Student: Dieses Jahr verbringe ich zwei Semester als Austauschstudent
5 an der Universität Hamburg.[1] Da ich aus einer Kleinstadt in Colorado komme, schien°
mir Hamburg zuerst riesengroß. Es war schwer zu verstehen, wie die Deutschen so
dicht zusammengedrängt° leben können.

most

advantages and disadvantages

der Teil = part

spend (time)

seemed

gigantic

dicht zusammengedrängt = crowded together

---

1. A deep-water port on the Elbe River, population 1.7 million.

Einkaufen auf dem Markt
(München)

Aber das heißt nicht, dass Hamburg mir nicht gefällt. Im Gegenteil! Ich finde es fantastisch, dass es in der Stadt so viel zu tun gibt. Wenn ich Lust habe, kann ich jeden
10 Tag ins Konzert, ins Kino oder ins Museum gehen. Hamburg ist die zweitgrößte° Stadt der Bundesrepublik. Weil es eine Hafenstadt ist, gibt es seit Jahrhunderten Verbindungen° mit dem Ausland.

    Wenn das Stadtleben mir zu viel wird, dann ist es sehr leicht mein Fahrrad zu nehmen, in die Bahn zu steigen und aufs Land zu fahren. In der Lüneburger Heide[1]
15 südlich von° Hamburg kann man schöne Radtouren machen. Dieser Kontrast zwischen Stadt und Land scheint mir typisch für Deutschland. Das Land ist den Einwohnern° der Städte sehr wichtig als Erholung° vom Stress des Alltags.

second largest

ties

south of

inhabitants / relaxation
important

„Ich wohne gern hier"

Beate Kreuz, Sozialarbeiterin in München[2]: Ich arbeite mit Jugendlichen°. Sie haben
20 oft keinen Schulabschluss° und können keine Arbeit finden. Ich sehe also jeden Tag die Probleme der Großstadt. Trotz dieser Probleme wohne ich sehr gerne hier. Obwohl die Wohnungsnot° schlimm ist, habe ich eine Wohnung in einem alten Gebäude finden können. Ich kann mit der S-Bahn° überall hinfahren° und brauche gar kein Auto. Im Sommer gehen wir in der Isar schwimmen oder im Englischen Garten[3] Rad
25 fahren und im Winter fahren wir in den Alpen Ski. In der Kaufinger Straße gibt es eine große Fußgängerzone, wo viele gern einen Schaufensterbummel machen. An jeder Ecke gibt es ein elegantes Geschäft, aber in meinem Beruf sehe ich so viel Arbeitslosigkeit°, dass mich der Konsumzwang° und die hohen° Preise ärgern. Trotzdem kann man auch ohne sehr viel Geld in der Tasche relativ gut leben.

mit Jugendlichen = mit jungen Leuten / diploma
Despite
housing shortage *bad*
Stadtbahn = commuter rail service / **überall hin-** = everywhere

unemployment / pressure to buy / high

---

1. **Die Lüneburger Heide** (*heath*) is an extensive nature preserve on the North German plain between Hamburg and Hannover.
2. **München**: capital city of Bavaria (**Bayern**), population 1.2 million.
3. **Die Isar**: a tributary of the Danube. **Englischer Garten**: large park in the center of Munich designed by the American-born Benjamin Thompson, Count Rumford (1753–1814).

30 **Aufbauarbeit° im Osten**

Carsten Oberosler, 52; Steinmetz° in Dresden: Seit Generationen wohnen meine Vorfahren° in Sachsen°, aber meine Eltern sind erst nach dem Krieg nach Dresden[1] gekommen. Wie mein Vater bin ich Steinmetz und habe auch jahrelang° an der Restauration meiner Heimatstadt° gearbeitet.

35   Dresden war immer ein kunsthistorisches Juwel° Deutschlands, aber die eine Bombennacht° im Februar 1945 hat die ganze Innenstadt° zerstört. Bis heute haben wir immer noch nicht alles wiederaufgebaut° und dazu° bedroht° die katastrophale <u>Luftverschmutzung</u> Menschen und Gebäude. Ich bin aber optimistisch, weil die Stadt seit der Vereinigung Deutschlands 1990 endlich mehr Geld für die <u>wichtige</u> Restaura-

40 tionsarbeit bekommt.

reconstruction work
stone cutter
Vorfahren = Eltern, Großeltern usw. / Saxony / for years / home town

jewel   pronunciation: **Ju-wél**
night of bombing / center of the city / reconstructed / in addition / threatens
air pollution
important

Nach dem Lesen

■ **A** ■   **Antworten Sie auf Deutsch.**

1. Woher kommt Mark Walker?
2. Wie <u>gefällt</u> ihm die Stadt Hamburg?   *pleases*
3. Was können die Menschen in der Stadt machen, wenn ihnen der Stress des Alltags zu viel wird?
4. Was ist Beate Kreuz von Beruf?
5. Warum braucht sie gar kein Auto?
6. Was macht sie in ihrer Freizeit im Sommer? im Winter?
7. Welche Probleme des Stadtlebens sieht sie in ihrer Arbeit?
8. Was ist Herr Oberosler von Beruf?
9. Warum ist seine Arbeit in einer Stadt wie Dresden besonders wichtig?

■ **B** ■   **Wie ist es bei Ihnen zu Hause?**   Sie haben über drei deutsche Städte gelesen. Jetzt beschreiben Sie einem deutschen Freund den Ort, wo Sie wohnen. Geben Sie z.B. Informationen über diese Themen:

> Größe (*size*)
> Lage und Umgebung (*location and surroundings*)
> Industrie
> Kultur (Museen, Konzerte, Kinos usw.)
> Geschäfte   *businesses*
> Hochschulen

BEISPIEL: Boston ist eine Großstadt mit vielen Unis und Colleges. Es ist eine Hafenstadt und ist historisch sehr interessant. ...

Lab Manual Kap. 8, Diktat.

Workbook Kap. 8, I–O.

Seals of the five new federal states created from the former German Democratic Republic; from left to right:
Mecklenburg-Vorpommern
Sachsen-Anhalt
Thüringen
Sachsen
Brandenburg

1. **Dresden** on the Elbe River is the capital of the federal state of Saxony (**Sachsen**). Under the 18th-century Saxon kings it reached its zenith as a center of art and culture. It is renowned for its beautiful public buildings and art treasures.

Situationen aus dem Alltag

■ **Unterwegs in der Stadt**

Gebäude und Orte (*Buildings and places*)

This vocabulary focuses on an everday topic or situation. Words you already know from **Wortschatz** sections are listed without English equivalents; new supplementary vocabulary is listed with definitions. Your instructor may assign some supplementary vocabulary for active mastery.

die **Apotheke, -n**	*pharmacy*
die **Brücke, -n**	*bridge*
das **Café, -s**	*café*
die **Haltestelle, -n**	*streetcar or bus stop*
das **Kaufhaus, ̈er**	*department store*
die **Kirche, -n**	*church*
die **Konditorei, -en**	*pastry café*
die **Post**	*post office*
das **Rathaus, ̈er**	*city hall*

Verkehrsmittel (*Means of transportation*)

der **Bus, -se**	*bus*
das **Taxi, -s**	*taxicab*
die **Straßenbahn**	*streetcar*
die **U-Bahn**	*subway*

U-Bahn: short for **Untergrundbahn**.

Fragen wir nach dem Weg. (*Let's ask for directions.*)

Entschuldigung, wie komme ich **zur Post?**

... **zum Bahnhof?**

Das ist gleich in der Nähe.

Das ist nicht weit von hier.

Gehen Sie über die Straße und dann **geradeaus.**

... **nach links.**

... **nach rechts.**

... **um die Ecke.**

Asking directions is a communicative goal.

■ **A** ■ **Partnerarbeit: Wie komme ich zu ... ?** Partner A ist fremd in dieser Stadt. Er oder sie benutzt den Stadtplan, um nach dem Weg zu fragen. Partner B ist hier zu Hause und sagt Partner A den Weg durch die Stadt. Dann tauschen Sie die Rollen (**tauschen** = *exchange*).

1. Sie stehen vor der Post und wollen zum Marktplatz.
2. Sie sind im Museum und müssen zum Hotel zurück, um zu Mittag zu essen.
3. Sie sind in der Fußgängerzone und haben Hunger. Sie brauchen Hilfe (*help*), um ein Restaurant zu finden.

Gruppendiskussion: Was machen wir denn morgen? Mit einer Studentengruppe machen Sie eine Reise durch Deutschland. Heute Abend sind Sie in einer Großstadt angekommen und übernachten im Hotel Sommerhof (siehe Stadtplan). Besprechen Sie, was Sie morgen machen wollen.

> Wohin wollen wir gehen?
> Was gibt es dort zu tun oder zu sehen?
> Wo wollen wir essen?
> Was machen wir denn am Abend?
> Wie kommen wir hin (*get there*)? Zu Fuß, mit einem Taxi oder mit der Straßenbahn?

■ **In der Konditorei**

Am Tisch

1. die **Serviette, -n**
2. die **Gabel, -n**
3. der **Teller, -**
4. das **Messer, -**

5. der **Löffel, -**
6. das **Glas, ¨er**
7. die **Speisekarte, -n**

Was gibt's zum Essen und zum Trinken?

Das wissen Sie schon:

das **Bier**	die **Kartoffel, -n**	die **Tasse**
das **Brot**	der **Käse**	das **Wasser**
das **Brötchen, -**	der **Nachtisch** *dessert*	der **Wein**
die **Flasche, -n**	die **Pommes frites**	die **Wurst**
der **Kaffee**	der **Salat**	

A **Konditorei** is a bakery-café serving pastries and sometimes light fare such as cold cuts and egg dishes.

Auf der Speisekarte der Konditorei finden Sie auch:

die **Butter**	*butter*
das **Ei, -er**	*egg*
das **Eis**	*ice cream*
das **Kännchen, -**	*small (coffee or tea) pot*
der **Kuchen, -**	*cake*
die **Milch**	*milk*
die **Portion, -en**	*serving of, order of*
der **Saft, ̈e**	*juice*
die **Sahne**	*cream*
der **Schinken**	*ham*
der **Tee**	*tea*

Kaffee Hag is decaffeinated coffee; **Glühwein** is hot mulled wine; **Zitrone natur** is fresh lemonade; **Konfitüre** = **Marmelade**.

❖ *Café-Konditorei Reidel*

Warme Getränke

Tasse Kaffee	2,30
Kännchen Kaffee . . .	4,60
Tasse Mocca	4,40
Kännchen Mocca . . .	5,40
Tasse Kaffee Hag. . . .	2,40
Kännchen Kaffee Hag . .	4,80
Tasse Kakao mit Sahne . .	2,40
Kännchen Kakao mit Sahne .	4,80
Glas Tee mit Milch oder Zitrone .	2,30
Glas Tee mit Rum . . .	4,50
Glas Pfefferminztee . . .	2,30
Glas Grog von Rum 4 cl . .	5,00
Glas Glühwein 0,21 . . .	4,50
Glas heiße Zitrone	2,60

Eis und Eisgetränke

Portion gemischtes Eis . .	3,20
Portion gemischtes Eis mit Sahne	3,90
Früchte-Eisbecher ‚Florida' . .	6,50
Eis-Schokolade	4,00

Kalte Getränke

Flasche Mineralwasser . . .	2,10
Flasche Coca Cola . . .	2,10
Flasche Orangeade . . .	2,10
Pokal Apfelsaft	2,40
Glas Orangensaft . . .	2,80
Glas Tomatensaft . . .	2,80
Glas Zitrone natur . . .	2,60

[handwritten: goblet]

Frühstück

Kleines Gedeck	6,00

  1 Kännchen Kaffee, Tee od. Schokolade, 2 Brötchen, Butter, Konfitüre

Großes Gedeck	7,90

  1 Kännchen Kaffee, Tee od. Schokolade, 2 Brötchen, Butter, Konfitüre, 1 gek. Ei, 1 Scheibe *[handwritten: slice]* Schinken od. Käse

Ergänzung zum Frühstück

[handwritten: supplement]

1 gekochtes Ei	1,00
1 Portion Konfitüre	0,80
1 Portion Butter	0,80
1 Scheibe Käse	1,60
1 Scheibe Schinken	1,80
1 Brötchen oder 1 Scheibe Brot	0,60

Talking about food and ordering in a restaurant are communicative goals.

■ C ■ **Gruppenarbeit: In der Konditorei (*3 oder 4 Personen*)** Sie sitzen zusammen in der Café-Konditorei Reidel und bestellen etwas zu essen und trinken. Jemand in der Gruppe spielt den Kellner oder die Kellnerin. Die anderen bestellen von der Speisekarte.

View Module 4 of the ***Neue Horizonte*** video (13:19) and do the activities in **Videoecke 4** in your Workbook/Laboratory Manual/Video Manual.

Mit dem Bus durch Berlin

Most German cities have superb public transportation systems that make it easy to get around. Berlin, for instance, has a comprehensive system of subways, buses, streetcars, and commuter trains. These pages from a brochure give information about touring the city with the double-decker buses of the **BVG** (Berlin's public transportation authority). The map of bus line 100 (**die Hunderter Linie**) through the heart of Berlin (**Berlin Mitte**) and the accompanying photos show points of interest along the route. These include the Brandenburg Gate (**das Brandenburger Tor**) and Museum Island (**die Museumsinsel**).

⑧ Brandenburger Tor

Wahrzeichen für die Stadt Berlin und seit dem Mauerfall auch Symbol für die Einheit Deutschlands. 1788-91 wurde das Brandenburger Tor von Langhans nach antikem Vorbild erbaut. 1793 wurde Schadows Quadriga mit der Siegesgöttin aufgestellt.

⑨ Staatsoper Unter den Linden

Die Lindenoper feierte 1992 ihr 250-jähriges Jubiläum. Mendelssohn-Bartholdy, Furtwängler und Richard Strauss feierten hier große künstlerische Triumphe. Der 1742 eingeweihte Knobelsdorf-Bau ist ein Zeugnis des norddeutschen Rokoko.

testimony ?

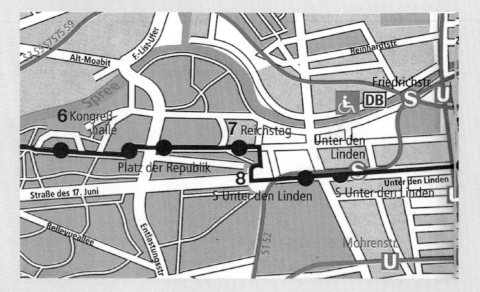

Berliner Dom

Im Stil der Neorenaissance wurde die Hof-
kirche der Hohenzollern in den Jahren 1893
bis 1905 erbaut. Im Krieg stark zerstört,
wurde der größte Kirchenbau Berlins 1993
nach 18jähriger Renovierung wiedereröff-
net. Hörenswert sind die Konzerte auf der
historischen Orgel des Doms.

TIP

Museumsinsel

Zwischen dem Alten Museum und dem
Bodemuseum erstreckt sich auf einer Insel
zwischen Spree und Kupfergraben einer
der weltweit bedeutendsten Museums-
komplexe. Unter anderem befindet sich
hier auch das Pergamonmuseum. Attrak-
tionen sind der beeindruckende Perga-
mon-Altar und das berühmte Markttor von
Milet. Nehmen Sie sich Zeit für einen
Spaziergang in einer Welt von Kunst und
Geschichte.

K A P I T E L   9

Unsere Umwelt

Communicative Goals

- Using adjectives to describe things
- Giving the date
- Discussing ecology and recycling
- Talking about sports

Cultural Goal

- Learning about German and global environmental issues

Chapter Outline

- **Lyrik zum Vorlesen**
  Jürgen Werner, „Die Lorelei 1973"

- **Grammatik**
  Attributive adjectives and adjective endings
  Word order of adverbs: Time/manner/place
  Ordinal numbers and dates

- **Lesestück**
  Unsere Umwelt in Gefahr

- **Situationen aus dem Alltag**
  Der Sport

- **Almanach**
  Seid ihr schlaue Umweltfüchse?

Lab Manual Kap. 9,
Dialoge, Fragen, Hören

Sie gut zu!

Haus also = *apartment house,
building*.

Discussing recycling is a
communicative goal.

Recycling in unserem Wohnhaus

Frau Berg trifft Herrn Reh auf der Treppe.

FR. BERG: Mensch, wohin mit dem riesengroßen Sack?

HR. REH: In den Keller. Die neuen Container sind da. Jetzt können wir Altglas und
Altpapier hier im Haus sammeln.

FR. BERG: Na, endlich! Jetzt brauche ich meinen Müll nicht mehr zum Recycling zu
schleppen.

HR. REH: Ja, das ist jetzt nicht mehr nötig. Wenn alle mitmachen, dann ist das ein
großer Fortschritt.

Ein umweltfreundliches Geburtstagsgeschenk

DANIEL: Was hat dir Marianne zum Geburtstag geschenkt?

FRANK: Ein neues Fahrrad, weil wir unseren Zweitwagen verkauft haben.

DANIEL: Wieso denn?

FRANK: Er war ja sowieso kaputt, und da wir in die Stadt umgezogen sind, kann ich
mit dem Rad zur Arbeit fahren.

DANIEL: Da sparst du aber viel Geld.

FRANK: Ja, und ich habe auch ein gutes Gefühl, weil ich etwas gegen die
Luftverschmutzung mache.

Treibst du Sport?

Talking about sports is a
communicative goal.

JUNGE: Sag mal, treibst du gern Sport?

MÄDCHEN: Klar. Ich verbringe das ganze Wochenende auf dem Tennisplatz. Spielst du
auch Tennis?

JUNGE: Ja, das ist mein Lieblingssport, aber ich bin kein guter Spieler.

MÄDCHEN: Da kann ich dir einen wunderbaren Tennislehrer empfehlen.

Notes on Usage: Adverb **da** and flavoring particle **aber**

***The adverb* da**   At the beginning of a clause, the adverb **da** often means *then, in
that case, under those circumstances, for that reason*:

> **Da** sparst du aber viel Geld.
> **Da** kann ich dir einen wunderbaren Tennislehrer empfehlen.

***The flavoring particle* aber**   As a flavoring particle, **aber** is often used to intensify a
statement. It adds the sense of *really, indeed*.

> Da sparst du **aber** viel Geld.   *Then you'll **really** save a lot of
>   money.*

The particle **aber** can add a note of surprise or admiration:

> Mensch, das ist **aber** teuer!   *Wow, that's **really** expensive!*

■ Wortschatz 1

Verben

empfehlen (empfiehlt), hat empfohlen to recommend
mit·machen to participate, cooperate
sammeln to collect
schleppen (*colloq.*) to drag, lug (along), haul
treffen (trifft), hat getroffen to meet
treiben, hat getrieben to drive, force, propel
  Sport treiben to play sports
um·ziehen, ist umgezogen to move, change residence

Substantive

der **Container, -** large trash container
der **Fortschritt, -e** progress
der **Geburtstag, -e** birthday
  zum Geburtstag for (your/her/my/etc.) birthday
der **Junge, -n, -n** boy
der **Keller, -** cellar, basement
der **Müll** trash, refuse
der **Sack, ¨e** sack

der **Sport** sport
der **Tennisplatz, ¨e** tennis court
der **Zweitwagen, -** second car

das **Gefühl, -e** feeling
das **Geschenk, -e** present
das **Mädchen, -** girl
das **Papier, -e** paper
das **Recycling** recycling; recycling center
das **Tennis** tennis
das **Wohnhaus, ¨er** apartment building

die **Treppe** staircase, stairs
  auf der Treppe on the stairs
die **Umwelt** environment
die **Verschmutzung** pollution

Adjektive und Adverbien

ganz whole, entire
  das ganze Wochenende all weekend, the whole weekend
kaputt (*colloq.*) broken, kaput; exhausted

The word **kaputt** comes from a French cardplaying term, *être capot: "to lose all the tricks, be wiped out."*

klar clear; (*colloq.*) sure, of course
nötig necessary
schmutzig dirty
sportlich athletic
umweltfreundlich environmentally safe, non-polluting
zweit- second

zweit- must have an adjective ending. See pp. 221–224 below. It can also be a prefix, as in **Zweitwagen.**

Aktion Saubere Landschaft e. V.
Oskar-Walzel-Straße 17, 5300 Bonn

Recycling in Our Apartment Building

Ms. Berg meets Mr. Reh on the stairs.

MS. B: Wow, where to with that huge sack?

MR. R: To the cellar. The new trash containers are here. Now we can collect (old) glass and waste paper here in the building.

MS. B: At last! Now I don't have to haul my trash to the recycling center anymore.

MR. R: Yes, that's not necessary anymore. If everyone participates, then that's great progress.

An Ecological Birthday Present

D: What did Marianne give you for your birthday?

F: A new bicycle, because we sold our second car.

D: How come?

F: It was kaput anyway, and since we've moved to the city, I can ride my bike to work.

D: Then you're saving a lot of money.

F: Yes, and it also feels good to be doing something about air pollution.

Do You Play Sports?

BOY: Hey, do you like to play sports?

GIRL: Sure. I spend all weekend on the tennis court. Do you play tennis too?

BOY: Yes, that's my favorite sport, but I'm not a good player.

GIRL: Then I can recommend a wonderful tennis instructor to you.

Andere Vokabeln

Lieblings- (*noun prefix*) favorite
   Lieblingssport favorite sport
was für ... ? what kind of . . . ?
wieso? How come? How's that?
   What do you mean?

Nützlicher Ausdruck

na endlich! at last! high time!

Gegensätze

nötig ≠ unnötig necessary ≠
   unnecessary
schmutzig ≠ sauber dirty ≠ clean

Mit anderen Worten

dreckig (*colloq.*) = **schmutzig**

Variationen

■ A ■   Persönliche Fragen

1. Ist man in Ihrem Studentenwohnheim umweltfreundlich? Was macht man da für die Umwelt?

   environment

2. Auch als Hobby kann man Dinge sammeln, z.B. Briefmarken (*stamps*), Münzen (*coins*) oder CDs. Sammeln Sie etwas? Was?
3. Frau Berg hat früher ihren Müll zum Recycling geschleppt. Was müssen Sie jeden Tag (z.B. in Ihrem Rucksack) mitschleppen?
4. Zum Geburtstag hat Frank ein neues Fahrrad bekommen. Was würden Sie gern zum Geburtstag bekommen?
5. Besitzt Ihre Familie einen Zweitwagen? Braucht sie wirklich zwei Wagen?

   own

6. Fährt jemand in Ihrer Familie mit dem Rad zur Arbeit? Wenn nicht, warum nicht?
7. Meinen Sie, dass die Luftverschmutzung hier ein Problem ist? Wie ist die Luft bei Ihnen zu Hause?
8. Treiben Sie Sport? Wie oft in der Woche?
9. Was ist Ihr Lieblingssport? Lieblingsfilm? Lieblingsbuch? Und Ihre Lieblingsstadt?

■ B ■   Warum ich Geld brauche.   Sagen Sie, warum Sie Geld brauchen.

BEISPIEL: Warum brauchen Sie Geld?
        Ich brauche Geld, *um* ein Rad *zu* kaufen.

das Hobby
die Hobbys

Ich habe am achten Dezember
Geburtstag

C **Welche Farbe hat das?** Sagen Sie, welche Farbe diese Dinge haben.

BEISPIEL: Welche Farbe hat Georgs Hemd?
Es ist rot.

Welche Farbe hat/haben ...

der Wald?	der Wein?
der Kaffee?	das Hemd dieses Jungen?
das Meer?	diese Landkarte?
die Wände dieses Zimmers?	die Bäume im Sommer? im Herbst?
die Bluse dieser Studentin?	Ihr Pulli?

Lyrik zum Vorlesen

Lab Manual Kap. 9, Lyrik zum Vorlesen.

Many words are not glossed here because they are the same as in Heine's poem. Some new active vocabulary comes from **Wortschatz 2** of this chapter.

Albtraum (*nightmare*) is an old word related to English *elf* and suggesting a terrifying vision. It has nothing to do with the mountains (**die Alpen**).

Um diese Parodie zu verstehen muss man „Die Loreley" von Heinrich Heine schon kennen. Lesen Sie noch einmal Heines Gedicht (*poem*) auf Seite 193 und dann diesen Text.

Die Lorelei 1973

Ich weiß nicht, was soll es bedeuten,
dass ich so traurig bin;
ein Albtraum° aus unseren Zeiten,   nightmare
er geht mir nicht aus dem Sinn.

Die Luft ist schwül° und verdunkelt,   close, heavy
und dreckig fließt der Rhein;   *dirty*
kein Gipfel des Berges funkelt,   *summit, glistens*
wo sollt' auch die Sonne sein?   *should the sun shine?*

Am Ufer° des Rheines sitzt sie,   bank
die deutsche Chemie-Industrie;
dort braut° sie gefährliche Gifte°,   brews / poisons *dangerous*
die Luft macht erstickend° sie.   suffocating

Sie kümmert sich nicht um° den Abfall°,   **kümmert ...** = doesn't care about / garbage
der° aus den Rohren° fließt;   / that / pipes
er kommt aus dem chemischen Saustall°,   pigsty
wo er in den Rhein sich ergießt°.   **sich ...** = pours

Dem Schiffer im Tankerschiffe,
ihm macht das Atmen Müh'°;   **ihm ...** = has trouble breathing
er schaut nicht die Felsenriffe,   *show*
er schaut nur die dreckige Brüh'°.   slop *dirty* (*broth*)

Ich weiß, die Wellen verschlingen
einst° nicht nur Schiffer und Kahn;   some day
und das hat mit ihren Giften
die Industrie getan.

Jürgen Werner (geboren 1939)

Grammatik

■ Predicate adjectives versus attributive adjectives

Adjectives in both English and German are used in one of two ways:

- They may follow "linking" verbs such as *to be, to become, to remain*, and *to seem* (**sein, werden, bleiben, scheinen**), in which case they are called *predicate adjectives* because they constitute the second part of the predicate. Most of the adjectives you have encountered in this book have been predicate adjectives.

Das Rad ist **neu**.	*The bicycle is **new**.*
Meine Großeltern werden **alt**.	*My grandparents are getting **old**.*
Der Kaffee ist **heiß**.	*The coffee is **hot**.*

Predicate adjectives in German have *no endings.*

- Adjectives may also occur *before* a noun. In this position they are called *attributive adjectives.*

das **neue** Rad	*the **new** bicycle*
meine **alten** Großeltern	*my **old** grandparents*
heißer Kaffee	***hot** coffee*

German attributive adjectives *always* have endings.

EIN NEUES DENKEN FÜR EINE NEUE ZEIT

■ The noun phrase

Attributive adjectives occur in noun phrases. A noun phrase consists of a noun and the words directly associated with it. English and German noun phrases have similar structures. They typically consist of three types of words: *limiting words, attributive adjectives*, and *nouns*.

Limiting words are the **der**-words and **ein**-words you already know:

der-*words*	ein-*words*	
der	ein	
dieser	kein	
jeder	mein	
welcher	dein	
alle	sein	*Possessive adjectives*
	ihr	
	unser	
	euer	
	ihr	

These words are called "limiting words" because they *limit* the noun in some way rather than describing it: *dieses* **Fahrrad** (***this*** bicycle, *not that one*), *meine* **Großeltern** (***my*** grandparents, *not yours*).

Here are some examples of noun phrases. Note that the noun phrase does not necessarily contain both a limiting word and an attributive adjective.

limiting word +	attributive adjective +	noun	
das	neue	Fahrrad	*the new bicycle*
jede		Woche	*every week*
alle	deutschen	Studenten	*all German students*
	heißer	Kaffee	*hot coffee*
meine	kleine	Schwester	*my little sister*

German adjective endings have acquired the reputation of being a formidable obstacle for the learner. However, the system is conceptually quite simple and just requires practice until it becomes automatic in spoken German. To be able to use attributive adjectives, you need to know only two sets of endings—called the *primary endings* and the *secondary endings*—and three rules for their use. Half of the system is already familiar to you: the primary endings are simply the endings of the **der**-words that show gender, number, and case.

Alle is usually plural and takes the primary plural endings. Adjectives that follow it take the secondary plural endings: **alle deutschen Studenten**. When **alle** is followed by a second limiting word, however, they both take the same primary ending: **alle meine Freunde**, **alle diese Leute**.

Primary Endings				
	masc.	neut.	fem.	plur.
nom.	-er	-es	-e	-e
acc.	-en	-es	-e	-e
dat.	-em	-em	-er	-en
gen.	-es	-es	-er	-er

There are only two secondary endings, **-e** and **-en**. They occur in the following pattern:

Secondary Endings				
	masc.	neut.	fem.	plur.
nom.	-e	-e	-e	-en
acc.	-en	-e	-e	-en
dat.	-en	-en	-en	-en
gen.	-en	-en	-en	-en

Note that the **-en** occurs *throughout the plural* as well as *throughout the dative and genitive cases.*

■ Rules for the use of adjective endings

1. Noun phrases with adjectives must have a primary ending, either on the limiting word, or on the adjective itself. When the limiting word takes a primary ending, the adjective that follows it takes a secondary ending.

limiting word with primary ending	+	attributive adjective with secondary ending	+ noun	
dies**es**		schön**e**	Bild	*this beautiful picture*
mit mein**er**		gut**en**	Freundin	*with my good friend*

2. If the noun phrase has no limiting word or has an **ein**-word without an ending, then the attributive adjective takes the primary ending.[1]

no limiting word or **ein**-word without ending	+	attributive adjective with primary ending	+ noun	
		alt**e**	Häuser	*old houses*
		heiß**er**	Kaffee	*hot coffee*
ein		alt**es**	Haus	*an old house*

The following examples contrast noun phrases with and without limiting words. Note how the primary ending shifts from the limiting word to the adjective when there is no limiting word:

dies**e** neu**en** Tennisplätze →   neu**e** Tennisplätze
mit mein**em** österreichisch**en** Geld →   mit österreichisch**em** Geld
welch**es** deutsch**e** Bier →   deutsch**es** Bier

3. Attributive adjectives in succession have the same ending.

ein groß**es** alt**es** Haus   *a large old house*
groß**e** alt**e** Häuser   *large old houses*
gut**er** deutsch**er** Wein   *good German wine*

Pay special attention to the three instances in which **ein**-words have no endings. They are the *only* instances in which **ein**-word endings differ from **der**-word endings.

masculine nominative	*neuter nominative and accusative*
ein alt**er** Mann	ein klein**es** Kind
but	*but*
d**er** alt**e** Mann	dies**es** klein**e** Kind

---

1. There is one exception to rule 2: In the masculine and neuter genitive singular, the attributive adjective not preceded by a limiting word takes the *secondary ending* **-en** rather than the primary ending.

    trotz tief**en** Schnee**s**   *in spite of deep snow*
    wegen schlecht**en** Wetter**s**   *because of bad weather*

Such phrases are quite rare. Moreover, note that the primary ending *is* present on the noun itself.

Adjectives whose basic forms end in unstressed **-er** (**teuer**) or **-el** (**dunkel**) drop the **-e-** when they take endings.

Die Theaterkarten waren **teuer**.	Das waren aber **teure** Karten!
Ist diese Farbe zu **dunkel**?	Ich mag **dunkle** Farben.

Let's summarize. The first table below shows the complete declension of an adjective following a **der**-word; the second, following an **ein**-word. The highlighted forms in the second table show the only instances in which the **ein**-word endings differ from the **der**-word endings. The third table shows adjective endings in noun phrases without a limiting word.

Adjective Endings Following a *der*-word			
masculine	**neuter**	**feminine**	**plural**
nom. dies**er** jung**e** Mann	dies**es** jung**e** Kind	dies**e** jung**e** Frau	dies**e** jung**en** Leute
acc. dies**en** jung**en** Mann	dies**es** jung**e** Kind	dies**e** jung**e** Frau	dies**e** jung**en** Leute
dat. dies**em** jung**en** Mann	dies**em** jung**en** Kind	dies**er** jung**en** Frau	dies**en** jung**en** Leute**n**
gen. dies**es** jung**en** Mann**es**	dies**es** jung**en** Kind**es**	dies**er** jung**en** Frau	dies**er** jung**en** Leute

Adjective Endings Following an *ein*-word			
masculine	**neuter**	**feminine**	**plural**
nom. ein jung**er** Mann	ein jung**es** Kind	ein**e** jung**e** Frau	mein**e** jung**en** Leute
acc. ein**en** jung**en** Mann	ein jung**es** Kind	ein**e** jung**e** Frau	mein**e** jung**en** Leute
dat. ein**em** jung**en** Mann	ein**em** jung**en** Kind	ein**er** jung**en** Frau	mein**en** jung**en** Leute**n**
gen. ein**es** jung**en** Mann**es**	ein**es** jung**en** Kind**es**	ein**er** jung**en** Frau	mein**er** jung**en** Leute

Adjective Endings Without a Limiting Word			
masculine	**neuter**	**feminine**	**plural**
nom. kalt**er** Wein	kalt**es** Wasser	kalt**e** Milch	kalt**e** Suppen
acc. kalt**en** Wein	kalt**es** Wasser	kalt**e** Milch	kalt**e** Suppen
dat. kalt**em** Wein	kalt**em** Wasser	kalt**er** Milch	kalt**en** Suppen
gen. kalt**en** Weines	kalt**en** Wassers	kalt**er** Milch	kalt**er** Suppen

exception   *exception*

Neue Mode:
Alte Häuser

■ 1 ■ **Übung: Welcher Tisch ist das?** *(Mit offenen Büchern)* Below is a list of some people and classroom objects, arranged by gender, as well as a list of adjectives that you can use to describe them. Your instructor will ask you about them. Describe them with adjectives as in the example.

BEISPIEL: Welches Bild ist das?
Das ist *das neue Bild.*

Masculine	*Neuter*	*Feminine*	*Plural*	*Adjectives*
Bleistift	Bild	Gruppe	Bücher	alt
Junge	Buch	Hose	Jeans	billig
Kugelschreiber	Fenster	Jacke	Schuhe	blau, rot,
Mantel	Foto	Kamera	Studenten	grün *usw.*
Pulli	Glas	Landkarte		bunt *colorful*
Radiergummi	Heft	Studentin		fleißig *hard-working*
Stadtplan	Hemd	Tafel		freundlich
Student	Kleid	Tasche		groß
Stuhl	Mädchen	Tür		herrlich *great*
	Papier	Uhr		höflich *polite*
	Poster	Zeitschrift *magazine*		kaputt *broken*
	Wörterbuch	Zeitung		kurz
				langweilig *boring*
				neu
				schrecklich *terrible*
				toll *great!*
				typisch
				wunderbar

chewing gum/der Kaugummi ← (Radiergummi)

faul – lazy

■ 2 ■ **Übung: Sehen Sie den Tisch?** Now your instructor asks whether you see certain objects or people. You're not sure which ones are meant, so you ask for more information.

BEISPIEL: Sehen Sie den Tisch?
Meinen Sie den *grünen* Tisch?

Fragewort

Was für ... ?   *What kind of ... ?*

Was für ein Artikel ist das?	*What kind of article is that?*
Was für einen Wagen hast du?	*What kind of car do you have?*
Mit **was für** Menschen arbeitest du zusammen?	*What kind of people do you work with?*

■ 3 ■   **Übung: Was für ein Buch ist das?**   Jetzt fragt Ihr Professor zum Beispiel, was für ein Buch das ist. Sie beschreiben das Buch.

> BEISPIEL: Was für ein Buch ist das?
> Das ist ein interessantes Buch.

■ 4 ■   **Partnerarbeit: Nicht wahr?**   Respond to each other's impressions. One partner asks, the other responds, then switch roles.

> BEISPIEL: Das Haus ist schön, nicht wahr?
> Ja, das ist ein schönes Haus.   (*oder*)
> Nein, das ist kein schönes Haus.

tavern
smart

1. Die Kneipe ist alt, nicht?
2. Der Junge ist klug, nicht wahr?
3. Das Hotel ist teuer, nicht wahr?
4. Der Automechaniker ist gut, nicht?

5. Das Kind ist müde, nicht wahr?
6. Die Buchhandlung ist fantastisch, nicht?
7. Das Bett ist bequem, nicht?   *comfortable*
8. Der Tag ist warm, nicht?

Now create your own sentences on the same pattern.

what kind of book

■ 5 ■   **Übung: Was für ein Buch brauchen Sie?**   Jetzt möchte Ihre Professorin wissen, was für Sachen Sie brauchen, tragen usw. Sagen Sie es ihr.

> BEISPIELE: A: Was für ein Buch brauchen Sie?
> B: Ich brauche ein neues Buch.
>
> A: Was für Schuhe tragen Sie heute?
> B: Heute trage ich alte Turnschuhe.

■ 6 ■   **Übung: Wir haben keinen neuen Wagen.**   Ihr Professor fragt Sie nach (*about*) etwas. Sie antworten, dass Sie es nicht haben.

> BEISPIEL: Ist Ihr Wagen neu?
> Nein, ich habe keinen neuen Wagen.

*keine langweiligen
Bücher*

1. Ist Ihr Fahrrad neu?
2. Sind diese Bücher langweilig?
3. Ist der Tennislehrer wunderbar?
4. Ist der Kaffee heiß?

5. Ist die Wurst frisch?
6. Sind Ihre Freunde sportlich?
7. Sind diese Kleider schmutzig?
8. Ist Ihr Zimmer groß?
9. Ist Ihr Mantel neu?

Schwerindustrie im
Ruhrgebiet.

■ 7 ■   Übung: Was machen Sie lieber?   Der Professor fragt Sie, was Sie lieber
machen.

BEISPIEL: Dieser Zug fährt langsam, aber dieser fährt schnell.
            Mit welchem Zug fahren Sie lieber?
            Ich fahre lieber mit dem langsamen Zug.

1. Dieser Kaffee ist heiß, aber dieser ist kalt. Welchen trinken Sie lieber?
2. Dieses Hemd ist rot und dieses ist gelb. Welches gefällt Ihnen besser?   *Dieses rote H.*
3. Diese Kartoffeln sind groß, aber diese sind klein. Welche nehmen Sie?   *diese kleinen*
4. Dieser See ist warm, aber dieser ist kühl. In welchem würden Sie lieber   *diesem warmen See*
   schwimmen?
5. Diese Stadt ist schön, aber diese ist hässlich. In welcher würden Sie lieber   *diese schöne*
   wohnen?
6. Dieses Zimmer ist hell, aber dieses ist dunkel. Welches gefällt Ihnen?   *Das helle Zimmer*
7. Dieses Hotel ist alt, aber dieses ist neu. In welchem würden Sie lieber   *im alten Hotel*
   übernachten?
8. Diese Brezeln sind frisch, aber diese sind alt. Welche würden Sie lieber essen?   *Ich esse lieber die frische B.*

Word order of adverbs: Time/manner/place

You learned in **Kapitel 1** that adverb sequence in German is time before place.

	time	*place*
Ich fahre	**morgen**	**nach Kopenhagen**.
Wir bleiben	**heute**	**zu Hause**.

If an adverb or adverbial phrase of manner (answering the question **wie?** or **mit
wem?**) is also present, the sequence is *time—manner—place*.

	time	*manner*	*place*
Ich fahre	morgen	**mit der Bahn**	nach Kopenhagen.
Sie bleibt	heute	**allein**	zu Hause.

Place can be either location (**zu Hause**) or destination (**nach Kopenhagen**). Notice that prepositional phrases such as these function as adverbs.

A good mnemonic device is that adverbs answer the following questions in alphabetical order:

wann? (morgen)   **wie?** (mit der Bahn)   **wo(hin)?** (nach Kopenhagen)

Workbook Kap. 9, I.

■ 8 ■ **Gruppenarbeit: Wie? Mit wem?**   Create your own answers to these questions. Follow the example sentences.

1. Wie können wir morgen nach Berlin fahren?
   Wie viele Möglichkeiten gibt es für eine Reise nach Berlin?

   BEISPIEL: Wir können morgen *mit der Bahn* nach Berlin fahren.

2. Mit wem gehen Sie abends ins Kino?

   BEISPIEL: Ich gehe abends *mit meinem Freund* ins Kino.

Ordinal numbers and dates

The ordinal numbers (i.e., *first*, *second*, *third*, etc.) are adjectives and in German take the usual adjective endings.

German numbers up to **neunzehn** add **-t-** to the cardinal number and then the appropriate adjective ending. Note the three irregular forms in boldface.

der, das, die	**erste**	1st	elfte	11th
	zweite	2nd	zwölfte	12th
	dritte	3rd	dreizehnte	13th
	vierte	4th	vierzehnte	14th
	fünfte	5th	fünfzehnte	15th
	sechste	6th	sechzehnte	16th
	siebte	7th	siebzehnte	17th
	achte	8th	achtzehnte	18th
	neunte	9th	neunzehnte	19th
	zehnte	10th		

German numbers **zwanzig** and above add **-st-** and the adjective ending to the cardinal number.

der, das, die	zwanzigste	20th
	einundzwanzigste	21st
	zweiundzwanzigste	22nd
	dreiundzwanzigste	23rd
	usw.	
	dreißigste	30th
	vierzigste	40th
	hundertste	100th
	tausendste	1000th

In German, an ordinal number is seldom written out in letters. It is usually indicated by a period after the numeral.

der **10**. November = der zehnte November

The ordinal numbers are capitalized here (**die Erste, der Zweite**) because they are used as nouns. See **Kapitel 11**, p. 280.

■ **9** ■   **Kettenreaktion: Ich bin die Erste. Ich bin der Zweite.**   Count off using ordinal numbers. Males say **der** ... , females say **die** ...

Immer auf der richtigen Höhe – damit die Kleinen am Tisch der Großen sitzen können.

Fürs vierte Jahr

Fürs erste Jahr

■ Dates in German

In German, the full date is given in the order: day, month, year.

> **den 1.2.1999**   *February 1, 1999*

To tell in what year something happened, English uses the phrase *in 1999.* The German equivalent is **im Jahre 1999** or simply **1999** (no **in**). Here is how to say on what date something occurs or occurred:

Das war **am zehnten** August.	*That was on the tenth of August.*
Wir fliegen **am Achtzehnten**.	*We're flying on the eighteenth.*

Here is how to ask for and give the date:

Den Wievielten haben wir heute?	*What's the date today?*
or	(literally: *"The how manyeth do we have today/is today?"*)
Der Wievielte ist heute?	
Heute haben wir **den Dreizehnten.**	
or	*Today is the thirteenth.*
Heute ist **der Dreizehnte**.	

Lab Manual Kap. 9,
Üb. 10, 11.

Workbook Kap. 9, J.

Giving the date is a communicative goal.

*Vorgestern — day /
übermorgen*

■ 10 ■ Übungen

A. Der Wievielte ist heute?
Heute ist der ...

3. August
9. Februar
1. Mai
20. Juli
2. Januar
8. April

B. Den Wievielten haben wir heute?
Heute haben wir den ...

5. März   *- en*
13. Juni
11. November
19. September
7. Dezember
28. Oktober

■ 11 ■ Übung   Wann kommt Frank? Er kommt am ...

4. Januar   *am Vierten*
30. September
5. April
25. Juli
31. Oktober
20. Februar
24. März

■ 12 ■ Partnerarbeit: Wann reist Susanne nach München?   Hier sehen Sie Susannes Terminkalender für Februar. Fragen Sie einander, wann sie alles macht.

appt:

*pronoun goes in
middle (but not
nouns)*

BEISPIEL: A: Wann besucht sie Heinz?
B: Sie besucht ihn am Ersten.

FEBRUAR	
1 Heinz besuchen	**9** im Computerzentrum arbeiten
2	**10** *terrible/nasty um das 5. m. zu sehen*
3 ins Theater gehen („Mutter Courage")	**11** ins Kino („Das schreckliche Mädchen")
4	**12** zum Recycling gehen
5	**13** Referat schreiben *das Referat am 13en*
6 mit Jörg und Katja essen gehen	...
7 schwimmen gehen (19 Uhr) *um 19 Uhr*	**20** Reise nach München
8	**21** in die Berge fahren

time manner place

general to specific

Vor dem Lesen

Tipps zum Lesen und Lernen

■ **Tipps zum Vokabelnlernen**

Identifying noun gender   Now that you have acquired a German vocabulary of several hundred words, you can begin to recognize some patterns in the gender and formation of nouns. You have already learned that agent nouns ending in **-er** are always masculine (**der Lehrer**) and that the ending **-in** always designates a female (**die Lehrerin**).

The gender of many nouns is determined by a suffix. Here are some of the most common suffixes that form nouns.

- Nouns with the following suffixes are *always feminine* and *always* have the plural ending **-en**:

  -ung, -heit, -keit, -schaft, -ion, -tät

- **-ung** forms nouns from verb stems:

lösen (*to solve*) →	**die Lösung, -en** (*solution*)
zerstören (*to destroy*) →	**die Zerstörung** (*destruction*)
verschmutzen (*to pollute*) →	**die Verschmutzung** (*pollution*)

- **-heit** and **-keit** form nouns from adjective stems and from other nouns:

frei →	**die Freiheit, -en**	(*freedom*)
freundlich →	**die Freundlichkeit**	(*friendliness*)
gesund →	**die Gesundheit**	(*health*)
Mensch →	**die Menschheit**	(*humanity*)

- **-schaft** forms collective and more abstract nouns from concrete nouns:

Studenten →	**die Studentenschaft**	(*student body*)
Land →	**die Landschaft, -en**	(*landscape*)
Freund →	**die Freundschaft, -en**	(*friendship*)

  Wirtschaft = (the) economy

- **-ion** and **-tät**: Words with these suffixes are borrowed from French or Latin. Most have English cognates:

die Diskussion, -en	**die Generation, -en**
die Universität, -en	**die Elektrizität**

- The suffixes **-chen** and **-lein** form diminutives. The stem vowel of the noun is umlauted wherever possible, and the noun automatically becomes *neuter*. The plural and singular forms are always identical.

die Karte →	**das Kärtchen, -**	(*little card*)
das Stück →	**das Stückchen, -**	(*little piece*)
das Brot →	**das Brötchen, -**	
die Magd (archaic: *maid*) →	**das Mädchen, -**	
die Frau →	**das Fräulein, -**	(*Miss; young woman*)
das Buch →	**das Büchlein, -**	(*little book*)

Übung: Raten Sie mal! (Take a guess!)   Was bedeuten diese Wörter?

1. die Möglichkeit   *possibility*
2. die Wanderung   *hiking*
3. die Ähnlichkeit   *similarity*
→ 4. die Mehrheit   *majority*
→ 5. die Meinung   *opinion*
6. die Lehrerschaft   *teaching staff*
7. die Wohnung   *apt, house*
8. die Schönheit   *beauty*
9. die Dummheit   *stupidity*
10. die Studentenschaft   *student body*

11. die Radikalität   *radicalism*
12. die Gesundheit   *health*
→ 13. die Schwierigkeit   *difficulty*
14. das Brüderlein   *little brother*
15. das Liedchen   *a song*
16. das Städtchen   *small city*
17. das Würstchen   *small sausage*
18. das Häuschen   *cottage*
19. die Kindheit   *childhood*
20. die Menschheit   *mankind, humanity*

Lab Manual Kap. 9, Üb. zur Betonung.

■ Leicht zu merken

aktiv	akt<u>i</u>v
akut	
das **Atom, -e**	At<u>om</u>
die **Basis**	
demonstrieren	demonstr<u>ie</u>ren
die **Elektrizität**	Elektriz<u>i</u>tät
die **Energie**	En<u>e</u>rgie
enorm	
die **Konsequenz, -en**	Konsequ<u>e</u>nz
der **Lebensstandard**	
die **Natur**	Nat<u>u</u>r
das **Ökosystem**	
das **Plastik**	
politisch	
produzieren	produz<u>ie</u>ren
das **Prozent** (%)	
radikal	radik<u>a</u>l
sortieren	sort<u>ie</u>ren *sort*
sowjetisch	sowj<u>e</u>tisch
der **Supertanker, -**	

MEHR LEBENSRAUM

■ Einstieg in den Text

The following text discusses environmental problems. These issues concern people all over the globe. They are particularly crucial in densely populated Europe.

Look over **Wortschatz 2**, then read the following hypotheses about the environment. Do you agree or disagree with them? Compare your responses to the opinions expressed in the reading.

	Das stimmt.	Das stimmt nicht.
1. Wir sind heute immer noch sehr abhängig von der Natur.	☐	☐
2. Die Schwerindustrie ist für die Umweltverschmutzung verantwortlich.	☐	☐
3. Die Atomenergie ist eine gute Alternative zum Öl.	☐	☐
4. Der Durchschnittsbürger (*average citizen*) kann im Alltag viel gegen die Umweltverschmutzung tun.	☐	☐
5. Die Politiker müssen viel mehr für die Umwelt tun.	☐	☐

■ Wortschatz 2

Verben

führen to lead
lösen to solve
retten to rescue, save
verschmutzen to pollute; to dirty
verschwenden to waste
werfen (wirft), hat geworfen to throw
  weg·werfen to throw away, discard

Substantive

der **Fisch, -e** fish
der **Politiker, -** politician
der **Unfall, ̈e** accident
der **Vogel, ̈** bird

das **Beispiel, -e** example
das **Kraftwerk, -e** power plant
  das **Atomkraftwerk** atomic power plant
das **Öl** oil
das **Tier, -e** animal

die **Chance, -n** chance
die **Dose, -n** (tin) can
die **Gefahr, -en** danger
die **Gesellschaft, -en** society *Company?*

die **Gesundheit** health
die **Jugend** (*sing.*) youth; young people
die **Kraft, ̈e** power, strength
die **Lösung, -en** solution
die **Menschheit** mankind, human race
die **Partei, -en** political party
die **Pflanze, -n** plant
die **Politik** politics; policy
die **Technik** technology
die **Ware, -n** product

Adjektive und Adverbien

bereit prepared, ready
eigen- own
erstaunlich astounding
gefährlich dangerous
gesund healthy
hoch (*predicate adj.*), **hoh-** (*attributive adj.*) high
  Das Gebäude ist **hoch.**
    aber
  Das ist ein **hohes** Gebäude.
jährlich annually
sauer sour; acidic
  der saure Regen acid rain
stark strong

Andere Vokabeln

mancher, -es, -e many a (*in plural* = some)
  manche Pflanzen some plants
solcher, -es, -e such, such a

Nützliche Ausdrücke

im Jahr(e) 1989 in 1989
nicht nur ... sondern auch not only . . . but also

im Jahre: Like the final **-e** in **nach/zu Hause**, this **-e** is an old dative ending.

Gegensätze

führen ≠ **folgen** (+ *dat.*) to lead ≠ to follow
gesund ≠ **krank** healthy ≠ sick
die **Gesundheit** ≠ die **Krankheit** health ≠ sickness
hoch ≠ **niedrig** high ≠ low
sauer ≠ **süß** sour ≠ sweet
stark ≠ **schwach** strong ≠ weak

KATZEN
würden
GREENPEACE
wählen!

choose

Lab Manual Kap. 9, Lesestück.

Learning about German environmental issues is the cultural goal of this chapter.

Unsere Umwelt in Gefahr

Das Problem: Der Mensch gegen die Natur?

Wir leben heute in Europa und Nordamerika in einer hoch industrialisierten° Welt. Wir lieben unseren Luxus° und brauchen die Technik, denn sie ist die Basis unseres hohen Lebensstandards. Aber unseren erstaunlichen Fortschritt haben wir teuer bezahlt°.

astonishing advances

5   Manchmal vergessen wir, dass wir immer noch von der Natur abhängig° sind.

Um unsere Lebensweise° möglich zu machen brauchen wir enorm viel Energie. Obwohl die Nordamerikaner und Westeuropäer nur zirka 15% der Weltbevölkerung° sind, verbrauchen° sie zirka 65% aller produzierten Energie. Spätestens° seit der Katastrophe im sowjetischen Atomkraftwerk in Tschernobyl am 26. April 1986 weiß

10 man aber, wie gefährlich diese Energiequelle° für unser Ökosystem sein kann. Ein zweites Beispiel ist die Exxon-Valdez-Katastrophe vom Jahre 1989; das Öl aus diesem verunglückten° Supertanker hat das Meer verschmutzt und Fische und Vögel weit und breit° in Gefahr gebracht. Die schlimmen Folgen° von solchen Unfällen können jahrelang fortdauern°. Leider aber sind alle unsere Hauptenergiequellen (Öl, Kohle°,

15 Atomkraft) schädlich° für die Natur und für unsere Gesundheit.

Aber nicht nur die Schwerindustrie muss für die Umwelt verantwortlich sein, sondern auch jeder einzelne° Mensch. Wir fahren zu viel Auto, wir essen zu viel in Fastfood-Restaurants, wir benutzen zu viele Spraydosen° und produzieren zu viel Müll. Die Konsequenzen sind: der saure Regen, Müllhalden° voll von unnötigen

20 Plastikverpackungen° und die Zerstörung der Ozonschicht°. Das Problem ist im dicht besiedelten° Deutschland besonders akut. Dort wirft jeder Bürger jährlich zirka 300 bis 400 kg Müll weg! Man möchte wirklich fragen: Sind wir Menschen denn die Feinde° der Natur?

Die Lösung: aktiv umweltfreundlich sein!

25 Besonders die junge Generation in Deutschland zeigt für diese Probleme starkes Engagement°. Manche finden bei den Grünen[1] eine radikale Alternative zu der Umweltpolitik der großen Parteien. Viele demonstrieren gegen neue Atomkraftwerke und suchen auch in ihrem eigenen Leben Alternativen zu der Wegwerfgesellschaft. Aber nicht nur die umweltbewusste° Jugend, sondern auch Deutsche aus allen

30 Altersgruppen° sind heute bereit ihr Leben zu ändern°, um Meere, Wälder, Tiere und Pflanzen zu retten.[2]

prepared, ready

Glossary (right margin):

- highly industrialized
- luxury
- **teuer ...** = paid a high price for / **von ...** = dependent on
- way of life
- world population
- consume / at the latest
- *dangerous*
- energy source
- grounded (*have an accident*)
- far and wide / consequences
- **jahrelang ...** = persist for years / coal / harmful
- *environment*
- individual
- aerosol cans
- trash dumps
- plastic packaging / ozone layer / **dicht besiedelt** = densely populated
- enemies
- *watchword, slogan especially*
- commitment
- *throw-away society*
- environmentally conscious
- age groups / change

1. **Die Grünen**, the environmental and anti-nuclear party, first won seats in the **Bundestag** in 1983. Although they lost these seats in the 1990 federal elections, they regained them in 1994 and are also represented at the state level in some **Länder**.
2. In 1990 the Federal Republic became the first nation to ban the production and use of ozone-depleting chlorofluorocarbons.

Im Schwarzwald

Waldsterben

Wie kann man denn ein umweltfreundliches Leben führen? Man kann z.B. mehr
Rad fahren oder zu Fuß gehen und weniger° Auto fahren. Man sollte° nur Waren ohne
unnötige Verpackung kaufen und den Hausmüll sortieren und zum Recycling bringen.
35 Man kann auch so wenig Wasser und Elektrizität wie° möglich verschwenden. Diese
Vorschläge° für den Alltag sind nur ein Anfang. Man muss natürlich auch von den
Politikern mehr Umweltbewusstsein° fordern°. Die Menschheit hat nicht mehr viel
Zeit. Nur wenn alle Länder politisch zusammenarbeiten, haben wir noch eine Chance
unsere Umwelt zu retten.

department store

less / should

so ... wie = as . . . as
suggestions *beginning*
environmental awareness /
  demand

save, rescue

Nach dem Lesen

Discussing ecology and recycling is a
communicative goal.

■ **A** ■   **Antworten Sie auf Deutsch.**

1. Von welchen Umweltkatastrophen haben Sie schon gehört?
2. Wann war die Katastrophe in Tschernobyl?
3. Wie können Umweltkatastrophen für die Natur gefährlich sein?
4. Wer soll denn für die Umwelt verantwortlich sein?
5. Nennen Sie unsere Hauptenergiequellen.
6. Kennen Sie alternative Energiequellen?
7. Wie kann unser modernes Alltagsleben für die Umwelt gefährlich sein?
8. Wie können wir ein umweltfreundliches Leben führen?

■ B ■   Gruppenarbeit: Unsere Wegwerfgesellschaft? *(4 oder 5 Personen)*

Jeden Tag benutzen wir viele Sachen. Aber wir verschwenden auch eine Menge, besonders Dinge aus Plastik. Machen Sie eine Liste von solchen Dingen aus Ihrem Alltag. Was haben Sie in den letzten Tagen wegwerfen müssen? Warum?

Liste: „Das haben wir in letzter Zeit weggeworfen."

Lab Manual Kap. 9, Diktat.

Workbook Kap. 9, K–Q.

Die Wälder sterben- nach den Wäldern sterben die Menschen.

Situationen aus dem Alltag

Talking about sports is a communicative goal.

This vocabulary focuses on an everyday topic or situation. Words you already know from **Wortschatz** sections are listed without English equivalents; new supplementary vocabulary is listed with definitions. Your instructor may assign some supplementary vocabulary for active mastery.

■   Der Sport

„Wer Sport treibt, bleibt fit!" hört man oft. Was meinen Sie? Treiben Sie Sport, um fit und gesund zu bleiben, oder nur, weil es Ihnen Spaß macht? Hier sind einige nützliche Wörter für eine Diskussion über Sport.

Substantive
das **Spiel**, -e   *game*
die **Mannschaft**, -en
die **Konkurrenz**   *competition*

Verben
gewinnen, hat gewonnen   *to win*
schlagen, hat geschlagen   *to beat*
trainieren   *to train*

■ A ■   Gruppenarbeit: Was spielst du gern?   Hier sind einige Piktogramme von den Olympischen Spielen. Welchen Sport treiben Sie gern?

> BEISPIEL: A: Ich schwimme gern. Und du?
>
> B: Ich _____ .

laufen
der **Läufer**
die **Läuferin**

schwimmen
der **Schwimmer**
die **Schwimmerin**

Ski fahren
der **Skifahrer**
die **Skifahrerin**

boxen
der **Boxer**

Volleyball spielen
der **Volleyballspieler**
die **Volleyballspielerin**

Fußball spielen
der **Fußballspieler**
die **Fußballspielerin**

Rad fahren
der **Radfahrer**
die **Radfahrerin**

(Eis)hockey spielen
der **Hockeyspieler**
die **Hockeyspielerin**

■ B ■   Gruppenarbeit: Sprechen wir über Sport (*2 oder 3 Personen*)

1. Welchen Sport treibst du?
2. Warum gefällt dir dieser Sport?
3. Treibst du an der Uni Sport? Hast du auch in der Schule Sport getrieben?

■ C ■   Klassendiskussion: Was meinen Sie?

1. Kann man fit bleiben, ohne Sport zu treiben?
2. In Deutschland gibt es viele Sportklubs, aber nur wenige (*few*) Universitätsmannschaften. Finden Sie es gut, dass es solche Mannschaften an amerikanischen Unis gibt? Warum?

Seid ihr schlaue Umweltfüchse?

[handwritten: crafty, cunning]
[handwritten underline under "schlaue"]

Der „Bund für Umwelt und Naturschutz Deutschland" ist eine Lobby von umweltfreundlichen Menschen. In einer Broschüre geben sie Tipps zum Schutz (*protection*) der Umwelt.

Umweltfüchse wissen, ...

- dass Wasser ein Lebensmittel ist. *[handwritten: food ?]*
- dass jeder Deutsche pro Tag zirka 150 Liter Trinkwasser benutzt.

Schlaue Umweltfüchse ...

- werfen keine Medikamente in die Toilette, sondern bringen sie zur Sammelstelle für Giftmüll.
- duschen lieber, als ein Vollbad zu nehmen, weil sie beim Duschen nur 50 bis 100 Liter Wasser benutzen, statt 200 Liter beim Baden.

Umweltfüchse wissen, ...

- dass die Bundesrepublik jedes Jahr einen Müllberg produziert, der so groß wie die Zugspitze ist.
- dass nur 11 Prozent dieses Mülls echter Müll sind. 89 Prozent wären recyclebar.

Schlaue Umweltfüchse ...

[handwritten: environmental]
- kaufen Recyclingprodukte, z.B. Umweltschutzpapier.
- sortieren ihren Müll und bringen Glasflaschen, Metall und Papier zu Containern oder direkt zum Recycling.

Recyclingcontainer.
(Garmisch-
Partenkirchen, Bayern)

UMWELTTIPS

für jeden Tag

trafic?

Haus · Garten · Verkehr

Bund für
Umwelt und
Naturschutz
Deutschland
e. V.

protection

BUND

Deutschland im 20. Jahrhundert

Communicative Goals

- Narrating events in the past
- Describing objects
- Telling how long ago something happened
- Telling how long something lasted

Cultural Goal

- Learning about the Weimar Republic

Chapter Outline

- **Lyrik zum Vorlesen**
  Bertolt Brecht, „Mein junger Sohn fragt mich"

- **Grammatik**
  Simple past tense
  Equivalents for *when*: als, wenn, wann
  Past perfect tense
  More time expressions

- **Lesestück**
  Eine Ausstellung historischer
  Plakate aus der Weimarer Republik

- **Situationen aus dem Alltag**
  Die Politik

- **Almanach**
  German Politics and the European Union

Dialoge

Lab Manual Kap. 10,
Dialoge, Fragen, Hören

Sie gut zu!

Damals *at that time*

Zwei Senioren sitzen nachmittags auf einer Bank.

HERR ZIEGLER: Wie lange wohnen Sie schon hier, Frau Planck?
FRAU PLANCK: Seit letztem Jahr. Vorher habe ich in Mainz gewohnt.
HERR ZIEGLER: Ach, das wusste ich ja gar nicht. Als ich ein Kind war, habe ich immer
              den ganzen Sommer dort bei meinen Großeltern verbracht. *spend time*
FRAU PLANCK: Damals vor dem Krieg war die Stadt natürlich ganz anders.

wissen

Was ist denn los?

JÜRGEN: Heinz, was ist denn los? Du siehst so besorgt aus.
HEINZ: Ach, Barbara hat mir vor zwei Wochen ihren neuen Kassettenrecorder
         geliehen ...
JÜRGEN: Na und? Du hast ihn doch nicht verloren, oder?
HEINZ: Keine Ahnung. Ich hatte ihn in meiner Tasche, aber vor zehn Minuten
         konnte ich ihn dann plötzlich nicht mehr finden. *suddenly*
JÜRGEN: So ein Mist! Meinst du, jemand hat ihn dir geklaut? *ripped it off*
HEINZ: Nee, denn mein Geldbeutel fehlt nicht. *missing*

Shit

no idea

The tag question ...**oder**? (here = *Did you*?) can follow either positive or negative statements. **Nicht wahr?** (p. 77) follows positive statements only.

Schlimme Zeiten

Als Hausaufgabe muss Steffi (10 Jahre alt) ihre Oma interviewen.

STEFFI: Oma, für die Schule sollen wir unsere Großeltern über die Kriegszeit
          interviewen.
OMA: Nun, was willst du denn wissen, Steffi?
STEFFI: Also ... wann bist du eigentlich geboren? *really*
OMA: 1935. Als der Krieg anfing, war ich noch ein kleines Mädchen.
STEFFI: Erzähl mir bitte, wie es euch damals ging.
OMA: Gott sei Dank lebten wir auf dem Land und zuerst ging es uns relativ gut,
       obwohl wir nicht reich waren.
STEFFI: Was ist dann passiert?
OMA: Das dauerte nur bis 1943. Dann ist mein Bruder in Russland gefallen und ein
       Jahr später starb meine Mutter.

Remember: English *in 1935* = **1935** (no *in*) or **im Jahre 1935**.

Note the restricted meaning of **fallen** in this context: *to die in combat.* Proverb: **Generale siegen, Soldaten fallen** (siegen = *to be victorious*).

Note on Usage: *doch*

In **Kapitel 4**, you learned that **doch** can soften a command to a suggestion. In a statement, **doch** adds emphasis in the sense of *surely, really*. In the second dialogue, Jürgen fears the worst and says to Heinz:

Du hast ihn **doch** nicht verloren, oder?   *(Surely) you haven't lost it, have you?*

Wortschatz 1

Verben

dauern to last; to take (time)
fallen (fällt), fiel, ist gefallen to fall; to die in battle
fehlen to be missing; to be absent
interviewen, hat interviewt to interview
leihen, lieh, hat geliehen to lend, loan; to borrow
passieren, passierte, ist passiert to happen
stehlen (stiehlt), stahl, hat gestohlen to steal
verlieren, verlor, hat verloren to lose

Substantive

der **Geldbeutel, -** wallet, change purse
der **Kassettenrecorder, -** cassette player
der **Monat, -e** month
der **Nachmittag, -e** afternoon
  am Nachmittag in the afternoon
der **Senior, -en, -en** senior citizen
die **Bank, ˙-e** bench

Adjektive und Adverbien

besorgt worried, concerned
damals at that time, back then
letzt- last
plötzlich sudden(ly)
reich rich
vorher before that, previously

Andere Vokabeln

als (*sub. conj.*) when, as
doch (*flavoring particle, see p. 277*)
nachdem (*sub. conj.*) after
nun now; well; well now

Nützliche Ausdrücke

(Ich habe) keine Ahnung. (I have) no idea.

den ganzen Sommer (Tag, Nachmittag usw.) all summer (day, afternoon, etc.)
Na und? And so? So what?
So ein Mist! (*crude, colloq.*) What a drag! What a lot of bull!
Wann sind Sie geboren? When were you born?

Gegensätze

besorgt ≠ unbesorgt
  concerned ≠ carefree
reich ≠ arm   rich ≠ poor
vorher ≠ nachher   before that ≠ after that

Mit anderen Worten

klauen (*colloq.*) = stehlen

Back Then

Two senior citizens are sitting on a bench in the afternoon.

z: How long have you lived here, Mrs. Planck?
p: Since last year. Before that, I lived in Mainz.
z: Oh, I didn't know that. When I was a child, I always spent the whole summer there with my grandparents.
p: Of course back then before the war the city was very different.

What's wrong?

j: Heinz, what's wrong? You look so worried.
h: Oh, Barbara ~~loaned~~ *lent* me her new cassette player two weeks ago . . .
j: So? You haven't lost it, have you?
h: No idea. I had it in my bag, but then ten minutes ago I suddenly couldn't find it.
j: What a drag! You think somebody ripped it off?
h: Nope, because my wallet's not missing.

Tough Times

As a homework assignment, Steffi (age 10) has to interview her grandmother.

s: Grandma, for school we're supposed to interview our grandparents about the war years.
o: Well, what do you want to know, Steffi?
s: Let's see . . . when were you born, anyway?
o: In 1935. When the war began I was still a little girl.
s: Please tell me what it was like for you back then.
o: Thank goodness we lived in the country, and at first things were relatively good, although we weren't rich.
s: What happened then?
o: That lasted only until 1943. Then my brother was killed in action in Russia and my mother died a year later.

Variationen

■ A ■ Persönliche Fragen

1. Heinz sieht besorgt aus, weil er etwas verloren hat. Haben Sie je etwas verloren? *Handschüh* *der Schlüssel* Was?
2. Was machen Sie, wenn Sie etwas nicht finden können?
3. Würden Sie jemand Ihren Kassettenrecorder leihen? Warum oder warum nicht?
4. Wissen Sie, wann und wo Ihre Eltern geboren sind? Ihre Großeltern?
5. Wie lange wohnen Sie schon in dieser Stadt?
6. Herr Ziegler hat als Kind seine Sommerferien bei seinen Großeltern verbracht. Was haben Sie als Kind im Sommer gemacht? *der See*

Describing objects is a communicative goal.

■ B ■ Partnerarbeit: Fundbüro (Lost and found)

Sie gehen zum Fundbüro, weil Sie etwas verloren haben. Unten ist eine Liste von Dingen im Fundbüro. Sagen Sie, was Sie verloren haben. Dann beschreiben Sie es.

BEISPIEL: A: Was haben Sie verloren?
B: Ich habe meine Kamera verloren.
A: Können Sie sie beschreiben? *ihn*
B: Es war eine _____ Kamera.

das Fahrrad   *das* Wörterbuch
der Kassettenrecorder   *der* Pulli
die Jacke   *die* Turnschuhe
der Koffer – *suitcase*   *der* Geldbeutel = *das Portemonnaie*
die Tasche

■ C ■ Übung: Was ist passiert?

Gestern war sehr viel los. Sagen Sie, was passiert ist.

BEISPIEL: Können Sie uns sagen, was gestern passiert ist?
Ja, gestern ...

■ D ■ Übung: Den ganzen Tag

How long did you do certain things? Answer that you did them all morning, all day, all week, all semester, and so on.

BEISPIEL: Wie lange sind Sie in Europa gewesen?
Ich war *den ganzen Sommer* da.

1. Wie lange haben Sie gestern Tennis gespielt?
2. Wie lange waren Sie in der Bibliothek?
3. Wie lange waren Sie mit Ihren Freunden zusammen?
4. Wie lange sind Sie im Bett geblieben?
5. Wie lange haben Sie an Ihrem Referat gearbeitet?

Bertolt Brecht fled Germany in 1933 to settle first in France, then in Scandinavia. This poem, written in Finland during World War II, is the sixth of the short cycle "1940." It reflects events of that year.

Lab Manual Kap. 10, Lyrik zum Vorlesen.

Mein junger sohn fragt mich

Mein junger Sohn fragt mich: Soll ich
    Mathematik lernen?   *Am I supposed to*

Wozu°, möchte ich sagen. Dass zwei   *would like*   what for?
    Stück Brot mehr ist als eines

Das wirst du auch so merken°.   **Das** ... = you'll notice that anyway

Mein junger Sohn fragt mich: Soll
    ich Französisch lernen?

Wozu, möchte ich sagen. Dieses Reich   **Reich** ... = empire will
    geht unter°. Und   collapse

Reibe° du nur mit der Hand den Bauch°   rub / belly
    und stöhne°   groan

Und man wird dich schon verstehen.

Mein junger Sohn fragt mich: Soll
    ich Geschichte lernen?

Wozu, möchte ich sagen. Lerne du nur
    deinen Kopf in die Erde stecken°   **deinen** ... = to stick your head in the sand

Da wirst du vielleicht übrig bleiben°. *be left over*   **wirst** ... = will survive

Ja, lerne Mathematik, sage ich
Lerne Französisch, lerne Geschichte!

    Bertolt Brecht (1898–1956)

Narrating events in the past is a communicative goal.

Like German present tense (see Kapitel 1, p. 29), German past tense lacks progressive and emphatic forms (English: *was living, did live*).

Simple past tense

The simple past tense is used in written German to narrate a series of events in the past. Most literary texts are written in the simple past. In spoken German, however, the *perfect* tense is more commonly used to relate past events. Exceptions are **sein**, **haben**, and the modal verbs, which are used most frequently with the simple past in both conversation and writing. You learned the simple past tense of **sein** in **Kapitel 6**.

Weak verbs and strong verbs form the simple past tense in different ways. About 90 percent of German verbs are weak, but the strong verbs introduced in *Neue Horizonte: A Brief Course* occur very frequently.

■ **Simple past of weak verbs** = *regular verbs (don't change their stem)*

The marker for the simple past of weak verbs is **-te**. Weak verbs form the simple past by adding endings to the verb stem as follows:

First- and third-person singular forms are identical: **ich wohnte**, **er wohnte**.

ich wohn-**te**	*I lived*	wir wohn-**ten**	*we lived*
du wohn-**test**	*you lived*	ihr wohn-**tet**	*you lived*
er, es, sie wohn-**te**	*he, it, she lived*	sie, Sie wohn-**ten**	*they, you lived*

Verbs whose stems end in **-d** or **-t** add **-e-** between the stem and these endings:

ich arbeit-**ete**	*I worked*	wir arbeit-**eten**	*we worked*
du arbeit-**etest**	*you worked*	ihr arbeit-**etet**	*you worked*
er, es, sie arbeit-**ete**	*he, it, she worked*	sie, Sie arbeit-**eten**	*they, you worked*

For weak verbs, the only form you need to know to generate all other possible forms is the infinitive: **wohnen, wohnte, hat gewohnt; arbeiten, arbeitete, hat gearbeitet.**

Lab Manual Kap. 10, Var. zur Üb. 1.

In short narratives like this, German uses the simple past rather than the perfect.

■ 1 ■ **Übung: Doras Einkaufstag** Here is a present-tense narrative of Dora's day in town. Retell it in the simple past tense.

Dora **braucht** Lebensmittel. Sie **wartet** bis zehn Uhr, dann **kauft** sie in einer kleinen Bäckerei ein. Sie **bezahlt** ihre Brötchen und **dankt** der Verkäuferin. Draußen **schneit** es und sie **hört** Musik auf der Straße. Sie **sucht** ein Restaurant. Also **fragt** sie zwei Studenten. Die Studenten **zeigen** ihr ein gutes Restaurant gleich in der Nähe. Dort **bestellt** sie etwas zu essen und eine Tasse Kaffee. Es **schmeckt** ihr sehr gut, aber die Menschen am nächsten Tisch **quatschen** zu laut und das **ärgert** sie ein bisschen.

gossip, talk, chat

Simple past of strong verbs

Page 247 lists the 50 strong verbs introduced so far. The new simple past tense forms are boldfaced. Give yourself plenty of time to learn these and practice them aloud with a friend.

Strong verbs do *not* have the marker **-te**. Instead, the verb stem is changed. The changed stem is called the *simple past stem*, e.g., nehmen, **nahm**, hat genommen. This new stem takes the following personal endings in the simple past tense:

ich nahm	*I took*	wir nahm-**en**	*we took*
du nahm-**st**	*you took*	ihr nahm-**t**	*you took*
er, es, sie nahm	*he, it, she took*	sie, Sie nahm-**en**	*they, you took*

Note that the **ich-** and the **er**, **es**, **sie**-forms of strong verbs have *no* endings in the simple past: **ich nahm**, **sie nahm**.

Principal parts of strong verbs

The simple past stem is one of the *principal parts* of a strong German verb. The principal parts are the three (or sometimes four) forms you must know in order to generate all other forms of a strong verb. You have now learned all of them.

infinitive	*3rd-person sing. present*	*simple past stem*	*auxiliary + past participle*
nehmen	**(nimmt)**	**nahm**	**hat genommen**

The table on p. 247 contains the principal parts of all the strong verbs you have learned so far. As an aid to memorization, they have been arranged into groups according to the way their stem-vowels change in the past tenses. Memorize their simple past stems and review your knowledge of the other principal parts. Verbs formed by adding prefixes to these stems are not included in the table, e.g., **abfahren**, **aufstehen**, **beschreiben**, **verstehen**.

Wahlplakat der Grünen, Rheinland-Pfalz.

Principal Parts of Strong Verbs

Infinitive	3rd-sing. pres.	Simple past	Perfect	English
anfangen	fängt an	**fing an**	hat angefangen	*to begin*
fallen	fällt	**fiel**	ist gefallen	*to fall; to die in battle*
halten	hält	**hielt**	hat gehalten	*to hold; to stop*
schlafen	schläft	**schlief**	hat geschlafen	*to sleep*
verlassen	verlässt	**verließ**	hat verlassen	*to leave*
einladen	lädt ein	**lud ein**	hat eingeladen	*to invite*
fahren	fährt	**fuhr**	ist gefahren	*to drive*
tragen	trägt	**trug**	hat getragen	*to carry; to wear*
essen	isst	**aß**	hat gegessen	*to eat*
geben	gibt	**gab**	hat gegeben	*to give*
lesen	liest	**las**	hat gelesen	*to read*
sehen	sieht	**sah**	hat gesehen	*to see*
vergessen	vergisst	**vergaß**	hat vergessen	*to forget*
empfehlen	empfiehlt	**empfahl**	hat empfohlen	*to recommend*
helfen	hilft	**half**	hat geholfen	*to help*
nehmen	nimmt	**nahm**	hat genommen	*to take*
sprechen	spricht	**sprach**	hat gesprochen	*to speak*
stehlen	stiehlt	**stahl**	hat gestohlen	*to steal*
sterben	stirbt	**starb**	ist gestorben	*to die*
treffen	trifft	**traf**	hat getroffen	*to meet*
werfen	wirft	**warf**	hat geworfen	*to throw*
bleiben		**blieb**	ist geblieben	*to stay*
entscheiden		**entschied**	hat entschieden	*to decide*
leihen		**lieh**	hat geliehen	*to lend*
scheinen		**schien**	hat geschienen	*to shine; to seem*
schreiben		**schrieb**	hat geschrieben	*to write*
steigen		**stieg**	ist gestiegen	*to climb*
treiben		**trieb**	hat getrieben	*to drive, propel*
finden		**fand**	hat gefunden	*to find*
klingen		**klang**	hat geklungen	*to sound*
singen		**sang**	hat gesungen	*to sing*
trinken		**trank**	hat getrunken	*to drink*
beginnen		**begann**	hat begonnen	*to begin*
schwimmen		**schwamm**	ist geschwommen	*to swim*
liegen		**lag**	hat gelegen	*to lie*
sitzen		**saß**	hat gesessen	*to sit*
fliegen		**flog**	ist geflogen	*to fly*
fließen		**floss**	ist geflossen	*to flow*
schließen		**schloss**	hat geschlossen	*to close*
verlieren		**verlor**	hat verloren	*to lose*
ziehen		**zog**	hat/ist gezogen	*to pull; to move*
anrufen		**rief an**	hat angerufen	*to call up*
gehen		**ging**	ist gegangen	*to go*
hängen		**hing**	hat gehangen	*to be hanging*
heißen		**hieß**	hat geheißen	*to be called*
kommen		**kam**	ist gekommen	*to come*
laufen	läuft	**lief**	ist gelaufen	*to run*
sein	ist	**war**	ist gewesen	*to be*
stehen		**stand**	hat gestanden	*to stand*
tun		**tat**	hat getan	*to do*

■ 2 ■ **Übung** Change the following sentences to the simple past tense.

1. Mir gefällt sein neues Fahrrad. *gefiel*
2. Barbara ruft um halb fünf an. *rief*
3. Sie schwimmt das ganze Jahr, um fit zu bleiben. *schwamm*
4. Stefan findet seinen Geldbeutel nicht. *fand*
5. Jede Woche schreibt sie uns eine Postkarte. *schrieb*
6. Der Film beginnt um 20.30 Uhr. *begann*
7. Er hilft mir gern mit meinen Hausaufgaben. *half*
8. Sie heißt Dora Schilling. *hieß*
9. Um acht gehen die Senioren miteinander essen. *gingen*
10. Er liegt immer gern im Bett und liest die Zeitung. *lag / las*
11. Ich finde es komisch, dass er nichts trinkt. *fand / trank*
12. Am Montag kommt Bert zurück. *kam*
13. Sie kommt um 10 Uhr an und bleibt den ganzen Tag da. *kam / blieb*
14. Sie sieht ihren Freund und läuft schnell zu ihm. *sah / lief*

In sentence 3, the infinitive construction **um fit zu bleiben** does not change tense.

Workbook Kap. 10, A–B.

Lab Manual Kap. 10, Var. zur Üb. 2. *Soror*

■ 3 ■ **Übung: Ein Brief** Complete this letter by filling in the verbs in the simple past tense. Some of the verbs are strong and some are weak.

Liebe Martine,

weißt du, was dem armen Ulrich vorgestern passiert ist? Er hat mich gestern angerufen und _erzählte_ (erzählen) es mir. Er _lernte_ (kennen lernen) im Park eine sympathische junge Studentin _kennen_. Sie _sah_ (aussehen) ganz elegant und reich _aus_. Zusammen _saßen_ (sitzen) sie auf einer Bank und _sprachen_ (they) (sprechen) über das Studium. Ulrich _trug_ (tragen) eine Jacke, aber weil es sehr heiß war, _legte_ (legen) er sie auf die Bank. Alles _schien_ (scheinen) gut zu gehen und Ulrich _lud_ (einladen) sie in ein Konzert _ein_. Sie _sagte_ (sagen) ja und _gab_ (geben) ihm ihre Adresse und Telefonnummer. Nach einer Stunde _stand_ (stehen) die Studentin auf und _ging_ (gehen) in die Bibliothek zurück. Am Abend _kam_ (kommen) er nach Hause und _suchte_ (suchen) seinen Hausschlüssel in der Tasche seiner Jacke. Aber dort _fand_ (finden) er keinen Schlüssel und auch sein Geld _war_ (sein) weg. Er _rief_ (rufen) die Nummer der Studentin an, aber sie _wohnte_ (wohnen) gar nicht da. So ein Mist, nicht?

Jetzt muss ich gehen. Viele Grüße,

What a drag!

deine

Annelies

■ **Simple past of modal verbs**

The modal verbs form their simple past with the **-te** marker, like the weak verbs. But those modals that have an umlaut in the infinitive *drop* it in the past tense.

müssen, **musste**			
ich muss**te**	*I had to*	wir muss**ten**	*we had to*
du muss**test**	*you had to*	ihr muss**tet**	*you had to*
er, es, sie muss**te**	*he, it, she had to*	sie, Sie muss**ten**	*they, you had to*

Similarly:

dürfen	ich **durfte**	*I was allowed to*
können	ich **konnte**	*I was able to*
mögen	ich **mochte**	*I liked*
sollen	ich **sollte**	*I was supposed to*
wollen	ich **wollte**	*I wanted to*

Note that **mögen** drops the umlaut and also has a consonant change in the simple past.

Workbook Kap. 10, C–D.

Lab Manual Kap. 10, Var. zur Üb. 4.

■4■   Übung

1. Sagen Sie, was Sie gestern machen mussten.   *Ich musste mein Hund spazieren gehen.*

   BEISPIEL: Ich musste gestern zwei Bücher lesen.

2. Jetzt sagen Sie, was Sie und Ihre Freunde gestern machen wollten.   *ich fuhrte nach SF, der Ballet zu sehen.*

   BEISPIEL: Wir wollten gestern Ski fahren gehen.

3. Was durften Sie als Kind nicht machen?   *spät in die Schule sein,*

   BEISPIEL: Ich durfte nie allein schwimmen gehen.
   must not

■ Simple past of mixed verbs

The mixed verbs (see p. 147) use the **-te** marker for the simple past but attach it to the *changed* stem, which you have already learned for the past participles:

wissen, **wusste**, hat gewusst			
ich wuss**te**	*I knew*	wir wuss**ten**	*we knew*
du wuss**test**	*you knew*	ihr wuss**tet**	*you knew*
er, es, sie wuss**te**	*he, it, she knew*	sie, Sie wuss**ten**	*they, you knew*

Remember that **wissen** is irregular in the present-tense singular: ich **weiß**, du **weißt**, er **weiß**.

Similarly:

bringen, **brachte**, hat gebracht
kennen, **kannte**, hat gekannt

■ Simple past of *haben* and *werden*

Only **haben** and **werden** are irregular in the simple past tense.

haben, **hatte**, hat gehabt			
ich hat**te**	*I had*	wir hat**ten**	*we had*
du hat**test**	*you had*	ihr hat**tet**	*you had*
er, es, sie hat**te**	*he, it, she had*	sie, Sie hat**ten**	*they, you had*

werden, **wurde**, ist geworden			
ich wurd**e**	*I became*	wir wurd**en**	*we became*
du wurd**est**	*you became*	ihr wurd**et**	*you became*
er, es, sie wurd**e**	*he, it, she became*	sie, Sie wurd**en**	*they, you became*

Workbook Kap. 10, E.

Lab Manual Kap. 10, Var. zur Üb. 5.

durfte

■5■ Übung   Retell the following short narrative in the simple past.

kannte   *wohnten*

Andreas **kennt** Mainz sehr gut, weil seine Großeltern dort **wohnen**. Als er 11 Jahre alt

wurde   *spend time*

wird, **darf** er allein mit dem Zug nach Mainz fahren. Er **verbringt** jeden Sommer dort.
Die Großeltern **wissen** alles über die Stadt, denn sie **leben** seit Jahren in Mainz. Er

verbrachte

bringt ihnen immer ein Geschenk mit und das **haben** sie immer gern.

brachte   *wussten*   *hatten*   *lebten*

■ Use of the simple past tense

In English there is a difference in *meaning* between past tense and perfect tense. Compare these sentences:

> I saw Marion in the restaurant.
> I have seen Marion in the restaurant.

I saw Marion refers to a unique event in the past, while *I have seen Marion* implies that Marion has been in the restaurant on several occasions and may be there again.

In German, there is *no difference in meaning between simple past and perfect tense*. They both simply convey that the action is in the past:

> Ich **sah** Marion im Restaurant.
> Ich **habe** Marion im
> Restaurant **gesehen**.   } *I saw Marion in the restaurant.*

The difference between German simple past and perfect tense is mainly one of *usage*: they are used under different circumstances. As you have already learned, the perfect tense is the *conversational past*, used in conversation to refer to events in the past. The simple past tense is regularly used in conversation only with frequently occurring verbs such as **sein**, **haben**, and the modal verbs.

> A: Wo **warst** du denn gestern?   *Where were you yesterday? I waited*
>   Ich habe auf dich gewartet.   *for you.*
> B: Ich **hatte** kein Geld mehr   *I didn't have any more money and had*
>   und **musste** nach Hause.   *to go home.*

The primary use of simple past tense is in *written* German (in letters, newspaper reports, short stories, novels, etc.) to narrate a series of events in the past. Here, for example, is the beginning of the fairy tale "Hänsel und Gretel":

Es war einmal ... is the formulaic beginning for most German fairy tales.

> Es **war** einmal ein armer   *Once upon a time there was a poor*
> Holzhacker. Er **wohnte** mit   *woodcutter. He lived at the edge of a*
> seinen zwei Kindern vor einem   *forest with his two children. Their*
> Wald. Sie **hießen** Hänsel und   *names were Hansel and Gretel. They*
> Gretel. Sie **hatten** wenig zu essen *had little to eat and their stepmother*
> und ihre Stiefmutter **wollte** sie   *wanted to get rid of them.*
> los werden.

■ Simple past after the conjunction *als*

Clauses introduced by the subordinating conjunction **als** (*when* or *as* referring to a point or stretch of time in the past) require the simple past tense.

> Hans hat uns oft besucht, **als** er in   *Hans often visited us when he lived*
> New York **wohnte**.   *in New York.*

> **Als** ich meinen Geldbeutel **suchte**,   *When I looked for my wallet I*
> konnte ich ihn nicht finden.   *couldn't find it.*

Lab Manual Kap. 10,
Var. zur Üb. 6.

■ **6** ■ **Übung: Es war schon spät**   Sagen Sie, dass es schon spät war, als etwas passierte.

> **BEISPIEL:** Das Konzert fing an.
> Es war schon spät, als das Konzert anfing.

1. Ich fand den Laden.
2. Er ging endlich.
3. Wir kamen in München an.
4. Sie fuhr ab.
5. Das Telefon klingelte.
6. Meine Freunde kamen vorbei.

■ **7** ■ **Partnerarbeit: Wie geht's weiter?**   Take turns completing the following sentences with an als-clause.

1. Jürgen konnte seinen Schlüssel nicht finden, als ...
2. Herr Ziegler hat jeden Sommer seine Großeltern besucht, als ...
3. Es ging der Großmutter nicht gut, als ...
4. Ute lief schnell ins Haus, als ...
5. Alle Schüler lachten, als ...

Now restate the sentences, beginning with your **als**-clause.

> **BEISPIEL:** *Als* Jürgen nach Hause kam, konnte er seinen
> Schlüssel nicht finden.

Equivalents for "when": als, wenn, wann

It is important to distinguish among three German subordinating conjunctions, each of which may be translated by English *when*.

- **als** = *when* (in the past); *as*
  Als refers to an event or state *in the past* and requires the simple past tense.

> **Als** wir in Wien waren, haben wir   *When we were in Vienna, we visited*
> Andreas besucht.   *Andreas.*

If necessary, remind students that **ob** = *if/whether*.

- **wenn** = *when/if; whenever*
  Wenn means *when* in reference to an event *in the present or future*. Since it can also mean *if*, clauses with **wenn** can be ambiguous.

> **Wenn** wir in Wien sind, besuchen   *When (If) we're in Vienna, we'll visit*
> wir Andreas.   *Andreas.*

Wenn also means *whenever* in reference to repeated action in the past or present. To avoid confusion between *whenever* and *if*, add the adverb **immer** if you mean *whenever*.

> **Wenn** Hans nach Wien kommt,   *Whenever Hans comes to Vienna, he*
> geht er **immer** ins Kaffeehaus.   *always goes to a coffee house.*

Note carefully the difference in meaning between **als** and **wenn** used with simple past tense.

> **Als** sie das sagte, wurde er rot.   *When she said that, he turned red.*
>
> **Wenn** sie das sagte, wurde er   *Whenever she said that, he always*
> immer rot.   *turned red.*

Workbook Kap. 10, F.

• **Wann** = *when, at what time*
Wann is always a question word, used both in direct questions and in indirect questions:

> **Wann** ist das passiert?
> *When did that happen?*

> Ich weiß nicht, **wann** das passiert ist.
> *I don't know when that happened.*

■ **8** ■ **Übung: Als, wenn oder wann?** (*Mit offenen Büchern*)

1. Mutti, ___*wann*___ darf ich spielen?
   ___*Wenn*___ du das Altglas in den Keller getragen hast.

2. ___*Wann*___ fängt das Konzert an?
   Ich weiß nicht, ___*wann*___ es anfängt.
   Karl kann es uns sagen, ___*wann*___ er zurückkommt.
   Wir haben viele Konzerte gehört, ___*als*___ wir Berlin besuchten.
   Das möchte ich auch tun, ___*wenn*___ ich nächstes Jahr in Berlin bin.

3. ___*Als*___ ich gestern an der Uni war, habe ich Angelika getroffen. Sie hat gesagt, sie kommt heute Abend mit.
   Gut! ___*Wenn*___ Angelika mitkommt, macht es mehr Spaß.
   Sag mir bitte noch einmal, ___*wann*___ die Party beginnt.

■ **9** ■ **Partnerarbeit: Wie sagt man das auf Deutsch?** Sagen Sie diese Dialoge auf Deutsch.

1. A: When did you meet Claudia? *kennen lernen*
   B: I met her when I was studying in Vienna. Whenever I'm there, I always write her a postcard. *traf sie studierte* *Wenn ich da bin / Ich schr/eine Karte immer schreibe*
   A: I don't know when I'll go to Vienna again. *Ich weis nicht wann ich wieder nach Wien gehen.*

Die ersten freien Wahlen in der ehemaligen DDR.

2. A: When I was young I hitchhiked a lot. *per Autostopp reiste, per Anhalten*
   B: When I go to Europe, I'll do that too. *tue ich das auch.*
   A: When are you going to Europe? *Wann fahren Sie nach Europe*
   B: When I have enough money. *Wenn ich genug Geld habe*

Past perfect tense

The past perfect tense is used for an event in the past that preceded another event in the past.

Als Hans aufstand, **hatte** Ulla schon **gefrühstückt**.	*When Hans got up, Ulla **had** already **eaten breakfast**.*

The form of the past perfect tense is parallel to that of the perfect tense, but the auxiliary verb (**haben** or **sein**) is in the past tense instead of the present (**haben** → **hatte**, **sein** → **war**).

ich **hatte gegessen**	*I had eaten*
du **hattest gegessen**	*you had eaten*
er **hatte gegessen**	*he had eaten*
wir **hatten gegessen**	*we had eaten*
ihr **hattet gegessen**	*you had eaten*
sie **hatten gegessen**	*they had eaten*
ich **war aufgestanden**	*I had gotten up*
du **warst aufgestanden**	*you had gotten up*
sie **war aufgestanden**	*she had gotten up*
wir **waren aufgestanden**	*we had gotten up*
ihr **wart aufgestanden**	*you had gotten up*
sie **waren aufgestanden**	*they had gotten up*

Look at the following timetable of morning events at Hans and Ulla's house, then at how they are combined in the sentences that follow.

8.00 Uhr: Ulla hat gefrühstückt.

9.00 Uhr: Hans ist aufgestanden.

10.00 Uhr: Ulla ist zur Uni gegangen.

11.00 Uhr: Hans hat gefrühstückt.

event 1 (8.00 Uhr)	event 2 (9.00 Uhr)
Ulla **hatte** schon **gefrühstückt**,	als Hans aufstand.
Ulla had already eaten,	*when Hans got up.*

The order of the clauses may of course be reversed:

event 2 (9.00 Uhr)	event 1 (8.00 Uhr)
Als Hans aufstand,	**hatte** Ulla schon **gefrühstückt**.
When Hans got up,	*Ulla had already eaten.*

The subordinating conjunction **nachdem** (*after*) is often used with the past perfect tense.

Nachdem Ulla gefrühstückt hatte, ging sie zur Uni.

After Ulla had eaten breakfast, she went to the university.

Distinguish between the preposition **nach** (+ noun in the dative) and the conjunction **nachdem** (+ clause with the verb in final position). Both are translated *after*. **Nach der Deutschstunde** … (after German class); **Nachdem wir das Essen bestellt hatten** … (*After we had ordered the meal* …).

Lab Manual Kap. 10, Var. zur Üb. 10.

Workbook Kap. 10, G.

■ **10** ■ **Übung: Als Ulla nach Hause kam** Sie spielen die Rolle von Hans. Sie sind heute vor Ulla nach Hause gekommen und hatten viel Zeit eine Menge zu ~ *a lot* machen. Sagen Sie, was Sie schon gemacht hatten, als Ulla um 23.00 Uhr endlich nach Hause kam.

BEISPIEL: Lebensmittel eingekauft
Als Ulla nach Hause kam, hatte ich schon
Lebensmittel eingekauft.

1. nach Hause gekommen   *was*
2. Kartoffeln gekocht
3. alles sauber gemacht
4. die Kinder abgeholt   *picked up*
5. einkaufen gegangen
6. den Kindern das Essen gegeben
7. die Zeitung gelesen
8. ein Glas Wein getrunken
9. die Kinder ins Bett gebracht
10. ein paar Briefe geschrieben
11. meine Kusine angerufen
12. ins Bett gegangen   *w*

More time expressions

Telling how long ago something happened is a communicative goal.

■ *vor* + dative = *ago*

The preposition **vor** is used with various time expressions in the dative case to mean *ago*.

die	**vor fünf Minuten**	*five minutes ago*
die	**vor einer Stunde**	*an hour ago*
der	**vor drei Tagen**	*three days ago* *vor einem Tag*
die	**vor vielen Wochen**	*many weeks ago*
der	**vor einem Monat**	*a month ago*
das	**vor hundert Jahren**	*a hundred years ago*

einem Tag

■ 11 ■   **Übung: Wann war das?**   Sagen Sie auf Deutsch, wann etwas passiert ist.

BEISPIEL: Wann ist das passiert?
(*two days ago*): Vor zwei Tagen.

1. a minute ago *eine~*
2. an hour ago *einer Stunde*
3. three years ago *drei Jahren*

4. five months ago *fünf Monaten*
5. ten days ago *zehn Tagen*
6. a couple of weeks ago *ein paar Wochen*

„Vor 60 Jahren hast du mich hier ins Kino eingeladen. Nächstes Jahr lade ich dich ein."

einladen = invite

■ 12 ■   **Partnerarbeit: Wann hast du zuletzt ... gemacht?**   Ask each other when you last did these things.

das **BEISPIEL:** A: Wann hast du zuletzt deine Großeltern besucht?
B: Ich habe sie vor drei Monaten besucht.

fast = almost

deine Oma besuchen
Geld ausgeben *spend*
einen Stadtbummel machen
einen langen Roman lesen

bist du *umgezogen?* *35 Jahren*
^ in ein neues Haus umziehen
Sport treiben *getrieben*
etwas für die Umwelt tun
einen Brief bekommen

(hat) transitive
er ist gekommen

■   **Duration ending in the past**

German and English differ in the way they show an action ending in the past versus an action continuing into the present. English makes this distinction by using different verb tenses:

We **lived** in Berlin for three years.   *Past tense* for a state ending in the past (i.e., we don't live there any more).

We **have lived** in Berlin for three years.   *Perfect tense* for a state continuing at the moment of speaking (i.e., we're *still* living there).

Telling how long something lasted is a communicative goal.

In German, however, both *the simple past* and *the perfect tense* are used for a state ending in the past.

Wir **wohnten** drei Jahre in Berlin. } *We **lived** in Berlin*
Wir **haben** drei Jahre in Berlin **gewohnt**. } *for three years.*

■ Duration beginning in the past but continuing in the present

For a state beginning in the past but continuing at the moment of speaking, German uses *present tense* and one of these adverbial phrases:

schon (+ accusative)   →   **schon drei Jahre**
seit (+ dative)   →   **seit drei Jahren**

Wir **wohnen schon drei Jahre** in Berlin. ⎫ *We **have lived** in*
Wir **wohnen seit drei Jahren** in Berlin. ⎭ *Berlin for three years.*

Note carefully the difference between verb tenses in the two languages!

> ### Note on Usage: **For a long time**
>
> Notice the different ways to express *for a long time*.
>
> Ich hoffe, du kannst **lange** bleiben.   *I hope you can stay **for a long time**.*
>   (continuing into the future)
>
> Ich wohne **schon lange** hier. ⎫ *I've lived here **for a long time**.*
> Ich wohne **seit langem** hier. ⎭ (continuing from the past)

Lab Manual Kap. 10, Üb. 13.

Workbook Kap. 10, H.

word order?

■ **13** ■ **Übung: Wie lange schon?**   Ihre Professorin möchte wissen, wie lange Sie etwas schon machen. Sagen Sie, Sie machen es schon zwei Jahre.

> BEISPIEL: Wie lange arbeiten Sie schon hier?
> Ich arbeite schon zwei Jahre hier.

Antworten Sie mit **schon**.   Antworten Sie mit **seit**. *dative*

sechs Monate

1. Wie lange studieren Sie schon hier?
2. Wie lange lernen Sie schon Deutsch?
3. Wie lange treiben Sie schon Sport?
4. Wie lange wohnen Sie schon im Studentenwohnheim?
5. Wie lange fahren Sie schon Rad?

viele Jahre

6. Seit wann kennen Sie mich?
7. Seit wann haben Sie kurze Haare?
8. Seit wann studieren Sie hier?
9. Seit wann sammeln Sie Altglas?
10. Seit wann spielen Sie ein Musikinstrument?

■ **14** ■ **Partnerarbeit: Wie sagt man das auf Deutsch?**   Übersetzen Sie diese Sätze mit Ihrem Partner.

1. We've known him for a year. *(das) Wir kennen ihn seit eine einem Jahr*
2. She's lived here for two weeks. *Sie wohnt seit zwei Wochen hier*
3. He's been lending me money for a long time. *Er leiht mir Geld vor langer Zeit*
4. Barbara has already been here five days. *B ist hier schon fünf Tagen*
5. She has studied in Halle for two semesters. *Sie studiert in Halle für 2 Semester*
6. For ten years there's been an excellent restaurant here. *Seit 10 Jahren ist ein guter R hier*
7. Michael has been interviewing her for three hours. *M interviewt sie seit 3 Stunden*
8. I've been hungry for two days. *Ich bin schon 2 Tagen hungrig.*

15 Partnerarbeit: Wie lange machst du das schon? Fragen Sie einander, wie lange oder seit wann Sie etwas machen. Unten (*below*) sind einige Ideen, aber Sie können auch Ihre eigenen Fragen stellen.

1. Wie lange studierst du schon hier? *Ich studiere schon sieben Monaten*
2. Seit wann lernst du Fremdsprachen? *Ich lerne F seit xx Jahren*
3. Wie lange lernst du schon Deutsch? *Ich lerne schon vielen Jahren Deutsch.*
4. Seit wann gibt es diese Uni? *Seit 114 Jahren gibt est*
5. Wie lange kannst du schon Auto fahren? *Ich kann schon vielen Jahren Auto f.*
6. Seit wann arbeitest du mit dem Computer? *Ich arbeite seit 23 Jahren mit*
7. Wie lange sind wir heute schon in der Deutschstunde? *Wir sind schon xx Minuten*

Vor dem Lesen

Lesestück

Other examples: **Katholizismus, Protestantismus, Kapitalismus, Protektionismus, Sozialismus, Anarchismus, Modernismus, Expressionismus, Futurismus.**

This is the origin of words like *hamburger, wiener, frankfurter, Budweiser,* and *pilsner* (from *Budweis* and *Pilsen,* German names for the Czech cities **České Budejovice** and **Plzeň**).

Lab Manual Kap. 10, Üb. zur Betonung.

Tipps zum Lesen und Lernen

■ **Tipps zum Vokabelnlernen**

The following reading mentions several concepts such as National Socialism, Communism, and anti-Semitism. English words ending in *-ism* denote a system of belief, a doctrine, or a characteristic. Their German equivalents end in the suffix **-ismus**. These words are all masculine in German and the stress is always on the penultimate syllable (**Optimismus**).

der Antisemitismus   der Kommunismus
der Extremismus   der Optimismus
der Idealismus   der Pessimismus

City names as adjectives The reading also mentions the *Weimar* Republic, the *Versailles* Treaty, and the *New York* Stock Exchange. When the names of cities are used as adjectives in German, they are capitalized and simply add the ending **-er** in all cases: **die Weimarer Republik, der Versailler Vertrag, die New Yorker Börse.**

■ **Leicht zu merken**

die **Demokratie, -n**	Demokratie
demokratisch	
der **Direktor, -en**	
die **Epoche, -n**	Epoche
extrem	
die **Form, -en**	
ideologisch	
illegal	illegal
die **Inflation**	Inflation
manipulieren	manipulieren
die **Methode, -n**	Methode
die **Monarchie, -n**	Monarchie
die **Opposition, -en**	Opposition
die **Republik, -en**	Republik
die **Situation, -en**	Situation
symbolisch	
terroristisch	terroristisch

Einstieg in den Text

In the following reading, you will encounter quite a bit of factual historical information about an important period in modern German history: the Weimar Republic. Much of the information will probably be new to you, but you already know enough German to be able to understand complex issues.

When reading the text through for the first time, keep the following basic information questions in mind as a guide:

Was war die Weimarer Republik?
Wann war diese historische Epoche?
Wer hat damals eine Rolle gespielt?
Warum war diese Zeit so wichtig?

Before reading, also examine the illustrations that accompany and are referred to in the reading. These convey an impression of the content of the reading and will help you to understand the issues discussed.

Was für Plakate sind das?
Aus welcher Zeit kommen sie?
Was zeigen die Bilder?
Welche Wörter oder Namen können Sie schon verstehen?

Wortschatz 2

Verben

erklären to explain
nennen, nannte, hat genannt to name, call
stören to disturb
unterbrechen (unterbricht), unterbrach, hat unterbrochen to interrupt
versuchen to try, attempt
wachsen (wächst), wuchs, ist gewachsen to grow
wählen to choose; to vote
zählen to count

Substantive

der **Arm, -e** arm *job (F)*
der **Schriftsteller, -** writer (*m.*)
der **Staat, -en** state
der **Wähler, -** voter

das **Plakat, -e** poster
das **Reich, -e** empire, realm
das **Volk, ¨er** people, nation, folk

die **Arbeitslosigkeit** unemployment
die **Ausstellung, -en** exhibition
die **Bedeutung, -en** meaning, significance
die **Dame, -n** lady
die **Idee, -n** idea
die **Schriftstellerin, -nen** writer (*f.*)
die **Wahl, -en** choice; election

Idea: **die Idee** is the most general equivalent: **Das ist eine gute Idee.** *Ahnung* means *inkling*: **Ich habe keine Ahnung.**

Adjektive und Adverbien

arbeitslos unemployed
ausländisch foreign
bekannt known; well known
hart hard; tough; harsh
unruhig restless, uneasy, troubled
schwer: heavy, hard, difficult

Andere Vokabel

bevor (*sub. conj.*) before

Nützliche Ausdrücke

zu Ende sein to end, be finished, be over
  1918 war der Krieg zu Ende.
  The war ended in 1918.
eine Frage stellen to ask a question

Fragen takes a direct object of person (**Ich habe ihn gefragt**).

Gegensätze

bekannt ≠ **unbekannt**
  known ≠ unknown
unruhig ≠ **ruhig**
  restless ≠ calm, peaceful

Eine Ausstellung historischer Plakate aus der Weimarer Republik

Im Hessischen Landesmuseum° gab es vor einiger Zeit° eine *exhibition* Ausstellung politischer Plakate aus der Weimarer Republik (1919–1933). Der Museumsdirektor führte eine Gruppe ausländischer Studenten durch die Ausstellung.

„Meine Damen und Herren, herzlich willkommen im Landesmuseum! Bevor wir
5 in die Ausstellung gehen, möchte ich Ihnen ein paar Worte über die Geschichte der Weimarer Republik sagen. Vielleicht ist Ihnen diese Epoche schon bekannt, aber wenn Ihnen etwas nicht klar ist, können Sie jederzeit° Fragen stellen – das stört mich gar nicht.

fact
Was war das eigentlich, die Weimarer Republik? So nennen wir den deutschen
10 Staat in der Zeit zwischen dem Ende des Ersten Weltkrieges 1918 und dem Anfang des Dritten Reiches[1] im Januar 1933. Es war Deutschlands erster Versuch° eine demokratische Staatsform zu entwickeln°. Unsere Plakate zeigen die extremen ideologischen Gegensätze° dieser Epoche. Aber sie zeigen auch, wie man gegensätzliche° Ideen oft mit ähnlichen Bildern darstellen° kann.“

15 Hier unterbrach ein Student mit einer Frage: „Entschuldigung, aber können Sie uns erklären, warum es die ‚Weimarer' Republik hieß? War Berlin nicht damals die Hauptstadt Deutschlands?“

Plakat is the term for informational posters, **Poster** for decorative posters (performers, vacation spots, etc.).

Hessian State Museum /
vor … = a while ago

Lab Manual Kap. 10, Lesestück.

at any time

Learning about the Weimar Republic is the cultural goal of this chapter.

attempt
develop
polarities / contradictory
represent   *similar*

German equivalents for *people*: **das Volk** (a people defined by a common language and culture: **das deutsche Volk**); **Menschen** (people in general: **die Menschen in dieser Stadt**); **Leute** (more restricted grouping: **die Leute hier im Zimmer**).

choose

fetters

The symbols on the snakes from left to right identify the following parties: the Social Democrats (SPD), the Nazis (NSDAP), and the Communists (KPD). The fourth snake behind the others probably represents the right-wing German National People's Party (DNVP).

---

1. **Das Dritte Reich**: The Nazis' own name for their regime (1933–1945). The first empire was the Holy Roman Empire (962–1806). The second empire (**das Deutsche Reich**, 1871–1918) collapsed at the end of the First World War.

„Sicher. Berlin blieb auch die Hauptstadt, aber die Politiker kamen 1919 in der Stadt Weimar zusammen, um die neue demokratische Verfassung zu beschließen°. In
20 Berlin war die politische Situation damals sehr unruhig und außerdem° hatte Weimar wichtige symbolische Bedeutung als die Stadt, wo die großen Schriftsteller Goethe und Schiller[1] früher gelebt und gearbeitet hatten.

Die ersten Jahre der Republik waren eine Zeit der Arbeitslosigkeit und der hohen Inflation. Deutschland hatte den Ersten Weltkrieg verloren und die Monarchie war zu
25 Ende.[2] Unter dem harten Versailler Friedensvertrag musste der neue demokratische Staat 20 Milliarden° Goldmark an die Siegermächte° (besonders an Frankreich) zahlen. Unser erstes Plakat, aus der Zeit vor 1925, zeigt den deutschen Reichsadler° durch den Versailler Vertrag gefesselt°.

Verfassung ... = ratify the constitution / moreover
back then

peace
billion / victors
imperial eagle
fettered

SPD poster for the Reichstag election of May 1924 ("The Answer to the Hitler Trial")

After the failed Nazi putsch in Munich in November 1923, Hitler received a light prison sentence of 5 years, and his National Socialist Party was officially banned. The SPD made a weak showing in the election, while both the Communists and the radical Right gained strength.

1. Johann Wolfgang von Goethe (1749–1832); Friedrich von Schiller (1759–1805).
2. Kaiser Wilhelm II (1859–1941) abdicated in November 1918 and went into exile in the Netherlands. The Treaty of Versailles officially ended the First World War in 1919.

Als die New Yorker Börse° 1929 stürzte°, wurde die Wirtschaftskrise° in den

30 Industrieländern Europas katastrophal. Man zählte im Februar 1930 schon mehr als° 3,5 Millionen arbeitslose Menschen in Deutschland.

Diese Wirtschaftskrise brachte die junge deutsche Demokratie in Gefahr, denn schon 1932 waren sieben Millionen Menschen arbeitslos. Es gab damals mehr als dreißig politische Parteien und besonders die antidemokratischen konnten schnell

35 wachsen. Auf diesem zweiten Plakat sieht man, wie die ‚starke Hand' der katholischen Zentrumspartei[1] die extremen Parteien erwürgt°. In den Wahlen nach 1930 stieg aber die Macht der Nationalsozialistischen Deutschen Arbeiterpartei (NSDAP) – der Nazis – bis sie die stärkste° im Reichstag[2] wurde. Ihr Führer Adolf Hitler benutzte den Antisemitismus und Antikommunismus um die Ängste des Volkes zu manipulieren.

40 Ein Plakat der Nazis zeigt den symbolischen ‚starken Mann', der° Deutschland retten soll. Die Opposition sehen Sie noch auf diesem Plakat von 1931, wo starke Arme versuchen, das Hakenkreuz° der Nazis zu zerreißen°."

Eine Studentin stellte eine Frage: „Ist denn Hitler nicht illegal an die Macht gekommen°?"

45 „Eigentlich nicht", antwortete der Museumsdirektor. „Nachdem die Wähler den Nazis die meisten Stimmen° gegeben hatten, musste man Hitler zum Reichskanzler ernennen°. Erst als er Kanzler geworden war, konnte er mit terroristischen Methoden die Republik in eine Diktatur verwandeln°. Deutschland ist also ein gutes Beispiel für die Zerstörung einer schwachen Demokratie durch wirtschaftliche Not° und politi-

50 schen Extremismus."

stock market / crashed / economic crisis / **mehr als** = more than	
danger	
back then	
especially	
strangles	*steigen = climbs*
strongest	*used*
who	*rescue*
swastika / rip apart	
an … = came to power *Actually*	
(*here*) votes	
zum … = appoint chancellor	
in … = transform into a dictatorship / **wirtschaftliche Not** = economic hardship	

destruction   *weak*

1. The conservative Center Party, consisting mainly of Catholic voters.
2. The name of the German Parliament until 1945, now called **der Bundestag**. The parliament building in Berlin is still called the **Reichstag**.

Nach dem Lesen

■ A ■ Antworten Sie auf Deutsch.

1. Warum besuchte die Studentengruppe das Museum?
2. Aus welcher Zeit waren die Plakate dieser Ausstellung?
3. Wer führte die Gruppe durch die Ausstellung?
4. Was für Plakate haben die Studenten im Museum gesehen?
5. Warum hieß der deutsche Staat damals die „Weimarer" Republik?
6. Wie war die Situation in Deutschland nach dem Ersten Weltkrieg? Beschreiben Sie die Probleme.
7. Warum war die junge Demokratie in Gefahr?
8. Wann wurde Hitler Reichskanzler?
9. Wie ist er an die Macht gekommen?

Lab Manual Kap. 10, Diktat.

Workbook Kap. 10, Üb. I–O.

■ B ■ Gruppendiskussion: Bilder erzählen Geschichte. Im Lesestück finden Sie fünf politische Plakate aus der Weimarer Republik. Besprechen Sie diese historischen Bilder.

1. Lesen Sie den Text auf dem Plakat vor. *read aloud*
2. Beschreiben Sie das Bild so ausführlich (*completely*) wie möglich.
3. Interpretieren Sie die Bilder: Was symbolisiert z.B. der Adler auf dem ersten Plakat? die Hand auf dem zweiten? die Kette auf dem letzten? usw.

Situationen aus dem Alltag

This vocabulary focuses on an everyday topic or situation. Words you already know from **Wortschatz** sections are listed without English equivalents; new supplementary vocabulary is listed with definitions. Your instructor may assign some supplementary vocabulary for active mastery.

■ Die Politik

In dem Lesestück haben Sie nicht nur etwas über Geschichte, sondern auch etwas über Politik gelernt. Was hat denn diese politische Diskussion mit unserem Leben zu tun? Wir sind alle politische Menschen und die Politik spielt eine Rolle in unserem Alltag, ob wir es wollen oder nicht.

Spielen wir jetzt ein bisschen mit der Sprache und den Bildern der Politik. Zuerst einige Wörter (viele sind Ihnen schon bekannt):

Politik also means *policy*: **Außenpolitik** (*foreign policy*), **Energiepolitik**, **Umweltpolitik** usw.

die **Freiheit**
der **Frieden** *peace*
der **Krieg, -e**
die **Politik**
der **Politiker**/die **Politikerin**
die **Regierung, -en**   *government in power, administration*

der **Staat, -en**
die **Umwelt**
das **Volk, ¨er**
die **Wahl, -en**   *Vote*
wählen
der **Wähler, -**

■ **A** ■   **Gruppenarbeit: Wir sind politisch aktiv (*in kleinen Gruppen*)**   Gründen
Sie (*found*) eine neue politische Partei.

Der Name unserer Partei: _____
Unser Parteiprogramm:
    Wir sind für _____ , _____ usw.
    Wir sind gegen _____ , _____ usw.
Wir sehen viele Probleme in der modernen Welt:
_____
Unsere Lösungen sind:
_____
Unsere Parole (*slogan*) für die Wahlen:
_____

■ **B** ■   **Gruppenarbeit**   Ihre politische Partei braucht auch ein Symbol für ihr
Wahlplakat. Wie Sie gerade gelesen haben, waren Tiere wichtige Symbole auf den   *animals*
Plakaten in der Weimarer Republik. Sie können ein Tier als Symbol Ihrer Partei
wählen, denn Tiere können Ideen symbolisieren.

der Adler, -	*eagle*
der Bär, -en, -en	*bear*
der Elefant, -en, -en	*elephant*
der Esel, -	*donkey*
der Fuchs, ¨e	*fox*
der Löwe, -n, -n	*lion*
die Schlange, -n	*snake*
die Taube, -n	*dove*

■ **C** ■   **Gruppenarbeit: Wahlkampagne**   (Election campaign)   Jetzt zeigen Sie
den anderen Studenten Ihr Wahlplakat. Erklären Sie, warum man Ihre Partei wählen
soll. Die „Wähler" können natürlich Fragen stellen oder kritisieren.

Unser Plakat zeigt ...
Wählt unsere Partei, weil ...

■ **D** ■   **Gruppenarbeit: Zur Diskussion**   Ist es wichtig für Politiker die
Geschichte ihres Landes zu kennen? Was meinen Sie?

View Module 5 of the ***Neue Horizonte*** video (18:18) and do the activities in
Videoecke 5 in your Workbook/Laboratory Manual/Video Manual.

German Politics and the European Union

On December 2, 1990, with the addition of the five new **Länder** (*states*) from the former German Democratic Republic, a united Germany held its first free elections in fifty-eight years. The last had been in November 1932, just before Hitler's seizure of dictatorial powers. In order to prevent the profusion of small parties that had weakened the Reichstag during the Weimar Republic, the framers of the post-war **Grundgesetz** (*Basic Law* or constitution of the Federal Republic of Germany) in 1949 added a requirement that a party must receive at least 5% of the popular vote to be represented in the **Bundestag** (*Federal Parliament*). This provision has effectively excluded small extremist parties of both the Right and the Left.

Stimmzettel

für die Wahl zum Deutschen Bundestag im Wahlkreis 63 Bonn

am ....

Sie haben 2 Stimmen

hier 1 Stimme
für die Wahl
eines/einer Wahlkreis-
abgeordneten

hier 1 Stimme
für die Wahl
einer Landesliste (Partei)
- maßgebende Stimme für die Verteilung der
Sitze insgesamt auf die einzelnen Parteien -

Erststimme

1 **Schmitz,** Mathias
Werkmeister   **CDU**   Christlich Demokratische Union Deutschlands
Bonn,
Hohe Str. 30 ◯

2 **Kolven,** Franz
Studienrat   **SPD**   Sozialdemokratische Partei Deutschlands
Bonn,
Aachener Str. 29 ◯

3 **Dr. Jansen,** Hildegard
Ärztin   **F.D.P.**   Freie Demokratische Partei
Bonn,
Wiener Platz 15 ◯

4 **Anger,** Martin
Kaufmann   **GRÜNE**   DIE GRÜNEN
Bonn,
Römerstr. 209 ◯

5 **Müller,** Dietrich
Journalist   **DKP**   Deutsche Kommunistische Partei
Bonn-Beuel,
Rheinstr. 63 ◯

7 **Linzbach,** Josef
Bundesbeamter   Wählergruppe Linzbach
Bonn,
Neumarkt 15 ◯

Zweitstimme

1 ◯ **CDU** Christlich Demokratische Union Deutschlands
Karl Minzenbach, Ute Krings, Paul Lammerich, Heinz Mewisson, Dr. Kurt Küppers

2 ◯ **SPD** Sozialdemokratische Partei Deutschlands
Hans Schmitz, Brigitte Nolden, Fritz Bilgenbach, Udo Walbröhl, Max Palm

3 ◯ **F.D.P.** Freie Demokratische Partei
Bruno Meurer, Ernst Merten, Herbert Nettekoven, Renate Rottgen, Gustav Schlosser

4 ◯ **GRÜNE** DIE GRÜNEN
Manfred Bauer, Inge Böcker, Willi Geyer, Käthe Köhler, Axel Winter

5 ◯ **DKP** Deutsche Kommunistische Partei
Peter Adam, Ursula Bartsch, Rudolf Hoffmann, Arthur Schulz, Alfred Sommer

6 ◯ **NPD** Nationaldemokratische Partei Deutschlands
Jürgen Frank, Martina Gross, Otto Kraft, Alfons Sturm, Klaus Weber

11 States in WG
5   EG

The **CDU** (**Christlich-Demokratische Union**), with its Bavarian sister party the **CSU** (**Christlich-Soziale Union**), form the conservative end of the German political spectrum and have consistently received 45–50% of the popular vote. The **SPD** (**Sozialdemokratische Partei Deutschlands**) is the oldest party in the **Bundestag**, with a history stretching back to the beginnings of socialism in the 19th century. Today's SPD is dedicated to the welfare state, with only a minority supporting a program of more radical socialism. It traditionally receives 35–45% of the popular vote from industrial workers, students, and young professionals.

The small, liberal **FDP** (**Freie Demokratische Partei**) has had an influence out of proportion to its size because the larger parties need it as a coalition partner to achieve a majority in the **Bundestag**. The environmental and anti-nuclear party known as the Greens (**Die Grünen**) first won parliamentary representation in 1983 and has forced the traditional parties to adopt more environmentally-conscious platforms. The **PDS** (**Partei des Demokratischen Sozialismus**), successor to the former East German Communist Party, draws its votes largely from East Germans dissatisfied with the unemployment and social dislocations brought about by unification and integration into a free market economy.

Since the end of World War Two, the central concern of German foreign policy has been to insure Germany's integration into a peaceful Europe. The rabid nationalism that led to two disastrous wars in the first half of the 20th century was replaced by a firm commitment to European unity. France and Germany, archenemies since the 19th century, formed a coal and steel cooperative in 1950 that gradually grew into today's European Union. The 1992 Treaty of Maastricht commits the Union's 13 member nations to a central banking system and a common currency (the Euro) by the year 2000 and to increased political coordination, especially in the areas of foreign policy and security.

Germans have been more divided in their attitude toward their Eastern European neighbors, but since the early 1970s, the major parties of both the Right and the Left have recognized the need for increasing contact and dialogue with the East. Since the break-up of the Soviet Union in the late 1980s, many of its former satellite states are eager to apply for membership in both the European Union and NATO. Because of its history of division between West and East, its central location, and its strong economy, Germany will continue to play a leading role in the unification of Europe.

Wahlplakat in München

Deutschland nach der Mauer

Communicative Goals

- Learning the parts of the body
- Describing morning routines
- Designating nationalities and saying where people are from

Cultural Goal

- Understanding Germany's role in Europe today

Chapter Outline

- **Lyrik zum Vorlesen**
  Hoffmann von Fallersleben, „Das Lied der Deutschen"

- **Grammatik**
  Reflexive verbs
  Dative pronouns with clothing and parts of the body
  Adjectives and pronouns of indefinite number: *einige, mehrere,* etc.
  Adjectival nouns
  More on *bei*
  Designating decades: The 90s, etc.

- **Lesestück**
  Deutschland im europäischen Haus

- **Situationen aus dem Alltag**
  Morgens nach dem Aufstehen

- **Almanach**
  Zeittafel, 1939–heute

Dialoge

Lab Manual Kap. 11, Dialoge, Fragen, Hören Sie gut zu!

Das Brandenburger Tor: The Brandenburg Gate is a triumphal arch built in the late 18th century. From 1961–1989 the Berlin Wall ran just west of it.

die neuen Bundesländer: The 5 new federal States created, after unification, from the former German Democratic Republic: Sachsen-Anhalt, Mecklenburg-Vorpommern, Sachsen, Thüringen, Brandenburg. More information on unification is found in the **Lesestück** in this chapter. See also map of Germany inside the front cover.

Am Brandenburger Tor **aus den USA**: Note dative plural.

Helen aus den USA war 1989 in Berlin. Jetzt ist sie wieder in Berlin, um ihre Bekannte Anke zu besuchen. Zusammen stehen sie am Brandenburger Tor.

ANKE: Weißt du noch, wie es am 9. November 1989 hier an der Mauer aussah?
HELEN: Als die DDR die Grenze öffnete? Das vergess' ich nie!
ANKE: Die Menschen haben sich so gefreut, sogar die Polizeibeamten waren *even, in fact* freundlich! *enthusiasm*
HELEN: Du, von dieser Begeisterung merkt man aber heute nichts mehr. Man hört fast nur, wie schwierig und teuer die Vereinigung ist.
ANKE: Es stimmt: Deutschland ist wieder *ein* Land, aber es gibt noch starke Unterschiede zwischen den alten und den neuen Bundesländern. *differences* *federal states*

Ein Unfall: Stefan bricht sich das Bein

23.00 Uhr. Stefans Vater liegt schon im Bett. Seine Mutter spricht am Telefon. Plötzlich läuft sie ins Schlafzimmer.

MUTTER: Markus, zieh dich schnell an und komm mit! Etwas Schlimmes ist passiert!
VATER: Was ist denn los?
MUTTER: Stefan hat sich beim Radfahren verletzt! Ich fürchte, er hat sich das Bein gebrochen. *get hurt*
VATER: Um Gottes Willen! Beeilen wir uns!

Anna besucht Stefan im Krankenhaus

ANNA: Wie geht's dir denn, du Armer?
STEFAN: Hallo Anna! Schön, dass du gekommen bist.
ANNA: Fühlst du dich heute besser oder tut dir das Bein noch weh?
STEFAN: Ach, es geht. Ich kann mich schon selber waschen, aber ich darf noch nicht aufstehen.
ANNA: Schade! Schau mal, ich habe dir Schokolade und Blumen mitgebracht.
STEFAN: Oh, die sind hübsch! Danke, das ist aber lieb von dir!
ANNA: Nichts zu danken! Gute Besserung!

Gute Besserung

Note on Usage: **The definite article as pronoun**

In colloquial spoken German, the definite article can replace the personal pronoun. This is somewhat more emphatic than the personal pronoun and usually comes at the beginning of the sentence.

Die (= sie) sind hübsch! *Those are pretty.*

■ Wortschatz 1

Verben

sich[1] etwas an·sehen (sieht an), sah an, hat angesehen to take a look at something

sich an·ziehen, zog an, hat angezogen to get dressed

sich beeilen to hurry

brechen (bricht), brach, hat gebrochen to break

sich erkälten to catch a cold

sich freuen to be happy

sich fühlen to feel (*intrans.*)

fürchten to fear

sich etwas leisten können to be able to afford something

Das kann ich mir nicht leisten. I can't afford that.

merken to notice

öffnen to open

schauen to look

schneiden, schnitt, hat geschnitten to cut

sich setzen to sit down

sich verletzen to injure oneself, get hurt

sich verspäten to be late

sich etwas vor·stellen to imagine something

waschen (wäscht), wusch, hat gewaschen to wash

wehtun, tat weh, hat wehgetan (+ *dat. of person*) to hurt

Das tut (mir) weh. That hurts (me).

Compare: **Das tut mir weh** (*That hurts me*) with **Es tut mir Leid** (*I'm sorry*).

Substantive

der **Arzt, ¨e** doctor (*m.*)

der **Beamte, -n** (*adj. noun*) official, civil servant (*m.*)

der/die[2] **Bekannte, -n** (*adj. noun*) acquaintance, friend

der **Finger, -** finger

der **Kopf, ¨e** head

der **Mund, ¨er** mouth

der **Unterschied, -e** difference

der/die **Verwandte, -n** (*adj. noun*) relative

der **Zahn, ¨e** tooth

das **Auge, -n** eye

das **Bein, -e** leg

das **Bundesland, ¨er** federal state (*in Germany and Austria*)

das **Gesicht, -er** face

das **Krankenhaus, ¨er** hospital

das **Licht, -er** light

das **Ohr, -en** ear

das **Schlafzimmer, -** bedroom

das **Tor, -e** gate

die **Ärztin, -nen** doctor (*f.*)

die **Beamtin, -nen** official, civil servant (*f.*)

die **Begeisterung** enthusiasm

die **Blume, -n** flower

die **Deutsche Demokratische Republik (DDR)** the German Democratic Republic (GDR)

die **Grenze, -n** border

die **Mauer, -n** (*freestanding or outside*) wall

---

1. **Sich** is a reflexive pronoun. This will be explained on pp. 271–272.
2. Inclusion of both masculine and feminine articles indicates that this is an adjectival noun. See p. 280.

At the Brandenburg Gate

Helen from the USA was in Berlin in 1989. Now she's in Berlin again to visit her friend Anke. They're standing together at the Brandenburg Gate.

A: Do you remember what it looked like here at the Wall on November 9, 1989?

H: When the GDR opened the border? I'll never forget it!

A: People were so happy, even the police officers were friendly.

H: You know, these days you don't see that enthusiasm anymore. Almost all you hear is how difficult and expensive unification is.

A: You're right: Germany is one country again, but there are still great differences between the old and the new *Bundesländer*.

An Accident: Stefan Breaks His Leg

11:00 P.M. Stefan's father is already in bed. His mother is talking on the telephone. Suddenly she runs into the bedroom.

M: Markus, get dressed quickly and come along! Something bad has happened.

F: What's wrong?

M: Stefan hurt himself riding his bike! I'm afraid he's broken his leg.

F: For heaven's sake! Let's hurry!

Anna Visits Stefan in the Hospital

A: How are you, you poor guy?

S: Hi, Anna! Nice of you to come.

A: Do you feel better today or does your leg still hurt?

S: Oh, it's all right. I can wash myself already, but they won't let me get up yet.

A: Too bad. Look, I've brought you chocolate and flowers.

S: Oh, those are pretty. Thanks, that's really nice of you!

A: Don't mention it. Get well soon!

die **Polizei** (*sing. only*) police
die **Schokolade** chocolate
die **Vereinigung** unification

Contrast **die Mauer** (*free-standing wall*) with **die Wand** (*interior wall*). The two words tell the cultural story of Roman innovations in building techniques. **Mauer** (from the Latin *murus*) was made of stone and capable of having windows (**Fenster** from Latin *fenestra*), whereas the Germanic **Wand** is related to the verb **winden**, and described a wall of woven twigs.

Adjektive und Adverbien

ander- other, different
genau exact, precise
hübsch pretty, handsome
mehrere several, a few
wenige few

Andere Vokabel

sich (*third-person reflexive pronoun, see pp. 313–314*)

Nützliche Ausdrücke

Gute Besserung! Get well soon!
schade too bad
  Das ist schade! That's a shame! Too bad! What a pity!
Schau mal. Look. Look here.
Weißt du noch? Do you remember?

Gegensätze

sich anziehen ≠ **sich ausziehen**
  to get dressed ≠ to get undressed

Mit anderen Worten

schnell machen (*colloq.*) = **sich beeilen**

Variationen

■ **A** ■ Persönliche Fragen

1. Helen besucht ihre Bekannte in Berlin. Haben Sie Bekannte oder Verwandte im Ausland? Wo leben sie? Haben Sie sie schon einmal besucht? *every when = überall*

2. Helen sagt, sie vergisst den 9. November 1989 nie. Gibt es einen Tag, den Sie nie vergessen können? Was ist an diesem Tag passiert?

3. Stefan hatte einen Unfall beim Radfahren. Haben Sie je einen Unfall gehabt? Mit dem Rad oder dem Auto?

4. Er hat sich verletzt. Ist Ihnen so was als Kind passiert? Wenn ja, wie?

5. Sind Sie je im Krankenhaus gewesen? Warum? Haben Ihnen Ihre Freunde etwas mitgebracht? Was denn?

6. Anna bringt Stefan Schokolade und Blumen mit. Was bringen Sie mir, wenn ich im Krankenhaus bin?

■ **B** ■ Übung: Ich habe etwas Interessantes gemacht!   Choose from the list of adjectives below to characterize something you have done. Then say what it was you did.

BEISPIEL: A: Ich habe einmal etwas _____-es gemacht.
          B: Wieso? Was hast du denn gemacht?
          A: Ich habe (*oder* bin) _____ .

blöd *stupid*	toll *great, terrific*	wahnsinnig *incredibly*	intelligent
interessant	gefährlich	neu	furchtbar *terrible*
wunderbar	schwierig *difficult*	langweilig	schlimm *bad*
	dangerous		

■ C ■   Partnerarbeit: Wie geht's denn weiter?   Take these two lines from the second dialogue and compose your own continuation. Then perform your dialogue for the class.

A: Zieh dich schnell an und komm mit!
B: Was ist denn los?
A: _____
B: _____
A: _____
B: _____

Lyrik zum Vorlesen

The famous "Lied der Deutschen," also known as the "Deutschlandlied," is one of the most fervently nationalistic—and controversial—political songs ever composed. Although the first stanza is commonly associated with German military expansionism, the author was, ironically, an opponent of repressive government. His anti-authoritarian sentiments cost him his post as professor at the University of Breslau. The text proclaims abstract concepts ("unity, law, freedom") and calls for a unification of all German-speaking territories into one state. The idealistic dreams of unity were appropriate for Hoffmann's generation, which had survived the ravages of the Napoleonic Wars and was frustrated by the division of Germany into many small states.

Hoffmann wrote the text in 1841 to a favorite popular tune by Joseph Haydn in praise of the Austrian Emperor, "Gott erhalte Franz den Kaiser" (*God Preserve Kaiser Franz*, [1797]). Haydn also used this melody in his magnificent *Kaiserquartett* (Opus 76, No. 3, second movement). The song did not become the German national anthem until 1922, when it was chosen by the young Weimar Republic. In 1945 it was banned by the allied military government. In 1952, when no satisfactory substitute could be found, the third stanza alone became the national anthem of the Federal Republic of Germany.

Lab Manual Kap. 11, Lyrik zum Vorlesen.

die Maas = the Meuse River (Belgium); **die Memel** = the Nemunas River in Lithuania; **die Etsch** = the Adige River in South Tirol (Italy); **der Belt** = strait between two Danish islands in the Baltic Sea.

Das Lied der Deutschen

Deutschland, Deutschland über alles,
Über alles in der Welt,
Wenn es stets° zu Schutz und Trutze°
Brüderlich zusammenhält;
Von der Maas bis an die Memel,
Von der Etsch bis an den Belt:
Deutschland, Deutschland über alles,
Über alles in der Welt!

= **immer** / **Schutz ...** = protection and defiance

Deutsche Frauen, deutsche Treue°,
Deutscher Wein und deutscher Sang°
Sollen in der Welt erhalten°
Ihren alten, schönen Klang°,
Uns zu edler Tat begeistern°
Unser ganzes Leben lang:
Deutsche Frauen, deutsche Treue,
Deutscher Wein und deutscher Sang!

loyalty
song
preserve
sound
Uns ... begeistern = inspire us to noble deeds

Berlin, Potsdamer Platz: größte Baustelle (*construction site*) der Welt

Einigkeit° und Recht° und Freiheit	unity / justice
Für das deutsche Vaterland!	
Danach lasst uns alle streben°	**lasst ...** = let us strive
Brüderlich mit Herz und Hand!	
Einigkeit und Recht und Freiheit	
Sind des Glückes Unterpfand°:	**des ...** = guarantees of happiness
Blüh° im Glanze° dieses Glückes,	flourish / glow
Blühe, deutsches Vaterland!	

August Heinrich Hoffmann von Fallersleben (1798–1874)

Grammatik

Reflexive verbs

■ Reflexive verbs and pronouns

In most sentences with objects, the subject and the object are two different people or things.

> subj.   obj.
> **Ich** habe **ihn** verletzt.   *I injured **him**.*

Sometimes, however, a verb's subject and object are the *same* person or thing. The verb is then called *reflexive*. The object of a *reflexive verb* is always a pronoun called a *reflexive pronoun*.

> subj.   obj.
> **Ich** habe **mich** verletzt.   *I hurt **myself**.*

Reflexive pronouns in English end in -self or -selves, e.g., *myself, himself, herself, themselves*. German has both accusative and dative reflexive pronouns. Reflexive pronouns are identical to personal pronouns except in the third person and the formal second person, where the reflexive pronoun is **sich**.

Reflexive Pronouns		
	accusative	dative
ich	**mich**	**mir**
du	**dich**	**dir**
er, es, sie	sich	sich
wir	uns	uns
ihr	euch	euch
sie, Sie	sich	sich

Note on spelling: **sich** is not capitalized when used with the polite **Sie: Fühlen Sie sich heute besser?**

In the plural, the reflexive pronouns often denote reciprocity and are the equivalent of English *each other*.

Wir treffen **uns** morgen.	*We'll meet **each other** tomorrow.*
Kennt ihr **euch**?	*Do you know **each other**?*
Sie kennen **sich** seit langem.	*They've known **each other** for a long time.*
Wir verstehen **uns** gut.	*We understand **each other** well.*
	(= We're on the same wavelength.)

Note on Usage: *einander* (each other)

Plural reflexive pronouns used reciprocally may be replaced by the reciprocal pronoun **einander** (*each other*).

Kennt ihr **euch**? = Kennt ihr **einander**?

Remember that **einander** can also combine with prepositions.

miteinander	*with each other*
zueinander	*to each other*

■ Verbs with accusative reflexive pronouns

A transitive verb is a verb that takes a direct object (e.g., **sehen**, **tragen**, **verletzen**). An intransitive verb cannot take a direct object (e.g., **sein**, **werden**, **schlafen**).

Any transitive verb may be used reflexively. Here is a sample conjugation using **sich verletzen**.

Ich habe **mich** verletzt.	*I hurt **myself**.*
Du hast **dich** verletzt.	*You hurt **yourself**.*
Sie hat **sich** verletzt.	*She hurt **herself**.*
Wir haben **uns** verletzt.	*We hurt **ourselves**.*
Ihr habt **euch** verletzt.	*You hurt **yourselves**.*
Sie haben **sich** verletzt.	*They hurt **themselves**. (You hurt yourself / yourselves.)*

■ **1** ■ **Übung: Wer hat sich verletzt?** Die ganze Klasse war im Bus, als der Busfahrer einen kleinen Unfall hatte. Sagen Sie, wer sich verletzt hat.

BEISPIEL: Ich habe mich verletzt.

Note on Usage: *selber* and *selbst* as intensifiers

The words **selber** and **selbst** are often used to intensify or emphasize a reflexive pronoun:

Soll ich das Kind waschen?	*Should I wash the child?*
Nein, sie kann sich **selber** waschen.	*No, she can wash herself.*

■ **2** ■ **Übung: Er kennt nur sich selbst.** Answer these questions by saying that the person knows, sees, etc. only him- or herself.

BEISPIEL: <u>Wen</u> kennt er denn?   *whom?*
            Er kennt nur sich selbst.

1. Wen sieht sie denn?   *sich*
2. Wen versteht er denn?   *sich*
3. Wen lieben Sie denn?   *sich*
4. Wen brauche ich denn?

5. Wen haben Sie denn <u>verletzt</u>?   *hurt*
6. Wen hat er <u>geärgert</u>?   *annoy*
7. Wen haben sie <u>gerettet</u>?   *rescue*

Proverb: **Liebe dich selbst, so hast du keine Rivalen.**

■ **3** ■ **Partnerarbeit: Wir verstehen uns.** Use each of the verbs below in the following routine:

BEISPIEL: A: *Verstehst* du mich?
              B: Ja, ich verstehe dich. Verstehst du mich?
              A: Ja, ich verstehe dich auch.
        A & B: Wir verstehen uns! (Wir verstehen einander!)

verstehen	brauchen	morgen <u>treffen</u> *meet*
sehen	kennen	am Wochenende besuchen

■ **German reflexive verbs that are not reflexive in English**

Many German reflexive verbs are not reflexive in English. Their English equivalents often use *get*. Here are some examples.

sich anziehen	*to get dressed*
sich waschen	*to get washed*
sich setzen	*to sit down*

zog an/anziehen

Sie wäscht **sich**.	*She's getting washed.*
Er zog **sich** an.	*He got dressed.*
Bitte, setzen Sie **sich**.	*Please sit down.* (literally: *Please seat yourselves.*)

Täglich sich waschen

■ **4** ■ **Übung: Bitte, setzen Sie sich!** Your instructor will tell you to stand up or sit down. Then say what you have done.

BEISPIEL: A: Bitte stehen Sie auf!
          B: (*Student/in steht auf.*) Ich bin aufgestanden.
          A: Bitte setzen Sie sich.
          B: (*Student/in setzt sich.*) Ich habe mich gesetzt.

■ Verbs requiring the accusative reflexive

Verbs like **anziehen** and **waschen** may be used either reflexively (**ich wasche mich**) or nonreflexively (**ich wasche den Wagen**). Some German verbs, however, must *always* be used with an accusative reflexive pronoun. Their English equivalents are *not* reflexive.

An analogous English verb is *to enjoy oneself. I enjoyed myself at the party* means I enjoyed the *party*, not literally *myself.* German: **sich amüsieren.**

 **Lab Manual** Kap. 11, Var. zur Üb. 5.

sich beeilen	*to hurry*	**sich fühlen**	*to feel*
sich erkälten	*to catch cold*	**sich verspäten**	*to be late*
sich freuen	*to be happy*		

■ 5 ■ **Gruppenarbeit: Wann freust du dich besonders? (3 oder 4 Personen)**

especially

Alle müssen sagen, wann sie sich besonders freuen. Die Bilder geben Ihnen einige Ideen, aber Sie dürfen auch frei antworten.

BEISPIEL: Ich freue mich, wenn die Sonne scheint. Wann freust du dich?

das Geschenk   *Tennis treiben*

■ 6 ■ **Gruppenarbeit: Warum musst du dich beeilen?**   Jetzt sind Sie alle in Eile. Sagen Sie einander warum.

BEISPIEL: Ich muss mich beeilen, weil ich zur Uni muss. Warum musst du dich beeilen?

der Zug nehmen

■ 7 ■ **Gruppenarbeit: Warum hast du dich verspätet?**   Jeder verspätet sich manchmal. Erzählen Sie der Klasse, warum Sie sich einmal verspätet haben. Unten sind einige Möglichkeiten, aber Sie dürfen auch frei antworten.

BEISPIEL: Ich habe mich einmal verspätet, weil ...

krank sein	Fahrrad kaputt
spät aufstehen	die Deutschstunde vergessen
sich verletzen *hurt*	die Uhr verlieren *watch lost*
einen Unfall haben	einen Freund im Krankenhaus besuchen

■ Verbs with dative reflexive pronouns

Verbs with dative objects   Verbs such as **helfen** that require a dative object take a dative reflexive pronoun when they are used reflexively.

Ich kann **mir selber** helfen.   *I can help **myself**.*

Reflexive indirect object   The subject and *indirect* object of a verb can be the same person. In this case the indirect object is a *dative* reflexive pronoun.

Ich kaufe **mir** Blumen.	*I'm buying **myself** flowers.*
Du kaufst **dir** Blumen.	*You're buying **yourself** flowers.*
Sie kaufen **sich** Blumen.	
Er kauft **sich** Blumen.	*He's buying **himself** flowers.*
Wir kaufen **uns** Blumen.	*We're buying **ourselves** flowers.*
Ihr kauft **euch** Blumen.	*You're buying **yourselves** flowers.*
Sie kaufen **sich** Blumen.	
Sie kaufen **sich** Blumen.	*They're buying **themselves** flowers.*

The dative reflexive makes explicit the fact that the subject is the beneficiary of its own action. It may be omitted without changing the basic meaning of the sentence.

Ich kaufe mir eine Jacke.	*I'm buying myself a jacket.*
Ich kaufe eine Jacke.	*I'm buying a jacket.*

Lab Manual Kap. 11, Var. zur Üb. 8.

■ 8 ■   **Übung: Einkaufsbummel**   Jetzt gehen wir zusammen einkaufen. Jeder hat DM 200 und darf sich etwas kaufen. Erzählen Sie den anderen, was Sie sich kaufen. Die Bilder geben Ihnen einige Ideen, aber Sie dürfen sich natürlich auch andere Sachen kaufen.

> **BEISPIEL:**   A: Was kaufen Sie sich, Robert?
> B: Ich kaufe mir ein neues Hemd und eine Zeitung.

■ Verbs requiring the dative reflexive

There are some German verbs that must *always* be used with the dative reflexive pronoun. They all require a *direct object* (in the accusative) as well. Their English equivalents are *not* reflexive.

German: dative reflexive	*English: not reflexive*
sich etwas ansehen	*to take a look at, look over*
Ich wollte **mir** den Wagen ansehen.	*I wanted to take a look at the car.*
sich etwas leisten können	*to be able to afford*
Kannst du **dir** ein neues Fahrrad leisten?	*Can you afford a new bicycle?*
sich etwas vorstellen	*to imagine*
Das kann ich **mir** nicht vorstellen.	*I can't imagine that.*

Since the pronoun **sich** is both accusative and dative, how do you know which it should be with any particular reflexive verb? When a **Wortschatz** entry in this book includes the direct object **etwas**, it indicates that the reflexive pronoun is dative. If you look up **ansehen**, for example, you find **sich etwas ansehen**. This tells you that **etwas** is accusative and **sich** is dative. Any noun or pronoun in the accusative can replace **etwas**.

A parallel English structure is *to cook oneself something* (**sich etwas kochen**). I'm cooking myself (*ind. obj.*) an egg (*dir. obj.*). = **Ich koche mir ein Ei.**

sich (*dative*) **etwas** (*accusative*) ansehen

Ich möchte **mir** das **Auto** ansehen.

to be able to afford

■9■ Kettenreaktion: Die armen Studenten Wie alle Studenten haben Sie nie genug Geld. Sagen Sie, was Sie sich nicht leisten können und dann fragen Sie weiter.

> BEISPIEL: A: Ich kann mir keine Europareise leisten. Was kannst du dir nicht leisten?
> B: Ich kann mir ...

Lab Manual Kap. 11, Var. zur Üb. 10.

■10■ Partnerarbeit: Was wollen wir uns heute nachmittag ansehen? Sehen Sie sich den Stadtplan auf Seite 237 an. Sie verbringen den Nachmittag zusammen in dieser Stadt. Sagen Sie einander, was Sie sich ansehen möchten.

> BEISPIEL: A: Ich möchte mir den Dom und _____ ansehen. Und du?
> B: Ich möchte mir lieber _____ ansehen.

Dative pronouns with clothing and parts of the body

Learning the parts of the body is a communicative goal.

Unlike English, German does not usually use possessive forms with parts of the body, or with articles of clothing when they are being put on or taken off. German uses the personal dative instead.

Note that plural **die Haare** is more common than singular: **Sie hat dunkle Haare.**

Die Mutter wäscht **dem Kind** die Hände.	*The mother washes **the child's** hands.*
Meine Freundin schneidet **mir** die Haare.	*My girlfriend cuts **my** hair.*
Sie zog **ihm** den Mantel an.	*She put the coat on **him**.*

If the subject is performing the action on itself, the dative pronoun is of course *reflexive.*

Ich habe **mir** die Hände gewaschen.	*I washed **my** hands.*
Sie zog **sich** den Mantel an.	*She put on **her** coat.*
Ich schneide **mir** selber die Haare.	*I cut **my** hair myself.*
Stefan hat **sich** das Bein gebrochen.	*Stefan broke **his** leg.*

Workbook Kap. 11, A–E.

■ 11 ■ **Übung: Körperteile**   Review your knowledge of parts of the body by identifying them in the picture below.

Rätsel (Riddle)
Was ist das? Hat Arme, aber keine Hände, läuft und hat doch keine Füße. — *flows — der Rhein*

die **Katze, -n**   *cat*   der **Hund, -e**   *dog*

AUCH FÜSSE HABEN GEFÜHLE

feelings

Lab Manual Kap. 11, Var. zur Üb. 12.

■ **12** ■ **Übung: Wo tut es Ihnen weh?** Stefan tut das Bein noch ein bisschen weh. Wo tut es Ihnen weh?

> **BEISPIEL:** Wo tut es Ihnen weh?
> Mir tut der Kopf weh. *mir tun die Augen weh.*

■ **13** ■ **Übung** Sagen Sie Ihrem Professor, **wann** Sie sich heute angezogen haben, und dann, **was** Sie sich angezogen haben.

> **BEISPIEL:** A: Um wie viel Uhr haben Sie sich heute angezogen?   *ausgezrhvrtak 4!*
> B: Ich habe mich um halb acht angezogen.
> A: Was haben Sie sich angezogen?
> B: Ich habe mir *Pulli* , *Hose* und *Jacke* angezogen.

Ich ziehe **mich an**. = *I'm getting dressed.*
Ich ziehe **mir** ein Hemd an. = *I'm putting on a shirt.*

Adjectives and pronouns of indefinite number

You have already learned as individual vocabulary words a group of adjectives used with plural nouns to indicate indefinite amounts.

wenige	*few*
einige	*some*
mehrere	*several*
andere	*other(s)*
viele	*many*

These adjectives are *not* limiting words. They are treated just like descriptive adjectives: when not preceded by a limiting word, they take *primary* endings.

For **limiting words**, see p. 221; for **primary and secondary endings**, see p. 222.

> **Andere** Leute waren da. — *Other people were there.*
> Ich habe **viele** Freunde in Bonn. — *I have a lot of friends in Bonn.*

When a limiting word precedes them, they take *secondary* endings.

> **Die anderen** Leute waren da. — *The other people were there.*
> **Meine vielen** Freunde schreiben mir oft. — *My many friends often write to me.*

Remember that descriptive adjectives following the adjective of indefinite number *always* have the *same* ending as the adjective of indefinite number.

> Ander**e** jung**e** Leute waren da. — *Other young people were there.*
> Die ander**en** jung**en** Leute waren da. — *The other young people were there.*

■14■ **Gruppenarbeit: Viele oder wenige?** Choose a word from each column and state your opinion about a group of people. Begin with **Ich würde sagen, ...** *would say*

BEISPIEL: Ich würde sagen, viele sportliche Frauen sind gesund.

A	B	C	D
viele	jung	Menschen	Sport treiben
wenige	sportlich	Amerikaner	gesund sein
	reich	Professoren	Müll recyclen *der Müll*
	arm	Studenten	glücklich sein
	stark	Frauen	Deutsch sprechen
	nice sympathisch	Männer	gut verdienen *earn*
	verrückt *crazy*	Eltern	gern trampen
	kreativ		

Lab Manual Kap. 11, Var.
zur Üb. 15.

Workbook Kap. 11, F.

limiting word

■15■ **Übung** Supply the correct adjective endings.

1. Darf ich mir einig_e_ schön_e_ Postkarten ansehen?
2. Sie hat schon mehrer_er_ deutsch_er_ Bücher gelesen. *several*
3. Viel_e_ jung_e_ amerikanisch_e_ Schüler verstehen das nicht.
4. Haben Sie auch die ander_en_ neu_en_ Arbeiter kennen gelernt?
5. Ich habe mit viel_en_ interessant_en_ Menschen gesprochen. *dative*
6. Deine viel_en_ neu_en_ Ideen gefallen mir sehr.
7. Das sind die Probleme der ander_en_ jung_en_ Journalisten. *genitive pl.*
8. Ich kenne einig_e_ gut_e_ Restaurants in Hamburg.

■ **Indefinite pronouns**

When these words are not followed by nouns, they function as indefinite pronouns referring to human beings:

Viele sagen das.	*Many (people) say that.*
Einige gehen ins Kino, **andere** ins Theater.	*Some (people) are going to the movies, others to the theater.*

■16■ **Übung: Einige und andere** Not everyone in your class likes doing the same things. Answer the following questions by saying that *some of you* (**einige**) like doing one thing, *others* (**andere**) prefer something else.

BEISPIEL: A: Gehen Sie gern ins Kino?
B: *Einige* gehen gern ins Kino.
C: *Andere* gehen lieber _____ .

1. Spielen Sie gern Tennis?
2. Sprechen Sie gern über Politik?
3. Essen Sie gern Wurst?
4. Fahren Sie gern Ski?
5. Lesen Sie gern Zeitung?
6. Arbeiten Sie gern in der Bibliothek?
7. Trinken Sie gern Kaffee zum Frühstück?
8. Sitzen Sie gern vor dem Fernseher?

Adjectival nouns

■ Adjectival nouns referring to people

In English, adjectives such as *sick*, *rich*, and *famous* occasionally function as nouns referring *collectively* to a group of people.

> *Florence Nightingale cared for **the sick**.*
> *Lifestyles of **the rich and famous**.*

Adjectival nouns are more frequent in German than in English. Moreover, they can refer to individuals, not just to collective groups as in English. Masculine adjectival nouns denote men, feminine ones denote women, while plural adjectival nouns are not gender specific.

der Alte   *the old man*
die Alte   *the old woman*
die Alten *the old people*

Colloquial **mein Alter/meine Alte** can mean *my father/my mother* or *my husband/my wife* (compare English *my old man/old lady*).

Realia on p. 229 has good examples of adjectival nouns in nominative and accusative plural.

Like other nouns in German, adjectival nouns are capitalized, but <u>they *receive adjective endings*</u> as though they were followed by the nouns **Mann**, **Frau**, or **Menschen**. Here are some examples that include these nouns in brackets to make the structure clear. *Note the adjective endings!* As in any noun phrase, these endings will change depending on whether or not the adjectival noun is preceded by a limiting word.

Die Alte [Frau] lag im Bett.   *The old woman was lying in bed.*
Kennst du **den Großen** [Mann] da?   *Do you know that tall man there?*
Hier wohnt **ein Reicher** [Mann].   *A rich man lives here.*
Er wollte **den Armen** [Menschen] helfen.   *He wanted to help the poor.*

In principle, any adjective can be used as an adjectival noun. Here are some common ones you should learn:

Only the masculine form **der Beamte** is an adjectival noun. The feminine form is **die Beamtin**.

der/die Deutsche is the *only* noun of nationality that is adjectival.

der/die **Alte, -n**   *old man/woman*
der/die **Arme, -n**   *poor man/woman*
→ der **Beamte, -n**   *official, civil servant*   *die Beamtin, -nen*
der/die **Bekannte, -n**   *acquaintance, friend*
der/die **Deutsche, -n**   *German (man/woman)* — *not changed for gender*
der/die **Grüne, -n**   *member of the Greens (the environmental* — *& other political party)*   *nationalities*
der/die **Kleine, -n**   *little boy/girl or short man/woman*
der/die **Kranke, -n**   *sick man/woman*
→ der/die **Verwandte, -n**   *relative*
(from **verwandt** = *related*)

Lab Manual Kap. 11, Üb. 17.

Workbook Kap. 11, G.

■ **17** ■ **Übung**   Complete each sentence with the appropriate form of **mein Bekannter** (*my acquaintance, friend* [m.]).

BEISPIEL: Das ist _____ .
          Das ist *mein Bekannter*.

1. Heute zum Mittagessen treffe ich *mein Bekannten*
2. Ich gehe oft mit ____ Volleyball spielen.   *meinem B -en*

3. Das ist die Frau *meines Bekannten*
4. _____ heißt Robert. *Mein B-er*

Now use a form of **meine Bekannten** (*my friends*).

5. Das sind *meine B*
6. Kennen Sie *meine B*
7. Helfen Sie bitte _____! *meinen B-en (dative)*
8. Das sind die Kinder *meiner Bekannten*

Now use a form of **die Deutsche** (*the German* [f.]).

9. Wie heißt denn _____? *die D e*
10. Meinst du _____? *die D e*
11. Ich trampe mit _____ nach Italien. *der Deutschen (dative)*
12. Ist das der Rucksack _____? *der D en?*

Now use a form of **die Alten** (*the old people*).

13. Das haben wir von _____ gelernt. *den Alten*
14. Morgen kommen _____. *die Alten*
15. Wer trägt denn die Koffer _____? *der Alten (gen)*
16. Machen wir etwas Schönes für *die* Alten? *(acc)*

Now use a form of **unser Verwandter** (*our relative* [m.]).

17. Helmut ist _____.
18. Kennst du _____? *unseren Verwandten*
19. Du sollst mit _____ sprechen. *unserem V-en*
20. Die Tochter _____ besucht uns morgen. *unseres V-en*

■ **Neuter adjectival nouns referring to qualities**

Neuter adjectival nouns are abstract nouns designating qualities (e.g., *something good*, *nothing new*). They occur only in the singular, most frequently after the indefinite pronouns **etwas**, **nichts**, **viel**, and **wenig**. Note that since these pronouns are *not* limiting words, the following adjectival noun has the *primary* neuter ending **-es**.

etwas Herrliches	*something marvelous*
nichts Neues	*nothing new*
viel Gutes	*much that is good*
wenig Interessantes	*little of interest*

Etwas Unglaubliches wird passieren:

Sie sitzen im Auto und

FAHREN.

■ 18 ■   Rollenspiel: Was haben Sie mir mitgebracht? (*Mit offenen Büchern*)

Ihre Professorin hatte einen Unfall und liegt im Krankenhaus. Sie besuchen sie und bringen ihr Geschenke mit. (*First choose an adjective from the left-hand column to describe your present, then tell her what it is.*)

BEISPIEL: A: Ich habe Ihnen etwas _____ -es mitgebracht.
           B: Oh, wie schön! Was denn?
           A: Ein-_____ .

Workbook Kap. 11, H.

neu	FS Pflanze
schön	M Kassettenrekorder
teuer	N frische Brötchen
interessant	F Schokolade
herrlich	N Fotos von unserer Reise
klein	N Stück von der Berliner Mauer
lecker	FS Flasche Wein
umweltfreundlich	F Zeitschriften
wunderbar	F Blumen

great terrific

delicious tasty

Neuter adjectival nouns can also occur after the definite article **das**. In this case, they are abstract nouns signaling the *quality* designated by the adjective. There are several English equivalents for this.

Das Moderne gefällt mir.   *I like modern things.*
                                        I like what is modern.

Sie sucht immer **das Gute**.   *She's always seeking the good.*
                                        She's always seeking what's good.

Compare the adjective endings in **etwas Modernes** (*something modern*) and **das Moderne** (*what is modern; modern things*).

More on bei

In **Kapitel 5** you learned that the dative preposition **bei** has the spatial meanings *in the home of* or *at*. Frequently, however, **bei** is used to set a scene. It then has the meanings *during, while . . . ing,* or *at* (an activity or someone's home or business). In this meaning, **bei** is often used with verbal nouns (p. 178).

Er hat sich **beim Radfahren** verletzt.   *He injured himself while riding his bicycle.*
Marion ist jetzt **bei der Arbeit**.   *Marion's at work now.*
Ich lese oft **beim Essen**.   *I often read while eating.*
Ich war gestern **beim Arzt**.   *I was at the doctor's yesterday.*

Lab Manual Kap. 11, Var. zur Üb. 19.

■ **19** ■ **Übung: Wann passiert das?** Sagen Sie, wann etwas passiert oder nicht passiert. <u>Benutzen</u> Sie **bei** in Ihrer Antwort. *use*

BEISPIEL: Ich falle nie, wenn ich Ski fahre.
Ich falle nie beim Skifahren.

1. Mein Mitbewohner <u>stört</u> mich, wenn ich lese. *disturb* — *beim Lesen*
2. Wir treffen uns oft, wenn wir Rad fahren. — *beim Radfahren*
3. <u>Höfliche</u> Kinder singen nicht, wenn sie essen. *Polite* — *beim Essen*
4. Wenn wir spazieren gehen, können wir miteinander sprechen. — *beim Spazierengehen*
5. Ich höre gern Musik, wenn ich Auto fahre. — *beim Auto fahren*
6. Wenn ich arbéite, ziehe ich mir die Schuhe aus. — *Beim arbeiten*

■ **20** ■ **Übung** Antworten Sie mit **bei**.

BEISPIEL: Wie hat er sich denn verletzt? (*while skiing*)
Beim Skifahren.

1. Wie haben Sie sich erkältet? (*while swimming*) — *beim Schwimmen*
2. Wo sind Sie morgens um zehn? (*at work*) — *bei der Arbeit*
3. Wann lernt man viele Menschen kennen? (*while hitchhiking*) — *beim Autostoppeisen Trampen*
4. Wann sprechen Sie nicht viel? (*when driving a car*) — *beim Autofahren*
5. Wo ist denn Ihre Frau? (*at the doctor's*) — *beim Arzt*
6. Wie hast du so viel Geld verloren? (*playing cards*) — *beim Kartenspielen*

Designating decades: The 90s, etc.

These examples show how German designates decades (**das Jahrzehnt, -e**).

die 20er (= zwanziger) Jahre	*the 20s (twenties)*
aus den 60er-Jahren	*from the 60s*
in den 90er-Jahren	*in the 90s*

Note that the cardinal number adds the ending **-er**. <u>No other adjective ending is used, regardless of case.</u>

■ **21** ■ **Übung: Alte Briefmarken** (stamps) Aus welchen Jahrzehnten kommen diese deutschen Briefmarken?

20-er

90er

40er

70er

Lesestück

Designating nationalities and talking about where people are from are communicative goals.

Vor dem Lesen

Tipps zum Lesen und Lernen

Tipps zum Vokabelnlernen

Country names; nouns and adjectives of nationality   The only designation of nationality that is an adjectival noun is **der/die Deutsche**. Some other nouns of nationality have a masculine form ending in **-er** and a feminine in **-erin**. You already know some of these:

(handwritten: all N unless F or pl)

Country	Male native	Female native	Adjective
Amerika	der Amerikaner	die Amerikanerin	amerikanisch
England *(N)*	der Engländer	die Engländerin	englisch
Italien	der Italiener	die Italienerin	italienisch
Kanada *(N)*	der Kanadier	die Kanadierin	kanadisch
Österreich	der Österreicher	die Österreicherin	österreichisch
die Schweiz	der Schweizer	die Schweizerin	schweizerisch

Other nouns of nationality are N-nouns in the masculine that add **-in** (and sometimes an umlaut) in the feminine.

Country	Male native *(GDA)*	Female native	Adjective
China	der Chinese, -n, -n	die Chinesin	chinesisch
Frankreich	der Franzose, -n, -n	die Französin	französisch
Russland	der Russe, -n, -n	die Russin	russisch

Remember that when stating a person's nationality, Germans do *not* use the indefinite article.

Sind Sie Deutsche?	*Are you a German?*
Nein, ich bin Französin.	*No, I'm French.*

■ **A** ■   **Gruppenarbeit: Woher kommst du?**   Sie sind auf einer internationalen Studentenkonferenz. Sie bekommen vom Professor ein Stück Papier. Auf dem Papier steht der Name Ihrer Heimat (*native country*). Jetzt fragen Sie einander, woher Sie kommen.

> **BEISPIEL:** A: Woher kommst du denn?
> B: Ich komme aus England.
> A: Ach, du bist Engländerin!

Lab Manual Kap. 11, Üb. zur Betonung.

Workbook Kap. 11, I.

■ **Leicht zu merken**

die **Demokratisierung**
die **Demonstration, -en**   Demonstra<u>ti</u>on
existieren   exist<u>ie</u>ren
die **Integration**   Integra<u>ti</u>on
investieren   invest<u>ie</u>ren
der **Kapitalismus**   Kapital<u>i</u>smus
der **Kommunismus**   Kommun<u>i</u>smus
der **Manager, -**
die **Million, -en**   Mill<u>i</u>on
modernisieren   modern<u>i</u>sieren
Osteuropa
der **Protest**   Prot<u>e</u>st
die **Reform, -en**
reformieren   reform<u>ie</u>ren
das **Regime, -s**
die **Revolution, -en**   Revolu<u>ti</u>on
(das) **Rumänien**
separat   sepa<u>ra</u>t
die **Sowjetunion**   Sowjetun<u>i</u>on
stabil   stab<u>il</u>
das **Symbol, -e**   Symb<u>o</u>l
zentral   zent<u>ra</u>l
die **Zone, -n**

■ **Einstieg in den Text**   *Way in?*

Word features such as prefixes and suffixes can help you build on your existing vocabulary and recognize new words in context.

The negating prefix **un-**   The prefix **un-** attached to a noun or adjective forms the antonym of that word. Guess the meanings of these words from the **Lesestück:**

die **Unsicherheit** (line 3)   *uncertainty*
ungelöste Probleme (line 36)   *unsolved*

The suffix **-los**   The suffix **-(s)los** is attached to nouns and forms adjectives and adverbs, e.g., **arbeitslos**. It is the equivalent of the English suffix *-less*. Guess the meanings of these words from the **Lesestück:**

gewaltlos (from **Gewalt**: *force, violence*) line 27   *nonviolent?*
hoffnungslos (from **Hoffnung**: *hope*) line 38   *hopeless*

Past participles as adjectives   Past participles of verbs are often used as attributive adjectives. They take regular adjective endings.

bauen → **gebaut-**   *to build* → *built*
Das ist das neu **gebaute**   *That's the newly built dormitory.*
   Studentenwohnheim.

The reading contains the following participles used as adjectives:

besiegen	*to defeat*	→	**besiegt-** (line 9)
entnazifizieren	*to denazify*	→	**entnazifiziert-** (lines 9–10)
vereinen	*to unite*	→	**vereint-** (lines 32–33)
lösen	*to solve*	→	**ungelöst-** (line 36)

■ **B** ■ **Übung** Wie heißt das Adjektiv (mit Endung!)? Und wie heißt der neue Satz auf Englisch?

BEISPIEL: Jemand hat diese Waren gestohlen.
Die Polizei hat die *gestohlenen* Waren gefunden.
The police found the stolen goods.

1. Ich habe Altpapier gesammelt und jetzt schleppe ich das _____ *gesammelten* Altpapier zum Recycling.
2. Eine Fabrik hat diesen Fluss verschmutzt und jetzt darf man in dem _verschmutztem_ Wasser nicht schwimmen.
3. Der Krieg hat viele deutsche Städte zerstört. Jetzt hat Deutschland seine _zerstörtene_ _____ Städte wieder aufgebaut.
4. Wir hatten eine schöne Reise nach Schottland geplant, aber leider konnten wir *geplante* uns die _____ Reise nicht leisten.
5. Ich habe meiner Mutter ein schönes Zimmer reserviert, aber das _reserviertenes_ Zimmer war ihr zu klein.

■ Wortschatz 2

Verben

ändern to change (*trans.*)
  Sie hat ihr Leben geändert. She changed her life.
sich ändern to change (*intrans.*)
  Ihr Leben hat sich geändert. Her life changed.
auf·geben (gibt auf), gab auf, hat aufgegeben to give up
aus·wandern to emigrate
rufen, rief, hat gerufen to call, shout
vereinen to unite
verschwinden, verschwand, ist verschwunden to disappear

Substantive

der Hass hatred
der Nachbar, -n, -n neighbor
der Schlüssel, - key
der Teil, -e part
der Tod death

das Mitglied, -er member

die Brücke, -n bridge
die Bundesrepublik Deutschland (BRD) the Federal Republic of Germany (FRG)
die Heimat homeland; native country
die Macht, ⸚e power, might
die Regierung, -en government in power, administration
die Wirtschaft economy
die Zukunft future

Adjektive und Adverbien

beid- both
berühmt famous
europäisch European
offen open
tief deep
tot dead

verschieden various, different
wirtschaftlich economic

Compare **verschieden** (*various, different*) and **ander-** (*other, different*): **Ich kenne viele verschiedene Lieder** (*I know many different songs*) vs. **Ich kenne andere Lieder als du** (*I know different songs than you*).

Gegensätze

auswandern ≠ **einwandern** to emigrate ≠ to immigrate
der Hass ≠ **die Liebe** hatred ≠ love
offen ≠ **geschlossen** open ≠ closed
der Tod ≠ **das Leben** death ≠ life
die Zukunft ≠ **die Vergangenheit** future ≠ past

Deutschland im europäischen Haus

Understanding Germany's role in Europe today is the cultural goal of this chapter.

Lab Manual Kap. 11, Lesestück.

Im Jahre 1989 ging mit dem Fall° der Berliner Mauer eine Epoche der europäischen Geschichte zu Ende: Die Nachkriegszeit war endlich vorbei°. Besonders für die Länder Osteuropas sind die 90er-Jahre eine Zeit der Unsicherheit, aber auch der neuen Hoffnungen. Mit seiner zentralen Lage° zwischen Ost und West und seiner starken
5 Wirtschaft ist Deutschland in vieler Hinsicht° der Schlüssel zum neuen „europäischen Haus".[1]

fall
over
uncertainty (handwritten)
location
in ... = in many respects

Historischer Hintergrund°: 1945 bis 1989

1945 teilten die vier Alliierten° – Amerika, England, Frankreich und die Sowjetunion – das besiegte° Hitlerreich in vier Zonen auf°, mit dem Ziel später einen neuen entnazi-
10 fizierten° Staat zu bilden°. Aber bald änderte sich das politische Klima. Es begann der sogenannte° Kalte Krieg zwischen dem Kommunismus im Osten und dem Kapitalismus im Westen. Anstatt eines vereinten Landes gründete° man 1949 die Bundesrepublik Deutschland (BRD) und die Deutsche Demokratische Republik (DDR), zwei separate und sehr verschiedene Staaten.

15   Weil die Grenze zwischen Ost- und Westberlin bis 1961 offen blieb, konnten zirka 2,7 Millionen Menschen aus der DDR in den Westen auswandern.[2] Die DDR verblutete°. Um einen langsamen Tod zu verhindern° baute die ostdeutsche Regierung 1961 eine Mauer mitten durch° Berlin. Die Berliner Mauer, das berühmte Symbol des Kalten Krieges, existierte 28 Jahre, bis die zwei Supermächte USA und Sowjetunion
20 endlich ihre Feindschaft° aufgaben.

background
allies
defeated / **teilten ... auf** = divided / denazified / form / *Change* (handwritten)
so-called
founded

was bleeding to death / to prevent / **mitten ...** = through the middle of
enmity

November 1989: Die Grenze öffnet sich

In den 80er Jahren leitete die „Glasnost-Politik"[3] Michael Gorbatschows in der Sowjetunion eine Reform ein°, die° sich schnell auf die anderen Länder Osteuropas ausweitete°. Im Sommer 1989 gab es in Leipzig, Dresden und vielen anderen Städten
25 der DDR riesengroße friedliche° Demonstrationen gegen den kommunistischen Staat.

leitete ... ein = initiated / that
sich ... ausweitete = spread
peaceful

DDR-Wagen kurz vor der Wiedervereinigung. Was bedeutet „BRDDR"?

---

1. The common "European House" was envisioned by the former Soviet President Mikhail Gorbachev.
2. Although Berlin was located in the middle of the Soviet Occupation Zone, it too was divided among the Allies because of its importance as the capital. Air and highway corridors linked it to the West.
3. Mikhail Gorbachev initiated the internal reforms in the former Soviet Union known as *perestroika* (restructuring) and *glasnost* (openness). These changes eroded the Communist Party's centralized control and hegemony.

„Wir sind das Volk", riefen die Demonstranten° und später: „Wir sind *ein* Volk". Diese Demonstrationen leiteten die erste erfolgreiche gewaltlose Revolution der deutschen Geschichte ein°. Die Regierung musste die Grenze öffnen. Im März 1990 kamen dann die ersten freien Wahlen in der DDR und im Oktober die Vereinigung der beiden Teile
30 Deutschlands.

demonstrators

leiteten ... ein = initiated

parts

Deutschland im neuen Europa   *member*

Als Wirtschaftsmacht und größtes° Mitglied der Europäischen Union[1] spielt das vereinte Deutschland eine wichtige Rolle als Brücke zwischen Ost und West. Deutschland ist selber ein Spiegel der großen Unterschiede in Europa. Wie sieht denn die Zukunft
35 des europäischen Hauses aus?

biggest

differences

   Es gibt natürlich noch ungelöste Probleme. Die Umwelt in Osteuropa war durch die Industrie viel mehr beschädigt° als° im Westen. Auch waren die meisten° Fabriken in den neuen Bundesländern° und in anderen osteuropäischen Ländern hoffnungslos veraltet° und konnten mit der westeuropäischen Industrie nicht mehr konkurrieren°.
40 Man musste sie entweder schließen oder° sehr viel investieren um sie zu modernisieren und umweltfreundlicher zu machen. Das bedeutete im Osten mehr Arbeitslosigkeit und Ressentiments° gegen die Manager aus dem Westen, die° die Marktwirtschaft° einführen° sollten.

damaged / than / most
federal states
antiquated / compete
entweder ... oder = either . . .
   or
resentment / who
market economy / introduce

   Die wirtschaftliche Situation in Osteuropa war nach der Auflösung° der
45 Sowjetunion so prekär°, dass viele Menschen ihre Heimat verließen und nach Deutschland auswanderten.[2] Besonders die sogenannten° „Aussiedler" – d.h.

dissolution
precarious
so-called

Im BMW-Werk

1. The European Union, a political and economic alliance of western European nations.
2. Until 1993 Germany had the most liberal asylum laws in the world. In January 1993 alone, 36,000 foreigners applied for asylum. Through a constitutional amendment that redefined application criteria, applications were reduced to 13,000 in January 1994.

Menschen deutscher Abstammung° aus Ländern wie Rumänien und Russland –
stellten sich ein besseres° Leben in Deutschland vor. Obwohl die meisten° Deutschen
diesen Menschen helfen wollen, gibt es auch eine rechtsradikale Minderheit°, die°
50 Hass und Gewalt gegen Ausländer propagiert°. Im Ausland erwecken° solche Neonazis
natürlich alte Ängste und Erinnerungen an die Hitlerzeit.
      Es dauert wahrscheinlich noch lange, bis diese alten Ängste und die neuen
politischen Probleme überwunden° sind. Aber die Demokratisierung und Integration
Osteuropas mit dem Westen sind nicht mehr aufzuhalten°. Zwischen den neuen
55 Nachbarn im Osten und den reichen Demokratien im Westen steht die politisch
stabile und wirtschaftlich starke Bundesrepublik. Es ist sicher, dass sie in der
Europäischen Union eine führende° Rolle zu spielen hat.

deutscher ... = of German descent / better / most

rechtsradikale ... = radical right minority / who / spreads / awaken

overcome
sind ... = can no longer be stopped

leading

Nach dem Lesen

■ A ■   Antworten Sie auf Deutsch.

1. Wer hat zuerst von einem „europäischen Haus" gesprochen? Was bedeutet das?
2. Warum ist Deutschlands Rolle so wichtig im neuen Europa?
3. Wie kam es zu zwei deutschen Staaten?
4. Warum waren die beiden deutschen Staaten so verschieden?
5. Warum hat die Regierung der DDR die Mauer mitten durch Berlin gebaut?
6. Wie hat die friedliche Revolution in der DDR begonnen?
7. Wann hat die DDR-Regierung die Grenze ganz geöffnet?
8. Warum wollten Menschen aus Osteuropa nach Deutschland auswandern?

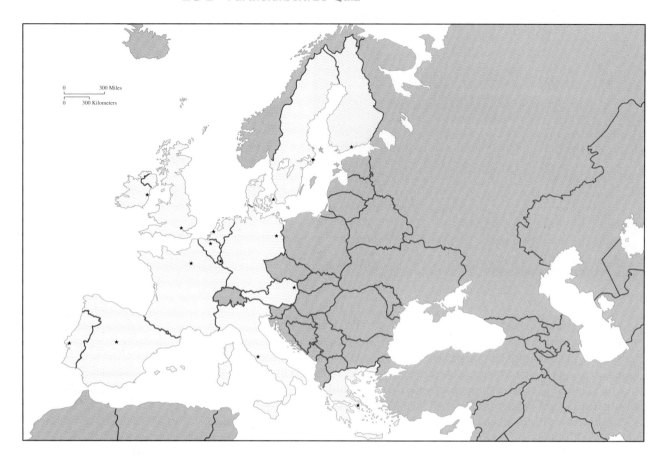

1. Tragen Sie die Namen der EU-Mitgliedstaaten und ihrer Hauptstädte auf die
   Karte ein. (**eintragen**: *to enter*)

   member

Mitgliedstaaten		*Hauptstädte*	
Belgien	Italien	Athen	London
Dänemark	Luxemburg	Berlin	Luxemburg
Deutschland	Niederlande	Brüssel	Madrid
Finnland	Österreich	den Haag	Paris
Frankreich	Portugal	Dublin	Rom
Griechenland	Schweden	Helsinki	Stockholm
Großbritannien	Spanien	Kopenhagen	Wien
Irland		Lissabon	

Lab Manual Kap. 11,
Diktat.

Workbook Kap. 11, J–P.

2. Welche Kurzbeschreibung passt (*fits*) zu welchem Land?

   a. Wurde erst 1995 Mitglied der EU. Landessprache: Deutsch.
   b. Hat im 16. Jahrhundert Mexiko, Süd- und Mittelamerika kolonisiert.
   c. Der kleinste EU-Staat.
   d. Hier hatten die westliche Philosophie und die Demokratie ihren Anfang.
   e. Im 17. und 18. Jahrhundert eine große See- und Handelsmacht; hatte in
      Afrika, Indonesien und Nordamerika Kolonien.
   f. Halbinsel im Mittelmeer; historisches Zentrum eines alten Weltreichs.

Situationen aus dem Alltag

■ Morgens nach dem Aufstehen

Das Wochenende war herrlich, aber jetzt ist es wieder Montag. Sie müssen sich für den Tag fertig machen und gehen ins Badezimmer. Sie müssen eine <u>Menge</u> Reflexivverben benutzen um die Morgenroutine zu beschreiben.

■ A ■ Übung: Welcher Satz gehört zu welchem Bild?

Er kämmt sich die Haare.   Er rasiert sich.   Sie schminkt sich.
Sie badet sich.   Sie putzt sich die Zähne.   Er duscht sich.

■ B ■ Übung: Was ist Ihre Morgenroutine?   In welcher <u>Reihenfolge</u> (*order*) machen Sie sich morgens fertig? Antworten Sie mit ganzen Sätzen.

With this chapter you have completed the third quarter of *Neue Horizonte: A Brief Course*. For a concise review of the grammar and idiomatic phrases in chapters 8–11, you may consult the **Zusammenfassung und Wiederholung 3** (*Summary and Review 3*) of your Workbook. The review section is followed by a self-correcting test.

⑤ frühstücken
   Sachen in die Tasche packen
① aufstehen
   zur Uni gehen
⑦ sich rasieren oder sich schminken   *put on make up*
⑥ sich die Zähne putzen   *Tee*
   eine zweite Tasse Kaffee trinken
④ sich <u>anziehen</u>   *get dressed*
② sich duschen oder baden
③ sich die Haare kämmen

1. Zuerst stehe ich auf.
2. Dann _____
3. _____
4. _____
5. _____
6. _____
7. _____
8. _____
9. _____
10. _____

Zeittafel, 1939–heute

1948 Währungsreform im Westen. Berlin-Blockade durch die Sowjets, Berliner Luftbrücke.

1945 9. Mai Kapitulation Deutschlands. Der Zweite Weltkrieg ist zu Ende.

1949 Gründung der BRD und der DDR, Deutschland in zwei Staaten geteilt.

1955 BRD wird Mitglied der NATO, DDR wird Mitglied des Warschauer Paktes

1950

1960

1947 Marshall-Plan bringt den Westzonen ökonomische Hilfe. Der Wiederaufbau beginnt.

1946 Erste demokratische Kommunalwahlen seit 1933.

1953 Protestdemonstrationen in Ostberlin gegen zu hohe Arbeitsnormen.

standardize?

invasion

1939 Deutscher Einmarsch in Polen; Anfang des Zweiten Weltkriegs.

Almanach

1989 Spätsommer Tägliche Flucht vieler DDR-Bürger über <u>Ungarn</u>. Erich Honecker tritt zurück. Millionen demonstrieren in Ostberlin, Leipzig und anderen Städten. *Hungary*

9. November Die <u>Regierung</u> öffnet die Grenzen.

1990 März Erste demokratische Wahlen in der DDR.

Juli Währungsunion der beiden deutschen Staaten. *currency*

Oktober Deutsche Vereinigung.

Dezember Erste gesamtdeutsche demokratische Wahlen seit 1932.

1961 Bau der Mauer zwischen Ost- und West-Berlin

70er Jahre Willy Brandts Ostpolitik. Normalisierung der Beziehungen zwischen BRD und DDR.

1994 Die letzten alliierten Truppen verlassen Berlin.

1970 **1980** **1990** **1994** **1995**

1963 Besuch des US-Präsidenten John F. Kennedy an der Mauer.

1982 Beginn der Kanzlerschaft Helmut Kohls.

1987 750-Jahr-<u>Feier</u> in beiden Teilen der Stadt Berlin.

1991 Berlin wird wieder die Hauptstadt Deutschlands.

1995 Österreich wird Mitglied der Europäischen Union.

Erinnerungen

Dialoge

Lab Manual Kap. 12, Dialoge, Fragen, Hören

Sie gut zu!

Idiotensicher

HANS-PETER: Du, Karin, hast du das Buch mit, das ich dir geliehen habe?

KARIN: Ach, tut mir Leid. Ich hab's wieder zu Hause gelassen. Ich arbeite noch an meinem Referat.

HANS-PETER: Ist ja egal. Du darfst es ruhig noch behalten. Hast du noch viel zu tun?

KARIN: Nein, ich bin fast fertig. Ich benutze zum ersten Mal meinen neuen Computer. Die Software ist wirklich <u>idiotensicher</u>. *idiotproof*

Klatsch *Gossip*

PETRA: Wer war denn der Typ, mit dem Rita gestern weggegangen ist?

JÖRG: Der Mann, der so komisch angezogen war?

PETRA: Genau, den meine ich. *Image*

JÖRG: Das war der Rudi. Stell dir vor, sie hat sich mit ihm <u>verlobt!</u> *engaged*

PETRA: Wenigstens sah er intelligenter aus als ihr letzter Freund.

Vor der Haustür

Notice two N-nouns: **Nachbar** and **Herr**.

Frau Schwarzer, die neulich ins Haus eingezogen ist, redet <u>nach</u> der Arbeit mit ihrem Nachbarn Herrn Beck.

FRAU SCHWARZER: Ach Herr Beck, ich wollte Sie etwas fragen. Wo kann ich am billigsten meinen VW reparieren lassen? *how vay*

HERR BECK: In der nächsten Querstraße gibt's den besten Mechaniker in der Gegend, aber der ist leider nicht der Billigste. *short on money*

FRAU SCHWARZER: Hmm ... Im Augenblick bin ich etwas <u>knapp bei Kasse</u>. Ich glaub', ich mache es diesmal lieber selber.

HERR BECK: Na, viel Spaß. Also, dann wünsche ich Ihnen einen schönen Abend noch.

FRAU SCHWARZER: Danke, gleichfalls!

Guten Abend is a greeting. **(Ich wünsche Ihnen einen) schönen Abend noch** is said when parting.

Notes on Usage: *es* and *etwas*

In spoken German, the pronoun **es** is often contracted to **'s**.

Ich **hab's** wieder zu Hause gelassen.
In der nächsten Querstraße **gibt's** den besten Mechaniker.

etwas Note three different meanings:

Ich habe **etwas** vergessen.	*something*
Ich bin **etwas** müde.	*somewhat, a little*
Hast du **etwas** Geld?	*some*

Wortschatz 1

Verben

behalten (behält), behielt, hat behalten to keep, retain
erinnern an (+ *acc.*) to remind of
sich erinnern an (+ *acc.*) to remember
lassen (lässt), ließ, hat gelassen to leave (something or someone), leave behind; to let, allow; to cause to be done
reden to talk, speak
reparieren to repair
sich verloben mit to become engaged to
weg·gehen, ging weg, ist weggegangen to go away, leave
wünschen to wish

Substantive

der **Augenblick, -e** moment
  im Augenblick at the moment
der **Besuch, -e** visit
der **Computer, -** computer
der **Klatsch** gossip
der **Typ, -en** (*slang*) guy

der Typ: Used colloquially for males (**ein sympathischer Typ**). For both male and female: **Er/sie ist nicht mein Typ.**

das **Mal, -e** time (*in the sense of "occurrence"*)
  jedes Mal every time
  zum ersten Mal for the first time
die **Erinnerung, -en** memory
die **Gegend, -en** area, region
die **Nacht, ⸚e** night
  in der Nacht at night
  Gute Nacht. Good night.
die **Querstraße, -n** cross street
die **Software** software

Adjektive und Adverbien

diesmal this time
einmal once
etwas somewhat, a little
fertig done, finished
idiotensicher foolproof
intelligent intelligent
knapp scarce, in short supply
  knapp bei Kasse short of money
komisch peculiar, odd; funny
mit along with (someone)
nächst- nearest; next
neulich recently
ruhig (*as sentence adverb*) feel free to, go ahead and
  Du kannst ruhig hier bleiben. Feel free to stay here.

Remember the basic meaning of **ruhig**: peaceful, calm. Cf. the cartoon on p. 70.

übermorgen the day after tomorrow
vorgestern the day before yesterday

Andere Vokabeln

als (*with adj. or adv. in comparative degree*) than
  intelligenter als more intelligent than
na well . . .

Nützliche Ausdrücke

(Einen) Augenblick, bitte! Just a moment, please!
Danke, gleichfalls. Thanks, you too. Same to you.
Viel Spaß! Have fun!

Gegensätze

sich erinnern ≠ vergessen to remember ≠ to forget
reden ≠ schweigen, schwieg, hat geschwiegen to speak ≠ to be silent
reparieren ≠ kaputtmachen to repair ≠ to break
weggehen ≠ zurückkommen to go away ≠ to come back
die Nacht ≠ der Tag night ≠ day

Proverb: **Reden ist Silber, Schweigen ist Gold.**

Foolproof

H.-P: Karin, do you have the book with you that I lent you?

K: Oh, sorry. I left it at home again. I'm still working on my paper.

H.-P: Doesn't matter. Go ahead and keep it. Do you still have a lot to do?

K: No, I'm almost done. I'm using my new computer for the first time. The software is really foolproof.

Gossip

P: Who was the guy Rita left with yesterday?

J: The man who was dressed so funny?

P: Exactly. He's the one I mean.

J: That was Rudi. Just imagine, she's gotten engaged to him!

P: At least he looked more intelligent than her last boyfriend.

At the Front Door

Ms. Schwarzer, who has recently moved into the building, is talking after work to her neighbor, Mr. Beck.

MS. S: Oh Mr. Beck, I wanted to ask you something. Where can I get my VW repaired most cheaply?

MR. B: In the next cross street there's the best mechanic in the area, but he's unfortunately not the cheapest.

MS. S: Hmm . . . At the moment I'm somewhat short of cash. I think I'll do it myself this time.

MR. B: Well, have fun. Then I'll wish you a good evening.

MS. S: Thanks, you too.

Variationen

■ A ■ Persönliche Fragen

1. Schreiben Sie Ihre Referate mit dem Computer?
2. Leihen Sie Ihren Freunden Bücher oder nicht? Wie ist es mit CDs, Ihrem Fahrrad, oder mit Kleidern?
3. Was haben Sie heute zu Hause gelassen?
4. Jörg sagt, dass Rudi komisch angezogen war. Ziehen Sie sich manchmal komisch an? Was tragen Sie dann?
5. Wie alt soll man sein, bevor man sich verlobt? Was meinen Sie?
6. Besitzen Sie einen Wagen? <u>Was für</u> einen?   *what kind?*
7. Sind Sie ein guter Mechaniker? Können Sie Ihr Auto selber reparieren?

■ B ■ Übung: Was braucht man?

Um ihr Referat zu schreiben, <u>braucht</u> Karin Bücher, einen Computer und vielleicht auch ein Wörterbuch. Was braucht man um ...

einen Brief zu schreiben? *Bleistift Papier, Briefmarke (f.)*
das Frühstück zu machen? *Saft (m) Bröt(n) Milch, Tee Haferbrei (m) oder Muesli?*
vacation eine <u>Urlaubs</u>reise zu machen? *Wagen oder Flugzeug (n), Geld, Kleider, Bücher*
eine Fremdsprache zu lernen? *einen Professor, Bücher, CD*
einkaufen zu gehen? *Geld, Wagen, Tasche, eine Liste*
eine Radtour zu machen? *ein Rad, ein (m) Rucksack, Wasser, Jacke*
eine Wanderung in den Bergen zu machen? *gute Schuhe, Wasser*

■ C ■ Übung: Das Beste in der Gegend

Herr Beck weiß, wer der beste Mechaniker in der Gegend ist. Wissen Sie, wo man das Beste in der Gegend findet? Wo ist hier in unserer Gegend ...

das beste griechische Restaurant? das beste französische Restaurant?
das beste Kleidergeschäft?
das beste Hotel?
die beste Kneipe? *pub—*
die beste Pizza?
das beste Sportgeschäft? *shop*
der beste Supermarkt? *JJ+F*

■ D ■ **Übung: Sie dürfen das ruhig machen.** Sie sagen, Sie würden gern etwas machen. Der/Die Nächste sagt, Sie dürfen es ruhig machen (oder) Sie können es ruhig machen.

BEISPIEL: Ich würde gern deinen Kuli benutzen. *Kugelschreiber – ball point*
Klar, du darfst ihn *ruhig* benutzen.

The sentence adverb **ruhig** goes immediately after the inflected verb and all personal pronouns.

1. Ich würde gerne deinen Wagen bis 3 Uhr behalten.
2. Heute Abend würde ich dich gerne besuchen.
3. Ich würde gern etwas Wichtiges sagen. *important*
4. Ich würde meine Freunde gerne einladen. *invite*
5. Ich würde gern etwas essen.
6. Meinen Wagen würde ich gerne hier lassen.
7. Ich würde mir gerne die Kirche ansehen. *look at*
8. Ich würde gern meine Freundin Gertrud mitbringen.

Lyrik zum Vorlesen

Joseph von Eichendorff was one of the foremost poets of the Romantic movement in Germany. Reverence for nature, longing for one's beloved, and nostalgia for one's homeland are all typical themes for the Romantics. The poem "Heimweh" (*Homesickness*) is from Eichendorff's story ***Aus dem Leben eines Taugenichts*** (*From the Life of a Good-for-Nothing*), in which the hero, in Italy, yearns for Germany and his beloved.

Lab Manual Kap. 12, Lyrik zum Vorlesen.

Heimweh

Wer in die Fremde° will wandern   = ins Ausland
Der muss mit der Liebsten° gehn,   beloved
Es jubeln° und lassen die andern   rejoice
Den Fremden alleine stehn.

Zeichnung (*drawing*) von Ludwig Richter (19. Jhdt.)

Was <u>wisset</u> ihr, dunkele <u>Wipfel°</u>   treetops
Von der alten, schönen Zeit?
Ach, die Heimat hinter den Gipfeln°,   peaks
Wie liegt sie von hier so <u>weit!</u>   *wide, broad*

Am liebsten° <u>betracht</u>° ich die Sterne°,   most of all / contemplate /
Die schienen, wie° ich ging zu ihr,   stars / = **als**
Die Nachtigall° hör ich so gerne,   nightingale
Sie sang vor der Liebsten <u>Tür</u>.

Der Morgen, das ist meine Freude°!   joy
Da steig ich in stiller° <u>Stund</u>'   quiet
Auf den höchsten° Berg in die Weite°,   highest / distance
Grüß dich, Deutschland, aus Herzens
    Grund°!   **aus** ... = from the bottom of
                                                                 my heart

Joseph von Eichendorff (1788–1857)

Grammatik

Comparing things is a communicative goal.

Comparison of adjectives and adverbs

When adjectives or adverbs are used in comparisons, they can occur in three stages or degrees.

- Positive degree (*basic form*)

  so interessant wie = *as interesting as*

     Jörg ist **so interessant wie** Dieter.   *Jörg is **as interesting as** Dieter.*
     Jutta läuft **schnell**.   *Jutta runs **fast**.*

- Comparative degree (*marker*: **-er**)

  interessanter als = *more interesting than*

     Jörg ist **interessanter als** Helmut.   *Jörg is **more interesting than** Helmut.*
     Jutta läuft **schneller als** ich.   *Jutta runs **faster than** I do.*

- Superlative degree of attributive adjectives (*marker*: **-st**)

  der interessanteste Schüler = *the most interesting pupil*
  die schnellste Läuferin = *the fastest runner*

- Superlative degree of adverbs and predicate adjectives
  (*marker*: **am _____ -(e)sten**)

  am interessantesten = *most interesting*

     Von allen Schülern ist Jörg   *Of all the pupils, Jörg is **most***
        am interessantesten.   ***interesting**.*
     Jutta läuft **am schnellsten**.   *Jutta runs **fastest**.*

> ## Die schnellsten Männer
> ## der Welt starten nicht in Monza,
> ## sondern im Büro.

Formation of comparative degree

- To form the comparative degree of any adjective or adverb, add the marker **-er** to the basic form:

Basic form	+ -er	=	*Comparative degree*
schnell-	-er		**schneller**
dunkel-	-er		**dunkler**
interessant-	-er		**interessanter**

rk. English adjectives longer than two syllables form their comparative with *more*: *interesting—more interesting*. German does not follow this pattern. Simply add **-er** to make the comparative, no matter how long the adjective is: **interessant— interessanter**.

- Attributive adjectives add the regular adjective endings *after* the comparative **-er**-ending.

Basic form	+ -er-	+ *Adjective ending*
schnell-	-er-	-en
interessant-	-er-	-es

Wir fuhren mit dem **schnelleren** Zug.	*We took the faster train.*
Ich lese ein **interessanteres** Buch.	*I'm reading a more interesting book.*

- **als** = *than* when used with the comparative.

Das Buch ist interessanter **als** der Artikel.	*The book is more interesting than the article.*

sp Spelling note: Adjectives ending in **-el** and **-er** drop the **-e-** in the comparative:
dunkel → **dunkler**
teuer → **teurer**

lab Lab Manual Kap. 12, Üb. 1; Var. zur Üb. 3.

■ 1 ■ Übung Everyone is praising Jörg, but you respond that you are *more* everything than he is.

BEISPIEL: A: Jörg ist interessant.
B: Aber ich bin interessanter als er.

1. Jörg ist hübsch.
2. Er ist ruhig.
3. Er läuft schnell.
4. Er ist ehrlich.
5. Jörg ist fleißig. *hardworking*
6. Er ist freundlich.
7. Er steht früh auf.
8. Er ist sportlich.

■ 2 ■ Übung: Vergleichen wir! (Let's compare!) Antworten Sie mit einem ganzen Satz.

BEISPIEL: A: Was fährt schneller als ein Fahrrad?
B: Ein Auto fährt schneller als ein Fahrrad.

1. Was fährt langsamer als ein Zug?
2. Was schmeckt Ihnen besser als Salat?
3. Was ist moderner als eine Schreibmaschine (*typewriter*)?
4. Wer ist reicher als Sie?
5. Welches Auto ist teurer als ein Volkswagen?
6. Welche Energiequelle (*energy source*) ist umweltfreundlicher als Öl? *Wasserkraft*
7. Welche Stadt ist sauberer als New York?
8. Welche Länder sind kleiner als Deutschland?

foot 300 ■ Kapitel 12

Hier sehen Sie einen der größten
Kohlendioxidfresser der Welt.

■ 3 ■ **Übung: Im Kaufhaus** Sie sind Verkäufer im Kaufhaus. Ihr Professor spielt
einen Kunden. Nichts scheint ihm zu gefallen. Sie versuchen ihm etwas Schöneres,
Billigeres usw. zu zeigen.

> BEISPIEL: A: Dieses Hemd ist mir nicht dunkel genug.
> B: Hier haben wir dunklere Hemden.

1. Diese Blumen sind mir nicht schön genug.
2. Diese Brötchen sind mir nicht frisch genug.
3. Diese Taschen sind mir nicht leicht genug.
4. Diese Bücher sind mir nicht billig genug.
5. Diese Fahrräder sind mir nicht leicht genug.
6. Diese Computer sind mir nicht schnell genug.

■ **Formation of the superlative**

The superlative is formed in the following ways:

Adverbs All adverbs form their superlative using the following pattern:

> **am** _____-**(e)sten**
> **am schnellsten** *most quickly*

> Jutta läuft **am schnellsten**. *Jutta runs **fastest**.*
> Hans hat **am schönsten** gesungen. *Hans sang **most beautifully**.*

Note on spelling: An extra -**e**- is added when the basic form ends in -**d**, -**t**, -**s**, -**ß**, or -**z**: **am mildesten, am heißesten**.

German has no superlative marker like English *most*. No matter how long an adverb is,
simply add -**sten**: **am interessantesten** = *most interestingly*.

Attributive Adjectives With attributive adjectives, add the regular adjective endings
after the superlative -**(e)st**-, for example:

Basic form	+	*-(e)st-*	+	*Adjective ending*
interessant-		-est-		-e
schnell-		-st-		-en

> Die **interessanteste** Studentin *The **most interesting** student is
> heißt Marianne. named Marianne.*
> Wir fuhren mit dem **schnellsten** Zug. *We took the **fastest** train.*

Predicate Adjectives   Predicate adjectives in the superlative may occur either in the **am** _____ **-sten** pattern or with the definite article and regular adjective endings.

Albert ist **am interessantesten**.   *Albert is **most interesting**.*
Albert ist **der Interessanteste**.   *Albert is **the most interesting person**.*
Diese Bücher sind die   *These books are **the most interesting**
  interessantesten.   **(ones)**.*

You can use the superlative only with the *definite* article, never with the *indefinite* article: **der tiefste See**, but not **ein tiefster See**.

Workbook Kap. 12, A.

Lab Manual Kap. 12, Var. zu Üb. 4, 6.

■ **4** ■   **Übung: Ich mache das am besten!**   A visitor is praising the whole class. You then praise yourself in the superlative.

> BEISPIEL: A: Sie laufen alle schnell.
> B: Aber ich laufe am schnell<u>sten</u>.

1. Sie sind alle freundlich.
2. Sie sind alle sehr <u>fleißig</u>. *industrious, hardworking*
3. Sie singen alle sehr schön.
4. Sie sind alle elegant <u>angezogen</u>.
5. Sie sind alle sehr sportlich.
6. Sie denken alle sehr kreativ.

Die besten Restaurants in Deutschland

■ **5** ■   **Gruppenarbeit: Ich bin der/die _____ -ste!**   Here are some adjectives you can use to describe yourself. Choose the one that you think you exemplify the best of anyone in the class. (Don't take this too seriously!) Then say, **Ich bin der/die _____ -ste.**

> BEISPIEL: Ich bin der/die Schönste hier!

aktiv	elegant	hungrig
altmodisch	faul	modern
blöd *stupid*	fleißig	radikal
clever	höflich *polite*	wahnsinnig

clever in German means *sly, ingenious*.

■ **6** ■   **Übung: Im Laden**   Sie sind wieder Verkäufer und Ihre Professorin spielt eine <u>Kundin</u>. Sie sucht etwas und Sie sagen, Sie haben das Neueste, Billigste usw.

> BEISPIEL: A: Ich suche billige Weine.
> B: Hier sind die *billig<u>sten</u>* Weine.

1. Ich suche neue Schuhe.
2. Ich suche schöne Bilder.
3. Ich suche interessante Bücher.
4. Ich suche moderne Stühle.
5. Ich suche leichte Fahrräder.
6. Ich suche elegante Kleider. *dresses*
   Kleidung clothing

■ Umlaut in comparative and superlative

Some comparative and superlative adjectives have two possible forms: **roter/röter, nasser/nässer, gesunder/gesünder. Gesund** is the only two-syllable adjective where umlaut is possible.

Many one-syllable adjectives and adverbs whose stem vowels are **a**, **o**, or **u** (but *not* **au**) are umlauted in the comparative and superlative degrees. Here is a list of adjectives and adverbs you already know. Some occur in easy-to-remember pairs of opposites.

old	alt	älter	am ältesten
young	jung	jünger	am jüngsten
dumb	dumm	dümmer	am dümmsten
smart	klug	klüger	am klügsten
cold	kalt	kälter	am kältesten
warm	warm	wärmer	am wärmsten
short	kurz	kürzer	am kürzesten
long	lang	länger	am längsten
strong	stark	stärker	am stärksten
weak	schwach	schwächer	am schwächsten
sick	krank	kränker	am kränksten
healthy	gesund	gesünder	am gesündesten
poor	arm	ärmer	am ärmsten
hard, harsh	hart	härter	am härtesten
often	oft	öfter	am öftesten
red	rot	röter	am rötesten
black	schwarz	schwärzer	am schwärzesten

Lab Manual Kap. 12, Var. zur Üb. 7.

■ 7 ■ **Gruppenarbeit: kalt / kälter / am kältesten** The first student reads a sentence, and the next two respond with the comparative and superlative.

BEISPIEL: A: Meine Wohnung ist kalt.
B: Meine Wohnung ist noch kälter. *even*
C: Aber meine Wohnung ist am kältesten.

1. Mein Bruder ist stark.
2. Mein Auto ist alt.
3. Mein Referat ist lang.
4. Mein Freund ist krank.

5. Meine Schwester ist jung.
6. Mein Zimmer ist warm.
7. Mein Besuch war kurz.
8. Mein Beruf ist hart. *job, profession*

■ Irregular comparatives and superlatives

Some of the most frequently used adjectives and adverbs in German have irregular forms in the comparative and superlative.

Note: The superlative of **groß** adds **-t** (**größt-**) rather than **-est** to the stem.

Positive	*Comparative*	*Superlative*	
groß	größer	am größten	*big/bigger/biggest*
gut	besser	am besten	*good, well/better/best*
hoch, hoh-	höher	am höchsten	*high/higher/highest*
nahe	näher	am nächsten	*near/nearer/nearest; next*
viel	mehr	am meisten	*much, many/more/most*
gern	lieber	am liebsten	*like to/prefer to/most of all like to*

- The three degrees of **gern** are used to say how much you like to do things.

Ich gehe **gern** ins Kino.	*I like to go to the movies.*
Ich gehe **lieber** ins Theater.	*I'd rather (or) I prefer to go to the theater.*
Ich gehe **am liebsten** ins Konzert.	*Most of all, I like to go to concerts.*

Wenig, the antonym of **viel**, functions in the same way:
Ich esse **wenig** Brot.
Ich habe **wenige** Freunde.
Ich habe **weniger** Freunde als du.

- **Viel** means *much* or *a lot of* and it has *no adjective endings*. **Viele** means *many* and *does* have regular plural endings.

Ich esse **viel** Brot.	*I eat a lot of bread.*
Ich habe **viele** Freunde.	*I have many friends.*

The comparative degree **mehr** *never* has adjective endings.

Du hast **mehr** Freunde als ich.	*You have more friends than I.*

The superlative degree **meist-** *does* take endings; in addition, it is used with the definite article, in contrast to English *most.*

Die meisten Studenten essen in der Mensa.	***Most** students eat in the cafeteria.*

> **WENIGER IST MEHR.**

■ 8 ■ **Übung: gut, besser, am besten**   Rank the items on the right according to the criteria on the left.

Workbook Kap. 12, B–C.

Lab Manual Kap. 12, Var. zu Üb. 8, 9.

BEISPIEL: schnell fahren   Bus, Fahrrad, Zug
Ein Fahrrad fährt schnell, ein Bus fährt schneller und ein Zug fährt am schnellsten.

1. gut schmecken   Schokolade, Wurst, Kartoffelsalat
2. hoch sein   Berg, Haus, Dom
3. nahe sein   das Studentenwohnheim, die Mensa, die Bibliothek
4. viel wissen   Schüler, Professoren, Studenten

■ 9 ■ **Gruppenarbeit: Was sind Ihre Präferenzen?**   Rank your preferences, as in the example.

BEISPIEL: trinken   Tee, Kaffee, Milch
Ich trinke gern Milch. Ich trinke lieber Kaffee. Aber am liebsten trinke ich Tee.

1. lesen   Zeitungen, Gedichte *poetry*, Romane
2. hören   Rockmusik, Jazz, klassische Musik
3. wohnen   in der Stadt, auf dem Land, am Meer
4. spielen   Fußball, Tennis, Volleyball
5. bekommen   Briefe, Geschenke *gifts*, gute Noten
6. essen   Pommes frites, Sauerkraut, Bauernbrot
7. schreiben   Briefe, Referate, Postkarten

▪ Comparisons

genauso ... wie = *just as ... as*
nicht so ... wie = *not as ... as*

Heute ist es **genauso kalt wie** gestern.
Aber es ist **kälter als** vorgestern.

*Today is **just as cold as** yesterday.*
*But it's **colder than** the day before yesterday.*

Stuttgart ist **nicht so groß wie** Berlin.
Aber es ist **größer als** Tübingen.

*Stuttgart is **not as large as** Berlin.*
*But it's **bigger than** Tübingen.*

immer _____**-er** (shows progressive change)

Das Kind wird **immer größer**.
Sie liest **immer mehr** Bücher.

*The child's getting **bigger and bigger**.*
*She's reading **more and more** books.*

Lab Manual Kap. 12, Var. zu Üb. 10, 11.

■ **10** ■ **Gruppenarbeit: Damals und jetzt** Vergleichen wir (*Let's compare*) damals und jetzt. Jeder sagt, wie es früher war und wie sich alles immer mehr ändert.

BEISPIEL: Früher hatte man mehr Zeit, heute ist man immer mehr in Eile.
Früher war das Lebenstempo langsamer, jetzt wird es immer schneller.
Früher kostete das Studium ...

Workbook Kap. 12, D–G.

■ **11** ■ **Übung: Vergleiche** (Comparisons) Bring in pictures or photos that you have drawn, taken, or found in books or magazines. Find similarities and differences in these pictures and compare them in German for the class.

BEISPIELE: Diese Bäume sind höher als diese hier, aber dieser Berg ist genauso hoch wie der andere.

Diese Mutter sieht nicht so jung aus wie diese hier, aber dieses Kind ist genauso alt wie das Kind da.
Das dritte Kind ist das älteste.

Relative pronouns and relative clauses

A relative clause is a subordinate clause that modifies or further clarifies a noun. Relative clauses are introduced by relative pronouns. Compare the following sentences:

Das ist das **neue** Buch.   *That's the **new** book.*

           rel. pron.
Das ist das Buch,   ***das***   du mir geliehen hast.
That's the book   ***that***   *you lent me.*

The relative clause **das du mir geliehen hast**, like the descriptive adjective **neue**, modifies **Buch** by telling *which* book is being talked about.

The relative pronouns in English are *who, whom, whose, that,* and *which*. The German relative pronoun is identical in most cases to the definite article, which you already know. Study the following table and note especially the forms in bold, which are *different* from the definite article.

Compare declension of definite article on p. 202. There are only three relative pronouns that are not identical to forms of the definite article: **denen**, **dessen**, and **deren**. These forms are printed in boldface in the table.

Relative Pronouns			
masc.	**neut.**	**fem.**	**plur.**

	masc.	neut.	fem.	plur.
nom.	der ⎫	das	die	die
acc.	den ⎭			
dat.	dem	dem	der	**denen**
gen.	**dessen**	**dessen**	**deren**	**deren**

Sentences having a relative clause can be thought of as a combination of two separate sentences that share a common element (a noun and the pronoun representing it). This element in the main clause is called the *antecedent* because it *antecedes* (i.e., precedes) the relative pronoun. In the relative clause, the relative pronoun *relates* (i.e., refers) back to the antecedent. Here are some examples. Note how the antecedent and the relative pronoun always denote the same person or thing.

masc.
sing.
antecedent · nom.

1. Das ist **der Typ**. **Er** war im Kino.

   Das ist der Typ, **der** im Kino war.
   rel. pron.
   That's the guy who was at the movies.

fem.
sing.
antecedent · dat.

2. Kennst du **die Frau**? Ich arbeite mit **ihr**.

   Kennst du die Frau, mit **der** ich arbeite?
   rel. pron.
   Do you know the woman [whom] I work with?

masc.
sing.
antecedent · gen.

3. Das ist **der Autor**. Die Romane **des Autors** sind berühmt.

   Das ist der Autor, **dessen** Romane berühmt sind.
   rel. pron.
   That's the author whose novels are famous.

acc.
antecedent · plur.

4. Hast du **die Bücher**? Ich habe **sie** dir geliehen.

   Hast du die Bücher, **die** ich dir geliehen habe?
   rel. pron.
   Do you have the books [that] I lent you?

■ Rules for relative clauses

1. The relative pronoun is *never* omitted in German, as it often is in English (examples 2 and 4 above).

2. The relative pronoun *always* has the same gender and number as its antecedent.

3. The case of a relative pronoun is determined by its function in the relative clause.

fem.	fem.
sing.	sing.
nom.	dat.

   Das ist **die Frau**, mit **der** ich arbeite.

4. If the relative pronoun is the object of a preposition, the preposition *always precedes* it in the relative clause (example 2 above). In English the preposition often comes at the end of the relative clause (e.g., *the woman I work* **with**). This is *never* the case in German (die Frau, **mit** der ich arbeite).

5. The relative clause is *always a subordinate clause* with verb-last word order. The relative clause is *always* set off from the rest of the sentence by commas.

6. The relative clause is usually placed immediately after its antecedent.

   Das Buch, **das** du mir geliehen hast, hat mir geholfen.   *The book that you lent me helped me.*

Lab Manual Kap. 12, Üb. 12, 14.

Workbook Kap. 12, H–K.

■ 12 ■ **Kettenreaktion**   Student A liest den ersten Satz auf Deutsch vor. Studentin B gibt eine englische Übersetzung und liest dann den nächsten Satz vor usw.

1. Das ist der Mann, der hier wohnt.
2. Das ist der Mann, den ich kenne.
3. Das ist der Mann, dem wir helfen.   *helfen takes dative*
4. Das ist der Mann, dessen Frau ich kenne.

5. Das ist das Fahrrad, das sehr leicht ist.
6. Das ist das Fahrrad, das sie gekauft hat.
7. Das ist das Fahrrad, mit dem ich zur Arbeit fahre.
8. Das ist das Fahrrad, dessen Farbe mir gefällt.

9. Das ist die Frau, die Deutsch kann.
10. Das ist die Frau, die wir brauchen.
11. Das ist die Frau, der wir Geld geben.
12. Das ist die Frau, deren Romane ich kenne.

Der Mann,
der alles kann.

13. Das sind die Leute, die mich kennen.
14. Das sind die Leute, die ich kenne.
15. Das sind die Leute, denen wir helfen.
16. Das sind die Leute, deren Kinder wir kennen.

Informationen, die Sie nicht über Ihr Telefon bekommen:
Frankfurter Allgemeine

■ **13** ■ **Übung**   Lesen Sie jeden Satz mit dem richtigen Relativpronomen vor.

1. Die Donau ist ein Fluss, _der_ durch Österreich fließt.   (*that*)
2. Der Berg, _den_ man am Horizont sieht, ist die Zugspitze.   (*that*)
3. Kennst du den Herrn, _dem_ dieser Wagen gehört?   (*to whom*) > *dative*
4. Der Professor, _dessen_ Bücher dort liegen, kommt gleich zurück.   (*whose*)
5. Das ist ein Schaufenster, _das_ immer bunt aussieht.   (*that*)   *colorful*
6. Mir schmeckt jedes Abendessen, _das_ du kochst.   (*that*)
7. Das Kind, _dem_ ich geholfen habe, ist wieder gesund.   (*whom*)   *dative*
8. Sie kommt aus einem Land, _dessen_ Regierung undemokratisch ist.   (*whose*)   *govt.*
9. Die Studentin, _die_ neben mir saß, war im zweiten Semester.   (*who*)
10. Beschreiben Sie mir die Rolle, _die_ ich spielen soll.   (*that*)   *acc.*
11. Christa, _der_ der Computer gehört, leiht ihn dir gerne.   (*to whom*)   *dative*
12. Die Touristengruppe, _deren_ Gepäck dort steht, ist aus England.   (*whose*)
13. Wer sind die Leute, _die_ dort vor der Mensa stehen?   (*who*)
14. Da sind ein paar Studenten, _die_ du kennen lernen sollst.   (*whom*)
15. Es gibt viele Menschen, _denen_ dieser Arzt geholfen hat.   (*whom*)   *dative*
16. Sind das die Kinder, _deren_ Hund gestorben ist?   (*whose*)

■ **14** ■ **Übung**   Antworten Sie wie im Beispielsatz.

BEISPIEL: Arbeiten Sie für *diesen* Chef?
            Ja, *das* ist der Chef, für den ich arbeite.

1. Sind Sie durch *diese* Stadt gefahren?   *durch die ich gefahren bin*
2. Haben Sie in *diesem* Hotel übernachtet?   *in dem ich h*
3. Haben Sie mit *diesen* Amerikanern geredet?   *mit denen ich geredet habe*
4. Haben Sie an *dieser* Uni studiert?   *an der ich studiert habe*
remember 5. Erinnern Sie sich an *diesen* Roman?   *an den ich mich erinnere*
6. Kommen Sie aus *dieser* Stadt?   *aus der ich komme*
7. Wohnen Sie bei *dieser* Familie?   *bei der ich wohne*
8. Spricht er mit *diesen* Menschen?   *mit denen er spricht*
9. Steht unser Wagen hinter *diesem* Gebäude?   *hinter dem unser Wagen steht*
10. Bekommst du Briefe von *diesen* Freunden?   *von denen du Briefe bekommt*
11. Spielst du für *diese* Mannschaft?   *für die ich spiele*

In Europa ist nur die Wolga in Russland länger als die Donau (2.850 km). Die Zugspitze (2.692 m) ist der höchste Berg Deutschlands.

Rosen an einer alten Mauer
(Schloss Langenburg, Baden-
Württemberg).

These sentences are paired as
conversational exchanges. The relative
clauses in numbers 4 and 10 begin
with prepositions. In numbers 11 and
14, the relative pronoun is in the
genitive case.

■ 15 ■   **Übung**   Machen Sie aus den zwei Sätzen *einen* Satz. Machen Sie aus dem
zweiten Satz einen Relativsatz.

> **BEISPIEL:** Ich kenne die Frau. (Du meinst sie.)
> Ich kenne die Frau, die du meinst.

1. Suchst du die Schokolade? (Sie war hier.)
2. Nein, ich habe selber Schokolade. (Ich habe sie mitgebracht.)

3. Ist das die Geschichte? (Horst hat sie erzählt.)
4. Ja, er erzählt Geschichten. (Man muss über seine Geschichten lachen.)

5. Das ist ein Buch. (Ingrid hat es schon letztes Jahr gelesen.)
6. Meinst du das Buch? (Es ist jetzt sehr bekannt.)

7. Ist das der Mann? (Sie haben ihm geholfen.)
8. Nein, ich habe einem anderen Mann geholfen. (Er war nicht so jung.)

9. Kennst du die Studenten? (Sie wohnen in der Altstadt.)
10. Ja, das sind die Studenten. (Mit ihnen esse ich zusammen in der Mensa.)

11. Wie heißt der Junge? (Sein Vater ist Professor.)
12. Er hat einen komischen Namen. (Ich habe ihn vergessen.)

13. Ist die Frau berufstätig? (Du wohnst bei ihr.)
14. Ja, sie ist eine Frau. (Ihre Kinder wohnen nicht mehr zu Hause.)

■ 16 ■   **Partnerarbeit: Ist das ein neuer Mantel?**   Fragen Sie einander, ob Ihre
Kleider und andere Sachen neu sind. Antworten Sie, dass Sie alles letztes Jahr gekauft
haben. Benutzen Sie einen Relativsatz in Ihrer Antwort.

> **BEISPIEL:** Ist das ein neuer Mantel?
> Nein, das ist ein Mantel, *den* ich letztes Jahr kaufte.

■ The relative pronoun *was*

A relative clause following the pronoun antecedents **das**, **etwas**, **nichts**, **viel**, **wenig**, and **alles** begins with the relative pronoun **was**. Note again that English often leaves out the relative pronoun, whereas German requires it.

Stimmt **das, was** er uns erzählte?	*Is what he told us right?*
	(literally: *Is that right what he told us?*)
Gibt es noch **etwas, was** Sie brauchen?	*Is there something else [that] you need?*
Nein, Sie haben **nichts, was** ich brauche.	*No, you have nothing [that] I need.*
Alles, was er sagt, ist falsch.	*Everything [that] he says is wrong.*

Was must also begin a relative clause whose antecedent is a neuter adjectival noun (see p. 323–324):

Was war **das Interessante, was** du mir zeigen wolltest?	*What was the interesting thing [that] you wanted to show me?*
Ist das **das Beste, was** Sie haben?	*Is that the best [that] you have?*

Was also begins a relative clause whose antecedent is an entire clause (English uses *which*):

Rita hat sich verlobt, was ich nicht verstehen kann.	*Rita got engaged, which I can't understand.*

Lab Manual Kap. 12, Var. zu Üb. 17, 18.

■ 17 ■ Übung: Etwas, was mir gefällt. / Etwas, was mich ärgert. Ihre Professorin sagt etwas und möchte Ihre Reaktion hören. Ist das etwas, was Sie ärgert, oder etwas, was Ihnen gefällt?

> BEISPIEL: Die Umwelt ist sehr verschmutzt.
> Das ist etwas, was mich ärgert!

1. Das Studium wird immer teurer.
2. Der Kalte Krieg ist zu Ende.
3. Ihr Mitbewohner spielt abends laute Rockmusik.
4. Heute Abend in der Mensa gibt es Pizza zum Abendessen.
5. Die Ferien beginnen bald.
6. Morgen kommen viele Verwandte zu Besuch.

■ 18 ■ Partnerarbeit: Was war das Tollste, was du je gemacht hast? Below are cues for asking each other questions such as, "What's the greatest thing you've ever done?" Take turns asking each other the questions.

> BEISPIEL: toll / machen
> A: Was war das Tollste, was du je gemacht hast?
> B: Ich habe 1989 auf der Berliner Mauer gesessen.

1. schwierig / machen
2. schön / sehen
3. gefährlich / machen
4. dumm / sagen
5. erstaunlich / hören
6. gut / essen
7. interessant / lesen
8. toll / bekommen

The verb lassen

Caution! Do not confuse these principal parts: **lassen (lässt), ließ, hat gelassen** and **lesen (liest), las, hat gelesen** (*to read*).

The verb **lassen** has several meanings in German:

- *to leave (something or someone), leave behind*

Lassen Sie uns bitte allein.	*Please leave us alone.*
Hast du deinen Mantel im Restaurant **gelassen**?	*Did you leave your coat in the restaurant?*

- *to allow, let:* **lassen** + infinitive

Man **lässt** uns **gehen**.	*They're letting us leave.*
Lass doch die Kinder **spielen**!	*Let the children play!*

- *to have or order something done:* **lassen** + infinitive

In the following sentences **lassen** shows that the subject is not performing an action, but rather having it done by someone else.

Sie **lässt** ihren Wagen **reparieren**.	*She's having her car fixed.*

The accusative case shows who performs the action:

Sie lässt **den Mechaniker** ihren Wagen reparieren.	*She's having the mechanic fix her car.*

A dative reflexive pronoun shows explicitly that one is having something done for one's own benefit.

Ich lasse **mir** ein Haus bauen.	*I'm having a house built (for myself).*

When **lassen** is used with a dependent infinitive, it takes the double infinitive construction in the perfect tense. The structure is parallel to that of the modal verbs (see page 176).

double infinitive

Die Beamtin hat mich nicht **reden lassen**.
The official didn't let me speak.

Ich habe den Wagen **reparieren lassen**.
I had my car repaired.

Lab Manual Kap. 12, Var. zu Üb. 19, 21.

Workbook Kap. 12, L, M.

■ 19 ■ **Übung: Warum ist das nicht hier?** Sagen Sie, wo Sie diese Menschen oder Dinge gelassen haben. Rechts gibt es einige Möglichkeiten, aber Sie können auch frei antworten.

> **BEISPIEL:** Warum haben Sie heute keine Jacke?
> Ich habe sie zu Hause gelassen.

1. Warum sind Ihre Kinder nicht hier?	in der Schweiz
2. Warum tragen Sie heute keine Brille (*glasses*)?	im Rucksack
3. Warum haben Sie Ihr Referat nicht mit?	bei der Großmutter
4. Warum haben sie Ihren Ausweis nicht mit?	auf dem Bett
5. Warum haben Sie Ihren Wagen nicht mit?	zu Hause
6. Warum ist Ihre Tochter nicht hier?	in der Manteltasche

■ **20** ■ **Partnerarbeit: Wo hast du das gelassen?** Hat Ihre Partnerin heute etwas nicht mitgebracht? Fragen Sie sie, wo sie es gelassen hat.

> **BEISPIEL:** A: Wo hast du heute deine grüne Jacke gelassen?
> B: Ich habe sie im Zimmer gelassen.

■ **21** ■ **Übung: Er hat es machen lassen.** Manchmal will man etwas nicht selber machen, sondern man will es lieber machen lassen. Was haben diese Leute machen lassen?

> **BEISPIEL:** Hat Fritz das Mittagessen selber gekocht?
> Nein, er hat es kochen lassen.

1. Hat Herr von Hippel sein Haus selber gebaut?
2. Hat Frau Beck ihren Wagen selber repariert?
3. Hat Oma ihren Koffer selbst getragen?
4. Hat deine Freundin sich die Haare selber geschnitten?
5. Hat Frau Schwarzer den Brief selbst abgeschickt (*sent off*)?
6. Hat Günter das Referat selbst geschrieben?
7. Hat Robert seine Schuhe selber geputzt (*cleaned*)?

Notes on Usage: **German equivalents for English *to leave***

The equivalent you choose for the English verb *to leave* depends on whether it means *to go away* (intransitive) or *to leave something behind* (transitive), and also on what or whom you are leaving.

- Intransitive: **gehen, weggehen, abfahren** (= *leave by vehicle*)

Ich muss jetzt **gehen**.	*I have to leave now.*
Er **ging weg**, ohne etwas zu sagen.	*He left without saying anything.*
Um elf **fuhr** sie mit dem Zug **ab**.	*She left by train at eleven.*

- Transitive: **lassen** (= *leave something somewhere*); **verlassen** (= *leave a person or place for good*)

Ich habe meine Tasche zu Hause **gelassen**.	*I left my bag at home.*
Viele wollten ihre Heimat nicht **verlassen**.	*Many did not want to leave their homeland.*

■ **22** ■ **Übung: Wie sagt man das auf Deutsch?**

1. Jörg left the house at seven.
2. Jörg left at seven.
3. Jörg's train left at seven.
4. Jörg left his book in the Mensa.
5. Jörg, please leave the room.
6. Jörg left his car in front of the hotel.
7. Jörg wants to leave school.

Time phrases with Mal

The English word *time* has two German equivalents, **die Zeit** and **das Mal**.
Zeit denotes time in general.

> Ich brauche mehr **Zeit**. *I need more time.*

Mal denotes an occurrence.

Wie viele Male = wie oft

Das erste **Mal** habe ich das Buch nicht verstanden.	*I didn't understand the book the first time.*
Wie viele **Male** hast du es gelesen?	*How many times did you read it?*

Learn the following idioms with **Mal**.

das erste Mal	*the first time*
zum ersten Mal	*for the first time*
zum zweiten Mal	*for the second time*
zum letzten Mal	*for the last time*
diesmal	*this time*
jedes Mal	*every time*
das nächste Mal	*(the) next time*

Saying how often things happen is a communicative goal.

Note on Usage: The suffix *-mal*

Note that **-mal** added as a suffix to cardinal numbers forms adverbs indicating repetition.

einmal	*once*
zweimal	*twice*
zwanzigmal	*twenty times*
hundertmal	*a hundred times*
zigmal	*umpteen times*

Workbook Kap. 12, N.

■ 23 ■ Übung: Wie oft haben Sie das schon gemacht?   Fragen Sie einander, wie oft Sie etwas schon gemacht haben.

BEISPIEL: A: John, wie oft hast du schon dein Lieblingsbuch gelesen?
B: Ich habe es schon viermal gelesen.

1. Wie oft hast du schon deinen Wagen reparieren lassen?
2. Wie oft bist du dieses Jahr schon nach Hause gefahren?
3. Wie oft bist du dieses Semester schon ins Kino gegangen?
4. Wie oft hast du dieses Semester schon Referate schreiben müssen?
5. Wie oft hast du dieses Semester schon deinen besten Freund angerufen?
6. Wie oft bist du schon am Wochenende weggefahren?

■ 24 ■ Übung: Wie sagt man das auf Deutsch?

1. Please give me more time.
   Unfortunately, I don't have more time for you.

2. I'm trying it for the first time.
   The next time it's easier.

3. I need time and money.
   You say that every time.

ZEIT IN IHRER SCHÖNSTEN FORM.

■ **25** ■ **Gruppenarbeit: Was haben Sie zum ersten Mal hier erlebt?** Wenn man Student wird, erlebt (*experiences*) und lernt man viel Neues. Sagen Sie, was Sie hier an der Uni oder am College zum ersten Mal getan, erlebt, gelernt, gesehen, angefangen oder versucht haben.

> **BEISPIEL:** Ich habe *zum ersten Mal* etwas über Astronomie gelernt.
> Ich habe *zum ersten Mal* über Politik diskutiert.

Proverb: **Morgenstund' hat Gold im Mund** (*The early bird catches the worm*).

Parts of the day

German divides up the day in the following way:

gestern	früh *oder* Morgen	yesterday	morning
	Nachmittag		afternoon
	Abend		evening
heute	früh *oder* Morgen	this	morning
	Nachmittag		afternoon
	Abend		evening
morgen	früh	tomorrow	morning
	Nachmittag		afternoon
	Abend		evening

In addition, remember:

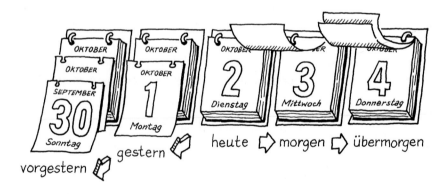

Workbook Kap. 12, O.

■ **26** ■ **Übung: Gestern, heute und morgen** Fragen Sie einander, wann Sie verschiedene Dinge zum letzten Mal gemacht haben.

> **BEISPIEL:** A: Wann hast du zum letzten Mal Kaffee getrunken?
> B: Gestern Abend. (*oder*) Heute früh.

1. Wann hast du zum letzten Mal deinen besten Freund gesehen?
2. Wann bist du zum letzten Mal einkaufen gegangen?

3. Wann hast du zum letzten Mal Hausaufgaben gemacht?
4. Wann bist du zum letzten Mal ins Kino gegangen?
5. Wann hast du zum letzten Mal telefoniert?

Jetzt fragen Sie, wann Sie verschiedene Dinge das nächste Mal machen.

6. Wann besuchst du das nächste Mal deine Eltern?
7. Wann gehst du das nächste Mal ins Konzert?
8. Wann gehst du das nächste Mal ins Museum?
9. Wann fährst du das nächste Mal Rad?
10. Wann triffst du das nächste Mal deine Freunde?

Lesestück

Lab Manual Kap. 12,
Üb. zur Betonung.

Similarly: **irgendwer**
(= **irgendjemand**), **irgendwas**
(= **irgendetwas**), **irgendwohin**,
irgendwoher.

Vor dem Lesen

Tipps zum Lesen und Lernen

■ **Tipps zum Vokabelnlernen**

The prefix **irgend-**   With question words like **wo**, **wie**, and **wann**, the prefix **irgend-** creates indefinite adverbs as does the English word *some* in *somewhere, somehow, sometime,* etc.

irgendwo	*somewhere (or other), anywhere*
irgendwie	*somehow (or other)*
irgendwann	*sometime (or other), any time*

Hast du meine Zeitung **irgendwo** gesehen?   *Have you seen my newspaper anywhere?*

Kommen Sie **irgendwann** vorbei?   *Will you come by sometime?*

Meinen Schlüssel habe ich **irgendwie** verloren.   *Somehow or other I've lost my key.*

Im Lesetext für dieses Kapitel schreibt Anna Seghers:

Der Dom hat die Luftangriffe … **irgendwie** überstanden.   *The cathedral survived the air raids somehow or other.*

■ **Einstieg in den Text**

Like the poems in **Lyrik zum Vorlesen**, the following reading, "Zwei Denkmäler" by Anna Seghers, was written not for students learning German but rather for an audience of German speakers. Nonetheless, you have now learned enough German to read an authentic text with a little help from marginal glosses.

"Zwei Denkmäler" is not a story, but rather an essay *about* a story that Seghers never finished but could not "get out of her head" (**Das geht mir heute nicht aus dem Kopf**). She focuses on two monuments (**Denkmäler**)—one of grand cultural significance, the other of individual suffering.

Now that you have learned how relative clauses work in German, you will notice how frequent they are in expository prose like "Zwei Denkmäler." During your first reading of the text, be on the lookout for the eight relative clauses it contains. List each antecedent and relative clause. Here is the first one:

1. ... eine Erzählung, die der Krieg unterbrochen hat.
   . . . a story that the war interrupted.

2. _____

3. _____

etc.

Anna Seghers

Zwei Denkmäler

Applying your knowledge of twentieth-century Germany to an authentic German literary text is the cultural goal of this chapter.

Anna Seghers is the pseudonym of Netty Reiling, who was born in Mainz in 1900. She studied art history and sinology. Because of her membership in the Communist Party, she was forced to flee Germany in 1933. She sought asylum in France and Mexico. Much of her writing in exile reflects the turbulent existence of a refugee and committed antifascist. In 1947 she moved to the GDR, where she died in 1983.

The opening sentence of Seghers's essay establishes the historical context of an exile from Hitler's Germany, writing during World War II about the horrors of World War I.

The writer addresses loss on many levels: of human life during wartime, of a literary manuscript, and of the memory of one woman's sacrifice. She suggests, however, that in the story she wanted to write, Frau Eppstein's daughter would have preserved that memory.

Lab Manual Kap. 12, Lesestück.

In der Emigration° begann ich eine Erzählung, die der Krieg unterbrochen hat. Ihr Anfang ist mir noch in Erinnerung geblieben. Nicht Wort für Wort, aber dem Sinn nach°. Was mich damals erregt° hat, geht mir auch heute nicht aus dem Kopf. Ich erinnere mich an eine Erinnerung.

5   In meiner Heimat, in Mainz am Rhein, gab es zwei Denkmäler, die ich niemals° vergessen konnte, in Freude und Angst, auf Schiffen, in fernen Städten. Eins° ist der Dom. Wie ich als Schulkind zu meinem Erstaunen° sah, ist er auf Pfeilern° gebaut, die tief in die Erde hineingehen° – damals kam es mir vor°, beinahe° so hoch wie der Dom hochragt°. Ihre Risse sind auszementiert worden° sagte man, in vergangener° Zeit, da,

10 wo das Grundwasser Unheil stiftete°. Ich weiß nicht, ob das stimmt, was uns ein Lehrer erzählte: Die romanischen[1] und gotischen[2] Pfeiler seien haltbarer° als die jüngeren.

Dieser Dom über der Rheinebene° wäre mir in all seiner Macht und Größe geblieben°, wenn ich ihn auch nie wieder gesehen hätte°. Aber ebensowenig° kann ich

15 ein anderes Denkmal in meiner Heimatstadt vergessen. Es bestand nur aus° einem einzigen flachen Stein, den man in das Pflaster° einer Straße gesetzt hat. Hieß die Straße Bonifaziusstraße? Hieß sie Frauenlobstraße? Das weiß ich nicht mehr. Ich weiß nur, dass der Stein zum Gedächtnis° einer Frau eingefügt wurde°, die im Ersten Weltkrieg durch Bombensplitter umkam°, als sie Milch für ihr Kind holen wollte.

20 Wenn ich mich recht erinnere, war sie die Frau des jüdischen Weinhändlers° Eppstein. Menschenfresserisch°, grausam war der Erste Weltkrieg, man begann aber erst an seinem Ende mit Luftangriffen° auf Städte und Menschen. Darum hat man zum Gedächtnis der Frau den Stein eingesetzt, flach wie das Pflaster, und ihren Namen eingraviert°.

25 Der Dom hat die Luftangriffe des Zweiten Weltkriegs irgendwie überstanden°, wie auch° die Stadt zerstört worden ist°. Er ragt° über Fluss und Ebene. Ob der kleine flache Gedenkstein° noch da ist, das weiß ich nicht. Bei meinen Besuchen habe ich ihn nicht mehr gefunden.

In der Erzählung, die ich vor dem Zweiten Weltkrieg zu schreiben begann und im

30 Krieg verlor, ist die Rede von° dem Kind, dem die Mutter Milch holen wollte, aber nicht heimbringen° konnte. Ich hatte die Absicht°, in dem Buch zu erzählen, was aus diesem Mädchen geworden ist.

here: in exile

dem ... = the sense of it / excited

niemals = **nie**
one of them
astonishment / pillars
go into / **kam ...** = it seemed to me / **beinahe** = fast
looms up / **Risse ...** = cracks have been patched
past / **Grundwasser ...** = groundwater caused damage
seien haltbarer = were more durable
Rheinebene = Rhine plain
wäre ... = would have remained / **wenn ...** = even if I had never seen it again
ebensowenig = no less
bestand ... = consisted of only
Pflaster = pavement
zum Gedächtnis = in memory of
eingefügt wurde = had been set in / **durch ...** = was killed by shrapnel
Weinhändler = wine merchant
Menschenfresserisch = cannibalistic
Luftangriffe = air raids
engraved
survived / **wie auch** = obwohl / **zerstört ...** = was destroyed / **ragt** = looms
Gedenkstein = commemorative stone
ist ... = the story is about
heimbringen = nach Hause bringen
Absicht = intention

---

1. **romanisch**   Romanesque style (mid-11th to mid-12th century), characterized by round arches and vaults.
2. **gotisch**   Gothic style (mid-12th to mid-16th century), characterized by pointed arches and vaults.

Nach dem Lesen

■ A ■ Antworten Sie auf Deutsch.

1. Was hat Anna Seghers' Erzählung unterbrochen?
2. Welche Stadt war Anna Seghers' Heimatstadt?
3. Was konnte sie nie vergessen?
4. Über welche Denkmäler schreibt sie?
5. Vergleichen Sie diese zwei Denkmäler.
6. An wen sollte der Stein erinnern?
7. Hat Anna Seghers den Stein wieder gefunden?
8. Wann begann sie die Erzählung zu schreiben?
9. Was wollte sie erzählen?

Workbook Kap. 12, P–R.

Lab Manual Kap. 12, Diktat.

■ B ■ Gruppenarbeit: Denkmäler und historische Gebäude

Hier sehen Sie Fotos von berühmten Denkmälern und Gebäuden. Sehen Sie sich zusammen die Bilder an und beschreiben Sie sie auf Deutsch. Welche Denkmäler und Gebäude sind Ihnen schon bekannt? An welche Personen oder Ereignisse (*events*) erinnern sie? Was ist Ihre Reaktion auf diese Denkmäler?

1. Kaiser-Wilhelm-Gedächtniskirche (Berlin)   2. Vietnam-Krieg-Denkmal (Washington)

3. Arc de Triomphe (Paris)

4. Mozarts Geburtshaus (Salzburg)

5. Reste (*remains*) der Berliner Mauer

Situationen aus dem Alltag

■ „Das geht mir nicht aus dem Kopf"

In der kurzen Erzählung „Zwei Denkmäler" erinnert sich die Schriftstellerin an etwas, was vor vielen Jahren passiert ist. Sie sagt, sie erinnert sich „an eine Erinnerung". Am Anfang dieses Kapitels haben Sie das Gedicht „Heimweh" von Eichendorff gelesen, in dem er auch über Erinnerungen an die Heimat und die Geliebte spricht. Sprechen wir jetzt ein bisschen über unsere eigenen Erinnerungen.

Neue Vokabeln

die **Erfahrung, -en**	*experience*	das **Heimweh**	*homesickness*
die **Gegenwart**	*present (time)*	der **Ort, -e**	*place; small town*

This vocabulary focuses on an everday topic or situation. Words you already know from **Wortschatz** sections are listed without English equivalents; new supplementary vocabulary is listed with definitions. Your instructor may assign some supplementary vocabulary for active mastery.

Diese Wörter und Ausdrücke kennen Sie schon.

Ich bin in _____ (Heimatort) geboren.

sich erinnern an
alte Freunde
umziehen
die Vergangenheit
verlassen
wieder sehen

Berlin um 1900

■ A ■ **Gruppendiskussion: Wo haben Sie als Kind gewohnt?** Leben Sie noch in der Stadt, wo Sie geboren sind, oder sind Sie umgezogen? Gefällt es Ihnen besser, wo Sie jetzt wohnen? Besuchen Sie manchmal Ihren Geburtsort? Was wollen Sie dort sehen? Was hat sich dort geändert?

Discussing personal memories is a communicative goal.

■ B ■ **Partnerarbeit: Ich erinnere mich an etwas Besonderes.** Erzählen Sie einander eine wichtige Erinnerung aus Ihrer Kindheit. Gibt es z.B. einen besonderen Menschen, an den Sie sich erinnern? Oder einen Lieblingsort oder ein Gebäude, wo Sie Zeit verbracht haben? Warum geht es Ihnen nicht aus dem Kopf?

View Module 6 of the *Neue Horizonte* video (22:44) and do the activities in **Videoecke 6** in your Workbook/Laboratory Manual/Video Manual.

Four Modern Writers

A particular kind of memory has haunted German and Austrian writers of the past fifty years: the refusal to forget the Third Reich and the Second World War. For contemporary Germans, the act of recalling and interpreting this painful history has been termed **Vergangenheitsbewältigung**: *surmounting* (or) *overcoming the past*. These four writers all experienced National Socialism and war as children. They began writing after 1945 and earned international reputations. For them, there can be no question of repressing the past, for their literary works honor its memory, confront German guilt, and engage in **Trauerarbeit**, the *work of mourning*.

Günter Grass (b. 1927)

Günter Grass, the son of a grocer in Danzig (today Gdansk, Poland), was drafted out of school at the very end of the war and served briefly as a tank gunner. After the war he apprenticed to a stonecutter in Düsseldorf, and then studied graphic art and sculpture in Berlin. His first novel, *Die Blechtrommel* (*The Tin Drum*, 1959), was an instant international success. In it, the dwarf narrator Oskar Matzerath recounts with an outsider's black humor and wicked satire his life among the lower middle class of Danzig before, during, and after the war. Grass has continued to use his native city of Danzig/Gdansk as a setting for his fiction and to be an active voice for German-Polish reconciliation.

Ingeborg Bachmann (1926–1973)

Ingeborg Bachmann was born in Klagenfurt, Austria, and studied philosophy at the University of Vienna. Although she first gained fame as a lyric poet, she also wrote radio plays and short stories, an opera libretto, and the novel *Malina* (1972), which is the first volume of an unfinished trilogy entitled *Todesarten* (*Kinds of Death*). In her late prose Ingeborg Bachmann brilliantly exposes the tyranny and psychic violence that continue to lurk beneath the cultivated exterior of post-war Viennese society.

Jurek Becker (1937–1997)

Jurek Becker, born in Lodz, Poland, to Jewish parents, managed to survive imprisonment in Nazi concentration camps along with his father. Believing that anti-Semitism had been eliminated in Germany but not in Poland, they remained in what was to become the German Democratic Republic after the war. Becker's first novel, *Jakob der Lügner* (*Jakob the Liar*, 1969), is the story of a Jew who owns a clandestine radio and sustains the hopes of his fellow ghetto inhabitants by inventing stories of Allied victories. In *Bronsteins Kinder* (1986) he explores the complex relationship between a Holocaust survivor and his son.

Christa Wolf (b. 1929)

Christa Wolf's parents were shopkeepers in Landsberg, today Gorzów (Poland). She worked as an editor in the German Democratic Republic before publishing her first fiction in 1961. Since then, her works have been widely translated. Her autobiographical novel *Kindheitsmuster* (*Patterns of Childhood*, 1976) is an extended reflection on the psychic damage done to a child educated as a true believer in Nazism. *Kassandra* (1983) retells the story of the Trojan War from a feminist and antiheroic point of view.

Die Schweiz

Communicative Goals

- Talking about the future
- Telling people you'd like them to do something
- Introducing yourself and others

Cultural Goal

- Learning about Switzerland

Chapter Outline

- **Lyrik zum Vorlesen**
  Eugen Gomringer, „nachwort"

- **Grammatik**
  Verbs with prepositional complements
  Pronouns as objects of prepositions: *da-* and *wo*-compounds
  Future tense
  Wanting X to do Y

- **Lesestück**
  Zwei Schweizer stellen ihre Heimat vor

- **Situationen aus dem Alltag**
  Wie stellt man sich vor?

- **Almanach**
  Profile of Switzerland

Dialoge

Lab Manual Kap. 13, Dialoge, Fragen, Hören Sie gut zu!

Ski is pronounced (and alternatively spelled) **Schi**. Note the colloquial contraction **vorm = vor dem**.

Skifahren in der Schweiz

Kurz vor dem Semesterende sprechen zwei Studentinnen über ihre Ferienpläne.

accusative

BRIGITTE: Ich freue mich sehr auf die Semesterferien!

JOHANNA: Hast du vor wieder Ski zu fahren?

BRIGITTE: Ja, ich werde zwei Wochen in der Schweiz verbringen. Morgen früh flieg' ich nach Zürich.

JOHANNA: Da bin ich ja ganz baff! Früher hast du doch immer Angst vorm Fliegen gehabt!

BRIGITTE: Stimmt, aber ich habe mich einfach daran gewöhnt.

coop living

In der WG: Bei Nina ist es unordentlich.

UTE: Nina, hör mal zu, wann wirst du deine Sachen endlich aufräumen?

NINA: Ich mach' das gleich. Seid mir nicht böse–ich musste mich heute Morgen wahnsinnig beeilen.

LUTZ: Ja, das sagst du immer. Jetzt haben wir aber die Nase voll. Alle müssen doch mitmachen.

NINA: Ihr habt Recht. Von jetzt an werde ich mich mehr um die Wohnung kümmern.

Am Informationsschalter in Basel

TOURIST: Entschuldigung. Darf ich Sie um Auskunft bitten?

BEAMTIN: Gerne. Wie kann ich Ihnen helfen?

TOURIST: Ich bin nur einen Tag in Basel und kenne mich hier nicht aus. Was können Sie mir empfehlen?

BEAMTIN: Es kommt darauf an, was Sie sehen wollen. Das Kunstmuseum lohnt sich besonders. Wenn Sie sich für das Mittelalter interessieren, dürfen Sie die neue Ausstellung nicht verpassen.

TOURIST: Das interessiert mich aber sehr. Wie komme ich denn dahin?

BEAMTIN: Direkt vor dem Bahnhof ist die Haltestelle. Dort müssen Sie in die Straßenbahnlinie 2 einsteigen. Am Museum steigen Sie dann aus.

TOURIST: Das werde ich schon finden. Vielen Dank für Ihre Hilfe.

BEAMTIN: Bitte sehr.

Note on Usage: *nicht dürfen*

The equivalent for English *must not* is **nicht dürfen**.

Die Ausstellung dürfen Sie nicht verpassen.	*You mustn't (really shouldn't) miss the exhibit.*

Wortschatz 1

Verben

Angst haben vor (+ *dat.*) to be afraid of

auf·räumen to tidy up, straighten up

sich aus·kennen to know one's way around
  Ich kenne mich hier nicht aus. I don't know my way around here.

bitten, bat, hat gebeten um to ask for, request

sich freuen auf (+ *acc.*) to look forward to

sich gewöhnen an (+ *acc.*) to get used to

interessieren to interest

sich interessieren für to be interested in

sich kümmern um to look after, take care of; to deal with

sich lohnen to be worthwhile, worth the trouble

verpassen to miss (*an event, opportunity, train, etc.*)

sich vor·bereiten auf (+ *acc.*) to prepare for

vor·haben to plan, have in mind

warten auf (+ *acc.*) to wait for

zu·hören (+ *dat.*) to listen (to)
  Hören Sie gut zu! Listen carefully.
  Hör mir zu. Listen to me.

Substantive

der **Schalter, -** counter, window

das **Mittelalter** the Middle Ages

die **Auskunft** information

die **Haltestelle, -n** (streetcar or bus) stop

die **Hilfe** help

die **Linie, -n** (streetcar or bus) line

die **Straßenbahn, -en** streetcar

Adjektive und Adverbien

böse (+ *dat.*) angry, mad (at); bad, evil
  Sei mir nicht böse. Don't be mad at me.

direkt direct(ly)

unordentlich disorderly, messy

Nützliche Ausdrücke

von jetzt an from now on

Es kommt darauf an. It depends.
  Es kommt darauf an, was Sie sehen wollen. It depends on what you want to see.

Wie komme ich dahin? How do I get there?

Gegensätze

böse ≠ **gut** evil ≠ good

sich interessieren ≠ **sich langweilen** to be interested ≠ to be bored

unordentlich ≠ **ordentlich** disorderly, messy ≠ orderly, neat

Mit anderen Worten

baff sein (*colloq.*) = **sehr staunen, sprachlos sein**

schlampig (*colloq.*) = **unordentlich**

Skiing in Switzerland

Shortly before the end of the semester, two students are talking about their vacation plans.

B: I'm really looking forward to the semester break!

J: Do you plan to go skiing again?

B: Yes, I'll spend two weeks in Switzerland. Tomorrow morning I fly to Zürich.

J: I'm flabbergasted! Before, you were always afraid of flying!

B: True, but I've simply gotten used to it.

In the Group Apartment: Nina's Place is Messy

U: Listen, Nina, when are you finally going to straighten up your things?

N: I'll do it right away. Don't be mad at me—I was in a big rush this morning.

L: Yeah, you always say that. Now we're really fed up. Everybody has to pitch in.

N: You're right. From now on I'll take more care of the apartment.

At the Information Window in Basel

T: Excuse me. May I ask you for information?

O: Sure. How can I help you?

T: I'm only in Basel for a day, and I don't know my way around here. What can you recommend to me?

O: It depends on what you want to see. The art museum is especially worthwhile. If you're interested in the Middle Ages, you mustn't miss the new exhibit.

T: That interests me a lot. How do I get there?

O: Right in front of the station is the streetcar stop. You have to get the number 2 streetcar. Then get out at the museum.

T: I'll find it all right. Thanks for your help.

O: You're welcome.

Variationen

■ A ■ Persönliche Fragen

1. Brigitte freut sich auf die Semesterferien. Freuen Sie sich auf etwas?
2. Sie hat vor Ski zu fahren. Was haben Sie am Wochenende vor?
3. Fahren Sie in den Semesterferien irgendwohin?

4. Bei Nina sieht's schlampig aus. Wie sieht es bei Ihnen im Zimmer aus?
5. Die anderen in der WG sind Nina böse, weil sie nicht aufräumt. Wann werden Sie böse?

6. Der Tourist kennt sich in Basel nicht aus, aber zu Hause kennt er sich natürlich sehr gut aus. In welcher Stadt kennen Sie sich besonders gut aus?
7. Der Tourist interessiert sich für das Mittelalter. Wann war denn das Mittelalter?
8. Der Tourist will die Ausstellung nicht verpassen. Haben Sie je etwas Gutes verpasst? Was denn?
9. Was machen Sie, wenn Sie sich in einer fremden Stadt nicht auskennen?

■ B ■ Übung: Wie sagt man das mit anderen Worten?

1. Wenn man sehr wenig Geld hat, ist man _____ .
2. Wenn man zu viel von etwas gehabt hat, sagt man: „Ich habe _____ voll."
3. Jemand, der besonders müde ist, nennt man _____ .
4. Wenn Sie sich bei einer Vorlesung sehr gelangweilt haben, dann haben Sie sie _____ gefunden.
5. Etwas, was sehr groß ist, kann man auch _____ nennen.
6. Ein anderes Wort für *dumm* ist _____ .

■ C ■ Übung: Es kommt darauf an. (It depends.)   Ihr Professor spielt die Rolle eines Freundes, dem Sie verschiedene Dinge empfehlen sollen. Sie sagen ihm jedes Mal, es kommt darauf an.

> BEISPIEL: Können Sie mir etwas *in der Stadt* empfehlen?
> Es kommt darauf an, *was Sie sehen wollen.*

1. etwas auf der Speisekarte
2. ein gutes Buch
3. eine neue CD
4. ein Reiseziel
5. ein ruhiges Hotel
6. einen guten Wein
7. einen guten Kassettenrekorder
8. einen neuen Beruf

■ D ■ Rollenspiel: Am Informationsschalter (*Gruppen von 3 Studenten*)

Zwei von Ihnen sind Touristen und kennen sich in dieser Stadt nicht aus. Der/die Dritte arbeitet am Infoschalter und gibt Auskunft. Vergessen Sie nicht „Sie" zueinander zu sagen. Fangen Sie so an:

TOURISTEN: Entschuldigung, dürfen wir Sie um Auskunft bitten?
BEAMTER/BEAMTIN: Gerne. Wie kann ich Ihnen helfen?

Alpendorf im Winter
(Kanton Graubünden)

Lyrik zum Vorlesen

Eugen Gomringer was born to Swiss parents in Bolivia. True to his typically polyglot Swiss background, he has written poems in German, Swiss-German dialect, French, English, and Spanish. Gomringer is a leading exponent of concrete poetry (**konkrete Poesie**), which rejects metaphor, radically simplifies syntax, and considers the printed page a visual as much as a linguistic experience. The following poem consists entirely of nouns followed by relative clauses in strict parallelism. Readers must work out the interrelationships for themselves. Pay particular attention to the verb tenses as you read this poem aloud.

Lab Manual Kap. 13,
Lyrik zum Vorlesen.

nachwort°   afterword

das dorf°, das ich nachts hörte   village
der wald, in dem ich schlief

das land, das ich überflog°   flew across
die stadt, in der ich wohnte

das haus, das den freunden gehörte
die frau, die ich kannte

das bild, das mich wach hielt°   kept awake
der klang°, der mir gefiel   sound

das buch, in dem ich las
der stein, den ich fand

der mann, den ich verstand
das kind, das ich lehrte°   taught

der baum, den ich blühen° sah   blooming
das tier, das ich fürchtete

die sprache, die ich spreche
die schrift°, die ich schreibe   writing

     Eugen Gomringer (geboren 1925)

Erstbesteigung (*first ascent*) des
Matterhorns (4.478 m) im Jahre 1865

Verbs with prepositional complements

Many verbs use a prepositional phrase to complete, expand, or change their meaning. Such phrases are called *prepositional complements*.

Ich spreche.	*I'm speaking.*
Ich spreche **mit ihm**.	*I'm speaking **with him**.*
Ich spreche **gegen ihn**.	*I'm speaking **against him**.*

In the examples above, English and German happen to use parallel prepositions. In many cases, however, they do not. For example:

Er wartet **auf** seinen Bruder.	*He's waiting **for** his brother.*
Sie bittet **um** Geld.	*She's asking **for** money.*

For this reason, you must learn the verb and the preposition used with it *together*. For instance, you should learn **bitten (bat, hat gebeten) um**, *to ask for*.

Here is a list of the verbs with prepositional complements that you have already learned in this and previous chapters.

Sometimes the complete verbal idea also involves a noun, as in **Angst haben vor.** Notice that most equivalent English verbs also have prepositional complements (*to look forward to, to wait for*), but some do not (*to remember, to request*).

Angst haben vor (+ *dat.*)   *to be afraid of*

Hast du Angst vorm Fliegen?	*Are you afraid of flying?*

bitten um   *to ask for, request*

Sie bat mich um Geld.	*She asked me for money.*

erinnern an (+ *acc.*)   *to remind of*

Das erinnert mich an etwas Wichtiges.	*That reminds me of something important.*

sich erinnern an (+ *acc.*)   *to remember*

Sie hat sich an meinen Geburtstag erinnert.	*She remembered my birthday.*

sich freuen auf (+ *acc.*)   *to look forward to*

Ich freue mich auf die Ferien!	*I'm looking forward to the vacation!*

sich gewöhnen an (+ *acc.*)   *to get used to*

Sie konnte sich nicht an das kalte Wetter gewöhnen.	*She couldn't get used to the cold weather.*

sich interessieren für   *to be interested in*

Interessieren Sie sich für moderne Kunst?	*Are you interested in modern art?*

sich kümmern um   *to look after, take care of; to deal with*

Ich werde mich mehr um die Wohnung kümmern.	*I'll take more care of the apartment.*

sprechen (schreiben, lesen, lachen usw.) über (+ *acc.*)   *to talk (write, read, laugh, etc.) about*

Er hat über seine Heimat gesprochen.	*He talked about his home.*

sich verloben mit   *to get engaged to*

Rita hat sich mit Rudi verlobt.	*Rita got engaged to Rudi.*

sich vor·bereiten auf (+ *acc.*)   *to prepare for*

Notice: Perfect tense of **sich vorbereiten** is **hat sich vorbereitet** (no -**ge**-).

Wir haben uns auf seinen Besuch gut vorbereitet.	*We prepared well for his visit.*

warten auf (+ *acc.*)   *to wait for*

Auf wen warten Sie denn?	*Whom are you waiting for?*

■ **Notes on verbs with prepositional complements**

1. When a prepositional phrase is a verbal complement, it constitutes the second part of the predicate (see p. 69) and therefore comes at the end of the sentence or clause.

Sie **schrieb** mir letzte Woche **über ihre neue Stelle**.	*She wrote me about her new job last week.*

2. When the preposition used with a verb is a two-way preposition, you must memorize the verb and the case it takes (dative or accusative). Don't just learn **warten auf**, *to wait for*, but rather **warten auf** + *accusative, to wait for*.

3. The two-way prepositions **auf** and **über** almost always take the accusative case when used as verbal complements in a non-spatial sense.

Spatial
Er wartet auf **der** Straße.
He's waiting on the street.

Das Bild hängt über **meiner** Tür.
The picture hangs above my door.

Non-spatial
Er wartet auf **die** Lehrerin.
He's waiting for the teacher.

Ich sprach über **meine** Heimat.
I talked about my homeland.

4. Some verbs have both a direct object *and* a prepositional complement.

      d.o.   *prep. compl.*
Er bittet die **Beamtin um Auskunft**.

He asks the official for information.

      d.o.   *prep. compl.*
Das erinnert **mich an meine Heimat**.

That reminds me of my homeland.

5. Be careful not to confuse prepositional complements (**erinnern *an***) and separable prefixes (***an*kommen**). Although separable prefixes sometimes look like prepositions, they are not, because they have no object.

Prepositional complement

      object
Er erinnert mich **an meinen Bruder**.

      object
Wartest du **auf mich**?

Separable prefix

Der Zug kommt um 9 Uhr **an**.

Wann stehst du **auf**?

Fragewörter

To ask a question using a verb with a prepositional complement, German forms a question word by attaching the prefix **wo-** to the preposition: **wo-** + **vor** = **wovor**. (If the preposition begins with a vowel, the prefix is **wor-**: **wor-** + **auf** = **worauf**.)

Wovor hast du Angst?   *What* are you afraid *of*?
Worauf wartest du denn?   *What* are you waiting *for*?
Wofür interessieren Sie sich?   *What* are you interested *in*?

Lab Manual Kap. 13, Var. zu Üb. 1–4, 5–6.

Workbook Kap. 13, A, B.

■ **1** ■   **Kettenreaktion: Wovor hast *du* denn Angst?**   Jeder hat manchmal Angst. Es gibt viele Sachen, vor denen man Angst haben kann. Sagen Sie, wovor Sie Angst haben, und fragen Sie dann weiter. Die Liste gibt Ihnen einige Beispiele, aber Sie können auch frei antworten.

BEISPIEL: A: Ich habe Angst vor großen Hunden. Wovor hast *du* denn Angst?
            B: Ich habe Angst vor ...

große Hunde	komplizierte Technik
tiefes Wasser	Klausuren
ein Besuch beim Zahnarzt	das Leben in der Großstadt
das Fliegen	eine Umweltkatastrophe

Basel.
Die Stadt am Rhein.

■ 2 ■   **Übung: Darf ich Sie um etwas bitten?**   Jeder braucht etwas und bittet die Professorin darum. Was brauchen Sie?

> BEISPIEL: A: Darf ich Sie um Hilfe bitten?
> B: Natürlich. Ich helfe Ihnen gerne.

■ 3 ■   **Kettenreaktion: Worauf wartest *du* denn?**   Sie stehen an einer Straßenecke und warten auf etwas. Sagen Sie, worauf Sie warten, und dann fragen Sie weiter.

> BEISPIEL: A: Ich warte auf die Staßenbahn, Linie 2. Worauf wartest *du* denn?
> B: Ich warte auf _____ .

■ 4 ■   **Kettenreaktion: Worauf freust *du* dich?**   Sagen Sie, worauf Sie sich besonders freuen, und dann fragen Sie weiter.

> BEISPIEL: A: Ich freue mich auf die Semesterferien. Worauf freust *du* dich?
> B: Ich freue mich auf _____ .

■ 5 ■   **Kettenreaktion: Wofür interessierst *du* dich?**   Nicht alle interessieren sich für die gleichen Dinge. Sagen Sie, wofür Sie sich besonders interessieren, und dann fragen Sie weiter.

> BEISPIEL: A: Ich interessiere mich für das Mittelalter. Wofür interessierst *du* dich?
> B: Ich interessiere mich für _____ .

■ 6 ■   **Übung: Woran konnten Sie sich nicht gewöhnen?**   Wenn man anfängt zu studieren, ist es manchmal schwer sich an das Neue zu gewöhnen. Sagen Sie, woran Sie sich am Anfang nicht so leicht gewöhnen konnten.

> BEISPIEL: A: Woran konnten Sie sich hier am Anfang nicht gewöhnen?
> B: Ich konnte mich nicht an das Klima gewöhnen.

Pronouns as objects of prepositions: da-*compounds and* wo-*compounds*

■ *da*-compounds

When noun objects of prepositions are replaced by pronouns (e.g., **für meinen Freund** → **für ihn**), a distinction is made in German between nouns referring to people and nouns referring to inanimate objects.

- Nouns referring to people are replaced by personal pronouns, as in English.

Steht Christof hinter Gabriele?	*Is Christof standing behind Gabriele?*
Ja, er steht **hinter ihr**.	*Yes, he's standing **behind her**.*
Sprichst du oft mit den Kindern?	*Do you often talk with the children?*
Ja, ich spreche oft **mit ihnen**.	*Yes, I often speak **with them**.*
Wartet ihr auf Manfred?	*Are you waiting for Manfred?*
Ja, wir warten **auf ihn**.	*Yes, we're waiting **for him**.*

Da-compounds simplify things: they do not reflect case, number, or gender of the nouns they replace.

- Nouns referring to inanimate objects, however, are *not* replaced by personal pronouns. Instead, they are replaced by the prefix **da-** attached to the preposition (**da- + mit = damit**). If the preposition begins with a vowel, the prefix is **dar-** (**dar- + auf = darauf**).

Steht dein Auto vor oder hinter dem Haus?	*Is your car in front of the house or behind it?*
Es steht **dahinter**.	*It's **behind it**.*
Was machen wir mit diesen alten Maschinen?	*What shall we do with these old machines?*
Ich weiß nicht, was wir **damit** machen.	*I don't know what we'll do **with them**.*
Wie lange warten Sie schon auf den Zug?	*How long have you been waiting for the train?*
Ich warte schon 10 Minuten **darauf**.	*I've been waiting **for it** for 10 minutes.*

cell phone=**das Handy**

Damit haben Sie das ganze Büro in der Hand

Lab Manual Kap. 13, Üb. 7, 8.

■ **7** ■   Übung   Antworten Sie wie im Beispielsatz.

> BEISPIEL: A: Stand er neben dem Fenster?
>
> B: Ja, er stand daneben.

1. Interessieren Sie sich für Fremdsprachen?
2. Hast du nach dem Konzert gegessen?
3. Fangt ihr mit der Arbeit an?
4. Hat er lange auf die Straßenbahn gewartet?
5. Hat sie sich an das Wetter gewöhnt?
6. Hat sie wieder um Geld gebeten?
7. Bereitest du dich auf die Deutschstunde vor?
8. Liegt meine Zeitung unter deinem Rucksack?
9. Erinnerst du dich an die Ferien?
10. Haben Sie vor der Bibliothek gewartet?

■ **8** ■   Partnerarbeit   Diesmal kommt es darauf an, ob das Objekt ein Mensch ist. Wenn nicht, dann müssen Sie mit **da-** antworten.

> BEISPIEL: A: Steht Ingrid neben *Hans-Peter*?
>
> B: Ja, sie steht *neben ihm.*
>
> A: Steht Ingrid neben dem *Wagen*?
>
> B: Ja, sie steht *daneben.*

1. Hast du dich an das Wetter gewöhnt?
2. Bist du mit Ursula gegangen?
3. Erinnerst du dich an deine Großeltern?
4. Können wir über dieses Problem sprechen?
5. Wohnst du bei Frau Lindner?
6. Demonstrierst du gegen diesen Politiker?
7. Demonstrierst du gegen seine Ideen?
8. Interessierst du dich für Sport?
9. Gehst du mit Karin essen?
10. Hat er dir für das Geschenk gedankt?

■ **wo-compounds**

With questions beginning with a prepositional phrase, the same distinction between animate and inanimate objects is made. To ask a question about a person, German uses the *preposition* + **wen** or **wem**.

Auf wen warten Sie denn?   *Whom are you waiting for?*
Mit wem spielen die Kinder?   *Whom are the children playing with?*

When asking about a thing, use the **wo**-compounds you have already learned.

Worauf warten Sie denn?   *What are you waiting for?*
Womit spielt das Kind?   *What is the child playing with?*

Workbook Kap. 13, C–G.

Lab Manual Kap. 13,
Var. zur Üb. 9.

■ 9 ■   **Gruppenarbeit** (*Mit geschlossenen Büchern*)   Only student A has an open book. A reads each sentence aloud; B asks C for information about what was said, as in the examples.

BEISPIELE: A: Ich habe auf einen Brief gewartet.
　　　　　　　 B: Worauf hat sie gewartet?
　　　　　　　 C: Auf einen Brief.

　　　　　　　 A: Ich habe auf meine Kusine gewartet.
　　　　　　　 B: Auf wen hat er gewartet?
　　　　　　　 C: Auf seine Kusine.

1. Ich freue mich auf die Semesterferien.
2. Ich habe mit Professor Hauser gearbeitet.
3. Ich habe mich mit Rita/Rudi verlobt.
4. Ich muss mich um die Wohnung kümmern.
5. Ich interessiere mich für deutschen Wein.
6. Ich habe keine Angst vor Polizeibeamten.
7. Ich erinnere mich an meinen komischen Onkel.
8. Ich kann mich nicht an diese harte Arbeit gewöhnen.

■ 10 ■   **Partnerarbeit: Persönliche Fragen**   Stellen Sie einander diese Fragen.

BEISPIEL: Wofür interessierst du dich besonders?
　　　　　　Für das Mittelalter. Und du?
　　　　　　Für _____ .

1. Wofür interessierst du dich besonders?
2. Wovor hast du manchmal Angst?
3. Worauf freust du dich besonders?
4. Worauf musst du dich im Moment vorbereiten?
5. Woran kannst du dich nicht gewöhnen?

Hildegard von Bingen
1098–1179

Hildegard von Bingen was a Benedictine nun and abbess. An early German mystic and author of numerous theological and spiritual works as well as sacred vocal music, Hildegard also wrote tracts on diet and health that are still read today.

Future tense

■ Formation: *werden* + infinitive

Talking about the future is a communicative goal.

The future is a compound tense, using an inflected form of the verb **werden** plus a dependent infinitive in final position:

ich	**werde schlafen**	*I shall sleep*	wir	**werden schlafen**	*we shall sleep*
du	**wirst schlafen**	*you will sleep*	ihr	**werdet schlafen**	*you will sleep*
sie	**wird schlafen**	*she will sleep*	sie, Sie	**werden schlafen**	*they, you will sleep*

Note: **Werden** as the auxiliary (helping) verb for future tense corresponds to *shall* or *will* in English. Do not confuse it with the modal verb **wollen**.

Er **wird** schlafen.   *He **will** sleep.*
Er **will** schlafen.   *He **wants to** sleep.*

Here is how the future tense of a modal verb is formed. Note that the order of the modal and its dependent infinitive is the reverse of English.

Wir werden es **tun müssen**.

*We will **have to do** it.*

■ Use of future tense

As you already know, German usually uses *present tense* to express future meaning, especially when a time expression makes the future meaning clear.

Sie kommt morgen zurück.   *She's coming back tomorrow.*

Future tense makes the future meaning explicit, especially in the absence of a time expression such as **morgen**.

Sie wird selbstverständlich **zurückkommen**.   *Of course she will come back.*

Lab Manual Kap. 13, Var. zur Üb. 11.

Workbook Kap. 13, H.

■ 11 ■   **Übung: Noch nicht, aber bald.**   Sagen Sie, dass etwas noch nicht passiert ist, aber bald passieren wird.

BEISPIEL: A: Hast du schon gegessen?
          B: Noch nicht, aber ich werde bald essen.

1. Hat es schon geregnet?
2. Hast du schon aufgeräumt?
3. Seid ihr schon Ski gefahren?
4. Ist er schon aufgestanden?
5. Haben sie sich schon vorbereitet?
6. Haben Sie das schon machen müssen?
7. Hat Susi schon angerufen?
8. Seid ihr schon essen gegangen?

Wanting X to do Y

Telling people you'd like them to do something is a communicative goal.

To express the idea that a person wants something to happen or be done, English uses a direct object and an infinitive phrase.

> *d.o.*   *infin. phrase*
> She would like **the music to stop**.
> I don't want   **him**   **to think that**.

German uses **wollen** or **möchten** followed by a **dass**-clause to express the same idea.

> Sie möchte, **dass die Musik aufhört**.
> Ich will nicht, **dass er das glaubt**.

Lab Manual Kap. 13,
Üb. 12; Var. zur Üb. 13.

Workbook Kap. 13, I.

■ **12** ■   **Übung: Der Chef will das so.**   Sie arbeiten für einen Chef, der sehr streng (*strict*) ist. Heute zeigen Sie einem neuen Lehrling das Büro. Er fragt immer, ob man alles so machen *muss*. Sagen Sie ihm, der Chef *will*, dass man es so macht.

> **BEISPIEL:** *Müssen* wir schon um acht im Büro sein?
>   Ja, der Chef will, dass wir schon um acht im Büro sind.

1. *Müssen* wir den ganzen Tag hier bleiben?
2. *Muss* ich immer pünktlich sein?
3. *Dürfen* wir erst um *zehn* Kaffee trinken?
4. *Müssen* wir diese alten Computer benutzen?
5. *Müssen* wir auch samstags arbeiten?
6. *Muss* man immer eine Krawatte tragen?

■ **13** ■   **Übung: Ich möchte etwas ändern.**   Diese Situationen gefallen Ihnen nicht. Sagen Sie, wie Sie sie ändern möchten. Mehrere Antworten sind möglich.

> **BEISPIEL:** Die Musik ist Ihnen zu laut.
>   Ich möchte, dass sie leiser wird.
>   ... , dass sie aufhört.

1. Draußen regnet es.
2. Das Wetter ist Ihnen zu kalt.
3. Ihre Mitbewohner quatschen zu viel.
4. Ihr kleiner Bruder stört Sie bei der Arbeit.
5. Man verschwendet zu viel Glas und Papier.
6. Ihre Mitbewohner sind Ihnen zu schlampig.

Lesestück

Vor dem Lesen

Tipps zum Lesen und Lernen

■   **Tipps zum Vokabelnlernen**

German equivalents for only   When *only* is an adjective (meaning *sole* or *unique*), use **einzig-**. Otherwise use **nur**.

> Er ist der **einzige** Mechaniker   *He's the **only** mechanic in the area.*
>   in der Gegend.
> Ich habe **nur** fünf Mark in der   *I have **only** five marks in my pocket.*
>   Tasche.

1. I have only one pencil.
2. My only pencil is yellow.
3. A cup of coffee costs only DM 1,00.
4. That was the only restaurant that was open.

Lab Manual Kap. 13, Üb. zur Betonung.

■ **Leicht zu merken**

die **Barriere, -n**	Barriere
(das) **Chinesisch**	
der **Dialekt, -e**	Dialekt
konservativ	konservativ
neutral	neutral
die **Neutralität**	Neutralität
offiziell	offiziell
das **Prozent**	
romantisch	
stabil	stabil
die **Stabilität**	Stabilität

■ **Einstieg in den Text**

In dem Lesestück auf Seite 338 sagt der Schweizer Dr. Anton Vischer, dass er sich manchmal über die Klischees ärgert, die er im Ausland über seine Heimat hört. Wenn man an die Schweiz denkt, denkt man z.B. automatisch an Schokolade, Schweizer Käse und gute Uhren. Diese Klischees sind Ihnen vielleicht auch bekannt. Aber interessanter ist sicher das Neue, was er über seine Heimat erzählt.

Nachdem Sie den Text gelesen haben, machen Sie sich eine Liste von wenigstens fünf neuen Dingen, die Sie über die Schweiz gelernt haben.

■ **Wortschatz 2**

Verben

antworten auf (+ *acc.*) to answer (something); to respond to

sich ärgern (**über** + *acc.*) to get annoyed (at), be annoyed (about)

auf·wachsen (**wächst auf**), **wuchs auf, ist aufgewachsen** to grow up

Use **antworten** + *dat.* for answering people (**Antworten Sie mir.**). Use **antworten auf** for answering questions (**Antworten Sie auf meine Frage.**).

denken, dachte, hat gedacht to think

denken an (+ *acc.*) to think of

sich erholen (**von**) to recover (from); to get well; to have a rest

reagieren auf (+ *acc.*) to react to

sich etwas überlegen to consider, ponder, think something over

Das muss ich mir überlegen. I have to think it over.

vor·stellen to introduce; to present

Darf ich meine Tante vorstellen? May I introduce my aunt?

sich wundern (**über** + *acc.*) to be surprised, amazed (at)

Substantive

der **Ort, -e** place; town
der **Rechtsanwalt, -̈e** lawyer (*m.*)
der **Schweizer, -** Swiss (*m.*)

das **Gespräch, -e** conversation
das **Werk, -e** work (of art), musical
    composition

die **Firma, Firmen** firm, company
die **Rechtsanwältin, -nen**
    lawyer (*f.*)
die **Schweizerin, -nen** Swiss (*f.*)
die **Schwierigkeit, -en** difficulty

Adjektive und Adverbien

froh happy
stolz auf (+ *acc.*) proud of

Andere Vokabel

beides (*sing.*) both things

Nützliche Ausdrücke

eines Tages some day (*in the
    future*); one day (*in the past or
    future*)
in Zukunft in the future

Gegensatz

froh ≠ **traurig** happy ≠ sad

Zwei Schweizer stellen ihre Heimat vor

Lab Manual Kap. 13, Lesestück.

Learning about Switzerland is the cultural goal of this chapter.

Dr. Anton Vischer (45 Jahre alt), Rechtsanwalt aus Basel[1]

„In meinem Beruf bin ich für die Investitionen° ausländischer Firmen verantwortlich und reise darum viel im Ausland. Dort höre ich oft die alten Klischees über meine Heimat. Wenn man sagt, dass man aus der Schweiz kommt, denken viele Menschen

5 automatisch an saubere Straßen, Schokolade, Uhren, Käse und an die Schweizer Garde[2] im Vatikan. Darüber ärgere ich mich immer ein bisschen. Ich möchte lieber, dass andere wissen, was für eine politische Ausnahme° die Schweiz in Europa bildet°. Ich werde versuchen Ihnen etwas davon zu beschreiben.

    Schon seit dem 13. Jahrhundert hat die Schweiz eine demokratische Verfassung°[3].

10 Sie gehört also zu° den ältesten und stabilsten Demokratien der Welt. In beiden Weltkriegen ist die Schweiz neutral geblieben und sie hat ihre Neutralität und ihre politische Stabilität bis heute bewahrt°.

    Einige werden unsere Gesellschaft wohl zu konservativ finden. In einem Kanton[4] war das Wahlrecht° der Frauen sogar bis 1992 beschränkt°. Aber man darf nicht ver-

15 gessen, dass es in der Schweiz durchaus° auch einen Platz für soziale Kritik° gibt. Das zeigen die Werke unserer bekanntesten Schriftsteller wie Max Frisch und Friedrich Dürrenmatt[5].

investments

exception / constitutes

constitution
**gehört ... = ist
  also eine von**
hat ... bewahrt = preserved

suffrage / restricted
definitely / criticism

---

1. Basel (*French* Bâle), Swiss city on the Rhine.
2. The Vatican's Swiss Guards, founded in 1505 by Pope Julius II, are the remnant of the Swiss mercenaries who served in foreign armies from the 15th century on. The Vatican guards are recruited from Switzerland's Catholic cantons.
3. In 1991, Switzerland celebrated the 700th anniversary of the Oath of Rütli, the defense pact among the three original cantons against the Austrian Habsburgs. Wilhelm Tell is the legendary hero of this period of Swiss resistance to foreign power.
4. Switzerland is composed of twenty-three cantons, each with considerable autonomy. Women in the canton of Appenzell could not vote in local elections until 1992.
5. Max Frisch (1911–1991) and Friedrich Dürrenmatt (1921–1990) both wrote novels, essays, and plays.

„In den Bergen kann man sich körperlich und seelisch erholen."

Jemand fragte mich einmal, ob ich stolz bin, Schweizer zu sein. Darauf habe ich
sofort mit Ja reagiert, aber in Zukunft werde ich mir die Antwort genauer überlegen.
20 Ich werde einfach sagen, ich bin *froh* Schweizer zu sein, denn meine Heimat ist das
schönste Land, das ich kenne. Da ich meine Freizeit immer auf Bergtouren verbringe,
ist mein Leben mit der Alpenlandschaft eng verbunden°. Für mich sind die Alpen der
einzige Ort, wo ich mich körperlich und seelisch° erholen kann. Das klingt vielleicht
romantisch, aber eigentlich bin ich ein ganz praktischer Mensch."

eng verbunden = closely
connected / **körperlich ...** =
physically and emotionally

25 *Nicole Wehrli (24 Jahre alt), Dolmetscherin° aus Biel*

interpreter

„Ich bin in der zweisprachigen° Stadt Biel – auf Französisch Bienne – aufgewachsen,
direkt an der Sprachgrenze zwischen der französischen und der deutschen Schweiz.
Bei uns können Sie manchmal auf der Straße Gespräche hören, in denen die
Menschen beides – Französisch *und* Deutsch – miteinander reden. In der Schule
30 habe ich dann Latein°, Englisch und Italienisch gelernt. Sie werden sich also nicht
wundern, dass ich mich für Fremdsprachen interessiere. Eines Tages möchte ich sogar
mit Chinesisch anfangen.

bilingual

Latin

Die Eidgenossenschaft[1] ist wohl ein Unikum° in Europa, denn sie ist viersprachig.
Die Sprachbarrieren waren lange Zeit ein großes Hindernis° für die politische Vereini-
35 gung der Kantone und machen uns heute noch manchmal Schwierigkeiten. 69% der
Bevölkerung° hat Deutsch als Muttersprache, 18% spricht Französisch, 12%
Italienisch und etwa° ein Prozent Rätoromanisch[2]. Unser „Schwyzerdütsch"[3]

something unique
obstacle

population
approximately

1. **Eidgenossenschaft** = Confederation. *Confoederatio Helvetica*: the official (Latin) name for
modern Switzerland, hence CH on Swiss cars.
2. Rhaetoromansch, or simply Romansch. It is a Romance language, a linguistic remnant of the
original Roman occupation of the Alpine territories, spoken by about 40,000 rural Swiss in the
canton of Grisons (**Graubünden**). Long under threat of extinction, it was declared one of the four
national languages in 1938.
3. **Schweizerdeutsch** (*Swiss-German dialect*). **Hochdeutsch** (*High German*) is the official, standardized language of German-speaking countries. It is the language of the media, the law, and
education, and is based on written German (**Schriftdeutsch**). Educated native speakers are bi-
dialectal, knowing their local dialect and High German, which they may speak with a regional
accent.

können die meisten Deutschen nicht verstehen. Da unsere Kinder Schriftdeutsch° standard written German
erst in der Schule lernen müssen, ist es für sie oft so schwer wie eine Fremdsprache.
40 Die geschriebene und offizielle Sprache in den Schulen bleibt Schriftdeutsch, aber
nach dem Unterricht° reden Lehrer und Schüler Schwyzerdütsch miteinander.“ **nach ...** = after class

Nach dem Lesen

■ A ■   **Antworten Sie auf Deutsch.**

1. Was ist Dr. Vischer von Beruf?
2. Welche Klischees hört er über die Schweiz, wenn er im Ausland ist?
3. Wie reagiert er darauf?
4. Seit wann hat die Schweiz eine demokratische Verfassung?
5. Was macht Herr Vischer in seiner Freizeit?
6. Warum ist die Stadt Biel, wo Nicole Wehrli aufgewachsen ist, besonders interessant?
7. Was war eine große Schwierigkeit bei der Vereinigung der Schweiz?
8. Wie viele Schweizer sind deutschsprachig?
9. Warum haben manche Deutschen Schwierigkeiten die Schweizer zu verstehen?

Kinder mit Schlitten (*sleds*) in der Altstadt von Basel.

„Mi Wält"

Lab Manual Kap. 13, Nach dem Lesen, Teil B.

■ **B** ■ In diesem Kapitel haben Sie über den Schweizer Dialekt – das Schwyzer-dütsch – gelesen. Hier ist der Anfang eines Märchens auf Schwyzerdütsch mit einer Übersetzung ins Schriftdeutsche. Das Märchen kommt aus dem Kanton Aargau, westlich von Zürich. „Der Ma im Mond"[1] erzählt von einem Mann, der am Sonntag Holz (*wood*) stiehlt. Gott bestraft (*punishes*) ihn, indem er ihn zum Mann im Mond (*moon*) macht (*by making him . . .*).

Der Ma im Mond

Weisch, wer dört oben im Mond lauft? Das isch emol en usöde Ma gsi, de het nid umegluegt ob's Sunntig oder Wärchtig gsi isch; goht einisch am ene heilige Sunntig is Holz und fangt a e Riswälle zsämestäle; und won er fertig gsi isch, und die Wälle bunde gha het, nimmt er si uf e Rügge und isch e heimlige Wäg us, won er gmeint het, das ihm kei Mönsch begägni. Aber wer em do begägnet, das isch der lieb Gott sälber gsi.

1. From: *Kinder- und Hausmärchen aus der Schweiz.* Collected and edited by Otto Sutermeister, with drawings by J. S. Weißbrod. Aarau: H. R. Sauerländer, 1873.

Der Mann Im Mond

Weißt (du), wer dort oben° im Mond läuft? Das ist einmal ein böser Mann gewesen, der hat sich nicht umgesehen°, ob es Sonntag oder Werktag° gewesen ist; (er) geht einmal an einem heiligen° Sonntag ins Holz° und fängt an, ein Reisigbündel° zusammenzustehlen; und als er fertig gewesen ist und das Bündel gebunden hat°, nimmt er
5 es auf den Rücken° und ist einen heimlichen Weg° hinausgegangen, wovon er gemeint hat, dass ihm kein Mensch begegnet°. Aber wer ihm dort begegnet, das ist der liebe Gott selber gewesen.

up there

sich ... = didn't pay attention / weekday / holy / woods / bundle of sticks / tied up

back / secret path
begegnen (+ dat.) = to encounter

Lab Manual Kap. 13, Diktat.

Workbook Kap. 13, J–N.

Situationen aus dem Alltag

■ Wie stellt man sich vor?

Wie stellt man sich oder einen Bekannten auf Deutsch vor? Es kommt auf die Situation an. Unten sind vier verschiedene Situationen, aber zuerst ein paar Bemerkungen (*comments*).

Unter jungen Menschen ist es nicht so formell: Man sagt einfach seinen Namen und **Hallo** oder **Tag**, wie zum Beispiel in *Situation 1* (unten). Wie Sie schon wissen, sagen Studenten sofort **du** zueinander.

Wenn man ältere Menschen zum ersten Mal kennen lernt, ist es formeller (*Situationen 2* und *3*). Man sagt **angenehm** oder **freut mich** oder **sehr erfreut** (alle drei = *pleased to meet you*). Natürlich sagt man **Sie** statt **du.**

In allen Situationen ist es höflich einander die Hand zu geben (*shake hands*). Das machen die Europäer viel öfter als die Amerikaner.

Introducing yourself and others is a communicative goal.

1. Die Studentin Sonja stellt ihrem Freund Wolfgang ihre Freundin Margaret aus Amerika vor.

    SONJA: Hallo Wolfgang! Darf ich vorstellen? Das ist meine Freundin Margaret aus Chicago.

    WOLFGANG: (*gibt ihr die Hand*) Hallo Margaret!

    MARGARET: Hallo Wolfgang.

    WOLFGANG: Nett, dich kennen zu lernen.

    MARGARET: Danke, gleichfalls.

2. Bernd, 20, stellt seiner Mutter einen Freund vor.

    BERND: Mutter, ich möchte dir meinen Freund Theo vorstellen.

    FRAU RINGSTEDT: Freut mich, Sie kennen zu lernen, Theo.

    THEO: Angenehm, Frau Ringstedt. (*Sie geben sich die Hand.*)

3. Der amerikanische Austauschstudent Michael Hayward stellt sich einem Professor in der Sprechstunde (*office hour*) vor.

MICHAEL HAYWARD: Guten Tag, Professor Mohr. Darf ich mich vorstellen? Mein Name ist Hayward. (*Gibt ihm die Hand.*)

PROF. MOHR: Guten Tag, Herr Hayward. Bitte nehmen Sie Platz.

4. Zwei Geschäftsleute treffen sich auf einer Konferenz.

FRAU MÜLLER: Guten Tag, mein Name ist Müller.

HERR BEHRENS: Freut mich, Frau Müller. Behrens.

■ ■ ■ **Gruppenarbeit: Rollenspiele**

1. Darf ich mich vorstellen?
Sie sind alle zusammen auf einer Studentenparty, wo sie einander noch nicht kennen. Stehen Sie alle auf und stellen Sie sich einander vor.

2. Ich möchte euch meine Freunde vorstellen.
Zwei Studenten spielen die Rollen der Eltern. Ein dritter Student bringt zwei Freunde nach Hause und stellt sie den Eltern vor.

3. Now pretend that you're all business people at a convention. Introduce yourselves to each other. (In this kind of situation, people usually give only their last names.)

Profile of Switzerland

Area: 41,288 square kilometers; 15,941 square miles (approximately the same area as the states of Massachusetts, Connecticut, and Rhode Island combined)

Population: 7,240,400; density 175 people per square kilometer (454 per square mile)

Currency: Swiss franc (**Schweizer Franken**); 1 sfr = 100 Rappen or Centimes

Major Cities: Berne (**Bern**, capital, pop. 130,000), Zürich (largest city, pop. 322,000), Basel, Geneva (**Genf**), Lausanne

Religions: 48% Roman Catholic, 44% Protestant, 8% other

Switzerland has one of the highest per capita incomes in the world, as well as one of the highest standards of living. The literacy rate is 99.5%. The beauty of the Swiss Alps has made tourism Switzerland's main service industry; the alpine rivers provide inexpensive hydroelectric power.

Switzerland has not sent troops into foreign wars since 1515. It guards its neutrality even to the extent of staying out of the European Union and the United Nations. It is, however, a member of several special U.N. agencies. The second headquarters of the U.N. are in Geneva, which is also the seat of the International Red Cross and the World Council of Churches.

Marktplatz und altes Rathaus (Basel)

In der zweisprachigen Stadt Biel / Bienne

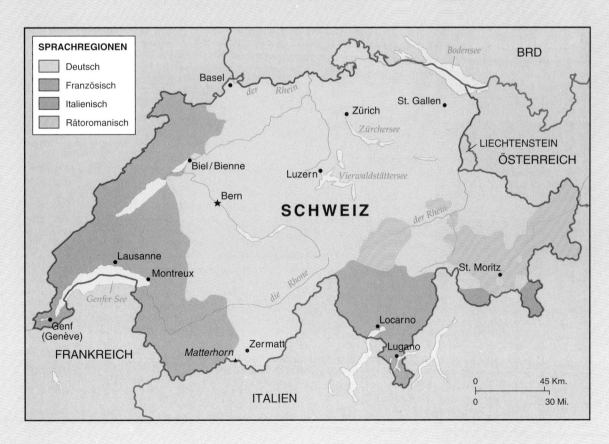

SPRACHREGIONEN

- Deutsch
- Französisch
- Italienisch
- Rätoromanisch

Bodensee

BRD

Basel

der Rhein

Zürich

St. Gallen

Zürchersee

LIECHTENSTEIN

ÖSTERREICH

Biel / Bienne

Luzern

Vierwaldstättersee

der Rhein

Bern

SCHWEIZ

St. Moritz

Lausanne

Montreux

die Rhone

Genfer See

Locarno

Genf
(Genève)

Zermatt

Lugano

Matterhorn

FRANKREICH

ITALIEN

0   45 Km.

0   30 Mi.

Österreich

Vienna, Karlsplatz subway station (architect: Otto Wagner).

Communicative Goals

- Getting a room in a hotel
- Expressing wishes contrary to fact
- Talking about contrary-to-fact situations
- Making suggestions
- Making polite requests

Cultural Goal

- Learning about Austria

Chapter Outline

- **Lyrik zum Vorlesen**
  Ernst Jandl, „ottos mops"

- **Grammatik**
  General subjunctive: Present tense
  Other uses of the general subjunctive
  Conditions contrary to fact
  Wishes contrary to fact
  Hypothetical statements and questions
  Polite requests

- **Lesestück**
  Zwei Österreicher stellen sich vor

- **Situationen aus dem Alltag**
  Im Hotel

- **Almanach**
  Profile of Austria

Lab Manual Kap. 14,
Dialoge, Fragen, Hören
Sie gut zu!

Austrian currency: **100 Groschen = 1 Schilling**.

Getting a room in a hotel is a communicative goal of this chapter.

heute Nacht = *tonight*, but also *last night* if said early in morning.

Most hotels in Europe include breakfast in the room price.

Note: **im ersten Stock** is the equivalent of American *on the second floor*.

Heurige are taverns in and around Vienna, each originally belonging to a vineyard and serving wine (called **Heuriger**) pressed from the current harvest (**heuer** = *this year*). **Grinzing**, a suburb of Vienna, has many **Heurige**.

Auf Urlaub in Österreich

Nach einem langen Tag in Salzburg will das Ehepaar Dietrichs aus Potsdam zum Abendessen ausgehen.

RICHARD: Ursula, hast du noch österreichisches Geld?

URSULA: Nein. Wieso, hast du auch keine Schillinge mehr?

RICHARD: Leider nicht. Wenn es nicht so spät wäre, könnte ich noch bei der Bank wechseln.

URSULA: Das macht ja nichts. An der Hotelkasse kannst du wechseln oder wir zahlen im Restaurant entweder mit Kreditkarte oder mit Reiseschecks.

An der Rezeption

TOURIST: Grüß Gott! Hätten Sie noch ein Zimmer frei für heute Nacht?

ANGESTELLTER: Wünschen Sie ein Einzelzimmer oder ein Doppelzimmer?

TOURIST: Am liebsten hätte ich ein Einzelzimmer mit Dusche.

ANGESTELLTER: Das könnte ich Ihnen erst morgen geben. Im Moment ist nur ein Doppelzimmer mit Bad frei.

TOURIST: Was würde das denn kosten?

ANGESTELLTER: 500 Schilling mit Frühstück.

TOURIST: Dürfte ich mir das Zimmer ansehen?

ANGESTELLTER: Selbstverständlich. (*Gibt ihm den Schlüssel.*) Das wäre Zimmer Nummer 14 im ersten Stock.

Ausflug zum Heurigen

Zwei Freunde im ersten Semester in Wien wollen den neuen Wein probieren.

ANDREAS: Hast du heute Abend etwas Besonderes vor?

ESTHER: Nein, warum?

ANDREAS: Dann könnten wir endlich nach Grinzing zum Heurigen fahren.

ESTHER: Ja, höchste Zeit! Und es wäre auch schön dort zu essen.

ANDREAS: Gute Idee! Ich hab' schon Riesenhunger.

ESTHER: Dann sollten wir gleich losfahren.

Bach-Hengl
SEIT 1685

WEINGUT   **GRINZING**   **HEURIGER**

GRINZING,   MUSIK   BUFFET
SANDGASSE 9,   PRÄMIERTE
TEL. 32 24 39   FLASCHENWEINE

■ Wortschatz 1

Verben

aus·gehen ging aus, ist ausgegangen to go out
los·fahren (fährt los), fuhr los, ist losgefahren to depart, start, leave
probieren to sample, try
wechseln to change (money)

Substantive

der/die **Angestellte, -n** employee
der **Ausflug, -̈e** outing, excursion
der **Scheck, -s** check
   der **Reisescheck, -s** traveler's check
der **Schilling** Austrian shilling
der **Stock** floor (*of a building*)
   der **erste Stock** the second floor
   im ersten Stock on the second floor

das **Bad, -̈er** bath
   ein Bad nehmen to take a bath
das **Badezimmer, -** bathroom
das **Doppelzimmer, -** double room
das **Ehepaar, -e** married couple
das **Einzelzimmer, -** single room
das **Erdgeschoss** first floor, ground floor

die **Bank, -en** bank
die **Dusche, -n** shower
die **Kasse, -n** cash register; cashier's office
die **Kreditkarte, -n** credit card
die **Nummer, -n** number
die **Rezeption** (hotel) reception desk

Adjektiv

österreichisch Austrian

Andere Vokabel

entweder ... oder (*conj.*) either ... or

Nützlicher Ausdruck

höchste Zeit high time

Gegensatz

entweder ... oder ≠ **weder ... noch** either ... or ≠ neither ... nor

Mit anderen Worten

der Riesenhunger = sehr großer Hunger

On Vacation in Austria

After a long day in Salzburg, Mr. and Mrs. Dietrichs from Potsdam want to go out to dinner.

R: Ursula, do you have any more Austrian money?
U: No. Why? Don't you have any more shillings either?
R: Unfortunately not. If it weren't so late, I could still change money at the bank.
U: That doesn't matter. You can change money at the hotel cashier, or we'll pay in the restaurant, either with credit card or with traveler's checks.

At the Reception Desk

T: Hello, would you still have a room free for tonight?
E: Do you want a single or a double room?
T: I'd prefer a single room with shower.
E: I couldn't give you that until tomorrow. At the moment there is only a double room with bath available.
T: What would that cost?
E: Five hundred shillings with breakfast.
T: May I please have a look at the room?
E: Of course. (*Hands him the key*). That would be room number 14 on the second floor.

Outing to a *Heuriger*

Two friends in their first semester in Vienna want to try the new wine.

A: Have you got anything special planned for tonight?
E: No, why?
A: Then we could finally go to Grinzing to a *Heuriger*.
E: Yes, high time! And it would be nice to eat there too.
A: Good idea! I'm already famished.
E: Then we ought to leave right away.

Variationen

■ A ■ Persönliche Fragen

1. Haben Sie je Geld wechseln müssen? Wo?
2. Zahlen Sie im Restaurant mit Kreditkarte, Scheck oder Bargeld (*cash*)?
3. Haben Sie je in einem Hotel übernachtet? Wo war das?
4. Würden Sie lieber in Jugendherbergen oder in Hotels übernachten, wenn Sie nach Österreich reisen? Warum?
5. Haben Sie ein Doppel- oder ein Einzelzimmer im Studentenwohnheim?
6. Grinzing ist ein Ausflugsort in der Nähe von Wien. Kennen Sie in Ihrer Gegend einen schönen Ausflugsort?

German dormitories have only singles and doubles. A triple would be called **ein Dreibettzimmer**.

■ B ■ Übung: Was ist ein Riese?

Ein berühmter Riese in der Bibel hieß Goliath. Sie kennen schon das Wort „riesengroß". So nennt man etwas sehr Großes. Jetzt wissen Sie auch, wenn man sehr hungrig ist, sagt man: „Ich habe Riesenhunger!" Also:

1. Einen riesengroßen Hunger nennt man auch *einen Riesenhunger.*
2. Einen sehr sehr großen Koffer nennt man auch _____ .
3. Eine ganz große Freude ist _____ .
4. Wenn viele Menschen zusammen demonstrieren, dann hat man _____ .
5. Wenn ein Supertanker einen Unfall hat und sein Öl ins Meer fließt, dann ist das _____ .
6. Ein sehr großes Hotel kann man auch _____ nennen.

Das Wiener Riesenrad

■ C ■ Partnerarbeit: Wie wäre das?

(How would that be?) Ihr Partner schlägt Ihnen etwas vor. Reagieren Sie darauf mit Ihren eigenen Worten: **Das wäre ...!** (Switch roles for second column.)

BEISPIEL: A: Sollen wir einen Ausflug machen?
　　　　　　B: Ja, das wäre toll!

ins Kino gehen?	uns die Stadt ansehen?
Geld wechseln?	zu Hause sitzen?
Freunde einladen?	das Zimmer aufräumen?
Ski fahren gehen?	im Restaurant essen?
Theaterkarten kaufen?	eine Radtour machen?

■ **D** ■ **Übung: entweder ... oder**   Sagen Sie, Sie machen entweder **dies** oder **das**.

BEISPIEL: Was trinken Sie heute Abend?
Ich trinke entweder Tee oder Kaffee.

1. Wohin fahren Sie im Sommer?
2. Was möchten Sie gern essen?
3. Mit wem wollen Sie Tennis spielen?
4. Welche Fremdsprache werden Sie nächstes Jahr lernen?
5. Wer war denn das?
6. Wissen Sie, in welchem Stock Ihr Hotelzimmer ist?
7. Wie kann man im Hotel zahlen?
8. Wann wollen Sie das nächste Mal Ski fahren gehen?

Lyrik zum Vorlesen

The Austrian poet Ernst Jandl was born in Vienna. In the following poem, he shows that it is possible to tell a whole story using only one vowel. Reading it aloud will be a good review of the German long and short **o**! Like many other modern poets, Jandl does not capitalize nouns.

Lab Manual Kap. 14, Lyrik zum Vorlesen.

ottos mops°   mutt
ottos mops trotzt°   won't obey
otto: fort° mops fort   go away
ottos mops hopst° fort   hops
otto: soso

otto holt koks°   charcoal briquettes
otto holt obst
otto horcht°   listens
otto: mops mops
otto hofft

ottos mops klopft°   knocks
otto: komm mops komm
ottos mops kommt
ottos mops kotzt°   pukes
otto: ogottogott

Ernst Jandl (geboren 1925)

Caricature by Wilhelm Busch (1832–1908), German painter, satirist, humorist. As an artist and poet, Busch paved the way for modern comics. He told stories with line drawings captioned with his own humorous texts, the most famous of which is **Max und Moritz** (1865). This drawing is from 1870.

Grammatik

The *imperative* (Kap. 4) is also a grammatical mood.

General subjunctive: Present tense

Language offers you the possibility of presenting information in various ways. On the one hand, you can present something as a fact. On the other hand, you can present it as hypothetical, conjectural, or contrary to fact. Both German and English have two different sets of verb forms for these two possibilities, called the *indicative* and the *subjunctive* moods (from Latin *modus*, "manner, mode, way").

Up to now, you have been using the *indicative mood* to talk about what is definite, certain, and real.

Barbara **ist** nicht hier.	*Barbara **isn't** here.*
Ich **habe** Zeit.	*I **have** time.*

The *subjunctive mood* (**der Konjunktiv**) is used to talk about hypothetical, uncertain, or unreal situations, and also to make polite statements and requests.

Wenn Barbara nur hier **wäre**!	*If only Barbara **were** here!*
Wenn ich mehr Zeit **hätte** ...	*If I **had** more time . . .*
Würden Sie mir bitte helfen?	***Would** you please help me?*

You've been using **würde**, the subjunctive form of **werden**, since Kap. 7.

A common subjunctive form in English is *were* in *if I were you*.

English *present* subjunctive is signalled by what look like *past-tense* forms or by ***would*** + a verb.

*If they **lived** nearby, we **would** visit them.*	(condition contrary to fact)
*If only I **had** more time!*	(wish contrary to fact)
*I **would like** to have a room.*	(polite request)

Note that the verbs *lived* and *had* in the examples above are identical to the past in *form*, but have present-tense meaning.

*If they **lived** nearby . . .*	(right now)
*If only I **had** more time!*	(right now)

■ Present subjunctive of weak verbs

The present tense of the general subjunctive in German is also based on past indicative forms. In the case of *weak* verbs (see p. 245), the present subjunctive is *identical* to the simple past indicative you have already learned.

wenn ich wohn**te**	*if I lived*	wenn wir wohn**ten**	*if we lived*
wenn du wohn**test**	*if you lived*	wenn ihr wohn**tet**	*if you lived*
wenn sie wohn**te**	*if she lived*	wenn sie, Sie wohn**ten**	*if they, you lived*

In Austria **Servus** means both *hello* and *so long*. It originally meant "Your servant" in Latin.

Servus in Österreich®

Österreich ■ 351

Expressing wishes contrary to fact is a communicative goal.

Note on Usage: Wishes contrary to fact

A contrary-to-fact wish is expressed in German by a **wenn**-clause in the subjunctive (verb last) with an added **nur**.

> Wenn ich **nur** näher **wohnte**!   *If only I **lived** closer!*

The **nur** is placed after all personal and reflexive pronouns, but before **nicht**:

> Wenn du es mir **nur** sagtest!   *If only you'd tell it to me!*
> Wenn es **nur** nicht so spät wäre.   *If only it weren't so late.*

Lab Manual Kap. 14, Üb. 1.

■ 1 ■   **Übung: Wenn es nur anders wäre!**   Sie hören eine Situation im Indikativ. Sie wünschen im Konjunktiv, dass es anders wäre.

> BEISPIEL: A: Hans-Peter wohnt nicht hier. *Hans-Peter doesn't live here.*
> B: Wenn er nur hier wohnte!   *If only he lived here!*

1. Petra kauft das nicht.
2. Georg beeilt sich nicht.
3. Der Urlaub dauert nicht länger.
4. Ich erhole mich nicht.
5. Die Gäste setzen sich nicht.
6. Maria macht die Tür nicht zu.
7. Robert bestellt nicht genug Bier.
8. Meine Freunde besuchen mich nicht.
9. Meine Großeltern wohnen nicht bei uns.
10. Inge wechselt ihr Geld nicht.

■ Present subjunctive of strong verbs

The present subjunctive of strong verbs is also based on their past indicative forms (see p. 246), but these forms are *modified* according to the following three-step procedure.

Remember that you can only add an umlaut to **a**, **o**, **u**, and **au**.

Step 1: Take the simple past stem of the verb:

> fahren → **fuhr-**   gehen → **ging-**   laufen → **lief-**   sein → **war-**

Step 2: Add an umlaut to the stem vowel whenever possible:

> **führ-**   **ging-**   **lief-**   **wär-**

Step 3: Add the following personal endings:

ich	wär**e**	*I would be*	wir	wär**en**	*we would be*
du	wär**est**	*you would be*	ihr	wär**et**	*you would be*
er	wär**e**	*he would be*	sie, Sie	wär**en**	*they, you would be*

Note the difference between the present subjunctive endings and the past indicative endings of strong verbs:

Present subjunctive (would go)		Past indicative (went)	
ich	ginge	ich	ging
du	gingest	du	gingst
sie	ginge	sie	ging
wir	gingen	wir	gingen
ihr	ginget	ihr	gingt
sie, Sie	gingen	sie, Sie	gingen

Only the **wir-** and the plural **sie-**endings are the same.

A complete list of the principal parts of strong and irregular verbs is found on pp. 371–372.

Workbook Kap. 14, A–B.

Lab Manual Kap. 14, Üb. 3.

■ **2** ■ **Übung** Review the simple past stems of these strong verbs.

BEISPIEL: laufen *lief*

scheinen	finden
kommen	gehen
anfangen	fahren
gefallen	sein
tun	schlafen
aussteigen	bekommen

■ **3** ■ **Übung: Wenn es nur anders wäre!** Jetzt hören Sie eine Situation im Indikativ. Sie wünschen im Konjunktiv, dass es anders wäre.

BEISPIEL: Meine Gäste gehen nicht nach Hause.
Wenn sie nur nach Hause gingen!

1. Gabi läuft nicht schnell.
2. Die Sonne scheint nicht.
3. Robert kommt nicht um zwölf.
4. Karin geht nicht mit uns spazieren.
5. Wir sind nicht alt genug.
6. Das Kind schläft nicht länger.
7. Wir bekommen kein Doppelzimmer.
8. Laura findet ihre Kreditkarte nicht.
9. Die Uhr geht nicht richtig.
10. Unsere Freunde fahren nicht nach Australien.
11. Der Film fängt nicht an.
12. Die Wohnung gefällt uns nicht.
13. Das tut Marie nicht gern.
14. Hier steigen wir nicht aus.

Ohne Musik wäre das Leben ein Irrtum.
Friedrich Nietzsche

■ Present subjunctive of modal verbs

To form the present subjunctive of modal verbs, take the past indicative, *including endings* (see pp. 248–249), and add an umlaut to the stem vowel of *only* those verbs that have an umlaut in their infinitive.

Infinitive		*Past indicative*	
dürfen	*to be allowed*	**ich durfte**	*I was allowed*

Present Subjunctive					
ich	**dürfte**	*I would be allowed*	wir	**dürften**	*we would be allowed*
du	**dürftest**	*you would be allowed*	ihr	**dürftet**	*you would be allowed*
er	**dürfte**	*he would be allowed*	sie, Sie	**dürften**	*they, you would be allowed*

Similarly:

Past indicative		*Present subjunctive*	
ich konnte	*I was able to*	ich **könnte**	*I could, would be able to*
ich mochte	*I liked*	ich **möchte**	*I would like to*
ich musste	*I had to*	ich **müsste**	*I would have to*

The present subjunctive of **sollen** and **wollen**, however, is *not* umlauted, and so looks just like the past indicative.

ich sollte	*I was supposed to*	ich **sollte**	*I ought to*
ich wollte	*I wanted to*	ich **wollte**	*I would want to*

Lab Manual Kap. 14, Var. zur Üb. 4; Üb. 5.

■ **4** ■ **Übung: Hören Sie gut zu!** (*Mit geschlossenen Büchern*) Listen to each pair of sentences, then say which one is past indicative and which present subjunctive. Then, with open books, repeat each sentence aloud and give the English equivalent.

1. Durfte sie das machen? / Dürfte sie das machen?
2. Wir könnten ihn abholen. / Wir konnten ihn abholen.
3. Sie müsste das wissen. / Sie musste das wissen.
4. Mochte er das Frühstück? / Möchte er das Frühstück?

■ **5** ■ **Übung: Wenn es nur anders wäre!** Ihre Professorin beschreibt wieder eine Situation im Indikativ. Sie wünschen im Konjunktiv, dass es anders wäre.

BEISPIEL: Christine kann kein Englisch.
Wenn sie nur Englisch *könnte*!

1. Wir können kein Französisch.
2. Die Gäste müssen nach Hause.
3. Wir dürfen nicht länger bleiben.
4. Esther will nicht nach Grinzing.
5. Die Kinder können nicht mitfahren.
6. Unsere Freunde müssen abfahren.
7. Sie dürfen nicht alles sagen.
8. Andreas will nicht helfen.

Making suggestions is a communicative goal.

Workbook Kap. 14, C.

> **Note on Usage:** **Using the subjunctive to make suggestions**
>
> Wir **könnten** zusammen ausgehen.
> *We **could** go out together.*
>
> Wir **sollten** eigentlich hier bleiben.
> *We really **ought** to stay here.*

■ 6 ■ **Partnerarbeit: Was könnten wir heute machen?** Partner A sagt etwas Schönes, was Sie machen **könnten**. Partner B sagt aber, Sie **sollten** eigentlich etwas anderes machen.

> BEISPIEL: A: Wir *könnten* zusammen spazieren gehen.
> B: Aber wir *sollten* eigentlich das Zimmer aufräumen.

Hier sind einige Möglichkeiten:

etwas Schönes	*etwas Wichtiges*
spazieren gehen	das Zimmer aufräumen
Karten spielen	Hausaufgaben machen
italienisch essen	Lebensmittel einkaufen
Musik hören	uns auf die Klausur vorbereiten

Ohne Zeitung hätten Sie weniger zu sagen.

DIE ZEITUNGEN IN DEUTSCHLAND.

Making polite requests is a communicative goal.

Lab Manual Kap. 14, Var. zu Üb. 7–8.

■ **Present subjunctive of *haben*, *werden*, and *wissen***

To form the present subjunctive of the verbs **haben**, **werden**, and **wissen**, take the past indicative, including endings (see p. 249), and add an umlaut to the stem vowel:

Past indicative		*Present subjunctive*	
ich hatte	*I had*	ich **hätte**	*I would have*
ich wurde	*I became*	ich **würde**	*I would become, I would*
ich wusste	*I knew*	ich **wüsste**	*I would know*

> **Note on Usage:** **Polite requests: Subjunctive + *gern***
>
> **Ich hätte gern** ein Einzelzimmer mit Bad.
> ***I would like to have** a single room with bath.*
>
> **Ich wüsste gern,** wo die Kasse ist.
> ***I would like to know** where the cashier is.*

■ 7 ■ **Kettenreaktion: Was hätten Sie gern?** Sagen Sie, was Sie gern hätten.

> BEISPIEL: Ich hätte gern ein frisches Brötchen. Und du?
> Ich hätte gern ein-_____ .

■ 8 ■ **Kettenreaktion: Was wüssten Sie gern?** Sagen Sie, was Sie gern wüssten.

> BEISPIEL: Ich wüsste gern, wo ich Geld verdienen könnte. Und du?
> Ich wüsste gern, _____ .

■ Present subjective with *würden* + infinitive

In **Kapitel 7** you learned how to use the subjunctive construction **würden** + *infinitive* to express intentions, opinions, preferences, and polite requests. This construction is an alternative to the one-word present subjunctive forms you have been learning in this chapter.

There is no difference in meaning between the following clauses:

Er **käme** ...
Er **würde kommen** ... } *He would come ...*

The present subjunctive with **würden** often replaces the one-word form of weak verbs which is indistinguishable from the past indicative:

Ich kaufte das nicht. { *I didn't buy that. (past indic.)*
I wouldn't buy that. (pres. subj.)

is replaced by:

Ich **würde** das nicht **kaufen**. *I wouldn't buy that.*

Spoken German also replaces the one-word form of many strong verbs with **würden** + *infinitive* (but *not* in the case of the frequently used verbs **sein**, **haben**, and the modals).

Ich **tränke** Wein ...   is replaced by
Ich **würde** Wein **trinken ...**   *I'd drink wine ...*

Lab Manual Kap. 14, Var. zur Üb. 9.

■ 9 ■ Übung: Was würden Sie machen?   Sagen Sie, was Sie in diesen Situationen machen würden.

BEISPIEL: Was würden Sie machen, wenn Sie diese Woche frei
hätten?
Ich würde nach Hause fahren.

Was würden Sie machen ...

1. wenn Sie 500 Schilling hätten?
2. wenn Sie Hunger hätten?
3. wenn Sie Durst hätten?
4. wenn Sie Musik hören wollten?
5. wenn Sie Wanderlust hätten?
6. wenn Sie knapp bei Kasse wären?
7. wenn Sie Spaß haben wollten?
8. wenn Sie sich das Studium nicht leisten könnten?

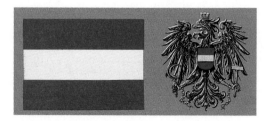

Other uses of the general subjunctive

Talking about contrary-to-fact situations is a communicative goal.

■ **Conditions contrary to fact: "If *X* were true, then *Y* would be true."**

In **Kapitel 8** you learned about conditional sentences containing a **wenn**-clause (see p. 196). When the conditional sentence is describing a situation that is contrary to fact, the verbs must be in the subjunctive. Note the difference between the following sentences:

Indicative

Wenn der Junge schon dreizehn **ist**, **darf** er den Film sehen.	*If the boy is already thirteen he's allowed to see the movie.*

(*Implication*: The speaker doesn't know whether the boy is thirteen or not.)

Subjunctive

Wenn der Junge schon dreizehn **wäre**, **dürfte** er den Film sehen.	*If the boy were already thirteen, he would be allowed to see the movie.*

(*Implication*: The speaker knows the boy is not yet thirteen.)

A **wenn**-clause states the condition contrary to fact: "If X were true . . ."

Wenn wir jetzt in Deutschland wären ...	*If we were in Germany now . . .*
Wenn ich mehr Geld hätte ...	*If I had more money . . .*

The main clause (with an optional **dann** as the first word) draws the unreal conclusion: ". . . then Y would be true."

... (dann) würden wir sehr schnell Deutsch lernen.	*. . . (then) we would learn German very quickly.*
... (dann) müsste ich nicht so viel arbeiten.	*. . . (then) I wouldn't have to work so much.*

Putting them together:

> **Wenn wir jetzt in Deutschland wären, würden wir sehr schnell Deutsch lernen.**
> **Wenn ich mehr Geld hätte, dann müsste ich nicht so viel arbeiten.**

Conditional sentences may begin either with the **wenn**-clause (as in the two previous examples) *or* with the conclusion clause.[1]

> Wir **würden** sehr schnell Deutsch lernen, wenn wir jetzt in Deutschland **wären**.
> Ich **müsste** nicht so viel arbeiten, wenn ich mehr Geld **hätte**.

---

1. The **wenn** is sometimes omitted from the **wenn**-clause. Its verb is then placed at the *beginning* of the clause. Compare the similar structure in English that omits *if*:

Hätte er das Geld, (dann) würde er mehr kaufen. ***Had** he the money, he would buy more.*

Lab Manual Kap. 14, Üb. 10.

Workbook Kap. 14, D–G.

■ **10** ■ Übung: Aber wenn es anders wäre ... (*Mit offenen Büchern*) Ihr Professor beschreibt eine Situation im Indikativ. Sie sagen im Konjunktiv, wie es wäre, wenn die Situation *anders* wäre. (Note that the logic of these sentences demands changing positive to negative and vice versa.)

> **BEISPIEL:** Weil es so kalt ist, können wir nicht schwimmen.
> Aber wenn es *nicht* so kalt *wäre, könnten* wir schwimmen.

1. Weil es so weit ist, können wir nicht zu Fuß gehen.
2. Weil ich keine Lust habe, mache ich es nicht.
3. Weil dieses Buch langweilig ist, lesen wir es nicht.
4. Weil der Dom geschlossen ist, können Sie ihn nicht besuchen.
5. Weil ich keine Zeit habe, kann ich kein Bad nehmen.
6. Weil sie nicht aus Österreich kommt, sagt sie nicht „Grüß Gott".
7. Weil ich keinen Hunger habe, bestelle ich nichts.
8. Weil sie sich nicht für diesen Film interessiert, geht sie nicht mit.

■ **11** ■ Übung (*Mit offenen Büchern*) Wiederholen Sie, was Sie schon in **Übung 10** gemacht haben, aber diesmal beginnen Sie *nicht* mit **wenn**.

> **BEISPIEL:** Wir kommen zu spät, weil du nicht schneller fährst.
> Aber wir würden nicht zu spät kommen, wenn du schneller fahren würdest.

1. Wir bleiben hier, weil er uns braucht.
2. Ich muss jetzt wechseln, weil ich kein österreichisches Geld habe.
3. Wir gehen spazieren, weil die Sonne scheint.
4. Wir trampen nach Italien, weil wir keinen Wagen haben.
5. Ich lese die Zeitung nicht, weil ich so müde bin.
6. Er kann mir nicht danken, weil er meinen Namen nicht weiß.
7. Wir sehen uns nicht, weil er nicht mehr vorbeikommt.

Wenn ich fliegen könnte...

■ **Wishes contrary to fact**

There are two ways to form contrary-to-fact wishes:

> Wenn sie nur hier wäre!   *If only she were here!*
> Ich wünschte, sie wäre hier.   *I wish she were here.*

When you use the second expression, notice that *both* verbs are in the subjunctive (**wünschte, wäre**). The second clause of this construction *never* begins with **dass** but *always* has verb-second word order.

Workbook Kap. 14, H.

Lab Manual Kap. 14, Var. zur Üb. 12.

■ **12** ■   **Gruppenarbeit: Buttje, Buttje, in der See**   Es gibt ein bekanntes norddeutsches Märchen („Der Fischer und seine Frau"), in dem ein großer Butt (*flounder*) einem Fischer seine Wünsche erfüllt (*grants*). Der Fischer ruft ihn immer wieder aus der See mit den Worten: „Buttje, Buttje, in der See", und sagt ihm, was er sich wünscht. Jetzt sagen Sie einander, was Sie sich wünschen. Antworten Sie, ob Sie den Wunsch erfüllen können oder nicht.

> **BEISPIEL:** A: Ich wünschte, ich könnte wie ein Vogel fliegen!
> B: Das kann ich dir leider nicht erfüllen!

■   **Hypothetical statements and questions**

German also uses subjunctive for hypothetical statements and questions, where English uses *would*, *could*, or *ought to*.

Du **solltest** daran denken.	*You **ought to** think of that.*
Wir **könnten** nach Grinzing fahren.	*We **could** drive to Grinzing.*
Das **wäre** schön!	*That **would be** nice!*
Was **würde** das kosten?	*What **would** that cost?*

Lab Manual Kap. 14, Var. zur Üb. 13.

■ **13** ■   **Partnerarbeit: Wie wäre das?**   Sie wollen heute irgendetwas zusammen machen. Partner A macht einen Vorschlag (*suggestion*). Partner B reagiert darauf.

> **BEISPIEL:** A: Wir *könnten* eine Wanderung machen.
> B: Ja, das *wäre* schön! (*oder*) Nein, das *wäre* mir zu schwierig.

Alt und Jung ruhen sich auf einer Bank aus. (Tirol, Österreich)

■ Polite requests

Note the difference in the tone of the following two requests:

> **Can** *you do this for me?* vs. **Could** *you do this for me?*

It is more polite to soften the request with the subjunctive, as in the second sentence. German uses the subjunctive in the same way as English to make polite requests. These are sometimes in the statement form you have already used.

Ich **hätte** gern eine Tasse Kaffee.	*I'd like to have a cup of coffee.*
Ich **wüsste** gern, wo der Bahnhof ist.	*I'd like to know where the train station is.*

Sometimes polite requests are questions.

Könnten Sie mir bitte helfen?	*Could you please help me?*
Würden Sie mir bitte den Koffer tragen?	*Would you please carry my suitcase?*
Dürfte ich eine Frage stellen?	*Might I ask a question?*

Workbook Kap. 14, I.

Lab Manual Kap. 14, Var. zur Üb. 14; Üb. 14.

■ 14 ■ Übung: Könnten Sie das bitte machen? Benutzen Sie den Konjunktiv statt des Indikativs um höflicher zu sein.

> BEISPIEL: Können Sie mir bitte ein Einzelzimmer zeigen?
> Könnten Sie mir bitte ein Einzelzimmer zeigen?

1. Können Sie mir bitte sagen, wann der Zug nach Berlin abfährt?
2. Haben Sie Zeit eine Tasse Kaffee mit mir zu trinken?
3. Darf ich mich hier setzen?
4. Tragen Sie mir bitte die Koffer? (Benutzen Sie *würden*!)
5. Ist es möglich eine Zeitung zu kaufen?
6. Können Sie mir meinen Platz zeigen?
7. Haben Sie ein Einzelzimmer mit Dusche?
8. Wissen Sie, wo man Karten kaufen kann?

Lesestück

Vor dem Lesen

Tipps zum Lesen und Lernen

■ Tipps zum Vokabelnlernen: Adverbs of time

The suffix *-lang*   To form the German equivalents of the English adverbial phrases *for days, for hours*, etc., add the suffix **-lang** to the plural of the noun.

minuten**lang**	*for minutes*	monate**lang**	*for months*
stunden**lang**	*for hours*	jahre**lang**	*for years*
tage**lang**	*for days*	jahrhunderte**lang**	*for centuries*
wochen**lang**	*for weeks*		

Also learn the phrase

eine Zeit lang   *for a time, for a while*

In diesem Kapitel lesen Sie über Österreich. Das Lesestück spricht von der historischen Rolle Österreichs als Weltreich:

> „Die Habsburger Dynastie regierte **jahrhundertelang** über Deutsche, Ungarn, Tschechen, Polen, Italiener, Serben und **eine Zeit lang** sogar über Mexikaner."

You can guess the meaning of **jahrzehntelang**.

Compare the Note on Usage on p. 256.

Workbook Kap. 14, J.

■ ■ ■   **Übung: Wie lange hat's gedauert?**   Ihre Professorin möchte wissen, ob etwas lange gedauert hat. Wählen Sie ein Zeitadverb mit **-lang** für Ihre Antwort.

> BEISPIEL: A: Haben Sie lange im Zug zwischen Paris und Berlin gesessen?
> B: Ja, *stundenlang*.

Hat das elegante Abendessen lange gedauert?
Haben Sie lange auf den Bus warten müssen?
War's letzten Sommer sehr heiß?
War der Chef lange am Telefon?
Sind Sie manchmal schlechter Laune?
Waren die alten Römer lange Zeit in Nordeuropa?

Lab Manual Kap. 14, Üb. zur Betonung.

■ Leicht zu merken

analysieren	analysieren
die **Dynastie, -n**	Dynastie
der **Humor**	Humor
die **Ironie**	Ironie
der **Kontakt**	Kontakt
kreativ	kreativ
literarisch	literarisch
die **Melancholie**	Melancholie
der **Patient, -en, -en**	Patient
philosophieren	philosophieren
produktiv	produktiv
die **Psychoanalyse**	Psychoanalyse

■ Einstieg in den Text

The two Austrians in the following reading selection use subjunctive mood mainly for conjectural and hypothetical statements. Below is one example of each type. After reading through the text once, write down other examples of subjunctive mood used for these purposes; be sure you understand them and can give English equivalents.

Hypothetical statements
Ich ... könnte ... bei meinen Eltern wohnen und an der Musikhochschule in Wien studieren.

Conjecture
... ohne Johann Strauß würde die Welt wahrscheinlich keine Walzer tanzen.

■ Wortschatz 2

Verben

erwarten to expect
sich konzentrieren auf (+ *acc.*) to concentrate on
statt·finden, fand statt, hat stattgefunden to take place
tanzen to dance
träumen to dream

Substantive

der **Künstler, -** artist (*m.*)
der **Spiegel, -** mirror
der **Witz, -e** joke; wit

das **Klavier, -e** piano
die **Gegenwart** present (time)
die **Gelegenheit, -en** opportunity, chance
die **Hochschule, -n** university; institution of higher learning
die **Künstlerin, -nen** artist (*f.*)

Hochschule corresponds roughly to college, not high school (generically called **die Oberschule**). **Musikhochschule** = *conservatory*; **Technische Hochschule** = engineering college.

Adjektive und Adverbien

außerdem (*adv.*) besides, in addition
begeistert von enthusiastic about, ecstatic about
ernst serious
  etwas ernst nehmen to take something seriously
gemütlich cozy, comfortable; quiet, relaxed
witzig witty, amusing
zunächst first (of all), to begin with

Zwei Österreicher stellen sich vor

Marie-Therese Werdenberg, Musikstudentin in Salzburg

Lab Manual Kap. 14,
Lesestück.

„Ich heiße Marie-Therese Werdenberg und bin Musikstudentin. Ich komme aus Wien
und könnte freilich° dort bei meinen Eltern wohnen und an der Musikhochschule in
Wien studieren. Aber ich studiere lieber in Salzburg, weil ich mich hier besser auf das
5 Klavierspielen konzentrieren kann. In Wien gäbe es zwar mehr Konzerte, in die man
gehen könnte, aber hier ist es ruhiger und gemütlicher. Außerdem finden hier im
Sommer die berühmten Festspiele[1] statt und da habe ich die Gelegenheit mit vielen
Musikern° in Kontakt zu kommen.

    Ja, was wäre Österreich ohne seine Musiktradition? Und umgekehrt°: Was wäre
10 die Musikgeschichte ohne Österreich? Salzburg ist Mozarts Geburtsort°. Auch Haydn,
Schubert, Bruckner, Mahler und Schönberg sind alle in Österreich geboren.
Beethoven und Brahms – beides deutsche Komponisten° – haben in Wien ihre
wichtigsten Werke geschrieben. Und ohne Johann Strauß würde die Welt wahrscheinlich keine Walzer° tanzen.

15   Aber ich sollte nicht nur über Musik reden, bloß° weil das meine Leidenschaft° ist.
Die Kulturgeschichte Österreichs hat der Welt eine ganze Menge gegeben. In Wien um
1900 gab es z.B. ein besonders produktives und faszinierendes° Kulturleben. Die
literarischen Werke von Hugo von Hofmannsthal und Arthur Schnitzler sind ein
Spiegel dieser sehr kreativen Zeit. In der Malerei° arbeiteten Künstler wie Gustav Klimt
20 und Oskar Kokoschka. Um diese Zeit gründete° Sigmund Freud die Psychoanalyse. Ich
könnte noch viele Namen nennen, aber dann müssten wir fast den ganzen Tag hier
sitzen.“

° = **natürlich**

Learning about Austria is the cultural
goal of this chapter.

° = **Menschen, die Musik,
   machen** / vice versa

° = **Ort, wo man geboren ist**

° = **Menschen, die Musik
   komponieren**

° waltzes

° = **nur** / passion

° = **sehr interessantes**

° painting
° founded

Oskar Kokoschka (1886–1980),
Selbstbildnis (*self-portrait*, 1917)

1. The **Salzburger Festspiele** are an annual summer festival of drama and classical
music.

Blick auf Salzburg

Dr. Ulrich Kraus, Psychologe° aus Wien

psychologist

„Mein Name ist Kraus und ich bin Psychologe. Mit meinen Patienten und ihren
25 Problemen habe ich mehr als genug zu tun; erwarten Sie also nicht von mir, dass ich
den Durchschnittsösterreicher° analysiere. Ich könnte aber mindestens° versuchen
diesen Menschen — den *homo austriacus* — ein bisschen zu beschreiben.

average Austrian /
= **wenigstens**

Zunächst etwas Geschichte: Ich möchte Sie daran erinnern, dass wir Österreicher
auf eine sehr alte und große Tradition stolz sind. Die Habsburger Dynastie regierte°
30 jahrhundertelang über Deutsche, Ungarn, Tschechen, Polen, Italiener, Serben und
eine Zeit lang sogar über Mexikaner.[1] Was man vom englischen Weltreich sagt, könnte
man auch von Österreich sagen: Die Sonne ging nicht unter° über diesem Reich.

ruled

ging ... unter = set
more modest

Heute spielt unser kleines Land eine viel bescheidenere° politische Rolle. Und
dieser Kontrast zwischen Vergangenheit und Gegenwart hat zu unserem Humor und
35 unserer Selbstironie beigetragen°. Manchmal habe ich das Gefühl, wir Österreicher
sind unglücklich über unsere verlorene Größe, aber wir sind wenigstens glücklich,
dass wir unglücklich sind. Verstehen Sie diese witzige Melancholie, die sich selbst
nicht ganz ernst nimmt?

contributed

Viele Österreicher würden den Unterschied zwischen sich und den Deutschen so
40 ausdrücken: Die Deutschen sind fleißig, aber die Österreicher gemütlich. Die Wiener
Kaffeehäuser könnten nicht existieren, wenn der Österreicher nicht gern stundenlang
vor seinem Mokka[2] säße und träumte. Er philosophiert gern darüber, wie die Welt sein
könnte. Darum nennt man Österreich manchmal das Land des Konjunktivs: ‚Alles
würde hier besser gehen, wenn wir nur ...' oder ‚Das wäre möglich, wenn ... '"

1. The Habsburgs ruled the Holy Roman Empire from 1278 to 1806, and Austria (later Austria-
Hungary) until 1918. The empire came to include Germans, Hungarians, Czechs, Poles, Italians,
and Serbs. In 1864 Archduke Maximilian, brother of the Austrian Emperor, was made Emperor of
Mexico. He was executed in 1867 by republican troops.
2. A strong aromatic coffee served in demitasse cups, named after a city in Yemen. The drink was
introduced into Vienna during the Turkish siege of the city in 1683. Viennese cafés serve dozens
of different types of coffee, each with its own name.

Im Café Central, Wien

Poster designed by Oskar Kokoschka for a 1908 art show of the Viennese "Secession Movement"

Nach dem Lesen

■ A ■ Antworten Sie auf Deutsch.

1. Woher kommt die Musikstudentin im ersten Teil des Textes und was macht sie in Salzburg?
2. Warum studiert sie lieber dort als in Wien?
3. Nennen Sie einen berühmten Menschen, der in Salzburg geboren ist.
4. Kennen Sie andere berühmte Namen aus der Musikgeschichte Österreichs?
5. Warum war Wien um 1900 besonders interessant? Wer hat damals dort gelebt und gearbeitet?
6. Was wissen Sie von der Geschichte Österreichs?
7. Beschreiben Sie den größten Unterschied für die Österreicher zwischen der Vergangenheit und der Gegenwart ihres Landes.
8. Welche Unterschiede findet Dr. Kraus zwischen den Deutschen und seinen Landsleuten?
9. Warum nennt man Österreich manchmal das Land des Konjunktivs?

■ B ■ Gruppenarbeit: Im Café   In einem Wiener Café darf man nicht einfach „eine Tasse Kaffee" bestellen, denn man hat eine riesengroße Auswahl von verschiedenen Kaffeegetränken. Von der Liste unten wählen Sie Ihren Lieblingskaffee. (Wenn Sie keinen Kaffee trinken wollen, gibt's natürlich auch Tee und Cola.) Lieben Sie Ihren Kaffee mit oder ohne Zucker? stark oder schwach? mit oder ohne Schlag (*whipped cream*)?

Kleiner Schwarzer	Demitasse of espresso.
Kleiner Brauner	**Kleiner Schwarzer** with a dash of milk.
Großer Schwarzer	Double shot of espresso.
Großer Brauner	A big **kleiner Brauner**.
Espresso	The universally-known strong black brew. If you'd like a weak one, ask for it "stretched": **gestreckt**.
Verlängerter	**Espresso gestreckt**, i.e., diluted with a shot of hot water.
Mokka	Synonymous with **Brauner** — a **Mokka** can be **klein** or **groß**.
Kapuziner	Dark coffee, the color of a Capuchin monk's robes.
Franziskaner	Dark coffee with a little more milk, the color of a Franciscan's robes.

Nussbraun	A little lighter: "nut brown."
Nussgold	Lighter still.
Gold	Very light.
Schwarzer	Black coffee (**klein** or **groß**).
Konsul	Black coffee with a dash of cream.
Melange	Espresso with steamed milk, sometimes with whipped cream (**Schlag** or **Schlagobers**).
Cappuccino	Espresso with foamed milk and a sprinkling of cinnamon.
Milchkaffee	Half coffee, half hot milk.
Einspänner	**Großer Mokka** with **Schlag** and a sprinkling of cocoa. Served in a tall glass.
Fiaker	Named after Vienna's horse-drawn carriages and their raucous drivers. Strong, black coffee laced with hot kirsch liqueur topped with Schlag and maraschino cherry.
Pharisäer	Strong black coffee with whipped cream, served with small liqueur glass of rum.
Türkischer	Black Turkish coffee served with traditional copper utensils.
Kaisermelange	Cup of black coffee served with raw egg yolk and brandy on the side.
Eiskaffee	Iced coffee with vanilla ice cream. Topped with **Schlag**.

■ **C** ■ **Gruppenarbeit (*3 Personen*)** Jetzt sitzen wir gemütlich zusammen, trinken unseren Kaffee und spekulieren ein bisschen. Unten sind einige Situationen. Besprechen Sie miteinander, was Sie in diesen Situationen tun würden.

> **BEISPIEL:** krank sein
> Was würdest du tun, wenn du krank wärest?
> Ich würde zunächst ins Bett gehen. Dann …

Lab Manual Kap. 14, Diktat.

Workbook Kap. 14, K–Q.

reich sein	viel Zeit haben
in Europa sein	jetzt Ferien haben
kein Student sein	Hunger haben
wenig Geld haben	Politiker sein

Situationen aus dem Alltag

This vocabulary focuses on an everyday topic or situation. Words you already know from **Wortschatz** sections are listed without English equivalents; new supplementary vocabulary is listed with definitions. Your instructor may assign some supplementary vocabulary for active mastery.

■ Im Hotel

Auf Seite 367 sehen Sie die Rezeption in einem Hotel. Hier ist eine Liste von Vokabeln, die Ihnen zum größten Teil (*for the most part*) schon bekannt sind.

Die Hotelgäste
sich an·melden   *to register*
das **Gepäck**
der **Koffer**, -

der **Reisepass, -pässe**   *passport*
ein Zimmer reservieren
ein Taxi bestellen

An der Rezeption
der/die **Angestellte**
die **Kasse**
der **Zimmerschlüssel, -**
der **Stadtplan, -̈e**
der **Stadtführer, -**   *city guidebook*
der **Speisesaal**   *dining room*
der **Lift**   *elevator*

Im Hotelzimmer
das **Bad**
die **Dusche**
das **Telefon (telefonieren)**
sich um·ziehen   *to change clothes*

■ **A** ■   **Gruppenarbeit**   Beschreiben Sie dieses Bild. Wer steht wo? Wer tut was?

With this chapter you have completed the fourth quarter of **Neue Horizonte: A Brief Course**. For a concise review of the grammar and idiomatic phrases in chapters 12–14, you may consult the **Zusammenfassung und Wiederholung 4** (*Summary and Review 4*) of your Workbook. The review section is followed by a self-correcting test.

■ **B** ■ **Rollenspiele** (*Gruppen von 3 Personen*) Spielen Sie diese Situationen zusammen. Improvisieren Sie.

1. *An der Rezeption* Zwei Touristen kommen gerade vom Flughafen im Hotel an. Sie haben schon ein Zimmer reserviert. Sie melden sich an der Rezeption an und stellen Fragen über das Zimmer.

2. *Eine Stunde später* Die Touristen haben sich jetzt geduscht und umgezogen. Jetzt wollen sie ausgehen und sich die Stadt ansehen. An der Rezeption bitten sie um Auskunft. Der Angestellte gibt ihnen viele Informationen über die Stadt, z.B. über das kulturelle Leben, Verkehrsmittel, Restaurants usw. Bei ihm bekommen sie auch Stadtführer, Stadtpläne und Broschüren (*brochures*). Sie müssen auch Geld wechseln.

View Modules 7–8 of the **Neue Horizonte** video (27:32/32:33) and do the activities in **Videoecken 7–8** in your Workbook/Laboratory Manual/Video Manual.

Profile of Austria

Area:	83,855 square kilometers; 32,376 square miles (slightly smaller than the state of Maine)
Population:	8,132,500; density 97 people per square kilometer (251 people per square mile)
Currency:	Schilling; 1 öS = 100 Groschen
Major Cities:	Vienna (**Wien**, capital, pop. 1,597,000), Graz, Linz, Salzburg, Innsbruck
Religion:	85% Roman Catholic, 6% Protestant, 9% other

Austria consists of nine states (**Bundesländer**). It became a member of the European Union in 1995. In addition to basic industries such as machinery, iron and steel, and textiles and chemicals, tourism provides an important source of income. The literacy rate is 98%.

Austria plays a vital role in the United Nations, and Vienna is an important point of contact between eastern and western Europe. With the opening of the "UNO City" in 1979, Vienna became the third seat of the United Nations. It is also the headquarters for OPEC (the Organization of Petroleum Exporting Countries).

Straßenkonzert vor dem Stephansdom, Wien

Endlich ist der Frühling da. (Innsbruck mit Blick auf die Nordkette)

Burgenland Kärnten Niederösterreich

Oberösterreich Salzburg Steiermark

Tirol Vorarlberg Wien

Principal Parts of Strong and Irregular Verbs

The following table contains the principal parts of all the strong, mixed, and irregular verbs in *Neue Horizonte: A Brief Course*. With a few exceptions, only the basic stem verbs are listed, e.g., **gehen**, **bringen**, and **kommen**. Verbs formed by adding a prefix—e.g., **weggehen**, **verbringen**, and **ankommen**—change their stems in the same way as the basic verb.

infinitive	3rd person sing. present	simple past	perfect	English
anfangen	fängt an	fing an	hat angefangen	begin
beginnen		begann	hat begonnen	begin
bieten		bot	hat geboten	offer, provide
bitten		bat	hat gebeten	ask for, request
bleiben		blieb	ist geblieben	stay
brechen	bricht	brach	hat gebrochen	break
brennen		brannte	hat gebrannt	burn
bringen		brachte	hat gebracht	bring
denken		dachte	hat gedacht	think
dürfen	darf	durfte	hat gedurft	may, be allowed to
einladen	lädt ein	lud ein	hat eingeladen	invite
empfehlen	empfiehlt	empfahl	hat empfohlen	recommend
entscheiden		entschied	hat entschieden	decide
essen	isst	aß	hat gegessen	eat
fahren	fährt	fuhr	ist gefahren	drive
fallen	fällt	fiel	ist gefallen	fall
finden		fand	hat gefunden	find
fliegen		flog	ist geflogen	fly
fließen		floss	ist geflossen	flow
geben	gibt	gab	hat gegeben	give
gehen		ging	ist gegangen	go
gewinnen		gewann	hat gewonnen	win
haben	hat	hatte	hat gehabt	have
halten	hält	hielt	hat gehalten	hold, stop
hängen[1]		hing	hat gehangen	be hanging
heißen		hieß	hat geheißen	be called
helfen	hilft	half	hat geholfen	help
kennen		kannte	hat gekannt	know, be acquainted with
klingen		klang	hat geklungen	sound
kommen		kam	ist gekommen	come
können	kann	konnte	hat gekonnt	can, be able to
lassen	lässt	ließ	hat gelassen	leave; let; allow to; cause to be done
laufen	läuft	lief	ist gelaufen	run

---

1. When it is transitive, **hängen** is weak: **hängte**, **hat gehängt**.

infinitive	3rd person sing. present	simple past	perfect	English
leihen		lieh	hat geliehen	*lend*
lesen	liest	las	hat gelesen	*read*
liegen		lag	hat gelegen	*lie*
mögen	mag	mochte	hat gemocht	*like*
müssen	muss	musste	hat gemusst	*must, have to*
nehmen	nimmt	nahm	hat genommen	*take*
nennen		nannte	hat genannt	*name, call*
raten	rät	riet	hat geraten	*guess*
rufen		rief	hat gerufen	*call, shout*
scheinen		schien	hat geschienen	*shine, seem*
schlafen	schläft	schlief	hat geschlafen	*sleep*
schlagen	schlägt	schlug	hat geschlagen	*hit, beat*
schließen		schloss	hat geschlossen	*close*
schneiden		schnitt	hat geschnitten	*cut*
schreiben		schrieb	hat geschrieben	*write*
schreien		schrie	hat geschrien	*shout, yell*
schweigen		schwieg	hat geschwiegen	*be silent*
schwimmen		schwamm	ist geschwommen	*swim*
sehen	sieht	sah	hat gesehen	*see*
sein	ist	war	ist gewesen	*be*
singen		sang	hat gesungen	*sing*
sitzen		saß	hat gesessen	*sit*
sollen	soll	sollte	hat gesollt	*should*
sprechen	spricht	sprach	hat gesprochen	*speak*
stehen		stand	hat gestanden	*stand*
stehlen	stiehlt	stahl	hat gestohlen	*steal*
steigen		stieg	ist gestiegen	*climb*
sterben	stirbt	starb	ist gestorben	*die*
tragen	trägt	trug	hat getragen	*carry, wear*
treffen	trifft	traf	hat getroffen	*meet*
treiben		trieb	hat getrieben	*drive, propel*
trinken		trank	hat getrunken	*drink*
tun		tat	hat getan	*do*
vergessen	vergisst	vergaß	hat vergessen	*forget*
vergleichen		verglich	hat verglichen	*compare*
verlassen	verlässt	verließ	hat verlassen	*leave*
verlieren		verlor	hat verloren	*lose*
verschwinden		verschwand	ist verschwunden	*disappear*
wachsen	wächst	wuchs	ist gewachsen	*grow*
waschen	wäscht	wusch	hat gewaschen	*wash*
werden	wird	wurde	ist geworden	*become*
werfen	wirft	warf	hat geworfen	*throw*
wiegen		wog	hat gewogen	*weigh*
wissen	weiß	wusste	hat gewusst	*know (a fact)*
wollen	will	wollte	hat gewollt	*want to*
ziehen		zog	hat/ist gezogen	*pull; move*

German–English Vocabulary

The following list contains all the words introduced in *Neue Horizonte: A Brief Course* except for definite and indefinite articles, personal and relative pronouns, possessive adjectives, cardinal and ordinal numbers, and words glossed in the margins of the **Lesestücke**. The code at the end of each entry shows where the word or phrase is introduced in the text:

12-1	Kapitel 12, Wortschatz 1
9-2	Kapitel 9, Wortschatz 2
Einf.	Einführung (Introductory Chapter)
2-G	Kapitel 2, Grammatik
5-TLL	Kapitel 5, Tipps zum Lesen und Lernen (*in the section* Leicht zu merken)
10-SA	Kapitel 10, Situationen aus dem Alltag

Strong and irregular verbs are listed with their principal parts: **nehmen (nimmt), nahm, hat genommen**. Weak verbs using **sein** as their auxiliary are shown by inclusion of the perfect: **reisen, ist gereist**.

Separable prefixes are indicated by a raised dot between prefix and verb stem: **ab·fahren**. This dot is *not* used in German spelling.

When a verb has a prepositional complement, the preposition follows all the principal parts. If it is a two-way preposition, the case it takes with this verb is indicated in parentheses: **teil·nehmen (nimmt teil), nahm teil, hat teilgenommen** *an* (+ *dat.*).

Adjectival nouns are indicated thus: der / die **Verwandte, -n**.

Masculine N-nouns like **der Student** and irregular nouns like **der Name** are followed by both the genitive singular and the plural endings: der **Student, -*en*, -en**; der **Name, -*ns*, -n**.

Adjectives followed by a hyphen may only be used attributively: **eigen-**.

If an adjective or adverb requires an umlaut in the comparative and superlative degrees, or if these forms are irregular, this is indicated in parentheses: **arm (ärmer); gern (lieber, am liebsten)**.

The following abbreviations are used here and throughout *Neue Horizonte: A Brief Course*.

acc.	accusative	*m.*	masculine
adj.	adjective	*neut.*	neuter
adj. noun	adjectival noun	*pers.*	person
adv.	adverb	*pl.*	plural
colloq.	colloquial	*prep.*	preposition
conj.	conjunction	*sing.*	singular
coor. conj.	coordinating conjunction	*sub. conj.*	subordinating conjunction
dat.	dative		
f.	feminine	*trans.*	transitive
gen.	genitive	*usw.*	(= *und so weiter*) etc.
intrans.	intransitive		

A

der **Abend, -e** evening, 7-2
  am Abend in the evening, 7-2
  Guten Abend! Good evening, *Einf.*
das **Abendessen, -** supper, evening meal, 8-1
  zum Abendessen for supper, 8-1
abends (in the) evenings, 5-2
aber (1) but (*coor. conj.*), 1-1; (2) (*flavoring particle*), 9-1
ab·fahren (fährt ab), fuhr ab, ist abgefahren to depart, leave (by vehicle), 7-1
ab·holen to pick up, fetch, get, 5-2
das **Abi** (*slang*) = **Abitur**, 5-1
das **Abitur** final secondary school examination, 5-1
ach oh, ah, 2-1
das **Adjektiv, -e** adjective
der **Adler, -** eagle, 10-SA
das **Adverb, -ien** adverb
ähnlich (+ *dat.*) similar (to), 3-2
  Sie ist ihrer Mutter ähnlich. She's like her mother.
die **Ähnlichkeit, -en** similarity, 11-2
die **Ahnung** notion, inkling, hunch
  (Ich habe) keine Ahnung. (I have) no idea. 10-1
aktiv active, 9-TLL
aktuell current, topical, 5-2
akut acute, 9-TLL
alle (*pl.*) all; everybody, 2-2
allein alone, 4-1
alles everything, 6-2
der **Alltag** everyday life, 8-2
der **Almanach, -e** almanac
die **Alpen** (*pl.*) the Alps, 4-TLL
als (1) when (*sub. conj.*), 10-1; (2) as a, 5-1; (3) than (*with comparative degree*), 12-1
also (1) well . . . 1-1; (2) thus, 3-2
alt (älter) old, 2-2
die **Alternative, -n** alternative, 2-TLL
altmodisch old-fashioned, 4-2
die **Altstadt, ̈-e** old city center, 8-TLL
(das) **Amerika** America, 3-2

der **Amerikaner, -** American (*m.*), 1-2
die **Amerikanerin, -nen** American (*f.*), 1-2
amerikanisch American, 3-2
an (*prep. + acc. or dat.*) to, toward; at, alongside of, 6-1
analysieren to analyze, 14-TLL
ander- other, different, 11-1
ändern to change (*trans.*), 11-2
  sich ändern to change (*intrans.*), 11-2
anders different, 2-2
der **Anfang, ̈-e** beginning, 6-1
  am Anfang at the beginning, 6-1
an·fangen (fängt an), fing an, hat angefangen to begin, start, 5-1
der **Anfänger, -** beginner, 5-TLL
angenehm pleased to meet you, 13-SA
der/die **Angestellte, -n** (*adj. noun*) employee, 14-1
die **Anglistik** English studies, 6-SA
die **Angst, ̈-e** fear, 3-2
  Angst haben to be afraid, 3-2
  Angst haben vor (+ *dat.*) to be afraid of, 13-1
an·kommen, kam an, ist angekommen to arrive, 5-1
  an·kommen auf (+ *acc.*) to depend on, be contingent on
  Es kommt darauf an. It depends. 13-1
sich an·melden to register (at a hotel, at the university, etc.), 14-SA
an·rufen, rief an, hat angerufen to call up, 5-1
sich etwas an·sehen (sieht an), sah an, hat angesehen to take a look at something, 11-1
anstatt (*prep. + gen.*) instead of, 8-G
die **Antwort, -en** answer, 6-2
antworten (+ *dat.*) to answer (a person), 6-2
  antworten auf (+ *acc.*) to answer (something), respond to, 13-2
sich an·ziehen, zog an, hat angezogen to get dressed, 11-1

der **Anzug, ̈-e** suit, 3-SA
die **Apotheke, -n** pharmacy, 8-SA
der **Appetit** appetite
  Guten Appetit! *Bon appétit!*, Enjoy your meal! 8-SA
(der) **April** April, *Einf.*
die **Arbeit** work, 2-2
arbeiten to work, 1-1
der **Arbeiter, -** worker (*m.*), 5-2
die **Arbeiterin, -nen** worker (*f.*)
arbeitslos unemployed, 10-2
die **Arbeitslosigkeit** unemployment, 10-2
ärgern to annoy; offend, 8-2
  sich ärgern (über + *acc.*) to get annoyed (at), be annoyed (about), 13-2
arm (ärmer) poor, 10-1
der **Arm, -e** arm, 10-2
der **Artikel, -** article, 2-1
der **Arzt, ̈-e** doctor (*m.*), 5-SA; 11-1
die **Ärztin, -nen** doctor (*f.*), 5-SA; 11-1
der **Aspekt, -e** aspect, 8-TLL
das **Atom, -e** atom, 9-TLL
das **Atomkraftwerk** atomic power plant, 9-2
auch also, too, 1-1
auf (*prep. + acc. or dat.*) onto; on, upon, on top of, 6-1
→ die **Aufgabe, -n** task, assignment
auf·geben (gibt auf), gab auf, hat aufgegeben (*trans. & intrans.*) to give up, quit, 11-2
auf·hängen to hang up, 7-1
auf·hören (mit) to cease, stop (doing something), 5-1
auf·machen to open, 5-1
auf·räumen to tidy up, straighten up, 13-1
der **Aufsatz, ̈-e** essay
das **Aufsatzthema, -themen** essay topic
auf·stehen, stand auf, ist aufgestanden (1) to stand up; to get up; (2) to get out of bed, 5-1
auf·wachen, ist aufgewacht to wake up (*intrans.*), 7-1

auf·wachsen (wächst auf), wuchs auf, ist aufgewachsen to grow up, 13-2

das Auge, -n eye, 11-1

der Augenblick, -e moment, 12-1
  (Einen) Augenblick, bitte. Just a moment, please. 12-1
  im Augenblick at the moment, 12-1

(der) August August, Einf.

aus (prep. + dat.) out of; from, 5-1

der Ausdruck, ⸚e expression

der Ausflug, ⸚e outing, excursion, 14-2

aus·geben (gibt aus), gab aus, hat ausgegeben to spend (money), 6-2

aus·gehen, ging aus, ist ausgegangen to go out, 14-1

ausgezeichnet excellent, 8-1

sich aus·kennen, kannte aus, hat ausgekannt to know one's way around, 13-1

die Auskunft information, 13-1

das Ausland (sing.) foreign countries, 7-2
  im Ausland abroad (location), 7-2
  ins Ausland abroad (destination), 7-2

ausländisch foreign, 10-2

aus·packen to unpack, 11-SA

aus·sehen (sieht aus), sah aus, hat ausgesehen to appear, look (like), 5-2

außer (prep. + dat.) besides; in addition to, 5-1

außerdem (adv.) besides, in addition, 14-2

aus·steigen, stieg aus, ist ausgestiegen to get out (of a vehicle), 7-2

die Ausstellung, -en exhibition, 10-2

der Austauschstudent, -en, -en exchange student, 6-1

aus·wandern, ist ausgewandert to emigrate, 11-2

der Ausweis, -e I.D. card, 6-2

aus·ziehen, zog aus, ist ausgezogen to move out, 6-1

sich ausziehen to get undressed, 11-1

das Auto, -s car, 2-2

die Autobahn, -en expressway, high-speed highway, 7-SA

automatisch automatic, 6-TLL

der Automechaniker, - auto mechanic, 5-1

der Autostopp hitchhiking
  per Autostopp reisen to hitchhike, 7-2

B

der Bäcker, - baker, 5-1

die Bäckerei, -en bakery, 5-1

das Bad bath, 14-1
  ein Bad nehmen to take a bath, 14-1

sich baden to take a bath, 11-SA

das Badezimmer, - bathroom, 14-1

baff sein (colloq.) to be flabbergasted, speechless, 13-1

die Bahn railroad, railway system, 7-2

der Bahnhof, ⸚e train station, 7-1

bald soon, 3-1

die Bank, ⸚e bench, 10-1

die Bank, -en bank, 14-1

der Bär, -en, -en bear, 10-SA

barbarisch barbaric, 4-TLL

die Barriere, -n barrier, 13-TLL

die Basis basis, 9-TLL

bauen to build, 8-2

der Bauer, -n, -n farmer, 5-1

das Bauernbrot dark bread, 5-1

der Baum, ⸚e tree, 4-2

der Beamte, -n (adj. noun) official, civil servant (m.), 11-1

die Beamtin, -nen official, civil servant (f.), 11-1

bedeuten to mean, signify, 1-2

die Bedeutung, -en meaning, significance, 10-2

sich beeilen to hurry, 11-1

begeistert von enthusiastic about, 14-2

die Begeisterung enthusiasm, 11-1

beginnen, begann, hat begonnen to begin, 4-1

behalten (behält), behielt, hat behalten to keep, retain, 12-1

bei (prep. + dat.) (1) at the home of; near; at, 5-1; (2) during, while ___-ing, 11-G

beid- (adj.) both, 11-2

beide (pl. pronoun) both (people), 14-2

beides (sing. pronoun) both things, 13-2

das Bein, -e leg, 11-1

das Beispiel, -e example, 9-2
  zum Beispiel for example, 1-2

bekannt known; well known, 10-2

der/die Bekannte, -n (adj. noun) acquaintance, friend, 11-1

bekommen, bekam, hat bekommen to receive, get, 4-1

belegen to take (a university course), 6-2

benutzen to use, 7-2

bequem comfortable, 7-2

bereit prepared, ready, 9-2

der Berg, -e mountain, 3-1

bergig mountainous, 4-SA

berichten to report, 5-2

der Beruf, -e profession, vocation, 2-2
  Was sind Sie von Beruf? What is your profession? 5-SA

berufstätig employed, 2-2

berühmt famous, 11-2

beschreiben, beschrieb, hat beschrieben to describe, 4-2

besitzen, besaß, hat besessen to own, 2-2

besonders especially, 5-2

besorgt worried, concerned, 10-1

besprechen (bespricht), besprach, hat besprochen to discuss, 3-2

besser better, 12-G

die Besserung: Gute Besserung! Get well soon! 11-1

best- best, 12-G

bestellen to order, 8-1

der Besuch, -e visit, 12-1

besuchen to visit, 3-1

die Betriebswirtschaft management, business, 6-SA

das **Bett, -en** bed, 6-1

   ins Bett gehen to go to bed, 7-1

bevor (*sub. conj.*) before, 10-2

bezahlen to pay, 6-2

die **Bibliothek, -en** library, 6-1

das **Bier, -e** beer, 4-2

das **Bild, -er** picture; image, 5-2

billig inexpensive, cheap, 6-2

die **Biologie** biology, 6-SA

bis (*prep. + acc.*) until, *Einf.*; by, 1-1

   bis dann until then, 1-1

ein bisschen a little; a little bit; a little while, 3-1

bitte (sehr) (1) you're welcome, 2-1; (2) please, 3-2; (3) here it is, there you are, 5-1

bitten, bat, hat gebeten um to ask for, request, 13-1

   Er bittet mich um das Geld. He's asking me for the money.

blau blue, 3-2

bleiben, blieb, ist geblieben to stay, remain, 2-2

der **Bleistift, -e** pencil, *Einf.*

blitzschnell quick as lightning, 3-2

blöd dumb, stupid, 5-1

die **Blume, -n** flower, 11-1

die **Bluse, -n** blouse, 3-SA

der **Boden, ¨** ground

böse (+ *dat.*) angry, mad (at); bad, evil, 13-1

boxen to box, 9-SA

brauchen to need, 2-1

braun brown, 3-2

die **BRD** (= **Bundesrepublik Deutschland**) the FRG (= the Federal Republic of Germany), 2-2

brechen (bricht), brach, hat gebrochen to break, 11-1

die **Brezel, -n** soft pretzel, 5-1

der **Brief, -e** letter, 6-2

der **Briefträger, -** letter carrier, mailman, 5-TLL

die **Brille** (*sing.*) (eye)glasses, 3-SA

bringen, brachte, hat gebracht to bring, 6-1

das **Brot, -e** bread, 5-1

das **Brötchen, -** roll, 4-1

die **Brücke, -n** bridge, 8-SA; 11-2

der **Bruder, ¨** brother, 2-1

das **Buch, ¨er** book, *Einf.*

das **Bücherregal, -e** bookcase, 6-SA

die **Buchhandlung, -en** bookstore, 5-2

die **Bude, -n** (*colloq.*) (rented) student room, 6-2

der **Bummel, -** stroll, walk, 8-1

   einen Bummel machen to take a stroll, 8-1

die **Bundesrepublik Deutschland** the Federal Republic of Germany, 2-2

bunt colorful, multicolored, 3-2

der **Bürger, -** citizen, 6-2

das **Büro, -s** office, 1-1

der **Bus, -se** bus, 7-SA

die **Butter** butter, 8-SA

C

das **Café, -s** café, 8-SA

campen to camp, 5-TLL

die **CD, -s** CD (compact disc), 6-SA

   der **CD-Spieler** CD player, 6-SA

die **Chance, -n** chance, 9-2

der **Chef, -s** boss (*m.*), 5-1

die **Chefin, -nen** boss (*f.*), 5-1

die **Chemie** chemistry, 6-SA

(das) **China** China, 11-TLL

der **Chinese, -n, -n** Chinese (*m.*), 11-TLL

die **Chinesin, -nen** Chinese (*f.*), 11-TLL

chinesisch Chinese (*adj.*), 11-TLL

der **Computer, -** computer, 6-SA; 12-1

der **Container, -** container, 9-1

D

da (1) there, 1-1; (2) then, in that case, 9-1; (3) since (*sub. conj., causal*), 8-G

   da drüben over there, 2-1

dahin: Wie komme ich dahin? How do I get there? 13-1

damals at that time, back then, 10-1

die **Dame, -n** lady, 10-2

der **Dank** thanks

   vielen Dank thanks a lot, 2-1

danke thanks, thank you, *Einf.*; 1-1

Danke, gleichfalls. You too. Same to you. *Einf.*; 12-1

danken (+ *dat.*) to thank, 7-1

   Nichts zu danken! Don't mention it! 2-1

dann then, 1-1

darf (*see* **dürfen**)

darum therefore, for that reason, 3-2

das sind (*pl. of* **das ist**) those are, 2-2

dass that (*sub. conj.*), 8-1

dauern to last; to take (time), 10-1

die **DDR** (= **Deutsche Demokratische Republik**) the GDR (= the German Democratic Republic), 11-1

die **Decke, -n** blanket, 6-SA

die **Demokratie, -n** democracy, 10-TLL

demokratisch democratic, 10-TLL

die **Demokratisierung** democratization, 11-TLL

die **Demonstration, -en** demonstration, 11-TLL

demonstrieren to demonstrate, 9-TLL

denken, dachte, hat gedacht to think, 13-2

   denken an (+ *acc.*) to think of, 13-2

das **Denkmal, ¨er** monument, 12-2

denn (1) (*flavoring particle in questions*), 2-1; (2) (*coor. conj.*) for, because, 7-G

deutsch (*adj.*) German, 2-2

(das) **Deutsch** German language, 3-2

   auf Deutsch in German, 1-2

der/die **Deutsche, -n** (*adj. noun*) German (person), 1-2

die **Deutsche Demokratische Republik** German Democratic Republic (GDR), 11-1

die **Deutsche Mark (DM)** German mark, 5-1

(das) **Deutschland** Germany, 1-2

die **Deutschstunde, -n** German class, 3-1

(der) **Dezember** December, *Einf.*

der **Dialekt, -e** dialect, 13-TLL

der **Dialog, -e** dialogue

der **Dichter, -** poet

(der) **Dienstag** Tuesday, *Einf.*

dieser, -es, -e; (*pl.*) **diese** this, these, 5-1

diesmal this time, 12-1

das **Ding, -e** thing, 7-2

direkt direct(ly), 12-1

der **Direktor, -en** director, 10-TLL

die **Diskussion, -en** discussion, 2-2

DM *see* **Deutsche Mark**

doch (1) (*stressed, contradictory*) yes I do, yes I am, yes he is, etc., 3-1; (2) (*unstressed flavoring particle with commands*), 4-1; (3) (*unstressed flavoring particle with statements*), 10-1

der **Dom, -e** cathedral, 8-1

(der) **Donnerstag** Thursday, *Einf.*

das **Doppelzimmer, -** double room, 14-1

das **Dorf, ¨er** village, 5-2

dort there, 2-1

die **Dose, -n** (tin) can, 9-2

draußen outside, 1-1

dreckig (*colloq.*) dirty, 9-1

dritt- third, 9-G

drüben over there, 2-1

dumm (dümmer) dumb, 5-1

dunkel dark, 3-2

durch (*prep. + acc.*) through, 4-1

dürfen (darf), durfte, hat gedurft may, to be allowed to, 3-1

Was darf es sein? What'll it be? May I help you? 5-1

der **Durst** thirst

Durst haben to be thirsty, 8-1

die **Dusche, -n** shower, 14-1

sich duschen to take a shower, 11-SA

duzen to address someone with **du**, 1-2

die **Dynastie, -n** dynasty, 14-TLL

E

die **Ecke, -n** corner, 8-2

an der Ecke at the corner, 8-2

um die Ecke around the corner, 8-2

egal wo, wer, warum usw. no matter where, who, why, etc., 7-2

Das ist (mir) egal. It doesn't matter (to me). I don't care. 7-1

das **Ehepaar, -e** married couple, 14-1

ehrlich honest, 3-2

das **Ei, -er** egg, 8-SA

eigen- own, 9-2

eigentlich actually, in fact, 3-2

die **Eile** hurry

in Eile in a hurry, 1-1

einander (*pronoun*) each other, 1-2

der **Eindruck, ¨e** impression, 8-2

einfach simple, easy, 5-1

einige some, 6-2

ein·kaufen to shop for; to go shopping, 5-2

ein·laden (lädt ein), lud ein, hat eingeladen to invite, 8-1

einmal once, 4-1

noch einmal once again, once more, 4-1

eins one, 1-2

ein·schlafen (schläft ein), schlief ein, ist eingeschlafen to fall asleep, 7-1

ein·steigen, stieg ein, ist eingestiegen to get in (a vehicle), 7-2

der **Einstieg, -e** entrance, way in

einverstanden Agreed. It's a deal. O.K. 5-1

ein·wandern, ist eingewandert to immigrate, 11-2

das **Einzelzimmer, -** single room, 14-1

ein·ziehen, zog ein, ist eingezogen to move in, 6-1

einzig- single, only, 12-2

das **Eis** (1) ice; (2) ice cream, 8-SA

der **Elefant, -en, -en** elephant, 10-SA

elegant elegant, 8-TLL

die **Elektrizität** electricity, 9-TLL

die **Elektrotechnik** electrical engineering, 6-SA

der **Elektrotechniker, -** electrician; electrical engineer (*m.*), 5-SA

die **Elektrotechnikerin, -nen** electrician; electrical engineer (*f.*), 5-SA

die **Eltern** (*pl.*) parents, 2-1

empfehlen (empfiehlt), empfahl, hat empfohlen to recommend, 9-1

das **Ende, -n** end, 6-2

am Ende at the end, 6-1

Ende Februar at the end of February, 6-2

zu Ende sein to end, be finished, be over, 10-2

endlich finally, 1-1

die **Energie, -n** energy, 9-TLL

der **Engländer, -** Englishman, 11-TLL

die **Engländerin, -nen** Englishwoman, 11-TLL

englisch English, 11-TLL

(das) **Englisch** English language, 3-2

enorm enormous, 9-TLL

entscheiden, entschied, hat entschieden to decide, 3-2

Entschuldigung! Pardon me! Excuse me. 1-1

enttäuschen to disappoint, 6-2

entweder ... oder either . . . or, 14-1

die **Epoche, -n** epoch, 10-TLL

die **Erde** earth, 12-2

das **Erdgeschoss** ground floor, first floor, 14-1 (*see* **Stock**)

die **Erfahrung, -en** experience, 12-SA

erfreut pleased

Sehr erfreut. Pleased to meet you. 13-SA

sich erholen (von) (1) to recover (from), get well; (2) to have a rest, 13-2

erinnern an (+ *acc.*) to remind of, 12-1

sich erinnern an (+ *acc.*) to remember, 12-1

die **Erinnerung, -en** memory, 12-1

sich erkälten to catch a cold, 11-1

erklären to explain, 10-2

ernst serious, 14-2

    etwas ernst nehmen to take something seriously, 14-2

erst (*adv.*) not until; only, 5-1

erst- (*adj.*) first, 9-G

erstaunlich astounding, 9-2

erwarten to expect, 14-2

erzählen to tell, recount, 6-2

die Erzählung, -en story, narrative, 12-2

der Esel, - donkey, 10-SA

essen (isst), aß, hat gegessen to eat, 2-1

das Essen food; meal, 2-2

etwas (1) (*pronoun*) something, 3-1; (2) (*adj. & adv.*) some, a little; somewhat, 12-1

(das) Europa Europe, 3-2

der Europäer, - European, 3-2

europäisch European, 11-2

existieren to exist, 11-TLL

extrem extreme, 10-TLL

F

die Fabrik, -en factory, 5-2

das Fach, ̈er area of study; subject, 6-SA

fahren (fährt), fuhr, ist gefahren to drive, go (by vehicle), 3-1

die Fahrkarte, -n ticket (for bus, train, streetcar, etc.), 7-2

das Fahrrad, ̈er bicycle, 8-2

fallen (fällt), fiel, ist gefallen (1) to fall; (2) to die in battle, 10-1

falsch false, incorrect, wrong, *Einf.*

die Familie, -n family, 2-1

fantastisch fantastic, 2-1

die Farbe, -n color, 3-2

fast almost, 2-2

faul lazy, 5-2

(der) Februar February, *Einf.*

fehlen to be missing; to be absent, 10-1

feiern to celebrate, 6-2

das Fenster, - window, *Einf.*

die Ferien (*pl.*) (university and school) vacation, 6-2

fern distant, far away, 12-2

fern·sehen (sieht fern), sah fern, hat ferngesehen to watch TV, 5-2

der Fernseher, - television set, 2-2

fertig (mit) (1) done, finished (with), 12-1; (2) ready, 5-1

der Film, -e film, movie, 6-TLL

finanzieren to finance, 6-TLL

finden, fand, hat gefunden to find, 2-2

    Das finde ich auch. I think so, too. 3-2

der Finger, - finger, 11-1

die Firma, Firmen (*pl.*) firm, company, 13-2

der Fisch, -e fish, 9-2

fit in shape, *Einf.*; 3-1

flach flat, 4-2

die Flasche, -n bottle, 7-1

das Fleisch meat, 2-1

fleißig industrious, hard-working, 5-2

fliegen, flog, ist geflogen to fly, 1-1

fließen, floss, ist geflossen to flow, 4-2

der Flughafen, ̈ airport, 7-SA

das Flugzeug, -e airplane, 7-2

der Fluss, ̈e river, 4-2

folgen, ist gefolgt (+ *dat.*) to follow, 9-2

die Form, -en form, 10-TLL

formell formal, 1-TLL

der Fortschritt, -e progress, 9-1

das Foto, -s photograph, 6-TLL; 7-2

    ein Foto machen to take a picture, 7-2

die Frage, -n question, 2-1

    eine Frage stellen to ask a question, 10-2

der Fragebogen questionnaire

fragen to ask, 1-1

    fragen nach to inquire, ask about, 8-SA

(das) Frankreich France, 5-2

der Franzose, -n, -n Frenchman, 11-TLL

die Französin, -nen Frenchwoman, 11-TLL

französisch French, 5-2

die Frau, -en woman; wife, 1-1

Frau Kuhn Mrs./Ms. Kuhn, *Einf.*

das Fräulein, - young (unmarried) woman *Einf.*

    Fräulein Schmidt Miss Schmidt, *Einf.*

frei free; unoccupied, 2-1

die Freiheit, -en freedom, 7-2

(der) Freitag Friday, *Einf.*

die Freizeit free time, leisure time, 5-2

fremd (1) strange; (2) foreign, 3-2

die Fremdsprache, -n foreign language, 3-2

die Freude, -n joy, 12-2

freuen

    Das freut mich. I'm glad. *Einf.*

    (Es) freut mich. Pleased to meet you. *Einf.*; 13-SA

    sich freuen to be happy, 11-1

    sich freuen auf (+ *acc.*) to look forward to, 13-1

der Freund, -e friend (*m.*), 2-1

die Freundin, -nen friend (*f.*), 3-1

freundlich friendly, 1-2

der Frieden peace, 6-2

frisch fresh, 5-1

froh happy, glad, 13-2

früh early, 3-1

der Frühling spring, 4-2

das Frühstück breakfast, 4-1

    zum Frühstück for breakfast, 4-1

frühstücken to eat breakfast, 4-1

sich fühlen to feel (*intrans.*), 11-1

führen to lead, 9-2

für (*prep. + acc.*) for, 1-1

furchtbar terrible, *Einf.*

fürchten to fear, 11-1

der Fuchs, ̈e fox, 10-SA

der Fuß, ̈e foot, 3-2

    zu Fuß on foot, 3-2

der Fußball soccer; soccer ball, 5-2

der Fußgänger, - pedestrian, 8-2

die Fußgängerzone, -n pedestrian zone, 8-2

G

die Gabel, -n fork, 8-SA

ganz entire, whole, 9-1

    ganz gut pretty good, 1-1

den ganzen Sommer (Tag, Nachmittag usw.) all summer (day, afternoon, etc.)

gar

   gar kein no . . . at all, not a . . . at all, 8-2

   gar nicht not at all, 3-2

der Gast, -̈e guest; patron, 8-1

das Gebäude, - building, 8-1

geben (gibt), gab, hat gegeben to give, 2-2

   es gibt (+ acc.) there is, there are, 2-2

das Gebirge, - mountain range, 4-TLL

geboren born

   Wann sind Sie geboren? When were you born? 10-1

der Geburtstag, -e birthday, 9-1

   Wann hast du Geburtstag? When is your birthday? Einf.

   zum Geburtstag for (one's) birthday, 9-1

das Gedicht, -e poem

die Gefahr, -en danger, 9-2

gefährlich dangerous, 9-2

gefallen (gefällt), gefiel, hat gefallen (+ dat. of person) to please, appeal to, 7-1

das Gefühl, -e feeling, 9-1

gegen (prep. + acc.) (1) against, (2) around, about (with time), 4-1

die Gegend, -en area, region, 12-1

der Gegensatz, -̈e opposite

das Gegenteil: im Gegenteil on the contrary, 8-2

die Gegenwart present (time), 12-SA; 14-2

gehen, ging, ist gegangen (1) to go; (2) to walk, 1-1

   Es geht. It's all right. 4-1

   Es geht nicht. Nothing doing. It can't be done.

   Wie geht es Ihnen/dir? How are you? Einf.

   Wie geht's? How are you? Einf.

gehören (+ dat. of person) to belong to (a person), 7-1

gelb yellow, 3-2

das Geld money, 2-2

der Geldbeutel, - wallet, change purse, 10-1

die Gelegenheit, -en opportunity, chance, 14-2

das Gemüse vegetables, 2-1

gemütlich cozy, comfortable; quiet, relaxed, 14-2

genau exact, precise, 11-1

genauso ... wie just as . . . as, 12-G

die Generation, -en generation, 8-TLL

genug enough, 3-1

die Geographie geography, 4-TLL

geographisch geographical, 4-TLL

das Gepäck luggage, 7-1

gerade just, at this moment, 6-2

geradeaus straight ahead, 8-2

die Germanistik German studies, 6-SA

gern(e) (lieber, am liebsten) gladly, with pleasure, 4-1

   etwas gern haben to like something, 4-1

   gern + verb like to, 4-1

   lieber + verb prefer to, would rather, 4-1

   Lieber nicht. I'd rather not. No thanks. Let's not. 4-1

das Geschäft, -e business; store, 5-2

die Geschäftsfrau, -en businesswoman, 5-SA

der Geschäftsmann, Geschäftsleute (pl.) businessman, 5-SA

das Geschenk, -e present (gift), 9-1

die Geschichte, -n (1) story; (2) history, 6-2; 6-SA

geschlossen closed (see schließen), 11-2

die Geschwister (pl.) siblings, 2-SA

die Gesellschaft, -en society, 9-2

das Gesicht, -er face, 11-1

das Gespräch, -e conversation, 13-2

gestern yesterday, 6-1

   gestern Abend yesterday evening, 12-G

gestern früh yesterday morning, 12-G

gesund healthy, 9-2

die Gesundheit health, 9-2

gewinnen, gewann, hat gewonnen to win, 9-SA

sich gewöhnen an (+ acc.) to get used to, 13-1

das Glas, -̈er glass, 8-1

glauben (+ dat. of person) (1) to believe; (2) to think, 4-1

   Ich glaube nicht. I don't think so. 8-1

   Ich glaube schon. I think so. 8-1

gleich right away, immediately, 5-1

das Gleis, -e track, 7-1

das Glück (1) happiness; (2) luck, 6-2

   Glück haben to be lucky, 6-2

glücklich happy, Einf.

der Gott, -̈er god

   Gott sei Dank thank goodness, 4-1

   Grüß Gott hello (in southern Germany and Austria), Einf.

   Um Gottes Willen! For heaven's sake! Oh my gosh! 3-1

das Gramm gram, 8-1

die Grammatik grammar

grau gray, 3-2

grausam terrible, gruesome; cruel, 12-2

die Grenze, -n border, 11-1

griechisch Greek, 8-1

groß (größer, am größten) big, tall, 2-1

die Größe, -n size; greatness, 12-1

die Großeltern (pl.) grandparents, 2-2

die Großmutter, -̈ grandmother, 2-2

die Großstadt, -̈e large city (over 500,000 inhabitants), 8-2

der Großvater, -̈ grandfather, 2-2

grün green, 3-2

die Gruppe, -n group, 1-2

grüßen to greet, say hello, 1-2

   Grüß Gott hello (in southern Germany and Austria), Einf.

gut (besser, am besten) good, well, *Einf.*; 1-1
  ganz gut pretty good, 1-1
  Guten Abend! Good evening! *Einf.*
  Guten Morgen! Good morning! *Einf.*
  Gute Reise! Have a good trip! 1-1
  Guten Tag! Hello! *Einf.*
  Ist gut. (*colloq.*) O.K. Fine by me. 5-1
das **Gymnasium,** *pl.* **Gymnasien** secondary school (prepares pupils for university), 3-2

H

das **Haar, -e** hair, 6-2
  sich die Haare kämmen to comb one's hair, 11-SA
haben (hat), hatte, hat gehabt to have, *Einf.*; 2-1
der **Hafen, ꞉** port, harbor, 8-2
halb (*adv.*) half
  halb acht seven-thirty, *Einf.*
Hallo! Hello! *Einf.*
halten (hält), hielt, hat gehalten (1) to stop (*intrans.*); (2) to hold, 3-1
die **Haltestelle, -n** (streetcar or bus) stop, 8-SA; 13-1
die **Hand, ꞉e** hand, 5-1
der **Handschuh, -e** glove, 3-SA
hängen (*trans.*) to hang, 7-1
hängen, hing, hat gehangen (*intrans.*) to be hanging, 7-1
hart (härter) hard; tough; harsh, 10-2
der **Hass** hatred, 11-2
hassen to hate, 3-2
hässlich ugly, 1-1
Haupt- (*noun prefix*) main, chief, primary, most important, 4-TLL
das **Hauptfach, ꞉er** major field (of study), 6-2
die **Hauptstadt, ꞉e** capital city, 4-TLL
das **Haus, ꞉er** house; building, 1-2

nach Hause home (as destination of motion), 3-1
  zu Hause at home, 2-2
die **Hausaufgabe, -n** homework assignment, 3-2
die **Hausfrau, -en** housewife, 2-2
das **Heft, -e** notebook, *Einf.*
die **Heimat** native place or country, homeland, 11-2
das **Heimweh** homesickness, 12-SA
heiß hot, *Einf.*
heißen, hieß, hat geheißen to be called, 2-1
  das heißt that means, in other words, 6-2
  Ich heiße ... My name is . . . *Einf.*
  Wie heißen Sie? What's your name? *Einf.*
heiter cheerful, 14-2
hektisch hectic, 7-TLL
helfen (hilft), half, hat geholfen (+ *dat.*) to help, 7-1
hell bright, light, 3-2
das **Hemd, -en** shirt, 3-2
der **Herbst** fall, autumn, 4-2
der **Herr, -n, -en** gentleman, 1-1
  Herr Lehmann Mr. Lehmann, *Einf.*
herrlich great, terrific, marvelous, *Einf.*
Herzlich willkommen! Welcome! Nice to see you! 6-2
heute today, *Einf.*
  heute Abend this evening, tonight, 1-1
  heute Morgen this morning, 5-1
  heute Nachmittag this afternoon, 12-G
hier here, 1-1
die **Hilfe** help, aid, 13-1
hinter (*prep.* + *acc.* or *dat.*) behind, 6-1
historisch historic, 8-TLL
hoch (*predicative adj.*), **hoh-** (*attributive adj.*) **(höher, am höchsten)** high, 4-2
  höchste Zeit high time, 14-1
das **Hochland** highlands, 4-TLL

die **Hochschule, -n** university, institute of higher learning, 14-2
hoffen to hope, 7-2
hoffentlich (*adv.*) I hope, 4-1
höflich polite, 1-2
hoh-, höher (*see* **hoch**)
holen to fetch, get, 12-2
hören to hear, 3-2
der **Horizont, -e** horizon, 7-TLL
die **Hose, -n** trousers, pants, 3-2
das **Hotel, -s** hotel, 4-1
hübsch pretty, handsome, 11-1
der **Hügel, -** hill, 4-2
hügelig hilly, 4-SA
der **Humor** humor, 14-TLL
der **Hund, -e** dog, 11-G
hundert hundred, 2-G
der **Hunger** hunger, 8-1
  Hunger haben to be hungry, 8-1
hungrig hungry, 4-1
der **Hut, ꞉e** hat, 3-SA

I

die **Idee, -n** idea, 10-2
ideologisch ideological, 10-TLL
idiotensicher foolproof, 12-1
illegal illegal, 10-TLL
immer always, 1-2
  immer größer bigger and bigger, 12-G
  immer noch still, 4-2
in (*prep.* + *acc.* or *dat.*) in, into, 1-1
der **Indikativ** indicative
die **Industrie, -n** industry, 5-TLL
die **Inflation** inflation, 10-TLL
die **Informatik** computer science, 6-SA
der **Ingenieur, -e** engineer (*m.*), 5-SA
die **Ingenieurin, -nen** engineer (*f.*), 5-SA
die **Insel, -n** island, 4-TLL
das **Instrument, -e** instrument, 7-TLL
die **Integration** integration, 11-2
intelligent intelligent, 12-1
interessant interesting, 3-1
interessieren to interest, 13-1
  sich interessieren für (+ *acc.*) to be interested in, 13-1

international international, 3-TLL
interviewen to interview, 10-1
investieren to invest, 11-TLL
irgend- (*prefix*)
  irgendwann sometime or other, any time, 12-G
  irgendwie somehow or other, 12-G
  irgendwo somewhere or other, anywhere, 12-G
die **Ironie** irony, 14-TLL
(das) **Italien** Italy, 4-2
der **Italiener, -** Italian (*m.*), 11-TLL
die **Italienerin, -nen** Italian (*f.*), 11-TLL
italienisch Italian, 11-TLL

J

ja (1) yes; (2) (*unstressed flavoring particle*), 1-1
die **Jacke, -n** jacket, 3-2
das **Jahr, -e** year, 5-1
  im Jahr(e) 1996 in 1996, 9-2
jahrelang (*adv.*) for years, 14-TLL
die **Jahreszeit, -en** season
das **Jahrhundert, -e** century, 8-2
jahrhundertelang (*adv.*) for centuries, 14-TLL
jährlich annually, 9-2
(der) **Januar** January, *Einf.*
je ever, 6-2
die **Jeans** (*pl.*) jeans, 3-TLL
jeder, -es, -e each, every, 5-1
jemand somebody, someone, 2-2
jetzt now, 3-1
  von jetzt an from now on, 13-1
der **Journalist, -en, -en** journalist, 5-TLL
jüdisch Jewish, 12-2
die **Jugend** (*sing.*) youth; young people, 9-2
die **Jugendherberge, -n** youth hostel, 7-2
(der) **Juli** July, *Einf.*
jung (jünger) young, 2-2
der **Junge, -n, -n** boy, 9-1
(der) **Juni** June, *Einf.*
Jura (study of) law, 6-SA

K

der **Kaffee** coffee, 8-1

kalt (kälter) cold, *Einf.*
die **Kamera, -s** camera, 7-TLL
kämmen to comb
  sich die Haare kämmen to comb one's hair, 11-SA
(das) **Kanada** Canada, 5-TLL; 6-1
der **Kanadier, -** Canadian (*m.*), 11-TLL
die **Kanadierin, -nen** Canadian (*f.*), 11-TLL
kanadisch Canadian (*adj.*), 11-TLL
das **Kännchen, -** small (coffee or tea) pot, 8-SA
der **Kapitalismus** capitalism, 11-TLL
das **Kapitel, -** chapter
kaputt (*colloq.*) (1) broken, kaput; (2) exhausted, 9-1
  kaputt·machen to break, 12-1
die **Karte, -n** (1) card; (2) ticket; (3) map, 4-1
die **Kartoffel, -n** potato, 8-1
der **Käse** cheese, 2-1
die **Kasse, -n** cashier; cashier's office, 14-1
der **Kassettenrecorder, -** cassette player, 10-1
katastrophal catastrophic, 8-TLL
die **Katastrophe, -n** catastrophe, 6-2
die **Katze, -n** cat, 11-G
kaufen to buy, 4-1
das **Kaufhaus, ̈-er** department store, 8-SA
kein not a, not any, no, 3-1
  kein ... mehr no more . . . , not a . . . any longer, 4-1
der **Keller, -** cellar, basement, 9-1
der **Kellner, -** waiter, 5-SA; 8-1
die **Kellnerin, -nen** waitress, 5-SA; 8-1
kennen, kannte, hat gekannt to know, be acquainted with, 2-1
kennen lernen to get to know; to meet, 5-1
die **Kettenreaktion, -en** chain reaction
das **Kilo** (*short for* das **Kilogramm**), 8-1
das **Kilogramm** kilogram, 8-1
der **Kilometer, -** kilometer

das **Kind, -er** child, 1-1
die **Kindheit, -en** childhood, 9-TLL
das **Kino, -s** movie theater, 6-2
die **Kirche, -n** church, 8-SA
klar (1) clear; (2) (*colloq.*) sure, of course, 9-1
die **Klasse, -n** class; grade, 1-2
der **Klatsch** gossip, 12-1
klauen (*colloq.*) to rip off, steal, 10-1
die **Klausur, -en** written test, 6-2
das **Klavier, -e** piano, 14-2
das **Kleid, -er** dress (*pl.* = dresses *or* clothes), 3-2
der **Kleiderschrank, ̈-e** clothes cupboard, wardrobe, 6-SA
die **Kleidung** clothing, 3-SA
klein little, small; short, 2-1
die **Kleinstadt, ̈-e** town (5,000 to 20,000 inhabitants), 8-2
das **Klima** climate, 4-2
klingeln to ring, 7-1
klingen, klang, hat geklungen to sound, 8-1
das **Klischee, -s** cliché, 2-2
klischeehaft (*adj.*) clichéd, stereotyped, 13-SA
klug (klüger) smart, bright, 5-1
knapp scarce, in short supply, 12-1
  knapp bei Kasse short of cash, 12-1
die **Kneipe, -n** tavern, bar, 6-2
kochen to cook, 2-2
der **Koffer, -** suitcase, 7-1
(das) **Köln** Cologne, 8-1
die **Kolonie, -n** colony, 4-TLL
komisch peculiar, odd; funny, 12-1
kommen, kam, ist gekommen to come, *Einf.*; 1-1
  kommen aus to come from, *Einf.*
der **Kommunismus** Communism, 11-TLL
die **Konditorei, -en** pastry café, 8-SA
der **Konflikt, -e** conflict, 2-TLL
der **Konjunktiv** subjunctive
die **Konkurrenz** competition, 9-SA

können (kann), konnte, hat gekonnt can, be able to, 3-1

    Ich kann Deutsch. I can speak German. 3-G

die Konsequenz, -en consequence, 9-TLL

konservativ conservative, 13-TLL

der Kontakt, -e contact, 14-TLL

der Kontrast, -e contrast, 4-TLL

sich konzentrieren auf (+ *acc.*) to concentrate on, 14-2

das Konzert, -e concert, 6-TLL

der Kopf, ∵e head, 11-1

    Das geht mir nicht aus dem Kopf. I can't forget that. 12-2

der Korrespondent, -en, -en correspondent, 5-TLL

(das) Korsika Corsica, 5-TLL

kosten to cost, 5-1

    Wie viel kostet das bitte? How much does that cost, please? 5-1

kostenlos free of charge, 6-2

die Kraft, ∵e power; strength, 9-2

das Kraftwerk, -e power plant, 9-2

krank (kränker) sick, *Einf.*

das Krankenhaus, ∵er hospital, 11-1

der Krankenpfleger, - nurse (*m.*), 5-SA

die Krankenschwester, -n nurse (*f.*), 5-SA

die Krankheit, -en sickness, 9-2

die Krawatte, -n tie, 3-SA

kreativ creative, 14-TLL

die Kreditkarte, -n credit card, 14-1

die Kreide chalk, *Einf.*

der Krieg, -e war, 6-2

der Kuchen, - cake, 8-SA

der Kugelschreiber, - ballpoint pen, *Einf.*

kühl cool, *Einf.*

die Kultur, -en culture, 4-TLL

sich kümmern um (+ *acc.*) to look after, take care of, deal with, 13-1

der Kunde, -n, -n customer (*m.*), 5-1

die Kundin, -nen customer (*f.*), 5-1

die Kunst, ∵e art, 8-1

die Kunstgeschichte art history, 6-SA

der Künstler, - artist (*m.*), 5-SA; 14-2

die Künstlerin, -nen artist (*f.*), 5-SA; 14-2

kurz (kürzer) short; for a short time, 4-1

die Kusine, -n cousin (*f.*), 2-SA

die Küste, -n coast, 4-TLL

L

das Labor, -s laboratory, 6-SA

lachen to laugh, 3-2

der Laden, ∵ shop, store, 5-1

die Lampe, -n lamp, 6-SA

das Land, ∵er country, 4-2

    auf dem Land in the country, 8-2

    aufs Land to the country, 8-2

die Landkarte, - map, *Einf.*

die Landschaft, -en landscape, 4-2

der Landwirt, -e farmer (*m.*), 5-SA

die Landwirtin, -nen farmer (*f.*), 5-SA

die Landwirtschaft agriculture, 6-SA

lang(e) (länger) long; for a long time, 4-1

langsam slow, *Einf.*; 3-2

sich langweilen to be bored, 13-1

langweilig boring, 3-1

lassen (lässt), ließ, hat gelassen (1) to leave (something or someone), leave behind; (2) to let, allow; (3) to cause to be done, 12-1

laufen (läuft), lief, ist gelaufen (1) to run; (2) (*colloq.*) to go on foot, walk, 3-1

die Laune mood

    guter/schlechter Laune in a good/bad mood, *Einf.*

laut loud, *Einf.*

leben to live, be alive, 2-2

das Leben life, 4-2

die Lebensmittel (*pl.*) groceries, 5-2

der Lebensstandard standard of living, 9-TLL

die Leberwurst, ∵e liverwurst, 8-1

lecker tasty, delicious, 8-1

leer empty, 5-1

legen to lay, put down, 6-1

der Lehrer, - teacher (*m.*), *Einf.*

die Lehrerin, -nen teacher (*f.*), *Einf.*

der Lehrling, -e apprentice, 5-1

leicht (1) light (in weight); (2) easy, 3-1

Leid: Das tut mir Leid. I'm sorry about that. *Einf.*; 7-1

leider unfortunately, *Einf.*; 3-1

leihen, lieh, hat geliehen (1) to lend, loan; (2) to borrow, 10-1

leise quiet, soft, *Einf.*

leisten: sich etwas leisten können to be able to afford something, 11-1

die Leitfrage, -n guiding question

lernen to learn, 3-2

lesen (liest), las, hat gelesen to read, 2-1

    lesen über (+ *acc.*) to read about, 2-1

das Lesestück, -e reading selection

letzt- last, 10-1

    letzte Woche last week, 6-2

die Leute (*pl.*) people, 2-1

das Licht, -er light, 11-1

lieb dear; nice, sweet, 6-2

    Lieber Fritz! Dear Fritz, (salutation in letter), 6-TLL

die Liebe love, 11-2

lieben to love, 3-2

lieber preferably, would rather (*see* **gern**), 4-1

Lieblings- (*noun prefix*) favorite, 9-1

liebsten: am liebsten most like to, like best of all to (*see* **gern**), 4-1

das Lied, -er song, 4-2

liegen, lag, hat gelegen to lie; to be situated, 4-2

der Lift, -s elevator, 14-SA

lila violet, lavender, 3-SA

die Linguistik linguistics, 6-SA

die Linie, -n (streetcar or bus) line, 13-1

links to the left; on the left, 8-2

die Liste, -n list

der **Liter** liter, 8-1

literarisch literary, 14-TLL

der **Löffel, -** spoon, 8-SA

sich lohnen to be worthwhile, worth the trouble, 13-1

das **Lokal, -e** neighborhood restaurant or tavern, 8-1

los: Was ist los? (1)What's the matter? (2)What's going on? 3-1

lösen to solve, 9-2

los·fahren (fährt los), fuhr los, ist losgefahren to depart, start, leave, 14-1

die **Lösung, -en** solution, 9-2

der **Löwe, -n, -n** lion, 10-SA

die **Luft** air, 4-SA; 8-2

die **Luftverschmutzung** air pollution, 8-2

die **Lust** desire
  Ich habe keine Lust. I don't want to. 3-1
  Lust haben (etwas zu tun) to want to do (something), 8-1

die **Lyrik** poetry

M

machen (1) to make; (2) to do, 1-1
  Das macht (mir) Spaß. That is fun (for me). 7-1
  Das macht zusammen ... All together that comes to . . . 5-1
  Es macht (doch) nichts. It doesn't matter. 7-1

die **Macht, ̈e** power, might, 11-2

das **Mädchen, -** girl, 9-1

mag (*see* **mögen**)

(der) **Mai** May, *Einf.*

mal (*flavoring particle with commands; see p. 104*), 4-1

das **Mal, -e** time (in the sense of occurrence), 12-1
  das nächste Mal (the) next time, 12-G
  jedes Mal every time, 12-1
  zum ersten Mal for the first time, 12-G

man one (*indefinite pronoun*), 1-2

der **Manager, -** manager, 11-TLL

mancher, -es, -e many a, 9-2
  manche (*pl.*) some, 9-2

manchmal sometimes, 2-2

manipulieren to manipulate, 10-TLL

der **Mann, ̈er** (1) man; (2) husband, 2-1

die **Mannschaft, -en** team, 5-2

der **Mantel, ̈** coat, 3-2

das **Märchen, -** fairy tale, 4-2

die **Mark** (die **Deutsche Mark— DM**) mark (the German mark), 5-1

(der) **März** March, *Einf.*

die **Mathematik** mathematics, 6-SA

die **Mauer, -n** (freestanding or exterior) wall, 11-1

der **Mechaniker, -** mechanic, 5-1

die **Medizin** (field of) medicine, 6-SA

das **Meer, -e** sea, 4-2

mehr more, 2-2
  nicht mehr no longer, not any more, 2-2

mehrere several, 11-1

meinen (1) to be of the opinion, think, 1-2; (2) to mean, 2-1

die **Meinung, -en** opinion

meist- most (*see* **viel**)

meistens mostly, usually, 5-2

die **Melancholie** melancholy, 14-TLL

die **Menge, -n** quantity; crowd
  eine Menge a lot, lots of, 6-2

die **Mensa** university cafeteria, 1-1

der **Mensch, -en, -en** person, human being, 6-1
  Mensch! Man! Wow! 3-1

die **Menschheit** mankind, human race, 9-2

merken to notice, 11-1
  leicht zu merken easy to remember

das **Messer, -** knife, 8-SA

die **Methode, -n** method, 10-TLL

die **Milch** milk, 8-SA; 12-2

mild mild, 4-TLL

die **Million, -en** million, 11-TLL

die **Minute, -n** minute, 3-1

minutenlang (*adv.*) for minutes, 14-TLL

Mist: So ein Mist! (*crude & colloq.*) (1) What a drag. (2) What a lot of bull. 10-1

mit (*prep. + dat.*) with, 2-1; (*adv.*) along with, 12-1

der **Mitbewohner, -** fellow occupant, roommate, housemate (*m.*), 3-1

die **Mitbewohnerin, -nen** fellow occupant, roommate, housemate (*f.*), 3-1

mit·bringen, brachte mit, hat mitgebracht to bring along, take along, 6-1

miteinander with each other, together, 1-2

das **Mitglied, -er** member, 11-2

mit·kommen, kam mit, ist mitgekommen to come along, 5-1

mit·machen to participate, cooperate, pitch in, 9-1

mit·nehmen (nimmt mit), nahm mit, hat mitgenommen to take along, 7-2

das **Mittagessen** midday meal, lunch, 5-2

das **Mittelalter** the Middle Ages, 13-1

(der) **Mittwoch** Wednesday, *Einf.*

die **Möbel** (*pl.*) furniture, 6-SA

möbliert furnished, 6-SA

modern modern, 4-2

modernisieren to modernize, 11-TLL

mögen (mag), mochte, hat gemocht to like, 4-1
  möchten would like to, 3-1
  Das mag sein. That may be. 16-G

möglich possible, 6-1

der **Moment, -e** moment
  im Moment at the moment, 1-1

die **Monarchie, -n** monarchy, 10-TLL

der **Monat, -e** month, 10-1

monatelang (*adv.*) for months, 14-TLL

(der) **Montag** Monday, *Einf.*

morgen tomorrow, *Einf.*; 1-1
  morgen Abend tomorrow evening, 12-G
  morgen früh tomorrow morning, 12-G
  morgen Nachmittag tomorrow afternoon, 12-G
der Morgen, - morning, 1-1
  Guten Morgen! Good morning! 1-1
morgens (*adv.*) in the morning(s), 4-1
das Motorrad, ¨er motorcycle, 5-1
müde tired, weary, *Einf.*
der Müll trash, refuse, 9-1
(das) München Munich, 8-2
der Mund, ¨er mouth, 11-1
munter wide-awake, cheerful, *Einf.*
das Museum, *pl.* **Museen** museum, 8-1
die Musik music, 3-2
die Musikwissenschaft musicology, 6-SA
müssen (muss), musste, hat gemusst must, to have to, 3-1
die Mutter, ¨ mother, 2-2
die Muttersprache, -n native language, 5-2
die Mutti, -s mama, mom, 2-2
die Mütze, -n cap, 3-SA

N

na well . . . 12-1
  Na endlich! At last! High time! 9-1
  Na und? And so? So what? 10-1
nach (*prep. + dat.*) (1) after, 5-1; (2) to (with cities and countries), 1-1
  nach Hause home (as destination of motion), 3-1
der Nachbar, -n, -n neighbor (*m.*), 11-2
die Nachbarin, -nen neighbor (*f.*), 11-2
nachdem (*sub. conj.*) after, 10-1
nachher (*adv.*) later on, after that, 4-1
der Nachmittag, -e afternoon, 10-1

am Nachmittag in the afternoon, 10-1
nachmittags (in the) afternoons, 5-TLL
nächst- next; nearest, 12-1
  nächstes Semester next semester, 2-1
die Nacht, ¨e night, 1-1
  Gute Nacht. Good night. 12-1
  in der Nacht in the night, at night, 12-1
der Nachtisch, -e dessert, 8-1
  zum Nachtisch for dessert, 8-1
nachts at night, 5-TLL
nah(e) (näher, am nächsten) near, 8-1
die Nähe nearness; vicinity
  in der Nähe (von or **+ gen.)** near, nearby, 7-2
der Name, -ns, -n name, 5-1
die Nase, -n nose, 5-1
  Ich habe die Nase voll. I'm fed up. I've had it up to here. 5-1
nass wet, damp, 4-2
die Natur nature, 9-TLL
natürlich natural, naturally; of course, 1-1
der Nebel fog, mist, 4-SA
neben (*prep. + acc.* or *dat.*) beside, next to, 6-1
das Nebenfach, ¨er minor field (of study), 6-2
neblig foggy, misty, *Einf.*
nee (*colloq.*) no, 6-1
nehmen (nimmt), nahm, hat genommen to take, 2-1
nein no, *Einf.*
nennen, nannte, hat genannt to name, call, 10-2
nett nice, 6-1
neu new, 3-2
neulich recently, 12-1
neutral neutral, 13-TLL
die Neutralität neutrality, 13-TLL
nicht not, *Einf.*; 1-1
  gar nicht not at all, 3-2
  nicht mehr no longer, not any more, 2-2
  nicht nur ... sondern auch not only . . . but also, 9-2

nicht wahr? isn't it? can't you? doesn't she? etc., 3-1
nichts nothing, 3-1
  Nichts zu danken! Don't mention it! 2-1
  Es macht nichts. It doesn't matter. 7-1
nie never, 1-2
niedrig low, 6-2
niemand nobody, no one, 2-2
noch still, 2-2
  noch ein another, an additional, 2-2
  noch einmal once again, once more, 4-1
  noch etwas something else, anything more, 8-1
  noch immer still, 4-2
  noch jemand someone else
  noch kein- not a . . . yet, not any . . . yet, 4-1
  noch nicht not yet, 4-1
(das) Nordamerika North America, 2-TLL
der Norden the north, 4-2
normal normal, 2-TLL
die Note, -n grade, 5-1
nötig necessary, 9-1
(der) November November, *Einf.*
die Nummer, -n number, *Einf.*; 14-1
nun (1) now; (2) well . . . , well now, 10-1
nur only, 2-1
nützlich useful

O

ob (*sub. conj.*) if, whether, 8-1
oben (*adv.*) above; on top
das Obst fruit, 2-1
obwohl (*sub. conj.*) although, 8-2
oder (*coor. conj.*) or, 1-2
offen open, 11-2
offiziell official, 13-TLL
öffnen to open, 11-1
oft (öfter) often, 1-2
ohne (*prep. + acc.*) without, 4-1
  ohne ... zu without . . . -ing, 8-G
das Ohr, -en ear, 11-1
das Ökosystem, -e ecosystem, 9-TLL

(der) **Oktober** October, *Einf.*

das **Öl** oil, 9-2

die **Oma, -s** grandma, 2-2

der **Onkel, -** uncle, 2-2

der **Opa, -s** grandpa, 2-2

die **Opposition, -en** opposition, 10-TLL

optimistisch optimistic, 3-TLL

ordentlich tidy, orderly, 13-1

der **Ort, -e** (1) place; (2) small town, 12-SA; 13-2

der **Osten** the east, 4-2

(das) **Österreich** Austria, 4-1

der **Österreicher, -** Austrian (*m.*), 11-TLL

die **Österreicherin, -nen** Austrian (*f.*), 11-TLL

österreichisch Austrian, 14-1

(das) **Osteuropa** Eastern Europe, 11-TLL

P

ein paar a couple (of), a few, 6-2

packen to pack, 7-TLL

die **Pädagogik** (field of) education, 6-SA

das **Papier, -e** paper, *Einf.*; 9-1

die **Partei, -en** political party, 9-2

der **Partner, -** partner, 5-TLL

die **Party, -s** party, 6-TLL

passieren, ist passiert to happen, 10-1

der **Patient, -en, -en** patient, 14-TLL

die **Pause, -n** break; intermission, 3-1

eine Pause machen to take a break, 3-1

Pech haben to have bad luck, be unlucky, 6-2

per by (means of)

per Autostopp reisen to hitchhike, 7-2

die **Person, -en** person

persönlich personal

pessimistisch pessimistic, 3-TLL

die **Pflanze, -n** plant, 9-2

die **Philosophie** philosophy, 6-TLL; 6-SA

philosophieren to philosophize, 14-TLL

die **Physik** physics, 6-SA

das **Plakat, -e** (political) poster, 10-2

planen to plan, make plans, 7-1

das **Plastik** plastic, 9-TLL

der **Platz, ̈e** (1) place; (2) space; (3) city square, 6-1; (4) seat, 7-2

plötzlich suddenly, 10-1

die **Politik** (1) politics; (2) policy, 9-2

der **Politiker, -** politician (*m.*), 5-SA; 9-2

die **Politikerin, -nen** politician (*f.*), 5-SA

die **Politikwissenschaft** political science, 6-SA

politisch political, 9-TLL

die **Polizei** (*sing. only*) the police

die **Pommes frites** (*pl.*) French fries, 3-2

die **Portion, -en** order, helping (of food), 8-SA

die **Post** (1) post office; postal service, 8-SA; (2) mail

das **Poster, -** poster, *Einf.*

die **Postkarte, -n** postcard, 5-2

praktisch practical, 6-TLL

der **Präsident, -en, -en** president, 10-SA

der **Preis, -e** price, 8-2

prima terrific, great, *Einf.*; 1-1

privat private, 6-TLL

probieren to sample, try, 14-1

das **Problem, -e** problem, 2-2

produktiv productive, 14-TLL

produzieren to produce, 9-TLL

der **Professor, -en** professor (*m.*), *Einf.*

die **Professorin, -nen** professor (*f.*), *Einf.*

das **Programm, -e** program, 6-TLL

der **Programmierer, -** programmer (*m.*), 5-SA

die **Programmiererin, -nen** programmer (*f.*), 5-SA

der **Protest, -e** protest, 11-TLL

das **Prozent** percent, 13-TLL

die **Prüfung, -en** examination

die **Psychoanalyse** psychoanalysis, 14-TLL

die **Psychologie** psychology, 6-SA

der **Pulli, -s** (*slang*) = **Pullover**, 3-2

der **Pullover, -** pullover, sweater, 3-2

pünktlich punctual, on time, 7-2

sich putzen to clean, 11-SA

Q

Quatsch! Nonsense! Baloney! 5-1

quatschen (*colloq.*) (1) to talk nonsense; (2) to chat, 7-2

die **Querstraße, -n** cross street, 12-1

R

das **Rad, ̈er** (1) wheel; (2) bicycle, 8-2

Rad fahren (fährt Rad), fuhr Rad, ist Rad gefahren to bicycle, 8-2

der **Radiergummi** eraser, *Einf.*

radikal radical, 9-TLL

das **Radio, -s** radio, 6-SA

sich rasieren to shave, 11-SA

raten (rät), riet, hat geraten to guess

Raten Sie mal! Take a guess!

das **Rathaus, ̈er** town hall, 8-SA

reagieren auf (+ *acc.*) to react to, 13-2

die **Reaktion, -en** reaction

realistisch realistic, 5-TLL

Recht: Recht haben (hat Recht), hatte Recht, hat Recht gehabt to be right, 4-1

rechts (*adv.*) to the right; on the right, 8-2

der **Rechtsanwalt, ̈e** lawyer (*m.*), 5-SA; 13-2

die **Rechtsanwältin, -nen** lawyer (*f.*), 5-SA; 13-2

das **Recycling** recycling; recycling center, 9-1

reden to talk, speak, 12-1

das **Referat, -e** (1) oral report; (2) written term paper, 6-2

ein Referat halten to give a report, 6-SA

ein Referat schreiben to write a paper, 6-SA

die **Reform, -en** reform, 11-TLL

reformieren to reform, 11-TLL

der **Regen** rain, 4-SA

der **Regenschirm, -e** umbrella, 3-SA

die **Regierung, -en** government in power, administration (U.S.), 10-SA; 11-2

das **Regime** regime, 11-TLL

die **Region, -en** region, 4-TLL

regnen to rain, *Einf.*; 1-1

regnerisch rainy, 4-SA

reich rich, 10-1

das **Reich, -e** empire; realm, 10-2

die **Reise, -n** trip, journey, 3-2

  eine Reise machen to take a trip, 3-2

  Gute Reise! Have a good trip! 1-1

der **Reiseführer, -** guide book, 5-1

reisen, ist gereist to travel, 5-2

  per Autostopp reisen to hitchhike, 7-2

der **Reisepass, ̈e** passport, 14-SA

der **Reisescheck, -s** traveler's check, 14-1

das **Reiseziel, -e** destination, 7-2

relativ (*adj. and adv.*) relative, 2-TLL

reparieren to repair, 12-1

die **Republik, -en** republic, 10-TLL

reservieren to reserve, 7-1

das **Restaurant, -s** restaurant, 8-1

die **Restauration, -en** restoration, 8-TLL

retten to save, rescue, 9-2

die **Revolution, -en** revolution, 11-TLL

die **Rezeption** hotel reception desk, 14-1

der **Rhein** the Rhine River, 4-TLL

richtig right, correct, *Einf.*

der **Riese, -n, -n** giant

riesen- (*noun and adj. prefix*) gigantic

  riesengroß huge, gigantic, 8-2

  Ich habe Riesenhunger. I'm famished (*or*) hungry as a bear. 14-2

der **Rock, ̈e** skirt, 3-SA

die **Rolle, -n** role, 2-2

der **Roman, -e** novel, 5-2

romantisch romantic, 13-TLL

rosa pink, 3-SA

rot (röter) red, 3-2

der **Rucksack, ̈e** rucksack, backpack, 7-2

rufen, rief, hat gerufen to call, shout, 11-2

ruhig (1) calm, peaceful, 10-2; (2) (*as sentence adverb*) "feel free to," "go ahead and," 12-1

(das) **Rumänien** Romania, 11-TLL

der **Russe, -n, -n** Russian (*m.*), 11-TLL

die **Russin, -nen** Russian (*f.*), 11-TLL

russisch Russian, 11-TLL

(das) **Russland** Russia, 8-2

S

die **Sache, -n** (1) thing; item, 8-1; (2) matter, affair

der **Sack, ̈e** sack, 9-1

der **Saft, ̈e** juice, 8-SA

sagen to say; to tell, 1-2

die **Sahne** cream, 8-SA

der **Salat, -e** (1) salad; (2) lettuce, 8-1

sammeln to collect, 9-1

(der) **Samstag** Saturday, *Einf.*

der **Satz, ̈e** sentence; clause

sauber clean, 9-1

sauer (*colloq.*) (1) ticked off, sore, *Einf.*; (2) sour, acidic, 9-2

schade too bad, 11-1

  Das ist schade! That's a shame! What a pity! 11-1

schaffen to handle, manage, get done, 3-1

der **Schalter, -** counter, window, 13-1

schauen to look, 11-1

  Schau mal. Look. Look here. 11-1

das **Schaufenster, -** store window, 5-2

der **Scheck, -s** check, 14-1

scheinen, schien, hat geschienen (1) to shine; (2) to seem, 1-1

schenken to give (as a gift), 5-1

schicken to send, 6-2

das **Schiff, -e** ship, 12-2

der **Schilling, -e** Austrian shilling, 14-1

der **Schinken** ham, 8-SA

schlafen (schläft), schlief, hat geschlafen to sleep, 3-1

das **Schlafzimmer, -** bedroom, 11-1

schlagen (schlägt), schlug, hat geschlagen (1) to hit; (2) to beat, 9-SA

schlampig (*colloq.*) messy, disorderly, 13-1

die **Schlange, -n** snake, 10-SA

schlecht bad, *Einf.*; 1-1

schleppen (*colloq.*) to drag, lug (along), haul, 9-1

schließen, schloss, hat geschlossen to close, 5-2

schlimm bad, 5-2

der **Schluss, ̈e** end, conclusion

  zum Schluss in conclusion, finally

der **Schlüssel, -** key, 6-SA; 11-2

schmecken (1) to taste (*trans. and intrans.*); (2) to taste good, 8-1

sich schminken to put on make-up, 11-SA

schmutzig dirty, 9-1

der **Schnee** snow, 4-2

schneiden, schnitt, hat geschnitten to cut, 11-1

schneien to snow, *Einf.*

schnell fast, *Einf.*; 3-2

  schnell machen (*colloq.*) to hurry, 11-1

das **Schnitzel, -** cutlet, chop, 8-1

die **Schokolade** chocolate, 11-1

schon (1) already, yet; (2) (*flavoring particle, see* p. 73), 3-1

  schon lange for a long time, 10-G

schön beautiful, 1-1

schrecklich terrible, 4-2

schreiben, schrieb, hat geschrieben to write, 3-2

Wie schreibt man das? How do you write (spell) that? *Einf.*

der **Schreibtisch, -e** desk, 6-1

der **Schriftsteller, -** writer (*m.*), 10-2

die **Schriftstellerin, -nen** writer (*f.*), 10-2

der **Schuh, -e** shoe, 3-2

die **Schule, -n** school, 1-2

der **Schüler, -** grade school pupil or secondary school student (*m.*), *Einf.*

die **Schülerin, -nen** grade school pupil or secondary school student (*f.*), *Einf.*

das **Schulsystem, -e** school system, 3-TLL

schwach (schwächer) weak, 9-2

schwarz (schwärzer) black, 3-2

schweigen, schwieg, hat geschwiegen to be silent, 12-1

die **Schweiz** Switzerland, 4-2

der **Schweizer, -** Swiss (*m.*), 13-2

die **Schweizerin, -nen** Swiss (*f.*), 13-2

schweizerisch Swiss, 11-TLL

schwer (1) heavy; (2) hard, difficult, 3-1

die **Schwester, -n** sister, 2-1

schwierig difficult, 5-1

die **Schwierigkeit, -en** difficulty, 13-2

das **Schwimmbad, ˝er** swimming pool, 8-SA

schwimmen, schwamm, ist geschwommen to swim, 4-1

der **See, -n** lake, 4-1

sehen (sieht), sah, hat gesehen to see, 2-1

sehr very, 1-1

sein (ist), war, ist gewesen to be, *Einf.*; 1-1

seit (*prep. + dat., sub. conj.*) since, 5-1

  seit 5 Jahren for (the past) 5 years, 5-1

  seit langem for a long time, 10-G

die **Seite, -n** page; side

der **Sekretär, -e** secretary (*m.*), 5-SA

die **Sekretärin, -nen** secretary (*f.*), 5-SA

selber (*or*) **selbst** (*adv.*) by oneself (myself, yourself, ourselves, etc.), 6-2

selbstverständlich "It goes without saying that . . ." 4-1

selten seldom, 1-2

das **Semester, -** semester, 2-1

  nächstes Semester next semester, 2-1

die **Semesterferien** (*pl.*) semester break, 6-2

das **Seminar, -e** (university) seminar, 4-1

der **Senior, -en, -en** senior citizen, 10-1

separat separate, 11-TLL

(der) **September** September, *Einf.*

die **Serviette, -n** napkin, 8-SA

setzen to set (down), put, 7-1

  sich setzen to sit down, 11-1

sich (*3rd person reflexive pronoun*) himself, herself, themselves, (*formal 2nd person*) yourself, yourselves, 11-1

sicher certain, sure, 2-1

siebt- seventh, 9-G

siezen to address someone with **Sie**, 1-2

singen, sang, hat gesungen to sing, 3-2

die **Situation, -en** situation, 10-TLL

sitzen, saß, hat gesessen to sit, 6-2

(das) **Skandinavien** Scandinavia, 8-TLL

Ski fahren (fährt Ski), ist Ski gefahren (*pronounced* "Schifahren") to ski, 8-2

so (1) like this, 1-2; (2) so, 7-2

  so lange (*adv.*) for such a long time, 6-1

sofort immediately, right away, 6-2

die **Software** software, 12-1

sogar even, in fact, 2-2

der **Sohn, ˝e** son, 2-1; 2-SA

solcher, -es, -e such, such a, 9-2

die **Solidarität** solidarity, 1-TLL

sollen (soll), sollte, hat gesollt should, be supposed to, 3-1

der **Sommer** summer, 4-2

das **Sommersemester** spring term (usually May–July), 6-SA

sondern (*coor. conj.*) but rather, instead, 7-1

  nicht nur ... sondern auch not only . . . but also, 9-2

(der) **Sonnabend** Saturday, *Einf.*

die **Sonne** sun, 1-1

sonnig sunny, *Einf.*

(der) **Sonntag** Sunday, *Einf.*

sonst (*adv.*) otherwise, apart from that, 6-2

  Sonst noch etwas? Will there be anything else? 5-1

sortieren to sort, 9-TLL

sowieso anyway, 7-1

die **Sowjetunion** Soviet Union, 11-TLL

sozial social, 2-TLL

der **Sozialarbeiter, -** social worker, 8-TLL

die **Soziologie** sociology, 6-SA

sparen to save (money *or* time), 7-2

der **Spaß** fun

  Das macht (mir) Spaß. That is fun (for me). 7-1

  Viel Spaß. Have fun. 12-1

spät late, 3-1

  Wie spät ist es? What time is it? *Einf.*

später later, 4-1

spazieren gehen, ging spazieren, ist spazieren gegangen to go for a walk, 5-2

die **Speisekarte, -n** menu, 8-SA

der **Speisesaal** (hotel) dining room, 14-SA

der **Spiegel, -** mirror, 6-SA; 14-2

das **Spiel, -e** game, 9-SA

spielen to play, 1-1

spontan spontaneous, 7-TLL

der **Sport** sport, 3-TLL; 9-1

  Sport treiben to play sports, 9-1

sportlich athletic, 9-1

die **Sprache, -n** language, 3-2

sprechen (spricht), sprach, hat gesprochen to speak, talk, 2-1 sprechen über (+ *acc.*) to talk about, 2-1

der **Staat, -en** state, 10-2

stabil stable, 11-TLL

die **Stabilität** stability, 13-TLL

die **Stadt, ̈e** city, 4-2

der **Stadtbummel, -** stroll through town, 8-1

der **Stadtführer, -** city guidebook, 14-SA

der **Stadtplan, ̈** city map, 5-2

stark (stärker) strong, 9-2

statt (*prep.* + *gen.*) instead of, 8-G

statt·finden, fand statt, hat stattgefunden to take place, 14-2

staunen to be amazed, surprised, 6-2

stehen, stand, hat gestanden to stand, 5-1

stehlen (stiehlt), stahl, hat gestohlen to steal, 10-1

steigen, stieg, ist gestiegen to climb, 8-2

steil steep, 3-1

der **Stein, -e** stone, 12-2

die **Stelle, -n** job, position, 2-2

stellen to put, place, 7-1

eine Frage stellen to ask a question, 10-2

sterben (stirbt), starb, ist gestorben to die, 5-2

die **Stimme, -n** voice, 5-2

stimmen to be right (*impersonal only*), 1-2

das stimmt that's right, that's true

Stimmt schon. That's right. 3-2

stinklangweilig (*colloq.*) extremely boring, 3-1

das **Stipendium, *pl.* Stipendien** scholarship, stipend, 6-2

der **Stock** floor (of a building), 14-2

der erste Stock the second floor (*see* **Erdgeschoss**), 14-1

im ersten Stock on the second floor, 14-1

stolz auf (+ *acc.*) proud of, 13-2

stören to disturb, 10-2

die **Straße, -n** street; road, 1-1

der **Straßenatlas** road atlas, 7-1

die **Straßenbahn, -en** streetcar, 8-SA; 13-1

der **Stress** stress, 5-2

stressig stressful, 5-2

das **Stück, -e** piece, 5-1

ein Stück Kuchen a piece of cake, 8-G

sechs Stück six (of the same item), 5-1

der **Student, -en, -en** university student (*m.*), *Einf.*; 1-2

der **Studentenausweis, -e** student I.D., 6-2

das **Studentenwohnheim, -e** student dormitory, 6-1

die **Studentin, -nen** university student (*f.*), *Einf.*; 1-2

studieren to attend a university; to study (a subject); to major in, 1-2

studieren an (+ *dat.*) to study at, 6-SA

das **Studium** university studies, 6-2

der **Stuhl, ̈e** chair, *Einf.*

die **Stunde, -n** (1) hour; (2) class hour, 3-1

stundenlang (*adv.*) for hours, 14-TLL

das **Substantiv, -e** noun

suchen to look for, seek, 2-1

der **Süden** the south, 4-2

super super, 4-1

der **Supermarkt, ̈e** supermarket, 5-TLL

der **Supertanker, -** super tanker, 9-TLL

die **Suppe, -n** soup, 1-1

süß sweet, 9-2

das **Symbol, -e** symbol, 11-TLL

symbolisch symbolic, 10-TLL

sympathisch friendly, congenial, likeable, 7-2

das **System, -e** system, 3-TLL

T

die **Tafel, -n** blackboard, *Einf.*

der **Tag, -e** day, 1-1

eines Tages some day (in the future); one day (in the past or future), 13-2

Guten Tag! Hello! *Einf.*

jeden Tag every day, 5-2

Tag! Hi! Hello! *Einf.*

tagelang (*adv.*) for days, 14-TLL

das **Tal, ̈er** valley, 4-2

die **Tante, -n** aunt, 2-2

tanzen to dance, 14-2

die **Tasche, -n** (1) pocket, (2) shoulder bag, 3-SA; 7-2

die **Tasse, -n** cup, 8-1

die **Taube, -n** dove, pigeon, 10-SA

tausend thousand, 2-G

das **Taxi, -s** taxicab, 8-SA

die **Technik** technology, 9-2

der **Tee** tea, 8-SA

der **Teil, -e** part, 11-2

teilen to divide, 11-2

das **Telefon, -e** telephone, 6-SA; 7-2

telefonieren to telephone, make a phone call, 14-SA

die **Telefonnummer, -n** telephone number, *Einf.*

der **Teller, -** plate, 8-SA

das **Tempo** pace, tempo, 6-2

das **Tennis** tennis, 9-1

der **Tennisplatz, ̈e** tennis court, 9-1

der **Teppich, -e** rug, 6-SA

der **Termin, -e** appointment, 6-2

terroristisch terrorist (*adj.*), 10-TLL

teuer expensive, 6-2

der **Text, -e** text

das **Theater, -** theater, 3-TLL

die **Thermosflasche, -n** thermos bottle, 7-1

das **Ticket, -s** (airline) ticket, 7-TLL

tief deep, 11-2

das **Tiefland** lowlands, 4-TLL

das **Tier, -e** animal, 9-2

der **Tipp, -s** tip, hint, suggestion

der **Tisch, -e** table, *Einf.*

die **Tochter, ̈** daughter, 2-2

der **Tod** death, 11-2

todmüde (*colloq.*) dead tired, 4-1

toll (*colloq.*) great, terrific, 3-2

das **Tor, -e** gate, 11-1

tot dead, 11-2

die **Tour, -en** tour, 8-TLL

der **Tourist, -en, -en** tourist (*m.*), 1-TLL

die **Touristin, -nen** tourist (*f.*), 1-2

die **Tradition, -en** tradition, 11-TLL

traditionell traditional, 2-TLL

tragen (trägt), trug, hat getragen (1) to carry; (2) to wear, 3-1

trainieren to train, 9-SA

trampen, ist getrampt to hitchhike, 7-2

träumen to dream, 14-2

traurig sad, 13-2

treffen (trifft), traf, hat getroffen to meet, 9-1

treiben, trieb, hat getrieben to drive, force, propel, 9-1

　Sport treiben to play sports, 9-1

die **Treppe** staircase, stairs, 9-1

　auf der Treppe on the stairs, 9-1

trinken, trank, hat getrunken to drink, 4-2

trocken dry, 4-2

trotz (*prep. + gen.*) in spite of, despite, 8-G

trotzdem (*adv.*) in spite of that, nevertheless, 8-2

Tschüss! So long! *Einf.*

das **T-Shirt, -s** T-shirt, 3-SA

tun, tat, hat getan to do, 3-1

　Das tut mir weh. That hurts (me). 11-1

　Es tut mir Leid. I'm sorry (about that). 7-1

die **Tür, -en** door, *Einf.*

der **Turnschuh, -e** sneaker, gym shoe, 3-2

der **Typ, -en** (1) type; (2) (*slang*) guy, 12-1

typisch typical, 1-1

U

die **U-Bahn** (= **Untergrundbahn**) subway train, 8-SA

üben to practice, *Einf.*

über (1) (*prep. + acc.*) about, 2-1; (2) (+ *acc.* or *dat.*) over, across; above, 6-1

überall everywhere, 2-2

sich etwas überlegen to consider, ponder, think something over, 13-2

übermorgen the day after tomorrow, 12-1

übernachten to spend the night, 7-2

übersetzen to translate, *Einf.*

übrigens by the way, 1-1

die **Übung, -en** exercise

die **Uhr, -en** clock; watch, *Einf.*

　9 Uhr 9 o'clock, *Einf.*; 5-1

　Wie viel Uhr ist es? What time is it? 7-1

um (1) at (with times), 1-1; (2) around (the outside of), 4-1

　um ... zu in order to, 8-1

um·steigen, stieg um, ist umgestiegen to transfer, change (trains, buses, etc.), 7-SA

die **Umwelt** environment, 3-2

umweltfreundlich environmentally safe, non-polluting, 9-1

um·ziehen, zog um, ist umgezogen to move, change residence, 9-1

　sich um·ziehen, hat sich umgezogen to change clothes, 14-SA

unbekannt unknown, 10-2

unbesorgt unconcerned, carefree, 10-1

und (*coor. conj.*) and, 1-1

der **Unfall, ¨e** accident, 9-2

ungemütlich unpleasant, not cozy, 14-2

die **Uni, -s** (*colloq.*) = **Universität**

die **Universität, -en** university, 5-TLL; 6-1

　an der Universität/Uni at the university, 6-1

unmöglich impossible, 6-1

unnötig unnecessary, 9-1

unordentlich messy, disorderly, 13-1

unruhig restless, troubled, 10-2

unten (*adv.*) below, on the bottom

unter (+ *acc.* or *dat.*) (1) under, beneath; (2) among, 6-1

unterbrechen (unterbricht), unterbrach, hat unterbrochen to interrupt, 10-2

der **Unterschied, -e** difference, 11-1

unterwegs on the way, en route; on the go, 4-1

unwichtig unimportant, 2-2

uralt ancient, 3-2

der **Urlaub, -e** vacation (from a job), 4-1

die **USA** (*pl.*) the USA, 5-TLL

usw. (= **und so weiter**) etc. (= and so forth), 1-1

V

die **Variation, -en** variation

der **Vater, ¨** father, 2-1

der **Vati, -s** papa, dad, 2-2

(das) **Venedig** Venice (Italy), 7-1

verantwortlich für responsible for, 6-2

das **Verb, -en** verb

verboten forbidden, prohibited

verbringen, verbrachte, hat verbracht to spend (time), 7-2

verdienen to earn, 2-2

vereinen to unite, 11-2

die **Vereinigung** unification, 11-1

die **Vergangenheit** past (time), 11-2

vergessen (vergisst), vergaß, hat vergessen to forget, 5-2

vergleichen, verglich, hat verglichen to compare, 12-2

verkaufen to sell, 4-1

der **Verkäufer, -** salesman, 5-SA

die **Verkäuferin, -nen** saleswoman, 5-SA

der **Verkehr** traffic, 7-SA

das **Verkehrsmittel, -** means of transportation, 8-SA

verlassen (verlässt), verließ, hat verlassen to leave (a person or place), 5-1

sich verletzen to injure oneself, get hurt, 11-1

verlieren, verlor, hat verloren to lose, 10-1

sich verloben mit (+ *dat.*) to become engaged to, 12-1

verpassen to miss (an event, opportunity, train, etc.), 13-1

verrückt crazy, insane, 7-2

verschieden different, various, 11-2

verschmutzen to pollute; to dirty, 9-2

die **Verschmutzung** pollution, 9-1

verschwenden to waste, 9-2

verschwinden, verschwand, ist verschwunden to disappear, 11-2

sich verspäten to be late, 11-1

verstehen, verstand, hat verstanden to understand, 3-1

versuchen to try, attempt, 10-2

der/die **Verwandte, -n** (*adj. noun*) relative, 11-1

der **Vetter, -n** cousin (*m.*), 2-SA

viel (mehr, am meisten) much, a lot, 1-1

viele many, 1-2; (*pronoun*) many people, 8-2

vielen Dank many thanks, 2-1

vielleicht maybe, perhaps, 1-1

das **Viertel** quarter, *Einf.*

Viertel vor/nach sieben quarter to/past seven, *Einf.*

der **Vogel, ¨** bird, 9-2

die **Vokabel, -n** word

das **Volk, ¨er** people, nation, folk, 10-2

das **Volkslied, -er** folk song, 4-2

voll full, 5-1

von (*prep. + dat.*) from, 4-2; of; by, 5-1

vor (*prep. + acc. or dat.*) in front of, 6-1

vor einem Jahr a year ago, 10-G

vorbei·kommen, kam vorbei, ist vorbeigekommen to come by, drop by, 5-2

vor·bereiten to prepare

sich vor·bereiten auf (+ *acc.*) to prepare for, 13-1

vorgestern the day before yesterday, 12-1

vor·haben (hat vor), hatte vor, hat vorgehabt to plan, have in mind, 13-1

vorher (*adv.*) before that, previously, 10-1

vor·lesen (liest vor), las vor, hat vorgelesen to read aloud

die **Vorlesung, -en** university lecture, 6-1

das **Vorlesungsverzeichnis, -se** university course catalogue, 6-1

der **Vorschlag, ¨e** suggestion

vor·stellen to introduce, present, 13-2

sich vor·stellen to introduce oneself, 13-2

sich etwas vor·stellen to imagine something, 11-1

das **Vorurteil, -e** prejudice, 13-SA

W

wachsen (wächst), wuchs, ist gewachsen to grow, 10-2

der **Wagen, -** car, 3-1

die **Wahl, -en** (1) choice; (2) election, 10-2

wählen (1) to choose; (2) to elect, 10-2

der **Wähler, -** voter, 10-2

wahnsinnig (*adv. colloq.*) extremely, incredibly, 3-1

wahr true, 3-1

nicht wahr? isn't it? can't you? doesn't she? etc., 3-1

während (*prep. + gen.*) during, 8-G

die **Wahrheit, -en** truth, 13-SA

wahrscheinlich probably, 1-2

der **Wald, ¨er** forest, 4-2

die **Wand, ¨e** (interior) wall, *Einf.*

die **Wanderlust** wanderlust, 7-TLL

wandern, ist gewandert to hike, wander, 4-2

die **Wanderung, -en** hike, 5-2

wann? when? *Einf.*

die **Ware, -n** product, 9-2

warm (wärmer) warm, *Einf.*

warten to wait, 4-1

warten auf (+ *acc.*) to wait for, 13-1

Warte mal! Wait a second! Hang on! 4-1

warum? why? 1-1

was? what? *Einf.*

was für? what kind of? 9-1

Was ist los? What's the matter? What's going on? 3-1

waschen (wäscht), wusch, hat gewaschen to wash, 11-1

das **Wasser** water, 4-1

wechseln to change (money), 14-1

der **Wecker, -** alarm clock, 6-SA

weder ... noch neither . . . nor, 14-1

weg (*adv.*) away, gone, 4-1

wegen (*prep. + gen.*) because of, on account of, 8-G

weg·gehen, ging weg, ist weggegangen to go away, leave, 12-1

weg·werfen (wirft weg), warf weg, hat weggeworfen to throw away, 9-2

wehtun, tat weh, hat wehgetan (+ *dat. of person*) to hurt, 11-1

weil (*sub. conj.*) because, 8-G

der **Wein, -e** wine, 4-2

weinen to cry, 3-2

weiß white, 3-2

weit far, far away, 8-1

welcher, -es, -e which, 7-1

die **Welt, -en** world, 3-2

wem? (*dat.*) to whom? for whom? 5-1

wen? (*acc.*) whom? 2-1

wenig little bit, not much, 1-1

wenige few, 11-1

wenigstens at least, 2-2

wenn (*sub. conj.*) (1) if, 8-G; (2) when, whenever, 10-G

wer? (*nom.*) who? *Einf.*

werden (wird), wurde, ist geworden to become, get (*in the sense of* become), 4-1

werfen (wirft), warf, hat geworfen to throw, 9-2

das **Werk, -e** work (of art), musical composition, 13-2

wessen? whose? 2-1

der **Westen** the west, 4-2

das **Wetter** weather, *Einf.*; 1-1

die **WG, -s** (= **Wohngemeinschaft**) communal living group, shared apartment, 6-1

wichtig important, 2-2

wie (1) how, *Einf.*; (2) like, as, 1-1

Wie bitte? I beg your pardon? What did you say? *Einf.*

wie lange? how long? 3-1

wieder again, 1-1

wiederholen to repeat, *Einf.*

die **Wiederholung, -en** repetition; review

wieder sehen (sieht wieder), sah wieder, hat wieder gesehen to see again, meet again, 12-2

Auf Wiedersehen! Good-bye! *Einf.*

(das) **Wien** Vienna, 1-1

wieso? How come? How's that?; What do you mean? 9-1

wie viel? how much? 5-1

Wie viel Uhr ist es? What time is it? 7-1

wie viele? how many? 2-1

Wievielt-: Den Wievielten haben wir heute? What's the date today? 9-G

wild wild, 4-TLL

willkommen welcome, 6-2

Herzlich willkommen! Welcome! Nice to see you!, 6-2

der **Wind** wind, 4-SA

windig windy, *Einf.*

der **Winter, -** winter, 4-1

im Winter in the winter, 4-1

das **Wintersemester** fall term (usually Oct.–Feb.), 6-SA

wirklich real, 6-1

die **Wirtschaft** economy, 11-2

wirtschaftlich economic, 11-2

die **Wirtschaftswissenschaft** economics, 6-SA

der **Wischer, -** (blackboard) eraser, *Einf.*

wissen (weiß), wusste, hat gewusst to know (a fact), 2-1

Weißt du noch? Do you remember? 11-1

die **Wissenschaft, -en** (1) science; (2) scholarship; field of knowledge, 6-SA

der **Witz, -e** (1) joke; (2) wit, 14-2

witzig witty, amusing, 14-2

wo? where? *Einf.*

die **Woche, -n** week, 5-1

das **Wochenende, -n** weekend, 5-2

am Wochenende on the weekend, 5-2

Schönes Wochenende! (Have a) nice weekend! *Einf.*

wochenlang (*adv.*) for weeks, 14-TLL

woher? from where? *Einf.*

wohin? to where? 3-1

wohl probably, 6-2

wohnen to live, dwell, 1-1

die **Wohngemeinschaft, -en** communal living group, shared apartment, 6-1

das **Wohnhaus, ¨er** apartment building, 9-1

die **Wohnung, -en** apartment, 6-2

die **Wolke, -n** cloud, 4-SA

wolkig cloudy, *Einf.*

wollen (will), wollte, hat gewollt to want to, intend to, 3-1

worden (*special form of the past participle of* **werden** *used in the perfect tenses of the passive voice*)

das **Wort** word (*2 plural forms:* die **Worte** = words in context; die **Wörter** = unconnected words, as in a dictionary), 5-2

das **Wörterbuch, ¨er** dictionary, 5-2

der **Wortschatz** vocabulary

das **Wunder, -** miracle

wunderbar wonderful, 7-1

sich wundern (über + *acc.*) to be surprised, amazed (at), 13-1

wunderschön very beautiful, 1-1

wünschen to wish, 12-1

die **Wurst, ¨e** sausage, 8-1

Das ist mir Wurst (*or* **Wurscht**). I don't give a darn. 7-1

Z

zahlen to pay, 8-1

Zahlen bitte! Check please! 8-1

zählen to count, 10-3

der **Zahn, ¨e** tooth, 11-SA

sich die Zähne putzen to brush one's teeth, 11-SA

zeigen to show, 5-1

die **Zeile, -n** line (of text)

die **Zeit, -en** time, 3-2

höchste Zeit high time, 14-1

eine Zeit lang for a time, for a while, 14-2

die **Zeitschrift, -en** magazine, 5-2

die **Zeitung, -en** newspaper, 2-1

zentral central, 11-TLL

zerstören to destroy, 8-2

die **Zerstörung** destruction, 9-TLL

ziehen, zog, hat gezogen to pull, 6-1

das **Ziel, -e** goal, 7-2

ziemlich fairly, quite, 1-2

zigmal (*adv.*) umpteen times, 12-G

das **Zimmer, -** room, 2-1

das **Zimmerschlüssel, -** room key, 14-SA

zirka circa, 4-TLL

die **Zone, -n** zone, 11-TLL

zu to; too, 1-1; (*prep.* + *dat.*) to, 5-1

zu Fuß on foot, 3-1

zu Hause at home, 2-2

zueinander to each other, 1-2

zuerst first, at first, 8-1

der **Zug, ¨e** train, 7-1

zu·hören (+ *dat.*) to listen (to), 13-1

die **Zukunft** future, 11-2

in Zukunft in the future, 13-2

zuletzt last of all, finally, 8-1

zu·machen to close, 5-1

zurück back, 1-1

zurück·kommen, kam zurück, ist zurückgekommen to come back, 1-1

zusammen together, *Einf.*; 4-1

die **Zusammenfassung** summary

zweimal twice, 12-G

zweit- second, 9-1

der **Zweitwagen, -** second car, 9-1

zwischen (*prep.* + *acc.* or *dat.*) between, 2-2

English–German Vocabulary

Strong and irregular verbs are marked by an asterisk: *brechen, *können, *bringen. Their principal parts can be found in the appendix *Principal Parts of Strong and Irregular Verbs*, pages 371–372.

A

able: be able to *können

about über (*prep. + acc.*)
   it's about X es geht um X

above oben (*adv.*); über (*prep. + dat. or acc.*)

abroad im Ausland (*location*); ins Ausland (*destination*)

absent: be absent fehlen

accident der Unfall, ⸚e

account: on account of wegen (*+ gen.*)

acidic sauer

acid rain der saure Regen

acquaintance der/die Bekannte, -n (*adj. noun*)

acquainted: be acquainted with *kennen

across über (*prep. + dat. or acc.*)

act: He acts as if . . . Er tut, als ob . . .

active aktiv

actually eigentlich

acute akut

address with *du* duzen

address with *Sie* siezen

adjective das Adjektiv, -e

administration, government in power die Regierung, -en

adverb das Adverb, -ien

affair, matter die Sache, -n

afford: be able to afford something sich etwas leisten können

afraid: be afraid (of) Angst haben (vor + *dat.*)

after nach (*prep. + dat.*); nachdem (*sub. conj.*)
   after all schließlich
   after that danach (*adv.*)

afternoon der Nachmittag, -e
   in the afternoon am Nachmittag

(in the) afternoons nachmittags

this afternoon heute Nachmittag (*adv.*)

afterwards, after that nachher (*adv.*)

again wieder

against gegen (*prep. + acc.*)

ago vor (*+ dat.*)
   a year ago vor einem Jahr

agreed einverstanden

agriculture die Landwirtschaft

ah ach

aid die Hilfe

air die Luft
   air pollution die Luftverschmutzung

airplane das Flugzeug, -e

airport der Flughafen, ⸚

alarm clock der Wecker, -

alive: be alive leben

all alle (*pl.*)
   all summer (day, afternoon, etc.) den ganzen Sommer (Tag, Nachmittag usw.)

allow *lassen

allowed: be allowed to *dürfen

almanac der Almanach, -e

almost fast

alone allein

along with mit (*adv.*)

alongside of an (*prep. + acc. or dat.*)

a lot viel (mehr, am meisten); eine Menge

Alps die Alpen (*pl.*)

already schon

also auch

alternative die Alternative, -n

although obwohl (*sub. conj.*)

always immer

ambivalent ambivalent

amazed
   be amazed staunen
   be amazed (at) sich wundern (über + *acc.*)

America (das) Amerika

American amerikanisch (*adj.*); der Amerikaner, -; die Amerikanerin, -nen

among unter (*prep. + acc. or dat.*)

amusing witzig

analyze analysieren

ancient uralt

and und (*coor. conj.*)

anecdote die Anekdote, -n

anger der Ärger

angry (at) böse (*+ dat.*)

animal das Tier, -e

annoy ärgern
   get annoyed sich ärgern

annoyance der Ärger

annually jährlich

another, an additional noch ein

answer die Antwort, -en

answer (a person) antworten (*+ dat.*)

answer (something) antworten auf (*+ acc.*)

anything
   Anything more? (Sonst) noch etwas?
   Will there be anything else? Sonst noch etwas?

anyway sowieso

anywhere irgendwo

apart from that sonst

apartment die Wohnung, -en
   apartment building das Wohnhaus, ⸚er

appear *aus·sehen

appointment der Termin, -e

apprentice der Lehrling, -e

April (der) April
architecture die Architektur
area die Gegend, -en
arm der Arm, -e
around, about (with time) gegen
    (*prep. + acc.*)
around (the outside of) um (*prep.
    + acc.*)
arrive ˚an·kommen
arrogance die Arroganz
art die Kunst, ¨e
    art history die Kunstgeschichte
article der Artikel, -
artist der Künstler, -; die
    Künstlerin, -nen
as wie
    as a als
ask fragen
    ask a question eine Frage
        stellen
    ask for ˚bitten um
aspect der Aspekt, -e
assignment die Aufgabe, -n
astounding erstaunlich
at bei (*prep. + dat.*); an (*prep. + acc.
    or dat.*); (*with times*) um
    (*prep. + acc.*)
    At last! Na endlich!
    at least wenigstens
athletic sportlich
atom das Atom, -e
atomic power plant das
    Atomkraftwerk, -e
attempt versuchen
attention: pay attention
    auf·passen
August (der) August
aunt die Tante, -n
Austria (das) Österreich
Austrian österreichisch (*adj.*); der
    Österreicher, -; die
    Österreicherin, -nen
author der Autor, -en; die Autorin,
    -nen
autobiographical
    autobiographisch
automatic automatisch
auto mechanic der
    Automechaniker, -; die
    Automechanikerin, -nen

automobile das Auto, -s; der
    Wagen, -
autumn der Herbst
away weg (*adv.*)

B

back zurück (*adv.*)
backpack der Rucksack, ¨e
bad schlecht; schlimm; böse (*evil*)
baker der Bäcker, -; die Bäckerin,
    -nen
bakery die Bäckerei, -en
ballpoint pen der Kugelschreiber, -
Baloney! Quatsch!
banana die Banane, -n
bank die Bank, -en
bar, tavern die Kneipe, -n
barbaric barbarisch
barely kaum
barrier die Barriere, -n
basement der Keller, -
basis die Basis
bath das Bad
    take a bath ein Bad ˚nehmen
bathroom das Badezimmer, -
be ˚sein
bear der Bär, -en, -en
beat ˚schlagen
beautiful schön
    very beautiful wunderschön
because weil (*sub. conj.*)
    because, for denn (*coor. conj.*)
    because of wegen (*+ gen.*)
become, get ˚werden
bed das Bett, -en
    get out of bed ˚auf·stehen
    go to bed ins Bett ˚gehen
bedroom das Schlafzimmer, -
beer das Bier, -e
before bevor (*sub. conj.*)
    before that vorher (*adv.*)
begin ˚an·fangen; ˚beginnen
    to begin with zunächst (*adv.*)
beginner der Anfänger, -
beginning der Anfang, ¨e
    at/in the beginning am Anfang
behind hinter (*prep. + acc. or
    dat.*)
believe glauben (*+ dat. of person*)
belong to (a person) gehören
    (*+ dat.*)

below unten (*adv.*); unter (*prep.
    + acc. or dat.*)
bench die Bank, ¨e
beneath unter (*prep. + acc. or dat.*)
beside neben (*prep. + acc. or dat.*)
besides außer (*+ dat.*)
best best-
    like best of all to am liebsten
        (*+ verb*)
better besser
between zwischen (*prep. + acc. or
    dat.*)
bicycle das Fahrrad, ¨er; das Rad,
    ¨er (*colloq.*)
    ride a bicycle Rad ˚fahren
big groß (größer, größt-)
bill die Rechnung, -en
biology die Biologie
bird der Vogel, ¨
birthday der Geburtstag, -e
    for one's birthday zum
        Geburtstag
    When is your birthday? Wann
        hast du Geburtstag?
black schwarz (schwärzer)
blackboard die Tafel, -n
blanket die Decke, -n
blouse die Bluse, -n
blue blau
book das Buch, ¨er; buchen (*verb*)
bookcase das Bücherregal, -e
bookstore die Buchhandlung, -en
border die Grenze, -n
bored: be bored sich langweilen
boring langweilig
    extremely boring
        stinklangweilig (*colloq.*)
born geboren
borrow ˚leihen
boss der Chef, -s; die Chefin, -nen
both beid-
    both (people) beide (*pl.
        pronoun*)
    both (things) beides (*sing.
        pronoun*)
bottle die Flasche, -n
bottom: at the bottom unten (*adv.*)
box boxen
boy der Junge, -n, -n
bread das Brot, -e
    dark bread das Bauernbrot

break, intermission die Pause, -n
    take a break eine Pause
      machen
break *brechen; kaputt machen
    break out *aus·brechen
breakfast das Frühstück, -e
    eat breakfast frühstücken
    for breakfast zum Frühstück
bridge die Brücke, -n
bright (light) hell
bright (intelligent) klug (klüger)
bring *bringen
    bring along *mit·bringen
    bring back *zurück·bringen
broken kaputt (colloq.)
brother der Bruder, ⸚
brown braun
brush one's teeth sich die Zähne
    putzen
build bauen
building das Gebäude, -
burn *brennen
bus der Bus, -se
business das Geschäft, -e
    business (field of study) die
      Betriebswirtschaft
    business people die
      Geschäftsleute
    businessman der
      Geschäftsmann
    businesswoman die
      Geschäftsfrau
but aber (coor. conj.)
    but rather sondern (coor. conj.)
butter die Butter
buy kaufen
by
    by (a certain time) bis (prep. +
      acc.)
    by oneself (myself, yourself, etc.)
      selbst or selber (adv.)
    by the way übrigens

C

café das Café, -s
    pastry café die Konditorei, -en
cafeteria (at the university) die
    Mensa
cake der Kuchen, -
call *rufen
    be called *heißen

call up *an·rufen
calm, peaceful ruhig
camera die Kamera, -s
camp campen
can, be able to *können
Canada (das) Kanada
Canadian kanadisch (adj.); der
    Kanadier, -; die Kanadierin,
    -nen
cap die Mütze, -n
capitalism der Kapitalismus
car das Auto, -s; der Wagen, -
card die Karte, -n
care
    I don't care. Das ist mir egal.
career die Karriere, -n
carefree unbesorgt
caricature die Karikatur, -en
carry *tragen
cartoon der Cartoon, -s
cash das Bargeld
cashier, cashier's office die Kasse,
    -n
cassette player der
    Kassettenrecorder, -
cat die Katze, -n
catalogue (university) das
    Vorlesungsverzeichnis, -se
catastrophe die Katastrophe, -n
catastrophic katastrophal
cathedral der Dom, -e
cause to be done *lassen
    (+ infinitive)
CD (compact disk) die CD, -s
    CD player der CD-Spieler, -
cease auf·hören (mit)
celebrate feiern
cellar der Keller, -
central zentral
century das Jahrhundert, -e
    for centuries jahrhundertelang
certain, sure sicher; bestimmt
chain die Kette, -n
    chain reaction die
      Kettenreaktion, -en
chair der Stuhl, ⸚e
chalk die Kreide
chance die Gelegenheit, -en; die
    Chance, -n
change ändern (trans.); sich
    ändern

change (clothes) sich
    *um·ziehen
change (money) wechseln
change (trains, buses, etc.),
    transfer *um·steigen
change purse der Geldbeutel, -
chapter das Kapitel, -
chat quatschen (colloq.)
cheap billig
check der Scheck, -s (bank check);
    die Rechnung, -en (restaurant
    bill)
    Check please! Zahlen bitte!
check kontrollieren
cheerful munter; heiter
Cheers! Prost! or Prosit!
cheese der Käse
chemistry die Chemie
chief Haupt- (noun prefix)
child das Kind, -er
childhood die Kindheit, -en
China (das) China
Chinese (das) Chinesisch; der
    Chinese, -n, -n; die Chinesin, -
    nen
chocolate die Schokolade
choice die Wahl, -en
choose wählen
chop, cutlet das Schnitzel, -
church die Kirche, -n
circa zirka
citizen der Bürger, -
city die Stadt, ⸚e
    capital city die Hauptstadt, ⸚e
    city guidebook der Stadtführer, -
    city map der Stadtplan, ⸚e
    large city (over 500,000
      inhabitants) die Großstadt,
      ⸚e
    old city center die Altstadt, ⸚e
    small city (5,000 to 20,000
      inhabitants) die Kleinstadt,
      ⸚e
civil servant der Beamte (adj.
    noun, m.); die Beamtin,
    -nen (f.)
claim to *wollen
class die Klasse, -n
    class hour die Stunde, -n
clean sauber (adj.); putzen (verb)
clear klar; deutlich

clerk der Verkäufer, -; die Verkäuferin, -nen

cliché das Klischee, -s

clichéd (adj.), stereotyped klischeehaft

climate das Klima

climb *steigen

clinic die Klinik, -en

clock die Uhr, -en

close *schließen, zu·machen
closed geschlossen

cloth das Tuch

clothes die Kleider (pl.)
clothes cupboard der Kleiderschrank, ¨e

clothing die Kleidung

cloud die Wolke, -n

cloudy wolkig

coat der Mantel, ¨

coffee der Kaffee

cold kalt (kälter)
catch a cold sich erkälten

collect sammeln

Cologne (das) Köln

colony die Kolonie, -n

color die Farbe, -n

colorful bunt

comb kämmen
comb one's hair sich die Haare kämmen

come *kommen
All together that comes to . . . Das macht zusammen ...
come along *mit·kommen
come back *zurück·kommen
come by *vorbei·kommen
I come from . . . Ich komme aus ...
Where do you come from? Woher kommst du?

comfortable bequem

communal living group die Wohngemeinschaft, -en; die WG, -s

Communism der Kommunismus

compare *vergleichen

compatriots die Landsleute (pl.)

competition die Konkurrenz

complain: I can't complain. Ich bin zufrieden.

computer der Computer, -
computer science die Informatik

concentrate on sich konzentrieren auf (+ acc.)

concerned besorgt

concert das Konzert, -e

conclusion der Schluss, ¨e
in conclusion zum Schluss

conflict der Konflikt, -e

confront konfrontieren

congenial sympathisch

Congratulations! Herzlichen Glückwunsch!

consequence die Konsequenz, -en

conservative konservativ

consider something sich etwas überlegen

contact der Kontakt, -e

contingent: be contingent on, depend on *an·kommen auf (+ acc.)

contrary: on the contrary im Gegenteil

contrast der Kontrast, -e

conversation das Gespräch, -e

cook kochen

cool kühl

cooperate mit·machen

corner die Ecke, -n
around the corner um die Ecke
at/on the corner an der Ecke

correct richtig

correspondent der Korrespondent, -en, -en

Corsica (das) Korsika

cost kosten

count zählen

counter, window der Schalter, -

country das Land, ¨er
in the country auf dem Land
to the country aufs Land

couple
a couple (of) ein paar
married couple das Ehepaar, -e

cousin die Kusine, -n (f.); der Vetter, -n (m.)

cozy, relaxed gemütlich

cram pauken (student slang)

crazy verrückt

cream die Sahne

creative kreativ

critical kritisch

cross street die Querstraße, -n

crowd die Menge, -n

cruel grausam

cry weinen

culture die Kultur, -en

cup die Tasse, -n

current aktuell (adj.)

customer der Kunde, -n, -n; die Kundin, -nen

cut *schneiden

cutlet das Schnitzel, -

D

dad der Vati, -s

damp nass

dance tanzen

danger die Gefahr, -en

dangerous gefährlich

dark dunkel

darn
Darn it all! Verflixt nochmal!
I don't give a darn. Das ist mir Wurst (or Wurscht).

date: What's the date today? Der Wievielte ist heute? Den Wievielten haben wir heute?

daughter die Tochter, ¨

day der Tag, -e
day after tomorrow übermorgen
day before yesterday vorgestern
for days tagelang
in those days damals
one day (in the past or future) eines Tages
some day (in the future) eines Tages

dead tot

deal with sich kümmern um

dear lieb

death der Tod, -e

December (der) Dezember

decide *entscheiden

deep tief

delicious lecker

democracy die Demokratie

democratic demokratisch

democratization die Demokratisierung

demonstrate demonstrieren

demonstration die Demonstration, -en

depart *ab·fahren; *los·fahren

department store das Kaufhaus, ⁻er

depend on *an·kommen auf (+ *acc.*)

describe *beschreiben

desire die Lust

desk der Schreibtisch, -e

despite trotz (+ *gen.*)

dessert der Nachtisch, -e; die Nachspeise, -n

   for dessert zum Nachtisch

destination das Reiseziel, -e

destroy zerstören

destruction die Zerstörung

dialect der Dialekt, -e

dialogue der Dialog, -e

dictionary das Wörterbuch, ⁻er

die *sterben

   die in battle *fallen

difference der Unterschied, -e

different, other ander- (*attributive adj.*); anders (*predicate adj.*)

   different, various verschieden

difficult schwer; schwierig

difficulty die Schwierigkeit, -en

dining room das Esszimmer, -

   dining room (hotel) der Speisesaal

direct(ly) direkt

director der Direktor, -en

dirty schmutzig; dreckig (*colloq.*)

disappear *verschwinden

disappoint enttäuschen

disappointment die Enttäuschung, -en

discount die Ermäßigung, -en

discuss diskutieren; *besprechen

discussion die Diskussion, -en

disorderly schlampig (*colloq.*); unordentlich

dissertation die Dissertation, -en; die Diss (*university slang*); die Doktorarbeit

distant fern

disturb stören

divide teilen

do machen; *tun

doctor der Arzt, ⁻e; die Ärztin, -nen

dog der Hund, -e

done fertig

donkey der Esel, -

door die Tür, -en

dove die Taube, -n

draftsman der Zeichner, -

drag schleppen (*colloq.*)

draw zeichnen

drawing die Zeichnung, -en

dream träumen

dress das Kleid, -er

dress, get dressed sich *an·ziehen

drink das Getränk, -e; *trinken (*verb*)

drive (a vehicle) *fahren

   drive, force *treiben

drop by *vorbei·kommen

dry trocken

dumb, stupid dumm (dümmer); blöd

during während (+ *gen.*)

   during, while . . . -ing bei ...

duty die Pflicht, -en

dwell wohnen

dynasty die Dynastie, -n

E

each jed-

   each other einander

eagle der Adler, -

ear das Ohr, -en

early früh

earn verdienen

earth die Erde

east der Osten

easy, simple einfach; leicht

eat *essen

economic wirtschaftlich

economics die Wirtschaftswissenschaft

economy die Wirtschaft

ecosystem das Ökosystem, -e

educated gebildet

education (as field of study) die Pädagogik

egg das Ei, -er

either . . . or entweder ... oder

elect wählen

election die Wahl, -en

electrical engineer der Elektrotechniker, -; die Elektrotechnikerin, -nen

electrical engineering die Elektrotechnik

electrician der Elektrotechniker, -; die Elektrotechnikerin, -nen

electricity die Elektrizität

elegant elegant

elephant der Elefant, -en, -en

elevator der Lift, -s

emancipation die Emanzipation

emigrate aus·wandern

empire das Reich, -e

employed berufstätig

employee der/die Angestellte, -n (*adj. noun*)

empty leer

end das Ende, -n; der Schluss, ⁻e

   at the end am Ende

   at the end of February Ende Februar

end, be finished, be over zu Ende *sein

energy die Energie

engaged: become engaged to sich verloben mit

engineer der Ingenieur, -e; die Ingenieurin, -nen

English (*adj.*) englisch

   English (language) (das) Englisch

   English studies die Anglistik

Englishman der Engländer, -

Englishwoman die Engländerin, -nen

enormous enorm

enough genug

en route unterwegs

enthusiasm die Begeisterung

enthusiastic about begeistert von

entire ganz

entrance, way in der Einstieg, -e

environment die Umwelt

   environmentally safe, non-polluting umweltfreundlich

epoch die Epoche, -n

equal gleich

equal rights die Gleichberechtigung (*sing.*)

    enjoying equal rights gleichberechtigt

eraser der Radiergummi (*pencil*); der Wischer, - (*blackboard*)

especially besonders

essay der Aufsatz, ⁼e

    essay topic das Aufsatzthema, -themen

etc. usw. (= und so weiter)

Europe (das) Europa

    Eastern Europe (das) Osteuropa

European europäisch (*adj.*); der Europäer, -; die Europäerin, -nen

even, in fact sogar

evening der Abend, -e

    evening meal das Abendessen

    good evening guten Abend

    in the evening am Abend

    (in the) evenings abends

    this evening, tonight heute Abend

ever je

every jed-

    every time jedes Mal (*adv.*)

everybody alle (*pl. pron.*)

everyday (*adj.*) alltäglich

everyday life der Alltag

everyone jeder (*sing. pron.*)

everything alles

everywhere überall

evil böse (*adj.*)

exact genau

examination die Prüfung, -en; das Abitur (*final secondary school exam*); das Abi (*slang*)

example das Beispiel, -e

    for example zum Beispiel

excellent ausgezeichnet

exchange student der Austauschstudent, -en, -en

excursion der Ausflug, ⁼e

Excuse me. Entschuldigung.

exercise die Übung, -en

exhausted kaputt (*colloq.*)

exhibition die Ausstellung, -en

exist existieren

expect erwarten

expensive teuer

experience die Erfahrung, -en

explain erklären

expression der Ausdruck, ⁼e

expressway die Autobahn, -en

extreme extrem

extremely wahnsinnig (*colloq. adv.*)

eye das Auge, -n

eyeglasses die Brille (*sing.*)

F

face das Gesicht, -er

fact

    in fact eigentlich

    in fact, even sogar

factory die Fabrik, -en

fairly ziemlich

fairy tale das Märchen, -

fall, autumn der Herbst

    fall term das Wintersemester

fall *fallen

    fall asleep *ein·schlafen

false, incorrect falsch

family die Familie, -n

famous berühmt

fantastic fantastisch

far, far away weit; fern

farmer der Bauer, -n, -n; der Landwirt, -e; die Landwirtin, -nen

fast schnell

father der Vater, ⁼

favorite Lieblings- (*noun prefix*)

fear die Angst, ⁼e; Angst haben (vor + *dat.*); fürchten

February (der) Februar

Federal Republic of Germany (FRG) die Bundesrepublik Deutschland (BRD)

fed up: I'm fed up. Ich habe die Nase voll.

feel sich fühlen (*intrans.*)

feeling das Gefühl, -e

fetch holen

    fetch, pick up ab·holen

few wenige

    a few ein paar

film der Film, -e

finally endlich; schließlich; zum Schluss; zuletzt

finance finanzieren

find *finden

Fine by me. Ist gut. (*colloq.*)

finger der Finger, -

finished with fertig mit

firm, company die Firma, *pl.* Firmen

first erst- (*adj.*); zuerst (*adv.*)

    at first zuerst

    first (of all) zunächst

fish der Fisch, -e

flabbergasted baff (*colloq.*)

flat flach

floor (of a building) der Stock

    ground floor, first floor das Erdgeschoss

    on the second floor im ersten Stock

    second floor der erste Stock

flow *fließen

flower die Blume, -n

fly *fliegen

fog der Nebel

foggy neblig

folk das Volk, ⁼er

    folk song das Volkslied, -er

follow folgen, ist gefolgt (+ *dat.*)

food das Essen; die Speise, -n (*dish, menu item*)

foolproof idiotensicher

foot der Fuß, ⁼e

    on foot zu Fuß

for für (*prep.* + *acc.*)

    for, because denn (*coor. conj.*)

    for a long time lange; seit langem, schon lange

    for years seit Jahren

forbidden verboten

force, propel *treiben

foreign ausländisch

    foreign, strange fremd

    foreign countries das Ausland (*sing.*)

    foreign language die Fremdsprache, -n

    foreign worker der Gastarbeiter, -; die Gastarbeiterin, -nen

foreigner der Ausländer, -; die Ausländerin, -nen

forest der Wald, ⁼er

forget *vergessen

I can't forget that. Das geht mir nicht aus dem Kopf.

fork die Gabel, -n

form die Form, -en

formal formell

formulate formulieren

fox der Fuchs, ⸚e

France (das) Frankreich

free

  free, unoccupied frei

  free of charge kostenlos

  free time die Freizeit

freedom die Freiheit, -en

French (*adj.*) französisch

French fries die Pommes frites (*pl.*)

Frenchman der Franzose, -n, -n

Frenchwoman die Französin, -nen

fresh frisch

Friday (der) Freitag

friend der Freund, -e; die Freundin, -nen

friendly freundlich; sympathisch

from aus (+ *dat.*); von (+ *dat.*)

front: in front of vor (*prep. + dat. or acc.*)

fruit das Obst

frustrate frustrieren

frustration die Frustration, -en

full voll

fun der Spaß

  Have fun. Viel Spaß.

  make fun of sich lustig machen über (+ *acc.*)

  That is fun (for me). Das macht (mir) Spaß.

funny, peculiar komisch

furnished möbliert

furniture die Möbel (*pl.*)

future die Zukunft

  in the future in Zukunft

G

game das Spiel, -e

garage die Garage, -n

garden der Garten, ⸚

gate das Tor, -e

gaze der Blick, -e

gaze, look blicken

gender das Geschlecht, -er

generation die Generation, -en

gentleman der Herr, -n, -en

geographical geographisch

geography die Geographie

German deutsch (*adj.*); der/die Deutsche, -n (*adj. noun*)

  German class die Deutschstunde, -n

  German Democratic Republic (GDR) die Deutsche Demokratische Republik (DDR)

  German (language) (das) Deutsch

  German mark, Deutschmark die Deutsche Mark

  German studies die Germanistik

  in German auf Deutsch

  German-speaking deutschsprachig

Germany (das) Deutschland

get, receive *bekommen

  get, become *werden

  get, fetch holen

  get, pick up ab·holen

  get in (a vehicle) *ein·steigen

  get out (of a vehicle) *aus·steigen

  get there: How do I get there? Wie komme ich dahin?

  get up, get out of bed *auf·stehen

giant der Riese, -n, -n

gigantic riesengroß; riesen- (*noun and adj. prefix*)

girl das Mädchen, -

give *geben

  give (as a gift) schenken

  give up *auf·geben

glad froh

  I'm glad. Das freut mich.

gladly, with pleasure gern(e) (*adv.*)

glance der Blick, -e

glass das Glas, ⸚er

glasses die Brille (*sing.*)

glove der Handschuh, -e

go *gehen

  go (by vehicle) *fahren

  go away *weg·gehen

  go out *aus·gehen

  let's go! los!

on the go unterwegs

goal das Ziel, -e

god der Gott, ⸚er

gone weg

good gut (besser, best-)

  Good-bye! Auf Wiedersehen!

  Good evening! Guten Abend!

  Good morning! Guten Morgen!

  Have a good trip! Gute Reise!

  pretty good ganz gut

gossip der Klatsch

government in power die Regierung, -en

grade, class die Klasse, -n

  grade (on a test, paper, etc.) die Note, -n

gram das Gramm

  500 grams das Pfund

grammar die Grammatik

granddaughter die Enkelin, -nen

grandfather der Großvater, ⸚

grandma die Oma, -s

grandmother die Großmutter, ⸚

grandpa der Opa, -s

grandparents die Großeltern (*pl.*)

grandson der Enkel, -

graphic artist der Zeichner, - ; die Zeichnerin, -nen

gray grau

great, terrific herrlich; prima, toll (*colloq.*)

greatness die Größe

Greece (das) Griechenland

Greek griechisch (*adj.*)

green grün

greet grüßen

groceries die Lebensmittel (*pl.*)

group die Gruppe, -n

grow *wachsen

  grow up *auf·wachsen

gruesome grausam

guess *raten

  Take a guess! Raten Sie mal!

guest der Gast, ⸚e

guide book der Reiseführer, -

guy der Typ, -en (*slang*)

gym shoe der Turnschuh, -e

H

hair das Haar, -e

half halb (*adv.*)

ham der Schinken
hand die Hand, ⸚e
handsome hübsch
hang hängen (*trans.*); *hängen (*intrans.*)
    hang up auf·hängen
happen passieren, ist passiert
happiness das Glück
happy glücklich, froh
    be happy sich freuen
harbor der Hafen, ⸚
hard hart (härter)
    hard, difficult schwer
hard-working fleißig
harsh hart (härter)
hat der Hut, ⸚e
hate hassen
hatred der Hass
haul schleppen
have *haben
    have in mind *vor·haben
    have to, must *müssen
head der Kopf, ⸚e
health die Gesundheit
healthy gesund (gesünder)
hear hören
heaven: For heaven's sake! Um Gottes Willen!
heavy schwer
hectic hektisch
hello Grüß Gott! (*in southern Germany and Austria*); Guten Tag!; Hallo!
    say hello to grüßen
help die Hilfe; *helfen (+ *dat.*)
helping, portion die Portion, -en
here hier (*location*); her (*destination*)
    Here it is. Bitte.
Hi! Tag!
high hoch (*pred. adj.*), hoh- (*attributive adj.*) (höher, höchst-)
    High time! Höchste Zeit! Na endlich!
highway die Autobahn, -en
hike die Wanderung, -en; wandern
hill der Hügel, -
hilly hügelig
hint der Tipp, -s

historic historisch
history die Geschichte, -n
hit *schlagen
hitchhike per Autostopp reisen; trampen
hitchhiking der Autostopp
hold *halten
home (as destination of motion) nach Hause
    at home zu Hause
    in the home of bei (+ *dat.*)
homeland die Heimat
homesickness das Heimweh
homework assignment die Hausaufgabe, -n
honest ehrlich
hope hoffen
    I hope hoffentlich (*adv.*)
horizon der Horizont, -e
hospital das Krankenhaus, ⸚er
hot heiß
hotel das Hotel, -s
hour die Stunde, -n
    for hours stundenlang
house das Haus, ⸚er
housemate der Mitbewohner, -; die Mitbewohnerin, -nen
housewife die Hausfrau, -en
how? wie?
    How come? Wieso? *or* Wie kommt das?
    how long? wie lange?
    how many? wie viele?
    how much? wie viel?
however aber
human being der Mensch, -en, -en
human race die Menschheit
humor der Humor
hunch die Ahnung, -en
hunger der Hunger
hungry hungrig
    be hungry Hunger haben
hurry die Eile; sich beeilen, schnell machen (*colloq.*)
    in a hurry in Eile
hurt *wehtun (+ *dat. of person*)
    get hurt sich verletzen
    That hurts (me). Das tut (mir) weh.
husband der Mann, ⸚er

I

ice das Eis
    ice cream das Eis
    ice hockey das Eishockey
idea die Idee, -n
    (I have) no idea. Ich habe keine Ahnung.
I.D. card der Ausweis, -e
ideological ideologisch
if wenn (*sub. conj.*)
    if, whether ob (*sub. conj.*)
illegal illegal
image das Bild, -er
imagine something sich etwas vor·stellen
immediately gleich; sofort
immigrate ein·wandern
important wichtig
    most important Haupt- (*noun prefix*)
impossible unmöglich
impression der Eindruck, ⸚e
incorrect, false falsch
incredibly wahnsinnig (*colloq. adv.*)
indicative der Indikativ
industrious fleißig
industry die Industrie, -n
inexpensive billig, preiswert
inflation die Inflation
information die Auskunft
injure oneself sich verletzen
inkling die Ahnung, -en
insane verrückt
instead sondern (*coor. conj.*)
    instead of anstatt (+ *gen.*); statt (+ *gen.*)
instrument das Instrument, -e
integration die Integration
intelligent intelligent
intend to *wollen
interest interessieren
    be interested in sich interessieren für
interesting interessant
intermission die Pause, -n
international international
interrupt *unterbrechen
interview interviewen
into in (*prep. + acc.*); hinein- (*prefix*)

introduce vor·stellen
    introduce oneself sich vor·stellen
invent *erfinden
invest investieren
invite *ein·laden
irony die Ironie
Italian italienisch (*adj.*); der Italiener, -; die Italienerin, -nen
Italy (das) Italien

J

jacket die Jacke, -n
January (der) Januar
jeans die Jeans (*pl.*)
Jewish jüdisch
job, position die Stelle, -n
joke der Witz, -e
journalist der Journalist, -en, -en
journey die Reise, -n
joy die Freude, -n
juice der Saft, ̈e
July (der) Juli
June (der) Juni
just, at the moment gerade
    just as . . . as genau so ... wie

K

kaput kaputt (*colloq.*)
keep *behalten
key der Schlüssel, -
kilogram das Kilogramm; das Kilo (*colloq.*)
kilometer der Kilometer, -
kitchen die Küche, -n
knife das Messer, -
know (a fact) *wissen
    get to know kennen lernen
    know, be acquainted with *kennen
    know one's way around sich *aus·kennen
known bekannt

L

lab(oratory) das Labor, -s
lady die Dame, -n
lake der See, -n
    at the lake am See

lamp die Lampe, -n
landscape die Landschaft, -en
language die Sprache, -n
last letzt-
    last of all zuletzt
last, take time dauern
late spät
    be late sich verspäten
    I'm late. Ich bin spät dran.
later on nachher (*adv.*)
laugh lachen
lavatory die Toilette, -n
lavender lila
law das Gesetz, -e
    (study of) law Jura
    under the law, in the eyes of the law vor dem Gesetz
lawyer der Rechtsanwalt, ̈e; die Rechtsanwältin, -nen
lay, put down legen
lazy faul
lead führen
learn lernen
leave (something or someone), leave behind *lassen
    leave (a person or place) *verlassen
    leave (by vehicle) *ab·fahren; *los·fahren
    leave, go away *weg·gehen
lecture (university) die Vorlesung, -en
left: to the left, on the left links (*adv.*)
leg das Bein, -e
leisure time die Freizeit
lend *leihen
let *lassen
let's go! los!
letter der Brief, -e
lettuce der Salat, -e
library die Bibliothek, -en
lie, be situated *liegen
life das Leben
light das Licht, -er
light (in color) hell
    light (in weight) leicht
like *mögen; wie (*conj.*)
    I like that. Das gefällt mir.
    like something etwas gern haben; etwas mögen

    like this so
    like to (do something) gern (+ *verb*)
    would like to möchten
likeable sympathisch
limnology die Limnologie
line (of text) die Zeile, -n
    line (streetcar or bus) die Linie, -n
linguistics die Linguistik
lion der Löwe, -n, -n
list die Liste, -n
listen (to) zu·hören (+ *dat.*)
liter der Liter
literary literarisch
little klein (*adj.*); wenig (*pronoun*)
    a little etwas
    a little; a little bit; a little while ein bisschen
live leben
    live, dwell wohnen
lively munter
liverwurst die Leberwurst, ̈e
loan *leihen
long lang(e) (länger)
    for a long time lange; (*stretch of time continuing in the present*) schon lange, seit langem
    for such a long time so lange
    no longer nicht mehr
look schauen, blicken
    look, appear *aus·sehen
    look after auf·passen auf (+ *acc.*); sich kümmern um
    look for, seek suchen
    look forward to sich freuen auf (+ *acc.*)
    Look here. Schau mal.
    take a look at something sich etwas *an·sehen
lose *verlieren
lots of eine Menge; viel
loud laut
love die Liebe; lieben
low niedrig
luck das Glück
    be lucky Glück haben
    be unlucky, have bad luck Pech haben
lug (along) schleppen (*colloq.*)

luggage das Gepäck
lunch, midday meal das Mittagessen

M

magazine die Zeitschrift, -en
mail die Post
mailman der Briefträger, -
main Haupt- (*noun prefix*)
major field (of study) das Hauptfach, -̈er
major in (a subject) studieren
make machen
make-up: put on make-up sich schminken
mama, mom die Mutti, -s
man der Mann, -̈er
  Man! Mensch!
manage schaffen (*colloq.*)
management (field of study) die Betriebswirtschaft
manager der Manager, -
manipulate manipulieren
mankind die Menschheit
many viele (*adj.*)
  many a manch-
  many people viele (*pl. pron.*)
  many things vieles (*sing. pron.*)
map die Karte, -n; die Landkarte, -n
March (der) März
mark (the German mark) die Mark
marriage die Ehe, -n
marvelous herrlich; sagenhaft
math die Mathe (*slang*)
mathematics die Mathematik (*sing.*)
matter, affair die Sache, -n
matter
  It doesn't matter. Es macht (doch) nichts.
  It doesn't matter to me. Das ist mir egal.
  no matter where, who, why, etc. egal wo, wer, warum usw.
  What's the matter? Was ist los?
May (der) Mai
may, be allowed to *dürfen
  That may be. Das mag sein.
maybe vielleicht

meal das Essen
mean, signify bedeuten
  mean, think meinen
  that means, in other words das heißt
  What do you mean? Wieso?
meaning die Bedeutung, -en
meat das Fleisch
mechanic der Mechaniker, -
medicine die Medizin
meet (for the first time) kennen lernen
  meet again wieder *sehen
  meet (by appointment) *treffen
melancholy die Melancholie
member das Mitglied, -er
mention: Don't mention it. Nichts zu danken.
menu die Speisekarte, -n
messy schlampig (*colloq.*); unordentlich
method die Methode, -n
Middle Ages das Mittelalter (*sing.*)
might die Macht
mild mild
milk die Milch
million die Million, -en
minor field (of study) das Nebenfach, -̈er
minute die Minute, -n
  for minutes minutenlang
miracle das Wunder, -
mirror der Spiegel, -
Miss Fräulein
miss (an event, opportunity, train, etc.) verpassen
missing: be missing fehlen
mist der Nebel
misty neblig
modern modern
modernize modernisieren
mom, mama die Mutti, -s
moment der Augenblick, -e; der Moment, -e
  at the moment im Augenblick; im Moment
  at the moment, just gerade
  Just a moment, please. (Einen) Augenblick, bitte.
monarchy die Monarchie, -n
Monday (der) Montag

money das Geld
month der Monat, -e
  for months monatelang
monument das Denkmal, -̈er
mood die Laune, -n
  in a good/bad mood guter / schlechter Laune
more mehr
  not any more nicht mehr
morning der Morgen, -
  Good morning! Guten Morgen!
  in the morning(s) morgens (*adv.*); vormittags (*adv.*)
  this morning heute Morgen
most meist-
  most like to am liebsten (+ *verb*)
mostly meistens
mother die Mutter, -̈
motorcycle das Motorrad, -̈er
mountainous bergig
mouth der Mund, -̈er
move, change residence *um·ziehen
  move in *ein·ziehen
  move out *aus·ziehen
movie der Film, -e
  movie theater das Kino, -s
Mr. Herr
Mrs. Frau
Ms. Frau
much viel (mehr, meist-)
  not much wenig
Munich (das) München
museum das Museum, *pl.* Museen
music die Musik
musicology die Musikwissenschaft
must *müssen

N

name der Name, -ns, -n; *nennen
  My name is . . . Ich heiße ...
  What's your name? Wie heißen Sie? *or* Wie ist Ihr Name?
napkin die Serviette, -n
nation, folk das Volk, -̈er
nationality die Nationalität, -en
native
  native language die Muttersprache, -n

native place or country die Heimat
natural natürlich
nature die Natur
near nah (näher, nächst-)
   near, nearby in der Nähe (von *or* + *gen.*)
nearness die Nähe
necessary nötig
need brauchen
neighbor der Nachbar, -n, -n; die Nachbarin, -nen
neither . . . nor weder ... noch
neutral neutral
neutrality die Neutralität
never nie
nevertheless trotzdem
new neu
newspaper die Zeitung, -en
next nächst-
nice nett; lieb
night die Nacht, ⸚e
   Good night. Gute Nacht.
   in the night, at night in der Nacht; nachts
no nein; nee (*colloq.*)
   no, not a kein (*negative article*)
   no more X kein X mehr
nobody, no one niemand
Nonsense! Quatsch!
normal normal
north der Norden
North America (das) Nordamerika
nose die Nase, -n
not nicht
   not a kein (*negative article*)
   not a . . . at all gar kein
   not an X any longer kein X mehr
   not any kein
   not any more, no longer nicht mehr
   not any X yet noch kein X
   not at all gar nicht
   not much wenig
   not only . . . but also nicht nur ... sondern auch
   not yet noch nicht
notebook das Heft, -e
nothing nichts
notice merken
notion die Ahnung, -en

noun das Substantiv, -e
novel der Roman, -e
November (der) November
now jetzt; nun
   from now on von jetzt an
number die Nummer, -n
nurse der Krankenpfleger, - (*m.*); die Krankenschwester, -n (*f.*)

O

object, thing die Sache, -n
objective objektiv
o'clock Uhr (3 o'clock = 3 Uhr)
October (der) Oktober
odd komisch
of von (*prep.* + *dat.*)
   of course natürlich
   of course, sure klar (*colloq.*)
offend ärgern
offer ⸰bieten
office das Büro, -s
official offiziell (*adj.*); der Beamte (*adj. noun, m.*); die Beamtin, -nen (*f.*)
often oft (öfter)
oh ach
oil das Öl
O.K. Ist gut; okay (*colloq.*)
old alt (älter)
old-fashioned altmodisch
on auf (*prep.* + *acc. or dat.*)
once einmal
   once again, once more noch einmal
one (*indefinite pronoun*) man
oneself: by oneself (myself, yourself, etc.) selber, selbst
only nur (*adv.*)
   only, single einzig- (*adj.*)
onto auf (*prep.* + *acc. or dat.*)
open offen (*adj.*); öffnen (*verb*)
opinion die Meinung, -en
   be of the opinion, think meinen
opportunity die Gelegenheit, -en
opposite der Gegensatz, ⸚e
opposition die Opposition, -en
optimistic optimistisch
or oder (*coor. conj.*)
order die Portion, -en (*of food*); bestellen
   in order to um ... zu

orderly ordentlich
other ander-
otherwise sonst
outing der Ausflug, ⸚e
out of aus (*prep.* + *dat.*)
outside draußen (*adv.*)
over über (*prep.* + *dat. or acc.*)
   over there drüben; da drüben
own eigen- (*adj.*); ⸰besitzen

P

pace das Tempo
pack packen
page die Seite, -n
pants die Hose, -n
papa der Vati, -s
paper das Papier, -e
   write a paper ein Referat schreiben
   written term paper das Referat
Pardon me. Entschuldigung.
   I beg your pardon? Wie bitte?
parents die Eltern (*pl.*)
part der Teil, -e
   take part in ⸰teil·nehmen an (+ *dat.*)
participate mit·machen
partner der Partner, -
party die Party, -s
   party (political) die Partei, -en
passport der Pass, ⸚e; der Reisepass, ⸚e
past (time) die Vergangenheit
patience die Geduld
patient der Patient, -en, -en
patron der Gast, ⸚e
pay bezahlen; zahlen
peace der Frieden
peaceful, calm ruhig
peculiar komisch
pedestrian der Fußgänger, -
   pedestrian zone die Fußgängerzone, -n
pen (ballpoint) der Kugelschreiber, -
pencil der Bleistift, -e
people die Leute (*pl.*)
   people, nation, folk das Volk, ⸚er
percent das Prozent
perfect perfekt
perhaps vielleicht

person der Mensch, -en, -en; die Person, -en
personal persönlich
pessimistic pessimistisch
pharmacy die Apotheke, -n
philosophize philosophieren
philosophy die Philosophie
photograph das Foto, -s
physics die Physik (*sing.*)
piano das Klavier, -e
pick up ab·holen
picture das Bild, -er
    take a picture ein Foto machen
piece das Stück, -e
pigeon die Taube, -n
pink rosa
pity: What a pity! Das ist schade!
place der Ort, -e; der Platz, ⁚e
place, put stellen
plan *vor·haben
    plan, make plans planen
plant die Pflanze, -n
plastic das Plastik
plate der Teller, -
play spielen
    play sports Sport *treiben
please bitte
please, appeal to *gefallen (+ *dat.*)
Pleased to meet you. Sehr erfreut. *or* Es freut mich.
Pleasure to meet you. Angenehm.
pocket die Tasche, -n
poem das Gedicht, -e
poet der Dichter, -; die Dichterin, -nen
poetry die Lyrik
police die Polizei (*sing. only*)
policy die Politik
polite höflich
political politisch
    political science die Politikwissenschaft
politician der Politiker, -; die Politikerin, -nen
politics die Politik
pollute verschmutzen
    non-polluting, ecologically beneficial umweltfreundlich
pollution die Verschmutzung
ponder something sich etwas überlegen

poor arm (ärmer)
popular beliebt
port der Hafen, ⁚
portion die Portion, -en
position, job die Stelle, -n
possible möglich
postage stamp die Briefmarke, -n
postal service die Post
postcard die Postkarte, -n
poster das Poster, -
    poster (political) das Plakat, -e
post office die Post
pot: small (coffee or tea) pot das Kännchen, -
potato die Kartoffel, -n
power die Kraft, ⁚e; die Macht, ⁚e
    power plant das Kraftwerk, -e
practical praktisch
practice üben
precise genau
prefer (to do something) lieber (+ *verb*)
preferably lieber
prejudice das Vorurteil, -e
prepared, ready bereit
prepare for sich vor·bereiten auf (+ *acc.*)
present (gift) das Geschenk, -e
    present (time) die Gegenwart
president der Präsident, -en, -en
pretty hübsch
pretzel die Brezel, -n
previously vorher
price der Preis, -e
primary Haupt- (*noun prefix*)
private privat
probably wahrscheinlich; wohl
problem das Problem, -e
produce produzieren
product, ware die Ware, -n
productive produktiv
profession der Beruf, -e
    What is your profession? Was sind Sie von Beruf?
professor der Professor, -en; die Professorin, -nen
program das Programm, -e
programmer der Programmierer, -; die Programmiererin, -nen
progress der Fortschritt, -e
prohibited verboten

propel *treiben
protect (from) schützen (vor + *dat.*)
protest der Protest, -e
proud of stolz auf (+ *acc.*)
provide *bieten
psychoanalysis die Psychoanalyse
psychology die Psychologie
public öffentlich
pull *ziehen
pullover der Pullover, -; der Pulli, -s (*colloq.*)
punctual pünktlich
pupil der Schüler, -; die Schülerin, -nen
put stellen
    put down, lay legen
    put down, set setzen

Q

quantity die Menge, -n
quarter das Viertel, -
    quarter to/past Viertel vor/nach
question die Frage, -n
    ask a question eine Frage stellen
    guiding question die Leitfrage, -n
    it's a question of es geht um
questionnaire der Fragebogen
quick as lightning blitzschnell
quiet leise
quit, to give up *auf·geben
quite ziemlich
quotidian alltäglich

R

radical radikal
radio das Radio, -s
railroad, railroad system die Bahn
rain der Regen; regnen
rainy regnerisch
rather
    I'd rather not. No thanks. Lieber nicht.
    would rather (do something) lieber (+ *verb*)
reaction die Reaktion, -en
react to reagieren auf (+ *acc.*)
read *lesen

read aloud *vor·lesen
reading selection das Lesestück,
   -e
ready, finished fertig
   ready, prepared bereit
real wirklich
really? echt? (*slang*)
realm das Reich, -e
reason der Grund, ⁻e
receive *bekommen
recently neulich
reception desk die Rezeption
recommend *empfehlen
recover (from) sich erholen von
recycling das Recycling
red rot (röter)
reform die Reform, -en;
   reformieren
refuse, trash der Müll
regime das Regime
region die Gegend, -en; die
   Region, -en
register (at a hotel, the university,
      etc.) sich an·melden
   register for, take (a university
      course) belegen
relative relativ (*adj.* and *adv.*);
   der/die Verwandte, -n (*adj.
   noun*)
remain *bleiben
remember sich erinnern an
   (+ *acc.*)
   Do you remember? Weißt du
   noch?
remind of erinnern an (+ *acc.*)
rent (from somebody) mieten
repair reparieren
repeat wiederholen
repetition die Wiederholung, -en
report berichten
   give a report ein Referat *halten
   oral report das Referat, -e
republic die Republik, -en
request *bitten um
rescue retten
reserve reservieren
respond to antworten auf (+ *acc.*)
responsible for verantwortlich für
rest: have a rest sich erholen
restaurant das Restaurant, -s; das
   Lokal, -e

restless unruhig
restoration die Restauration
retain *behalten
review die Wiederholung
revolution die Revolution, -en
Rhine River der Rhein
rich reich
right, correct richtig
   be right Recht *haben (*with
   person as subject*); stimmen
   (*impersonal only*)
   right away sofort; gleich
   That's right. Das stimmt.
   Stimmt schon.
   to the right, on the right rechts
   (*adv.*)
ring klingeln
rip off, steal klauen (*colloq.*)
river der Fluss, ⁻e
road die Straße, -n
   road atlas der Straßenatlas
role die Rolle, -n
roll das Brötchen, -
Romania (das) Rumänien
romantic romantisch
room das Zimmer, -
   dining room das Esszimmer, -
   double room das
   Doppelzimmer, -
   living room das Wohnzimmer, -
   rented student room die Bude,
   -n (*colloq.*)
   single room das Einzelzimmer, -
roommate der Mitbewohner, -; die
   Mitbewohnerin, -nen
rubble die Trümmer (*pl.*)
rucksack der Rucksack, ⁻e
rug der Teppich, -e
ruins die Trümmer (*pl.*)
run *laufen
Russia (das) Russland
Russian russisch (*adj.*); der Russe,
   -n, -n; die Russin, -nen

S

sack der Sack, ⁻e
sad traurig
salad der Salat, -e
salesman der Verkäufer, -
saleswoman die Verkäuferin, -nen

sample probieren
satisfied zufrieden
Saturday (der) Samstag, (der)
   Sonnabend
sausage die Wurst, ⁻e
save, rescue retten
   save (money or time) sparen
say sagen
   What did you say? Wie bitte?
scarce, in short supply knapp
scarf das Tuch, ⁻er
schilling (Austrian currency) der
   Schilling, -e
scholarship die Wissenschaft
   scholarship, stipend das
   Stipendium, *pl.* Stipendien
school die Schule, -n; das
   Gymnasium, *pl.* Gymnasien
   (*prepares pupils for university*)
   elementary school pupil or
   secondary school student
   der Schüler, -; die Schülerin, -
   nen
   school system das Schulsystem,
   -e
science die Wissenschaft, -en
sea das Meer, -e
seat der Platz, ⁻e
second zweit-
   second car der Zweitwagen, -
secretary der Sekretär, -e; die
   Sekretärin, -nen
see *sehen
   Let's see. Zeig mal her.
   see again wieder *sehen
seek, look for suchen
seem *scheinen
seldom selten
self: by oneself (myself, yourself,
      etc.) selbst *or* selber (*adv.*)
sell verkaufen
semester das Semester, -
   semester break die
   Semesterferien (*pl.*)
seminar das Seminar, -e
send schicken
senior citizen der Senior, -en, -en
sentence der Satz, ⁻e
separate separat
September (der) September
serious ernst

take something seriously etwas ernst *nehmen

set (down) setzen

seventh siebt-

several mehrere, einige

sex, gender das Geschlecht, -er

shame: That's a shame! Das ist schade!

shape: in shape fit

shared apartment die Wohngemeinschaft, -en; die WG, -s

shave sich rasieren

shine *scheinen

ship das Schiff, -e

shirt das Hemd, -en

shoe der Schuh, -e

shop, store der Laden, ¨

shop for, go shopping ein·kaufen

short kurz (kürzer); klein (*short in height*)

short of cash knapp bei Kasse

should *sollen

shoulder bag die Tasche, -n

show zeigen

shower die Dusche, -n

take a shower sich duschen

siblings die Geschwister (*pl.*)

sick krank (kränker)

sickness die Krankheit, -en

side die Seite. -n

significance die Bedeutung, -en

silent: be silent *schweigen

similar (to) ähnlich (+ *dat.*)

similarity die Ähnlichkeit, -en

simple, easy einfach; leicht

since (causal) da (*sub. conj.*)

since (temporal) seit (*prep. + dat. & sub. conj.*)

sing *singen

single, only einzig- (*adj.*)

single, unmarried ledig

sister die Schwester, -n

sit *sitzen

sit down sich setzen

situated: be situated *liegen

situation die Situation, -en

size die Größe, -n

skeptical skeptisch

ski Ski *fahren

skirt der Rock, ¨e

sleep *schlafen

slow langsam

small klein

smart klug (klüger)

snake die Schlange, -n

sneaker der Turnschuh, -e

snow der Schnee; schneien

so so

So long! Tschüss!

so that damit (*sub. conj.*)

So what? Na und?

soccer der Fußball

soccer ball der Fußball, ¨e

social gesellschaftlich; sozial

social worker der Sozialarbeiter, -; die Sozialarbeiterin, -nen

society die Gesellschaft, -en

sociology die Soziologie

soft, quiet leise

software die Software

solidarity die Solidarität

solution die Lösung, -en

solve lösen

some etwas (*sing.*); einige (*pl.*); manche (*pl.*)

somebody jemand

somehow or other irgendwie

someone jemand

something etwas

sometime or other irgendwann

sometimes manchmal

somewhat etwas

somewhere or other irgendwo

son der Sohn, ¨e

song das Lied, -er

soon bald

sore, ticked off sauer (*colloq.*)

sorry: I'm sorry about that. Das tut mir Leid.

sound *klingen

soup die Suppe, -n

sour, acidic sauer

south der Süden

Soviet Union die Sowjetunion

space der Platz, ¨e

Spain (das) Spanien

speak reden; *sprechen

I can speak German. Ich kann Deutsch.

speechless baff (*colloq.*)

speed das Tempo

spell: How do you spell that? Wie schreibt man das?

spend (money) *aus·geben

spend (time) *verbringen

spend the night übernachten

spite

in spite of trotz (+ *gen.*)

in spite of that, nevertheless trotzdem (*adv.*)

spontaneous spontan

spoon der Löffel, -

sport der Sport

play sports Sport *treiben

spouse die Ehefrau, -en (*f.*); der Ehemann, ¨er (*m.*)

spring der Frühling

spring term das Sommersemester

square: city square der Platz, ¨e

stability die Stabilität

stable stabil

staircase die Treppe, -n

stairs die Treppe, -n

stand *stehen

stand up *auf·stehen

standard of living der Lebensstandard

start *an·fangen

start, depart (by vehicle) *los·fahren

state der Staat, -en; das Bundesland, ¨er (federal state)

stay *bleiben

steal stehlen

steal, rip off klauen (*colloq.*)

steep steil

stereotyped, clichéd klischeehaft

still (*adv.*) noch; noch immer; immer noch

stipend das Stipendium, *pl.* Stipendien

stone der Stein, -e

stop (for streetcar or bus) die Haltestelle, -n

stop *halten (*intrans.*)

stop (doing something) auf·hören (mit)

store das Geschäft, -e

store, shop der Laden, ¨

story die Geschichte, -n

story, narrative die Erzählung, -en

straighten up auf·räumen

strange, foreign fremd

street die Straße, -n

streetcar die Straßenbahn, -en

strength die Kraft, ¨e

stress der Stress

stressed out gestresst (*colloq.*)

stressful stressig

stroll der Bummel, -

    stroll through town der Stadtbummel, -

    take a stroll einen Bummel machen

strong stark (stärker)

student (at university) der Student, -en, -en; die Studentin, -nen

    student dormitory das Studentenwohnheim, -e

    student I.D. der Studentenausweis, -e

studies (at university) das Studium

study das Arbeitszimmer, -

study (a subject), major in studieren

    study at studieren an (+ *dat.*)

stupid blöd; dumm

subject, area of study das Fach, ¨er

    subject, topic das Thema, *pl.* Themen

subjective subjektiv

subjunctive der Konjunktiv

subway train die Untergrundbahn; die U-Bahn

success der Erfolg, -e

suddenly plötzlich

suggestion der Vorschlag, ¨e; der Tipp, -s

suit der Anzug, ¨e

suitcase der Koffer, -

summary die Zusammenfassung, -en

summer der Sommer

sun die Sonne

Sunday (der) Sonntag

sunny sonnig

super super

supermarket der Supermarkt, ¨e

super tanker der Supertanker, -

supper das Abendessen

    for supper zum Abendessen

supposed: be supposed to *sollen

sure, certain sicher; bestimmt

    sure, of course klar (*colloq.*)

surprise die Überraschung, -en; überraschen

    be surprised staunen

    be surprised (about) sich wundern (über + *acc.*)

sweater der Pullover, -; der Pulli, -s (*colloq.*)

sweet süß

swim *schwimmen

swimming pool das Schwimmbad, ¨er

Swiss schweizerisch (*adj.*); der Schweizer, -; die Schweizerin, -nen

Switzerland die Schweiz

symbol das Symbol, -e

symbolic symbolisch

sympathy das Mitleid

system das System, -e

T

T-shirt das T-Shirt, -s

table der Tisch, -e

take *nehmen

    take along *mit·bringen; *mit·nehmen

    take (a university course) belegen

    take place *statt·finden

talk reden; *sprechen

    talk nonsense quatschen (*colloq.*)

tall groß

task die Aufgabe, -n

taste; taste good schmecken

tasty lecker

tavern die Kneipe, -n; das Lokal, -e

taxicab das Taxi, -s

tea der Tee

teacher der Lehrer, -; die Lehrerin, -nen

team die Mannschaft, -en

technology die Technik

telephone das Telefon, -e; telefonieren

television set der Fernseher, -

    watch television *fern·sehen

tell sagen

    tell, recount erzählen

    tell me sag mal

tempo das Tempo

tennis das Tennis

    tennis court der Tennisplatz, ¨e

term paper das Referat, -e

terrace die Terrasse, -n

terrible furchtbar; grausam; schrecklich

terrific herrlich; prima; toll (*colloq.*)

terrorist terroristisch (*adj.*)

test die Prüfung, -en

    written test die Klausur, -en

text der Text, -e

than (*with comparative degree*) als

thank danken (+ *dat.*)

    thank goodness Gott sei Dank

thanks der Dank

    thanks, thank you danke

    thanks a lot, many thanks vielen Dank

that dass (*sub. conj.*)

theater das Theater, -

theme das Thema, *pl.* Themen

then dann

    then, in that case da (*adv.*)

there da, dort

    How do I get there? Wie komme ich dahin?

    there is, there are es gibt (+ *acc.*)

therefore darum

thermos bottle die Thermosflasche, -n

thing das Ding, -e

    thing, item die Sache, -n

think *denken; meinen, glauben

    I don't think so. Ich glaube nicht.

    I think so. Ich glaube schon.

    I think so too. Das finde ich auch.

    think of *denken an (+ *acc.*)

    think something over sich etwas überlegen

    What do you think of that? Was meinen/sagen Sie dazu?

third dritt-

thirst der Durst

thirsty Durst haben

this, these dies-

thought der Gedanke, -ns, -n

through durch (*prep. + acc.*)

throw *werfen

   throw away *weg·werfen

Thursday (der) Donnerstag

thus also

ticked off, sore sauer (*colloq.*)

ticket die Karte, -n; die Fahrkarte, -n (*bus, train, streetcar*); das Ticket, -s (*airline*)

tidy ordentlich

tidy up auf·räumen

tie die Krawatte, -n

time die Zeit, -en

   for a long time lange

   for a short time, briefly kurz

   for a time eine Zeit lang

   for such a long time so lange

   high time höchste Zeit

   on time, punctual pünktlich

   take time, last dauern

   What time is it? Wie spät ist es? *or* Wie viel Uhr ist es?

time (in the sense of "occurrence") das Mal, -e

   any time irgendwann

   at that time, back then damals

   for the first time zum ersten Mal

   the next time das nächste Mal

   this time diesmal (*adv.*)

   umpteen times zigmal

tin can die Dose, -n

tip der Tipp, -s

tired, weary müde

   dead tired todmüde

to (*prep.*) an (*prep. + acc. or dat.*); nach (+ *dat., with cities and countries*); zu (+ *dat., with people and some places*)

   to each other zueinander

today heute

together zusammen; miteinander

tomorrow morgen

   tomorrow afternoon morgen Nachmittag

   tomorrow evening morgen Abend

tomorrow morning morgen früh

tonight heute Abend

too auch; zu

   too bad schade

tooth der Zahn, ̈e

top: on top oben (*adv.*)

topic das Thema, *pl.* Themen

topical aktuell

tough hart (härter)

tour die Tour, -en

tourist der Tourist, -en, -en; die Touristin, -nen

toward an (*prep. + acc. or dat.*)

town (5,000 to 20,000 inhabitants) die Kleinstadt, ̈e

   small town der Ort, -e

   town hall das Rathaus, ̈er

track das Gleis, -e

tradition die Tradition, -en

traditional traditionell

traffic der Verkehr

train der Zug, ̈e

   train station der Bahnhof, ̈e

train (for a sport) trainieren

transfer *um·steigen

translate übersetzen

trash der Müll

   trash container der Container, -

travel reisen

travel agency das Reisebüro, -s

traveler's check der Reisescheck, -s

tree der Baum, ̈e

trip die Reise, -n; die Fahrt

   Have a good trip! Gute Reise!

   take a trip eine Reise machen

trousers die Hose, -n

true wahr; richtig

truth die Wahrheit, -en

try versuchen (*attempt*); probieren (*sample*)

Tuesday (der) Dienstag

twice zweimal

type der Typ, -en

typical typisch

U

ugly hässlich

umbrella der Regenschirm, -e

unconcerned unbesorgt

under unter (*prep. + acc. or dat.*)

understand *verstehen

undress, get undressed sich *aus·ziehen

uneducated ungebildet

unemployed arbeitslos

unemployment die Arbeitslosigkeit

unfortunately leider

unification die Vereinigung

unimportant unwichtig

unite vereinen

university die Universität, -en; die Uni, -s (*colloq.*); die Hochschule, -n

   attend a university studieren

   at the university an der Uni(versität)

   university studies das Studium

unknown unbekannt

unnecessary unnötig

unpack aus·packen

unpleasant ungemütlich

unpopular unbeliebt

until bis

   not until erst

upon auf (*prep. + acc. or dat.*)

USA die USA (*pl.*)

use benutzen

used to: get used to sich gewöhnen an (+ *acc.*)

useful nützlich

usually meistens

V

vacation (from university or school) die Ferien (*pl.*)

   be on vacation auf (*or*) im Urlaub sein

   go on vacation in Urlaub gehen/fahren

   take a vacation Urlaub machen

   vacation (from a job) der Urlaub, -e

valley das Tal, ̈er

variation die Variation, -en

various verschieden

vegetables das Gemüse (*sing.*)

Venice (Italy) (das) Venedig

verb das Verb, -en

very sehr

vicinity die Nähe
Vienna (das) Wien
view der Blick, -e
village das Dorf, ¨er
visit der Besuch, -e; besuchen
vocabulary der Wortschatz
voice die Stimme, -n
volleyball der Volleyball
voter der Wähler, -

W

wage der Lohn, ¨e
wait (for) warten (auf + *acc.*)
   Wait a second! Hang on! Warte
     mal!
waiter der Kellner, -
waitress die Kellnerin, -nen
wake up auf·wachen (*intrans.*)
walk der Bummel, -; *gehen;
   *laufen (*colloq.*)
   go for a walk spazieren *gehen
wall (freestanding or exterior) die
   Mauer, -n
   wall (interior) die Wand, ¨e
wallet der Geldbeutel, -
wander wandern
wanderlust die Wanderlust
want to *wollen
   I don't want to. Ich habe keine
     Lust.
   want to do something Lust
     haben, etwas zu tun
war der Krieg, -e
wardrobe der Kleiderschrank, ¨e
warm warm (wärmer)
wash *waschen
waste verschwenden
watch die Uhr, -en
watch zu·schauen (+ *dat.*)
   watch television *fern·sehen
water das Wasser
way der Weg, -e
   on the way unterwegs
weak schwach (schwächer)
wear *tragen
weary, tired müde
weather das Wetter
Wednesday (der) Mittwoch

week die Woche, -n
   for weeks wochenlang (*adv.*)
weekend das Wochenende, -n
   on the weekend am
     Wochenende
welcome willkommen (*adj.*)
   Welcome! Nice to see you!
     Herzlich willkommen!
   You're welcome. Bitte (sehr).
well . . . also . . . ; na . . . ; nun . . .
well (*adv.*) gut
   get well sich erholen von
   Get well soon. Gute Besserung.
   well known bekannt
west der Westen
wet nass
what? was?
   what kind of? was für?
wheel das Rad, ¨er
when als (*sub. conj.*); wann
   (*question word*); wenn (*sub.
   conj.*)
whenever wenn (*sub. conj.*)
where? wo?
   from where? woher?
   to where? wohin?
whether, if ob (*sub. conj.*)
which? welch-?
while während (*sub. conj.*)
   for a while eine Zeit lang
   while . . . -ing bei . . .
white weiß
who? wer?
whole ganz
whose? wessen?
why? warum?
wild wild
win *gewinnen
wind der Wind
window das Fenster, -
   store window das
     Schaufenster, -
   window, counter der Schalter, -
windy windig
wine der Wein, -e
winter (der) Winter
   in the winter im Winter
wish wünschen

wit der Witz, -e
with mit
   with each other miteinander
without ohne
   without . . . -ing ohne . . . zu
witty witzig
woman die Frau, -en
   young unmarried woman das
     Fräulein, -
wonderful wunderbar
word das Wort; *two plural forms:*
   die Worte (*in context*), die
   Wörter (*unconnected*); die
   Vokabel, -n
work die Arbeit
   work (of art) das Werk, -e
work arbeiten
worker der Arbeiter, -; die
   Arbeiterin, -nen
world die Welt, -en
worried besorgt
worthwhile: be worthwhile, worth
   the trouble sich lohnen
Wow! Mensch!
write *schreiben
writer der Schriftsteller, -; die
   Schriftstellerin, -nen
wrong falsch

Y

year das Jahr, -e
   for years jahrelang
yellow gelb
yes ja
   yes I do, yes I am, etc. doch
yesterday gestern
   yesterday evening gestern
     Abend
   yesterday morning gestern früh
young jung (jünger)
   young people die Jugend (*sing.*)
youth die Jugend
   youth hostel die
     Jugendherberge, -n

Z

zone die Zone, -n

Index of Grammatical and Communicative Topics

etwas, 281, 295, 310
family members, 60–61, 62–63
flavoring particles, 36, 44, 65, 93, 217
food and drink, 212–213
Fragewörter. *See* question words
furniture, 160
future tense, 335

gefallen, 171
gehen
    + accusative preposition, 148
    + infinitive, 101
    meaning *to leave*, 312
    omission of, 72
genauso ... wie, 305
gender. *See* nouns, identifying gender of
genitive case, 201–203, 222
geography, physical, 107. *See also*
    countries
gern(e), 98–100, 304
greetings and partings, 2–3, 5, 8, 153,
    342–343

haben, 18
    as auxiliary, 141, 143, 176, 253
    gern ——, 99–100
    present tense of, 18, 52
    simple past tense of, 249
    subjunctive of, 355
Haupt-, 102
heißen, 4
hotels, 366–367
hypothetical statements and
    questions, 359

immer, 251, 305
imperative, 92–94
in, 148, 205
indefinite amounts, 278
indefinite adverbs, 315
indefinite articles
    in the accusative case, 48
    in the dative case, 118
    in the genitive case, 202
    in the nominative case, 32,
    omission of, 32, 134, 284
    See also **ein**-words
indefinite pronouns, 78, 278, 281
indirect objects, 116–117, 275. *See also*
    dative case
infinitives
    dependent, 173, 176, 176note, 311
    double, 176, 311
    formation of, 27
    gehen +, 101
    lassen +, 311

    with modal verbs, 71, 75
    omission of, 72
    with **um/ohne ... zu,** 200
    as verbal nouns, 178
    zu +, 199
information questions. *See* question
    words
inseparable prefixes, 124, 146
intensifiers, 273
interrogative pronouns, 7, 35, 49, 54,
    118, 227, 334
introducing oneself, 3–4, 342–343
irgend-, 315

ja, 34, 36

kein, 76, 97–98

landscape, 118
lassen, 311–312
leave, 311–312
leaving, 8, 311–312
letter-writing, 153
like, 98–100, 171
limiting words, 221–224, 278. *See also*
    der-words; **ein**-words
linking verbs, 33, 221
location, change of, 144

mal, 312–313
man, 78
measure, 204
mehr, 97–98, 304
memories, personal, 320
mixed verbs, 147, 176note, 249
möchte(n), 72, 99–100, 336
modal verbs, 69–71
    future tense of, 335
    negation of, 75
    perfect tense of, 176, 176note
    present tense of, 69–71
    + separable-prefix verbs, 123
    simple past tense of, 248–249
    subjunctive of, 354
    + verbal idea, 101
mögen, 99–100. *See also* **möchte(n)**
months, 18
mood, 351

nach, 121, 205
nachdem, 254
names, 62, 137
nationality, 9, 134, 280, 284. *See also*
    countries
negation
    with **kein,** 76, 97–98

    with prefix **un-,** 285
    and **sondern,** 169, 170
    word order with, 10, 74–75, 170
nicht, 10, 74–75, 76, 170
    —— **mehr,** 97–98
    —— **so wie,** 305
    —— **wahr?,** 77
    noch ——, 97
nicht?, 77
N-nouns, 152, 202
noch, 97–98
nominative case, 32–33. *See also*
    predicate nominative
noun phrases, 221–223
nouns
    adjectival, 228, 280, 281, 310
    agent, 126, 231
    capitalization of, 9
    compound, 56–57, 206
    identifying gender of, 30, 57, 231
    of measure, weight, and number,
    204
    of nationality, 134, 280, 284
    N-nouns, 152, 202
    plural of, 31, 32, 79
    prefixes for, 285
    proper, 202. *See also* names
    replacing, 332
    suffixes for, 36–37, 231, 257, 285
    verbal, 178, 282
number
    agreement of, 53
    indefinite, 278
numbers
    cardinal, 14, 55, 221, 283
    + **-mal,** 313
    ordinal, 228
    nouns of, 204
nur, 336, 352

ohne ... zu, 200
only, 336

past participles
    as adjectives, 285–286
    of mixed verbs, 176note
    with prefixes, 146
    of strong verbs, 143, 145, 174,
    246–247
    of weak verbs, 142, 174
past perfect tense, 253–254
past tense. *See* past perfect tense;
    perfect tense; simple past tense
perfect tense, 141–148
    auxiliary with, 141, 143
    double infinitive in, 176, 311

Credits

Text

Page 220: "Die Lorelei 1973" by Jürgen Werner from *Gegendarstellungen: Autoren korrigieren Autoren: lyr. Parodien.* Edited by Manfred Ach & Manfred Bosch (Andernach: Atelier-Verlag, 1974). Reprinted by permission of Atelier Verlag Andernach. 244: "Mein junger Sohn fragt mich" by Bertolt Brecht from *Gesammelte Werke,* Volume 9. Copyright © 1967, Suhrkamp Verlag Frankfurt am Main. Used by permission.

316–317: "Zwei Denkmäler" by Anna Seghers from *Atlaszusammengestellt von deutschen Autoren* (Berlin: Verlag Klaus Wagenbach, 1965). Copyright © by Anna Seghers. Reprinted by permission of Verlag Klaus Wagenbach. 327–328: "nachwort" by Eugen Gomringer from *The Book of Hours/Stundenbuch.* Reprinted by permission of Eugen Gomringer. 350: "ottos mops" by Ernst Jandl from *Der künstliche Baum,* 1970. Reprinted by permission of Luchterhand Literaturverlag GmbH.

Illustrations

Ruth J. Flanigan: 2–4, 6, 11–12, 14, 16–17, 24, 40–41, 48, 51, 63, 74, 78, 84, 92, 103, 115, 143, 150–152, 160, 175, 211–212, 230, 253, 274–277, 291, 314, 367.

Matthew Hansen: 114.

Joseph Scharl: 359. From *The Complete Grimm's Fairy Tales* by Jakob Ludwig Karl Grimm and Wilhelm Karl Grimm. Copyright © 1944 by Pantheon Books. Copyright renewed 1972 by Random House, Inc. Reprinted by permission of Pantheon Books, a division of Random House, Inc.

Marie Marcks: 70. © Marie Marcks, Heidelberg.

Deutsche Schule Washington, D.C.: 132. Reproduced by permission.

„Studienzeiten": 161. From Zeitschrift „Deutschland". Reproduced by permission.

Photographs

Page 1: Farrell Grehan/Photo Researchers, Inc. 7: David Simson/Stock Boston 12: (*left*) Kevin Galvin/Stock Boston; (*right*) Beryl Goldberg 15, 16: Andrew Brilliant; 21: Palmer & Brilliant 22: Beryl Goldberg 27: Ulrike Welsch 37: (*left*) Granitsas/The Image Works; (*right*) Beryl Goldberg 40: David Frazier 43: Bob Krist 46: Kees Van Den Berg/Photo Researchers, Inc. 54: Palmer & Brilliant 56: (*right*) Judy Poe 61: Andrew Brilliant 62, 64, 82: Ulrike Welsch 87: Wolfgang Kaehler 88: Tony Freeman/PhotoEdit 95: Mike Mazzaschi/Stock Boston 101: Wolfgang Kaehler 104: Vandystadt/ Photo Researchers, Inc. 105: COMSTOCK/Sven Martsen 108: (*left*) Judy Poe; (*center*) Ulrike Welsch; (*right*) Wolfgang Kaehler; (*below*) David Frazier 111: Jan Halaska/ Photo Researchers, Inc. 117: Palmer & Brilliant 127: Beryl Goldberg 129: Kevin Galvin/Stock Boston 133: Kevin Galvin 136: Beryl Goldberg 144: Palmer & Brilliant 154: Ulrike Welsch 157: Kevin Galvin 162: Carol Palmer 163: David Simson/Stock Boston 170: Kevin Galvin 177: Ulrike Welsch 178: Andrew Brilliant/Carole Palmer 181: Ulrike Welsch 188: Palmer & Brilliant 192: Pierre Valette 196: David Brilliant 208: Kevin Galvin 216: Ulrike Welsch 227: Helga Lade Fotoagentur 235: (*left*) Marvullo/The Stock Market; (*right*) W. Geiersperger/Interfoto 236: (*left*) Kevin Galvin/ Stock Boston; (*right*) Interfoto 238: Kevin Galvin 240: Owen Franken/Stock Boston